# Financial Information Analysis

# Financial Information Analysis

**Philip O'Regan**
*University of Limerick*

**JOHN WILEY & SONS, LTD**

Chichester • New York • Weinheim • Brisbane • Singapore • Toronto

*Other Wiley Editorial Offices*

John Wiley & Sons, Inc., 605 Third Avenue,
New York, NY 10158-0012, USA

WILEY-VCH Verlag GmbH, Pappelallee 3,
D-69469 Weinheim, Germany

Jacaranda Wiley Ltd, 33 Park Road, Milton,
Queensland 4064, Australia

John Wiley & Sons (Asia) Pte Ltd, 2 Clementi Loop #02-01,
Jin Xing Distripark, Singapore 129809

John Wiley & Sons (Canada) Ltd, 22 Worcester Road,
Rexdale, Ontario M9W 1L1, Canada

***Library of Congress Cataloging-in-Publication Data***

O'Regan, Philip
    Financial information analysis / Philip O'Regan.
    p. cm.
    ISBN 0–471–48923–9
    1. Financial statements. 2. Accounting. I. Title.
    HF5681.B2 074 2001
    657′.3–dc21                        2001026500

***British Library Cataloguing in Publication Data***
A catalogue record for this book is available from the British Library

ISBN 0–471–48923–9

Typeset in 10/12pt Times by Deerpark Publishing Services Ltd, Shannon, Ireland
Printed and bound in Great Britain by Biddles Ltd, Guildford and King's Lynn, UK
This book is printed on acid-free paper responsibly manufactured from sustainable forestation, for which at least two trees are planted for each one used for paper production.

# BRIEF CONTENTS

# CONTENTS

# ACKNOWLEDGEMENTS

This text has emerged from over a decade of teaching a course in Financial Information Analysis at the University of Limerick. While they may not have realized it, successive groups of students played a critical part in its development. I am grateful to them all.

I am also grateful to my colleagues in the Department of Accounting and Finance at the University of Limerick and, in particular, to the head of department, Professor Tom Kennedy, for their support.

John Heneghan and Pat Carroll provided important insights and feedback, while various reviewers were generous in their comments and observations. Likewise, Steve Hardman provided encouragement at times when it seemed easier to give up.

Finally, my wife Veronica, to whom this book is dedicated, was unstinting in her support as I worked on yet another 'last' book.

# PREFACE

## Creative Accounting

In the 1960s the term *military intelligence* was a popular oxymoron. But then came Desert Storm and we saw what creativity could do to a military strategy. Of course, before military intelligence took over, there was talk of averting war with economic intelligence.

But that would mean leaving liberation to the accountants. Bean counters, we call them. So low is the accountant's standing among so-called creative people that creative accounting is worse than an oxymoron. It's considered a crime. But history tells a different story:

In 1532 Francisco Pizarro came before the court of the Inca, seemingly in peace, but set on conquest. He noticed that certain members of the Inca court wore knotted ropes around their waists. Assuming these ropes were prayer beads, he ordered his men to ambush the men who wore them. Kill the priests, he thought, and their civilization will crumble. It worked. But not as planned. The knotted ropes contained the complete record of the empire's fortune. Pizarro wiped out their accountants, and with them went their empire...

Source: Peter Lloyd, Right Brain Works

Accounting information, as Pizarro discovered, is one of the most potent sources of influence and power in any society. This is especially so in those environments where accounting is recognized as a primary means of communication and control. In a world in which more and more people can expect to have to deal with complex financial information and an increasingly sizeable proportion of the population acquires shares, this importance can only increase.

This text reflects these developments by seeking to address the nature and role of accounting information in modern society, with specific reference to the UK. In particular, it focuses on one of the primary accounting documents, the Annual Report, which in the Anglo-American world is normally produced annually by every company. A primary aim is to equip readers with the skills needed to appreciate the information content of this, and other accounting documents.

The most significant feature of this text is that it attempts to place the discussion and analysis of the information contained in the Annual Report in as broad a context as possible. At its most basic this means recognizing that the Annual Report itself is only partly comprised of what is traditionally understood as accounting information, i.e. financial data in a recognizable financial statement. In fact, reflecting the limited capacity of accounting numbers to communicate the essence of any corporate entity, and responding to the information requirements of an increasingly large range of users, the Annual Report has become a substantial document containing a wealth of non-accounting information. For example, Directors' Reports, Chairman's Statements, commentaries on the environmental impact of corporate activity, as well as information presented in the form of graphs and tables now supplement the basic accounting statements.

At another level, this contextualization means that issues such as the role of governance cultures, the demand for and supply of accounting information and the regulatory, legislative and conceptual frameworks within which accounting information emerges are also investigated.

In seeking to broaden our understanding of the information content of the Annual Report, the text makes liberal use of extracts, quotations and articles from a variety of sources. This is done not only to supplement the narrative with original and incisive comment, but also to introduce readers to insights that often contradict the author's own viewpoint. The result is that the reader is challenged to confront issues and assimilate varying perspectives, rather than simply adopt one writer's prejudices.

## What is "Financial Information Analysis"?

Financial information is presented in various forms. Financial statements, such as the balance sheet, profit and loss account and cashflow statement that are found in an Annual Report, are probably the most common means by which financial information is made available.

These are complex documents, constructed according to detailed rules and regulations that reflect the accumulated wisdom of generations of accounting practice. In other words, they can often be extremely difficult to understand. It becomes necessary, therefore, to learn how to "read" them.

As employed in this text, the term "Financial Information Analysis" describes the processes and techniques used to identify and extract the critical information contained within financial statements and any supporting documentation. Thus, insights and skills developed by users of accounting information over many decades form a critical part of this text and are covered in considerable detail.

Significantly, however, the application of these techniques and processes is not presented as an end in itself. On the contrary, financial information analysis is viewed as a more holistic exercise that contributes to an informed and balanced decision-making process. This process includes the application of various techniques and skills. But it also seeks to understand the results these yield with reference to the broader strategic, commercial and social considerations that impact every commercial entity. Thus, the needs of a variety of users are considered, while the notion that any one interest group should dictate the financial reporting agenda is challenged.

## Fundamental Analysis

The perspective, techniques and skills adopted in this text can be broadly grouped under the heading "Fundamental Analysis". This is an approach that seeks to analyze and interpret a company by investigating its fundamental financial, strategic and human elements.

This distinguishes it from "Technical Analysis", an approach that focuses more on stock market measures and seeks to find indications of future share performance in historical patterns.

The text is divided into six sections as follows:

## I Context

The text begins with an identification and discussion of the various contexts within which corporate financial communication should be considered. The intention is to challenge readers to consider the various forces and influences that have conjoined to produce financial information in the forms in which it currently emerges.

Separate chapters are devoted to the following topics:

- Regulatory and legislative contexts;
- Conceptual context;
- Theoretical context;
- Governance context.

In discussing these, particular attention is paid to attempting to understand the international contexts within which the UK operates. These include the broader Anglo-American world in which the UK and US are the significant players, and the EU.

## II Content

The Annual Report is a substantial document containing a huge volume of information in various formats, only some of which are recognizably financial in nature. The second section of the text is devoted, therefore, to a detailed analysis of the reporting and disclosure requirements underpinning what should be included in an Annual Report.

These requirements are considered under two headings, reflecting the most obvious subdivision in the nature of the information contained in an Annual Report:

- Narrative Reports;
- Financial Statements.

## III Analysis

Since one of the primary functions of the text is to equip readers with the ability to identify and extract the key information from an Annual Report, a separate section is devoted to explaining one of the more popular and useful means by which this is traditionally achieved – Fundamental Analysis. Under headings that reflect the principal areas of concern for most large corporate entities, readers are introduced to the main techniques of Fundamental Analysis and encouraged to use these in analyzing financial information. They are also made aware of the limitations of this approach and, most importantly, of the fact that techniques such as these are merely a means to an end.

Reflecting the principal areas of corporate activity, this section includes chapters dealing with the following:

- Fundamental Analysis;
- Activity and Liquidity;
- Financing;
- Profitability and Return on Investment.

## IV Issues

This section deals with some of the more complex elements of financial accounting practice as these will need to be understood in order to analyze the financial statements of larger entities. These issues are considered in an international context and accounting practice in the UK is compared with that in the US and several continental European countries.

In addition, readers are alerted to some of the more common creative accounting techniques, as well as developments such as those occurring in the area of Corporate Social Reporting.

Chapters addressing the following issues are included in this section:

- Business Combinations;
- Taxation, Pensions, Leases and Foreign Currency;
- Creative Accounting;
- Corporate Social Reporting;
- International Accounting and Harmonization.

## V Interpretation

In this section readers are encouraged to bring together the various skills and contextual understandings gained so far. The purpose is not only to allow readers to see how these techniques can be applied, but also to highlight the fact that the process of interpreting such information involves more than merely the application of these skills.

There is one chapter in this section and it demonstrates the approach outlined thus far by presenting an analysis and interpretation of the Tesco plc 2000 Annual Report which is included as an appendix to the text.

## VI Challenges and Opportunities

The changing economic, social and political contexts induced by globalization and technological revolution have created a new set of challenges and opportunities for accountants and for those using accounting information. This final section seeks to identify some of these and to contour the outlines of the financial reporting culture that is beginning to emerge in response to these new dynamics.

This section includes chapters on:

- Alternative Approaches;
- Future Reporting.

## Unique features

This text employs several unique features in an attempt to communicate to readers the relevance and immediacy of the topic:

- The role of accounting information as an aid to the decision-making process is emphasized;
- Readers are not immediately confronted with masses of technical information. Thus, Section I introduces readers to fundamental theoretical and conceptual issues that need to be considered when approaching accounting information;
- Extracts from newspapers, journals and websites are employed liberally in order to elaborate on points made within the text, but also, on occasion, to illustrate alternative viewpoints;
- "In practice" inserts are used to demonstrate how various regulatory, legislative and other provisions translate into practice;
- Throughout, readers are referred to an Annual Report included in an appendix at the end of the text;

- "Review Questions" at the end of each chapter challenge readers to review the principal elements of the chapter;

- End-of-chapter "Case Studies", often incorporating detailed extracts from other sources, are intended to stimulate discussion as well as allow readers to investigate particular events and companies in more detail;

- Readers are referred to websites for supplementary reading and information;

- While UK accounting is placed firmly in the Anglo-American context to which it belongs, international comparisons constantly alert readers to the fact that alternative practices and perspectives exist;

- Interpretation is identified as an intuitive process that is assisted by techniques, contextual grounding and experience where the whole is often greater than the sum of the individual parts;

- The interests of stakeholders other than shareholders are discussed;

- The role of corporate governance in shaping and informing accounting practice is highlighted;

- The orientation of future corporate reporting is outlined;

- Non-financial measures of corporate performance and position, such as the Balanced Scorecard, are considered;

- Supplementary materials such as additional computational questions, answers to various questions included in the text, and illustrative examples are available on the associated website for this text.

With the permission of the company, the Tesco plc 2000 Annual Report is included as an appendix. Readers are referred to this throughout. Access to the company's website, where additional and supplementary information can be accessed, is encouraged.

# INTRODUCTION

## Your Money by Robert Barker

It was Wednesday, October 14, lunchtime, and there I was at my favorite pizzeria, flipping through an investment magazine as I awaited my order. "Hey," the guy behind me in line said. "You oughta be talking to me."

And so I met Ralph, my latest teacher in the ways of Wall Street. Ralph quickly told me he is a stock broker at one of the big, well-known brokerage firms. I introduced myself, told him that I write about investments, and soon we were talking over pizza and Cokes.

I made it plain that I invest only in funds (a good way to comply with Business Week's strict conflict-of-interest policy that ensures that what you read here isn't influenced by our personal investments). But before I could get through my second slice, Ralph said, "I know how I could make you money. Conoco." The oil giant (COC, $25.19) was set the following week to come public in a spin-off from its parent, DuPont (DD, $56.94). It would be the largest initial public offering in history, Ralph said, and he could get me 100, maybe 200 shares.

I said no thanks, but I had given him my business card, and when he phoned a couple of days later to see if I'd changed my mind, I decided to test this one broker's skills: For my order, how much help would this full-service broker offer me? Would he provide the kind of research a serious investor would need to make a decision?

So I asked Ralph to find out how the ratio of Conoco's expected market value to its annual sales, its price-sales ratio, compared with other, comparable oil companies. I told him I wasn't interested in comparing price-to-earnings ratios since the earnings number would be more of an accountant's work of art than would the top-line sales figure.

A few hours passed before Ralph faxed me a short letter with the views of his firm's oil analyst (bullish) and Conoco's expected p-e ratio, vs. those of Atlantic Richfield (ARC, $68.38), Texaco (TX, $59.50), and Phillips (P, $42.31). Nice, but not what I'd asked for. When I pressed him, Ralph soon threw up his hands. "I'm not an analyst. I'm in the sales end of it," he said. "Honestly, people don't ask for that kind of information, the technicalities. It's a good company. Good industry. That's all most people want to know."

Ralph pleaded with me not to identify him, lest I "ruin" his budding career. OK, but the whole incident did nothing to dispel my sense that while the "full-service" brokerage industry may linger for years, unless it does more for the paying customers, it will die.

Source: Business Week, October 30, 1998.

## Introduction

This opening vignette highlights a number of the themes that will be central to this text:

- For a start, notice how the potential investor asks for financial information and for this to be expressed in quite specific ways, for instance in the form of ratios such as price-to-earnings and price-to-sales. One of the primary purposes of this text is to explain how to compute and interpret such measures.

- Notice, too, the reference to the accountancy figures as "an accountant's work of art". Traditionally accounting data has been thought of as "correct" and "accurate" with little scope for imagination on the part of the preparers. It was, after all, a numerate discipline - so it had to be "right"! More recently, however, it has become obvious to the many users of accounting information that accounting rules allow considerable scope for subjective judgements to be employed by accountants and management. Indeed, it is now accepted that accounting practice owes more to a political process in which various interest groups lobby for their preferred treatment, than the discovery and implementation of any scientifically objective set of accounting rules. This in turn has focussed attention on the regulation of accounting and the need for a more mature understanding of the various factors that contribute to the formulation of accounting information and regulation. An appreciation of these factors will also be a central theme of this book.

- And look at what happened when the broker ignored the accounting information. For all of its faults, accounting information remains one of the most insightful and potent measures of corporate performance. While this text will highlight the need to supplement it with insights from other sources and acknowledge that it is open to manipulation, it will also demonstrate that interested parties ignore it at their peril.

## History and Development

Accounting has been described as the language of business. While this may sound a rather extravagant claim, it does express something of the importance of accounting in today's world. For example, without accounting data much that is taken for granted in our society, from simple calculations of profit to the operations of international stock markets, would be impossible.

The way in which accounting is practised today is a consequence of mankind's attempts to control the environment. Indeed, since earliest times mankind has felt the need to record events, and the emergence of some form of written record coincided with the development of basic recording skills. About 5,000 years ago writing and numbers were developed and with the large increase in trade and the growth of centres of habitation in the Middle East there came the need to record financial events. As the following extract illustrates, excavations in modern day Iran, Iraq and Egypt have uncovered evidence of the use of clay tablets as one means by which crude records were maintained around this time.

## Earliest Known Writing Uncovered in Egypt

Suhag Province, Egypt – Clay tablets just unearthed from the tomb of Egyptian King Scorpion I represent what is claimed to be the oldest discovered evidence of writing. German archaeologists say carbon dating places the age of the tablets at 3,300–3,200 BC. More than two-thirds of the translated hieroglyphic writings, on small pieces of clay tablets and the sides of jars, are tax accounting records.

Source: http://www.acaus.org/history/hsanc.html.

By the first century BC the need to account for wealth had developed to such an extent that the term "auditor" (a term still used today) had been adopted by the Romans to describe an individual who carried out such a task.

Accounting, therefore, emerged very early in the human record. This suggests that accounting for events is a basic social need. When people begin to organize they discover that accounting information is necessary for social control. It also shows that accounting develops in response to human needs, that is, accountants adapt their systems to accommodate social developments. Today that principle still applies, with accounting constantly being adapted and modified in response to the changing needs of business and society. Accounting is not an immutable science that possesses some absolute truths just waiting to be discovered by diligent researchers. It is a social discipline that responds to the needs of the society in which it functions.

Another important thing to note is that one of the consequences of recording financial events is that those who do so begin to play a key role in the allocation of wealth. For example, it is accountants who define and calculate profit, one of the parameters for the division of wealth in modern society. It is this that gives accounting as a discipline and accountants as a profession such importance and ensures that those involved in business and management must understand how the system operates.

## Early Modern Developments

The origins of modern accounting and bookkeeping can be traced to the late middle ages when increased trade led to the need to account for profit and wealth. Gradually the method of accounting began to be standardized. In Venice in 1494, a monk and friend of Leonardo da Vinci, Fra. Luca Pacioli, produced a text, *"Summa de Arithmetica, Geometrica, Proportioni et Proportionalita"*, ("Everything About Arithmetic, Geometry, and Proportions"), which contained a treatise on bookkeeping entitled *"Particularis de Computis et Scripturis"* ("Details of Accounting and Recording"). This was an outline of the mechanics of the double-entry bookkeeping system that had been used for several decades in and around Venice. Over five centuries later this system remains the basis of modern bookkeeping.

## The Industrial Revolution

The Industrial Revolution, particularly as experienced in Britain, changed the scale of business enterprise. Up to this point most businesses had been small family concerns. However, in response to investors needs new business entities called joint-stock companies emerged. These enabled a large number of individuals (called shareholders) to invest in a way which allowed them to limit potential personal losses. However, because it was impossible for all shareholders to be involved in the management of these limited companies, they usually appointed directors to manage the company on their behalf.

This meant that shareholders often knew very little about what was happening in their own companies. As a consequence the financial statements summarizing the company's performance became very important since only by understanding them could shareholders discover how their own money was being used.

## The Twentieth Century

The demand for accounting information increased dramatically throughout the twentieth century, driven not just by the requirements of international trade and global capital markets, but also, ironically, by the demands of two world wars. And as the need for financial information increased so did the influence of accounting and the accounting profession. The accounting function is now seen as a critical element of any developed, liberal, capitalist society, providing much of the information on which the financial and corporate worlds depend.

The advent of computers, the Internet and the "Information Age" have merely accentuated the importance of accounting information since financial data is now so prevalent and easily accessible that it has become one of the most powerful means of communication in the modern world. The new millennium, therefore, brings both challenges and opportunities.

## Forms of Accounting Information

Accounting information can be presented in a variety of forms, usually depending on the particular users in mind. For example, managers will often be presented with large amounts of financial detail in the form of budgets that enable them to plan and evaluate performance. Other forms of presentation include internal reports, asset schedules and forecasts. Information such as this is usually termed "internal" accounting information because it is intended primarily for use by management to assist in the efficient running of an organization.

The other principal category of financial information can be termed "external". This is because it is intended primarily to satisfy the statutory and public accountability responsibilities of a reporting entity whereby it releases information for more widespread consumption. The prime example of this type is the Annual Report. This is a statutorily required document which each UK company listed on the London Stock Exchange must issue within 6 months of its year-end. And it is also the primary focus of this text – the skills and insights provided over the course of the following chapters are intended to enable the analysis and interpretation of this document with a view to gaining an understanding of the company in question.

Typically an Annual Report will include:

- Accounting information:

  - Balance Sheet;
  - Profit and Loss Account;
  - Cashflow Statement;
  - Statement of Total Recognized Gains and Losses;
  - Notes to the accounts.

- Narrative reports:

  - Directors' Report;
  - Chairman's Statement;
  - Auditor's Report;
  - Other reports, such as the Operating and Financial Review.

As a principal means by which a company communicates with the various constituencies to which it is accountable, the Annual Report comprises a unique source of information about the company. Not surprisingly, therefore, it is the subject of considerable and detailed analysis and comment as the following extract, which is reporting on a report on Annual Reports, illustrates:

## The Company Report Report, by Jim Kelly

There is still great enthusiasm – at least within companies – for annual reports. The survey shows that they are continuing to evolve... They use personal rather than institutional language. They explain the company strategy every year. The worst reports make unsubstantiated claims, contain missing or conflicting information, and fail to address the concerns of shareholders.

Company finance directors are not the only people who think annual reports are important. Last week the annual Stock Exchange and Chartered Accountants' awards for the best reports were presented at the Mansion House, London. (The event could have been enlivened by nomination of the worst as well.) The winners were Kingfisher and Hodder Headline - the latter printing 6,000 reports for only 1,000 shareholders.

Both The Company Report Report and the Mansion House awards are based on the belief that the annual report and accounts are a primary source of financial communication. After all, there are no corresponding annual awards for interim or preliminary statements. The report goes further: 'Research confirms the importance of the annual report as a prime information source.'

Source: Financial Times, February 27, 1997.

There are, of course, other types of financial information available such as analysts' reports, prospectuses and media comment. And since the object is to consider information which will allow a comprehensive and contextual understanding of companies and their performance, it will be useful to refer to these in order to inform and supplement the information disclosed by the Annual Report.

Two of these other sources deserve particular mention:

- Interim reports: Annual Reports, as the title implies, are normally produced every year. However, a year is a long time for users to have to wait for information. For this reason UK companies listed on the Stock Exchange are required to issue half-yearly interim reports to shareholders either directly or by means of inserts in two national newspapers.

- Preliminary announcements: once draft accounts have been prepared, but before the Annual Report is actually issued, companies will normally make preliminary announcements about financial performance.

## Users of Accounting Information

The critical role which accounting plays in the liberal democratic market economies that predominate in today's world is reflected in the number and range of users of that information:

- **Shareholders and investors**: because of their large numbers, shareholders are not normally involved in the running of the business. For this reason it is particularly important that they receive prompt and accurate accounting information about their business so that they can assess how it has performed. The Annual Report has traditionally been intended to satisfy the information requirements of this group, although legislation now allows shareholders to opt to receive summary financial statements rather than the full Annual Report.

- **Financial analysts**: accounting information is prepared and presented in accordance with various regulations, concepts and terminology. Like any other language it is often incomprehensible to those who have not learned how to read it. Analysts play a key role in mediating between the preparers of accounts and those who need to understand them. They advise existing or potential shareholders such as insurance companies, pension funds, investment trusts and individuals, and are among the most sophisticated users of accounting information.

- **Management**: management, who will have access to all accounting data within a business, will be one of the principal users of accounting information. They will use it to assist them in checking past performance and also to help them in making decisions about the future activities of the business.

- **Employees**: accounting information is relevant to employees since they will want to know whether or not the company can offer safe employment and promotion. In recent years, with the advent of share option schemes and substantial numbers of shareholding employees, the relevance of accounting information to employees has taken on a new dimension.

- **Lenders**: lenders' primary concern is the security of their loans, so they will analyze the financial statements to determine whether the business will be able to repay amounts due. They will be particularly interested in the availability of cash and the value of any assets given as security against loans.

- **Taxation authorities**: the Inland Revenue use accounting information as a basis upon which to determine tax liability.

- **Others**: increasingly, members of the general public or pressure groups such as environmental protection organizations are using accounting information to pressure companies into changes in their operating practices.

---

### In practice:

*By means of share options and various government sponsored tax-efficient schemes it is now estimated that there are over 4 million employee shareholders in the UK.*

*Source: Accounting and Business, July 1999.*

The range of users is, therefore, substantial and growing. Indeed, as the following extract highlights, it is the large number of users which makes it so difficult for the Annual Report to satisfy all user needs:

## The Write Stuff

### Reporting results clearly in a jungle of regulations is no easy task.

...The main problem companies face when producing their annual report and accounts is that they have to be all things to all people. On one hand, the company's finance team has to make sure the report complies with an increasingly thick jungle of regulations governing what you are supposed to include and how you disclose it. On the other, the overall report and the information in it has to be as useful and as clear as possible to those who use the accounts.

And these users are a varied group. Investing in shares has become increasingly fashionable, and the number of small-time investors has exploded in recent years. An annual report now has to be produced in a way that is interesting and useful to private investors, and at the same time meets the needs of the ever-powerful institutional investors. On top of all this, there are increasing calls for compulsory reporting on social, environmental and ethical issues...

Source: Accountancy Age, July 13, 2000.

## Summary

If accounting is a language, indeed, a highly technical language, then financial analysis can be seen as a means of interpreting that language and of reducing it to more manageable concepts and expressions. It also acts as a mediating influence in disseminating information about commercial entities to a broader range of users.

In order to interpret it properly, however, it is necessary to understand some of the influences that shape both its form and the role it plays in modern society. This is the focus of Section I.

# SECTION I

# Contexts

One of the primary emphases of this text is that it is necessary to inform any interpretation of accounting information with as broad and rich a contextualization as possible. To coin a phrase, the three most important factors in enabling an informed understanding of accounting information are "context, context and context".

For this reason Section I is devoted to a discussion of four contexts which must be considered before any informed analysis and interpretation of accounting information is possible.

Chapter 1 looks at the regulatory and legislative frameworks that underpin accounting practice. The notion of accounting as the product of a "political" process is introduced. This is understood to mean that accounting rules result from a dynamic in which various interest groups compete to influence the decisions of regulators, whether professions, governments or others. If true, then this means that accounting regulations must be seen as deriving from political choices and preferences, rather than from laboratory-style research that somehow reveals "correct" and immutable schemes of accounting practice. This has major implications for any analysis of the information content of financial statements.

Chapter 2 develops the notion of accounting as a critical means of communication, albeit one which is still struggling to develop a set of unified principles and thought which would act as a base from which a more coherent and integrated set of practices might emerge.

Accounting information is, in many senses, simply a commodity. Chapter 3 extends the discussion, therefore, to attempt to answer the question "What is the role of accounting information in society?" Focusing specifically on the role of accounting information in the stock market, it looks at various theoretical approaches that seek to answer this question.

Having explored the role of accounting in the market, Chapter 4 changes the focus to the impact of corporate structure on the role and form of accounting information. Tracing the historical and commercial considerations that have resulted in the unique form of corporate governance that predominates in the Anglo-American world, this chapter considers the impact this has had on the nature and accessibility of accounting information.

# REGULATORY AND
# LEGISLATIVE CONTEXTS

[1]

When you have completed this chapter you will understand that:

- Accounting is closely regulated.
- Various entities such as governments, international organizations, capital markets and accountancy bodies have a role in the regulatory process.
- One way in which the regulatory role of governments is expressed is through legislation and this impacts directly upon accounting information.
- Stock Exchange rules represent another source of regulation.
- There are detailed provisions relating to the formation of a company in the UK.

## The Role of Governments in the Global Economy

...Among the great political achievements of the 20th century was the domesticating of *laissez-faire* capitalism's brute power, under democratic auspices. The nation-state accomplished this task in multiple ways. It pursued economic stabilization and steady growth through an active macro-economic policy. It regulated the more self-destructive tendencies of markets, especially banks and financial markets. It empowered trade unions and put a floor under labour, and later created environmental standards. It provided social income in various forms of social insurance. It financed the education and training of schoolchildren and workers. And it made direct public investments.

All of this made for a more socially bearable, as well as a more economically efficient, brand of capitalism. It tempered capitalism's extremes, both the volatility and the inequality. Increased stability also enhanced the political and economic bargaining power of ordinary people, which rooted the mixed economy in a majority politics. These political majorities then reciprocated by providing reliable constituencies for parties that believed in a mixed economy. So strong was this consensus during the post-war boom that even centre-right parties did not dare challenge the basic social entente or the conception of what was required to domesticate a market economy.

Despite new technology, what has changed is less the fundamental dynamic of markets than the venue of their regulation and with it the balance of political forces. If markets are global, their regulators must also be global. But we have no global government (nor, probably, should we) and only the very weakest of transnational institutions of governance. Corporations, it is said, gleefully, have outrun the writ of nation-states.

In principle, the shift to global *laissez-faire* is an unmitigated good because of the efficiency of the price system. From this perspective, the regulations and stabilizing policies are mere "distortions", whose elimination will produce only better alloca-tion of economic resources. But this view ignores the fact that the domestic policy interventions were necessitated in the first place by irredeemable market failures, in sectors of the economy where market forces could not by themselves optimize outcomes.

For example, financial markets still are prone to overshoot, and their speculative tendencies still risk spilling over into the real economy. A *laissez-faire* global mone-tary system still has an overall bias to deflation and slower-than-available growth. Curiously, the new architects of *laissez-faire* are not recommending the disman-tling of central banks; they are not proposing that the advanced countries turn their monetary policy over to some faceless global entity; they are not abandoning the supervision of securities exchanges and banks. And in the face of speculative mornings-after in Mexico and East Asia, they were quick to rely on central banks and international agencies for rescue operations. All of this is tribute to the fact that even the prophets of *laissez-faire* do not entirely believe in it. Indeed, even if all transactions were perfectly "transparent", herd instincts and speculative binges would continue to characterize financial flows. Since information is ever more quickly capitalized, the smart money has ever more of an incentive to get a jump on the pack. The speculative impulse never subsides, and with it survives the tendency of financial markets to overshoot...

Source: Kuttner, R. (2001), *The Role of Governments in the Global Economy*, in Hutton, W. and Giddens, A. eds., *On The Edge: Living with Global Capitalism*, Vintage, pp. 152–154. Reprinted by permission of the Random House Group Ltd.

## Introduction

A critique of *laissez-faire* ("unregulated") market economics, and the extent to which this philosophy has infused the process of globalization, may seem an unlikely way in which to begin a book about financial information analysis.

In fact, both market economics and globalization have forged new contexts within which accounting information must be considered. Traditionally seen in far-less ambitious settings, the realization that accounting is a critical means by which businesses communicate allows it to be viewed as but one element in an ongoing struggle between proponents of *laissez-faire* market economics and those more alert to the potential for volatility and inequality in an unregulated economy. Accounting must, therefore, be viewed first and foremost in such contexts. This allows the reasons for, and the agents of, its regulation to be properly assessed.

As the opening extract points out, for much of the 20th century government intervention and professional regulation were viewed as generally benign and disinterested influences. The result was the development of a complex regulatory process for accounting that embraced the law, governments, the profession and various other interested parties.

The latter decades of the 20th century, however, witnessed something of a reaction to this view. The Thatcherite Revolution in Britain and the Reaganite years in the US generally espoused a *laissez-faire* culture that sought to reassert the role of the market as the primary means by which information flows should be determined. In the process champions of this approach have sought to disengage the government and its regulatory tentacles from functions more properly considered the domain of the market.

The potential for this to transform the regulatory approach that had been constructed over the earlier decades of the century was considerable. However, while the market-based focus of recent decades has caused some reconsideration of the nature and extent of the regulatory process, it is still the case that the preparation and dissemination of accounting information is heavily controlled by the traditional parties such as government and the accounting profession.

## Regulatory Framework

The regulatory framework describes that system of rules and principles that controls and shapes the nature and content of financial information. Because of its critical importance in modern society, financial information has always attracted the interest of regulators. This has been true particularly since the early years of the last century. At that time the need to streamline and harmonize the flow of accounting information became apparent as the potential for accounting information to influence decisions of great importance became apparent.

The first section of this chapter outlines the regulatory apparatus as it has emerged in the Anglo-American world. It begins with an examination of the system that applies in the US, a model that has influenced the regulatory process in much of the developed world. It then deals with the system applying in the UK. Finally, it looks at the increasingly important role of the International Accounting Standards Committee (IASC).

## US

One of the catalysts shaping the regulatory environment of the 20th century was the crash of the Wall Street stock market on October 24, 1929. In the reaction to the supposedly unregulated market that was identified as a significant factor in this crash, the Roosevelt administration embarked upon a National Recovery Programme, known as the New Deal. This had as one of its core principles, the need for a greater regulation of capital markets. This was in line with the general thrust of US government commitment to control via regulation, as distinct from the interventionist model that led to extensive nationalization in contemporary Europe.

As part of this process the US government set up the Securities and Exchange Commission (SEC) and charged it with the task of regulating both the stock market itself and its constituent parts, one of which was the financial reporting process. As evidence of its seriousness the government appointed Joseph Kennedy, father of the future president, and soon to be ambassador to Great Britain, as the SEC's first chairman. When critics objected that Kennedy was a notorious speculator and, therefore, not acceptable, Roosevelt replied that these were the very credentials needed for the job.

Prior to the inauguration of the SEC there were little or no standards governing the content of corporate financial reports. The scope that this gave companies to produce financial reports to suit their own purposes was identified as a critical feature of the *laissez-faire* regime that had precipitated the crash. Under the Securities Act (1933) and the Securities Exchange Act (1934) all companies whose securities were traded publicly were required to file reports with the SEC. This had the effect of imposing a certain level of uniform disclosure on companies, intended to provide investors with the information necessary to make informed decisions about their investments.

---

**In practice:**

The following anecdote illustrates the relatively uncontrolled nature of financial reporting at the time of the Wall Street Crash in 1929:

*In 1928 a utilities company in the US prepared three sets of financial statements: one for internal use which showed a loss; one for shareholders which showed a small profit; and one for its bankers which not only showed a large profit but omitted any mention of various loans from other sources.*

---

Directly answerable to Congress, the SEC has developed into one of the most effective and potent regulatory agencies in the US. It is comprised of five commissioners, one of whom acts as chairman, and has a team of lawyers, accountants, analysts and others who monitor the companies under its aegis. In all a staff of approximately 3,000 monitors the 13,000 public companies within its remit. (There are almost 4 million US corporations in all.) A system of heavy penalties ensures, however, that much of the onus for securing compliance is placed directly upon companies themselves and their financial advisors.

Although it has occasionally issued standards, the SEC has been content to delegate to the private sector the task of determining Generally Accepted Accounting Principles (GAAP). In this process the American Institute of Certified Public Accountants (AICPA), as the pre-eminent accounting body in the US, has played an important role. In 1939, having worked closely with the New York Stock Exchange on a number of mutually important issues, the AICPA established the Committee on Accounting Procedure and the Committee on Accounting Terminology. These were crucial in developing a culture that recognized the importance of a uniform set of accounting practices devised by the accounting profession. Between 1939 and 1959 these committees issued 51 Accounting Research Bulletins which, to a limited extent, represented a broadly acceptable code of accounting practice.

By the late 1950s, however, the flaws inherent in a system which merely issued pronouncements in response to problems as they arose, as distinct from promulgating a set of principles which might form the basis on which to generate a more coherent GAAP, had become apparent. In 1959, therefore, the AICPA set up the Accounting Principles Board (APB) and the Accounting Research Division. These were charged with fostering an approach which would seek to establish just such a set of coherent, unifying principles, or theoretical framework. With limited success the APB pursued this agenda until 1973, by which time it was felt necessary to establish a new standard-setting regime.

### Financial Accounting Standards Board (FASB)

The FASB, which took over many of the functions of the APB, is an independent body governed by the Financial Accounting Foundation (FAF) which is itself comprised of representatives of nine organizations, including the AICPA, the Financial Executives Institute, the Security Industry Association, the Financial Analysts Federation, various not-for-profit organizations and others. Apart from appointing the seven-member FASB and the members of the Financial Accounting Standards Advisory Council (FASAC), which advises FASB on its agenda, the FAF is responsible for generating funding for the FASB as well as championing its role and its independence.

The stated purpose of the FASB is "to establish and improve standards of financial accounting and reporting for the guidance and education of the public, including issuers, auditors, and users of financial information". Implicit in this is a recognition of the fact that the number and range of users of accounting information has been increasing, and that accounting information needs to address the interests of this broader constituency.

The role of the FASB was reinforced when the SEC explicitly confirmed that 'principles, standards and practices promulgated by the FASB will be considered by the Commission as having substantial authoritative support'.

FASB differs from its predecessors in a number of ways:

- Its membership is smaller (seven), full-time, more independent and well-compensated;
- It is more autonomous from the accounting profession;
- There is no stipulation that it should consist only of members of the AICPA;
- Passage of a standard requires only a super-majority, i.e., five out of seven in favour.

The FASB issues two types of pronouncement: Statements of Financial Accounting Concepts (SFACs) which deal with fundamental accounting concepts and principles and provide a framework within which Statements of Financial Accounting Standards (SFAS) are formulated. While SFACs are critical in providing a coherent theoretical underpinning for accounting practice, only the provisions of SFASs are regarded as constituting GAAP.

One significant feature of the FASB has been its sensitivity to social and economic changes that have highlighted the responsibilities of standard-setting bodies to an increasingly large range of users. This has been reflected not only in the make-up of the Board, but also in the adoption of a more transparent due process through which issues are expected to pass before emerging as a SFAS. The stages in this process can be summarized as follows:

1. A topic is placed on the FASB agenda by FASAC.
2. A task force is set up to identify the relevant issues.
3. The FASB technical section then investigates the topic.
4. A Discussion Memorandum is released seeking responses from the public.
5. Public hearings are conducted.
6. An Exposure Draft (ED) is released.
7. The ED is re-evaluated in the light of responses.
8. The FASB membership vote on the ED and issue a SFAS if a sufficient majority is secured.

One particularly potent element of the new structure was the establishment of an Emerging Issues Task Force (EITF). Charged with identifying potentially contentious issues and alerting the FASB, as well as resolving technical issues, particularly where these are likely to give rise to variations in accounting practice, this has proved to be a very useful mechanism for dealing proactively with current issues before they have had an opportunity to generate too much confusion and disagreement.

### In practice:

That standard-setting is essentially a political process in which different groups lobby for their preferred outcome, rather than a scientific one in which "correct" accounting practices are "discovered" has already been alluded to. The following account of recent events in the US reinforces this point:

*US standard setter watching Washington and the world, by Glenn Cheney.*

*In Sebastian Junger's best-selling book, The Perfect Storm, a small fishing vessel is trapped, overwhelmed and consumed by a confluence of two massive Atlantic storms. In the US, the FASB may not be in danger of foundering, but two storms – one in Washington, DC, the other offshore – are converging, and FASB is in the middle. Just as it is pressed to devote even more attention to accounting standards – not just the nation's but the world's – the Board will have to be dedicating substantial efforts to defending private-sector standard setting in its nation's capital.*

*Last year, the US congress made it clear that private-sector standard setting was not comple-tely free of government domain. As the Board chiselled out a complex and widely criticized standard on business combinations, industry pressure inspired hearings in the US Senate and House of Representatives and a roundtable discussion with the senate banking committee. While both legislative chambers claimed to respect the FASB as a private-sector standard setter, the hearings were tinged with implications of congressional control if the standard deviated too far from the preferences of some companies, especially those of the banking and high-tech sectors.*

*...Asked if there was one thing he learned in 2000, FASB chairman Edmund L. Jenkins said: "I have learned that it is important to defend independent standard setting, that you can not take it for granted. You need to keep talking about the benefits of the capital market having sufficient information for investors to assess opportunities." With that lesson tucked in his syllabus, Jenkins expects to have FASB dedicate more time to political tactics in Washington. Unfortu-nately this will detract from efforts to fulfil the Board's real mission: to produce high-quality, non-partisan accounting standards...*

*Source: Accounting and Business, March 2001.*

# UK

By the late 1960s it had become apparent that the requirements governing the presen-tation and disclosure of financial statements in the UK were inadequate. While accountancy bodies such as the Institute of Chartered Accountants in England and Wales (ICAEW) made "recommendations" to members, accounting practice varied considerably.

At the initiative of the ICAEW, an Accounting Standards Steering Committee was formed with a view to developing a set of accounting standards. By 1971 the Institute of Chartered Accountants in Scotland (ICAS), the Institute of Chartered Accountants in Ireland (ICAI), the Association of Chartered Certified Accountants (ACCA), and the Chartered Institute of Management Accountants (CIMA), had joined the project. In 1976 this committee was reformed as the Accounting Standards Committee (ASC) under the sponsorship of the Consultative Committee of Accountancy Bodies (CCAB), a group comprising the five original sponsoring bodies plus the Chartered Institute of Public Finance Accountants (CIPFA).

### Accounting Standards Committee (ASC)

The ASC was charged with:

- Defining accounting concepts
- Narrowing differences in accounting practice; and
- Formulating best practice

By a due process which involved a degree of consultation with representatives of other interested parties, and the circulation of consultative documents called EDs, the ASC made recommendations to the CCAB, which, if it approved of them, issued these as Statements of Standard Accounting Practice (SSAPs). These were then binding on the members of the constituent bodies. Significantly, the ASC and the CCAB claimed to carry out these tasks "in the public interest", the presumption being that accountancy bodies were the ones most suited to fulfilling this role.

By the late 1980s, in the face of several high-profile corporate failures and the inability of the part-time ASC to respond more quickly to pressing issues, the CCAB appointed a committee chaired by Sir Ronald Dearing to review the standard-setting process.

The Dearing Report, issued in November 1988, contained a series of far-reaching proposals and recommendations. Specifically, it highlighted the need for:

- A standard-setting process which promoted compliance, reduced options and assisted interpretation by an emphasis on the production of standards which were based on core principles as distinct from the ASC approach of individual standards for individual issues.
- The development, following the model developed by the FASB, of a coherent conceptual framework (see Chapter 2).
- A reduction in the requirements to be met by small companies; and
- The gradual incorporation of public sector bodies within the framework.

In terms of structure, it recommended that overall responsibility for the standard-setting process be placed in the hands of a Financial Reporting Council (FRC) intended to guide the standard-setting process, ensure financing and act as a strong public champion of the standard-setting approach. It was to comprise of representatives from a number of interested parties under the chairmanship of a joint nominee of the Secretary of State for Trade and Industry and the Governor of the Bank of England. Accounting interests would be represented by members from practice, industry and the public sector, but there would also be an equal number of representatives from other interested bodies, such as the legal profession and bankers.

Mirroring the US scheme, it was envisaged that the FRC would devolve the task of devising accounting standards to a new Accounting Standards Board (ASB) under a full-time chairman and technical director, supplemented by a full-time secretariat. To address the lessons learned from the ASC's inability to deal promptly with the vast array of emerging issues it was proposed that an Urgent Issues Task Force (UITF) be set up with authority to issue non-mandatory, but authoritative, guidance on matters requiring to be addressed immediately.

Finally, to ensure prompt compliance, it was recommended that a Financial Reporting Review Panel (FRRP) be established to examine, with the support of the Stock Exchange, deviations from accepted accounting practice by large companies.

The Dearing Report received widespread support and the basic structure recommended was quickly in place. The FRC, initially under the chairmanship of Sir Ronald Dearing, and then Sir Sydney Lipworth, was established in 1990. In August 1990 the ASB, with David Tweedie as chairman, Allan Cook as technical director, and seven other members, came into being. This was followed shortly afterwards by the inauguration of the FRRP. The ASB, in turn, inaugurated the UITF.

### Accounting Standards Board (ASB)

One of the priorities of the ASB was to emphasize that, unlike its predecessor, it issued standards – called Financial Reporting Standards (FRSs) – in its own right. However, it was also anxious to avoid confusion over the status of SSAPs issued by the ASC. As a result it formally adopted the 22 extant SSAPs. It then set about issuing new standards in line with its stated aim to "establish and improve standards of financial accounting and reporting, for the benefit of users, preparers and auditors of financial information".

In pursuing this agenda, the ASB has decided to adopt policies designed to ensure that standards:

- Are the product of a research and consultative process which is sensitive to issues such as usefulness, timeliness and the relative costs and benefits of the proposed standard.

- Reflect national and international environments to the extent that they take cognizance of current UK law and EU directives.

- Support the IASC in its endeavours to harmonize international financial reporting.

- Are clearly expressed and supported by a coherent analysis and rationale.

- Result in information which *faithfully represents* the underlying commercial reality; and

- Reflect the desire for an evolutionary, as distinct from revolutionary, approach.

The procedure leading to the issuing of a standard reflects this determination to ensure as wide and informed a consultative process as possible. The sequence usually is:

1. Identification of issues by FRC.

2. Circulation of Discussion Paper by ASB which sets out issues, invites comment and encourages involvement.

3. Research and consultation leading to formulation of Exposure Draft (ED).

4. Circulation of Financial Reporting ED (FRED), an advanced draft of intended standard.

5. Adoption of FRS.

### Financial Reporting Review Panel (FRRP)

FRSs and SSAPs are authoritative statements detailing the manner in which specific types of events should be accounted for. It is assumed, therefore, that compliance with these standards is necessary in order to produce financial statements that present a "true and fair view". Only in very exceptional circumstances will a departure be either necessary or allowed.

In circumstances where the provisions of legislation have not been complied with, then the FRRP is authorized to intervene. However, it usually does not seek out such cases, waiting instead for matters to be drawn to its attention.

The FRRP, with support from the Department of Trade and Industry (DTI) and the Stock Exchange, provides a very effective disciplinary component of the regulatory structure. In fact, the bulk of cases that the FRRP has reviewed have been resolved by obtaining the agreement of the companies concerned to amend their accounts:

## Powers of Persuasion

There is a story, perhaps apocryphal, but widely repeated in the City, which illustrates the powers and limitations of the FRRP, the investigative wing of the regulatory structure which oversees company accounts in the UK.

...Edwin Glasgow QC, the panel's chairman, is in a meeting with the board of a company whose clearly defective accounts had been drawn to the panel's attention. The conversation has degenerated, so the story goes, into an arcane discussion of a particular technical point.

Glasgow, a lawyer who prides himself on a no-nonsense style, eventually suspects he is being blinded by science. "Do I get the impression, gentlemen", he says, "that, on the whole, you would rather discuss this matter with an accountant?" There are sage nods from the other side of the table. "Fine", says Glasgow, rising from his seat. "On the whole, I'd rather talk to a lawyer. I'll see you in court."

> The issue did not go to court – an illustration of the panel's power as a deterrent...
> The panel has its supporters and critics. The supporters believe it is a minor miracle
> of arm's length self-regulation. Its critics believe that it chooses easy targets, is
> afraid to test big issues it might lose in court, and works so slowly that by the
> time amended accounts are published investors have acted on misleading data.
>
> Source: Financial Times, February 20, 1997.

At an extreme, however, for example in cases where companies refuse to comply with requests to revise accounts, the FRRP can apply to the courts for an order requiring the directors of the company to conform. And, as the following "In practice" box explains, where it takes this action it usually achieves the desired result.

---

### In practice:

**FRRP threatens legal action**

*The FRRP threatened property and airport management group Wiggins with legal action after the company failed to amend its accounts to the oversight body's satisfaction.*

*Following what was only the third such warning from the FRRP, Wiggins agreed to amend its treatment of costs and timing of revenues for its 1999 and 2000 accounts, despite assurances from its advisers that its accounting practices were correct. The company had already restated its figures for the year ending March 31, 2000. The company agreed to issue revised accounts setting out the financial effect of any changes. These are due out this month. "The company will work closely with the Panel with a view to satisfying the Panel in relation to the issues which it has raised," it said in a statement last December, "and thereby avoiding the need for the Panel to consider seeking a ruling from the court."*

*Wiggins' share price dropped by 19% after the FRRP said it was taking legal action; however, it recovered somewhat when the company announced its intention to amend its accounts...*

*Source: Accountancy, February 2001.*

---

### Urgent Issues Task Force (UITF)

The UITF operates as a committee of the ASB comprised of experts in the area of financial reporting. The maximum number of members is 16. Its role is to complement the ASB by issuing binding pronouncements in situations in which there is uncertainty over the correct accounting procedure or the application of company law provisions.

Relying on principles enunciated by the ASB rather than specific provisions, it attempts to reach a voluntary consensus. These are then disseminated in the form of Abstracts, although it cannot issue such an Abstract if more than two members vote against. None of its pronouncements are to be interpreted as superseding an accounting standard. Instead, its remit envisages it dealing with serious divergences from accepted practice, or anticipating developments likely to give rise to such divergences. In recent years, in response to what was seen as precipitate action in many cases, the UITF has adopted a policy of issuing Abstracts in draft form for comment.

## International Accounting Standards Committee (IASC)

Increased international trade, coupled with the growing sense of globalization, resulted in pressure from various sources for a greater standardization of international accounting practice. This led in 1973 to the formation of the IASC, which by 1999 had representatives from accounting bodies in almost 100 countries, as well as other organizations with an interest in the financial reporting process.[1]

The IASC has by now developed into a very significant player in the regulatory environment. Essentially, it has set itself the task of developing and disseminating a globally acceptable set of accounting standards in relation to the financial reporting process as well as the harmonization of existing approaches. To this end it issues International Accounting Standards (IASs).

One of the principal criticisms of early IASs was that, in allowing great diversity of choice, they undermined the goal of comparability. US regulators were particularly keen to emphasize this point, hoping in the process to see FASB emerge as the global standard setter. The IASC responded that its initial priority was the elimination of unacceptable practices, a process that would have to precede any attempt to develop a global accounting standards regime.

As the following extract explains, however, the whole process of the development of standards for an international stage must also be considered within a political context. In particular, the skirmishing for supremacy between the IASC, FASB and EU has all the hallmarks of a battle between different accounting cultures and regimes:

## Accounting Worlds Apart? By Julia Irvine

In April this year, World Bank vice president Jules Muis delivered a personal and highly entertaining speech in Washington about the state of the world's accounting, auditing and financial architecture. It was, he said, an "expressionist account of an impressionist look" at the issues. Since the Asian crisis, two changes have taken place, he said: first, development economists have discovered quality accounting and auditing standards as economic fundamentals; and second, the world's most powerful have pondered the importance of robust accounting and auditing standards'. "It is like astronauts, having been away from home for too

---

[1] Another international forum for national standard setters is the G4+1 comprising representatives from US, UK, Canada, Australia and New Zealand. The IASC has observer status.

long, rediscovering mother earth; and then, getting closer to it, discovering that there is more to it than the deep blue sea; until they land on hard soil and discover the powers of gravitational force and of good and evil."

The pressure is on to build sound financial architecture, while at the same time dissecting the component parts – among them accounting and auditing – to ensure that they are of good quality. "In this landscape", he continued, "accounting is traditionally being seen as the language of business; and since language is power, and power is money, and money is what the capital market is all about, it is not void of self-interest and, believe it or not, emotion... Hence vested interest is born; and pressure to stick to the initial language builds up; and change aversion becomes a reality. Therefore, tribal disputes between competing schools of thought, driven by gatekeepers of financial markets, are part and parcel of that world our friend the astronaut returns to."

Mr Muis sets the context for the battle over who gets to set the world's accounting standards rather well – although describing it as a "tribal dispute" is questionable. Certainly, it is an issue for the accounting profession, but one with major economic and political consequences – whoever wins – that will cause significant reverberations around the world for many years to come. The two major contenders for the title may be the IASC and the US FASB, but they have become, in one sense, figureheads for a battle between the US and Europe for global dominance.

Source: Accountancy International, July 1999.

In 1995 the IASC received a substantial boost when it signed an agreement with the International Organization of Securities Commissions (IOSCO) to develop a set of new standards which, with the agreement of IOSCO, would form an acceptable basis for reporting purposes for companies with cross-border listings.

More recently, under the leadership of Sir Brian Carsberg, the IASC has adopted a different structure intended to broaden its governance and decision-making structure. As part of this process it will now be called The International Accounting Standards Board (IASB) and its standards will be called International Financial Reporting Standards (IFRS). It has also issued a range of standards that have gradually come to be seen as having international credibility. This, in turn, has led to a less hostile attitude from the US and EU as well as tentative approval from IOSCO.

As the following article outlines, this momentum is likely to be maintained with the appointment of Sir David Tweedie as new Board Chairman, and the EU's stated intention of requiring listed companies to comply with IASs by 2005:

## The Standard Bearer

...And how will it work? "The national standard setters will be the eyes and ears of IASC," he (Tweedie) responds. The IOSCO agreement, in principle, to international standards and Europe's stated intention that by 2005, all companies listed in Europe must comply with international standards, give the new board 5 years to arrive at standards which are globally accepted. He emphasizes that IASC is not intended as a dominating body but a partnership with national standard setters including the UK ASB. He regards enforcement as a challenge but emphasizes the growing confidence among analysts with international standards. "Standard setting is political accounting," he says and the new IASC's job is to meld different views into one set of standards. "We have got to get this IOSCO agreement stitched up," he adds, "so let us find out what are the core problems with the present standards and set up an improvement project. If there are minor differences which can be dealt with by a quick fix, let us do that."

The new Board must also consider, as a priority, the critical differences between standards in the major world economies and seek to make the best rules the global ones. He acknowledges there may be major disagreement on certain accounting issues, for example, stock options and concedes there is much to do very quickly. He counsels that the EU should rapidly make its views known to the new Board if it wishes to accomplish standards which accommodate the reservations implied by its recently suggested endorsement mechanism for European standards, but says, "if Europe tinkers, we do not have global standards".

He knows there is much to be done in developing economies and suggests that there will be a place for their accountants on the new 30 person advisory committee which will be consulted by the board of trustees. He says the professions too have a strong role in spotting the accountancy stars of the future and thinks that there could be room for adapted international standards for SMEs, with perhaps fewer disclosure requirements. His basic objective is very simple. One set of standards, accepted world-wide. He knows that without legal compulsion there must be buy-in from all stakeholders and he accepts that there will be "furious argument" over what the standards should be, but, "I am pretty sure we are going to succeed and it will save the financial market billions".

Time will tell and perhaps there is the hint of a last chance saloon in Tweedie's appointment. But even in the unlikely event that the price for success were becoming the most hated accountant in the world, it is pretty clear that he would regard this as a price worth paying.

Source: Accounting and Business, January 2001.

The role of the IASC, particularly as it relates to the issue of harmonization, is dealt with in more detail in Chapter 15.

## UK Legislative Framework

The regulation of company accounts by statute originated with the Joint Stock Companies Act, 1844. Modern company accounts are governed by more recent legislation, however. The Companies Act 1948 (CA48) laid down some of the basic principles relating to disclosure requirements that still apply today.

The Companies Act 1981 (CA81) was significant in a number of respects. Principal amongst these was the fact that it was a response to the EU Fourth Directive, which was an attempt by the EU to harmonize elements of company law throughout member states. It contained detailed specifications with regard to the format, content and publication of accounts. One of its legacies is the detailed format to which companies must conform when preparing and publishing their accounts in the Annual Report. This is discussed in more detail in Chapter 6.

In the wake of the consolidation of these various statutes into the Companies Act 1985 (CA85), this statute, as amended (somewhat confusingly) by the Companies Act 1989 (CA89), now forms the principal legislative framework for companies in the UK.

The question of the legal status of accounting standards was addressed in CA85 which provided that large companies were required to state whether or not the accounts had been prepared "in accordance with applicable accounting standards" and to detail and explain any departures. This was extended by CA89, which provides that:

- Accounts must state that they have been prepared in accordance with appropriate accounting standards.
- The term "accounting standards" as used by the act refers to "SSAPs issued by such body or bodies as may be prescribed by regulation"; and
- The Secretary of State or other interested parties may apply to the courts to order the revision of accounts considered defective.

While the detailed provisions of these acts as they relate to specific areas of accounting practice or disclosure requirements will be dealt with in later chapters, an analysis of these key pieces of company legislation makes it possible to identify a number of themes in the legislative framework that applies in the UK:

- There has been an increasing emphasis on greater disclosure by companies.
- Although they have decreased in recent years, attempts by the EU to impose harmonization in relation to company disclosures have had an impact, particularly in relation to the presentation, content and disclosure aspects of company reports.
- Statutory recognition has now been granted to accounting standards.
- The "true and fair" consideration (see Chapter 5) now forms a critical benchmark in assessing the disclosures made by a company.

## Nature of Companies

Companies are one of the most common forms of business entity in the UK. A company is defined as "a corporation that has an existence, rights and duties separate from its members (shareholders)".

Companies, other than those formed by Royal Charter or by act of parliament, are formed by registration under CA85. This involves the promoters of the company filing the following documents with the Registrar of Companies in England and Wales (or the Registrar of Companies in Scotland):

**Memorandum of Association**: This document essentially lays down the rules governing the company in its dealings with those outside of itself. The disclosure of the following is required:

- Name of the company
- Country in which Registered Office will be situated
- Objects of the company, i.e., the activities which the company may undertake
- Whether the liability of the members is limited or not
- The authorized share capital level and the nominal value of shares
- Whether it is a public company
- A list of the initial shareholders

**Articles of Association**: This contains the rules and regulations pertaining to the internal workings of the company, and should include details of the following:

- Share capital: the different classes of share, restrictions on transfer rights and the mechanism by which authorized share capital levels might be altered (see Chapter 9)
- Annual General Meetings: rules regarding the period of notice and procedures to be followed.
- Directors: information as to their duties, powers and the manner of their election, removal and retirement.
- Dividends.
- Procedures to be followed on winding-up.

Companies that submit these details to the Registrar of Companies will receive a Certificate of Incorporation at which point the company assumes a legal identity separate from its members.

### Limited Companies

Companies can be classified as either "Limited" or "Unlimited"[2]. However, most companies are limited companies, that is, the liability of the shareholders is limited. The two most common means by which this is achieved are:

- Guarantee: each member guarantees to provide a specified amount in the event of the company going into liquidation. This form is most commonly used by charities.

---

[2] Another form of company is a close company. Such a company is one that is under the control of five or less persons, together with their associates, or is under the control of its directors. The Stock Exchange requires listed companies to state whether or not the company is a close company. A listed company is deemed not to be a close company if more than 35% of its voting power is beneficially held by the public.

- Shares: the shareholder's liability is limited to any amount payable in respect of shares purchased. If, therefore, the shareholder has paid fully for any shares purchased, there is no further liability. It is the method most commonly adopted by companies. The most common types of shares are ordinary shares and preference shares (see Chapter 9).

### Private Companies

The vast bulk of companies are private limited companies, using the abbreviation Ltd. All such companies must prepare full statutory accounts for their shareholders, although those private companies classified as either small or medium may file less detailed information with the Registrar of Companies. Under Section 13(1) of CA89 companies are designated as small or medium, respectively if they satisfy two of the following criteria:

|  | Small | Medium |
| --- | --- | --- |
| Turnover not exceeding | £2.8 million | £11.2 million |
| Assets not exceeding | £1.4 million | £5.6 million |
| Number of employees not exceeding | 50 | 250 |

These financial thresholds are updated regularly in the light of inflation.

### Public Companies

A public company is one which:

- Is stated to be such in its Memorandum of Association.
- Is limited by shares or guarantee.
- Has a minimum issued share capital of £50,000, at least 25% of which has been fully paid up (with any share premium fully paid up).

The name of such a company must always end with the title Public Limited Company, abbreviated as "plc".

## Company Law Review

Conscious of the fact that legislation dating from the mid-19th century can no longer realistically be expected to meet the needs of 21st century business, the DTI has recently initiated a Company Law Review project. As the following extract highlights, the Review is likely to propose far-reaching change and dramatically impact the reporting practices and cultures of businesses.

## Put Gladstone to Rest: Review of Company Law Unveiled Last Week is Long Overdue writes Martin Scicluna

The company law review unveiled by the government last week provides a chance to create a legal framework that will take UK companies and their shareholders into the 21st century. The logic for reform is compelling. The growth in the economic wealth and influence of the corporate sector places company law at the heart of our economy. A sound, forward-looking legal framework is fundamental to national competitiveness.

The law as it stands falls well short of meeting those needs. The process of rule-setting is slow and inflexible – the law introduced by William Gladstone in 1844 has hardly changed, owing to a reluctance to recognize the developments of the last century. Changes made so far have merely added extra provisions to the existing framework. As a result, this lack of transparency affects the operation of market forces and the ability to make economic decisions...

Source: Financial Times; March 23, 2000.

The proposals of the Company Law Review in relation to financial reporting are discussed in more detail in Chapter 18.

## Stock Exchange Requirements

It is a common misconception that every plc is listed on the Stock Exchange. This is not necessarily the case, although only a plc can achieve such a listing. (Technically it is its securities, such as shares, as distinct from the plc itself, which is "listed".) In fact, there are over 13,000 plcs, but only about 2,500 of these are quoted on the London Stock Exchange.

The minimum requirements to which a company must conform in order to achieve a listing, i.e., to have its securities, such as its shares, debentures, unsecured loan stocks and warrants, admitted to the market, are listed in Part 4 of the Financial Services Act 1986. This implemented various EU Directives relating to the admission and regulation of listed companies across the EU. Together with the Stock Exchange's own rules, these are detailed in the London Stock Exchange's *Listing Rules*, also known as the "Yellow Book".

### Obtaining a Listing

There are various means by which a plc may obtain a listing. However, as a prerequisite, before allowing a plc to have its securities traded, the Stock Exchange must satisfy itself that these securities are marketable. There are, therefore, two minimum criteria that must be satisfied before a company can have its securities considered for listing:

- The expected total market value for the security must be at least £700,000 in the case of shares and £200,000 in the case of debt.
- At least 25% of the security must be in the hands of the general public.

If the plc satisfies the Stock Exchange under these headings then it can seek a listing. The principal ways in which a company can obtain a listing are summarized in Chapter 4 of the Yellow Book:

1. *Offer for sale*: this involves new and/or existing securities being issued to the public via a sponsoring bank or broker. The invitation can be either directly to the public, for example by newspaper advertisement in which case it is called an Offer for Subscription, or by means of a Tender Offer where interested parties are invited to tender at a price equal to or greater than a minimum issue price, with the shares then issued at one "striking price".

2. *Placing*: there is no offer to the public as securities are placed with clients of the sponsor.

3. *Intermediaries offer*: securities are offered to intermediaries who then allocate them to clients.

4. *Introduction*: this is a relatively unusual mechanism and involves a company which already has securities traded outside of the Stock Exchange being granted permission to have them traded on the Exchange. Companies already listed on overseas exchanges most commonly employ this method.

---

**In practice:**

**Tenon to raise £40 million through share offer**

*Accountancy consolidator Tenon – currently in negotiation about five more acquisitions – aims to raise £40.65 million through offering over 30 million shares at 130p per share... The placing and offer will raise around £39.2 million after expenses, and add to the firm's £17 milliom in the bank. Tenon is also seeking shareholder approval for the adoption of an approved employee share ownership plan.*

*The consolidator's chief executive Ian Buckley (added): "One year after the initial £50 million fund raising it is clear that the concept of becoming the service provider of choice for medium sized businesses and their owners throughout the UK is rapidly becoming a reality. We are greatly encouraged by the number of high quality firms that have approached us with a view to investing their businesses in Tenon. We are delighted with the enormous vote of confidence that we have received from existing and new institutional investors, evidenced by their participation in our Placing, despite the prevailing market conditions. All our existing UK Tenon Shareholders have an opportunity to participate through the Open Offer."*

*Tenon shares have been hovering around the 150p mark since its flotation last year...*

*Source: AccountingWEB, March 30, 2001.*

## Prospectus

Chapter 6 of the Yellow Book specifies the Listing Particulars. These are the details that must be supplied to the Stock Exchange before admittance, but after the two minimum criteria specified earlier have been satisfied. This information is usually included in the Prospectus, which is the document that invites prospective investors to participate. In the case of an Initial Public Offering (IPO) the Prospectus must be freely available at a UK address to any member of the public.

It should contain information relating to the following:

- General information on the company, its history, details of its activities, management and future prospects, including profit and dividend forecasts.
- The nature of the offer and the purposes to which the proceeds will be put.
- The company's share capital and existing indebtedness.
- The company's directors, secretary, auditor, advisers, solicitors, bankers and brokers.
- Profit and loss account and balance sheet for the previous 3 years.
- Subsidiary and associated companies.
- Share capital and share options.
- Directors' interests and service contracts.
- Material contracts.
- Pending litigation.
- Articles of Association.

Designed to ensure that a company makes available sufficient details regarding its history, performance and prospects to enable the public to make an assessment as to the value of its securities, a Prospectus provides very useful additional detail for any analyst or potential shareholder. Where such a document is available it should be referred to when attempting an analysis of a company.

## Continuing Obligations

The Yellow Book also provides details of the requirements imposed on companies once securities have been issued and trading has begun. For instance, companies are required to submit for approval to the Stock Exchange all circulars intended for distribution to holders of securities, as well as notices of meetings, proxy forms and advertisements intended for holders of bearer securities.

Companies must also provide the Stock Exchange with details of:

- Profit announcements
- Dividends
- Acquisitions

- Changes in directors; and
- Any other information necessary to allow the public to evaluate the position of the company

These rules also require that where forecasts are made that differ by 10% or more from the eventual outcome, an explanation of the difference must be provided. Additional disclosures are also required in respect of borrowings and investments.

Furthermore, if any information exists which can no longer be kept secret and which could result in significant share movements, then the company must inform the Companies Announcements Office immediately and disclose the relevant information.

## Disclosure Requirements

The Stock Exchange plays a significant role in determining the nature and content of a plc's Annual Report. This is because it imposes considerable disclosure requirements that are often over and above those imposed by legislation or required under accounting standards. For instance, in relation to each of the following categories, Stock Exchange rules require these disclosures:

- Shares and shareholders:

  - Any authority for the purchase of its own shares by the company and any purchases made other than through the market.
  - Participation of a parent company in any placing of shares.
  - Shares issued for cash other than pro-rata to existing shareholders.
  - Any dividends waived by shareholders.
  - Holdings, other than by directors, of more than 3% of any class of voting capital.

- Directors:

  - The beneficial and non-beneficial interests of each director in the company's shares and options.
  - Biographical details of each non-executive director.
  - Any emoluments waived by directors.

- Contracts:

  - Any significant contracts in which a director is materially interested.
  - Any significant contract with a corporate shareholder having 30% or more of the voting power.

---

**In practice:**

---

The increased disclosure that is required in respect of directors' remuneration reflects increasing public concern over the level of their remuneration. As the following report highlights, this is now of such public importance that the government intends to supplement the Stock Exchange's provisions:

**DTI to legislate over directors pay**

*Stephen Byers, the Trade and Industry Secretary has told Parliament that the DTI received 140 responses to its consultative document on directors' remuneration, with most respondents supporting the Government's proposals to promote a more effective linkage between performance and boardroom pay. As a result, the Government will now introduce secondary legislation under the Companies Act 1985 which will require quoted companies incorporated in Great Britain to publish a report on directors' remuneration as part of the company's annual reporting cycle.*

*Companies will be required to disclose within the report details of individual directors' remuneration packages, the role of the board's remuneration committee and the board's remuneration policy, including information on performance linkage, directors' service contracts and compensation payments. Byers went on to say that directors should be accountable to shareholders on remuneration, not least because boards of directors face a conflict of interest in relation to directors' remuneration. He said the Government continues to be concerned that many quoted companies are failing to respond adequately to the best practice recommendations on accountability, but it is also aware that the Company Law Review is looking at a number of issues in adjacent areas...*

*Source: AccountingWEB, March 9, 2001.*

---

Taken together with the disclosure requirements imposed by statue and accounting standards, therefore, the level of information that must be disclosed by a plc in its Annual Report is quite extensive. This reflects a general tendency in modern reporting culture to insist on greater and more focused disclosure by corporate entities.

## Alternative Investment Market (AIM)

The funding requirements and ambitions of smaller and medium public limited companies differ radically from those of larger entities. For this reason the London Stock Exchange has created the AIM which commenced trading in 1995.

This market is less demanding in its regulatory emphasis. Nevertheless, although the amount of documentation required is less onerous, companies seeking a listing must still supply a Prospectus that entails considerable disclosure and expense. They must also make price sensitive information available promptly as well as interim figures and details of directors' share dealings.

However, no minimum capitalization levels are imposed, and it is not necessary to employ a sponsoring merchant bank or broker. For this reason it is attractive to small or medium-sized family firms with the ambition and capacity to obtain a listing, but with no appetite for a listing on the larger official market.

## Summary

Accountants in the US, UK and elsewhere have traditionally played a key role in the regulation of accounting information. In the Anglo-American world this has usually taken the form of accounting standard-setting bodies being delegated authority to produce GAAP within a broader legislative and regulatory environment.

The large number and range of entities involved in the regulatory process attest to the significance of accounting information in modern society. These include:

- Standard-setting bodies: by means of accounting standards which delineate accounting practice.
- Parliament: by means of legislation.
- European Commission: by means of Directives and initiatives designed to facilitate a more harmonized perspective.
- Accounting bodies: by means of their direct involvement as preparers, auditors and disseminators of accounting information.
- Stock Exchange: by means of monitoring those companies whose securities are listed.
- International accounting entities: such as the IASC.
- Other interested parties: such as IOSCO.

The result, particularly in the case of large plcs, is that the Annual Report must include a vast amount of information intended to satisfy the information requirements of a wide range of users. And it is this that makes the Annual Report such a significant document when attempting to analyse the financial status, performance and prospects of any large corporate entity.

# Review Questions

## Question 1
In the article quoted earlier in this chapter, "The Standard Bearer", David Tweedie makes the comment that "Standard setting is political accounting". Explain what this means and discuss the implications of viewing the standard-setting process in this way.

## Question 2
"Accounting information emerges in the form that it does as a result of a process that is essentially political, i.e., it is determined by a process in which different interests lobby for their favoured practices. Those with the most influence, whether commercial, social or political, usually prevail. In no way, therefore, can accounting practice be considered 'scientific', in the sense that one can discover a 'correct' or 'immutable' set of principles and practices. Accountancy is an art not a science." Explain what this means.

## Question 3
Identify the principal characteristics of the US regulatory framework. Explain the role of the SEC in this system.

## Question 4
Outline the way in which the UK system of regulation has evolved over recent decades and identify similarities between the UK and US systems.

## Question 5
The IASC is emerging as a significant "player" in the global regulatory environment. Explain how this has happened and why the EU is not entirely happy with the way in which the influence of the IASC is developing.

## Question 6
Explain the role which legislation plays in determining the way in which accounting information is presented. In particular, identify the principal emphases of UK legislation as they relate to accounting information.

## Question 7
Distinguish between the following:
- Public and private companies
- Limited and unlimited companies
- Small, medium and large companies

## Question 8
The London Stock Exchange is playing an increasingly proactive role in the area of accounting disclosure. Identify some examples of this and assess the significance of the Stock Exchange's willingness to act in this way.

## Question 9
"In a free-market economy it is somewhat ironic that the form of accounting disclosures is so heavily regulated". Explain.

## Case Studies

### Case 1

David Tweedie has recently been replaced at the ASB by Mary Keegan. The following article outlines some of the issues she is likely to have to confront and places particular emphasis on the international context within which the ASB will now have to operate. In the context of the regulatory environment outlined earlier in this chapter, identify and discuss the role that the ASB is likely to play in the future.

## Interview – Keegan Aims for Convergence

*With her wide international experience as motivation, Mary Keegan, the ASB's new chairman, is eager to work towards global accounting convergence. In fact, it's part of the reason she took the job. By Peter Williams.*

It's already obvious that one item – the convergence of national accounting standards – is going to dominate the agenda of the ASB over the next few years. Mary Keegan, the incoming chairman of the ASB, knows this only too well. "I took the job because I am an ardent believer in the convergence of accounting standards to a global norm. Chairing the ASB gives me an opportunity to be part of that", she says.

Taking on the chairmanship of the ASB at this time is a logical progression for Keegan because, as a technical partner with PricewaterhouseCoopers, she has been active on the issue for the past few years. As a result, she already knows that the UK is in a unique position. "From the UK perspective, we have a chance to drive the convergence and ensure that those standards are good", she says.

Keegan also understands how much patience and determination it will take to make a contribution to this tortuous process. "Every time financial results are posted on the world-wide web you are presenting figures to a world-wide audience", she says. "For clarity you need to be able to use a common language, yet we are a long way from that."

In the past, standard setting has seemed an Anglo-Saxon affair, represented over the past few years by the G4 grouping (US, Canada, UK, Australia and New Zealand, the G4's fifth member). Keegan wants to create a more inclusive process that brings in accounting standard setter friends from continental Europe that she has made during her time with FEE, the European accounting organization. And, diplomatically, she refuses to cast the European Commission as the major obstacle. "Europe is an unknown quantity and we are still waiting for the EC regulation to see what the mechanism might be", she says.

All this talk of international standard setting can leave even the most internationally minded FD feeling a little left out, and, perhaps knowing this, Keegan makes clear her determination to keep consulting her wide network of contacts within UK business.

Of course, the international connections on Keegan's CV must have been a big plus during the interview process, but it can not have harmed her cause that she is a member of the technical committee of the Hundred Group of Finance Directors. Over the past few years, FDs have mainly been supportive of the work of the ASB, but that continuing support can not be taken for granted. Keegan is realistic enough to know she is not likely to win universal approbation all of the time but even so, her close contact with the Hundred Group surely will not do any harm when trying to keep relationships sweet.

This mostly good relationship with FDs has been built up at the same time that the ASB has adopted a stance of being tough on bad financial reporting and the causes of bad financial reporting, and Keegan says she will not relax on that approach.

However, she also wishes to maintain the UK tradition of avoiding the US cook-book approach to writing accounting standards. "There are always going to be occasions when people are testing the boundaries, but we do not want to be in a position where we have to redraw those boundaries. We do not want more rules", she says. "I would encourage the business and audit communities to ensure they police the existing boundaries."

Nevertheless, Keegan argues that accounting rules and standards must change to keep pace with the way business is changing. She cites the issue of sorting out the principles – and the practicalities – of revenue recognition as one example of this.

Keegan says that she is taking over the chair of the ASB while the organization is in a "position of strength". But it is clear that the ASB could be undergoing radical change in the next year or so, particularly if the idea of charging it with the role of becoming the UK's company law commission becomes a reality. In principle, Keegan says, she is keen on this idea, but it is clear that many of the practicalities have yet to be finalized.

But no matter how important the domestic scene, Keegan's main focus is still likely to be the international agenda – and she has her work cut out. Last month, the GAAP 2000 survey of the differences between International Accounting Standards and the standards in 53 countries showed that the world is still a long way away from the kind of convergence that she has in mind. How quickly and how effectively that gap is closed will go a long way to determining her success as the ASB's second chairman.

Source: Accountancy Age, February 1, 2001.

## Case 2

The three principal regulatory bodies dealt with in this chapter have excellent web sites. Access these at the following addresses and explore their contents.

   FASB: www.rutgers.edu/Accounting/raw/fasb/
   ASB: www.asb.org.uk/
   IASC: www.iasc.org.uk/

# CONCEPTUAL CONTEXT

When you have completed this chapter you will understand:

- The meaning and importance of a conceptual framework.

- How the development of accounting has been hampered by the lack of such a framework.

- How specific issues such as "recognition" and "measurement" can only be addressed in the context of such a framework.

- That considerable strides have been made in recent decades in addressing this deficiency.

## Van Dumholtz' Fleas

Assumptions structure one's thinking, and hence at times obstruct the seeing of certain "obvious" phenomena and ensure the seeing of certain "non-existent" phenomena....

For example, chemists before Lavoisier did not observe many of the phenomena associated with rust and oxidation, since their theoretical assumptions concerning phlogiston made it unlikely that these phenomena would be noticed. Biologists before Harvey, though they could not find any, were convinced there were holes between the left and right halves of the heart, since their theories pointed to such a conclusion.

Scientists often behave like Van Dumholtz does in the following story, though the esoteric nature of their concerns helps to keep this relatively secret.

Van Dumholtz has two large jars before him, one containing many fleas, the other empty. He gently removes a flea from the flea jar, places it on the table before the empty jar, steps back, and commands "Jump", whereupon the flea jumps into the empty jar. Methodically he gently removes each flea, places it on the table, says "Jump", and the flea jumps into the originally empty jar.

When he has transferred all the fleas in this way, he removes one from the now full jar, carefully pulls off its back legs, and places it on the table before the original jar. He commands, "Jump," but the flea does not move. He takes another flea from the jar, carefully pulls off its back legs, and places it on the table. Again he commands "Jump," but the flea does not move. Methodically he goes through this same procedure with the remaining fleas, and gets the same results.

Van Dumholtz beamingly records in his notebook: "A flea, when its back legs are pulled off, cannot hear."

Source: J.A. Paulos, *I Think, Therefore I Laugh*, Allen Lane, 2000, pp. 129–30

## Introduction

In the same way that these misfortunate fleas have arrived at their final hapless state, a variety of accounting practices have evolved over time. And with the "flawless" logic of Van Dumholtz, accountants have sought, *post facto*, to make sense of them by identifying common threads and themes – usually with little success.

One of the reasons for this failure is that accounting practices have evolved over a number of centuries in response to the demands of commerce and business, not as the logical outflow of an integrated discipline with a coherent "conceptual framework".

A conceptual framework may be described as "a unified and generally accepted set of theories and principles that provide a foundation from which specific practices and methods can be deduced". In other words it is fundamental set of principles, somewhat like a "constitution", or a coherent system of thought about a discipline. In the case of accounting it relates to that basic set of unifying principles, if any, which underlies accounting practice.

Although often misunderstood by practitioners and dismissed as an academic irrelevance, a conceptual framework would impact centrally upon the practice of accounting, the content and manner of its communication and, consequently, the social and economic impact of accounting information.

For instance, such a set of principles would be influential in determining how the discipline deals with issues such as:

- How transactions should be accounted for
- Which events should be accounted for
- What set of user-requirements financial accounting should aim to satisfy
- How financial information should be communicated to users

Unlike disciplines such as economics which can trace their origins to great theoretical works such as Adam Smith's *The Wealth of Nations*, and their subsequent impact to a series of theoretical models, such as those credited to Keynes, accounting cannot lay claim to such a prestigious pedigree.

Consigned during its formative years to the role of servant of business, it invariably responded to, rather than shaped, commercial demands. Thus, for example, rather than frame a set of principles which would allow them to determine what to include in a set of accounts, practitioners responded to capitalism's need for statements which measured wealth by devising the balance sheet, and changes in wealth by devising the profit and loss account. It was, in many senses, a case of "the cart before the horse".

While such a system could cope with the limited demands placed on it for a period, the increasing complexity of the commercial world has exposed accounting as a discipline that lacks the necessary conceptual framework to cope. In short, accounting stands indicted for its past failures, failures which open it to legitimate criticisms and which contain the potential to undermine the self-assumed "right" of accountants to regulate and control the supply of financial information to society and the market.

### In practice:

*"There are two competing views of accounting principles: one maintaining that accounting principles are based on what is generally done in practice and the other holding that a foundation of fundamental premises ('concepts') necessarily underlies and determines sound practice,"* explained Reed K. Storey, former FASB senior technical advisor. *"The latter view has been the source of significant advances in accounting theory for more than 20 years and has affected financial accounting standards and practice through the FASB's conceptual framework; accounting practice, however, has continued to be dominated by the former view."*

Source: FASB Special Report on Accounting Principles, 1998.

## US

As with most accounting initiatives of the 20th century, some of the earliest attempts to identify a coherent framework occurred in the US, gaining much of their impetus, as was the case with the regulatory process, from the events surrounding the Wall Street crash.

One of the first attempts at such a synthesis was undertaken by W.A. Paton and A.C. Littleton in the 1930s and 1940s. They were followed by Maurice Moonitz, appointed by the AICPA as its first Director of Accounting Research, and Robert Sprouse, who together published a number of research studies on the subject. At best their efforts met with indifference. At worst they inspired outright hostility from a community which questioned not only their methodology, but also the need for such a project.

Nevertheless, financial scandals which could be traced to certain accounting practices as well as sustained criticism of accounting's deficiencies compelled those within the Securities and Exchange Commission (SEC) and the profession to initiate a more comprehensive review. This led to the formation of two groups specifically charged with investigating the issue.

The *Study Group on Establishment of Accounting Principles*, chaired by Francis Wheat, was requested to focus on issues related to the organization and operations of the Accounting Principles Board (APB). Its report, issued in 1972, resulted in the disbanding of the APB and its replacement by the Financial Accounting Standards Board (FASB). This opened the way for a structure more sensitive to the need for a conceptual framework.

The *Study Group on Objectives of Financial Statements*, chaired by Robert Trueblood, was charged with initiating a process intended "to refine the objectives of financial statements". Specifically, the group was expected to address issuessuch as: Who are the primary users of financial accounting information?; What are their financial accounting information needs?; How could financial accounting information be best presented to satisfy the legitimate requirements of users?

In addressing these questions the Trueblood Committee identified a number of critical objectives and qualitative characteristics which should attach to financial reports intended to comply with the basic objective of financial statements which, significantly, was identified as being "to provide information useful for making economic decisions". In nominating these characteristics Trueblood provided the basis upon which the FASB could proceed to publish a statement dealing more specifically with an underlying conceptual framework.

## FASB Conceptual Framework Project

Following the criticisms that had accompanied the APBs efforts during its final years, and the loss of public confidence as a result of various financial reporting abuses, the FASB was seen by many within the profession as the final opportunity to retain the standard-setting regime in the private sector. As a result it set as one of its first goals the development of a set of accounting principles upon which a coherent set of accounting standards might be based.

Taking as its starting point the recommendations of the Trueblood committee, it issued a Discussion Memorandum, *Conceptual Framework for Accounting and Reporting*, which called for comment from interested parties. Two years later, in December 1976, it issued its *Tentative Conclusions on Objectives of Financial Statements* as well as a document which set out its aspirations for the whole conceptual framework project, *Scope and Implications of the Conceptual Project*. Six Statements of Financial Accounting Concepts (SFACs) dealing with central elements of the conceptual framework followed.[1]

---

[1] For a more complete analysis of these SFACs and of other elements of this chapter see Davies, M. et al, UK GAAP. 5th Ed., 1997, pp. 39–127.

*SFAC No. 1: Objectives of Financial Reporting by Business Enterprises* published in 1978 represents a seminal work in the development of a conceptual framework. Distinguishing between two classes of user, those with a direct interest such as investors, creditors, management and employees, and those with an indirect interest such as analysts, advisers and unions, it focuses primarily on the information needs of the first group, particularly investors and creditors.

Thus, while acknowledging that the traditional responsibilities of management persist, it identifies the principal objective of financial reporting as "the provision of information that is useful to present and potential investors and creditors and other users in making rational investment, credit and similar decisions'. One critical feature to emerge at this early stage, therefore, was the centrality of the concept of decision-usefulness of accounting information.

This statement has had a profound impact upon the way in which accounting practice and regulation has developed over the course of recent decades. A closer analysis of its constituent parts indicates several significant elements:

- The focus is placed firmly on the information needs of users, as distinct from the requirement that management account for their stewardship.
- Within the broad category of "user" investors and creditors are identified as the primary target group, and within the category of investor, potential investors are specifically acknowledged.
- The usefulness of accounting information is related to its capacity to assist in the decision-making process.

SFAC No. 1 was also important in extending financial reporting responsibilities to incorporate cash flow information. For instance, it explicitly listed prospective cash flows as one of the criteria which investors and creditors would find most useful in assessing the quality of their investment. However, it stopped short of requiring companies to include cash flow statements or forecasts in their reports.

*SFAC No. 2: Qualitative Characteristics of Accounting Information* also owed a considerable debt to the work of the Trueblood Committee.

It examined, classified and prioritized the various characteristics that make financial statements useful. In the process it identified a hierarchy of qualities which can be used to determine whether or not financial statements achieve their stated purpose. The scheme can be represented diagrammatically in Figure 2.1.

A number of observations can be made on this scheme:

- **Users**: the user-centred approach to financial statements is reflected in the fact that the requirements of users are prioritised.
- **Cost/Benefit Issue**: before considering the financial information itself it is necessary to determine whether the potential benefits to the user outweigh the costs of providing the information in the first place.

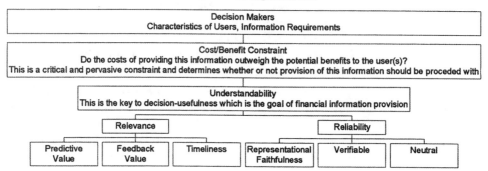

**Figure 2.1  Qualities of accounting information. Adapted from Figure 1 of SFAC No. 2.**

- **Understandability**: this is identified as a key requirement if the information is to contribute to the decision-making process.

- **Reliability and Relevance**: these are the primary qualities of useful information. The component parts of these elements all contribute to the capacity of the information to assist in enabling users to form opinions. As necessary, albeit secondary, qualities of financial information, SFAC 2 adds that it should be comparable with other financial information and consistent between and within accounting periods.

*SFAC No. 3: Elements of Financial Statements of Business Enterprises*, published in 1980, was replaced in 1985 by *SFAC No. 6: Elements of Financial Statements* (see below).

*SFAC No. 4: Objectives of Financial Reporting by Non-Business Organizations*, is not germane to this text.

*SFAC No. 5: Recognition and Measurement in Financial Statements of Business Enterprises*: Paralleling its work on the conceptual framework project, the FASB had also been engaged on a project relating to other fundamental issues. The work of this group was published in 1984 as SFAC No. 5. It dealt with two issues, "recognition" and "measurement", that had been identified as central concepts in accounting.

Recognition is defined as "the process of formally recording or incorporating an item into the financial statements of an entity as an asset, liability, revenue, expense, or the like". In other words, it refers to whether or not to include something in the financial recording process. Measurement refers to the capacity to identify attributes in an item, such as historical cost or current value. These two issues represent probably the most pressing conceptual challenges in accounting.

In determining whether or not to incorporate something the Statement outlines four criteria:

1. **Definition**: does the item satisfy the definition of an element of financial statements in SFAC No. 6?

2. **Measurability**: does the item have attributes that can be measured with sufficient reliability?

3. **Relevance**: will the item make a difference in user evaluation and decision-making?

4. **Reliability**: is the information verifiable, representationally faithful and neutral?

In many senses this statement was a considerable disappointment. In particular, it tended towards a description of current practices rather than a discussion of their relative merits and demerits. For example, when discussing measurement it described a range of methods such as historical cost, current cost and net realizable value without discussing the circumstances in which each might be appropriate. It represented, in some respects, a return to the rather technocratic approach that had undermined the credibility of the APB in the first place.

*SFAC No. 6: Elements of Financial Statements:* As the title implies, the Statement classified the various component parts of financial statements. Its principal contribution was that it provided definitions of a number of the more important elements of accounts, such as assets and liabilities, as well as various sub-categories within these:

- **Assets**: these are defined as "probable future economic benefits obtained or controlled by a particular entity as a result of past transactions or events".

- **Liabilities**: "probable future sacrifices of economic benefits arising from present obligations of a particular entity to transfer assets or provide services to other entities in the future as a result of past transactions or events".

- **Equity (net assets)**: "the residual interest in the assets of an entity after the deduction of its liabilities. Equity refers to the ownership interest in an enterprise".

- **Revenues**: "inflows or other enhancements of assets or settlements of its liabilities from delivering or producing goods, rendering services, or other activities that constitute the entity's ongoing major or central operations".

- **Expenses**: "outflows or other using up of assets or incurrences of liabilities from delivering or producing goods, rendering services, or other activities that constitute the entity's ongoing major or central operations".

All in all the FASB Conceptual Framework Project has had a significant impact. In stimulating discussion and identifying the need for a coherent conceptual basis upon which to construct accounting practice, it has served a useful purpose. It has also acted as a catalyst in motivating others such as the ASB and the International Accounting Standards Committee to undertake similar projects.

However, doubts persist amongst those who have long championed the need for such a framework. To many it has seemed that the process has never quite engaged on the fundamental issues of recognition and measurement and has, thereby, surrendered much of the advantage to those who favour a more pragmatic approach. In the nature of all such ambitious endeavours, however, the historical perspective may show the project to have been an important stepping-stone on the road to a more intellectually coherent and satisfying discipline.

## UK

Concern at the lack of a conceptual framework and the consequences that this had for the integrity of the standard-setting process were not unique to the US. A similar dynamic for change had developed in the UK. One of the more obvious consequences of this was the establishment of a new regulatory regime in the 1970s. Another was the formulation of SSAP 2, *Disclosure of accounting policies*, as one of the first acts of this new regime.

## SSAP 2

To a limited extent, SSAP 2, *Disclosure of Accounting Policies*, issued in November 1971, represented at least an acknowledgement of the role which fundamental concepts could and should play in the regulatory process. SSAP 2 does not specifically aspire to present a coherent conceptual framework. In fact, as the title suggests, its primary objective was to improve the quality and consistency of financial information disclosed to users. However, in formulating a set of accounting concepts that it took to be fundamental to all accounting practice, it did articulate a set of principles that still underlie accounting practice in the UK.

SSAP 2 approached its task in three stages, dealing first with fundamental concepts, then with accounting bases and finally, accounting practices.

### Fundamental Concepts

SSAP 2's main significance lay in the fact that it sought to identify those critical, unifying concepts that should underpin all accounting practice. In other words, it set out the basic principles which accountants should follow when preparing accounts. It identified four such concepts:

1. **Going concern:** assumes that a business (or enterprise) will continue in operational existence for the foreseeable future. This means that the financial statements are drawn up on the basis that there is no intention or necessity to liquidate the business or to curtail the scale of its operations.

2. **Accruals (matching):** states that costs and revenues should be matched against one another and be dealt with in the accounting period to which they *relate*.

3. **Consistency:** requires that a business be consistent in its accounting treatment of similar items, both *within* a particular accounting period and *between* one accounting period and the next.

4. **Prudence:** requires that revenues and profits not be included in the accounts unless it is likely that they will yield cash eventually. It also requires that in situations where losses are anticipated they should be accounted for as soon as possible. An example of the prudence concept being applied would be where a business has an estimate of a future loss of between £1,000 and

£1,500; in these circumstances the accountant should make provision for the highest estimate.

These concepts were accepted by CA85 as "accounting principles" and companies are now required to explain any departure from them.[2]

### Accounting Bases

Accounting bases are defined as the "methods developed for applying fundamental concepts to financial transactions". They have particular application when determining the accounting period in which revenues and expenses should be recognized and the amounts at which they should be included in the balance sheet.

Bases are, therefore, techniques that have been developed over time for ensuring that the fundamental concepts can be applied to particular events. Depreciation is one such technique.

### Accounting Policies

It will be necessary for management to choose from among the range of techniques available to it. An accounting policy, therefore, is "the specific accounting basis selected and consistently followed by a business enterprise as being, in the opinion of management, appropriate to its circumstances and best suited to present fairly its results and financial position". Where it has made choices such as this, management must then disclose details of those accounting policies adopted which it considers material to determining financial position in the accounting policies note which accompanies the financial statements.

For example, applying the fundamental concepts, most businesses will find it necessary to incorporate a charge for depreciation it the financial statements. Depreciation is an accounting basis since it is a method developed to ensure that the fundamental concepts are applied. There are, however, a number of depreciation techniques available. Management will, therefore, have to choose the one most

---

[2] It is generally accepted that CA85 added a fifth fundamental concept of its own, "non-aggregation" or "separate determination" which requires that each individual item be evaluated individually before being incorporated into the total for its class. Furthermore, many accountants would argue that another fundamental concept, "substance over form", was introduced by FRS 5, *Reporting the substance of transactions*. This requires that the economic substance of a transaction should be reflected in the accounts, rather than simply its legal form. There are also a number of other accounting principles outlined in SSAP 2 besides those fundamental concepts listed above: entity concept: states that the business is a separate entity from its owners and that the accounts must be kept from the perspective of the business, not from the perspective of the owner; materiality convention: requires that the financial statements should separately disclose items that are significant enough to affect evaluation or decisions; historical cost convention: means that items are included in accounts at their historical cost, i.e. at the amount that they originally cost the business.

appropriate to its circumstances. If, for example, it chooses the straight-line method for depreciation purposes, then this becomes its accounting policy.

## FRS 18 Accounting Policies

In December 2000 the ASB issued FRS 18, *Accounting Policies*, which has replaced SSAP 2 with effect from June 2001. While acknowledging that SSAP 2 was still fundamentally sound, it does reconsider the relative importance of the four fundamental concepts and gives greater weight to the going concern and accruals concepts. It also provides useful direction in relation to disclosures to be made where estimates are employed.

FRS 18 deals mainly with the selection, application and disclosure of accounting policies. Its objective is to ensure that for all material items:

- An entity adopts the accounting policies most appropriate to its particular circumstances for the purpose of giving a true and fair view.

- The accounting policies adopted are reviewed regularly to ensure that they remain appropriate, and are changed when a new policy becomes more appropriate to the entity's particular circumstances; and

- Sufficient information is disclosed in the financial statements to enable users to understand the accounting policies adopted and how they have been implemented.

Essentially FRS 18 requires that accounting policies adopted by reporting entities be consistent with accounting standards and legislation, and that choices made by reporting entities take into account the objectives of relevance, reliability, comparability and understandability. Its impact is unlikely to be profound as, to a large extent, it represents merely an updating of SSAP 2 in the light of conceptual developments over the last 30 years.

## Corporate Report

Commissioned by the Accounting Standards Steering Committee, the precursor of the ASC, this discussion paper took much of its inspiration from the Trueblood Committee in the US. Published in 1975, it sought to address three fundamental issues:

- *Types of organization* which should publish regular financial information: on this point, the Report concluded that economic entities of "significant size" (which it did not quantify) had a responsibility to report as part of their public accountability function.

- *Principal users* of such reports and their particular requirements: adopting the lead set in the US, the Corporate Report firmly established the necessity to address users and their respective needs as the primary focus of the corporate reporting function. It also categorized the various classes of user into seven sub-sections, each with specific but often overlapping needs, for example, evaluating performance, liquidity, funding requirements and future prospects.

- *Form of report* that best satisfies these requirements: the committee was of the opinion that the primary objective of a corporate report is to "communicate economic measurements of and information about the resources and performance of the reporting entity". To fulfil this objective it concluded that a report had to conform to various parameters which, echoing the Trueblood committee, included understandability, reliability, timeliness, comparability, objectivity and relevance.

The *Report* envisaged the publication of an annual report that not only provided financial information but was also sufficiently comprehensive that it completely described an organization's economic activity. While including basic financial statements such as the balance sheet, profit and loss account and funds-flow statement (the precursor to the cash flow statement), it proposed that such a report should also include narrative elements and other descriptive statements. With a view to satisfying the information needs of a broad range of users, it suggested that the following additional statements should be included in the Annual Report:

- Value-added statement
- Employment report
- Statement of foreign-currency transactions
- Statement of monetary exchanges with government
- Statement of future prospects
- Statement of corporate objectives

Significantly, the committee also advocated an extension of the social reporting aspect of corporate accountability that would require companies to acknowledge and report upon their performance as "corporate citizens". For example, companies would be required to report on their impact on the local communities in which they operated.

In stimulating discussion as to the nature and role of accounting information, the *Corporate Report* confirmed that the profession in the UK was alert to the difficulties inherent in a regulatory process that could not point to a coherent conceptual framework from which to operate. It was also an acknowledgement that the emphasis in financial reporting had moved from basic stewardship, i.e., the responsibility of management to manage and account for resources, to a user-oriented, decision-making perspective.

However, in its failure to deal comprehensively with fundamental issues such as measurement and valuation bases it fell foul of the same dynamic which would see SFAC No. 5, *Recognition and Measurement in Financial Statements of Business Enterprises*, fail to deal fully with the issue in the US some years later.

# Sandilands Report

On this valuation issue, however, the *Corporate Report* was to some extent overtaken by events, in particular the work of the Sandilands committee which had been commissioned by the Secretary of State for Trade and Industry in 1974 to consider whether company accounts should allow for price changes. This committee was expected to address the implications for accounting and the corporate reporting regime of the fact that the global economy was going through a period of seemingly intractable inflation.

Working from the now widely accepted paradigm of the primacy of user-oriented, decision-useful information, Sandilands proposed a gradual move towards a system of "current-cost-accounting". This was an approach based upon the notion of "value-to-the-business," where assets and liabilities were incorporated into the balance sheet at their value-to-the-business, and profit was to be calculated only after charging the value-to-the-business of any assets consumed in the process. The cumulative effect would have been to produce accounts that reflected a change in focus from crude measurements of profit based on historical costs to ones more concerned with the inclusion of assets and liabilities at values that reflected price changes.

Responding to this report the ASC embarked upon a frenzy of inflation accounting-related work that resulted eventually in the publication in 1980 of SSAP 16, *Current Cost Accounting*. This required companies to present current cost accounts either as their principal accounts or as supplements to the historic cost accounts. The standard encountered considerable opposition, however, both from within the profession and from industry. In 1985 it was withdrawn.

# Making Corporate Reports Valuable (MCRV)

Other reports, such as the *Macve Report*, continued to be commissioned by the various regulatory bodies in the US and the UK. But the reaction from the public, profession and government was disappointing. Aware of this, the Institute of Chartered Accountants of Scotland commissioned its Research Committee to undertake a fresh investigation into the corporate reporting regime. Uniquely, the committee was allowed to consider the process without reference to existing laws, traditional practice or other constraints.

Starting from the assumption that users need the same information as management, although usually in lesser quantities, *MCRV* identified four principal user groups, all with legitimate, if varying, requirements. These were:

- Equity investors
- Loan creditors
- Employees; and
- Business contacts such as creditors

The report then identified the following as issues on which a properly constituted financial report should be able to assist users:

- Understanding corporate objectives
- Explaining changes in corporate wealth
- Assessing future prospects
- Comprehending the economic environment within which the entity operates
- Providing information about ownership and control
- It was also suggested that management should be required to publish corporate financial plans as well as compare the entity's actual performance with previously published plans, explaining any variations in the process.

One of the most significant contributions of the *MCRV* was that it not only grappled with the challenges posed by problems of measurement, but actually made recommendations in the area. Dismissing the claims of historical cost and economic value as measures of economic reality, it proposed "net realizable value"[3] as the method that, albeit with important reservations, most comprehensively captured value.

Other significant conclusions of the report were:

- The substance of transactions, rather than merely their legal form, should be communicated.
- Increased disclosure should be considered as a way of satisfying user-requirements.
- There should be a greater focus on balance sheet valuations.

These aspirations caused the committee to completely reconsider the form in which information was communicated in the Annual Report. As a result *MCRV* proposed the following as the critical statements and elements of any report intended to achieve these purposes:

- **Statement of Assets and Liabilities**: this would include all assets and liabilities of the entity stated at net realizable value.
- **Operations Statement**: this was intended to determine the change in corporate wealth resulting from the trading activity of the entity.
- **Statement of Changes in Financial Wealth**: this would summarize changes in corporate wealth from all sources.
- **Distributions Statement**: this would detail any changes in wealth resulting from distributions, such as dividends, and would address capital maintenance concerns by ensuring an inflation adjustment during periods of rising prices.

---

[3] Net Realisable Value (NRV) can be defined as: "proceeds of sale less any additional unavoidable expenses of disposal."

- **Cash Flow Statement**: this would include details of all inflows and outflows subdivided into various subsections.

*MCRV* represented one of the most radical, yet thoughtful, reappraisals of the accounting and reporting functions. It challenged fundamentally some of the preconceptions on which corporate reporting had been based for decades. But it not only recited problems and discussed alternatives. In championing a value-based approach, it created the possibility of major changes in the way in which the accounting function interacted with its various environments. In so doing it has had a considerable impact upon the standard-setting process in the UK.

## Solomons Report

In 1987, responding to similar pressures to those that had resulted in the conceptual framework project in the US, the Research Committee of the ICAEW commissioned Prof. David Solomons, who had been an advisor to FASB, to undertake similar research in the UK.

Not surprisingly, his conclusions mirrored many of the findings of its US predecessor. In fact, its conclusions regarding the elements of financial statements reflected very closely SFAC No. 6, for example, in its definitions of assets and liabilities. Likewise, its summary of the qualitative characteristics of accounting information mirrored the thrust of SFAC No. 2 in emphasizing qualities such as decision-usefulness, timeliness, understandability, reliability and relevance.

One important aspect of the Solomons Report was a stated preference for a "balance sheet approach", i.e., one which favoured an asset and liability focus, as distinct from the traditional revenue-expense emphasis which it was felt allowed too much scope for profit manipulation.

Solomons concluded by devising a financial reporting model based upon the notion of "maintenance of real financial capital". This concept, which flowed from his balance sheet focus, considered income as the change in an entity's net worth. In other words, the primary focus was to be on determining the values at which to include assets and liabilities in the balance sheet. Income was then a by-product of this measure.

This model was useful in providing a definite rationale for a balance sheet approach. However, it was also helpful in pointing out potential difficulties with this emphasis. For instance, appropriate valuation bases and the ways in which intangible assets might be recognized and measured were highlighted as problematic, as were more specific issues such as the treatment of deferred taxation and pensions.

## ASB's Statement of Principles

The Dearing Report, which had recommended the changes in the standard-setting regime that had led to the ASB, also made recommendations in relation to the development of a conceptual framework. In fact, conscious of the difficulties which the absence of a clearly articulated conceptual basis posed, it had identified work in this area as a priority:

"(the) lack of a conceptual framework is a handicap to those involved in setting standards as well as to those applying them. Work on its development should, therefore, be pursued at a higher rate than hitherto but consistent with the perceived scope for progress... We believe that work in this area will assist standard-setters in formulating their thinking on particular accounting issues, facilitate judgements on the sufficiency of the disclosures required to give a true and fair view, and assist preparers and auditors in interpreting accounting standards and in resolving accounting issues not dealt with by specific standards."

Consequently, the ASB set as one of its priorities the formulation of such a framework, which it called its Statement of Principles (SoP). This emerged over a number of years in the form of Exposure Drafts (EDs) or chapters, each dealing with a component part of such a framework.

The first draft version of the SoP encountered significant opposition, however, as much for the manner of its formulation as its contents. As a consequence the ASB decided that, rather than proceed directly to the development of a final Statement, a revised draft would be prepared. In the interim it issued a Progress Paper intended to clarify certain points.

A Revised SoP was published in December 1999. However, there were few changes from the first draft. In fact, other than the addition of an extra chapter dealing with "Accounting for interests in other entities", together with proposals regarding the presentation of "profit", there were almost no significant variations from what had been produced some years previously.

The thinking behind the Statement of Principles, and the role such a framework is envisaged as playing, are summarized in the introduction to this revised draft:

## Purpose

1. This Statement of Principles for Financial Reporting sets out the principles that the Accounting Standards Board believes should underlie the preparation and presentation of general purpose financial statements.
2. The primary purpose of articulating such principles is to provide a coherent frame of reference to be used by the Board in the development and review of accounting standards and by others who interact with the Board during the standard-setting process.

3. Such a frame of reference should clarify the conceptual underpinnings of proposed accounting standards and should enable standards to be developed on a consistent basis by reducing the need to debate fundamental issues each time a standard is developed or revised. As such, it will play an important role in the development of accounting standards. It is expected that it will play a similar role in the development of Statements of Recommended Practice.

4. The Statement is being published because knowledge of the principles should assist preparers and users of financial statements, as well as auditors and others, to understand the Board's approach to formulating accounting standards and the nature and function of information reported in general purpose financial statements. The principles will also help preparers and auditors faced with new or emerging issues to carry out an initial analysis of the issues involved in the absence of applicable accounting standards.

Source: Statement of Principles, ASB, December 1999.

The Statement of Principles does not, in itself, comprise an accounting standard. Instead, it is envisaged that it will provide a common reference point for the ASB in formulating standards, for preparers in determining appropriate accounting treatment where accounting standards are silent, and for users in interpreting the information contained in financial reports.

The SoP consists of eight chapters as follows:

1. The objective of financial statements

2. The reporting entity

3. The qualitative characteristics of financial information

4. The elements of financial statements

5. Recognition in financial statements

6. Measurement in financial statements

7. Presentation of financial information

8. Accounting for interests in other entities

## Chapter 1: The Objective of Financial Statements

Reflecting the influence of the FASB project as well as the thrust of the Solomons Report and others, Chapter 1 frames the objectives of financial statements in terms of their ability "to provide information about the reporting entity's financial performance and financial position that is useful to a wide range of users for assessing the stewardship of management and for making economic decisions". Such users would include investors, lenders, creditors, employees, customers, government and the public. Significantly, however, it asserts that statements meeting the needs of owners and lenders will usually satisfy all users. Consequently, it is the investor perspective that predominates.

The chapter is also useful in emphasizing the importance of cash flow information as a crucial element in enabling an informed decision-making process.

## Chapter 2: The Reporting Entity

This chapter deals with those entities that the ASB believes should be required to prepare financial statements either as single entities or as part of a business combination or group. The basic premise is that an entity should prepare financial statements where there is a demand for such statements. This demand exists if there are people with legitimate interests in the entity's finances who would rely on financial statements as a source of information enabling them to make informed decisions.

## Chapter 3: The Qualitative Characteristics of Financial Information

Almost more than any other, this chapter reflects the influence of its US antecedents. Presenting the characteristics in a diagrammatic form that emphasizes the dynamic nature of the various inter-relationships, it highlights the qualities of relevance, reliability, comparability and understandability as critical components.

The chapter summarizes its provisions as follows:

"In deciding which information to include in financial statements, when to include it and how to present it, the aim is to ensure that financial statements yield information that is useful".

This chapter then considers the qualities of financial information that make it useful:

- "Information provided by financial statements needs to be relevant and reliable and, if a choice exists between relevant and reliable approaches that are mutually exclusive, the approach chosen needs to be the one that results in the relevance of the information provided being maximized.

- Information is relevant if it has the ability to influence the economic decisions of users and is provided in time to influence those decisions.

- Information is reliable if:

    (a) It can be depended upon by users to represent faithfully what it either purports to represent or could reasonably be expected to represent, and therefore reflects the substance of the transactions and other events that have taken place;

    (b) It is free from deliberate or systematic bias and material error and is complete; and

(c) In its preparation under conditions of uncertainty, a degree of caution has been applied in exercising the necessary judgements.

- Information in financial statements needs to be comparable.

- As an aid to comparability, information in financial statements needs to be prepared and presented in a way that enables users to discern and evaluate similarities in, and differences between, the nature and effects of transactions and other events over time and across different reporting entities.

- Information provided by financial statements needs to be understandable, although information should not be excluded from the financial statements simply because it would not be understood by some users.

- Information is understandable if its significance can be perceived by users that have a reasonable knowledge of business and economic activities and accounting and a willingness to study with reasonable diligence the information provided.

- Information that is material needs to be given in the financial statements and information that is not material need not be given.

- Information is material to the financial statements if its misstatement or omission might reasonably be expected to influence the economic decisions of users."

## Chapter 4: The Elements of Financial Statements

Again, following the approach of FASB, this chapter mirrors SFAC No. 6 in presenting definitions and discussions of the critical elements of financial statements. To this end it identifies seven such elements:

1. **Assets**: "rights or other access to future economic benefits controlled by an entity as a result of past transactions or events". The inclusion of the phrase "rights or other access" is significant in clarifying that it is not property *per se* which is the critical criterion, but the rights which result from ownership or other access.

2. **Liabilities**: "obligations of an entity to transfer economic benefits as a result of past transactions or events". Again, the definition is phrased in terms of obligations, in the same way that assets embrace "rights".

3. **Ownership interest**: "the residual amount found by deducting all of the entity's liabilities from all of the entity's assets".

4. **Gains**: "increases in ownership interest not resulting from contributions from owners".

5. **Losses**: "decreases in ownership interest not resulting from distributions to owners".

6. **Contributions from owners**: "increases in ownership interest resulting from transfers from owners in their capacity as owners".

7. **Distributions to owners**: "decreases in ownership interest resulting from transfers to owners in their capacity as owners".

## Chapter 5: Recognition in Financial Statements

This has been identified by the ASB as a core chapter as it deals with one of the fundamental issues in accounting. The Statement defines recognition as: "depicting an item both in words and by a monetary amount in the primary financial statement totals".

Recognition becomes an issue where a past event indicates that there has been a measurable change in assets or liabilities. This process falls into three stages:

- Initial recognition: for example, the purchase of a fixed asset
- Subsequent re-measurement: for example, the revaluation of a fixed asset
- De-recognition: for example, the sale of a fixed asset

Essentially, if a transaction or other event has created a new asset or liability or added to an existing asset or liability, then it should be recognized if:

- Sufficient evidence exists that the new asset or liability has been created or that there has been an addition to an existing asset or liability; and
- The item can be measured at a monetary amount with sufficient reliability.

In setting out recognition criteria such as these, this chapter represents a significant advance in the development of a conceptual framework in relation to recognition issues.

## Chapter 6: Measurement in Financial Statements

Traditionally accounting has employed the historical cost approach when assigning monetary values to transactions. In other words, it has used the amount at which the transaction was originally stated as the means of incorporating it into financial statements. While this has been modified slightly in the UK to the extent that most large entities now include certain items at historical cost and others at re-valued amounts, the accounting system has essentially remained faithful to the historical cost approach.

This is in spite of the fact that valid arguments can be put forward for alternative approaches, specifically those that attempt to incorporate some form of current value into financial statements. In discussing these alternatives this chapter contrasts the features of the historical cost approach with those of three alternatives:

1. **Entry value (replacement cost)**: this assigns a value to items, for example an asset, equivalent to the cost of replacing that asset.
2. **Exit value (net realizable value)**: this assigns a value to items, for example an asset, equivalent to the amount at which that asset could be disposed.
3. **Value-in-use**: this assigns a value to items, for example an asset, equivalent to the

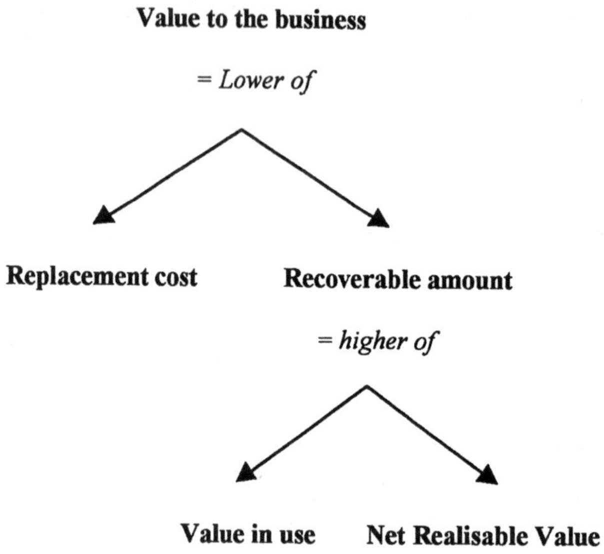

**Value to the business**

*= Lower of*

**Replacement cost**       **Recoverable amount**

*= higher of*

**Value in use**       **Net Realisable Value**

Figure 2.2   Value to the business.

discounted present value of the cash flows expected from that asset's continuing use and ultimate sale.

While historical cost has obvious advantages in terms of reliability, it suffers from the fact that it will often result in financial statement figures that bear little relation to current reality. As against this, current value methods, while resulting in figures that may be more up-to-date, are based on estimates of future realization and may often be so subjective as to be unsustainable.

Nevertheless, the chapter argues in favour of a gradual evolution towards a measurement system that involves a greater use of current values, although only to the extent that this does not completely compromise considerations of reliability and cost. To this end the chapter outlines a current value system which it calls "value to the business". It can be represented diagrammatically in Figure 2.2.

Not surprisingly, this has met with a mixed response. On the one hand supporters have argued that it is a move towards a form of current value accounting, implicit in which, they suggest, is a greater relevance to users. Critics on the other hand have pointed out that it is both vague in its definitions and unclear in its conceptualization. Furthermore, they point out that there has been little demand for change from users.

While accepting that it is not the function of financial statements to represent the total value of an entity, the chapter does reflect the balance sheet perspective that the ASB has adopted, particularly in its focus upon valuation as it applies to assets and liabilities. This reflects the fact that the profit and loss account is now viewed by many as merely a by-product of balance sheet changes.

## Chapter 7: Presentation of Financial Information

This chapter deals with the ways in which financial information can be presented so that those objectives set out in Chapter 1 can be met.

It is primarily concerned with issues such as levels of disclosure, detail, prominence and whether information should be included in the financial statements themselves, as notes to these statements or as supplementary information. To assist preparers in deciding on these issues it outlines those considerations that must be taken into account in determining how best to present financial information:

- **Focus**: the principal focus of financial statements should be the cash generating capacity and financial adaptability of the entity. This requirement is satisfied by means of a set of interrelated primary financial statements.

- **Aggregation**: financial statements summarize vast numbers of financial transactions. This means that the presentation of financial information often involves a high level of interpretation, simplification, abstraction and aggregation. Nevertheless, if carried out properly, these processes will not diminish the capacity of financial statements to assist users.

- **Classification**: this facilitates analysis and understanding by grouping items of a similar nature or function.

- **Structure**: financial information is presented in statements that have been structured in such a way as to indicate the financial performance, position or adaptability of an entity. The level of disclosure should be commensurate with the overall significance of the item.

- **Notes**: the notes to the accounts form an integral part of the accounts and should be considered in that context. They should provide additional detail to that provided in aggregate figures in the financial statements and, where appropriate, should provide an alternative perspective.

- **Supplementary information**: this is information other than that included in the financial statements and notes, for instance, management's analysis of, or commentary on, individual aspects of company performance, or information which is relevant but speculative.

## Chapter 8: Accounting for Interests in Other Entities

Since investments in other entities will be a material element in the overall activity and value of most large companies, these will need to be properly reflected in the financial statements. This will be explained in more detail in Chapters 6 and 11.

## Assessment of Statement of Principles

The Statement of Principles represents an attempt by the ASB to articulate a broadly acceptable conceptual framework that would provide the unifying theoretical base upon which a coherent system of accounting practice might be constructed.[4] Its principal features are:

- The subordination of concepts such as matching and prudence to recognition tests.
- A greater emphasis on the balance sheet and its constituent parts.
- A gradual evolution from the historical cost approach to one in which assets and liabilities are stated at "value to the business".
- A corresponding downgrading of the profit and loss account where increases or decreases in wealth are viewed as net changes in the carrying values of assets and liabilities in the balance sheet.
- Useful advances in identifying criteria to be applied for recognition and measurement purposes.

The Statement of Principles is still, however, encountering some opposition. On one level this has related to the integrity of a process that is seen as internally inconsistent and conceptually flawed. There is also fundamental disagreement as to the workability of its recognition tests and measurement proposals. The fact that in parallel the ASB has been issuing FRSs which it claims correspond to its Statement of Principles has also proven problematical in the face of counter-arguments that no such agreed framework exists as yet. Equally damning has been the observation that there may well be conflicts within and between various FRSs.

Those who support the project, however, have been equally robust in defending both the need for a coherent set of principles and the specifics of the ASB approach:

## An Ever-Stronger Influence

### The ASB's Statement of Principles has Already had a Major Impact on the Credibility of Financial Reporting, by Paul Ebling

...The ASB is not, of course, claiming that its principles are perfect, complete or carved in stone. Accounting thought is continually evolving, so the principles will need to be added to and refined, and occasionally they may also need to be amended. Some of the projects that the ASB is already working on may even cause such changes. For example, the accounting for equity project is looking again at the boundary that has been drawn between equity and liabilities; the work the ASB is carrying out on reporting financial performance may result in the identification of additional principles; and the work being carried out on financial instruments has involved re-examining various recognition and measurement principles.

---

[4] For an excellent analysis of the role and content of the SoP see: Rutherford, B.A., An Introduction to Modern Financial Reporting Theory, PCP, 2000.

## Building Out from the Bridgehead

Despite this ongoing process of refinement, the influence of the principles over accounting practice is likely to grow in the coming years. For example, now that the importance of the definitions of assets and liabilities has been established – through the ASB's work on off balance sheet finance and acquisition and "big bath" provisions – those definitions are shaping accounting practice in other areas, including leases, pensions and deferred tax. They are also likely to influence the conclusions the ASB reaches in its revenue recognition project on matters such as income received in advance of performance. Similarly, the SoP's measurement framework – which is already reflected in FRS 15, *Tangible Fixed Assets* – will, over the next few years, presumably also start to be reflected in the measurement of items for which there are active markets and financial instruments in general.

The SoP also has an international role, because its development is enabling the ASB to influence the international debate and has resulted in several of its newer standards being adopted as the international benchmarks. The principles in the SoP and other framework documents create a universal language that enables standard-setters around the world to analyse accounting problems in the same way and to resolve differences in ways that make sense in all jurisdictions. So, ignore those who claim that the SoP is a case of too little too late: it is made of the right stuff and shows perfect timing.

Paul Ebling was the ASB project director responsible for the Statement of Principles. The views expressed here are his own.

Source: Accountancy International, February 2000.

# IASC

At the same time as the FASB was engaged on its conceptual framework project, and prior to the ASB undertaking on its venture, the IASC had embarked on a conceptual framework project of its own. Its aspirations were complicated, however, by the fact that developing an international framework requires that the interests and biases of a variety of countries be negotiated. Thus, for instance, while Anglo-American regulators favour frameworks that emphasize the interests of the investor, continental European countries are less comfortable with this bias. In addition, the interests of developed and developing countries will often be diametrically opposed.

Nevertheless, in 1989 the IASC published its own ED, *Framework for the Presentation and Preparation of Financial Statements* which drew heavily on the US experience. This document dealt with a variety of issues that Trueblood in particular had identified. Specifically it addressed:

- **Objectives of financial statements**: essentially its conclusions were that financial statements should provide decision-useful information to a variety of users to inform and assist them when making economic decisions.

- **Qualitative characteristics of financial statements**: the principal characteristics were identified as reliability and relevance. However, comparability was also strongly emphasized, particularly in the sense that it interacted with other key factors.

- **Elements of financial statements**: in identifying assets, liabilities, and equity as critical elements, the IASC was closely following SFAC No. 6. Thus, when dealing with assets, it stated that "future economic benefit embodied in an asset is the potential to contribute, directly or indirectly, to the flow of cash and cash equivalents to the enterprise".

- **Recognition**: again this linked to the extent to which a transaction could be shown to have impacted upon the assets or liabilities of an entity.

- **Measurement**: the document was significant in recognizing that various measurement bases exist. However, like its US counterpart, it did not elaborate on circumstances in which one method might be preferable to another. In fact, it specifically stated that it did not see it as part of its function at that time to be prescriptive.

The dominant Anglo-American model, with its strong bias in favour of the interests of the private investor, has, therefore, been influential in shaping the thinking and approach of the IASC. This explains some of the reluctance of the EU to fully embrace IASs that was hinted at in Chapter 1 and is dealt with again in Chapter 15.

## Summary

The need for a conceptual framework is now broadly accepted. What is in dispute is the form it should take and the fundamental principles it should embrace. While much of the debate has become mired in detail it is helpful to remember that most difficulty revolves around the twin issues of recognition and measurement. And the solutions devised differ. For instance, while in the US the FASB has been widely criticized for opting to retain the historical cost approach, in the UK the ASB has been widely criticized for trying to adopt a more "current value" centred approach.

Nevertheless, some common ground has been established:

- It is now generally accepted that whatever framework is devised it must be sensitive to user requirements in an environment in which financial statements are now but one source of information.

- Recognition and measurement have been identified as fundamental issues to be addressed.

- Increased disclosure may provide one means of satisfying user requirements without impinging on the accounting process.

While some progress has been made, particularly in identifying recognition and measurement issues as critical elements of any framework, it is hard to deny that the aspirations of its early champions have been realized.

This may simply be a function of a process that seeks to synthesize in the hope of arriving at some form of "Holy Grail". However, it may also be a consequence of a regulatory process that has made definite political choices and is then required to operate within the intellectual straightjacket that this imposes. In persisting with an investor-focused model accounting regulators and practitioners may be accused of perpetuating a social model that favours capital at the expense of the common good.

# Review Questions

### Question 1
Outline what is meant by the phrase "conceptual framework" and explain what the practical impact of having such a framework might be for accounting.

### Question 2
Compare and contrast the experiences of accounting and economics in terms of the presence or absence of a conceptual framework.

### Question 3
Outline the history of the "search" for a conceptual framework in the US. In particular discuss the role of the Trueblood Committee in setting the agenda for conceptual framework projects both in the US and elsewhere.

### Question 4
Summarize the key elements of SFACs 1, 2, 5 and 6. Identify themes common to each as well as internal inconsistencies.

### Question 5
"In providing definitions for such key elements as assets and liabilities, SFAC 6 represented a seminal document in the development of an accounting framework". Explain.

### Question 6
Compare and contrast the IASC document, *Framework for the Presentation and Preparation of Financial Statements*, with its US equivalent.

### Question 7
To what extent could SSAP 2, *Disclosure of Accounting Policies*, be considered to have provided an adequate conceptual framework for the UK?

### Question 8
Identify the role of the *Corporate Report*, the *Sandilands Report*, and various other contributions in identifying both a need for, and the likely elements of, a conceptual framework for the UK.

### Question 9
Summarize the key elements of the various chapters of the Statement of Principles issued in 1999.

### Question 10
The introduction of the notion "value to the business" in Chapter 6 of the SoP represents a considerable break with previous official pronouncements on approaches to measurement. Outline the implications of this proposal with particular reference to the equivalent FASB and IASC provisions.

## Case Studies

### Case 1

Paul Ebling has already been quoted in the body of this chapter. As ASB project director for the SoP he is, not surprisingly, supportive of it. With this in mind, critically review the following article and discuss the key points he makes in its favour.

### A Matter of Principles: The UK's Statement of Principles Already has an Impressive Record and Should be Recognized as a Force for Good by Paul Ebling

In 1995, the UK Accounting Standards Board issued an ED of the Statement of Principles for Financial Reporting that attracted more comment than any of its other EDs, much of it highly critical. Last month it issued a revised draft, as well as an introductory booklet and a technical supplement – both of them are an essential read for anyone intending to respond to the revised draft. Together, these documents respond to the criticisms by exploding myths, rebutting arguments and, of course, making various technical changes.

#### Exploding Myths

One of the problems with the previous draft was that, on some important matters, the ASB did not communicate its views as successfully as it could have done. As a result, myths developed about the draft's content and meaning, which obscured much of the debate about its technical content.

In order to stop this problem recurring, the draft Statement has been extensively revised both to eliminate possible ambiguities and to present the key messages more clearly. The introductory booklet and technical supplement reinforce this work and also explode various myths, for example: "The draft Statement describes a novel approach to accounting". In fact, almost all the principles are already being used by the world's leading standard-setters, and have been for some time. The IASC's Framework for the Preparation and Presentation of Financial Statements, for instance – which is what the draft statement is based on – was issued 10 years ago. This framework was itself based on the FASB's Statements of Financial Accounting Concepts, most of which were issued more than 18 years ago.

"It is unrealistic to expect companies to comply with the Statement of Principles": it has never been the intention that the Statement would, when finalized, contain requirements or recommendations on how financial statements should be prepared or presented. The draft Statement is intended to be used for standard-setting. Company accounts will continue to be prepared under the requirements of company law and accounting standards.

"Using the principles to develop future standards will turn accounting practice on its head": since the ASB has been using the main principles as a frame of reference since it was set up, their effect can be judged by considering the accounting standards it has issued to date. Those standards have not turned accounting practice on its head; on the contrary, they have done much to restore the damage done to financial reporting by off balance sheet finance and other creative accounting devices.

"The draft Statement is looking to move accounting away from historical cost": most of the larger listed companies in the UK already carry some of their balance sheet items at current values. The draft Statement assumes that this practice will continue: it favours neither a current value system nor a historical cost system.

Various misconceptions about financial reporting are also addressed. For example, the supplement makes it clear that, contrary to the common perception, neither companies legislation nor case law suggests that the courts should or would take the view that a company's annual financial statements are prepared solely for its shareholders. It goes on to point out that, since companies are required to put a copy of their annual financial statements on the public record, the law appears to envisage that the public will use the statements. Similarly, those who argue that the draft Statement has no right to redefine prudence are reminded that SSAP 2 itself describes prudence and the other fundamental accounting concepts as being "capable of variation and evolution as accounting thought and practice develop".

## Rebutting Arguments

The supplement also sets out the rationale behind key aspects of the approach adopted in the draft Statement and, in doing so, seeks to rebut some of the criticisms that approach has attracted. Probably the two main criticisms it rebuts relate to: first, the absence of any role in the draft Statement for the realization notion (the supplement deals with this issue in some detail although, in essence, the point it makes is that, while realization is one way of determining whether a gain's existence is sufficiently certain to be recognized, nowadays there are better ways of achieving the same objective); and second, the draft Statement's approach in defining gains and losses by reference to movements in net assets. Although it has been claimed that this approach shifts the focus away from transactions and reduces the p&l account to a statement of residuals, the supplement makes it clear that the real issue is whether the matching notion should be allowed to justify deferring the recognition in the p&l account of expenses that involve no future economic benefits and of other losses. The supplement argues forcefully that it should not.

## Technical Changes

Various technical changes have also been made to the draft Statement. The two biggest are probably: the main focus of the material on measurement is now on describing a framework to guide the choice of an appropriate measurement basis for each balance sheet category; and the draft Statement no longer envisages the preparation of two performance statements – a p&l account and a statement of total recognized gains and losses – nor does it address the allocation of items between performance statements. Instead, it explains that these issues involve no fundamental principles and then points out that they are being dealt with in the ASB's review of FRS 3.

The draft Statement's principles have been shaping UK accounting standards for nearly 10 years now – a period in which the accounting abuses of the 1980s have been stamped out. It is on such successes that the Statement should be judged.

Source: Accountancy International, April 1999.

## Case 2

While the ASB's Statement of Principles has been broadly welcomed, there have been some criticisms. The following article views it as more of a political statement by the ASB than any genuine attempt to produce a conceptual framework. Discuss the validity of the main points made.

## It's not the principle that's important

*The benefits accruing from a coherent SoP appear to be outweighed by the difficulty of creating it, says Peter Williams. But the ASB cannot afford to drop it for political reasons.*

... it seems that the quest for this Holy Grail of accounting is no longer – even if it ever was – about setting out basic principles from which the work of the accounting standard setter can proceed. Instead it is more to do with the politicking of the international accounting standard-setting process. The UK belongs to a premier league club of international standard setters, called G4 + 1 (there are actually five members of G4, plus the IASC), and all the other countries have conceptual frameworks. Furthermore, part of the group's "constitution" states that they "share the view that financial reporting standards should be based on a conceptual framework". In other words, if the ASB is to stay in the premier league – which it desperately wants to do as internationalization becomes more important – it needs to be able to point to the existence of its own SoP framework.

Academics such as Professor Anthony Hopwood of Oxford University suggest that having the SoP in place will give the ASB and the standard-setting process greater authority and legitimacy. This line of thinking links in with the way that the ASB's sister body, the Financial Reporting Review Panel (FRRP) behaved in the years while it was establishing itself. (See "Yellow Brick Road to the FRRP", Financial Director, May 1999, page 14).

But while that tactic may have been necessary early on for the FRRP, it is hard to see how the SoP will make the ASB stronger in the eyes of its domestic audience. Over the years it has assiduously and skilfully fought and won battles on various issues – off-balance-sheet financing, goodwill, big bath provisions, the difference between debt and equity, etc., – and, in doing so, has already established its reputation and authority. In fact, if the SoP does anything, it is likely to diminish the ASB in the eyes of UK preparers and users. At the same time, the success and acceptance of the ASB's standards has diminished the need for an SoP. Dr Pelham Gore of Lancaster University describes one political function of an SoP as providing a "defensive shield". In the early days, it promises to bring benefits, and later on it can be used to defend standards by claiming consistency.

But to the pragmatic British mind, it seems odd that the ASB has succeeded in publishing 15 standards before completing the framework on which that work purports to be based. The ASB knows this and is trying its best to distance itself from its own SoP. Apart from the need to compete internationally, the most compelling reason why the ASB is still chasing an SoP is because the Dearing Report gave the new body three main tasks: to stamp out accounting abuses, to harmonize with international standards, and to develop a conceptual framework. But even if there was any great enthusiasm among the ASB for this particular project at first, it has withered now. Both Andrew Lennard, an ASB staff member and author of the first SoP, and Ken Wild, a board member, say that one of the main benefits of the SoP is for internal use. In preparing new standards the board can check from first principles what the answer should be.

But it is an indication of how bored or demoralized they are by the project that they are cheerfully admitting that if the SoP comes up with an answer which they intuitively think is the wrong one, they will pick another solution. In other words, the SoP would be little more than a private guide for the standard setters, which for reasons of openness they have chosen to publish. It will help to ensure consistency, but it will not be followed slavishly.

There is good precedent for this take it or leave it attitude. The US standard on pensions runs a coach and horses through its framework. And in general, the US situation should have provided a lesson for us. There, the debate over the conceptual framework dragged on from 1973–1985. The project was started in a flush of enthusiasm, with high hopes after a new accounting standard setting body was set up. But soon afterwards, the framework ran into the mire. Although the SoP has been re-ordered, it is not yet free from similar problems. As yet, its fundamental purpose is still not clear. The question of whether it is prescriptive or descriptive goes unanswered, so no one is sure if it is a blueprint for best practice or a collection of current practice. According to Gore, this vagueness is deliberate. The ASB is trying to leave itself plenty of escape routes should it need them later on. One such, for instance, is the lack of clarity over the role of current values as opposed to historical costs. One solution to this mess might be to refrain from publishing the SoP as an FRS.

Instead, along with a commitment to review it in 3–5 years time, the ASB could give it a similar status to the Financial Reporting Standard for Smaller Entities (FRSSE) which sits alongside, but is not part of, the canon of accounting standards. This way, the SoP would exist for political purposes but would not be a core feature of standard setting. A fudge like this is likely because the ASB cannot abandon the SoP and cannot – or will not – substantially rewrite it. Les Cullen, finance director of Inchcape plc, says that he certainly does not feel moved to man the barricades over the issue – either to cheer it on or bring it down. At this stage, the best the ASB can hope for is that most of Cullen's fellow finance directors feel the same.

Peter Williams is a chartered accountant and freelance journalist.

Source: Accountancy Age, November 3, 1999.

## Case 3

In January 2000 FASB issued a special report, *The Framework of Financial Accounting Concepts and Standards*, intended to explain how the FASB's conceptual framework has evolved. Access the report at http://www.summa.org.uk/raw/raw/fasb/welcome.htm and discuss its contents.

# THEORETICAL CONTEXT

When you have completed this chapter you will understand that:

- Accounting information is a commodity which can be traded in a market.

- There are various theories that seek to explain the role of accounting information in these markets.

- The dominant paradigm over the course of recent decades has been the market-based perspective.

- The most important of these market-based theories has been the Efficient Market Hypothesis (EMH), or Theory (EMT).

- EMH questions the usefulness and timeliness of accounting information contained in the Annual Report.

- More recently the dominance of EMH has been challenged.

## Moving into a Tricky Climate, by Philip Coggan

The age-old British festival of Bonfire Night seems to be in decline. Burning a Catholic in effigy is not as popular as it used to be, although, to please traditionalists, children are still encouraged to buy those explosive and highly flammable devices called fireworks. There has been a definite switch in affections towards the pagan/American festival of Halloween, in which children are encouraged to "trick or treat", otherwise known as demanding confectionery with menaces.

The stock market, too, seems to be in trick or treat mode. When a company makes an announcement, investors expect not just good news, but better-than-expected news. The merest hint of bad news prompts the stock market equivalent of smearing tomato ketchup on the doorstep – a rapid fall in the company's shares.

Take Vodafone, the UK market's biggest company. On Thursday, rumours started to sweep the market that the company was guiding down analysts who were making top-of-the-range profit forecasts. The shares fell 8.6%, single-handedly knocking more than 60 points off the FTSE 100 index. The initial focus was on UBS Warburg, the company's broker, which was in the process of adjusting down its Earnings Before Interest, Tax, Depreciation and Amortisation (EBITDA) forecast by less than 2%. The reason for this adjustment was Vodafone's success in attracting new subscribers in Germany – getting each new subscriber costs around £100. Other brokers downgraded their EBITDA forecasts but the cuts were hardly devastating, with Deutsche Bank accompanying its adjustment with a "strong buy" recommendation...

...The current, more tricky, climate has been prompted by a number of factors. The wave of profit warnings in the US and the surge in the price of oil have played their part. In the telecoms sector, investors have become concerned about the costs involved in paying for the third generation of mobile phones. The sector's debt rating has suffered (although Vodafone has avoided this problem by selling Orange for cash).

A year ago, the market's view of telecoms could be summed up as: "Wonderful business, rapid growth." Now it could be summed up as: "Nice growth but... will profits be squeezed by rising costs and falling prices? And will consumers actually want all the services available from third-generation phones?"

The twitchiness of the market about Vodafone's figures may also be a symptom of a wider trend. Life has become more difficult for the corporate sector at a time of globalisation, competition from the Internet and low inflation. It is very difficult for businesses to raise prices...

Source: Financial Times, November 3, 2000.

## Introduction

The question being addressed in this chapter is "What is the relationship between accounting information and the market?" specifically the stock market, which, as the opening vignette explains, is one of the principal markets for accounting information. Here suppliers of information meet those seeking to acquire it. In other words, the intention is to seek to understand the significance and impact of accounting information, in particular that incorporated in the Annual Report, by asking how it impacts upon market measures such as share price.

In order to consider this it is necessary first to explore some of the theoretical approaches that are more commonly employed to explain the role of such information. The significance of a theoretical model is that it can be employed to either explain something that has already happened or to predict what may happen. A theory's capacity in these regards will, however, be directly related to the degree to which it describes the "real" world. Herein lies one of the problems with theories: many incorporate such a range of assumptions that they no longer approximate to the reality they are trying to describe.

Nevertheless, simplifications such as these are often required in order to construct initial hypotheses. Subsequently, as empirical testing indicates, the model may be refined and should conform more to reality. Repeating this process then allows the model to be further refined.

When considering accounting information and the role it plays in the modern capital-market economy it is necessary to speculate about the nature of accounting information and the way in which the market assimilates it. A number of different approaches have been adopted. However, they can basically be divided into three streams of thought, each reflecting different approaches to information at the macro-economic level as disseminated through more general theoretical developments in economics and finance.

The first of these is the Classical approach which predominated in accounting circles until the 1970s. Since that time market-based theories have been dominant and the bulk of this chapter is devoted to explaining the impact of this paradigm. Finally, Positive Accounting Theory and the impact it has had on accounting thought and practice is considered.

In order to make its point this chapter introduces various concepts from finance theory. These are merely means to an end, however, and should not be allowed to distract from the fundamental issue being addressed. Thus, mathematical constructs outlined here can be safely ignored by the fainthearted. The goal should simply be to appreciate that an understanding of accounting information is fundamentally impacted by the theoretical perspective from which it is viewed.[1]

## Classical Theory

Finance theory in the decades following the Second World War inclined to the view that all financial instruments, for example shares, had a certain intrinsic value. This value, it was assumed, could be verified by financial analysis techniques which extracted the supporting data from the financial accounts of a business. The Classical (or Normative) approach, dominant in the academic accounting community particularly during the 1960s and early 1970s, reflected this perspective.

This approach assumes that it is possible to identify and measure the intrinsic value of a firm and evaluate the efficacy of the accounting function with that in mind. In other words, accounting practices are gauged in terms of how close they come to reporting the "true" economic reality about the firm.

Because there was a presumption that accounting can, in some sense, measure and report the "true" situation about a firm, the research emphasis was primarily on determining those accounting practices best suited to achieving this end. As a consequence a dynamic developed in which a preconceived notion of the intrinsic value of

---

[1] The structure of this chapter draws on White, G.I., et al. The Analysis and Use of Financial Statements, 2nd Ed., pp. 215–56.

a firm was constructed which was in turn confirmed by techniques which it was assumed could measure this value. Academic energy was devoted therefore to developing and promulgating accounting practices that were presumed to be correct, rather than to testing these assumptions by means of empirical research.

Indeed, it is possible to argue that this perspective persists in the regulatory regimes in both the UK and the US which, in the main, have held to the Normative paradigm that a measurable economic reality exists which can best be captured by accounting methods as promulgated by accounting standards.

## Market-Based Theory

It was partly as a reaction to this rather myopic approach, but also in response to developments in finance theory which moved the perspective to the decision needs of the user, that the Classical approach gradually gave way to the market-based paradigm.

While the Classical approach assumes that an underlying reality exists which accounting can best capture, market-based theory sees reality as something that the market determines, and in which process the accounting alternatives adopted make no difference. This approach posits that information can only be evaluated in the context of its effect upon users of that information, rather than in terms of any implicit reality that it purports to describe.

This perspective has had a number of fundamental implications for accounting and accounting research:

- One of the criticisms of the classical approach was that it could not be tested. Market-based theory, by definition, was based on an empirical testing of the actual usefulness of the information content of accounting disclosures.

- The focus was on the needs of users as distinct from preparers of accounting information.

- Rather than presuming the existence of "correct" accounting practices, it was now possible to test how different practices impacted upon the usefulness of the accounting information and whether specific accounting practices existed which most suited user needs.

## Portfolio Theory

This market-based approach was facilitated by developments in finance theory, such as the emergence of portfolio theory, particularly as mediated through the Capital Asset Pricing Model (CAPM).

A portfolio is simply a combination of various investments. Whether or not an investor chooses to invest in a security such as a share will depend on a variety of factors, for example, price, expected capital growth, dividends and tax planning considerations. However, the principal requirement will be that the investment should yield a return proportionate to the risk involved. In finance theory risk is normally taken to refer to the chance that a cash flow or other return will not materialize as expected. For example, if an investor anticipates a return of 8%, but there is a probability that the return will be less, then the investor is assuming a risk.

Naturally, it would be of considerable advantage in constructing a portfolio if the associated risk could be quantified. Yet this would require an assessment of the probability of all possible future return profiles. Obviously this would involve an element of guesswork and could never be achieved with complete confidence. However, it is generally accepted that recent past performance can be taken as a reasonable guide to probable future returns.

But, if even this somewhat tenuous connection is accepted, difficulties remain in assessing the nature of the information contained in such probabilities. One option is to compare the projected distribution of returns with those for another security. Typically the approach adopted is to express the projected returns in terms of some statistical technique. One particularly suitable method is to assess the profile in terms of the mean and the standard deviation. These are appropriate for this exercise because, assuming a normal distribution, the standard deviation from the mean, since it is a measure of dispersion, can be used as a measure of risk: a low standard deviation indicates a low anticipated variability from the expected mean, that is, a relatively low risk, while a high standard deviation implies a high risk.

The following extract narrates how Harry Markowitz, one of the pioneers of portfolio theory, developed his ideas:

"On the other hand, investors *can* manage the risks that they take. Higher risk should in time produce more wealth, but only for investors who can stand the heat. As these simple truths grew increasingly obvious over the course of the 1970s Markowitz became a household name among professional investors and their clients.

Markowitz's objective in 'Portfolio Selection' was to use the notion of risk to construct portfolios for investors who 'consider expected return a desirable thing *and* variance of return an undesirable thing,' The italicized 'and' that links return and variance is the fulcrum on which Markowitz builds his case.

Markowitz makes no mention of the word 'risk' in describing his investment strategy. He simply identifies variance of return as the 'undesirable thing' that investors try to minimize. Risk and variance have become synonymous. Von Neumann and Morgenstern had put a number on utility; Markowitz put a number on investment risk.

Variance is a statistical measurement of how widely the returns on an asset swing around their average. The concept is mathematically linked to the standard deviation; in fact, the two are essentially interchangeable. The greater the variance or the standard deviation around the average, the less the average return will signify about what the outcome is likely to be. A high-variance situation lands you back in the head-in-the-oven-feet-in-the-refrigerator syndrome".

Source: Peter L. Bernstein, Against the Gods, Wiley 1996, p. 252.

This capacity to measure risk is important, since portfolio theory is concerned with identifying portfolios of securities that reduce risk through diversification on the assumption that investors are risk-averse, i.e., faced with a choice between two securities that offer the same return, the investor will choose the one with the lowest risk. In terms of the statistical techniques just described this can be restated as "faced with a choice between two securities that offer the same return, the investor will choose the one with the lowest standard deviation".

In terms of portfolio theory this has further significance in that, as the number of shares in the portfolio increases, the standard deviation for the portfolio as a whole decreases. For example, if an investor decides to put half of his or her funds into a software company and the other half into a retail chain then any misfortunes (resulting in negative variations) in one may be offset to some extent by the fortunes of the other. In other words, it is possible to reduce risk, although never eliminate it, by means of diversification.

Furthermore, as the portfolio increases and the standard deviation of the portfolio as a whole accordingly decreases, the return attributable to this portfolio begins, more and more, to correspond to the return enjoyed by the market as a whole. Obviously, if the portfolio included all equities quoted on the market its return would correspond exactly to the market return.

---

**In practice:**

*Most investors will want to diversify their portfolio. This simply means that they will want to hold shares in a range of industries with different characteristics.*

*For instance, most will want to have a mixture of small company shares, some of which are often risky but offer quick growth, and large company shares with a history of more steady growth. Whatever the mix adopted the point is that the risk is being spread across different industries and securities. The intention is that all shares in the portfolio would not be exposed to a sudden downturn in one industry.*

*For example, those who invested entirely in new technology stocks and did not diversify suffered more in the recent Nasdaq downturn than those who had balanced their new technology investments with some shares in traditional, more stable industries.*

---

## CAPM

CAPM builds on portfolio theory, but extends it to incorporate a measure of the relationship between risk and return. Essentially it is concerned with demonstrating how the minimum return required of a security is a function of its riskiness.

It makes a number of assumptions:

- All investors are rational, wealth maximizes

- Investors are risk averse

- Standard deviation is the most appropriate measure of risk

- There are no transaction costs and information has no cost and is available to all

- All investors can borrow and lend at the risk-free rate, i.e., the rate enjoyed on risk free investments such as government bonds

- All investors have similar expectations about future returns

A portfolio of shares may commence with just one security, but the usual pattern will be for additional securities to be added over time. According to portfolio theory, as the number of securities in the portfolio increases the standard deviation (the measure of risk) decreases. In other words, the relevant risk to be considered when deciding whether or not to incorporate a security into a portfolio is not the total risk associated with it, *but the effect its incorporation would have on the riskiness of the portfolio as a whole.*

CAPM is a technique that allows this marginal effect to be measured by subdividing the risk element of a security into its component parts:

- The element that can be diversified away, i.e., unsystematic risk, for example, the risks particular to that firm such as its susceptibility to strikes. This will be diversified away by the fact that the portfolio will include other securities which will not be susceptible to such risk.

- The element that cannot be diversified away, i.e., the systematic (or market) risk. This is the element of risk deriving from considerations common to all firms in the market such as macro-economic issues, inflation, etc.

Since unsystematic risk will be diversified away in any balanced portfolio, CAPM posits that the only element of risk that needs to be assessed when deciding whether or not to include a security in a portfolio is its systematic risk. This is because it is the only element of risk which the portfolio will be rewarded for taking. A security with a high correlation to variations in the market, i.e., a high systematic risk, will do relatively little to reduce the risk element of a portfolio and, therefore, will be required to produce a high return. Correspondingly, a security with a low systematic risk is useful as a means of reducing the riskiness of a portfolio and, consequently, will only be required to yield a lower return.

The issue becomes, then, how to properly quantify the systematic risk element of a security, i.e., the degree of correlation to variations in the market.

The method used by CAPM to do this is an index, normally referred to as the beta ($\beta$) of a security. There are two bases to this index:

- **The risk-free security**: such a security, for example a government bond, carries no risk and, therefore, no systematic risk. It is assigned a beta of zero.

- **The market portfolio**: a market portfolio represents complete diversification and, as a result, only contains risks that can be specifically attributed to the market, i.e., it would be expected to replicate market movements exactly. This is assigned a beta of 1.

Every security will have a beta that can be expressed in terms of these bases. For example, a security with a $\beta$ of 0.8 can be said to be less volatile than the market as a whole, one with a $\beta$ of 1.1 is more volatile than the market as a whole, while one with a $\beta$ of 0.05 shows very little volatility.

The importance of CAPM is that it provides a useful model of expected returns, relating them to a measure of risk, $\beta$, which quantifies the degree of relationship between that security and the market. Ideally, what should be determined for a security is its future $\beta$. In practice, however, past betas are usually taken as an appropriate basis upon which to appraise required returns.

Since, therefore, both the return and the risk on the market portfolio are known it is possible to express the relationship between them as follows:

$$E(R_p) = R_f + \beta(E(R_m) - R_f)$$

where $E(R_p)$ is the expected return on the security; $R_f$ is the risk-free return; $E(R_m) - R_f$ is the risk premium on the market. This is the marginal return investors enjoy by taking market-related risk and in the UK it has traditionally been in the range of 6–9%; $\beta$, the riskiness of the security relative to the market.[2]

In reality many of the assumptions underlying the CAPM are transgressed. For example, a risk-free rate is difficult to identify because of inflation. It is also unrealistic to expect that all investors will have equal access and capacity to borrow and lend funds at this rate. Furthermore, there are obvious problems with calculating beta on the basis of past results. In addition, there are other difficulties with the model, since, for example, it only assesses the level of return, not its constituent parts, such as capital gains and dividends. For some investors these may be important considerations.

Notwithstanding this, analysts are concerned not so much with the underlying assumptions as with whether or not the model "works" in terms of explaining returns on the market. Empirical testing of CAPM yields somewhat ambiguous results. Nevertheless, until recently, the general consensus was that the model was relatively robust and does approximate to real world conditions, in that it demonstrates a strong relationship between systematic risk and rate of return.

Since it suggests that the expected return for a firm is not dependent upon risks that can be diversified away, with the obvious corollary that information regarding the prospects for a particular security is irrelevant, CAPM has had a major impact upon accounting theory and practice. Specifically, it questions the usefulness of company-specific accounting data to investors. In so doing it challenges the rationale

---

[2] For an excellent and more complete explanation of these models see Rees, *Financial Analysis*, 2nd ed., 1999.

for the production and analysis of such information. The real issue, CAPM suggests, is its systematic risk, expressed in terms of its beta.

## Arbitrage Pricing Theory (APT)

The limitations inherent in a single-index model such as CAPM as a mechanism for understanding the relationship between risk and return have led to a search for models with greater explanatory power. One alternative developed by Ross is APT which expresses the relationship between expected returns and a wide range of factors to which a security may be sensitive. In contrast to the single-index (beta) CAPM, APT is a multi-index model. Thus, while CAPM can only incorporate sensitivity to market returns in the form of beta, APT can include a multitude of factors such as interest rate and industry specific indices.

## Efficient Market Hypothesis (EMH)

CAPM and APT were important factors in the development of EMH which has had a profound effect on the way in which the relationship between accounting information and the market is viewed. Specifically, by changing the perspective from that of the information provider to the information consumer, EMH claims to explain how the market for accounting information operates.

An efficient market is defined as one where "stocks are valued fairly in the light of all available information." Such a market is assumed to immediately and rationally impound information relevant to the security. For example, as information that suggests increased profits becomes available the share price should increase to a level where the yield would be equivalent to that expected for shares with a similar risk profile. Likewise, information suggesting a decrease should lead to a drop in share price to a level that would yield an amount equivalent to that expected for shares with a similar risk profile.

EMH contends, therefore, that a market is efficient if share prices fully reflect all information available, i.e., it does not allow anyone to profit from such information since it is assumed that the market has immediately and rationally impounded the implications of that information into the price of the share. In other words, any new or additional information is quickly absorbed by the market and used to determine the appropriate value of the shares. The agreed price for a security is seen to be set by the market, therefore, in a manner which represents some form of weighted consensus as to the value of a share on a given day, since the market, if it is efficient, will fully reflect all available and relevant information. Thus, there is an assumption that the market will only react in an extreme manner to surprise announcements. In short, EMH considers the stock market the most efficient mechanism for determining value.

---

**In practice:**

*The Efficient Market Theory (EMT) is conventional economic wisdom: "the market knows best" how to use capital resources to promote maximum growth. Since the 1970s EMT has provided the justification for dismantling the ubiquitous post-war financial market regulations, arguing "liberalization" would produce lower real costs of capital and higher output and productivity growth compared to the growth rates experienced between the Second World War and 1973, when international capital flow controls were widely practised.*

*Source: The Guardian, March 15, 1999.*

---

The implications of this for accounting information and its disclosure, particularly as disseminated by means of the Annual Report, are enormous:

- EMH assumes that accounting information will be impounded in the share price when that information becomes available. By virtue of interim reports, preliminary announcements, profit warnings/forecasts, press briefings, leaks, insider information, insider trading and other means, such information will usually become available to the market prior to the publication of the Annual Report. (In fact, if anything, the market is most likely to respond to the preliminary announcement.) This raises fundamental questions about the usefulness and timeliness of one of the most important (and lucrative) documents produced by the accounting process. Obviously, by extension, it questions the usefulness of any analysis of the information contained in Annual Reports.

- EMH recognizes that accounting information is not the only information source used for decision making.

- EMH presumes, contrary to the Classical approach, that the market is a more efficient arbiter of value than accounting.

### Implications of EMH for Accounting Information

Because the existence of an efficient market could have such significance, extensive empirical research has been carried out in the US and, to a lesser extent, in the UK. Among those identified as likely to be impacted are:

- **Accounting regulators**: if the market can be shown to be capable of properly discerning attempts by management to mislead it by the use of "creative" accounting techniques, then the usefulness of regulations, intended, in part, to protect naïve investors, is open to question.

- **Accountants**: since EMH posits that the information contained in Annual Reports will already have been impounded in the share price by the time the Annual Report is published by virtue of interim reports, preliminary announcements, insider trading, etc., there is little point in companies producing Annual Reports.

- **Investors, fund managers and analysts**: if an efficient market exists then there is little point expending time and money on an analysis of financial information since possession of such information does not confer any advantage, as it will already have been impounded into the price of a security. Furthermore, it will not be possible to develop strategies that generate "abnormal returns" by identifying mis-priced shares.

---

### In practice:

*...Should we accept the EMH and its conclusions so quickly? Actually, we witness events each day that support the theory's truth. At least 80% of the mutual funds in existence, backed by mounds of research and a universe of stocks to choose from, have failed to beat the S&P 500 in 1, 3, 5, and 10 year averages. Most Wall Street analysts and fund managers inhale and exhale the financial conditions and future prospects of companies during every waking minute, and then in their dreams. They attend industry conferences, fly cross-country to visit factories, make long distance phone calls to CEOs, and then recalculate, buying and selling companies in a breathless reaction to new information (such that the stock price reflects its true value almost immediately). Yet whatever benefit they may gain from "getting to market before the rest of us" seems to barely cover the costs (including fees and capital gains taxes) of the effort...*

*Source: Mary Naber, Will Values-based investing affect your returns? Crosswalk.com.*

---

### Is the Market Efficient?

Obviously, these points are of particular significance to accountants since what is being assessed is the usefulness to users of incurring additional costs in acquiring and analysing accounting information such as that disclosed in the Annual Report. In essence, if EMH can be shown to be true, i.e., if an efficient market can be shown to exist, then the usefulness of analysing accounting information produced by companies is brought into question.

The question is, therefore, "Is the market efficient?" To answer this it is important to understand what is meant by the word "efficient". In the context of EMH what it means is that share prices quickly adjust to "fully reflect" available information. In other words, possession of that information does not enable the possessor to profit from it. However, it does not mean that every user of this information will interpret it and/or use it in the same way.

The efficiency or otherwise of a market can be tested in a number of ways:

1. **Allocative efficiency** posits that a market is efficient if it directs savings towards the most productive enterprises. If this is so, then the most efficient firms should find it easier to raise funds than others. It is assumed that the amount of information required to obtain funds, for example on the Stock Exchange, is such that allocative efficiency is assured.

2. **Operational efficiency** relates to the cost of transacting business in a market. On the Stock Exchange, for example, the lower the brokerage costs the greater the operational efficiency. Operational efficiency can be shown to exist in the larger Stock Exchanges such as those in the US and London where transaction costs are low, and to have been secured by the huge increase in the range and type of trading activity facilitated by the Internet. Because of limited research, the position is less clear in relation to exchanges in continental Europe and Asia.

3. **Information processing efficiency** relates to the extent to which the current share price reflects the future prospects of the firm. Where all known information is reflected in the share price, then, because all investors have the same chance, as there is no advantage to be had from having information which has already been impounded, the investment process is termed "fair game". This does not imply that there is no risk to individual investors, but that returns will be "fair" since they will be commensurate with the risk taken.

For example, suppose that a fund manager comes into possession of information that suggests the profits of a particular firm will far exceed even the most positive projections. In an inefficient market this manager could capitalize on the fact that this information is not yet available to smaller investors and purchase shares from them at a price that has not impounded this information. In an efficient market, however, no such opportunity would exist as it is assumed that the market would immediately and correctly impound this information in the share price.

Research is less conclusive about the existence of information processing efficiency.

**Forms of EMH**

Because research does not verify the existence of perfect information processing efficiency, it is necessary to test EMH in three forms, each reflecting the classification of information into categories, and positing the ability of the market to produce estimates of value corresponding to information availability:

- **Weak form:** In this form the information available is that relating to past share price movements only. The hypothesis is that past share price movements cannot be taken as a guide to future price movements. In other words, analysis of past share movements and trends is unlikely to yield better returns and as such is not a worthwhile activity. For example, if a company's share price has increased steadily over the previous few months, then this cannot be taken as an indication of future share movements, and the next change in price could, with equal probability, be either upwards or downwards. This randomness has given rise to the Random Walk Hypothesis, which says that share price movements over time approximate to a random, unpredictable walk. Empirical research has strongly supported the Random Walk Hypothesis, and so the EMH in its weak form is widely accepted, as the extract below illustrates:

## Can you Beat the Blindfolded Monkey?

Is financial acumen an oxymoron, like military intelligence? Or can the smartest money managers really fulfil their promise to beat average returns on the stock markets?

...Mr Malkiel's "A Random Walk Down Wall Street", first published nearly 30 years ago and now revised, is deservedly a perennial best-seller. It maintains that investors who buy and hold all the stocks in a broad stock market average – as index funds do – are likely to do better than investors who put their money into actively managed funds, not least because the higher charges and trading costs of professional money managers cut into investment returns.

Charts and tables are produced by Mr Malkiel to back his assertion. They show, for instance, that a person who invested $10,000 in 1969 in a Standard & Poor's 500-stock index fund would have seen its value increase to about $310,000 by mid-1998 – $140,000 more than $10,000 invested over the same period in the average actively managed fund. And in making these calculations, Mr Malkiel plays fair: he deducts the typical running expense (one-fifth of 1%) charged by an index fund. To the dismay of active equity managers, the ranks of the random-walk converts are swelling all the time, especially in the US where passive managers now handle most of the shares in public-sector pension funds.

Even so, Mr Malkiel does not stick to the letter of his own fundamentalist text: "The market prices stocks so efficiently that a blindfolded chimpanzee throwing darts at the Wall Street Journal can select a portfolio that performs as well as those managed by the experts." He concedes that some money managers do succeed, at least for a time, in beating the stock market averages. The difficulty lies in identifying them before, rather than after, they do it.

Source: Economist, 17 July 1999, review of B. Malkiel, A Random Walk Down Wall Street.

- **Semi-strong form**: In this form the information set available is taken to be all publicly available data, including that contained in the Annual Report. Because the share price is assumed to fully reflect all such information, there is assumed to be no advantage accruing to holders of this information. If verified, then this has major implications for both accountants, who provide such information, and financial analysts, who have traditionally applied various analytical techniques to accounting information in an attempt to identify mis-priced shares, which they could then exploit. This form has been widely tested by examining the way in which the market reacts to new information about a company and the evidence does suggest that it is fairly robust. Kaplan and Roll,[1] for instance, tested the impact on a company's share price of a change in depreciation methods which, while affecting earnings, had no effect on cash flows. Initially, the study showed, share prices rose but within 3 months share prices dropped once investors realized that these creative accounting practices were cosmetic. The significance of this was not only that the market was shown to respond rationally, but also that it appeared that it was the information they conveyed about future cash flows, not the accounting numbers as such, which was important to the investors. If the market is capable of extracting the significant information from accounts constructed according to complex accounting rules and standards then, supporters of EMH contend, the efficacy, necessity and costs to firms of such rules and standards are brought into question.

- **Strong form**: In this form the information available is all data, including private (insider) information. This form can best be tested by examining the market's reaction to information about the company that has previously been confidential. If the EMH in this form is correct then the market should not react at all to the mere release of this information, as the assumption is that all information relevant to the company has already become available, whether by press release, interim reports or other means, and been impounded in the share price. As a result, it should not be possible to make profits by availing of inside information. (In any case "insider dealing" is illegal in both the UK and the US.) In fact, studies tend to demonstrate that markets do react to the publication of such information. In other words, illegal or not, it would be possible to make abnormal returns by exploiting insider information. It would appear, therefore, that in its strong form EMH is not sustainable.

Throughout the 1970s and early 1980s EMH was the dominant paradigm in the literature and it was widely accepted that stock markets conformed, at least, to the semi-strong form of the thesis. Event studies, particularly those based on the US and UK stock markets, seemed to confirm that these markets were efficient to the extent that they priced information quickly and accurately and shares fully and fairly reflected all publicly available information as to the future net cash flows deriving from underlying assets. With the exception of a small number of individuals such as Warren Buffett, it was accepted that it was not possible to develop strategies that consistently outperformed the market.

Worryingly for supporters of EMH, however, studies began to identify an increasing number of anomalies that tended to challenge assertions that the market was efficient. For example, even the Kaplan and Roll study which seemed to support the semi-strong form, was forced to confront the fact that, while the market eventually adjusted for creative accounting practices, this did not happen immediately but over a period of several months.

Gradually, evidence of a number of such "anomalies" began to accumulate. For instance, researchers claimed to have identified a *small-firm-in-January* effect whereby those investing in December in firms with relatively small market capitalization and selling in January generated abnormally high risk-adjusted returns. Others claimed to have identified a *mean-reversion* tendency, which asserted that while markets tended to overreact to new information, they gradually reverted to a mean value.

Supporters of EMH countered that anomalies such as the *small-firm-in-January* effect amounted to nothing more than a *neglected-firm-effect* that, as EMH hypothesized, tend to be traded away once larger institutions begin to invest in these previously "anonymous" companies. This, they argue, illustrates one of the great paradoxes of EMH: it is those analysts actively searching for market-beating strategies and disgruntled company executives complaining about inefficiencies, who actually contribute to market efficiency by making available additional information which the market can then assimilate. Ironically, as the authors of the following extract contend, efforts to prove market inefficiency actually lead to the very efficiency that critics are working so hard to refute.

## The EMT Thrives on Criticism

No theoretical abstraction is likely to be entirely consistent with the complexity of the real world it attempts to explain and the theory of efficient markets is no exception to this rule. Quite apart from the problems of accurately testing the EMT, and determining just how anomalous an identified anomaly really is, there are no doubt real anomalies out there. But the EMT is practically alone among theories in that it becomes more powerful when people discover serious inconsistencies between it and the real world. If a clear efficient market anomaly is discovered, the behaviour (or lack of behaviour) that gives rise to it will tend to be eliminated by competition among investors for higher returns.

If, for example, it becomes clear that investors in general overreact to new information, as some studies suggest, such overreaction presents other investors with clear opportunities for profitable behaviour – and such behaviour will in turn reduce, if not eliminate, the overreaction. Similarly, if stock prices are found to follow predictable seasonal patterns unrelated to financially relevant considerations, this knowledge will elicit responses that have the effect of eliminating the very patterns they were designed to exploit...

The implication here is rather striking. The more empirical flaws that are discovered in the EMT, the more robust the theory becomes. Actual behaviour, when discovered to be incongruous with what is predicted by the theory, then adjusts to conform more closely to the theory. In the case of EMT, the Heisenberg principle – the idea that to study something is to change it – rather than confounding attempts to understand the real world, has the effect of bringing the real world more in line with our understanding. Those who do the most to ensure that the EMT remains fundamental to our understanding of financial economics are not its intellectual defenders, but those mounting the most serious empirical assault on it. Attempting to destroy the EMT by uncovering anomalies is no less difficult than attempting to destroy a hydra-headed monster by chopping off its heads. For every head that falls, two more grow back.

Source: D. R. Lee and J A Verbrugge, 'The EMT Thrives on Criticism', Journal of Applied Corporate Finance, 9, (1), 1996.

Notwithstanding arguments such as that made in this extract, the effect of market-based research highlighting some problems with EMH has been to temper some of the claims made in its name. Thus, some of those formerly advocating the infallibility of EMH now accept that the evidence is not unambiguous.

This scepticism has extended to many economists who have begun to question some of the fundamental assumptions underpinning theories such as EMH.

## Irrationality: Rethinking Thinking

"ARE economists human?" is not a question that occurs to many practitioners of the dismal science, but it is one that springs to the minds of many non-economists exposed to conventional economic explanations. Economists have typically described the thought processes of Homo sapiens as more like that of Star Trek's Mr Spock – strictly logical, centred on a clearly defined goal and free from the unsteady influences of emotion or irrationality – than the uncertain, error-prone groping with which most of us are familiar. Of course, some human behaviour does fit the rational pattern so beloved of economists. But remember, Mr Spock is a Vulcan, not a human.

Even economists are finally waking up to this fact. A wind of change is now blowing some human spirit back into the ivory towers where economic theory is made. It is becoming increasingly fashionable for economists, especially the younger, more ambitious ones, to borrow insights from psychologists (and some-times even biologists) to try to explain drug addiction, the working habits of New York taxi-drivers, current sky-high American share prices and other types of beha-viour which seem to defy rationality. Alan Greenspan, the chairman of the Federal Reserve, made a bow to this new trend when he wondered about the "irrational exuberance" of American stock markets way back in December 1996 (after an initial flutter of concern, investors ignored him).

Many economic rationalists still hold true to their faith, and some have fought back by devising rational explanations for the apparent irrationalities studied by the growing school of "behavioural economists". Ironically, orthodox economists have been forced to fight this rearguard action against heretics in their own ranks just as their own approach has begun to be more widely applied in other social sciences such as the study of law and politics.

The golden age of rational economic man began in the 1940s... By the late 1970s, economic rationality was not only the orthodoxy, it began to effect events in the real world. Macroeconomic policy, notably in America and Britain, fell into the hands of believers in the theory of "rational expectations". This said that, rather than forming expectations on the basis of limited information drawn from previous experience, people take into account all available information. This includes making an accurate assessment of government policy. Thus, when governments announced that they would do whatever was necessary to bring down inflation, people would adjust their expectations accordingly.

In the same way, Wall Street investment firms, too, increasingly fell under the spell of the "efficient markets hypothesis", an economic theory that assumes that the prices of financial assets such as shares and bonds are rationally based on all available information. Even if there are many stupid investors, went the theory, they would be driven out of the market by rational investors who could profit by trading against the investments of the foolish. As a result, economists scoffed at the notion that investors could consistently earn a higher return than the market average by picking shares. How times have changed. Some of those same economists have now become investment managers – although their performance has suggested that they should have paid heed to their earlier beliefs about the difficulty of beating the market.

During the 1980s, macroeconomic policies based on rational expectations failed to live up to their promise (although this was probably because people rationally refused to believe government promises). And the stock market crash of October 1987 shattered the confidence of many economists in efficient markets. The crash seemed to have occurred without any new information or reason. Thus, the door of the ivory tower opened, at first only slightly, to theories that included irrational behaviour. Today there is a growing school of economists who are drawing on a vast range of behavioural traits identified by experimental psychologists which amount to a frontal assault on the whole idea that people, individually or as a group, mostly act rationally...

Source: The Economist, December 18, 1999.

Not only economists, but others who approach matters from a behaviourist perspective, have begun to challenge some of the fundamental challenges upon which EMH is built. For example, some cognitive psychologists argue that, because decision-makers have limited ability to interpret, assimilate and act on information, thus compromising their ability to make rational choices, one of the fundamental tenets of EMH, rational behaviour, is undermined. Thus, while a high probability of optimal pricing still exists, it is not assured. Furthermore, cognitive psychologists point out, the presence of anomalies points to some element of irrationality.

Arrow (1982) suggests that a heuristic (rule-of-thumb) approach replaces the rational process as decision-makers seek to assimilate information.[2] This in turn offers scope for management to massage information in such a way as to induce the desired effect on share price. Arrow has also argued that this both encourages and explains the short-termism of many investors. The short-term hypothesis suggests that there is a prejudice against long-term investment since the average investor expects abnormally high rates of return, which in turn increases the cost of capital to firms making such investments. Investors are inclined as a result to focus on information relevant to the immediate prospects of the firm. Therefore, management is encouraged to make accounting disclosures that intentionally exaggerate short-term profitability at the expense of long-term returns.

The large number of examples of management manipulation of accounting disclosures in Terry Smith's *Accounting for Growth* (1996) has been put forward by supporters of the cognitive psychology thesis as evidence of the heuristic approach in operation on a wide scale in the UK market. Smith argued that management in companies such as Coloroll, Polly Peck and Maxwell Communications Corporation had employed dubious and creative accounting practices intended to hide fundamental weaknesses in these businesses. Complicit in this was a market which employed a heuristic approach to make sense of the vast amount of complex financial information being presented to them.

Champions of EMH counter, however, that until the case-study approach of studies such as Smith's are complemented by rigorous statistical analysis these claims can be dismissed as merely anecdotal. Furthermore, supporters of the EMH model claim that much of what is identified as anomalous is merely the time-lag effect of private information becoming public. In other words, all that is being challenged is the strong-form EMH, and even that somewhat dubiously. More plausibly they point out that, while the cognitive psychology model does conceivably pose some challenges, until it is tested by more rigorous research its claims are somewhat compromised.

Nevertheless, because it highlights mental processes, in particular emphasizing the heuristic approach, the insights of cognitive psychology offer the possibility of re-asserting the need for regulatory processes. This may well prove decisive in defending the role of accounting regulation as a means of protecting users from those intent upon exploiting their inability to act rationally.

## Positive Accounting Theory

The third main stream of accounting theory to have had a strong influence over the course of recent decades has been Positive Accounting Theory, sometimes called "contracting theory". As Watts explains in the following extract, it arose partly as a reaction to what were perceived to be deficiencies in the methodologies of the classical and market-based approaches.

"We have no theory of corporate financial statements, in the form of a group of internally consistent, interrelated hypotheses which have been subjected to formal tests and 'confirmed'. Prescriptions in the accounting literature are based on hypotheses about observed phenomena in capital markets, political process, and other areas. Rarely do any of the prescribers suggest that the hypotheses be tested formally, let alone perform such tests. Moreover, the hypotheses are often inconsistent with currently accepted theories in finance and economics.

Even that part of the accounting literature which relies on the empirically-based efficient market hypothesis and the capital-asset-pricing models of finance does not include any tests of hypotheses which directly explain why financial statements take their current form. Instead the emphasis in that finance-based literature is on stock market reaction to the content of financial statements.

The development of prescriptions and the development of theory are not incompatible. The development of prescriptions which are likely to achieve their objectives requires an underlying theory which explains observed phenomena: which predicts the effects of particular prescriptions. Thus, given the concentration on prescriptions, the lack of development of theory in financial accounting remains an enigma."

Source: Watts, R. L. (1977), Corporate Financial Statements, A Product of the Market and Political Process, *Australian Journal of Management*, 2, pp. 53–75. Copyright: The Australian Graduate School of Management.

The central hypothesis of Positive Accounting Theory is that accounting arose, not in response to market demands for information, but as a device by which the contracts which mediate relationships within a firm could be monitored.

In contrast to the Classical approach, which is predicated upon the notion of accounting as the best mechanism by which to capture the "correct" value of a firm, the Positive Approach assumes that there is no such "correct" value.

Consequently, it does not look on accounting as some external, neutral entity, but as a vibrant element of the firm which not so much describes that reality as helps to define and shape it. In other words, accounting data and systems are seen as a means of exerting control. Management, for example, can be employed on contracts that incorporate accounting measures such as profit as the basis for the bonus element of their remuneration packages. In this scenario, accounting methods and systems act as mechanisms by which resources are allocated within a firm.

From this understanding of the key role of accounting information within a firm it is postulated that managers have a vested interest in the effect of their actions on accounting information and disclosures. In other words, they will have incentives to change either their decisions or the firm's accounting policies in order to influence the accounting numbers. This will be most likely in circumstances where their remuneration is tied to performance. The effect of this insight has been to move the focus away from testing market reaction to accounting disclosures, and onto the study and observation of management behaviour in relation to the incentives underlying their choice of alternative accounting policies.

This paradigm found a natural ally in agency theory which is predicated on the belief that people are motivated primarily by self-interest. Management could, therefore, be assumed to act in ways that maximized the value of the firm only if this coincided with their own vested interests. Furthermore, unless owners were prepared to establish monitoring mechanisms, then management had incentives to minimize their input and increase their remuneration in ways that would be contrary to the interests of shareholders and creditors.

The significance of accounting measures and systems in this scenario is that they not only offer an obvious monitoring mechanism, but can also be employed as a "language" in which the contracts that are seen as integral to the operation of any set of relationships can be framed. The use of accounting information in this way allows it to be viewed as a medium through which relationships can be expressed and controlled, in other words as an efficient way in which to operate the firm.

One attraction of the Positive Accounting paradigm is that it acknowledges that accounting information, and the actors who interact with it, play out their roles in a "political" context and are subject to a variety of political pressures. As a result the public and political perception of financial information is important. This is particularly the case for large firms, especially those in the utility sector. There will, for example, be pressures on management of entities such as water companies to show that they are not making exorbitant profits at a time of water shortage. As was the case several years ago in the UK, failure to respond to these pressures may result in political pressures to impose windfall taxes on such profits. Likewise there will be pressures on management of certain companies to ensure that the figures for management remuneration are not excessive.

In such circumstances management may be tempted to employ creative accounting practices to "massage" profits. For example, water companies responded to these pressures by incorporating provisions for "environmental costs" which had the double advantage of reducing profits without any immediate cash flow impact, while simultaneously allowing management to respond to criticisms from the green lobby about their environmental record.

By concentrating on the incentives for management to act selfishly and opportunistically, Positive Accounting Theory has provided a useful means by which the political aspects of accounting policy choice can be investigated. Furthermore, by focusing on issues such as why firms choose particular accounting methods, it has provided a significant counter-balance to the market-based approach. It remains to be seen whether its case-specific methodology can survive closer scrutiny.

## Implications for Financial Information Analysis

The answer to the question "What is the relationship between accounting information and the market?" may not seem any clearer. However, the various theoretical frameworks that have sought to address this question have at least allowed some advances in our understanding.

By seeming to confirm that the market impounds all information immediately and fairly, the ascendancy for the last two decades of the market-based approach, particularly as manifested by EMH, posed great challenges for accountants and financial analysts. Essentially the usefulness of analysing accounting data was being fundamentally questioned.

However, the validity of Fundamental Analysis as a legitimate exercise has been reasserted in recent years as it has gradually dawned on those championing the market-based approach that various anomalies, coupled with the failure of empirical studies to confirm EMH in its strong form, demonstrate that it is not capable of capturing all of the various dynamics at work in a market.

Significantly, this has coincided with calls for a re-examination of the role of Fundamental Analysis by academics such as Ohlson who have re-established its academic credentials by virtue of longer-term studies.[3] In direct contrast to the fashion typical of the finance literature, where accounting figures are deconstructed to expose cash flows, Ohlson demonstrates the relationship between basic account-ing measures and ratios, such as return on equity and book values.

The view of accountants, many academics and, of course, analysts, therefore, is that even if it is not possible to develop a strategy which offers superior returns to the market over the long-term, Fundamental Analysis is a legitimate and rewarding exercise. It offers one means of identifying firms that offer abnormal returns, since an ability to understand the implications of various accounting alternatives provides a competitive advantage to the user.

It is also worth remembering that financial information analysis is not carried out solely with a view to assessing the reaction of markets or the impact of financial information on share price. From the start of this text it has been emphasized that the analysis of financial information is an important element in the decision-making process of a variety of users, not just investors. Thus, financial information analysis is a valid exercise to the extent that it allows more informed, balanced and strategic decisions by those who see accounting information as an important element in the information resource of a firm.

## Summary

One of the primary purposes of this text is to consider the information content of accounting disclosures, especially as incorporated in an Annual Report, and to do so in the context of the political, social and economic environments within which accounting operates.

In an attempt to understand one of these environments, this chapter has sought to answer the question "What is the relationship between accounting information and the market?" Until recently the effect of the dominant market-based paradigm has been to question the usefulness of accounting information and, consequently, its analysis, on the grounds that the market will have impounded into the share price the information contained in an Annual Report prior to its publication.

More recently, however, a dawning realization that EMH, while robust, is not infallible, and research that has highlighted the strong correlation between share returns and basic accounting measures when considered over a long period of time, have re-established the efficacy of Fundamental Analysis as a legitimate and potentially profitable exercise. So too have perspectives that challenge the notion that it is the needs of investors which should be the dominant concern of the preparers of accounting information. Indeed, it is to this theme that the following chapter turns.

# Review Questions

### Question 1
Explain why theory can be useful in aiding an understanding of the broader issues involved in any particular practice or series of events.

### Question 2
Identify and distinguish between the three dominant paradigms that have been prevalent within accounting over the course of recent decades.

### Question 3
Explain how changes in finance theory gradually impacted upon the way in which academics and practitioners began to think about the role of accounting information in the market.

### Question 4
Explain what is meant by each of the following terms:
- Diversification
- Efficient market
- Portfolio
- Beta
- Riskiness

### Question 5
CAPM builds upon portfolio theory and incorporates a measure of the relationship between risk and return. Explain how it achieves this.

### Question 6
"The contribution of APT was to provide a complex model that approximated more closely to reality. This gave it a credibility that CAPM lacked". Explain what this means.

### Question 7
Identify the challenges that EMH brings to the traditional understanding of the role of accounting information in the market. How does this affect the way in which accounting information is perceived by users?

### Question 8
Explain the distinction between the EMH in its weak, semi-strong and strong paradigms.

### Question 9
Identify the sources of recent challenges to the previously dominant EMH paradigm. In respect of each indicate whether these can be refuted by EMH or whether they represent fundamental challenges.

### Question 10
Summarize the contribution of Positive Accounting Theory to accounting thought.

## Case Studies

### Case 1

Read the following reviews and discuss the points made with particular reference to the arguments in favour of and against EMH.

## Can you Beat the Blindfolded Monkey? (continued)

Kenneth Stern ...puts his money on the jockey rather than the horse and so sets out, in "Secrets of the Investment All-Stars", to pick the brains of the world's most successful investment professionals. His title shows flair for clever marketing, but its implied promise to provide readers with the keys to financial success is not kept. Mr Stern's nine all-stars offer contradictory advice. John Bogle, the founder of the Vanguard Investment Group, champions the passive, or index, approach to investment. Louis Navellier, editor of Modern Portfolio Theory (MPT) Review, emphatically disagrees. "If we can not beat the market, why are we here?" he asks.

For Ron Elijah, managing director of Robertson Stephens Investment Management, "everything is about demographics." Anticipate the demands of the baby boomers, who are passing through the American economy like a piglet through a python, he says, and you will make money. Today this means investing in technology, health care and financial services (baby-boomers save for retirement). Tomorrow, presumably, the best bets will be cruise liners, retirement homes and funeral parlours.

The advice from the others on Mr Stern's team is just as diverse. But which of them is the most successful? How many of the nine have beaten the S&P 500 over, say, the past 20 years and by how much exactly? Mr Stern does not say. Not all the money managers he wanted to see wanted to see him, and he rewards those who granted him an interview with uncritical acclaim. Nonetheless, one of his nine, Mr Navellier, does offer what may be a timely caution about a strong dollar's effect on stock prices. In early 1988, he recalls, when professional investors could not get enough of the 50 biggest stocks, "we slowly watched earnings growth fizzle. Much of this had to do with a strong dollar. Multinational companies have a hard time selling overseas when the dollar is so expensive. The early warning signs were when stocks such as Boeing and Eastman Kodak came in with lower than expected earnings."

The experts disagree even more sharply in Mr Krass's collection of Wall Street classics. But that is hardly surprising. Its earliest essays by W.W. Fowler, Arthur Crump and Charles Dow date from the 19th century when insiders manipulated the stock market and the notorious Daniel Drew spoke truly when he said: "To speculate as an outsider is like trying to drive black pigs in the dark."

The more recent contributions in Peter Krass's collection include an essay by Warren Buffett, the famed Sage of Omaha whose investment approach, so-called focus investing, offers a third way between the indexers and active traders, and is the subject of a whole book by Robert Hagstrom. Mr Hagstrom summarizes the approach succinctly: "Choose a few stocks that are likely to produce above-average returns over the long haul, concentrate the bulk of your investments in those stocks, and have the fortitude to hold steady during any short-term market gyrations." It is a simple idea but until recently it enjoyed phenomenal success, delivering a compound annual return of nearly 25% over 34 years to investors in Mr Buffett's investment vehicle, Berkshire Hathaway.

Yet even Mr Buffett's reputation has slipped lately. At Berkshire Hathaway's annual meeting in May, the folksy sage ruefully confessed to the more than 10,000 shareholders who turned up that they would have done better in 1998 if he had "regularly snuck off to the movies during market hours". His expensive mistakes included selling shares in McDonalds, which subsequently soared, and holding on to shares in Walt Disney, which fell. Who knows, perhaps even Mr Buffett will fail eventually to beat Mr Malkiel's blindfolded chimpanzee.

Source: Economist, 17 July 1999 review of K. Stern, Secrets of the Investment all-stars; Peter Krass, ed., The book of Investing Wisdom: Classic Writings by Great Stockpickers and Legends of Wall Street; and R. Hagstrom, The Warren Buffett Portfolio.

## Case 2

One of the implications of EMH is that there is no advantage to users in analysing the accounting information contained in an Annual Report with a view to identifying mis-priced securities. This represents a challenge to the role of the financial analyst. However, EMH assumes that relevant information will have reached the market by some means and, ironically, one of the conduits for this is the analyst through regular briefings provided by companies.

Using the following account of analyst activities and briefings, discuss some of the issues raised.

## What Every Investor Should Know About Stock Analysis:

### Half Textbook, Half Expose, a New Book Explains it All.

Every 3 months, Wall Street throws an invitation-only dance called earnings season. On one side of the ballroom are the chief financial officers of companies that are about to report their earnings. On the other side are the analysts, whose job it is to guess those earnings. The dance comes to an end with the company usually announcing numbers that are amazingly close to what most of the analysts guessed.

From the point of view of the individual investor, this world seems about as real as Merlin's. Indeed, the predictive abilities of the analysts of Wall Street appear to be nothing less than magical, and individual investors often see the analysts as wizards, hunched over cauldrons of data, summoning a crystalline vision of the future.

The truth is a little bit more complicated. Analysts usually get their earnings predictions from hints dispensed by executives of the company being "analysed." An average CEO has a good idea of what the quarterly earnings will be well before the end of the quarter and will pass that on – one way or another – to the analysts that cover the company.

Of course, the system should not work that way. The sad thing about how Wall Street's analyst community operates is that it is possible to analyse a stock and come up with an investing recommendation by rigorously examining publicly available data, but most analysts do not. The brokerage houses that employ them see analysts as salespeople who can bring investment banking business to the firm, rather than as analysts.

UNLIKE BUFFETT. The best analysts still do the scut work. Take Warren Buffett. Although he is famous as a money manager, his skill as a stock-picker is based on his old-fashioned analytical expertise. You better believe he knows how to take apart a balance sheet, an income statement, and a cash-flow statement (the three primary financial statements every public company is required to file with the SEC). Although most sell-side analysts (those employed by brokerage houses) claim that they can do the same, you cannot tell it from their records. Analysts hardly ever put a sell recommendation on a stock because if they did, their employer might lose other business from that company.

Into this environment comes a new book, Security Analysis on Wall Street by Jeffrey C. Hooke. It is an unusual cross between a textbook for analysts-in-training and a tell-all expose of the analyst profession in its current state. Although the marketing machine promoting the book has attempted to cast it as the successor to Graham and Dodd's classic text Security Analysis, that's something of a silly stretch. The basic disciplines in that book (buy low and sell high) are true today, and will be forever. But this book has something even better than Graham and Dodd: it gives the reader an easy-to-understand glimpse into the process of stock analysis and does not hold anything back about the shady side of the profession.

For instance, Hooke goes into great detail about the inherent conflict-of-interest of sell-side analysts. "Brokerage firms are primarily in the business of generating banking fees, commissions, and trading profits," he writes. "Providing unbiased research to investors ranks low on their list." So why pay any attention to sell-side analyst reports in the first place? Because they still can provide important bits of information. You just have to know how to interpret them through the fog of the multiple conflicts-of-interests involved in the company-analyst relationship. And this book does a good job of teaching the individual investor how to do that.

MISPLACED INFO. Hooke does not stop at revealing the underside of the analyst community. The book also warns investors how companies often massage financial statements to make them say what they want them to. For instance, a debt-laden company might want to make its balance sheet look less leveraged by placing the lease costs that it pays on office space under the heading of rent. In fact, if the lease is non-cancellable, then the proper place for lease payments is under debt. While this might not seem like much, it can make all the difference when that company applies for credit from a bank. If the bank uncovers the misplacement, which is legal but misleading, it might not issue credit to the company, thereby harming its ability to function. In other words, you do not want to own stock in a company that does that kind of thing.

One thing the book makes clear is that every analysis is only as good as the data that's provided by the company. Analysts who cover companies such as Livent and Cendant, both of which were recently forced to restate earnings because of fraudulent data, have been attacked in the press for not uncovering the fraud themselves. But that criticism is unfair. Analysts have to assume that the numbers provided by the company are correct. If the numbers are incorrect, then it is a fraud perpetrated by the company, not by the analysts.

The book is divided into four sections. The first explains the investing environment in which the analyst plays a leading role. The second describes how an analyst prepares the research report. The third describes the process of coming up with investing priorities. The fourth goes into detail about eight different types of stocks (from highly speculative stocks to natural resources stocks to emerging-market stocks).

While a particularly studious individual investor would probably benefit from reading the book cover-to-cover, that is a job better left to an MBA student. For most individual investors, Hooke's tome is more valuable as a reference than as a textbook. The introduction and first section are required reading. The last section, which lists different categories of stocks and how to analyse them, could be an invaluable resource. For instance, if you have just been given a tip on a gas stock but do not know what to look for when researching it, Hooke will tell you how to determine a reserve production ratio or a lifting cost and place them into the industry's context, and why that's important for this type of stock.

The most important tool an individual investor can have is an ability to chip through all the rocks to find a nugget of gold. This book is an invaluable, although expensive, pickaxe.

Source: Business Week Online's Daily Briefing, September 17, 1998.

## References

1. Kaplan, R.S. and Roll, R. (1972), Investor evaluation of accounting information: some empirical evidence, *Journal of Business*, 45, pp. 225–257.
2. Arrow, K. (1982), Risk perception in psychology and economics, *Economic Enquiry.*
3. Ohlson, J.A. (1995), Earnings, book values and dividends in equity valuation, *Contemporary Accounting Research*, Spring, pp. 661–687.

# GOVERNANCE CONTEXT [4]

When you have completed this chapter you will understand:

- The role of corporate governance in determining the financial reporting culture.

- The interrelationship between governance and accountability.

- The dominant role which capital markets play in the Anglo-American corporate structure.

- That the corporate governance model in the UK is a product of unique economic, social, cultural and historical factors.

- That the UK governance model is undergoing a period of review and change.

- The more inclusive approach based on 'Stakeholder Theory'

## In Britain, An Investigation into "Tomorrow's Company"

An inquiry by some of Britain's most thoughtful corporate leaders has come to the conclusion that UK corporations need to change in order to become more competitive at a global level. The most important change, according to the Tomorrow's Company report, involves developing a new vision of the company's relationships with key stakeholder groups, and recognizing that the short-term needs of shareholders need not always come first...

Managers and directors at the UK's largest publicly-held companies have lived for decades with the notion that their paramount responsibility was to provide their shareholders with ever-increasing profits and ever-larger dividends, and that their fiduciary duties precluded making decisions that might distract them from this single-minded pursuit.

But in June, along came a report that challenged the conventional wisdom. The study, entitled Tomorrow's Company, was produced by the Royal Society for the Encouragement of Arts, Manufactures and Commerce, a uniquely British institution that pulled together leaders of the business community to examine a range of global competitiveness issues. One of its most provocative conclusions: that the prevailing focus on maximizing shareholder value was preventing many British enterprises from becoming truly world-class in their operations.

As an alternative, the RSA proposed a vision of the future in which corporate decision-makers sought to balance the needs of multiple stakeholders, recognizing the company's responsibilities to its employees, its customers and its community as well as to its owners, and seeking to achieve consensus between those stakeholder groups around a common vision of the organization's purpose, direction and character.

This call for a more inclusive view of the world in which business operates was unveiled to a decidedly mixed reception in the UK. Some managers and directors appeared to find the RSA's vision liberating; others were clearly uncomfortable with this attempt to change familiar rules. Academics and ideologues who had been critical of current corporate governance practices suggested that the Society had invested millions of dollars and thousands of man hours coming to conclusions that were mere common sense; defenders of the traditional capitalist model suspected a socialist conspiracy to turn management decisions over to organized labour and community activists.

Nevertheless, the report succeeded in stimulating a debate over the role of business in society, and the need for business to adapt to the changing expectations of society, and the participation of some of the UK's largest corporations; Cadbury Schweppes, Guinness, IBM, NatWest, Thorn EMI and Unipart were among the corporate sponsors, along with management consulting firm Bain and Co., accounting giant Coopers and Lybrand and reputation management consultancy Countrywide Communications; brought added credibility to the theories of those progressive business thinkers in Europe and the US whose work the Tomorrow's Company report largely echoes.

"The companies which will sustain competitive success in the future are those which focus less exclusively on shareholders and on financial measures of success, and instead include all their stakeholder relationships and a broader range of measurements, in the way they think and talk about their purpose and performance," says Mark Goyder, the RSA's program director and author of the report.

Source: http://www.prcentral.com/rmso95tomor.htm.

## Introduction

A decade ago the term "corporate governance" would have been rarely heard, let alone understood, in boardrooms in the UK. Apart from some academics and management gurus, few paid attention to a term which basically describes the way in which companies are structured or "governed".

However, a series of large and costly corporate scandals focused attention on the possibility that many of the problems could be traced to factors such as the nature of corporate structure. In particular, collapses such as that which occurred at Maxwell Communications Corporation (MCC), suggested that issues such as the failure, or inability, of boards of directors to control and monitor business, laxity in accounting standards and an ethos of contented indifference on the part of many business leaders, had also played important roles.

The term "governance" in this context is used to describe the way in which a company is structured and controlled. It can best be understood as the "balance of power" that exists to reflect the rights of owners, managers, financiers and other stakeholders together with the structures, whether legal, administrative or cultural, which accommodate that balance.

The system of corporate governance prevailing in a country has profound implications for financial reporting and the form and degree of financial disclosure. For example, it is one of the factors that explain the detailed disclosures relating to executive remuneration in large UK companies.

For historical, cultural, social and economic reasons corporate governance systems vary throughout the world. Thus, the structures in the UK, France and Germany are significantly different in spite of efforts by the EU to sponsor some element of harmonization. And these differences profoundly impact on both the role of financial reporting and the nature and content of financial disclosure in these countries.

Over the course of the last decade, as the implications for competitive advantage of the governance structure predominating in a country have come to be appreciated, the issue has received greater attention. For instance, it was one of the considerations that prompted many of those with macro-economic responsibility in the UK and US to speculate about the relative merits of models of governance operating in Germany and Japan, two countries whose economic growth since the Second World War suggested corporate structures from which much could be learned.

## Corporate Governance in the UK

The UK corporate governance regime is typical of the Anglo-American system of corporate structure. Indeed, the model of corporate structure characteristic of the English-speaking world originated in England and was disseminated throughout the British Empire.

The unique characteristics of the Anglo-American (or Anglo-Saxon) form of corporate governance can be traced to the growth in numbers and significance of Joint-Stock companies in the 18th century. These entities, whose emergence coincided with the advent of the Industrial Revolution, were designed to facilitate the raising of the huge sums of money necessary to finance the large-scale industrialization then beginning.

Prior to that the dominant business entity had been the sole-tradership. Typically, however, these sole-traders did not have the finance needed to benefit fully from the opportunities offered by industrialization. The genius of the Joint-Stock company was that it allowed those with finance to team up with those who had skill and vision.

By investing in a company these investors were deemed to own a "share" in the company, hence the term shareholder. Typically, several of these individuals would invest, thus providing a number, often hundreds, of such shareholders. By allowing external holders of capital to invest in these entrepreneurial enterprises with limited risk, these Joint-Stock companies acted as catalysts to British industry and, in part, help to explain the extent to which Britain enjoyed such an early advantage in the industrialization process.

Over time the market in which these investors purchased and sold their shares evolved into the Stock Exchange. In contrast to many continental European countries, therefore, where the principal form of business structure continued to be the sole-tradership or partnership, the Stock Exchange has for a long time played a critical role in the financial and governance structure in the English-speaking world, particularly in the UK and the US.

This structure had other implications. Shareholders saw their role primarily as providers of capital, not entrepreneurial or managerial skill. For this reason, and because it would be simply impractical for all shareholders to involve themselves at this level, they delegated the management task to others. A central feature of the British form of corporate governance, therefore, is this division between owners and those who manage the entity on their behalf. In this scheme of things the Board of Directors came to represent a crucial element in the governance structure as it was here that the often diverging interests of investors and managers were mediated.

---

**In practice:**

While shareholders are central to the governance structure in the UK, their influence has, until recently, been peripheral while that of the companies they own is critical.

*More power to the shareholder: It's time investors took an active role in ruling what is theirs, writes Simon Caulkin*

*…Despite symbolic importance and substantial potential powers, shareholders are the hollow centre of today's stakeholder corporation. This matters for two reasons.*

*First, publicly quoted (that is shareholder controlled) companies and their managers have accumulated power beyond the imaginings of those who framed the original Acts and regulations which remain the architecture of the system today. Fifty of the world's largest economic entities are companies; including customers and suppliers, up to 40 million people depend directly or indirectly on the 10 largest global firms. Privatization means shareholders, not the state, control swathes of routine but essential economic activity such as water, light, heating and transport. The UK's listed companies are worth more than its GDP.*

> *Second, the UK depends to an overwhelming degree on listed companies for goods and services, for investment returns to finance housing, insurance and particularly retirement provision. The entire economic edifice is built on the performance of the publicly quoted company; to an extent unique among developed countries.*
>
> *This is reflected in the dramatic growth of institutional shareholding. In the UK 60% of company shares are held by pension funds, insurers and other fund managers, compared with 34% in the US and 21% in Japan. Thanks in part to the Thatcher privatization's, the UK is nearest to what business analyst Peter Drucker was already in the late Seventies calling "pension fund socialism". As the authors of Fair Shares emphasize, the performance of UK firms is of paramount importance – the shareholder is, ultimately, us.*
>
> *Source: The Guardian, August 29, 1999.*

Because these owners were divorced from the operation of their own business, it became necessary to devise a mechanism by which they might be kept informed of the performance of the company. It was in response to this that the practice of management preparing accounts that were then distributed to the owners evolved. Consequently, the practice of distributing Annual Reports to owners needs to be considered first and foremost in this context: whatever about their usefulness or timeliness, Annual Reports are primarily a means of bridging the gulf between owners and managers that results from the corporate governance model peculiar to the English-speaking world.

As the number of shareholders grew and the quantities of money raised on the market increased so too did the significance of these accounts. As a result parliament took a greater interest in the process to the extent that the accounting and auditing functions are now the subject of considerable statutory control.

## Best Practice

This governance system has had profound implications for both accounting as a discipline and the accounting and auditing professions in general. For instance, as the providers of a critical information component of the corporate edifice, accountants assumed a role and status significantly greater than their continental counterparts. So too did the information they provided. To a large extent the influence of accountants in the Anglo-American world derives from their key role in constructing and controlling the accounting information that has traditionally bridged the communications gap between owners and managers.

Many of the problems and challenges facing accounting, however, stem directly from this same gulf. Specifically they derive from the realization that the nature and form of information supplied by accountants is no longer adequate to bridge it. This is especially the case as the numbers of those with an interest in this information increase. Furthermore, spectacular failures of the accounting and auditing functions in recent years have exposed both the inadequacies of the Anglo-American governance model, and the inability of accounting information as currently presented to satisfy the interests of an increasing numbers of stakeholders.

## Cadbury Report

Since the late 1980s, therefore, there has been considerable pressure on those responsible for the regulation of the accounting and governance functions to address these perceived inadequacies. One response was the commissioning by the FRC, the Stock Exchange and the accounting profession of an investigation into corporate governance practice in the UK. Under the chairmanship of Sir Adrian Cadbury, a committee on the Financial Aspects of Corporate Governance was formed and charged with reviewing governance practice with specific reference to the following:

- The responsibilities of executive and non-executive directors for reviewing and reporting on performance to shareholders and other financially interested parties.
- The frequency, clarity and form in which information should be provided.
- The case for audit committees, including their composition and role.
- The principal responsibilities of auditors and the extent and value of the audit.
- The link between shareholders, boards and auditors; and
- Any other relevant matters.

Cadbury's approach was to attempt to establish a framework within which good corporate governance and accountability might flourish. To this end the Committee's final report emphasized matters such as transparency, disclosure and accountability as critical unifying features of any mature governance system.

In its final form the Cadbury Report concentrated on four key areas:

1. **Board of Directors**: the importance of an efficient board was emphasized. There were specific recommendations in relation to their composition and the respective roles of executive and non-executive directors. It was observed that under the board system that applies in the UK the Chairman plays a key role in ensuring that best practice is encouraged. One part of this is making sure that there is a healthy level of accountability and division of responsibilities. Although it stopped short of recommending that the roles be split, the Report strongly advised that proper accountability would be facilitated by a system in which the same person did not hold the functions of Chairman and CEO.

2. **Executive directors**: with the accountability of executive directors in mind, the Report recommended that service contracts should not exceed 3 years without shareholders approval. Without pressing the point (the issue was addressed subsequently by the Greenbury Committee) it also argued for increased disclosure of directors' remuneration. Specifically, it recommended that a remuneration committee comprised mainly of non-executive directors should set directors' pay.

3. **Non-Executive directors**: one surprising element was an emphasis on the way in which non-executive directors could play a far more proactive and independent role in a healthy corporate governance regime. As the Report outlined, non-executive directors "should be independent of management and free from any business or other relationship that could materially interfere with the exercise of their independent judgement, apart from their fees and shareholding. Their fees should reflect the time which they commit to the company." It was also envisaged that they would dominate audit and remuneration committees.

4. **Reporting and controls**: finally, the Report addressed the respective responsibilities of directors and others in relation to the presentation of information about a company's performance and position. It specifically identified it as a responsibility of the board "to present a balanced and understandable assessment of the company's position". In achieving this the Report recognized that this can mean presenting not only audited accounting data but also additional narrative material covering the company's performance and future prospects. (In response to this, the Accounting Standards Board recommended that Annual Reports incorporate a new narrative statement, called the Operating and Financial Review, in which the directors provide more information on the principal issues underlying performance. This is considered in more detail in chapter 5).

The Report also made some other specific recommendations:

- Every company should establish an audit committee comprised of "at least three non-executive directors with written terms of reference which deal clearly with its authority and duties". This committee would then liase with the external auditor and ensure that the audit function was carried out "efficiently and objectively" without any undue pressure being exerted on the auditor. Since this recommendation was made, the audit committee has emerged as a critical element in the governance architecture of complying companies. In particular, it has come to be seen as a forum in which the competing interests of preparers and users can be addressed and the concerns of auditors can be expressed. The result has been the gradual acceptance of the audit committee as a key component in any developed corporate governance structure.

- On the question of responsibility for the preparation of accounts and the audit process, it recommended that "directors should explain their responsibility for preparing the accounts next to a statement by the auditors about their reporting responsibilities". This was intended to ensure that readers, particularly shareholders, understand the respective responsibilities of directors and auditors in relation to the production of accounts. In many eyes, however, it was seen as a sop to the Report's sponsoring bodies, intended to protect them from legal action.

- A further recommendation in relation to the effectiveness of the company's system of internal control has since been dealt with by the Turnbull Committee and is discussed below.

Not surprisingly, given the vested interests of the sponsoring bodies, the terms of reference of the Cadbury Committee focussed its attentions away from fundamental issues such as the nature of the corporate governance structure in the Anglo-American world with its strong alliance to capital markets. Nevertheless, the extent to which the role of the board and, in particular non-executive directors, was addressed was more radical than many had anticipated.

## The New Breed on the Board

### Who Runs Britain's Big Companies? As Alex Brummer and Roger Cowe Report, Boardrooms are More Transparent than they Used to Be

David Montgomery's fate as chief executive of the Mirror Group is the latest example of how power is shifting inside company boardrooms. The age of the all-conquering chief executive or chairman who could steamroller any decision through a bunch of great and good time-servers, happily collecting their £30,000 a year for simply turning up at board meetings, is rapidly passing at Britain's bigger companies.

A new breed of non-executive now populates upper corporate floors: it is likely to be composed of business people powerful in their own right, with a clearer understanding of complex financial issues and knowledge of how to exercise power in the interest of creating value for shareholders. Corporate "democracy" it is not but we seem to be entering a new age of boardroom pluralism... The emerging power of non-executives can be traced back to the scandals early this decade involving Robert Maxwell chairman of the Mirror Group, and the Polly Peck chief Asil Nadir. Together with other high-profile company collapses at the end of the 1980s they prompted concern verging on panic.

The City had always been resolutely wedded to self-regulation. Financiers had been happy to work within a loose legal framework which required little of directors other than to publish accounts every year. Other organizations from trade unions to charities and schools were subject to increasingly tight regulation but the governance of companies remained locked in a Victorian haze. Directors were there to manage, subject only to basic concepts of shareholder protection.

The rash of companies suddenly falling from grace in the late 1980s caused auditors to panic. They were in the firing line for having to attest whether or not annual accounts were "true and fair". Firms faced payments running to tens of millions of pounds to settle legal actions from disgruntled shareholders who argued that auditors should have sounded the alarm before companies crashed.

In an effort to make sure the buck stopped with company directors, the accountancy profession commissioned Sir Adrian Cadbury, former chairman of the chocolate company, to come up with some way of pinning the blame on the board when things went wrong. To everyone's surprise the mild-mannered, softly-spoken Sir Adrian went way beyond the nitty-gritty of company reporting and attacked the structure of company boards.

The Cadbury Code, which the Stock Exchange was reluctantly persuaded to make mandatory for every quoted company, specified a number of new requirements for the directors' annual report, such as a statement about companies' internal controls. But the real bombshell for most British boardrooms was a demand to curb the freedom of executive directors. Cadbury said every public company should have at least three non-executive directors, whose job it would be to ensure that the board operated properly in the interests of the company. And with an eye very firmly on Maxwell and Nadir, the Cadbury Code recommended that the top jobs at every company should be split between two directors. Ideally there would be a non-executive chairman leading the board, to whom a chief executive would report. Or there should be a non-executive deputy chairman in companies where the chairman was also the senior executive.

Source: The Guardian, January 27, 1999.

## Greenbury

The Cadbury Report represented only the first in a series of efforts by regulatory bodies to deal with corporate governance issues. Indeed, one consequence of the publicity surrounding its publication and adoption was that public pressure ensured that other, related issues would have to be dealt with.

For instance, while the general public is generally indifferent to the issues surrounding the corporate governance debate, one specific element of it, the level of executive remuneration, has the capacity to generate heated reaction. And this is stoked on a regular basis by media reports of excessive remuneration packages being awarded to CEOs and directors.

### Trimming the Fat Cats

**Public Hostility to Big Money in the Boardroom Can be Overcome But Only if it is Reflected By a Corresponding Profit in the Company: by Lisa Buckingham**

The British public, usually oblivious to what happens in the boardrooms of big firms, cares about how much executives get paid. During the 1990s, corporate fat cats have rarely been out of the limelight, the creatures, largely, of the Tories' financial free-for-all. Yet Labour now appears to be soft-pedalling, despite years of exasperation and often vituperative criticism of its predecessors' failure to address blatant examples of boardroom greed. Stephen Byers, trade and industry secretary, has made it clear he does not want rules on maximum earnings. Instead, he is to follow a more "realistic" path which on the surface looks like a distinct break with Labour's recent thinking on fat cattery. Next week he gives what is being billed as a seminal address to the powerbrokers of corporate ownership; in it he will emphasize how the government is not hostile to big money in Britain's board-rooms.

No one in Whitehall, he suggests, will bat an eyelid at £1.5 million a year for a new boss at Barclays Bank or £60 million of share options for Jan Leschly at drugs giant SmithKline Beecham, just so long as the performance of their companies is equally spectacular and shareholders, employees and the nation's economy are co-beneficiaries. It is a useful departure even if one born of necessity. British business is becoming more global and bosses here want to be paid as much as their counter-parts elsewhere. Indeed many come from elsewhere and many of their overseas employees earn significantly more than they do.

Byers' demand for a provable link between rewards and performance addresses the outrage perpetrated in British boardrooms over the past decade when many reaped windfall share option gains in the privatized utilities. Phenomenal rewards transformed mediocre managers into multi-millionaires. Nothing was owed to individual achievement and everything to the fact that companies had been priva-tized at a price which created a feeding frenzy in the City. Share prices soared, boosting the value of options granted to directors. Public disgust was intensified because taxpayers felt a residual ownership interest in electricity, water and gas.

Source: The Guardian, July 13, 1999.

In 1995 the Confederation of British Industry instituted the "Study Group on Directors' Remuneration" and charged it with producing a statement of best practice in relation to directors' remuneration. The chairman, Richard Greenbury, chairman of Marks and Spencer, made it quite clear that he did not intend a radical overhaul of the current system. Nevertheless, responding to considerable public pressure and some injudicious awards to the directors of several newly privatized utilities, the Greenbury Report produce some useful proposals.

The Greenbury Code, as it came to be called, made recommendations under four principal headings:

- **Remuneration committee**: reflecting the tenor of the Cadbury Report, it proposed that the remuneration of executive directors be decided by a remuneration committee made up of non-executive directors, the names of whom should be disclosed in the Annual Report.

- **Disclosure and approval provisions**: this committee should report annually on the criteria adopted in arriving at the remuneration levels of individual directors. This report was to be included in the Annual Report and should disclose details of the full remuneration packages, including pension contributions, share options and other entitlements.

- **Remuneration policy**: as a general principle, remuneration packages should reflect generally accepted rates and be consistent with industry standards. Perfor-mance-related pay elements, in particular share-based schemes, would be expected to be long-term in focus.

- **Service contracts and compensation**: the period of notice required under service contracts should generally be 1 year or less.

The provisions of the Code were given effect by the amendment of the Listing Rules of the Stock Exchange to include a section titled Best Practice Provisions: Directors Remuneration, which broadly corresponded to the Greenbury provisions.

---

### In practice:

In spite of Greenbury and concerted public and political pressure, directors continue to award themselves large remuneration packages.

*TUC Hits Out Over Directors Pay*

*The Trades Union Congress (TUC) has accused directors of not adhering to the Cadbury and Greenbury corporate governance reports and has recommended that remuneration committees should set directors pay, bringing them in line with employee pay rises. The recommendations came in a report published ahead of yesterday's launch of the TUC's week-long annual conference in Glasgow. The report follows research commissioned by the TUC, which shows that the difference between company directors' pay and staff earnings continues to polarize.*

*The research found that the highest paid director of a FTSE all share index member company earned just under 16 times that of the median pay of their employees. Director pay increased 72% between 1994 and 1999, averaging £410,000. While average employee earnings increased by just 18% in comparison for the same period, from £17,332–20,485…*

*…The report, Top Cats-the last closed shop, said that the four-fold rise in pay showed that remuneration committees have ignored the recommendation of the Combined Code: "to be sensitive to the wider scene, including pay and employment conditions elsewhere in the group especially when determining annual salary increases." It suggests that a wider pool of non-executive directors needs to be established in order to make director pay more competitive. It also suggests that employees should be represented on remuneration boards and that incentive targets for the company should be more challenging with schemes "rewarding only good and exceptional performances".*

*(A spokesman) said the UK needs "more than disclosure" of company boardroom proceedings in order to make pay fairer. "Naming and shaming has little effect. Directors will put up with a few days bad publicity for a mega-buck pay packet", he said. "This is Britain's last closed shop", he added. "Remuneration committees are dominated by a 'you scratch my back, I will scratch yours' world where top directors from one company set the pay of other top directors. No wonder they think the going rate is four times what everyone else gets. You can imagine the reaction if unions suggested that nurses and other vital public service workers could set their own pay".*

*Source: www.accountancymagazine.com, September 12, 2000.*

## Hampel

In November 1995 Sir Ronald Hampel, chairman of ICI, was appointed to chair a successor body to Cadbury. Its remit was to continue the work of its predecessor by seeking to "promote high standards of corporate governance in the interests of investor protection". The chairman interpreted this to mean that his task was primarily to "fine-tune" Cadbury.

Published in 1998, its main provisions merely reiterated many of the points made by Cadbury and Greenbury, albeit in somewhat stronger terms. The main recommendations were:

- The positions of Chairman and CEO should be filled by different people.
- Directors should be on contracts of 1 year or less.
- The remuneration committee should consist of non-executive directors only.
- Non-executive directors may be paid in the form of shares although this is not recommended.
- One senior non-executive director should be nominated with responsibility for liasing with shareholders and addressing their concerns.
- Directors should be required to undertake some form of training for their role.

The Cadbury, Greenbury and Hampel Reports were brought together to form what came to be known as the Combined Code, a code of best practice which was incorporated by the Stock Exchange into its Yellow Book effective for accounting periods ending after December 31, 1998. This Code, which is discussed below, would be first supplemented by the Turnbull Report.

## Turnbull

The Cadbury Report had highlighted the role of internal controls and risk management as significant elements in the corporate governance debate. In response, the ICAEW set up a committee under the chairmanship of Nigel Turnbull, chairman of the leisure group Rank, to issue recommendations. In September 1999 this committee issued its final report, Internal Control: Guidance for Directors on the Combined Code.

As the title suggests this report is mainly concerned with indicating to directors how the various elements of the Combined Code relating to internal control and risk management are to be implemented.

To the surprise of many, it did make some significant contributions to the whole corporate governance debate, particularly in the importance which it attaches to the whole area of risk management. In terms of corporate strategies and perspective it effectively assigns to the whole area of risk management a strategic and operational importance which had not previously been articulated.

The Turnbull Report is predicated on the notion that "internal control is embedded in the business processes" and assumes that a company's board adopts a risk-based approach to establishing a sound system of internal control. Consequently, it emphasizes that the internal control system plays a critical function in efficiently managing risks that are central to a company achieving its business objectives. In all of this it places effective financial controls and the maintenance of proper accounting records firmly at the centre.

The following extract summarizes many of the more salient points of Turnbull.

## What You Need to Know About the Latest Proposals on Corporate Governance, by Timothy Copnell

In what many hope is the final piece of the corporate governance jigsaw, the long-awaited proposals from the Turnbull working party, Internal Control: Guidance for Directors of Listed Companies Incorporated in the UK, were issued in April. The Combined Code, and the underlying Hampel recommendation that directors review all controls, were of course the triggers for preparing the guidance. However, the recognition that successful risk management has an essential role to play in adding value to business was, perhaps, the real driving force behind the proposals.

The proposals apply to all UK listed companies. They follow Hampel's lead by focusing on principles rather than prescriptive rules. This allows emphasis to be placed on what boards consider to be the key risks facing their business. However, it is a shame that the proposals do not offer more illustrative guidance. Companies looking for more practical help may be left wondering exactly what is meant by ethical, compliance, environmental and operational controls...

Those companies that are in the habit of providing shareholders with meaningful governance disclosures should have no problem with the new disclosures. However, they essentially amount to assurances that everything is under control, rather than a description of how the controls actually work. So companies looking to get away with as little as possible have the opportunity to disclose virtually nothing about their risk management process and system of internal control.

### The Heart of the Matter

At the heart of the proposals is the assertion that sound internal control is best achieved by a process firmly embedded in a company's operations. This leads to a requirement for boards, or relevant board committees, to regularly receive and review reports on control issues from management and/or others qualified to prepare them. Issues to be considered as part of the regular review process should include the identification, evaluation and management of key risks, the effectiveness of the related system of internal control, and the actions taken to remedy any weaknesses found. A cyclical approach is recommended. An approach in which all key risks are covered each year may well be better.

> In addition to the regular review, Turnbull proposes that directors undertake a specific annual review for the purposes of making the internal control disclosures required by the Listing Rules. This should include, for example, changes in the nature and extent of significant risks, the company's ability to respond effectively to change and the quality of the regular review process. Where regular reviews are not carried out, it is proposed that a comprehensive review of the internal control system be undertaken. This makes good sense as a transitional provision, but not as a permanent option. An appendix to the document sets out the "principal characteristics" for boards to consider when assessing internal control.
>
> Source: Accountancy International, June 1999.

This emphasis on risk, transparency and internal controls has succeeded in establishing them as part of the corporate governance equation. Issues pertaining to corporate governance can now be demonstrated to have the potential to impact directly upon more that merely the reporting and accountability responsibilities of an organization.

---

**In practice:**

*Companies Not Yet Complying With Turnbull*

*Most companies have a long way to go before they will be compliant with the Turnbull recommendations on corporate governance, according to research by KPMG. In a review of listed companies with accounting years ending in December, 98% were not compliant with the new guidance at the end of 1999; full compliance is expected for accounting periods ending on or after December 23, 2000. KPMG's technical accounting group senior manager Timothy Copnell said the figures are actually very encouraging. Turnbull procedures were published half-way through last year, but companies reluctance to rush into compliance shows that they realize Turnbull guidelines are "more than just a compliance issue".*

*Source: www.accountancymagazine.com, May 17, 2000.*

---

## Combined Code

The past decade has been a period of intense activity in relation to corporate governance issues. Corporate failures as well as international, competitive and regulatory pressures have combined to inspire a flurry of activity as already outlined. And one consequence has been a plethora of Reports addressing several areas of governance. The result is that the UK has been to the fore in initiating many innovative reforms.

## Britain Tops Shareholder Friendly Markets Poll

Britain has topped the poll of the world's most shareholder friendly markets for the fourth year, according to a corporate governance indicators survey by Davis Global Advisors, writes Lisa Buckingham.

The research, which measures markets according to guidelines that international investors regard as the most important, ranked the US second, followed by France. Germany "surged" up the points table thanks to new rules on transparency, but remained locked into fourth position because of take-over barriers and secrecy on executive pay. Japan was judged to have remained the market where companies were least likely to follow strategies which would create shareholder value.

Stephen Davis, the author of the review and president of Davis Global Advisors, said: "Corporations are reinventing themselves to compete for international investment capital. Boards which fall behind in this new accountability face court failure."

The measures against which companies are judged include adherence to best practice codes, the quality and balance of non-executive directors, independence of the board and the separation of the roles of chairman and chief executive, and the existence of board committees such as audit, remuneration and succession bodies. In addition the index looks at voting rights and issues, accounting standards, executive pay and take-over barriers.

Despite resistance to the advances in boardroom governance over the past decade, Britain stood head and shoulders above the other leading economies in the survey, scoring 8.3 points compared with 7 points for the US and just 3.5 points for Japan. The report found that Germany and Japan failed to measure up to OECD corporate governance standards, which roughly reflect the Cadbury code's.

Source: The Guardian, November 22, 1999.

In the main, the net effect of this concerted effort has been that many of the former abuses have been identified and rectified. It has also meant that the UK now possesses a more robust, if still imperfect corporate governance culture.

The adoption of the Combined Code by the London Stock Exchange, and its incorporation into its Yellow Book with effect for accounting periods ending after December 31, 1998, has meant that there are now significant disclosures to be made by listed companies in relation to their corporate governance cultures and practices.

Specifically, a UK company listed on the London Stock Exchange must now include the following in its Annual Report:

- **Appliance Statement**: a narrative statement of how it has applied the principles set out in the Combined Code, providing an explanation which enables its shareholders to evaluate how the principles have been applied.

- **Compliance Statement**: a statement as to whether or not it has complied throughout the accounting period with the provisions set out in the Combined Code. A company that has not complied with the Code provisions, or complied with only some of the Code provisions or (in the case of provisions whose requirements are of a continuing nature) complied for only part of an accounting period, must specify the Code provisions with which it has not complied, and give reasons for any non-compliance.

These application and compliance requirements represent a significant advance in the area of corporate governance and relevant disclosures. And they are in addition to the Operating and Financial Review, which the ASB has recommended be added to all Annual Reports.

However, more than mere disclosure, the effect of almost a decade of investigation, analysis and reports has been to provide the UK with arguably one of the most credible and mature corporate governance regimes in the world. And this is gradually being seen as a template for more widespread adoption.

---

**In practice:**

*Combined Code Widely Ignored*

*Many companies are not complying fully with the government's combined code on corporate governance, reports Pensions and Investment Research Consultants. Only 77% of companies have a wholly independent remuneration committee; just 51% have 1-year contracts or less for all executive directors; and a mere 27% said the board had considered whether to put remuneration committee reports to the vote at the agm.*

*This will come as disappointment to the government, as many of the 468 respondent companies failed to comply with recommendations laid out in its consultation document on corporate governance.*

*Also unimpressive were the responses on reporting issues: 29% of companies failed to identify either the chairman, chief executive or senior independent directors, and 29% did not provide enough biographical information on all directors facing election.*

*Source: Accountancy, February 2000.*

---

## Corporate Governance in Europe

The accounting and governance regimes applying on continental Europe, specifically in France and Germany, are outlined in Chapter 15.

## Stakeholder Theory

While the cumulative effect of these various reports would seem to suggest that over the course of the 1990s corporate governance practice in the UK has undergone a radical overhaul, critics argue that all that has happened has been some "tinkering at the edges".

One of the more coherent critiques comes from those who advocate a much broader understanding of the whole subject of how and for whom companies are run, an approach which extends the consideration of interested parties beyond the traditional one of investors to the more inclusive notion of "stakeholders".

Stakeholder theory is predicated on the notion that it is not the primary task of democracy to underpin the role of the market in society. In this scheme of things corporations are understood to be, first and foremost, corporate citizens with rights and corresponding obligations. These obligations extend beyond the obvious and oft-repeated duties to shareholders, to the less-frequently articulated duties to other interested parties.

One of the most compelling champions of the stakeholder approach in the UK is Will Hutton.

## Time for Labour to Put Some Spine into its Stake-holding Idea, by Will Hutton

Changes in government and changes in ideas go hand in hand. The outgoing administration loses internal coherence as it battles to marry incoming ideas with its outdated programme and rusting ideological anchors. The opposition gains in confidence and coherence. We saw it happening in the late 1970s with the rise of monetarism. In the mid-1990s it could be happening again with stakeholding.

For it was not the Thatcherites who launched British-style monetarism as they entered office in 1979. It was the Labour Chancellor, Denis Healey, who, after the 1976 crisis, began focusing on lowering the public-sector borrowing requirement, targeting money supply growth and lifting exchange and credit controls. The intellectual climate had been changing for 3 years before Mrs Thatcher took office. This, as much as her political prowess, laid the foundations of her success.

Historians will make similar remarks about the years up to 1996–7. British business and the unions have themselves begun the move towards
stakeholding as a principle of company relations. It was the "Tomorrow's Company" inquiry, published by the Royal Society of Arts in 1995 and backed by leading British companies, that first set out the merits of organizing a company as an inclusive social entity, to maximize creativity and trust. The job of a board is not to act exclusively as the agents of the shareholders, the report said; it is to act more as the long-term trustees of the business, furthering its productive capacity, reputation and the skills of its workforce and suppliers.

Furthermore, Sir Adrian Cadbury (over the constitution of company boards) and Sir Richard Greenbury (over executive pay) have chaired committees that developed voluntary codes which, whatever their compromises and shortcomings, begin to uphold elements of the stakeholding notion. Long-term corporate success is a more subtle business than simply maximizing shareholder value. There is a wider public interest to be protected. Best if it is voluntary, but most know that legislation will ultimately be needed.

Source: The Guardian, January 22, 1996.

As this extract suggests, one of the principal effects of stakeholder theory is to challenge business to recognize its responsibilities to a larger constituency. Typically this would include, in addition to shareholders and investors, the following:

- Employees
- Environmentalists
- Creditors
- Customers
- Local communities and interest groups

Once the field of potential stakeholders is extended in this fashion it becomes possible to completely reconsider not only the way in which a company should relate to them but also, at a very fundamental level, the suitability of the current corporate structure to meet this agenda.

Stakeholder theory and its implications for both corporate governance and financial reporting will be discussed further in Chapter 14. So too will the notion of the company as a "corporate citizen" with social and ethical responsibilities to the communities within which it operates.

## Summary

In an increasingly global, competitive and technology-driven environment, corporate governance is seen as a source of considerable competitive advantage. Consequently it has attracted the attentions of not only practitioners and company executives, but also of regulators. This has resulted in a raft of reports, recommendations and voluntary codes aimed at enforcing some element of accountability and uniformity.

Simultaneously, the fact that many European and Asian companies have been compelled to seek funds on the New York and London Stock Exchanges has highlighted the fact that it is the Anglo-American system of corporate governance that has proven most robust. This has resulted in a situation in which the Anglo-American corporate governance model, with all of its flaws, is being increasingly championed as the one that offers the most suitable basis upon which to proceed.

# Review Questions

## Question 1
Explain what is meant by the term "corporate governance" and identify specific reasons for divergences in corporate governance cultures.

## Question 2
Explain how corporate governance impacts upon notions of accountability and, consequently, upon the nature and form of accounting practice.

## Question 3
Identify the role, if any, which the following may play in the future in the area of international corporate governance practice:

- UK government
- EU
- SEC
- IASC
- Stock Exchanges
- International accounting bodies
- Shareholders
- Other stakeholders

## Question 4
Explain what is meant by "Best Practice" in the context of UK corporate governance. Identify the reasons why this became an issue in the 1990s.

## Question 5
Identify the principal contributions of the following reports to the corporate governance regime as it currently exists in the UK.

- Cadbury
- Greenbury
- Hampel
- Turnbull

## Question 6
"In focusing attention on risk management and in requiring management to integrate this into the governance and operational aspects of corporate life, Turnbull will be seen in a few years time as having had the most profound effect upon corporate governance, practice and accountability". Discuss

## Question 7
Explain what is meant by "Stakeholder Theory" and identify specific ways in which pressure from stakeholders other than shareholders has influenced corporate governance and reporting practice.

# Case Studies

## Case 1

The following report highlights how issues of corporate governance can have an impact upon all aspects of society, even soccer teams. Discuss the issues raised.

# Can Man United Win Again?

## Manchester United May Win the Trophies in the Stock Market; But Will Football Survive?

I do not suppose Ryan Giggs or Andy Cole have ever thought about globalization, shareholder value or corporate governance very much, any more than Manchester United's hundreds of thousands of fans have, but they had a first-hand initiation last week. Their club is becoming football's first ever version of basketball's Harlem Globetrotters as the game detaches itself from its roots in place, blood and fans' hearts, a destiny that is as inevitable as it is controversial. Ungoverned money has its own ineluctable logic, and Manchester United is showing the British public both the opportunities and the pitfalls...

...It is an open secret that Alex Ferguson and his team are uneasy about the march of events, but they are all beneficiaries of United's riches. But increasingly the rest of us are losers. European and global competitions are inevitable and potentially exciting; but they need to be built around structures that ensure that any good club can win. That might mean European and even world football, for example, borrowing from American football and allowing losing clubs the first chance of buying star players in the pre-season transfer market to even up the game. Global football needs to be globally governed in the interest of all the game.

But closer to home we have to take the financial pressure off our leading football clubs; and that means that the legal system in which they incorporate themselves has to be much more sophisticated than at present. Stephen Byers, the Trade and Industry Secretary, last week famously said he did not mind what top directors made if, like top football players, they had earned their wealth through good performance. The task was rather to make sure that shareholders set demanding performance criteria.

Byers aim is well-intentioned, but flawed; the problem is that the performance criteria that pension funds and insurance companies set is to boost the short-term share price. But if the shareholders set higher targets for United's board, then the process of its self-destruction will only accelerate. Shareholders in Manchester United should rather think of themselves as shareholders in a football club; they have wider responsibilities to football and Manchester as well as the right to share in the club's success and prosperity.

What is required is a more subtle and far-reaching approach to ownership, remuneration and performance setting embodied in British corporate law that reflects the responsibilities of ownership as well as the rights. Pension funds and insurance companies need to be accountable for their decisions; at present they have to explain nothing to their ultimate beneficiaries, you and me. And when they buy a share in a company, they buy the right to a flow of dividends, but they should also buy a reciprocal obligation to share in the decision-making and forego profits for the long-run health of the business.

In short, they should sit on company boards and remuneration committees and account for themselves in turn to their contributors and beneficiaries. In United's case it would mean shareholders' thinking much more constructively how this club can lead and shape the English game to everyone's advantage rather than just making its own directors and leading players stinking rich. Byers is an independent minded politician, and may surprise us yet with the direction of his thinking, but he needs to move fast. There is more to economic and social life than maximizing the share price; and football-mad Blairites might ponder if the future of the game they love is really safe in the hands of bloated, self-interested directors. United's compromises may yet have an influence well beyond football.

Source: Will Hutton, The Guardian, July 25, 1999.

## Case 2

One of the most imaginative reports on corporate practice in the UK as it is likely to evolve over the next decade came from an unlikely source, the Royal Society for the Encouragement of Arts, Manufactures and Commerce. Reflecting its essentially non-commercial background, the report it produced into "Tomorrow's Company", with a extract from which this chapter began, presented a unique and thought-provoking challenge.

Read the report, which can be accessed at http://www.prcentral.com/rmso95to-mor.htm and discuss the main observations it makes.

## Case 3

The various themes covered in this chapter are also dealt with in some detail in a report on a survey carried out by accountancy firm PricewaterhouseCoopers. This can be accessed and read at the following site: http://www2.pw.com/uk/conv_cult_exec_sum.htm.

## Case 4

The following is an extract from Section 1 of The Code of Best Practice. Read the provisions and discuss the implications for companies of complying with them.

# Section 1 Companies

## D. Accountability and Audit

## D.1 Financial Reporting

Principle: The board should present a balanced and understandable assessment of the company's position and prospects.

### Code Provisions

D.1.1 The directors should explain their responsibility for preparing the accounts and there should be a statement by the auditors about their reporting responsibilities.

D.1.2 The board's responsibility to present a balanced and understandable assessment extends to interim and other price-sensitive public reports and reports to regulators as well as to information required to be presented by statutory requirements.

D.1.3 The directors should report that the business is a going concern, with supporting assumptions or qualifications as necessary.

## D.2 Internal Control

Principle: The board should maintain a sound system of internal control to safeguard shareholders' investment and the company's assets.

### Code Provisions

D.2.1 The directors should, at least annually, conduct a review of the effectiveness of the group's system of internal controls and should report to shareholders that they have done so. The review should cover all controls, including financial, operational and compliance controls and risk management.

D.2.2 Companies which do not have an internal audit function should from time to time review the need for one.

## D.3 Audit Committee and Auditors

Principle: The board should establish formal and transparent arrangements for considering how they should apply the financial reporting and internal control principles and for maintaining an appropriate relationship with the company's auditors.

### Code Provisions

D.3.1 The board should establish an audit committee of at least three directors, all non-executive, with written terms of reference, which deal clearly with its authority and duties. The members of the committee, a majority of who should be independent non-executive directors, should be named in the report and accounts.

D.3.2 The duties of the audit committee should include keeping under review the scope and results of the audit and its cost effectiveness and the independence and objectivity of the auditors. Where the auditors also supply a substantial volume of non-audit services to the company, the committee should keep the nature and extent of such services under review, seeking to balance the maintenance of objectivity and value for money.

Source: The Cadbury Report.

## Case 5

The following article provides some very perceptive insights into the impact which new information flows and a revitalized stakeholder approach might have on the UK economy and society. Identify the main points made and discuss whether or not the conclusions reached are tenable.

## Born Free But Everywhere in Chains

### It is the Information Age, But Openness is Still Difficult to Find, and Nowhere More Than at Whitehall. Simon Caulkin reports

It is a surprise, but the UK is now the governance laboratory of the world. Admittedly, the pathbreaking Cadbury, Greenbury and Hampel committees were the direct product of the horrors that had gone before – the Maxwell and BCCI scandals, for example. Nor is the competition outstandingly strong. Nevertheless, the central point remains – the UK's practical experiments in corporate accountability and openness, although well short of perfection, put it squarely ahead of the field...

At one level, information is what makes competitive markets work. The more information and the more freely available it is, the better markets function. Conversely, the less freely information circulates, the easier markets are to rig. This is why there are rules against insider trading.

For the most dramatic illustration of the consequences of free-flowing information, look no further than the Internet. With the price of everything instantly available on the web, transaction and search costs approach vanishing point. Intermediaries and brokers can be dispensed with and costs and prices fall. Almost everything, from airline tickets to financial services to antique china, can be cyber-auctioned – the nearest thing to a perfect market that we are ever likely to see.

Within the company, equalizing information between the constituencies is what corporate governance is all about. In the normal course of business, information operates on the inside: managers and directors have a lot more of it than shareholders and can manipulate it for their own ends. Hence the increasing duty of disclosure to level the playing field.

In management terms, too, information has become a key operating resource. In the weightless economy, where an Internet start-up can find itself as valuable as General Motors, creating wealth has little to do with the classical combination of capital, land and labour. It is much more to do with what goes on in people's heads.

Business success can no longer be commanded by hoarding information and managing its flow from the top. As Konsuke Matsushita, founder of the eponymous Japanese firm, once put it: "Business is now so complex and difficult, the survival of the firm so hazardous in an environment increasingly unpredictable, competitive and fraught with dangers, that its continued existence depends on the mobilization of every ounce of intelligence." In turn, that requires the willing engagement and initiative of individual producers of ideas.

Information empowers people to work differently – and in so doing, as Tony Blair correctly analysed, it changes the relationship between stakeholders. This is why it is so powerful, and in some traditionalists' view, so dangerous. Although few big companies have yet had the courage to put open-book management – broadly, opening up the books to all employees – into action, that is the logical next step.

Enough small and medium-sized firms in the US and UK have tested the openness concept in practice to prove that commonly expressed fears – that employees cannot be trusted with information about sensitive issues like strategy or salary levels – are not just overblown, but diametrically wrong. It is partial information that is damaging (since employees gossip about strategy and salaries anyway). Freeing up information saves time and concentrates energy on real issues, not imaginary ones.

Fundamentally, stake-holding is meaningless without full information. In the US, companies routinely use the freedom of information laws to keep tabs on their competitors' relationships, and contracts, with government. They have also become a crucial working instrument for non-governmental organizations, which in practice are the only check on the global ambitions of the multinational companies. Information keeps people honest.

All these are good reasons why, subject to safeguards, most corporate and government information should be freely available unless they can prove that there are very good grounds for it not to be. This was the presumption in the first White Paper, and it should be reinstated. In the information age, freedom of information is indivisible: a governance and a business imperative as well as a political one.

Source: The Guardian, June 20, 1999.

# SECTION II

The Annual Report is one of the most important means of communication between a company and its stakeholders, particularly its shareholders. As a result it is a highly regulated document containing a mass of data in the form of both financial statements and narrative reports. From humble beginnings in the 19th century it has grown to become a large, glossy production often reaching over 100 pages in length.

While the financial statements and notes still represent the core of the Annual Report, recent decades have witnessed a significant increase in the number and range of non-financial data. Chapter 5 looks at these qualitative reports and narrative commentaries, which range from the heavily regulated Directors' Report and Auditor's Report, to the far less controlled Chairman's Statement and Operating and Financial Review.

Chapter 6 deals with the financial statements and attendant notes which, despite the rising importance of the qualitative elements, still constitute the core of the Annual Report. Because these statements are heavily regulated by both statute and accounting standards this chapter, of necessity, sets out a mass of technical information regarding formats, accounting principles and disclosure requirements. It is, therefore, somewhat out of kilter with the remainder of the text, which is more concerned with contextual rather than technical issues. Nevertheless, it is critical that the relevant provisions be understood as they underpin the way in which financial statements are constructed and the thinking behind their current configuration.

# NARRATIVE REPORTS [5]

When you have completed this chapter you will understand:

- The importance of the Annual Report as a primary means of communication between a company and its various stakeholders.
- The increasing importance of non-financial disclosures.
- The nature and purpose of the narrative elements of the Annual Report.
- That these narrative reports include some which are statutorily controlled and others which are not.
- That the structure of the Annual Report allows companies to employ various techniques intended to influence readers' impressions.

## Back to the Future Now?

### Investors Want Non-Financial Information Too; Companies Must Decide How Much They Can Afford to Disclose. By Kathy Leach

It is, perhaps, a paradox for the ICAEW's Financial Reporting Committee to be recommending that non-financial information should be included in annual reports. Its recent discussion paper, Inside Out: Reporting on Shareholder Value, is a contribution to the quest for corporate reporting that meets investors' needs. The paper calls for a more forward-looking and long-term perspective in a company's annual report, with more transparent reporting of key elements of the information used to manage the business.

The proposals are incremental, and companies can experiment with the recommended disclosures immediately. They build on and give a structure to a reporting practice that is beginning to emerge around the world. Illustrative examples from, inter alia, Cadbury Schweppes, Ericsson, Stakis, Skandia, Boots, WPP Group and Bank of Montreal are reproduced in the paper. There is nothing radically new in many of the individual disclosures, but the steering group responsible for the paper believes that putting them together will present a sharper image and differentiate a company in increasingly demanding capital markets. The proposals could be particularly helpful in awakening investors' interest in smaller companies.

The forward-looking, non-financial disclosure proposed is of the information management uses to plot and steer its course – that is, its strategy for value creation and the progress made towards achieving that strategy, as shown by management's key performance indicators and measures. Without such information, an investor embarks on an uncharted journey and cannot tell whether the ship is off course. But why is this important to investors when what they really want to know is their destination, i.e., the return they will get from investing in a company's shares?

The premise underpinning the discussion paper is that the economic value of a business is the present value of its expected future cash flows. The value created, or the return, over a period is therefore best represented by the change in its economic value, that is, the change in the net present value of its expected future cash flows.

## Qualitative, Not Quantitative

However, because the future is uncertain, changes in economic value cannot be captured in a single figure and reported as a matter of fact. The measurement of value created is inevitably subjective, and a system of financial reporting based on expectations of future cash flows would not currently be thought sufficiently reliable to be widely acceptable. So, an entirely quantitative, financial approach to reporting value creation is not practicable.

Many investors do, however, base share valuations on forecasts of future cash flows and want forward-looking information to feed into their valuation models. To help them, they look for softer, qualitative information from companies about their potential for creating value. The forward-looking perspective management adopts in the strategic planning process in general and by a "shareholder value" focus in particular, matches investors' desire for long-term, future-orientated information. The paper quotes extensive research evidence of investors' keen interest in disclosures about the development and implementation of a company's strategy.

Source: Accountancy International, December 1999.

# Introduction

While the information to be included in Annual Reports appears to be ever increasing, the statements and reports required can basically be classified into two types – financial and narrative. Historically, Annual Reports consisted almost entirely of financial statements supplemented by an Auditor's Report and a Directors' Report. However, as its importance as a primary means of communication between a company and its stakeholders has come to be appreciated, its form and content have changed.

Recent decades have witnessed, therefore, increased financial disclosure and the incorporation of more narrative reports both for their own sake, and as a means of supplementing the financial statements. This in turn has led to calls, such as that articulated by the ICAEW above, for even more narrative reports and a greater emphasis on using these to outline future strategies and ambitions.

---

**In practice:**

*Developments in Corporate Financial Disclosure Over the Period 1975–96: Evidence from UK Annual Reports, by Thomas Schleicher*

*UK annual reports have changed quite dramatically between the mid 1970s and today. The overall amount of information given has increased considerably, and this is equally true for the financial statements and the discussion section of the annual report. New financial statements have emerged with the funds flow/cash flow statement or more recently the statement of total recognized gains and losses, and existing statements now offer a greater level of disaggregation. Moreover, most companies now have separate sections for the business review, financial review and directors' remuneration.*

*As a consequence the annual report has gained considerably in size. The average number of pages in our sample has doubled over the 22-year period from 24–48 with the number of pages containing management's discussion rising from 8–20. Those discussion sections now represent an average of 40% of the annual report against 32% in 1975. In particular larger companies now often devote more pages to supplementary analysis than to the financial statements themselves.*

*Source: www.acca.org.uk/technical/research/schleicher.html.*

---

Financial disclosures, which still form the core of an Annual Report, will be covered in Chapter 6. This chapter will deal with those sections devoted to narrative reports.

## Narrative Reports

One of the principles of the Combined Code is that "the board should present a balanced and understandable assessment of the company's position and prospects". It is generally accepted that financial statements on their own are unlikely to achieve this. Consequently, various narrative sections that provide both additional information and a commentary on the company's position, performance and prospects have been added over time in order to supplement the financial information.

> **In practice:**
>
> *A recent FTSE-100 annual reports survey has calculated that in a "typical" 80 page Annual Report, the financial data take up around 31 pages, while the narrative and visual elements comprise the remaining 49. Of these, the Operating and Financial Review (OFR) takes up around 16 pages and information regarding directors and their remuneration about six.*

Typically these narratives would include:

- Chairman's Statement
- Directors' Report
- Auditor's Report
- Operating and Financial Review (OFR)

Of these only the Directors' Report and the Auditor's Report are required by law. However, because these two reports are subject to considerable legislative control, they offer little scope to those responsible for running the company to communicate more openly with users. As a result it has become usual for the Annual Report to open with a Chairman's Statement, which offers an opportunity for the Chairman to offer his or her own (often biased) perspective on the company's position and performance.

More recently, in response to the Combined Code and with the support of the Accounting Standards Board (ASB), the Annual Report of most large companies will also include an OFR. This provides management with an opportunity to comment on various aspects of the company's operating and financing functions.

As Chapter 18 will demonstrate, the likelihood is that under the twin impulses of new technology and a corporate governance culture which emphasizes the qualities of transparency and disclosure, the narrative sections of an Annual Report will continue to grow in terms of both quantity and scope.

The remainder of this chapter looks at each of the four principal narrative reports listed above in more detail.

## Chairman's Statement

There is no legal requirement to include a Chairman's Statement in the Annual Report. However, as the profile of the company chairman has increased in recent years, so too has the demand, and, on many chairmen's part, the desire, to comment in fairly general terms on the company's performance and prospects. The Chairman's Statement, therefore, provides a useful forum in which the chairman can set forth his or her thoughts on the company and, increasingly, discuss various macro-economic and political issues that impinge upon the company.

The Chairman's Statement normally appears at the front of the Annual Report and research shows that it is the most widely read section. In many senses it is a public relations document in which the chairman presents a personal perspective on how the company has performed and its future prospects. It is, as a result, often a rather bland document full of hyperbole and optimistic aspirations. Nevertheless, properly used, it can provide a useful conduit between the chairman, who in many instances plays a key role in shaping corporate ethos and objectives, and stakeholders.

## Content

There is no standard format for the Chairman's Statement. However, in most cases all or some of the following would appear:

- A brief account of the company's financial and operating performance over the previous year.
- Details of significant events which had a material effect on performance, for example, acquisitions or disposals.
- A summary of activities within key categories of the company.
- Reference to changes in board membership.
- Outline of new strategies, corporate goals or changes in focus or emphasis.
- An often over-optimistic assessment of future prospects.

The growing importance of the Chairman's Statement has meant that there are now calls for it too to be subject to some form of control with regard to its content, in particular in ensuring some element of consistency between its often self-congratulatory tone and the actual financial performance as disclosed in the remainder of the Annual Report.

---

**In practice:**

In presenting its Annual Report, Tesco plc distinguishes between statutorily required reports and statements, which it includes in one publication (this is provided at the rear of the text) and other elements which it publishes separately. The Chairman's Statement is included in the latter document and is provided here.

*Chairman's Statement*

*The Tesco Group has delivered another set of excellent results driven by our determination to be number one for customers wherever we are. In the UK we continued to lower prices and increase service for customers gaining us further market share despite the industry seeing very little growth. Internationally, we accelerated our expansion programme adding 16 new hypermarkets in six countries.*

*The Tesco Group has achieved another excellent set of results. Growth in all areas of our business contributed to an increase of 9.8% in Group sales, to £20.4 billion. Group profit before tax is up by 8.4% to £955 million and adjusted diluted earnings per share rose by 8.6% to 10.18 p. The Board has recommended a final net dividend of 3.14 p, making the total dividend for the year 4.48 p, maintaining cover at 2.27 times.*

*These results demonstrate both focused strategy and innovative management. In markets characterized by some of the toughest ever trading conditions, Tesco is one of the very few major retailers to deliver continued profit growth.*

*We have four parts to our strategy:*

***Strong UK core business****: While the industry saw very little growth over the past year, Tesco continued to increase market share through our policy of getting cheaper, offering better value and providing more choice and convenience for our customers.*

***Non-food business****: Tesco has gained rapid share of a market worth £75 billion in the UK where our goal is to be as strong in non-food as in food.*

***Following the customer****: As customers' shopping habits change – we change and respond by providing new products and services. Our e-commerce business has grown rapidly and to continue its development we will give it additional focus through setting up tesco.com, a 100% subsidiary. Tesco Personal Finance continues to grow and develop excellent products offering value and choice. In recognition of its excellent value TPF recently won the Best Direct Credit Card award.*

***International strategy****: Tesco has been successful in opening up new growth markets in Central Europe and Asia. These, together with our growing business in the Republic of Ireland, raised the proportion of total Group space outside the UK to 30% last year. We shall continue to pursue this strategy, believing that it is the best way forward for Tesco, and will accelerate our earnings growth.*

*Lesley James, our Human Resources Director, left the Group in April 1999, after 15 years with Tesco. We would all like to thank her for her contribution during that time. We also welcome Harald Einsmann, who was appointed as a Non-executive Director in April 1999.*

*For three of the last 4 years, Tesco was judged by its peers, to be the UK's most admired company. The judges said, "the feeling about Tesco remains that its strategy is crystal clear, well understood by staff and customers."*

*That accolade is due in no small measure to the efforts of the 220,000 Tesco people who are busy delivering that strategy. I would like to congratulate them all on another great year of progress, and to thank them for the part they have played, as individuals and teams, in making Tesco such a powerful force for growth.*

*John Gardiner, Chairman.*

## The Directors' Report

The Directors' Report is intended to provide a narrative supplement to the financial information contained in an Annual Report. It is a statutory report under CA85 (as amended). Consequently, certain information must be included. However, the directors are free to include additional information if they so wish. Furthermore, for companies listed on the Stock Exchange, the Listing Agreement will require additional disclosure as already outlined in Chapter 1. Finally, the Combined Code has specified particular items, such as directors' remuneration, that should be commented on by the directors and it is usual to see these alluded to in the Directors' Report or in a separate section.

The Directors' Report is intended to provide the directors of the company with an opportunity to comment on various aspects of the company's activities during the period in question. There is no set format for such a report and they vary widely in both content and format. However, the following areas must be addressed.

## Activities and Trading Results

By law the Directors' Report is required to contain details of:

- The principal activities of the company and its subsidiaries; and
- Any significant developments or changes that occurred during the period.

## Developments During the Period

One of the main functions envisaged for the Directors' Report is the provision of an opportunity for the directors to give a review of any significant developments that have occurred during the year and of the position of the company at the end of the period. This provides an important narrative supplement to the financial data. In addition, the directors are expected to provide their own assessment of possible future developments, together with an assessment of how these may affect the company. Any narrative would be expected to refer to, and be consistent with, the financial information.

This section should include comment on the following:

- Turnover and profits deriving from trading activities
- Exceptional items
- Taxation
- Foreign currency management
- Significant changes in activities
- Existing borrowings and proposals for funding future capital expenditure

- Details of "non-adjusting" post-balance sheet events
- Significant changes in fixed assets – in terms of both value and physical changes
- Research and development activities

In recent years, and particularly since the Cadbury Report and the advent of the OFR, it has become quite common for a number of the items listed here to be discussed, in varying detail, in that Review.

## Directors

As indicated in Chapter 1, one of the most sensitive areas in any Annual Report concerns the role, remuneration and interests of the directors of the company. Legislation and stock exchange rules require the disclosure of significant amounts of information under this heading.

At a minimum the following must be disclosed:

- Names of any individuals who held office as directors at any time during the period.
- The interest of those directors, (including that of their spouses, children and wards of court), in the shares and debentures of the company and its subsidiaries at the beginning and end of the period. Alternatively this information can be given in the notes to the accounts.
- Details of any loans, quasi-loans or credit facilities extended to directors, while, in certain circumstances, details must also be given of a director's service contract.
- The emoluments and remuneration of all directors – (this will often run to several pages).

Listed companies must also distinguish between directors' beneficial and non-beneficial holdings.

---

**In practice:**

*The combined effect of accounting standards, legislation, stock exchange rules and the Combined Code has been to increase the level of disclosure in relation to directors. These disclosures may often run to several pages with considerable space devoted to detailing directors remuneration in particular.*

*Refer to pages 12–16 of the Tesco plc 2000 Annual Report for an indication of the level of disclosure required.*

## Dividends

The Directors' Report should indicate whether a dividend is proposed and if so the amount proposed for each type and class of share.

## Substantial Holdings

Where any person or other entity owns or acquires 3% or more of the nominal value of any class of voting capital of a public company then, under the terms of the Listing Agreement of the Stock Exchange, this fact must be disclosed.

## Employees

One of the most interesting developments of recent decades has been the increasing focus upon the employees of a company as both stakeholders and users of accounts. As a result there is now a considerable amount of information in the Annual Report in relation to employees and employment conditions. For example, in the notes to the accounts the total average number of employees must be given, with a breakdown of this total into the various categories of company activity. In addition, the total for staff costs must be disclosed either on the face of the profit and loss account or as a note. Since 1980 the Directors' Report of a company which has more than an average total of 250 employees must also include a statement of its employment policy in relation to disabled persons. Significantly, companies are also voluntarily disclosing information relating to health and safety.

## Auditing

While the appointment of the auditor is the business of the shareholders at the AGM, it has become customary for the directors to indicate the willingness or otherwise of the existing auditors to continue. In the event of the existing auditors being unwilling to continue, then the Directors' Report provides the directors with an opportunity to comment on this situation.

## Donations

Where political or charitable donations exceed £200 per annum then the directors must disclose this fact in the Directors' Report. Where the donations are for a political purpose then the name of the recipients and the individual amounts must be disclosed. Given the relative sensitivity over the issue of political donations in recent years, where companies do not make any such contributions they have taken to explicitly stating so.

# Corporate Governance

The Combined Code has had a considerable influence on the content of the Directors' Report. For instance, many of the items previously included in the Directors' Report, such as information on developments during the period, can now be elaborated upon in the OFR.

In recognition of the importance now being attached to issues of corporate governance, the Combined Code requires that directors include Appliance and Compliance Statements, as outlined in Chapter 4. Essentially, these specify whether or not the company conforms to best practice. The Code, as supplemented by Turnbull, also requires directors to report on the company's internal control system and whether they believe the company to be a going concern or not. These statements can be included in the Directors' Report.

The Code also recommends that a statement of directors' responsibilities be included. This should specify:

- That it is the directors responsibility to prepare financial statements for each year which give a true and fair view of the state of affairs of the company as at the end of the financial year and of the profit or loss for that period.

- The responsibility of directors in relation to maintaining adequate accounting records, safeguarding the assets of the company and preventing or detecting fraud.

- That suitable, consistent and prudent accounting policies have been employed.

- That applicable accounting standards have been followed, subject to any material departures being disclosed and explained in the notes to the accounts.

---

**In practice:**

This following extract from the 1999 Cable and Wireless plc Annual Report is typical, but also interesting, in that it identifies specific areas where the company does not yet conform to best practice.

*Corporate Governance*

*Companies are directed and controlled by corporate governance. Good governance has been and remains the responsibility of the whole Board. The Combined Code – Principles of Good Governance and Code of Best Practice (the Combined Code) was published by the London Stock Exchange in June 1998. This statement describes how the Company applies the principles and complies with the provisions of the Combined Code.*

*Compliance*

*The Board confirms that the Company was fully compliant with all the provisions of Section 1 of the Combined Code throughout the period with the exception of: (1) Directors' service contracts, as set out on page 31, and (2) the requirement that all Directors seek re-election at intervals of not more than 3 years. Shareholders at the forthcoming Annual General Meeting are being asked to approve an amendment to the Company's Articles of Association to ensure that the Company complies with the latter aspect of the Combined Code in the future.*

While these statements are useful in having directors acknowledge their legal responsibilities in relation to the preparation of accounts, they are seen by many as merely an attempt to insulate auditors from litigation. It remains to be seen how effective they would be in serving this purpose.

## Auditor's Report

An audit has been defined as "an independent review, and expression of opinion on, the financial statements of an enterprise". It is a statutory requirement that an audit be carried out, although for companies with a turnover of between £90,000 and £350,000 an independent accountant's report now suffices. The purpose of an audit is to provide independent verification for the shareholders that "the financial statements have been properly prepared in accordance with the legislative and regulatory requirements, that they present the information in a true and fair manner and that they comply with best accounting practice". While the auditor is not expected to audit the Directors' Report, it is required that he or she draws the attention of the reader to any inconsistencies between it and the financial results.

In recent years, particularly in the wake of several large corporate collapses, the audit process has been the subject of intense criticism. In part this derives from a misunderstanding on the part of many users who are under the misapprehension that the audit is primarily a fraud detection exercise. Auditors counter that, while they would expect to uncover incidences of material fraud, this is not the main focus of an audit. This difference between what users expect of an audit and what auditors are actually providing has been termed the "expectations gap".

One case which exposed many of the frailties of the audit process, and which has long haunted the auditing profession, is the Maxwell Communications Corporation (MCC) case. This and similar cases in the late 1980s and early 1990s highlighted the need for change. As the following extract highlights, these debacles are still impacting on the nature and conduct of the audit.

# Coopers Gets Much of the "Maxwell blame"

## Auditors Failed to Carry Out "Adequate Investigation"

Coopers and Lybrand has come under heavy criticism for its role as auditor to Robert Maxwell's Mirror Group Newspapers in the Department of Trade and Industry report published today (30 March). In addition to the company's auditors, the report also comes down hard on investment bank Goldman Sachs, which acted for Maxwell over its trade shares, and Samuel Montagu, the bank that advised the group on its flotation. To a lesser extent, it criticizes lenders Morgan Stanley and Lehman Brothers, Salomon Brothers International, and law firms Clifford Chance and Linklater and Paines.

According to the 370-page review, which took 10 years to compile, the reporting accountants failed to carry out an "adequate investigation" into cash loans, the use of shares as collateral and the investments in related companies. It says that, given the way Maxwell ran his businesses and the pension funds, C&L "ought" to have: "investigated the way in which Maxwell had exercised control over the pension schemes; enquired into the audits of the pension schemes…and carried out additional audit procedures in relation to the pension funds' assets; considered the adequacy of the post balance-sheet events' audit work; and carried out additional procedures to provide adequate information about the pension funds."

The firm also gets most of the blame for failing to ascertain Maxwell's financial controls. It says C&L did not identify his direct personal control over the disposition of Mirror Group's funds or his sole signatory authority, or the way in which the central treasury operated. The company's directors were also criticized in this regard. C&L is also blamed for failing to bring certain share transactions to the pension scheme trustees' attention, despite being aware of the risks that Maxwell's control entailed and the share transactions. "(The firm) consistently agreed accounting treatment of transactions that served the interest of Maxwell and not those of the trustees or the beneficiaries of the pension scheme, provided it could be justified by an interpretation of the letter of the relevant standards or regulations."

Among the recommendations by report authors the Honourable Sir Roger Thomas and Raymond Turner FCA as to how legislation and regulation could be improved to avoid such a situation occurring again, are: to provide more guidance on the business empires' audit; to make non-executive directors more accountable, partly by separating the role of chairman and CEO and providing guidance on directors' duties; to build on the Occupational Pensions Regulatory Authority's work in providing more assistance to pension scheme trustees; to provide a guidance statement upon flotation on advisers roles and duties; to build on the Financial Services Authority's work to impose sanctions on companies that do not report fraud; to review securities markets' regulation; and to make the public aware that no amount of regulation will ever totally eliminate fraud.

"The most important lesson from all the events is that high ethical and professional standards must always be put before commercial advantage. The reputation of the financial markets depends on it…'

Source: www.accountancymagazine.com, posted March 30, 2001 by Joanna Malvern.

The profession has attempted to address many of the problems that gave rise to cases such as MCC. In 1991 the Consultative Committee of Accounting Bodies (CCAB), which is comprised of representatives of the six major accounting bodies in the British Isles, established the Auditing Practices Board (APB). This is charged with advancing standards of auditing and has proven a key element in attempts to revise audit practices and standards. It issues Statements of Auditing Standards (SASs) with which members of the six constituting bodies of the CCAB must comply.

Another way in which the auditing profession has attempted to counter criticism has been to embark on a process of educating the users of financial statements as to the precise nature and function of an audit and to inform the various interested parties of their respective roles. For example, directors must now acknowledge in the Directors' Report that it is their responsibility, and not the auditor's, to prepare the financial statements.

Other innovations have seen the emergence of the audit committee as a key element in the governance structure and a more explicit recognition of auditor's responsibilities in relation to the detection of fraud and error.

## True and Fair

The principal requirement of an audit is that the auditor expresses his or her opinion in relation to whether the accounts present a "true and fair" view of the performance of the company over the period and of its position at the balance sheet date. This is done in the Auditor's Report.

This phrase "true and fair" has never been defined in any legislation. As a result, it is the subject of considerable uncertainty. Case law has established, however, that it does not imply mathematical accuracy, as it would be unrealistic to expect that the financial performance and status of any corporate entity could ever be reduced to a set of figures that could be termed "correct". This is not surprising given the subjective nature of many of the valuations and judgements required when preparing any set of accounts.

Significantly, the phrase was incorporated into the provisions of the EU Fourth Directive, an important catalyst in harmonizing financial reporting within the EU. The provisions of this Directive were enacted in CA81, and are now contained in Section 226 and 227 of CA85, which reiterates that financial statements should give a true and fair view. CA81 also stipulated that ensuring that a true and fair view was provided was now to be an "overriding consideration". This means that companies are required to disclose more than the basic legal minimum if this is necessary in order to give a true and fair view.

## Reports

SAS 600, *Auditors Reports on Financial Statements*, details the format, content and standards pertaining to the Auditor's Report. The auditor has a number of options as to how to report:

1. **An unqualified report**: this certifies that the financial statements do give a "true and fair view".

2. **An unqualified report with reference to fundamental uncertainty**: provided these fundamental uncertainties are properly accounted for, however, the auditor may still be in a position to issue an unqualified opinion.

3. **A qualified opinion** can be issued in a number of scenarios:

   - **Disagreement** – this occurs where the auditors disagree with the directors' treatment or disclosure of one or more items in the financial statements. In such circumstances the auditor's report will explain the issues involved and state that except for this the accounts give a true and fair view.
   - **Adverse opinion** – this occurs where the effect of the item or items of disagreement are such as to lead the auditor to believe that the financial statements are misleading. In such circumstances the auditor's report would state that the accounts do not give a true and fair view.
   - **"Except for" limitation or scope** – this occurs where the scope of the audit has been limited by an inability to obtain acceptable explanations or evidence or because proper accounting records have not been maintained such that this prevents the auditor giving an unqualified report. Where the limitation is perceived to be so material, then it may be necessary for the Report to contain a disclaimer, indicating that the auditor was unable to form an opinion on whether the accounts give a true and fair view.

In addition to providing a clear expression of opinion on the financial statements, the auditor should reinforce this by including confirmation that:

1. They comply with standards.

2. The audit process has included:

   - An examination of evidence relating to the amounts and disclosures in the various financial statements.
   - An assessment of any material estimates and judgements made by directors.
   - An assessment of whether the various accounting policies adopted are appropriate, consistent and adequately disclosed.

3. The audit was planned and executed so as to obtain reasonable assurances that the financial statements are free from material mis-statement.

4. The overall impact of the manner of presentation of the financial statements has been evaluated.

> **In practice:**
>
> *Companies will be determined to ensure that they do not receive a qualified audit report as these can be very damaging to both share price and future prospects. Research has shown that qualified audit reports can result in substantial share price declines from which companies find it very hard to recover. In the event that a qualified audit report is being signalled by the auditor, the company, via its audit committee, will attempt to address the auditor's concerns and thus negate the need for such a report. In most cases this process leads to a successful resolution. However, in a small minority of cases auditors will find it necessary to proceed with the qualified report.*

## Internal Control

Another area of corporate activity with which the Cadbury Report and, more recently, the Turnbull Report, concerned themselves was that of internal control. These are the procedures instituted by a company intended, amongst other things, to safeguard against the incidence of fraud and error. The Report recommended that directors should report on the effectiveness of the company's internal control systems and that auditors should comment on this in their Report.

## *Operating and Financial Review (OFR)*

The Cadbury Report was determined to ensure that shareholders received financial statements supplemented and supported "by a coherent narrative that combined to provide a balanced and understandable presentation of the company's performance". For this reason it emphasized the responsibility of the directors to allude to both negative as well as positive developments. However, it was also keen to ensure that these narratives did not adopt a purely historic perspective. The need for some assessment of the company's future prospects was identified as critical. These considerations combined to cause the committee to recommend that an Annual Report should include a report intended to address these issues.

The ASB was simultaneously devising a Statement of Best Practice that included just such a proposal. Issued in 1993, it proposed the inclusion of an OFR, although not on a mandatory basis. Such a review was envisaged as a forum in which the entity's past performance and future prospects as a whole might be discussed in a manner which would augment and not simply refer to the financial figures.

As a result, the OFR not only reports on the year under review, but also identifies and explains those significant aspects that are relevant to any assessment of future prospects. Significantly, however, it is not intended to be a forecast of future results.

Typically, the OFR might include:

- Reference to comments in previous reviews which have not been borne out by subsequent events.
- Analysis, discussion and comment on, as distinct from mere reference to, financial data.
- Discussion of both the business as a whole and individual elements within it.
- Discussion of any underlying trends at a macro or micro level which have affected the business and which are expected to cease or to continue to affect business.
- Reference to and justification of any changes in accounting policies.
- An indication of how ratios and other information have been compiled or computed.

An increasing number of companies have begun to produce an OFR. However, the quality of many reports leaves much to be desired. The trend, nevertheless, suggests increasing conformity and that issues of accountability and transparency are being acknowledged and addressed. Some companies include a separate Chief Executive's Review as part of their Annual Report. This provides an opportunity for the CEO to communicate directly with readers. In circumstances where an OFR is not included, this may cover many of the relevant points.

The OFR, as the title suggests, is concerned with two aspects of corporate activity. These can be presented together or as separate parts.

## Operating Review

This section is primarily concerned with communicating the operational aspects of the principal elements of the business as well as the interrelationship between these segments. The main focus of this section, therefore, will be on "the identification and explanation of the commercial and operational dynamics underlying the business, with an emphasis upon those elements which have altered over the period or which it is anticipated will change in the foreseeable future".

The ASB Statement envisages that the Operational Review will be concerned with the following:

1. The most significant aspects of the operating activity of the business, for example:
   - New products or services.
   - Changes in market conditions, market share or macro-economic factors, such as exchange rates or the inflation rate.
   - New activities and acquisitions.
   - Discontinued activities and disposals.

2. A discussion of the main factors and issues that will significantly influence future results.

3. An outline of the extent to which the board of the company has attempted to

secure future revenues and profits by investing in, for example, research, development, training or capital projects.

4. A breakdown of the return attributable to shareholders, measured in terms of dividends and improvements in shareholders funds, with an analysis of the portions contributed by the various business units together with details of other items included in the statement of total recognized gains and losses.

5. An explanation of the dividend policy, dealing with the relationship between reported profit and dividends, together with comment on the earnings per share achieved and the basis of calculation of any other measures used.

6. A disclosure of any subjective judgements to which the financial statements are sensitive.

## Financial Review

The principal function of the Financial Review is to explain the essence of the company's financial structure, concentrating on its capital structure, liquidity, sources of finance and treasury policy. In addition, reference should be made to the financing of future capital projects.

Typically, the Financial Review might address the following:

- The capital structure of the business and related treasury policies.
- Cash generated from operations as well as other significant cash inflows during the period, with particular reference to any significant variations between segmental cash flows and segmental profits.
- The liquidity of the business at the end of the period together with details of the borrowings at the end of the period, a maturity profile of borrowings and committed borrowing facilities as well as a comment on the seasonality of borrowing requirements.
- Any significant constraints on the freedom of a group to transfer funds from one part of the group to another.
- Debt covenants which could restrict the use of credit facilities, together with details of any breach of covenant which has occurred or is expected to occur and measures proposed to remedy the situation.
- The ability of the business to remain a going concern.
- Details of any resources of the business which are not fully reflected in the balance sheet, for example intangible assets.

The Company Law Review has highlighted the potential for the OFR to play a far greater role in the reporting process in future. However, the suggestion that the OFR might now be more closely regulated has prompted a mixed reaction.

## ICAEW Throws its Weight Behind Statutory OFR

The ICAEW has supported the proposals for the OFR to become a part of the audited reports that companies are legally required to file. In its formal response to the Company Law Review's Strategic Framework, the institute said it believed "now may be an appropriate time to introduce some compulsion for public interest companies to publish an OFR". ASB chairman Sir David Tweedie and ICAEW council member Tony Bennewith have both expressed reservations about the proposal.

At an institute meeting, covering "the big picture" behind the Company Law Review, Roger Davis, chairman of the ICAEW Company Law taskforce, explained the thinking behind the endorsement. "Do we want to carry on being bean counters, or do we want to switch to being skilled in accountability right across the board?" Davis asked the meeting. Arguing that the profession has debated for some time historical cost accounting's deficiencies when it comes to measuring the value of intangible assets, the PricewaterhouseCoopers partner for professional affairs said, "The new OFR is an excellent idea to compensate for all those deficiencies and to have some kind of structure for reporting strategies, the drivers of business value and on stakeholders' interests."

The institute was conscious of the danger highlighted by Tweedie and Bennewith that legally mandated OFRs would lead to "boilerplate" reporting. The official ICAEW response suggested that the OFR should be linked to the statutory statement of directors' responsibilities. Davis envisaged that a second-level rule making body (probably the ASB) would set out a framework of basic headings that the OFR should cover. Similar guidelines for auditors would also need to be devised.

"If you accept that historical cost accounts have now got to the position where they are too far away from companies' market values and are not the main focus of users and market analysts, then something has to be done – and I do not want to hand it over to the legal profession," Davis said. "My recommendation is that by trying really hard to show the legislators how this can be done well, we can ensure the OFR meets the purpose for which it is designed."

Source: AccountingWEB, July 7, 2000.

## *Historical Summaries*

Although not required under statute or any regulation, it has been the practice for over a decade for companies to provide historical summaries as part of their Annual Reports.

These summaries are essentially tabular or graphical presentations of significant financial performance measures over a period of a few, normally 5, years. Their main function is to provide sufficient information to users to enable them to interpret current data over a longer time frame than would otherwise be provided by the Annual Report. Their main usefulness, therefore, is that they allow trends to be established, a critical factor in any considered evaluation of a company.

## *Summary*

The Annual Report is one of the most important documents produced by a company. Indeed, it represents the primary means of communication between a company and its stakeholders. Its format means that it supplements the financial statements with narrative comment and information that is important in enabling users to arrive at informed conclusions and decisions with regard to the company.

Because it is such an important document it is subject to considerable control and regulation. This applies not only to the financial statements, but also to the narrative elements, such as the Directors' Report and Auditor's Report, which are viewed as integral parts of the reporting package.

Indeed, increasingly the attentions of users are being directed to the narrative sections for important supplementary information as well as insights into future prospects, investment plans and corporate strategy. These points will be explored in more detail in Chapters 14 and 18.

# Review Questions

### Question 1
Explain why the narrative sections of Annual Reports have assumed such importance in recent years.

### Question 2
List the principal narrative elements of an Annual Report and for each indicate the principal component parts and the user group that would be most interested.

### Question 3
Only some of the narrative elements of an Annual Report are subject to legislative control with regard to content, etc. Is this appropriate or should each element of the Annual Report be subject to regulation?

### Question 4
To what extent have the various additional disclosure requirements resulting from recent legislation and standards succeeded in remedying the "information deficiency" identified by many users?

### Question 5
Consider the implications for auditors of increasing disclosure and reporting requirements.

### Question 6
"The OFR has meant a significant amount of additional information is now made available to readers of an Annual Report. The main importance of the OFR is that it requires management to not only disclose information but to comment upon it and give opinions as to its significance." Explain how the OFR significantly increases the information available to users regarding future prospects for a company.

### Question 7
To what extent do financial analysts allow their analysis to be informed by the information contained in the narrative portion of Annual Reports?

### Question 8
Explain how requirements in relation to narrative disclosures are likely to develop. For instance is it likely that there will be even greater disclosure requirements placed on companies? As a result is it possible that there might be resistance on the part of companies concerned at both the cost and the disclosure of sensitive information to competitors?

## Case Studies

### Case 1

The following Executive Summary reports on research into the way in which the content of Annual Reports has changed over the course of recent decades. Identify the main trends and the significance of these changes.

## Developments in Corporate Financial Disclosure Over the Period 1975–96: Evidence from UK Annual Reports, by Thomas Schleicher

### Executive Summary

UK annual reports have changed quite dramatically between the mid 1970s and today. The overall amount of information given has increased considerably, and this is equally true for the financial statements and the discussion section of the annual report. New financial statements have emerged with the funds flow/cash flow statement or more recently the statement of total recognized gains and losses, and existing statements now offer a greater level of disaggregation. Moreover, most companies now have separate sections for the business review, financial review and directors' remuneration. As a consequence the annual report has gained considerably in size. The average number of pages in our sample has doubled over the 22-year period from 24–48 with the number of pages containing management's discussion rising from 8–20. Those discussion sections now represent an average of 40% of the annual report against 32% in 1975. In particular larger companies now often devote more pages to supplementary analysis than to the financial statements themselves.

### Disclosure Index Methodology

To analyse the developments in reporting practice separately for various parts of the annual report we have constructed a disclosure index comprising 404 (equally-weighted) items and assigned each item to one of 12 sub-indices. These sub-indices cover the annual report in its entirety and include voluntary and mandatory items alike. The financial statements are divided into seven sub-indices (number of items in brackets):

(A) Accounting Policies (11)
(B) Profit and Loss Account (33)
(C) Balance Sheet (76)
(D) Segmental Reporting (14)
(E) Funds Flow/Cash Flow Statement (14)
(F) Inflation Accounting (31)
(G) Other Financial Statements (19).

Management's Discussion and Analysis (D&A) are allocated to five sub-indices:

(H)  OFR (82)
(I)  OFP (69)
(J)  Research and Development (10)
(K)  Social Responsibility (28)
(L)  Corporate Governance (17)

## Sample

The average values of the sub-indices presented in this report are based on analysing the annual reports of 20 stock market listed companies from the engineering and electronic equipment sectors. Between 1975 and 1993 every other year has been examined. Subsequently, the original study has been updated with results for year 1996. This update enables it to capture the most recent changes in financial reporting practice. For the year 1985 we also present sub-index means for a second sample of 53 companies across 18 level 4 (FT-SE) sectors. Comparing this sample with the 1985 results of the 20 engineering and electronic equipment companies should indicate whether our results are representative of the economy as a whole. We observe moderately higher disclosure levels in the large sample of 53 firms. Overall, we believe that the trends we identify are representative.

## Main Results

The disclosure quality in all parts of the annual report improves over the period 1975–96 (exception: inflation accounting), but the extent and timing of the improvements vary considerably across the different sub-indices. Not surprisingly, in the light of the recent reports from the Cadbury and Greenbury Committees, we find the largest increase for the Corporate Governance sub-index: 60% in 1996 against 13.83% in 1975, an increase of 46.17 percentage points over the whole period (Table 5.1). We also find large increases for the balance sheet and the profit and loss account mainly brought about by the introduction of statutory formats with the CA 81. Segmental disclosure more than doubled in 1991 as a consequence of SSAP 25.

**Table 5.1. Total change in sub-index means over the review period 1975–96**

| Sub-index (number of items) | 1975 (%) | 1996 (%) | Change |
| --- | --- | --- | --- |
| Accounting policies (11) | 51.62 | 88.18 | 36.56 |
| Profit and loss account (33) | 16.99 | 60.71 | 43.72 |
| Balance sheet (76) | 34.52 | 75.02 | 40.50 |
| Segmental reporting (14) | 24.76 | 59.61 | 34.85 |
| Funds/cash flow statement (14) | 39.70 | 62.50 | 22.80 |
| Inflation accounting (31) | 3.71 | 0.00 | −3.71 |
| Other financial statements (19) | 25.26 | 32.90 | 7.64 |
| OFR (82) | 17.93 | 30.12 | 12.19 |
| OFP (69) | 13.70 | 20.36 | 6.66 |

| | | | |
|---|---|---|---|
| Research and development (10) | 15.50 | 34.00 | 18.50 |
| Social responsibility (28) | 6.62 | 21.25 | 14.63 |
| Corporate governance (17) | 13.83 | 60.00 | 46.17 |
| Total disclosure index (404) | 20.10 | 41.36 | 21.26 |

The two sub-indices OFR and OFP are of particular interest from a theoretical point of view. This is true because almost all items are classified as voluntary pieces of information during the entire review period. Both indices should therefore closely reflect management's deliberate decision for a high or low disclosure strategy. We find only modest increases of 12.19 and 6.66 percentage points, but more importantly, in both cases the quality improvements occur largely in 1993 and 1996. If the additional disclosure is a direct response to the ASB statement "OFR" issued in July 1993, then the question emerges of how this observation can be reconciled with predictions in information economics. We will argue that information asymmetries are a problem that exists in both directions. Finance directors need guidance on what information is decision-relevant before they are able to communicate insider information.

## To Whom is This Study of Interest?

After explaining the construction of our disclosure index the study discusses in greater detail the developments in each sub-index. Changes in the financial statements are linked to new legal and professional requirements, and reasons are given for increased disclosure in the D&A sub-indices. Furthermore, we report which pieces of information are likely to be disclosed and point to areas where managers are more reluctant to give anything away. The discussion is conducted on the level of individual items, classes of information and sub-indices. This information should be of interest to:

Finance directors as a basis for an informed decision on their own communication strategy.

Financial analysts as a benchmark against which to measure the disclosure in researched annual reports; this information assists in identifying unusual openness/silences and can be addressed in private meetings with the firm.

Anyone involved in the standard setting process and in particular those who are charged with monitoring compliance with existing requirements.

Researchers as a basis for further investigation into causes and effects of increased disclosure.

Anyone who is interested in annual reports as a product of evolution.

Source: www.acca.org.uk/technical/research/schleicher.html.

## Case 2

One element of the Annual Report that has received comparatively little attention, but which forms an important component (as well as offering considerable scope for manipulation) is the pictorial or graphical representation of information and results. The following summary of research in this area highlights some important issues. Identify and discuss the more significant of these.

## Limited Graphical Reporting Choices: Communication or Manipulation? by Vivien Beattie and Michael John Jones

### Executive Summary

The corporate annual report remains the most widely used information source for individual investors. The technical accounting components are embedded within a powerfully designed annual report package geared towards "impression management". In an attempt to improve communicative effectiveness, companies have explored alternative presentational formats such as graphs. Graphs are particularly useful because large quantities of information can be easily and effectively reviewed, and trends become more apparent.

The primary purpose of this research is to determine whether the nature of graph use is dependent upon corporate performance (i.e., the so-called "manipulation hypothesis"). We focus upon time series data. The detailed objectives are:

- To document the use of financial graphs by top UK companies over a 5-year period and to identify general changes in the aggregate pattern of use. (For example, is more or less use being made of graphs over time?)
- To relate changes in aggregate financial graph use to aggregate measures of corporate profitability.
- To investigate whether the changes in individual companies' financial graph use (e.g., the introduction/cessation of financial graphs, changes in graph construction or design) can be explained by changes in individual corporate performance.
- To test empirically whether the level of financial graph use by individual companies (i.e., cross-sectional variation) can be explained by individual corporate performance and other corporate characteristics.

This research is based on the corporate annual reports of 137 top UK companies which were in continued existence during the 5-year period from 1988–92, a time period which encompasses the UK economic recession which started in 1990.

## Principal Findings Are as Follows

The use of graphs, particularly Key Financial Variable (KFV) graphs (i.e., turnover, profit before tax, earnings per share, and dividends per share), is associated positively with corporate performance:

- The percentage of companies using graphs falls continuously throughout the period from 80.3% in 1988 to 68.6% in 1992, with the largest decline coinciding with the largest fall in profitability.
- The mean number of graphs used over time mirrors corporate profitability very closely.
- The total number of KFV graphs rises marginally in 1989 and then falls quite rapidly, in line with the aggregate trend in corporate performance.
- There is a relative growth in the importance of DPS graphs vis-à-vis other KFV graphs.

As performance declines, changes in graph construction and design occur which are consistent with a desire by annual report preparers to manage the impression of performance conveyed:

- There is a decline in the prominence of KFV graphs in terms of both their location within the annual report and their physical size as the recession takes hold.
- Over the period, there is a marked shift from more creative graphical design types (i.e., 3D columns and pictograms) to simpler graphical types.
- Over the period, the popularity of 5-year trends (the norm) declines markedly.
- The overall mean measurement distortion (i.e., data trend exaggeration) across KFV graphs and years is +22.8%, with a significant minority (30.1%) of KFV graphs being materially distorted.
- The mean aspect ratio for KFV graphs is 38.4°, with nearly half of all graphs diverging more than 15° from the optimum for communicative effectiveness (45°).
- The use of design features which tend to enhance the impression conveyed (e.g., the use of colour changes to draw attention to the final year's result) decline as the recession takes hold.

Statistical testing relating the changes in individual companies' financial graph use to changes in individual corporate performance revealed that:

- The start/stop KFV graphs decision, the primary graphical choice, is strongly associated with both the direction and magnitude of change in performance indicators. Thus, companies are more inclined to start using graphs when financial performance improves and vice-versa.
- Where KFV graphs are used in the face of poor performance, they are presented less prominently in terms of size and position within the annual report.

The level of financial graph use by individual companies can be explained partly by individual corporate performance and company size. Companies in 1992 with better performance and of larger size were more likely to use at least one KFV graph.

Taken together, our findings provide strong evidence to suggest that the existence, construction, and design of KFV graphs in corporate annual reports are systematically influenced by corporate characteristics, in particular, by corporate performance. We therefore recommend that an explicit set of graphical reporting guidelines be introduced.

Source: www.acca.org.uk/technical/research/beattie.html.

## Case 3

This chapter includes an article broadly supportive of proposals to give the OFR statutory status. However, several regulators, such as Sir David Tweedie, are unhappy at this. The following article elaborates on some of Sir David's misgivings. Summarize the arguments for and against this proposal.

## Keep Lawyers Hands Off OFR, Warns Tweedie

ASB chairman, Sir David Tweedie has warned that plans to give the OFR statutory status could backfire. The ASB invented the OFR to give directors the opportunity to "tell the story" behind their financial accounts. The company law review proposes to make it a statutory element of financial statements.

Sir David told the audience at the IFA "Accountancy in the New Millennium" conference in London, "I have doubts about giving (the OFR) statutory status – we do not want the lawyers to get involved." The ASB chairman explained to AccountingWEB, "if the OFR gets into the hands of the legal profession there is a danger it would end up filled with meaningless boilerplate like the directors report". He also wondered how auditors would react when faced with general forecasts of business performance.

"We want more opinion, based on sensible facts. We have got to be careful not to wreck the OFR. We might end up getting less information, not more." said Sir David and added, "the DTI knows our views."

Source: AccountingWEB, June 13, 2000.

# FINANCIAL STATEMENTS $[6]$

When you have completed this chapter you will understand:

- The complex structures typical of many large business combinations.
- How these structures impact upon the nature and content of the Annual Report.
- The formatting regulations relating to financial statements included in an Annual Report.
- The accounting principles and disclosure requirements relating to the various elements of financial statements.
- Some of the current issues surrounding financial reporting in the UK.

(a)                                                    (b)

**Figure 6.1** **(a) Lenin and Trotsky celebrate the second anniversary of the Russian Revolution in the Red Square. (b) Lenin celebrates, but Trotsky has been airbrushed. Source: David King, The Commissar Vanishes, 1997.**

# Introduction

Financial statements, and in particular balance sheets, are often compared to photographs – they attempt to capture company performance in a snapshot. However, in the same way that ordinary photographs can be manipulated, so too can financial statements. Just as political circumstances in 1920s Russia made it expedient for Stalin to attempt to erase Trotsky from public memory, it is often tempting for companies to seek to construct their accounts in such a way as to communicate a particular message.

For this reason there are extensive and rigorous regulations relating to the presentation of financial information in an Annual Report. In particular, the ways in which the balance sheet and profit and loss account are to be presented are heavily controlled, allowing only limited scope for variability within strict formats.

This chapter deals with the rules covering the disclosure of financial information. This involves identifying the accounting and disclosure rules relating to items normally included in financial statements and in the accompanying notes. The provisions relating to the balance sheet are dealt with first, followed by those relating to the profit and loss account, statement of total recognized gains and losses and the cash flow statement. While the requirements outlined are quite extensive, they are intended to be indicative and not exhaustive.

Reference should be made throughout to the Tesco plc 2000 Annual Report for examples of how the provisions referred to are translated into practice.

Before this, however, the chapter looks at the implications of the fact that most large business entities are actually business combinations, i.e., they are comprised of a parent company and several others in some form of relationship with that parent.

# Corporate Structure

Most large business entities will comprise of a number of companies related to one overall parent company. This will have an effect on the information to be included in an Annual Report because accounting recognizes such a business combination (or group) as a separate entity for reporting purposes.

The nature of these inter-company relationships can be varied and complex and there may often be a deliberately ill-defined structure in place. This will be dealt with in more detail in Chapter 11. However, for the purposes of this chapter it is necessary to have some idea of the relationships that can exist between corporate entities.

The nature of these relationships include:

- Parent/wholly-owned subsidiary, where one company owns another entity (subsidiary) entirely.
- Parent/partly owned subsidiary, where one company controls (or has a dominant influence over) another, but does not own it entirely. That portion of the subsidiary owned by entities other than the parent company is called the "minority interest".

- Investor/associate company, where one company has a substantial participating interest (normally 20% or more) in another company.

- Investor/investee, where one company simply makes an investment in another.

In a situation in which this parent company is called P, a group structure might comprise any combination of the following permutations (Figure 6.2).

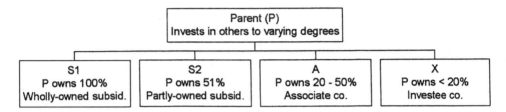

**Figure 6.2   A group structure.**

The Annual Report filed for P must recognize the fact that P has these relationships with other companies. This is usually satisfied by preparing an additional set of accounts – called group (or consolidated) accounts. The procedure for preparing group accounts will be covered in more detail in Chapter 11, but can be summarized as follows:

- P has one or more wholly-owned subsidiaries: combine results of these companies entirely with those of P.

- P has one or more partly-owned subsidiaries: combine results of these companies entirely with those of P, but reflect the claims of the minority interest on net assets and profit by indicating these claims under the heading "minority interest" in both the balance sheet and the profit and loss account, respectively.

- P has one or more associate companies: recognize the claim of P to a share of the total profits made by these associates proportionate to its investment and indicate the total value of the investment in the balance sheet as a proportion of the net assets of the associates.

- P has one or more investees: simply include these as short-term investments in the balance sheet and record any resulting income in the profit and loss account.

## Annual Report – Financial Statements

While a substantial part of an Annual Report will be made up of the narrative elements and reports, the financial statements and notes still constitute its core. Where the reporting entity is a group these will include:

**By statute:**

1. Balance sheet of the parent company as an individual company.

2. Profit and loss account of the parent company as an individual company. (Under S.230(3) CA85 this may be omitted if the parent company balance sheet discloses the parent company's profit for the year.)

3. Consolidated balance sheet for group as a whole.

4. Consolidated profit and loss account for the group as a whole.

5. Additional explanatory notes.

**By FRS:**

6. Cash flow statement for parent and group (FRS 1 revised).

7. Statement of total recognized gains and losses (FRS 3).

The remainder of this chapter deals with the formats, accounting principles and disclosure requirements appropriate to each of these financial statements in turn. For each element of each statement general accounting principles and disclosure requirements are outlined. The chapter is, therefore, quite detailed in its specifications. It is important, however, not to be so consumed in the detail that the overall picture, and the "true and fair" requirement, is overlooked.

## *Balance Sheet*

This is best described as a financial photograph. It is a statement that summarizes in financial terms the position of an entity at a moment in time.

The presentation and structure of the balance sheet is influenced by a number of considerations. However, the two principal shaping influences are statute, in particular Schedule 4 CA85 as amended, and accounting standards such as FRS 3, *Reporting Financial Performance*.

## **Formats**

Originally prescribed in CA81, which was a response to the EU Fourth Directive, Schedule 4 CA85 (as amended) sets out the two permitted formats for a balance sheet. Constructed as a series of sections (Roman letters) and sub-sections (Roman numerals), these formats allow little flexibility and preparers are expected to conform rigidly to the outlines. Only where further sub-headings apply (indicated by Arabic numerals) is there any scope for adaptation.

### Format 1[1]

This is the format adopted by the vast majority of UK companies and is commonly known as the "vertical format" because it lists all items sequentially (Table 6.1).

---

[1] Format 2 contains the same headings as Format 1, but presents them in horizontal fashion, with assets on one side and liabilities on the other.

## Table 6.1. Format 1 (vertical format)

A Called-up share capital not paid[a]
B Fixed assets
*I Intangible assets*
    1. Development costs
    2. Concessions, patents, trade marks and similar rights and assets
    3. Goodwill
    4. Payments on account
*II Tangible assets*
    1. Land and buildings
    2. Plant and machinery
    3. Fixtures, fittings, tools and equipment
    4. Payments on account and assets in course of construction
*III Investments*
    1. Shares in group undertakings
    2. Loans to group undertakings
    3. Participating interests
    4. Loans to undertakings in which the company has a participating interest
    5. Other investments other than loans
    6. Other loans
    7. Own shares
C Current assets
*I Stocks*
    1. Raw materials and consumables
    2. Work-in-progress
    3. Finished goods and goods for resale
    4. Payments on account
*II Debtors*
    1. Trade debtors
    2. Amounts owed by group undertakings
    3. Amounts owed by undertakings in which the company has a participating interest
    4. Other debtors
    5. Called-up share capital not paid[a]
    6. Prepayments and accrued income[a]
*III Investments*
    1. Shares in group undertakings
    2. Own shares
    3. Other investments
*IV Cash at bank and in hand*
D Prepayments and accrued income[a]
E Creditors: amounts falling due within 1 year
    1. Debenture loans
    2. Bank loans and overdrafts
    3. Payments received on account
    4. Trade creditors
    5. Bills of exchange payable
    6. Amounts owed to group undertakings
    7. Amounts owed to undertakings in which the company has a participating interest

**Table 6.1.** (*continued*)

8. Other creditors including taxation and social security
9. Accruals and deferred income[a]
F Net current assets (liabilities)
G Total assets less current liabilities
H Creditors: amounts falling due after more than 1 year
   1. Debenture loans
   2. Bank loans and overdrafts
   3. Payments received on account
   4. Trade creditors
   5. Bills of exchange payable
   6. Amounts owed to group undertakings
   7. Amounts owed to undertakings in which the company has a participating interest
   8. Other creditors including taxation and social security
   9. Accruals and deferred income[a]
I Provisions for liabilities and charges
   1. Pensions and similar obligations
   2. Taxation including deferred taxation
   3. Other provisions
J Accruals and deferred income[a]
K Capital and reserves
*I Called-up share capital*
*II Share premium account*
*III Revaluation reserve*
*IV Other reserves*
   1. Capital redemption reserve
   2. Reserve for own shares
   3. Reserves provided for by the articles of association
   4. Other reserves
*V Profit and loss account*

[a] These items may be presented in one of two places as indicated.

## General Comments

This outline indicates the general headings that must be employed when preparing a balance sheet for publication. The following points explain some of these provisions:

- Items indicated by a Roman letter (A, B, C, etc.) or numeral (I, II, III) must be shown on the face of the balance sheet and in the order indicated, unless they are not material or, as in the case of items A, D an J, can be shown elsewhere as sub-headings.

- Only in relation to those sub-headings assigned Arabic numerals (1, 2, 3, etc.) is there any real discretion as to presentation. For example, where the nature of the company's business requires it, their order may be rearranged or they may be disclosed by means of notes to the accounts. It is also permitted to combine two or more of them if either the individual items are not material to assessing the state of affairs, or such a combination would assist a user in making such an assessment.

- Any item may be shown in greater detail than the format specifies.
- Where specific items are not covered by the headings or sub-headings provided these may be added.
- Corresponding amounts must be shown for the previous year and must be comparable to current year figures.

The accounting principles and disclosure requirements relating to each of the headings and sub-sections required under Format 1 are now outlined in more detail.

## A. Called-Up Share Capital Not Paid

When a company issues shares it may or may not decide to call-up the entire amount due from those to whom it has decided to allot shares. This figure represents amounts called-up but not yet received from shareholders. If the amount is not material the option exists for this to be included as a sub-heading under Debtors.

## B. Fixed Assets

Chapter 4 of the Statement of Principles defines assets as "rights or other access to future economic benefits controlled by an entity as a result of past transactions or events". Fixed assets are defined by CA85 as those assets intended for use "on a continuing basis in the company's activities". All other assets will be classified as current.

These definitions mean that where a company enjoys the benefits and undertakes the risks associated with an asset, then it should be included in the balance sheet regardless of the legal position.

Consequently assets purchased under hire-purchase arrangements should be included, despite the fact that legal ownership normally does not transfer until the final payment. Assets leased out on terms whereby the company enjoys the benefits and undertakes the risks (finance leases) will also be included. The amount at which such assets should be capitalized (i.e., included in the balance sheet) is the present value of the minimum lease payments. They should be subject to the normal depreciation policy of the company for that class of asset.

Fixed assets are normally to be stated at cost of purchase (or cost of production where appropriate). Interest on capital borrowed to finance the purchase or production of a fixed asset may also be included. Revaluation of specific assets to current values is allowed, but in such circumstances the historical cost must also be disclosed.

Provision for decreases in value must be made where appropriate. Where the asset in question has a limited useful economic life then the depreciable amount must be written off over that period on a systematic basis. Where any reduction in value is reversed then it must be written back to the extent that it is no longer required.

## Disclosure

Every company is required to supplement the information provided on the face of the balance sheet with additional disclosures in a standard note to the accounts. This should contain information about the cost (or revalued amount) at the beginning and end of the period for each item listed as a fixed asset, together with the effect on that item of:

- Acquisitions
- Disposals
- Transfers
- Revisions due to changes in accounting bases

For each category information must also be provided regarding any provision for depreciation or diminution in value at the beginning and end of the period together with any provisions or adjustments made during the year in respect of disposals or other events.

## I. Intangible Assets

Intangible assets can be broadly defined as assets that do not have a physical substance. Examples include brand names, goodwill and patents. FRS 10, *Goodwill and Intangible Assets*, defines intangible assets as "non-financial fixed assets that do not have physical substance but are identifiable and are controlled by the entity through custody or legal rights". For an asset to be identifiable it must be possible to dispose of it separately from the rest of the business. If this is not possible then it is to be considered as goodwill which, where it has been purchased, is to be shown in the balance sheet. However, FRS 10 provides that internally developed intangible assets may only be shown in the balance sheet if they have a readily ascertainable market value.

Intangible assets having a finite life should be depreciated (the term used in relation to intangible assets is "amortized"). Usually the maximum term over which such intangible assets are to be amortized is 20 years, although if it can be established by means of annual impairment reviews that the value has not decreased then it need not be amortized. (Impairment reviews are reviews intended to ensure that assets are not carried at amounts exceeding their recoverable amount, which, as outlined in Chapter 2, is the higher of net realizable value and value in use.) However, this fact must be disclosed together with an explanation of the reasons for not amortizing as well as an assessment of the effect of not so doing.

As this text has attempted to highlight thus far, accounting practice does not exist in a vacuum. It is the result of a political process and can have immediate and widespread social effects. FRS 10, for instance, has impacted the way in which footballers are accounted for, and, hence, the values placed on them and their clubs.

## Accounting Treatment Fuels Football Transfer Boom

Treating football players as intangible assets under FRS 10 may have fuelled the boom in football player transfers, according to Deloitte and Touche. In its financial review of the 1998–9 football season, the firm pinpointed a 50% increase in transfer spending. The net outflow in transfer fees paid to foreign clubs doubled to £142.2 million.

FRS 10, which came into effect on March 23, 1999, required companies to show purchased players as assets on their balance sheets, and to amortize their transfer fees across the length of the player's contract rather than writing them off that year's profits. But under the standard, home-grown players like Paul Scholes and David Beckham are not shown as assets, giving clubs a financial incentive to wheel and deal.

"The club's did not like FRS 10 at first because they did not get the tax relief when they bought players," said Deloitte and Touche tax partner Richard Baldwin. "Cumulatively FRS10 added £507 million to the Premier League's balance sheets. It should make clubs look more profitable as they spread the expenses over the life of the contract. Sophisticated FDs at some of the clubs could exploit the situation to manage things like their PE (price/earning) ratios, but FRS10 is too subtle for most clubs." Baldwin suggested that the transfer boom probably had more to do with the "shop-window" affect of the 1998 World Cup, which took place just before the season reviewed. Overall, football's income rose 10% to £951 million in 1998–9, while wages and salaries rose 18% to £620 million.

Source: AccountingWEB, August 15, 2000.

There are specific disclosure requirements in relation to each of the sub-categories of intangible assets specified in Format 1 as follows.

### 1. Development Costs

Development costs relate to the costs of developing a product or service and can form a substantial part of the expenditure of many firms.

Opinion on how such expenditure should be treated is divided. On the one hand those arguing that it should be capitalized (i.e., put in the balance sheet) and depreciated, point out that it is essentially an investment in the future of the company. Those arguing that it should be immediately written off to the profit and loss account counter that any future returns are inherently uncertain and that to capitalize them would run counter to the prudence concept.

SSAP 13, *Accounting for research and development*, devised an essentially pragmatic solution. It basically requires that the bulk of research and development expenditure be charged to the profit and loss account immediately. However, it does allow development costs to be capitalized, i.e., included in the balance sheet as an intangible asset, under certain strict conditions:

- There is a clearly defined project
- The related expenditure is separately identifiable
- It is reasonably certain that the project is both technically feasible and commercially viable
- It is expected to be profitable, having considered all current and future costs; and
- The company has the resources to complete the project

The treatment of such expenditure has become particularly topical with the advent of "new economy" firms for whom expenditure on software development represents a significant outgoing. The ways in which various regulatory bodies are attempting to address the concerns of such businesses are discussed in Chapter 18.

## 2. Concessions, Patents, Licences, Trade Marks and Similar Rights and Assets

Patents, trade marks and similar rights can be capitalized and shown as intangible assets where they have been acquired for valuable consideration or created by the company itself. They will normally be included at cost, but may be included at replacement cost, i.e., the current cost of an equivalent asset. In any case they are depreciated over the period of their useful lives. Similarly, copyrights and licences, for example, those relating to software, can also be included as intangible assets.

Brands can often constitute a significant part of a company's value. However, unless brands are acquired through purchase then they are notoriously difficult to value. FRS 10 makes the following comments on them:

"It is not possible to determine a market value for unique intangible assets such as brands and publishing titles. Replacement cost may be equally difficult to determine directly. However, certain entities that are regularly involved in the purchase and sale of unique intangible assets have developed techniques for estimating their values indirectly and these may be used for initial recognition of such assets at the time of purchase. Techniques used can be based, for example, on 'indicators of value' – such as multiples of turnover – or on estimating the present value of the royalties that would be payable to license the asset from a third party."

Because they are considered to have indefinite lives, brands are not normally amortized. Under the provisions of FRS 10, however, those companies adopting this policy are required to carry out annual impairment reviews to ensure that assets are not being carried at amounts exceeding their recoverable value.

### 3. Goodwill

FRS 10 defines goodwill as "the difference between the cost of an acquired entity and the aggregate of the fair values of that entity's identifiable assets and liabilities." In other words, goodwill is the premium paid by one entity to acquire the net assets of another. For example, if company P acquires company S for £10 million at a time when the fair value of S's separable net assets amounts to £7 million, then goodwill of £3 million is deemed to have been acquired.

Historically it was the practice not to include goodwill on the face of the balance sheet, although SSAP 22, *Accounting for goodwill*, allowed this option. Most companies favoured the alternative course of eliminating goodwill against reserves since this meant that there was no asset remaining in the balance sheet that attracted an amortization charge every year, which would have the effect of reducing profits.

---

**In practice:**

*Sound and Vision Group*

*Following the issue of FRS 10, Goodwill and Intangible Assets, the directors thought it appropriate to reconsider the treatment of purchased goodwill in order to comply with recommended practice. The accounts for the year ended September 30, 1998 state that the previously eliminated goodwill of £2,797 million has been capitalized and brought into the balance sheet.*

*Additionally, the directors have carried out an impairment review of goodwill, resulting in a write-down of £1,985 million to £812,500 at September 1997. This was the net realizable value of the showrooms that were sold in the year ended September 30, 1998 and those held with a view to later sale.*

*Source: Accountancy International, June 1999.*

---

However, since the introduction of FRS 10 purchased goodwill must be capitalized. It now appears in the balance sheet as an intangible asset subject to amortization. This ensures that goodwill is charged against future profits, i.e., in those periods expected to benefit from the acquisition of this goodwill. This is consistent with FRS 10's stated aim of ensuring that "purchased goodwill and intangible assets are charged in the profit and loss account in the periods in which they are depleted".

In determining the amount of amortization, or whether goodwill should be amortized in the first place, FRS 10 introduces the concept of impairment reviews, in relation to which it provides the following.

"An asset is regarded as impaired if its recoverable amount (the higher of net realizable value and value in use) falls below its carrying value, i.e., the amount at which it is included in the accounts. Impairment reviews should be performed to ensure that goodwill and intangible assets are not carried at above their recoverable amounts. Where goodwill and intangible assets are amortized over a period that does not exceed 20 years, impairment reviews need be performed only at the end of the first full financial year following the initial recognition of the goodwill or intangible asset and, in other periods, if events or changes in circumstances indicate that its carrying value may not be recoverable in full. Where goodwill and intangible assets are not amortized, or are amortized over a period exceeding 20 years, impairment reviews should be performed each year.'

Impairment reviews have since been dealt with further in FRS 11, *Impairment of fixed assets and goodwill*, and this is covered later in this chapter. The treatment of goodwill as it arises in the context of the acquisition of one company by another is dealt with in more detail in Chapter 11.

### 4. Payments on Account

Where there have been payments on account in respect of the purchase of intangible assets then these must be disclosed.

Refer to Note 11 of the Tesco plc 2000 Annual Report for an example of the detail to be disclosed in relation to intangible assets.

## II. Tangible Assets

Tangible assets, unlike intangible assets, have a physical substance. Almost all companies will have such assets, although there are examples of some "new economy" firms which show "nil" under this heading.

In relation to the specific subsections under which tangible assets must be presented under Format 1 the following provisions apply.

### 1. Land and Buildings

This category must be further subdivided into freehold, long leasehold (i.e., with an unexpired lease period of more than 50 years remaining) and short leaseholds. In the case of land it is permissible to capitalize costs such as legal fees, landscaping and demolition costs. Where a building is purchased it should include all repair, alteration and improvement costs. If the building has been constructed then the balance sheet figure should include the cost of materials, all sub-contracted work, overheads and other costs such as professional fees. Where construction has been financed by borrowings then the cost should include capitalized interest charges. This amount must be separately disclosed by way of note. As is the case for all assets, where buildings have been revalued during the year the names of the valuers and the valuation bases employed must be disclosed, normally by way of note, as must the historical cost information that would apply if there had been no revaluation.

## 2. Plant and Machinery

Where appropriate, the requirements for land and buildings are also relevant to plant and machinery. The balance sheet figure must also include costs such as freight and installation costs.

## 3. Fixtures, Fittings, Tools and Equipment

This should include the cost of relatively permanent items only. It is acceptable to include in the balance sheet a fixed amount for items such as "tools" which are regularly being replaced and which are neither material to the company nor subject to material variation in either quantity or value.

## 4. Payments on Account and Assets in Course of Construction

Costs incurred in relation to assets in the course of production must include cost of materials, all sub-contracted work, overheads and professional fees.

Assets, and tangible fixed assets in particular, have recently been the subject of several standards issued by the Accounting Standards Board. These have addressed at a fundamental level several issues relevant to tangible assets such as valuation, presentation and disclosure.

FRS 11, *Impairment of fixed assets and goodwill*, ensures that reporting entities focus on the values at which fixed assets are carried in the balance sheet, in particular, on those assets which have been "impaired". As the FRS points out impairment is not a new concept and existing legislation and accounting rules meant that assets could not be held in the balance sheet at amounts exceeding their recoverable amounts. The principal achievement of FRS 11 "is that it puts in place a detailed and coherent methodology by which impairment can be both identified and calculated."

Recoverable amount is the higher of "net realizable value" and "value in use", an amount arrived at using a conservative discounting of future cash flows likely to arise over the life of the assets concerned. The rate used for this purpose must be a market rate that reflects the riskiness of the assets involved. This rate must be disclosed, although only where the exercise has resulted in the recognition of an impairment loss.

The first step in applying impairment tests will normally involve sub-dividing assets into "Income-Generating Units" (IGUs). This is often a difficult concept to apply since it requires the identification of units that can be said to form discrete revenue generating units. However this is done, the principle is that impairment tests should be carried out at the lowest possible level of aggregation.

As the following "In practice" box points out, there can be many and varied reasons for impairment:

**In practice:**

*Reasons for the Write-downs by Hans Nailor*

*...The nature of the exercise suggests that when impairment losses are recognized, the amounts involved are generally substantial. A review of disclosures relating to FRS 11-related asset write-downs shows that the directors have given the impact of the write-downs considerable attention in the presentation of their annual reports, which is one of FRS 11's objectives. Reasons given for impairment losses were:*

- *Economic crisis in Russia.*
- *Slump in oil prices (several companies in this sector were materially affected).*
- *Reduction in gas production and reserve estimates.*
- *Fall in metal prices; write-down of regulatory assets as a result of a Monopolies and Mergers Commission report*
- *Impairment of assets in businesses affected by rationalization programmes.*
- *Adopting FRS 11 methodology.*

*Most of the impairments we have identified related to tangible fixed assets (including land and buildings, plant and equipment, oil and gas assets, mines). Capitalized goodwill appears to have been largely unaffected thus far, which is to be expected, since most companies have begun to capitalize goodwill only on their most recent acquisitions in 1998.*

*Source: Accountancy International, December 1999.*

FRS 15, *Tangible Fixed Assets*, is another standard that has impacted on this section of the balance sheet. Its main purpose is to bring greater consistency to the treatment of fixed assets in terms of determination of cost, valuation and depreciation. On these points it deals with the following:

- Cost: clear rules are provided on what element of initial cost and subsequent expenditure can be capitalized.

- Depreciation: this must reflect the level of consumption of an asset, a fact which may require certain assets to be sub-divided. On certain long-term assets it is now possible to avoid depreciation. However, the rules to be applied are very strict and disclosure requirements extensive.

- Capitalizing finance costs is optional, but where an entity adopts such a policy it should be applied consistently.

---

**In practice:**

---

*FRS 15 Under Fire as Rank Profits Dive*

*UK leisure group Rank has blamed accounting standard FRS 15 and the sale of Universal Studios for a £42.1 million slide in half-year profits. The company said the need to depreciate assets under the tangible fixed assets standard, which came into force this year, cost it an extra £8.4 million. This, and charges for the disposal of its Universal film business, led to the 48% dive in profits, down from £80.5 million for the same period last year.*

*Rank said that operating profit before exceptional items and FRS 15 was 24% ahead of last year. Proforma profit before tax, and excluding FRS 15, the Universal sale and capitalized interest, was up 9% to £65.1 million. After a series of disposals, the firm believes that it is down to four "credible business groupings", but more restructuring is planned. The holiday arm of the group – which accounted for £4.8 million of the FRS 15 depreciation – is up for sale, with private firm Bourne Leisure tipped as a likely buyer.*

*Source: AccountingWEB, September 11, 2000.*

---

Because arbitrary revaluations have been extensively used by those seeking to distract attention from operational deficiencies, FRS 15 introduces the following provisions in relation to revaluations:

- Revaluing tangible fixed assets is optional.

- Where an entity does revalue it must apply the same revaluation policy to all tangible fixed assets of the same class, and should keep the valuations shown in the balance sheet up to date.

- Revalued assets should be given a full valuation involving a qualified external valuer at least every 5 years, an interim valuation by a qualified internal or external auditor in year three and further interim valuations in the intervening years where it is likely that there has been a material change in value.

Refer to Note 12 of the Tesco plc 2000 Annual Report for an example of the level of detail to be disclosed in relation to tangible assets.

## III. Investments

This section can include a variety of investments that can be classified as long-term. However, the sub-categories indicated under this heading suggest that the investments most likely to be included here will be investments made in the shares of other companies.

Companies invest in the shares of other companies for a variety of reasons. In some cases the intention will be to invest surplus cash for a short period of time. However, if these shares are likely to be retained for more than 1 year then they will be shown here, rather than under current assets.

As with other fixed assets, such investments should be shown at cost, unless net realizable value is lower, in which case provision must be made for loss in value. Such provision must be made where an investment has decreased in value, even temporarily. Where such losses are reversed, any provisions for loss in value must be written back.

Each category of listed investment must be subdivided between those listed on a recognized UK stock exchange and those listed elsewhere. The market value of listed investments must be disclosed by way of note.

The more detailed requirements relating to the various categories indicated under this heading are covered in Chapter 11.

## C. Current Assets

Current assets can be defined as resources likely to be held for the short-term. The most obvious examples are stock, debtors and cash.

## I. Stocks

Stocks will usually comprise one of the most valuable resources of a company and consequently its incorporation, disclosure and valuation receive considerable attention in statute and accounting standards. In fact, SSAP 9 (revised), *Stocks and Long Term Contracts*, is devoted specifically to this category.

The general valuation rule is that stock should be shown at the lower of cost and net realizable value. Net realizable value is defined as "anticipated selling price less completion, sales, marketing and distribution costs". "Cost" can often be more problematic. Except for businesses that simply purchase goods and then sell them on, questions as to what actually comprises cost will arise. For instance, for manufacturing firms it will often be difficult to determine how much overhead should be attributed to stock. This is also the case where raw materials are processed and at the end of year remain unfinished. Long-term contracts, where costs cannot always be matched to particular accounting periods, will also pose problems.

In response to this various "costing" methods have been developed. Thus, techniques such as First In First Out (FIFO), Last In First Out (LIFO), weighted average or other similar methods may be used to determine cost subject to the overriding consideration that the basis adopted must be one which, in the opinion of the directors, is appropriate to the company. LIFO, however, is not permitted under accounting standards. (These valuation methods are discussed in more detail in Chapter 8.)

Where raw materials and consumables are carried they may be included at a fixed amount where they are constantly being replaced and are neither material in amount nor variable in quantity or value.

# Disclosure

CA85 (as amended) requires stock to be disclosed under the following sub-headings where appropriate:

1. Raw materials and consumables

2. Work-in-progress

3. Finished goods and goods for resale

4. Payments on account for items not yet received

SSAP 9 allows a more extensive categorization, and it is acceptable for companies to adapt these sub-headings where to do so "would contribute to presenting a true and fair view":

- Goods or other assets purchased for resale

- Consumable stores

- Raw materials and components purchased for incorporation into products for sale

- Products and services in intermediate stages of completion

- Long term contract balances; and

- Finished goods

Any material difference between the figure shown on the balance sheet and market value, replacement cost or most recent purchase price must be disclosed by way of note.

In relation to specific elements of stock, the following provisions apply.

*Consignment stock*: this is covered specifically in an application note to FRS 5, *Reporting the substance of transactions* and is a special case in that it is stock which is subject to a reservation of title clause. In other words, it is held by one party but is owned until sold by another, for example, in cases where car manufacturers supply vehicles to dealers. FRS 5 requires that such items be shown in the accounts of whichever party takes the risks and rewards of ownership. In determining this FRS 5 identifies four considerations to be taken into account:

- The manufacturer's right of return

- The customer's right of return

- The stock transfer price and deposits; and

- The customer's right to use the stock

*Long-term contracts*: many large entities, particularly those engaged in industries such as construction, must deal with the added complications created by long-term contracts. They pose additional problems in terms of calculating the amount of profit to be taken, and the value of any closing stock, because costs and profits cannot always be neatly attributed to arbitrary accounting periods.

---

**In practice:**

*Brunel*

*The design engineering and distribution group refers in its interim report for the 6 months ended December 31, 1998 to the fact that, in the year ended June 30, 1998, the group took an order to supply two machines to China. At June 30, 1998 the machines were partially complete and, in accordance with SSAP 9, turnover of £1,515 million and profit of £485,000 were recognized in that year.*

*However, the customer has not yet decided to proceed with the order and, as a result, the turnover and profit previously taken have been reversed out.*

*Source: Accountancy International, June 1999.*

---

It would be unacceptable to force entities to wait until completion before incorporating some element of profit on such contracts. Consequently, SSAP 9 allows companies engaged in such long-term contracts to include turnover and profit from partly completed projects in their profit and loss account while the project is in progress. This is provided that the outcome can be determined prior to completion and reasonable prudence is exercised.

The normal apportionment basis is "percentage of completion", with the profit and loss account incorporating the difference between attributable turnover and related costs. Any resulting asset, i.e., payments due on foot of attributable turnover, should be treated as a debtor – "amounts receivable on contracts".

Long-term contract stock balances may also exist. These are calculated as costs incurred to date less amounts already accounted for as:

- Cost of sales
- Foreseeable losses
- Payments on account not matched by turnover

## II. Debtors

Debtors are amounts of money owed to the business. They should be included at net realizable value if this is lower than other valuations. Consequently it is necessary to make provisions for bad and doubtful debts, although such provisions are not required to be disclosed unless material.

Under CA85 Sch. 4 amounts included under this heading must distinguish between those due within the next 12 months and those due after that date.

In relation to the specific sub-sections under which this item must be disclosed, the following provisions apply:

1. **Trade debtors**: these are amounts due to the company arising from its trading activity, and will usually form the largest element of the Debtors figure.

2. **Amounts owed by group undertakings**: companies within a group will often trade with one another. As a result they will owe amounts to, and be owed monies by, one another at the end of accounting periods. The specifics of dealing with these balances are dealt with in more detail in Chapter 11.

3. **Amounts owed by undertakings in which the company has a participating interest**: this is also dealt with in detail in Chapter 11.

4. **Other debtors**: this refers to amounts due for reasons other than trading. Examples include amounts not yet received in respect of fixed asset sales and loans made to directors of the company not yet repaid.

5. **Called-up share capital not paid**: to the extent that this amount is not disclosed under Section A of the balance sheet it should be disclosed here.

6. **Prepayments and accrued income**: prepayments are amounts paid in advance in respect of expenses or services that will be consumed during a subsequent accounting period. Common examples are rent and insurance prepaid. Accrued income refers to income from non-trading sources which has been realized but not yet received.

In addition to these six specified categories, CA85 provides that information may also be included here in relation to items usually appearing as creditors for which a debit balance exists. Examples include pension prepayments, amounts receivable under finance leases and corporation tax recoverable.

## III. Investments

Investments categorized as current assets normally relate to short-term investments intended to generate income from available cash. Such investments are normally shown at the lower of cost and net realizable value, although CA85 (as amended) does allow them to be shown at market value (a technique known as "marking to market") or at any other method which directors consider appropriate.

In relation to the three sub-categories provided for in Format 1 the following provisions apply.

1. **Shares in group undertakings**: this relates to short-term investments in entities in which the company has control or dominant influence. This is covered in Chapter 11.

2. **Own shares**: companies cannot legally hold their own shares as an investment for their own benefit, whether short or long-term. However, they may retain them where they are held, for example, for employee share option schemes.

3. **Other investments**

Examples of investments of this type include:

- Listed and government securities.
- Certificates of deposit, which are deposits where a company agrees to deposit money with a bank for an agreed period of time in return for which the company receives a certificate which is a negotiable instrument and a higher rate of return than would normally be the case.
- Other deposits.

## Disclosure

Because of the flexibility allowed in terms of valuation of short-term investments the disclosure requirements by way of note are considerable:

- The valuation method and the reasons for adopting it must be disclosed.

- Any material difference between the figure shown on the balance sheet and market value or most recent purchase price must be disclosed.

- Notes to the accounts should show listed investments on the London Stock Exchange as a separate category from those listed on overseas markets.

## IV Cash at Bank and in Hand

Cash at bank and in hand includes cash and all near-cash items such as cheques, legal tender, credit card vouchers and similar items. However, it does not include deposits with building societies or time deposits with banks where there are restrictions on the right to withdraw funds at notice. Such items would be shown as investments.

## D. Prepayments and Accrued Income

These items will not normally be substantial. They can also be presented under sub-heading 6 of Debtors if this is considered more appropriate.

## E. Creditors: Amounts falling due within 1 year

This relates to amounts owed which must be paid within the following 12 months. They are short-term liabilities.

The following provisions relate to the sub-sections indicated under Format 1.

1. **Debenture loans**: a debenture is a medium or long-term source of finance, so the amount indicated under this heading would only be that portion which must be repaid within the next 12 months. Technically a debenture is a document that either creates or acknowledges a debt undertaken by the company. Debentures

are usually secured against the assets of the company under terms specified in a debenture deed or trust document. This can be by means of a fixed charge, i.e., on a particular asset, or a floating charge, i.e., on a class of asset.

2. **Bank loans and overdrafts**: only that portion of this source of funding due within the next 12 months should be disclosed under this heading.

3. **Payments received on account**: in some circumstances customers may pay deposits for goods or services that will not yet have been provided. The item appears as a creditor because such deposits create an obligation on the part of the company to supply the goods and services or refund the deposit.

4. **Trade creditors**: this represents the amount due by the company within the next 12 months in respect of goods and/or services received during the period just ended. This is usually one of the largest sources of funding availed of by companies since, during the interval between receipt of the goods and/or services and eventual payment, they effectively have the use of free funds.

5. **Bills of exchange payable**: these are acknowledgements of debt written by the supplier and signed by the company. They are negotiable instruments and can be traded by the bearer.

6. **Amounts owed to group undertakings**: companies within a group will often trade with one another. As a result they will owe amounts to, and be owed monies by, one another at the end of an accounting period. The specifics of dealing with these balances are dealt with in more detail in Chapter 11.

7. **Amounts owed to undertakings in which the company has a participating interest**: this is dealt with in Chapter 11.

8. **Other creditors including taxation and social security**: these are amounts owing which cannot be included under any of the other categories. Examples include:

   - Corporation tax
   - VAT
   - National Insurance
   - PAYE
   - Excise duties

9. **Accrued expenses and deferred income**: accrued expenses are amounts outstanding in respect of expenses or services consumed during the year. Common examples would be amounts unpaid in respect of salaries, advertising and stationery. Deferred income arises in circumstances where money has been received by a company without being earned. For example, a publishing house accepting advance magazine subscriptions will have received funds but will not have earned the money since the magazines will not yet have been supplied to customers. Since, technically, the company might be called upon to refund these subscriptions the amount appears as a short-term liability until the relevant issues are supplied.

## F. Net Current Assets (Liabilities)

This is the net difference between the totals for items C, D and E.

## G. Total Assets Less Current Liabilities

This is the net difference between total assets and "Creditors: amounts due within 1 year".

## H. Creditors: Amounts Falling Due After More Than 1 Year

The sub-headings here are exactly the same as those discussed under Section E above, emphasizing the fact that the only difference between them relates to time: this section relates to those creditors which are not payable until after 1 year.

### Disclosure

Disclosure provisions applying to creditors falling due after 1 year are the same as those applying to creditors due within 1 year, with the following additions:

- The amount which is not payable within 5 years together with details of repayment terms and rates of interest where relevant.
- The amount of any security given, together with an indication of the nature of the security.

## I. Provisions for Liabilities and Charges

Provisions can be defined as "amounts provided in relation to which there is some element of uncertainty, either in regard to amount or timing". Examples of items appearing under this heading include future pension and rationalization costs. Another common example is deferred taxation, which is discussed in more detail in Chapter 12. In recent years some companies have begun to make provision for future liabilities deriving from the environmental impact of their activities.

Historically, provisions have provided one of the most potent means of manipulating accounting figures. Typically, a business would create a provision in 1 year and, instead of reversing this provision when the anticipated event or loss failed to materialize, would use it as a fund against which subsequent costs could be written off.

FRS 12, *Provisions, contingent liabilities and contingent assets*, has effectively countered this practice by providing that a provision will only be recognized when:

- An entity has a present obligation as a result of past events.
- It is probable that a transfer of economic benefits will be required to settle the obligation; and
- A reliable estimate can be made of the amount of the obligation.

## Disclosure

In relation to any provisions made, the following disclosure requirements apply:

1. Details of any changes in provisions as follows:

   - The amount at the beginning and end of the year.
   - Transfers to and from provisions during the year.
   - The source and application of the amounts transferred.

2. Particulars of any pension commitments provided for as well as those pension contributions for which no provision has been made.

3. Separate disclosure must be made in respect of any commitment relating to pensions for past directors.

4. Where provisions are included under the heading "other provisions", full details of the nature and amounts of these must be provided if material.

5. Where provision has been made in respect of taxation then there must be disclosure by way of note of any amount not relating to deferred taxation.

## Contingent Liabilities

Provisions and contingencies have much in common. However, contingent liabilities are less certain to result in a transfer of economic benefits and it is not possible to arrive at a reliable estimate of the potential liability. In other words, they fail to satisfy the three recognition criteria set out above in respect of provisions.

A common example is losses that might occur as a result of a legal action against the company. Other examples include financial exposure deriving from guarantees and warranties given.

FRS 12 provides that only if the occurrence of a contingent liability becomes "probable" should it be provided for. If the likelihood of the contingency materializing remains only "possible", then the following disclosures should be made:

- An estimate of the likely financial effect
- An explanation of the uncertainties involved; and
- An assessment of the likelihood of any reimbursement

> **In practice:**
>
> *A number of large companies have been forced to create provisions in respect of various contingencies related to environmental and health issues in recent years. For example, one of the largest manufacturing conglomerates in the world, has recently provided over £560 million in respect of 66,000 asbestos-related personal injury claims.*

Where a contingent liability has not been provided for, CA85 requires that companies make the following disclosures:

- The amount, or estimated amount of the liability
- The legal nature of the liability
- Whether any valuable security has been offered by the company in connection with the liability and, if so, the nature of this security

## J. Accruals and Deferred Income

Items under this heading are more commonly presented under Creditors.

## K. Capital and Reserves

The amount of share capital that any company can issue is called its authorized share capital and is indicated in the Memorandum of Association. This amount must be shown either on the face of the balance sheet or by way of note. However, it is an information item only and is not included in calculations.

The issued share capital figure, which is the portion of the authorized share capital actually issued, appears on the face of the balance sheet and is included in calculations. A note to this item will normally refer to it as:

- **Allotted**: i.e., the company has decided who is to receive shares from those who applied.
- **Called-up**: i.e., the company has asked for those who have been allotted shares to pay the amount due.
- **Fully paid**: i.e., the amounts called-up have been paid. Amounts called-up but not paid would be indicated in Section A of the balance sheet. In the event of liquidation, shareholders would be required to pay in this amount.

### Share Values

Shares can have a number of values:

- **Nominal value** of a share is the original value assigned to a share when a company is formed. It is also called **par value**. In the UK shares cannot legally be issued at a price below this value, i.e., at a discount. Most shares will have a nominal value of £1. Other common values are 50p, 25p and £5. It is used as a basis upon which the amount to be distributed as dividends may be computed and expressed.

- **Issue price** of a share is the amount at which a share is made available to those who may wish to purchase. For example, a company may have £1 shares that it makes available to the public at a price of £1.15. In these circumstances the nominal value is £1 and the issue price is £1.15. The difference between these two values is known as **Share Premium**. Statute requires that the Share Premium element of any share issue be shown separately from the nominal value element in the balance sheet.

- **Market Value** is the price that a share can command on the open market. If the company is a public limited company then this will be the current stock market price. If it is a private company, then it is the amount which a family member, friend or investor would be willing to pay.

---

### In practice:

*The following extract from the 2000 Cable and Wireless plc Annual Report illustrates how Share Capital is presented*

|  | 2000 | 1999 |
|---|---|---|
| Note 22: called up share capital | | |
| Authorized | | |
| 2,734,520,636 ordinary shares of 25p each | £684 million | £684 million |
| (1999 – 2,734,520,636 ordinary shares of 25p each) | | |
| Special rights preference share of £1 | £1 | £1 |
| | | |
| Allotted, called up and fully paid | | |
| 2,440,220,758 ordinary shares of 25p each | £610 million | £603 million |
| (1999 – 2,410,726,458 ordinary shares of £1) | | |
| Special rights preference share of £1 | £1 | £1 |

*The Special Rights Preference Share is held by H. M. Government and carries no right to participate in the capital, beyond the sum of £1, or the earnings of the Company.*

*At an Extraordinary General Meeting of the Company held on March 13, 2000, shareholders approved the increase in the Company's authorized share capital from £683,630,160– 875,000,000 by the creation of an additional 765,479,360 ordinary shares of 25p each. The increase however, is conditional upon the exercise of options in connection with the acquisition by the Company of the minority interest in the business operations of Cable and Wireless Communications plc.*

# Reserves

Reserves arise from a variety of sources and can form a substantial part of the funding a company. In the UK there are strict rules as to the classification of reserves and the uses to which they can be put.

Reserves are sub-divided into two types:

1. Distributable
2. Undistributable

## Distributable Reserves

These are reserves that can be used as a source for the payment of dividends. The principal reserve of this type is the profit and loss account, sometimes called Revenue Reserve. This reserve results principally from the accumulation of profits.

## Undistributable Reserves

These are reserves that cannot be distributed in the form of dividends. There are several examples of this type:

- **Share Premium Account**: when shares are issued at a price higher than their nominal value an amount equivalent to this excess must be transferred to a Share Premium account (except in the case of a merger) and disclosed separately. Once such an account is created it is legally treated as part of share capital. This account can, however, be used to finance a bonus issue (see Chapter 9) or can have preliminary formation expenses or share issue costs charged against it.

- **Revaluation Reserve**: when assets are revalued in the balance sheet an amount equal to any increase in value of the asset should be credited (or debited in the event of a decrease) to such a reserve. Where previously revalued assets are disposed of, in other words when any revaluation is realized, this will necessitate a transfer from the revaluation reserve to the profit and loss so that the profit or loss on disposal of that asset can be determined.

- **Capital Redemption Reserve**: where a firm redeems its own shares using its distributable reserves then it must transfer to a Capital Redemption Reserve an amount equal to the amount by which the company's issued share capital has been diminished. This is in order to maintain the company's share capital and non-distributable reserves level. Where such redemption is financed by the proceeds of a new issue of shares then such a transfer is not necessary.

- **Reserves that cannot be distributed under the company's Memorandum of Association**: these are specific reserves which the company's own rules preclude it from distributing.

## Disclosure

Shares and Reserves will be dealt with in more detail in Chapter 9. This section is concerned with the disclosure requirements for this category. CA 85 (Sch 4, s 38–41) provides the following in relation to capital and reserves:

1. The level of authorized share capital for each class of share capital together with the aggregate nominal value of each class allotted should be disclosed.

2. Allotted share capital and called-up share capital paid up must be separately disclosed.

3. Where shares have been issued and allotted during the year the following must be disclosed.

   - The reason for the issue.
   - The class of shares issued.
   - For each class of share issued, the number, nominal value and consideration received.

4. Where the company has allotted redeemable shares it must disclose.

   - The earliest and latest dates for redemption.
   - Whether the company is obliged to redeem the shares, or merely has the option to do so.
   - Whether a premium is payable on redemption and, if so, the amount of this premium.

5. If the company has outstanding share options and warrants it must disclose:

   - The number, description and amount of the shares involved.
   - The period during which these rights can be exercised.
   - The price payable in respect of options.

6. The tax treatment of amounts taken to Revaluation Reserve must be disclosed.

7. Movements on all reserve accounts must be disclosed by way of notes.

## Additional Balance Sheet Disclosure Requirements

In addition to the disclosure requirements required in respect of the items indicated in Format 1 outlined above, it is necessary to make disclosure by way of notes to the accounts in relation to the following items.

### 1. Capital Expenditure Commitments

- The amounts of contracts entered into for capital expenditure not provided for in the accounts.

- The amounts of capital expenditure authorized by the board of directors but not yet contracted for.

## 2. Transactions in Which Directors Have a Material Interest

In relation to transactions or other arrangements (excluding service contracts or where the amount involved is less than £5,000 or 1% of the company's net assets), the notes must disclose:

- The name of the director and the nature of their interest
- The value of the director's interest

# Profit and Loss Account

CA85 recognizes four formats under which the profit and loss account may be presented. However, Formats 3 and 4 are merely horizontal versions of the vertical formats allowed under Formats 1 and 2. Consequently only Formats 1 and 2 will be considered here since the vertical format is the one more commonly adopted by businesses (Tables 6.2 and 6.3).

**Table 6.2. Format 1**

| | |
|---|---|
| 1 | Turnover |
| 2 | Cost of sales[a] |
| 3 | Gross profit (or loss) |
| 4 | Distribution costs[a] |
| 5 | Administrative expenses[a] |
| 6 | Other operating income |
| 7 | Income from shares in group undertakings[b] |
| 8 | Income from participating interests |
| 9 | Income from other fixed asset investments[c] |
| 10 | Other interest receivable and similar income[c] |
| 11 | Amounts written off investments |
| 12 | Interest payable and similar charges[d] |
| 13 | Tax on profit or loss on ordinary activities |
| 14 | Profit or loss on ordinary activities after taxation |
| 15 | Extraordinary income |
| 16 | Extraordinary charges |
| 17 | Extraordinary profit or loss |
| 18 | Tax on extraordinary profit or loss |
| 19 | Other taxes not shown under the above items |
| 20 | Profit or loss for the financial year |

[a] These items are to be stated after taking into account any necessary provisions for depreciation or diminution in value.

[b] The amount of any provisions for depreciation and diminution in value of tangible and intangible fixed assets falling to be shown under item 7(a) in Format 2 must be disclosed in a note to the accounts in any case where the profit and loss account is prepared under Format 1.

[c] Income and interest derived from group companies are to be shown separately from that derived from other sources.

[d] The amount payable to group companies must be shown separately.

**Table 6.3. Format 2**

| | |
|---|---|
| 1 | Turnover |
| 2 | Changes in stock of finished goods and work-in-progress |
| 3 | Own work capitalized |
| 4 | Other operating income |
| 5 | (a) Raw materials and consumables |
| | (b) Other external charges |
| 6 | Staff costs |
| | (a) wages and salaries |
| | (b) Social security costs |
| | (c) Other pension costs |
| 7 | (a) Depreciation and other amounts written off tangible and intangible fixed assets |
| | (b) Exceptional amounts written off current items |
| 8 | Other operating charges |
| 9 | Income from shares in group undertakings |
| 10 | Income from participating interests |
| 11 | Income from other fixed asset investments[a] |
| 12 | Other interest receivable and similar income[a] |
| 13 | Amounts written off investments |
| 14 | Interest payable and similar charges[b] |
| 15 | Tax on profit or loss on ordinary activities |
| 16 | Profit or Loss on ordinary activities after taxation |
| 17 | Extraordinary income |
| 18 | Extraordinary charges |
| 19 | Extraordinary profit or loss |
| 20 | Tax on extraordinary profit or loss |
| 21 | Other taxes not shown under the above items |
| 22 | Profit or loss for the financial year |

[a] Income and interest derived from group companies are to be shown separately from that derived from other sources.

[b] The amount payable to group companies must be shown separately.

## General Comments

1. The last 14 items in each format (items 7–20 in Format 1; items 9–22 in Format 2) are identical, indicating that the area of difference is to be found in the earlier part of the profit and loss account.

2. There are no letters or numerals assigned to different entries, so it is not required that any of the items listed be disclosed on the face of the profit and loss account.

3. The following three additional items must appear by statute:

   • The company's profit or loss on ordinary activities before taxation.
   • The amount set aside or proposed to be set aside to or withdrawn or proposed to be withdrawn from, reserves; and
   • The aggregate amount of any dividends paid and proposed.

4. Any item may be shown in greater detail and additional headings may be added for items not otherwise covered.

5. Corresponding amounts must be shown and these must be comparable to current year's figures.

The detailed requirements applicable to Format 1 are now outlined.

## 1: Turnover

There are detailed disclosure provisions relating to turnover:

- Turnover should exclude trade discounts, VAT and any other sales taxes.

- Group accounts must only show external sales, i.e., not intra-group sales. These may, however, be disclosed by way of a note to the accounts dealing with segmental activity.

- Having regard to the manner in which company operations are organized, turnover must be broken down by class of business and geographical market in a note. Immaterial amounts may be combined and classes or markets that do not differ substantially can be treated as one. Details such as these may, however, be omitted if their disclosure would be seriously prejudicial to the interests of the company.

## 2, 4 and 5: Costs

The bulk of costs, other than financing costs, should be included under one or other of these headings. The following provisions relate to disclosures which are normally made by way of notes to the accounts:

- **Staff costs**: notes to the accounts must show the average number of employees during the year, wherever located, and the average number of employees in categories considered appropriate by the directors.

- **Depreciation and amortization**: assets with useful economic lives must be written off systematically over those lives. This includes both tangible and intangible assets. Disclosure by way of note must be made of the following:

  - Depreciation or other amounts written off.
  - Amounts written back.

## 3: Gross Profit (or Loss)

This is the difference between turnover and cost of sales.

## 6: Other Operating Income

Any operating income which cannot be classified as turnover should be included here.

## 7 and 8: Income from Shares in Group Undertakings and Participating Interests

These are dealt with in detail in Chapter 11.

## 9 and 10: Income from Other Fixed Asset Investments and Other Interest Receivable

Examples of income to be disclosed under these headings include rents from lands where they form a substantial part of a company's income.

## 11: Amounts Written Off Investments

Where it has been necessary to write down the amount at which investments are shown, such amounts should be disclosed here.

## 12: Interest Payable and Similar Charges

Except in the case of loans from group companies, separate disclosure of interest or similar charges payable is required in respect of the following:

- Bank loans, overdrafts and other loans which are wholly repayable within 5 years, whether or not secured.
- Loans of any other kind whether or not secured.

## 13: Tax On Profit or Loss On Ordinary Activities

Taxation and its disclosure are dealt with in detail in Chapter 12.

## 14: Profit or Loss On Ordinary Activities After Taxation

This is simply the post-taxation profit or loss for the year on ordinary activities.

**Note:** CA 85 requires that "profit or loss on ordinary activities **before** taxation" should also be disclosed on the face of the profit and loss account. This would normally appear before item 13 above. CA 85 Sch. 4 requires that "profit or loss on ordinary activities before taxation" be disclosed for each class of business. SSAP 25, *Segmental Reporting*, requires that it also be broken down by geographical market. These latter two requirements are normally satisfied by way of notes.

## 15, 16, 17 and 18: Extraordinary Items

FRS 3, *Reporting Financial Performance*, issued in 1992, has had a significant impact upon the manner and form in which financial statements are presented. Prior to its issue the principal standard impacting on financial statement presentation was SSAP 6, *Extraordinary items and prior year adjustments*, issued in 1974.

SSAP 6 viewed the "profit on ordinary activities" figure as especially important, particularly when calculating Earnings per Share (EPS), an important measure of company performance (see Chapter 10). Consequently, it made efforts to ensure that it was not distorted by the inclusion of unusual figures such as "extraordinary" or "exceptional" items.

Much depended, therefore, on the respective definitions of "exceptional item" and "extraordinary item". The definitions under SSAP 6 were:

- **Exceptional items**: material items which derive from events or transactions which fall **within the ordinary activities** of the company, and which need to be disclosed separately by virtue of their size or incidence if the financial statements are to give a true and fair view.

- **Extraordinary items**: material items which derive from events or transactions that fall **outside the ordinary activities** of the company and which are therefore expected not to recur frequently or regularly. Reorganization costs and the costs of discontinuing activities were common examples.

While these seemed clear-cut, firms were able to stretch the definitions to suit their own purposes. Under SSAP 6 companies could manipulate the "profit on ordinary activities" figure by a simple reclassification of an item from "exceptional" to "extraordinary". Since an exceptional item was added (or deducted) before arriving at "profit on ordinary activities" and an extraordinary item appeared after it, such a reclassification had the effect of increasing (or decreasing) the profit figure on which EPS was based.

However, FRS 3 eradicated many of the abusive practices associated with this confusion. It did so by essentially eliminating extraordinary items and forcing firms to deal in a much more transparent manner with expenses that were previously categorized as exceptional. For instance, it reclassified discontinued operations as part of ordinary activities and provided for the separate disclosure of items such as fundamental reorganization and restructuring costs.

Under FRS 3, therefore, many costs previously classified as "extraordinary" must now be included under the statutory heading to which they belong and separately disclosed by way of note. They can no longer be included as a separate item after "profit or loss on ordinary activities after taxation".

The FRS makes exceptions in respect of the following three items, which may be shown separately on the face of the profit and loss account after "profit on ordinary activities before interest":

1. Profits or losses on the sale or termination of an operation

2. Costs of a fundamental reorganization or restructuring

3. Profits or losses on the disposal of fixed assets

## Other Items to Be Disclosed

Separate disclosure, usually by way of notes to the accounts, must be made in respect of the following:

- Auditor's remuneration, with details of audit and non-audit fees
- Plant and machinery hire expense

## *Cash Flow Statements*

In 1991 the ASB issued FRS 1, *Cash Flow Statements*. In 1996 this was revised to provide more detail, reflecting the increasing importance of the cash flow statement. FRS 1 (revised) requires all large companies, and encourages all small and medium sized companies, to include a cash flow statement with its final accounts.

A cash flow statement must contain details of cash flows under the following headings:

- Operating (Trading) Activity.
- Returns on Investments and Servicing of Finance (Preference dividends paid, Dividends received; Interest paid and received).
- Taxation.
- Capital Expenditure (Purchase and Sale of Fixed Assets).
- Acquisitions and Disposals.
- Equity (Ordinary) Dividends paid.
- Liquid Resources (Investments which can be quickly turned into cash).
- Financing Activity (Issue of Shares, Repayment of bank debts, etc.).

The figure shown at the end of the cash flow statement is the cash increase or decrease for the year resulting from all of these movements and should reconcile to the difference between the opening and closing cash balances shown on the Balance Sheet.

Notes to the cash flow statement are also required as follows:

- Reconciliation of operating (net) profit to cash flow from operating activities.
- Sub-totals for inflows and outflows where the standard headings do not give sufficient detail.

A cash flow statement would look like this:

*Cash flow statement of X Ltd year ending December 31, 20X1*

|  |  | £ | Note |
|---|---|---|---|
| Cash flow from operating activity |  | X | 1 |
| Returns on investments and servicing of finance |  |  |  |
|    Interest received/paid | X |  |  |
|    Preference dividends paid | X |  |  |
|    Dividends received | <u>X</u> | X |  |
| Taxation |  |  |  |
|    Corporation tax |  | X |  |
| Capital expenditure |  |  |  |
|    Purchases of fixed assets | X |  |  |
|    Sales of fixed assets | <u>X</u> | X |  |
| Acquisitions and disposals |  | X |  |
| Equity dividends paid |  | X |  |
| Management of liquid resources |  | X |  |
| Financing activity |  |  |  |
|    Share/loan movements |  | <u>X</u> |  |
| Increase/decrease in cash |  | <u>X</u> |  |

# Accounting Standards and Financial Information Presentation

FRS 3, *Reporting Financial Performance*, has had a major impact on the way in which financial statements, and in particular the profit and loss account, are presented. Essentially, it requires companies to identify the various constituent parts of its financial performance in such a way that users can make assessments of future prospects and cash flows. It achieves this by providing that all gains and losses recognized in the financial statements are included in either the profit and loss account or a new primary statement, "the statement of total recognized gains and losses". Gains and losses can no longer be moved through reserves, therefore, unless allowed by statute or accounting regulation.

## Continuing (including Acquisitions) and Discontinued Activities

One of the ways in which FRS 3 achieved this goal of highlighting the various constituent parts of financial performance was to introduce a layered format to the profit and loss account which requires the company to distinguish between:

a. Results of continuing operations (including the results of acquisitions).

b. Results of discontinued operations.

c. Profits or losses on the sale or termination of an operation, costs of a fundamental reorganization or restructuring and profits or losses on the disposal of fixed assets.

d. Extraordinary items, which, as outlined earlier, have effectively been eliminated.

The result is a format for the profit and loss account that corresponds to the following outline (Figure 6.3).

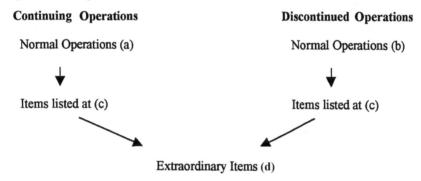

**Figure 6.3   Profit and loss account.**

The requirement that a profit and loss account present information in relation to both its continuing and its discontinued operations (i.e., those that have been disposed of during the year) had the most visible effect on the profit and loss account. The following specific provisions also apply:

- The subdivision of results between continuing and discontinued operations should be brought to the level of operating profit. The minimum disclosure allowed in this regard on the face of the profit and loss account is turnover and operating profit.

- Where the full statutory headings required under the formats outlined earlier are not given on the face of the profit and loss account, a note to the accounts must provide an analysis of the various cost headings required, for both continuing and discontinued operations.

- The analysis of continuing (including acquisitions) and discontinued operations need only proceed to the point of "profit on ordinary activities before interest". Since interest payable is usually a function of the company's overall financial requirements it is permissible at that point to combine the operating profit (loss) figures from continuing and discontinued operations.

- Comparative figures should be calculated on the basis of the status of those operations, i.e., as continuing or discontinued, during the current year. This will result in a need to restate previous year figures where, for example, one element of operation activities is classified during the current year as discontinued.

## Statement of Total Recognized Gains and Losses

One of the most important effects of FRS 3 was that it introduced a new primary financial statement, the statement of total recognized gains and losses. This must be included, therefore, where accounts are intended to give a "true and fair view".

This statement is designed to highlight those gains or losses that have been recognized, but are as yet unrealized. It has the effect, therefore, of forcing users to focus not simply on profit or loss but on other items that impact on reserves.

A statement of total recognized gains and losses will look like this:

*Statement of total recognized gains and losses for the year ended December 31, 20X1*

|  | 20X1 £ | 20X0 £ |
|---|---|---|
| Profit for financial year | X | X |
| Unrealized surplus (deficit) on revaluation of properties | X | X |
| Unrealized surplus (deficit) on trade investment | X | X |
|  | X | X |
| Gains (losses) on currency translation on foreign currency investments | X | X |
| Total recognized gains and losses | X | X |
| Prior year adjustment (see note) | X | |
| Total recognized gains and losses since last annual report | X | |

## Reconciliation of Movements in Shareholders Funds

In addition to the statement of total recognized gains and losses, FRS 3 requires that two additional statements be included in the notes to the accounts: the "reconciliation of movements in shareholders funds" and the "note of historical cost profits and losses". The latter must be presented immediately after the statement of total recognized gains and losses.

As the title implies the "reconciliation of movements in shareholders funds" reconciles all movements in the shareholders funds sections of the balance sheet with the total movements indicated in the statement of total recognized gains and losses, taking into account all capital movements during the period, such as capital contributed by owners, and dividends.

Such a note might look as look like this:

*Reconciliation of movements in shareholders funds for the year ended December 31, 20X1*

|  | 20X1 £ | 20X0 £ |
| --- | --- | --- |
| Profit for financial year | X | X |
| Dividends | (X) | (X) |
| Other recognized gains and losses relating to the year | X | X |
| New share capital subscribed | X | X |
| Net additions to shareholders funds | X | X |
| Opening shareholders funds | X | X |
| Closing shareholders funds | X | X |

## Note of Historical Cost Profits and Losses

Increasingly items are being included in the accounts at values other than historical cost. For example, properties will now regularly be included at revalued amounts. This note is essentially a restatement of the profit and loss account in such a way as to exclude the effect of any revaluation on profit or loss for the year. It is presented immediately after the statement of total recognized gains and losses.

## Prior Period Adjustments

These are defined as material adjustments applicable to prior periods arising from changes in accounting policies or from the correction of fundamental errors. They do not include normal recurring adjustments or corrections of accounting estimates made in prior periods.

The effect of all such adjustments must be disclosed at the end of the statement of total recognized gains and losses.

## Segmental Reporting

SSAP 25, *Segmental Reporting*, issued in June 1990, was introduced primarily in order to ensure that there was greater disclosure in relation to discrete elements of an entity's activity.

It recognizes that many firms conduct "several classes of business or operate in several geographical areas, with different rates of profitability, different opportunities for growth and different degrees of risk". Consequently, it is normally impossible for a user of the financial statements to appreciate this unless the financial statements provide some segmental analysis of the information they contain.

SSAP 25 is intended, therefore, to ensure that the segmental information reported by an entity is disclosed on a consistent basis, year by year.

---

**In practice:**

*Bodycote International 1999 Annual Report*

*Note 1: segmental information (extract)*

| By geographical destination: turnover | 1999 | 1998 |
| --- | --- | --- |
| | £,000 | £,000 |
| UK | 61,278 | 60,463 |
| Mainland Europe | 209,288 | 183,417 |
| North America | 80,198 | 65,037 |
| Rest of World | 4,616 | 11,051 |
| | 355,380 | 319,968 |

---

## Post-Balance Sheet Events

The Annual Report is issued several months after the financial year-end. In the interim, it is possible that circumstances could have changed for the company or information that clarifies the position of the company at the balance sheet date may have come to light. SSAP 17, *Accounting for post-balance sheet events*, recognizes these possibilities and provides guidance for companies in dealing with them.

Its approach is to divide such events into two types:

- **Adjusting events**: these are post balance sheet events which "provide additional evidence of conditions existing at the balance sheet date." Such events, for example, the confirmation of the amount of a bad debt where the amount had been uncertain at the balance sheet date, will impact the balance sheet, but need only be disclosed if material.

- **Non-adjusting events**: these are post balance sheet events which concern conditions which did not exist at the balance sheet date. An example would be an acquisition or disposal by the company. It is not relevant to the period under review but is significant because it may affect future prospects.

## *Reporting Performance – Recent Developments*

The question has been raised as to whether two statements, i.e., the profit and loss account and the statement of total recognized gains and losses, are necessary to report on performance. In response to this the G4 + 1, an international group of standard setters which includes the ASB, has issued proposals which, if implemented, would see performance presented in one Statement of Financial Performance.

As the following report explains, this proposal has been taken up by the ASB and forms the basis of FRED 22, *Revision of FRS 3, Reporting Financial Performance*, which is currently being debated.

## ASB Draft "Performance Statement Guide to Overhaul STRGL"

On the same day that it launched a radical new fair value approach to financial instruments, the ASB also issued an exposure draft that will overhaul how profit and loss accounts are presented. FRED 22 is a proposed revision of FRS 3 "Reporting Financial Performance" based around an international project to create a three-part single performance statement.

When it was introduced in 1992, FRS 3 established a new component in financial statements – the Statement of Total Recognized Gains and Losses (STRGL). The STRGL has come under fire from several directions, including the ICAEW's financial reporting committee. The STRGL is intended to separate gains and losses such as treasury activities from the operational P&L, but according to critics, most users ignore it and go straight to the bottom line.

Undeterred by the critics, the ASB has worked with other international standard setters to expand the STRGL into the new look performance statement outlined in FRED 22. ASB chairman Sir David Tweedie commented: "FRS 3 was a landmark standard for its time, but represents a job only half completed. It introduced the notion of continuing/discontinued income, effectively abolished extraordinary items and raised the visibility of gains and losses formerly dealt with by reserve accounting by requiring them to be passed through a new statement of recognized gains and losses. Our proposal today combines the profit and loss account and the statement of total recognized gains and losses and simplifies the presentation of the components of income, breaking slightly with the traditions of the past.

Readers of accounts will now see on one page results of a company's operations, its treasury and financing activities (themselves the spotlight of the Joint Working Group's paper on financial instruments) and all other gains and losses (such as revaluation of fixed assets and gains and losses on the pension scheme)." Sir David added: "The Board believes that showing components of performance so succinctly will benefit users by enabling them to identify rapidly the impact of the various different aspects of a company's interaction with its financial environment."

For most entities, the new single statement would be divided into three sections:

- Operating
- Financing and treasury; and
- Other gains and losses

The format would be adapted in certain special cases such as banking and insurance.

The exposure draft is based on a discussion paper from the G4 + 1 group of standards setters issued last year. In response to comments on that paper, the ASB has sharpened its definition of financial performance to comprise: "the return (an entity) obtains on the resources it controls, the components of that return and the characteristics of those components insofar as they can be captured by the accounting model". In mathematical terms, the ASB explains, "it is the change in net assets of the reporting entity" over the elapsed reporting period.

The draft standard also provides a more detailed list of the items that should be carried in each section of the performance statement. The consultation process highlighted confusion about what should go into the "other" section. The ASB added a new explanation that it should cover "holding gains" derived from assets that are incidental to an entity's trading activities. These gains and losses can be significant, the draft explains, but "should be segregated from the results of both the operating and financing activities". The draft makes explicit that the "other" section should include:

- Revaluation gains on fixed assets determined according to FRS 15 "Tangible Fixed Assets".
- Property disposals of continuing operations (again, following FRS 15).
- Actuarial gains and losses arising from defined benefit pension schemes, as set out in FRS 17 "Retirement Benefits", issued earlier in December.
- Profits and losses on disposal of discontinuing operations.
- Currency translation differences from foreign investments.
- Gains and losses arising from revaluations of investment properties (set out in SSAP 19).
- Previously recognized amounts from a warrant or licence that has lapsed (see FRS 4 "Capital Instruments").
- Other gains and losses thrown up by UITF abstracts or another accounting standard.

The ASB would argue that sophisticated financial analysts already strip out such items when examining operation performance; the new standard would make it easier for everyone else to do so...

Source: AccountingWEB, December 14, 2000.

Other factors forcing regulators to consider even more extensive reconfiguration of the way in which financial information is presented, for instance the consequences of new technologies or the new media available, are discussed in more detail in Chapter 18.

## Summary

The impact of both statute and accounting standards on the presentation of financial information in the Annual Report is considerable, particularly in terms of the level of disclosure now required in respect of a growing range of items. This merely confirms the general thrust of financial information presentation in recent decades: the emphasis has been more and more on disclosure as a means of satisfying user requirements. While sustainable in its own right, this has, however, often been at the expense of any resolution of the issues of recognition and measurement which should underlie the accountant's approach to financial information.

The disclosure requirements given in this chapter have been detailed and quite specific. In later chapters further disclosure requirements and accounting regulations relevant to particular areas, such as groups, taxation, foreign currency and pensions, will be outlined.

# Review Questions

### Question 1
In terms of group structure, describe the types of relationships which it is possible for one company to have with another.

### Question 2
List the primary financial statements that appear in Annual Reports. Comment on whether and/or how they complement one another.

### Question 3
List the principal constituent parts of the balance sheet. For each of these list several of the sub-headings found in Format 1.

### Question 4
Identify the impact of the following recent FRSs on disclosure requirements:

- FRS 10, *Goodwill and Intangible Assets*
- FRS 11, *Impairment of Fixed Assets and Goodwill*
- FRS 12, *Provisions, Contingent Liabilities and Contingent Assets*
- FRS 15, *Tangible Fixed Assets*

### Question 5
List the principal constituent parts of the profit and loss account. For each of these list several of the sub-headings found in Formats 1 and 2.

### Question 6
Explain the role of FRS 3 in shaping the format of financial statement presentation, and assess the likely impact of FRED 22, *Revision of FRS 3, Reporting Financial Performance*, if implemented.

### Question 7
Explain the thinking behind the introduction of the statement of total recognized gains and losses, and the arguments now being raised for its removal. Refer to the Tesco plc statement of total recognized gains and losses and highlight the specific items disclosed there that are not included in the profit and loss account.

### Question 8
Identify the additional information disclosed by a cash flow statement. Explain why this information might be of use to potential investors in deciding whether or not to invest in the shares of a reporting entity.

# Case Studies

## Case 1

You have been provided with the following trial balance by the accountant at Gladiator plc, a company located in Manchester. It is based on the books of the company at December 31, 20X1

|  | £,000 | £,000 |
|---|---|---|
| Turnover | | 15,610 |
| Returns outwards | | 278 |
| Purchases | 7,489 | |
| Returns inwards | 300 | |
| Carriage inwards | 140 | |
| Carriage outwards | 117 | |
| Debenture interest paid | 30 | |
| Salesmen's commissions and salaries | 970 | |
| Distribution expenses | 265 | |
| Administrative expenses | 868 | |
| Directors' remuneration | 632 | |
| Trade debtors | 2,799 | |
| Stock | 674 | |
| Cash at bank and in hand | 54 | |
| Plant and equipment | 4,300 | |
| Motors | 2,100 | |
| Fixtures and fittings | 200 | |
| Provision for depreciation of plant and equipment | | 875 |
| Provision for depreciation of motors | | 315 |
| Provision for depreciation of fixtures and fittings | | 100 |
| Goodwill | 3,000 | |
| Rent receivable | | 60 |
| Trade creditors | | 600 |
| Debentures (10% redeemable 20X5) | | 600 |
| Issued share capital: | | |
|   Ordinary £1 shares (Authorized, £100,000,000) | | 4,000 |
|   6% preference shares (Authorized, £5,000,000) | | 1,000 |
| Share premium | | 200 |
| Profit and loss account | | 300 |
| | 23,938 | 23,938 |

The following information has come to light since the trial balance was prepared:

1. Plant and Equipment includes specialist equipment costing £500,000 which was acquired during 20X1.
2. The following items must be provided for:
   - An audit fee of £50,000.
   - Debenture interest outstanding.
   - The preference dividend.
   - An ordinary dividend of 7p per share.
   - Corporation tax of £400,000.
3. Depreciation is to be provided at the following rates:
   - Plant and Equipment at 20% straight-line.
   - Motors at 20% reducing balance.
   - Fixtures and fittings at 12.5% reducing balance.

4. The company has decided that it is appropriate to amortize goodwill evenly over the next 20 years.
5. Closing stock was valued at £900,000 being the lower of cost and net realizable value.
6. Directors' remuneration is made up as follows: Chairman: £50,000; Chief Executive: £427,000 (including pension contributions of £100,000); Marketing Director: £150,000; Non-executive director: £5,000.

Prepare a profit and loss account for the year ended December 31, 20X1 and a balance sheet as at that date in Format 1 style of presentation together with the note relating to fixed assets.

(The answer to this question can be found on the website for this text.)

## Case 2

The following article considers the relative importance assigned to elements of the Annual Report by institutional investors. Consider the implications for regulators and for the reporting model of the conclusions of this research. (The ratios mentioned in this article will be covered in later chapters.)

### Research Reveals How Institutional Investors Make Their Decisions

**City Investors Look at the P&L and Cash Flow Rather Than the Balance Sheet. So Are they Getting a True Picture? By Peter Williams**

Contrary to the assumption of cynical FDs, recent research (Institutional Investors,

Accounting Information and the ASB[2] by Dr Richard Barker) suggests that accounting information is much used by institutional investors. However, it also suggests that various issues of recognition and measurement are not well understood – which is worrying because these investors should be the most sophisticated users of accounts.

Institutional investors make judgements on companies in terms of the quality of their financial information. Their main concern is the level of disclosure. The City does not think that creative accounting is a major problem, although you could argue that if issues of recognition and measurement are not understood then institutional investors do not stand much chance of spotting it.

The investor has four main statements on which to judge a company: profit and loss account, cash-flow statement, balance sheet and Operating and Financial Review (OFR). The research shows that, while P&L reform has succeeded in stopping users simply looking at the bottom line, there is little use of recognized gains and losses that are not included in normalized earnings. This means there are questions over the usefulness of the statement of total recognized gains and losses. The ASB and users of accounts agree that the cash flow statement is of secondary importance to the P&L. The cash flow is useful in assessing a company's financial position and quality of earnings but is less important as an input to cash flow-based valuation models.

The balance sheet is firmly in third place, mostly because analysts and fund managers regard information as useful only if it causes share prices to change. As data in the balance sheet is relatively stable it has little effect in that context. However, the City appears unconcerned about the interaction between earnings and balance sheet values and therefore does not appreciate the clever FD's ability to use the balance sheet as a medium for managing earnings.

Like the balance sheet, the OFR does not excite professional users. As institutional investors maintain regular contact with the company they believe they would be unlikely to read anything in the OFR which they did not already know. Disappointingly for the ASB, which introduced and promoted the OFR, it is viewed in the City as little more than a PR exercise, because it contains subjective and selective disclosures.

Given the City's view on the main components of accounts, perhaps it is not surprising that the research found the most commonly used financial ratios were those related to the P&L and cash flow (ratios such as interest cover and operating margin), rather than those based on balance sheet data (such as working capital efficiency).

What is striking about the research is how unsophisticated institutional investors can be when valuing companies they look at. Analysts and fund managers are highly consistent in their preferences. The most popular valuation models are still the price-earning ratio and the dividend yield.

For all the approbation they have received in recent years, discounting models, such as the Discounted Cash Flow (DCF) and the Dividend Discount Model (DDM), are thought to be of little importance for the simple purpose of making reliable forecasts beyond the near future.

---

[2] Cambridge University's Judge Institute of Management, published by the Scots ICA.

Barker says that presentation standards such as FRS1 (cash flow) and FRS3 (financial performance) have been effective. But recognition and measurement standards such as FRS10 (goodwill), FRS12 (provisions) and FRS15 (fixed assets) are more difficult to judge. The ASB is unlikely to back this conclusion. It holds, for instance, that FRS10 brings tangible benefits to any accounts user.

Beneath all this lies the old argument between the "balance sheets approach" (which is broadly the ASB's position) and a "transaction approach" which, generally, is seen as relating to existing accounting practices. Barker argues that where there is a conflict between the P&L recording a company's financial position and the balance sheet stating correctly a company's position then accounting standards should favour the former document.

On that basis, Barker has two recommendations: first the ASB should extend its improvements in the disclosure and presentation of financial statement data. This would mean more highly segmented and mandatory disclosure in the OFR, which should be audited, and greater segmental disclosure of earnings and cash flow. And second, the ASB should focus on earnings, as they play a primary role in equity valuation. In essence the research is suggesting that the way the ASB can help users who are not experts at reading accounts or understanding FRSs is to maximize the economic relevance of the aggregate data reported in the profit and loss account.

Source: Accountancy Age, March 14, 2001.

# SECTION III

# Analysis

Financial Information Analysis is an art. It is a highly subjective exercise where the experience and intuition of the user are critical factors. However, it is also a skill. It can be facilitated and assisted by learning various techniques that have been developed by those seeking to understand financial information.

Building on the previous section which dealt with the information content of an Annual Report, this section of the text identifies techniques and approaches that have been developed by accountants, investors, financial analysts and others to help in identifying and extracting significant information from accounting statements.

This section begins with a macro-discussion of the various techniques that have been developed over the past hundred years, concentrating in particular on the Fundamental Analysis and Technical Analysis approaches.

Adopting the Fundamental Analysis approach as its preferred methodology, the text then identifies and illustrates the techniques developed under this approach for dealing with specific financial issues such as Activity, Liquidity, Financing, Profitability and Return on Investment.

This section deals primarily with techniques. However, there are reminders throughout that these are only a means to an end and not an end in themselves. The goal of the analysis of financial information is to facilitate a robust, informed and contextual interpretation leading to sound decision-making.

This can only be achieved by allowing the results derived from mathematical techniques to be properly contextualised and related to both the wider commercial context and the firm-specific environment. The text will return to this point in Section V when the various techniques discussed in this section are brought together to illustrate their proper use.

# FUNDAMENTAL ANALYSIS [7]

When you have completed this chapter you will understand:

- The different approaches that have been developed to facilitate the extraction of information from financial statements.

- The nature and role of both fundamental analysis and technical analysis.

- That this text, while respecting the insights which technical analysis can bring, adopts the fundamental analysis paradigm.

- The usefulness, but also the limitations, of ratios as a means of analysis.

- The importance of context and trends in properly applying these techniques.

## Money: Share clubs – The diamonds and the dogs by David Stevenson

There are thousands of share clubs in Britain which meet regularly to pool and invest cash. For more than 2 years we have followed the fortunes of the Reservoir Dogs, a group of London friends. Here is a tip worth remembering: stock markets get it wrong – regularly. They overdo price corrections while ignoring perfectly good companies because such firms do not show up on the analysts' "radar".

Spending time sifting out the genuine dogs from the fallen angels with long-term potential, has served the Reservoir Dogs well already, having generated substantial profits on companies such as Brooke's Service Group and Lloyds TSB.

But how can you tell if the market has over-reacted to bad news or troubling rumours? Most share clubs need to do plenty of hard work and detailed analysis. We look for companies whose share price has slumped to a 52-week low, before identifying sectors we either like or hate. We are not desperately keen on building stocks, for example, because the whole sector has bombed. We also steer clear of engineers because too many companies are being hit by the heinous exchange rate.

We then look for other warning signals:
- Very recent profits warnings spook stock markets, especially if the company is in a fast-growing sector. Be honest – if an IT or electronics company cannot boost profits in this climate, what chance will it have in a recession?
- A price/earnings ratio that is still above average for the sector is troubling. Marks & Spencer's share price is at a historic low of 200p, for example, but it is still valued at a higher rate than more efficient peers such as Next, French Connection and Kingfisher.
- If the company's directors are selling the shares, this should sound warning bells. Just as troubling is a 52-week low accompanied by absolutely no director buying, if only because directors should display real faith in their company.

Other factors are also worth considering. If the company is producing a strong dividend yield, look at how well the dividend is covered by the profits. Find out what the earnings (profit) per share are, and then divide by the dividends per share. Any ratio below two, implying a dividend cover of two, should alert you to the possibility that a sharp downturn in profits could lead to a dividend cut, which could be disastrous for a stock whose share price is supported by investors looking for a yield...

Source: Independent on Sunday, October 29, 2000.

## Introduction

Price/earnings ratios, dividend yields, earnings per share... While these terms will not be explained until later chapters in this section, they are an indication that measures have been developed which help to capture various aspects of financial performance and position. Indeed, the main lesson to be learned from the experience of the Reservoir Dogs is that it is necessary to properly contextualize information in order to understand it, and that techniques such as these assist to that end.

As previous chapters have highlighted, the Annual Report contains a mass of financial information. The user of this information is confronted, therefore, by a huge volume of data, both quantitative and qualitative, out of which he or she must make some sense. The problem of having to deal with such a mass of data is compounded by the fact that information of this nature is relatively meaningless of itself. That is, it is presented in a way which rarely contextualizes it. In other words, unless the information is given some context it is not possible to assess its significance either in whole or in part.

In order to deal with these twin problems of mass of data and lack of contextualization, a number of approaches have been developed by accountants, analysts and others. These can broadly be classified into two categories:

1. Fundamental Analysis

2. Technical Analysis

These are simply ways of looking at information relating to a company and its shares. As the following extract explains, however, they approach this information from different perspectives.

## What is the Difference Between Technical Analysis and Fundamental Analysis?

There are basically two schools of thought when we talk about market analysis: technical analysis and fundamental analysis. Let us start with fundamental analysis.

Fundamental analysis is the study of the fundamentals of the market. "Great," you say, "What are fundamentals?" Fundamentals are all things that affect the supply and demand of the underlying commodity. For example, if you were analysing the price of wheat and you thought that the price of wheat was going to go up because there is a drought in the mid-western US, then you would be basing your analysis of the wheat market on fundamentals.

Technical analysis, on the other hand, is the study of the market based on a chart of its price data... If you were to look at the chart of the price of wheat over time and saw that the price of wheat is the lowest it has been in 20 years, then you are said to be using technical analysis. You do not need to know anything about the underlying commodity to be a technical analyst and that is one of the advantages of being a technical analyst.

If you wanted to study the fundamentals of Coffee, then you would want to know everything about coffee: how it is grown, what the planting cycles are, who the big buyers of coffee are, what are their plans in the future and how would that affect the demand for coffee and so on. The problem in researching coffee is that it takes a very long time to find out this information and then even more time to examine and interpret it. Technical analysts claim that all of the fundamentals, or things that affect the price of a commodity, are shown on the price chart anyway. This actually makes sense if we think about it in terms of the laws of supply and demand: if the supply of coffee goes up and the demand stays the same then the price will go down. This supply and demand relationship can be seen as a price drop on a price chart.

Source: http://www.learninvesting/courses/commodity105.htm.

There are, therefore, significant differences in the perspectives adopted by these two approaches. Nevertheless, while the following sections highlight these, it is important to remember that there are also similarities, for instance, in the emphasis on trends.

## *Fundamental Analysis*

Fundamental analysis describes the process of identifying the fundamental drivers of company performance and value and of applying techniques to extract, summarize and contextualize these. It involves attempting to understand the range of macro and micro contexts within which a company operates. Thus, a user adopting this approach will seek to gain information about the industry in general, the company's place within that industry, the macro-economic climate, inflation rates, recent wage disputes and any other pertinent information. In all of this financial data will be a key data set. However, it will not be considered in a vacuum: any insights which the financial data yield will be informed by the full range of information available.

The measurement techniques embraced by this approach, all of which will be dealt with over the course of this section, are outlined in the following extract, which is also useful in identifying at a very general level how a fundamental analyst might approach the task.

## Fundamentals Apply in Analysing Stocks: Doing the Math

Stock-picking is the primary job in managing most portfolios and the toolkit for this chore is called fundamental analysis. As the name implies, it involves getting down to basics. The approach is similar for both stocks and bonds. Fundamental questions deal with the actual or expected profitability of the issuer. Can it earn enough to sustain regular dividend payments or continue the flow of interest payments on bonds? And if the issuer is a company, can it expand its market position so that stockholders can share in the growth? As a general rule, there are two components to this line of inquiry: an analysis of different groups of issuers, and then an assessment of the best performers in the best group.

An analysis of sectors depends partly on broad economic trends. For example, resource stocks usually lead the market when the economy is coming out of recession. But part of this exercise involves looking at whether the resource sector is growing and how it is changing. For example, what is the impact on mining companies of a trend in the auto industry to replace galvanized metal with plastic? Are the mines finding new customers as demand from the old ones declines? If prospects for the sector look promising, the job then is to compare the players in that field. This rating often involves looking for the lowest-cost producers, but investors also need to consider their own time horizons.

A company can be a low-cost producer by cutting back on research and development, a strategy that can give a quick boost to profits in the short term but ultimately put the company at a competitive disadvantage.
Here are some things to watch for.

- Revenue, profit and cash flow: Are these rising with no serious breaks in the pattern?
- Profit margin: Is the company getting a reasonable return on its revenue and invested capital?
- Interest, asset and dividend coverage: Is the earnings flow strong enough to ensure that interest and dividends can be paid with no strain and is the asset base big enough in relation to the current debt load?

- Debt-to-equity ratio: Is the size of the ownership stake big enough to provide a proper balance against bonds and bank debt? (Acceptable standards for the debt-to-equity ratio will vary from industry to industry.)
- Product innovation: Is the company keeping up with its peers in research or, better still, is it out in front?
- Quality of management: Is there depth on the bench in the key areas of operations, marketing and finance?

Source: Financial Post; November 16, 1999.

There are two principal fundamental analysis techniques employed by proponents of this approach:

- Common-size statements

- Ratios (and percentages)

It is important to remember, however, that these are merely techniques. They facilitate the contextualization of firm-specific data and the comparison of the financial performance or position represented by that mathematical representation. They enable the informed user to interpret the firm's performance or position but only when placed in the context of, say, other firms, previous performance, budgets, or industry averages.

For instance, consider the following information extracted from the profit and loss account of company X plc:

Turnover: £11 million

Of itself this discloses very little information. It is impossible, for example, to determine whether or not this represents an increase or decrease over the previous year's performance. If it is discovered that turnover for the previous year was £10 million, then the user can begin to contextualize the information and to appreciate that turnover this year represented a 10% increase over the previous year. In other words, as financial information is made relative to other information its significance gradually emerges.

It can be argued, therefore, that financial data and their various representations, for example ratios, only acquire their real significance when placed in an appropriate context. This "appropriate context" will depend on the purposes for which the information is being analysed, but can range from industry averages to previous year's results to market expectations.

Furthermore, the significance ascribed to financial data may vary depending on the context in which it is placed. For example, the superficially "good" performance of X plc in improving its turnover by 10% is placed in a different light if it transpires that its nearest competitor managed to increase turnover by 60%. One of the attributes of sound financial analysis, therefore, is placing the information being analysed into appropriate contexts.

The ascription of value judgements such as "good", "poor", etc. to financial measures raises other issues. While ratios and other techniques reduce financial information to standard formats that facilitate comparison, individuals with their own sets of values, expectations and outlook carry out this comparison. In other words, their interpretation is not carried out in a value-free manner. What is "acceptable" to one will be "unacceptable" to another. It is important for each user of financial information to be aware, therefore, of his or her perspectives, prejudices and paradigms, not necessarily with a view to eradicating them, but with the intention of informing the interpretative process and enabling the user to appreciate that interpretations are neither value-free nor infallible.

---

### In practice:

Note the way in which ratios are used in the following extract to give a particular "spin" to the financial performance of one party to a take-over attempt:

**Cost/income ratio reduction key at Natwest**

*The Royal Bank of Scotland Group plc said the fundamental issue facing shareholders of National Westminster Bank plc is which management team is best placed to cut the bank's cost/income ratio. The Royal Bank, which, together with the Bank of Scotland, has launched an unsolicited offer for NatWest, claimed that group chief executive Sir George Mathewson had managed to cut the bank's cost/income ratio by 12 percentage points since 1993 to 12 pct. By way of contrast, the Bank of Scotland brought its cost/income ratio down by just 0.4 percentage points over the same period, the Royal Bank said.*

*It added that Sir Brian Pitman and Peter Ellwood managed to cut Lloyds TSB's ratio by 15 percentage points, whilst Fred Goodwin, now deputy chief executive at RBoS, and John Wright achieved a reduction of 11 percentage points at Clydesdale Bank. "Between 1992 and 1996, RBoS successfully transformed almost every part of its UK banking activities through a substantial business re-engineering programme," Mathewson said. "Our record in cost/income ratio reduction speaks for itself. We believe that we are ideally placed to address the issues facing NatWest," he added.*

*Source: Financial Times, February 4, 2000.*

---

## Common-Size Statements

One problem when attempting to assess a firm's performance over time is that firm size is in a constant state of flux. This makes inter-period comparison very difficult. Similar difficulties confront users attempting to compare performance between firms.

Common-size statements, by means of which financial data from one accounting period, or for a number of accounting periods, or for different firms, can be expressed as a percentage or ratio of a relevant base figure, remove some of these difficulties.

The following example illustrates the use of four successive common-size profit and loss accounts in which sales are taken as the base figure (100%) and all other amounts for the same year are expressed as a percentage of this base (Table 7.1).

**Table 7.1. The use of four successive common-size profit and loss accounts in which sales are taken as the base figure (100%) and all other amounts for the same year are expressed as a percentage of this base**

| £ (000s) | | | | | Common size percentage | | | |
|---|---|---|---|---|---|---|---|---|
| 1 | 2 | 3 | 4 | Years | 1 | 2 | 3 | 4 |
| 500 | 600 | 700 | 800 | Sales | 100 | 100 | 100 | 100 |
| 125 | 180 | 210 | 240 | Cost of sales | 25 | 30 | 30 | 30 |
| 100 | 90 | 112 | 136 | Selling expenses | 20 | 15 | 16 | 17 |
| 50 | 66 | 84 | 104 | Admin. expenses | 10 | 11 | 12 | 13 |
| 225 | 264 | 294 | 320 | Operating profit | 45 | 44 | 42 | 40 |
| 10 | 12 | 14 | 40 | Interest | 2 | 2 | 2 | 5 |
| 215 | 252 | 280 | 280 | Profit before tax | 43 | 42 | 40 | 35 |
| 75 | 96 | 98 | 96 | Corporation tax | 15 | 16 | 14 | 12 |
| 140 | 156 | 182 | 184 | Profit after tax | 28 | 26 | 26 | 23 |
| 40 | 48 | 56 | 80 | Dividends | 8 | 8 | 8 | 10 |
| 100 | 108 | 126 | 104 | Retained profits | 20 | 18 | 18 | 13 |

As Table 7.1 illustrates, there are several advantages to this approach:

- It makes it possible to relate each item to a common base, in this case Sales for the year.
- Relative changes over time can be easily identified. For instance, while the absolute figures show that Operating profit is increasing, as a percentage of Sales it has decreased.
- It provides users with a mechanism by which the financial and economic trends and characteristics of individual firms and whole industries may be discerned.
- It is easily graphed, thus increasing its usefulness in determining trends.

While this example demonstrates how the common-size technique can be employed in relation to one firm over a period of time, the common-size statement facilitates various other comparative approaches:

- **Cross-sectional**: the scaling effect of common size statements means that firms of different size can be reduced to a common comparative base. One of the problems with this, however, is that this very process may disguise the fact that size difference, and the economies of scale that result, may actually be the explanatory variable.
- **Segmental**: some differences between firms may derive from the fact that, while operating in the same industry, different segments may predominate within differ-

ent firms. This can often be resolved by reference to the segmental analysis that will be provided in the Annual Report.

- **Time-based**: perhaps their greatest usefulness is as a means of comparing firm performance over a number of years. Thus, as in the example above, common-size statements can be prepared for a period of, say, 4 years, and the firm's performance can be observed over that period in either a firm or industry context. Graphs constructed using data from common-size statements are another means of highlighting such trends.

Used with caution, common-size statements can prove very useful in facilitating the analysis and interpretation of financial performance and position.

## Ratios

The most important fundamental analysis technique is "ratio analysis". Ratios (or percentages) allow the reduction of financial data to a manner that facilitates comparison, and ultimately the interpretation of the significance of that financial data. Thus, they enable the comparison of firms of different size.

Although there are many different ratios, often with variations in the way in which they are framed, traditionally ratio analysis is considered under five categories, reflecting five different aspects of the risk/return relationship. These areas relate to:

1. **Activity**: the efficiency with which management manage the firm's assets (see Chapter 8).
2. **Liquidity**: the ability of a firm to meet its short-term cash obligations (see Chapter 8).
3. **Financing**: the long-term financing structure (see Chapter 9).
4. **Profitability**: profits relative to turnover and investment (see Chapter 10).
5. **Investment**: returns enjoyed by investors, particularly equity investors (see Chapter 10).

Examples of ratios under each category are shown in Table 7.2.

### Qualities of Ratios

The obvious attraction of ratios is that they reduce complex financial data to a form that allows for the easier understanding of that data. Thus, loss of detail is offset by simplicity. However, the ease with which ratios have traditionally been assumed to facilitate this needs to be considered in the light of some of the fundamental conceptual problems inherent in any such approach:

- **Accounting numbers and policies**: this text has already highlighted some of the weaknesses inherent in accounting practice, for example the often subjective

**Table 7.2. Examples of ratios**

| Category | Quantifies | Examples |
|---|---|---|
| Activity | Efficiency | Stock/debtors/creditors days |
| | | Asset turnover |
| Liquidity | Ability to satisfy debts | Current ratio |
| | | Quick ratio |
| Financing | Financial structure | Gearing |
| | | Debt/equity ratio |
| Profitability | Operating performance | Return on capital employed |
| | | Gross profit rate |
| | | Net profit rate |
| Investment | Return to owners | Earnings per share |
| | | Price/earnings ratio |
| | | Dividend yield |
| | | Dividend cover |

nature of many accounting policy choices. Reducing the accounting data to another form of expression does not eliminate these problems, in fact it perpetuates them.

- **Economies of scale**: one of the primary functions of ratio analysis is the removal of size as a factor in inter-firm comparison. However, this can obscure the fact that size may itself be an explanatory variable, in other words that size, by virtue, for example, of economies of scale, may actually explain some of the differences being investigated.

- **Industry benchmarks and norms**: the proper use of ratios requires their comparison with industry norms and other measures. However, for a variety of reasons there may be no benchmark against which firm-specific measures may be reasonably compared.

- **Timing factors**: the imposition of arbitrary accounting periods can often have a somewhat distorting effect on measures of financial performance and position. For example, the closing stock figures of a large retail entity that adopts a financial year end date of January 31, since this is a low stock-holding point in the wake of new year sales, will not accurately reflect the firm's normal stockholding activity.

- **Creative accounting**: creative accounting practices can also distort ratios since they manipulate the underlying accounting numbers. Some of the more prevalent forms of creative accounting are discussed in more detail in Chapter 13.

- **Statistical issues**: by their very nature ratios raise a number of computational issues which must be considered:

  - **Negative numbers**: the incidence of such numbers can be problematical and the problem will be compounded where both numerator and denominator are negative.

- **Small numbers**: the potential for distortion where small numbers are involved, particularly when dividing by a small number, are considerable.
- **Distributional characteristics**: the use of comparative bases and industry averages implies certain assumptions about the probability distributions of the population. These may not always be sustainable.
- **Relationship between numerator and denominator**: for ease of comparison it is usually assumed that the relationship between numerator and denominator is linear. However, this may not always be the case, for example where economies or diseconomies of scale exist.

## Use of Ratios

In spite of these difficulties, ratio analysis remains the most common method used by financial analysts and others. It is important to remember, however, that it is but one step in the process. Far more important than the calculation of ratios is their incorporation into the decision-making process.

This can best be illustrated by understanding the reduction of financial information to summary statistical form as but one element in a five-step process:

1. **Observation:** this involves being aware of the financial data to be interpreted. For example, it might simply mean identifying that the Annual Report forms the principal source of information available.

2. **Calculation:** this involves the reduction of the financial information to a common base such as ratios or percentages. This allows comparison between successive years or within industries.

3. **Analysis:** this involves placing the figures calculated at step 2 into some form of context, such as previous year figures, budgeted expectations or industry averages. At a very basic level this allows a simplistic evaluation of performance. For example, it may be possible after comparing current year ratios with previous year ratios to say there has been an "improvement" or "disimprovement" in performance.

4. **Interpretation:** this involves placing the results in a context that will highlight their real significance as far as the company is concerned. For example, ratios calculated at step 2 may relate to profitability. Analysis at step 3 may disclose that profitability has decreased when compared to previous year results. This stage would require that the significance of this development be explored. It may, for example, lead to questions about the strategic plans of the company or its long-term viability.

5. **Decision-making:** this is the final step in the process and represents the ultimate goal of the financial information analysis process.

---

### In practice:

The application of fundamental analysis to a company, in this case Cisco Systems, is illustrated in the following extract, which demonstrates how ratios enable comparison with competitors, thus facilitating effective decision-making.

*Fundamental Analysis*

*...A fundamentalist will compare the earnings growth rate as well as sales growth rates. Negative numbers are obviously viewed negatively. However, even positive numbers are scrutinized as a positive correlation between the earnings growth and sales growth is desirable. Earning increases on flat sales are not as impressive as earning increases on increased sales.*

*Debt is another parameter fundamentalists will examine. If a company is growing, but increasing its debt, the fundamentalist will be leery. The business may by putting all of its profits into an interest payment, rather than building up book value. Companies that have no debt and have increasing sales and earnings are most attractive.*

*Another parameter is the capitalization of the company. Capitalization is merely the price per share of the stock multiplied by the number of shares outstanding (in issue). A fundamentalist would be impressed by large capitalization as it takes more earnings and profits to make the percentages positive. A company with large capitalization with sales and earnings increasing together and no debt would be a dream stock for the fundamentalist, particularly if it happened to be selling below book value. Although such qualities would be rare, the fundamentalist sifts carefully through the financial pages.*

*A fundamental analysis of a security such as Cisco Systems, which was featured in the July Supplemental issue of the Women's Street Journal, might read like the following: Cisco Systems, ticker symbol CSCO, trades on the Nasdaq with 4194.4 million shares outstanding with a $251,664 million capitalization. CSCO boasts 0% debt. Sales in the last four quarters have increased an average of 27% with sales increasing at 42%. Although the lag in earnings increases is a tad negative, the 5-year earnings growth rate is a healthy 43% and the company has a particularly large market capitalization for such a high growth rate.*

*The earnings performance of Cisco Systems outperforms its major competitors: MMC Network, Emulex Corp, Brocade Communication Systems Inc. and Performance Technologies, by a comfortable margin. The company has increased its earnings growth rate to 40% for the year 2000.*

*Source: Women's Street Journal. http://www.womensstreetjournal.com/members/fundamental.htm.*

# Technical Analysis

Technical analysis derives from the notion that future share price can be determined by identifying trading patterns which tend to repeat in cycles. Unlike fundamental analysis, therefore, it does not seek to analyse macro-economic, industrial and firm-specific fundamentals. Instead, it focuses on patterns and trends disclosed by share movements.

Being a market-centred measure, this approach has much in common with the EMH perspective outlined in Chapter 3, particularly in ascribing to the market the ability to best capture "value". It owes its origins to the work of Charles Henry Dow, the originator with Edward Jones of the Dow Jones Industrial Average Index. Dow first articulated his theories in the Wall Street Journal in the 1890s. His ideas stemmed form his observations of the closing prices of shares and the conclusion that it was possible to construct a representative stock average which would act as a barometer for the market as a whole.

The following extract explains in more detail how technical analysis operates.

## Eye on the Web – The New Technical Analysis, by Stephen Eckett

Most technical analysis is based on the idea that prices of stocks (or any other freely traded commodity) form recognizable trading patterns, which sometimes are repeated over time. Such patterns can be identified by computers analysing data series (price histories), or might be discernible visually when the prices are plotted as charts.

The analysis might be simple when it involves such things as moving averages – which try to highlight general price trends; or it may be more complex, as in the case of stochastics or Bollinger Bands. In either case, the raw data – underlying prices – is taken as a straightforward, easily observable phenomena. That's not to say that mistakes cannot be made in the recording of such data, and this is certainly the bane of many investors looking for "clean" data, but fundamentally the data itself is considered simple and objective. After all, either Tesco shares closed at 2331/4p on September 19, 2000, or they did not. Right?

The price data captured each day is usually the stock's opening price, high and low price of the day and closing price (OHLC). Sometimes, for good measure, the volume traded may also be recorded. These are the fundamental building blocks of most technical analysis. Upon this data, simple line charts may be created (displaying just the closing prices), or bar or candlestick charts try to display as much price information as possible. And on top of these charts, the whole esoteric world of technical analysis is built. Battles may rage as to the perceived accuracy of various technical indicators, but the underlying data is held sacrosanct – or is it? For many technical indicators, much store is held by the exact closing price, but what happens when there isn't a closing price due to 24 h trading? Of course, a reference price can be taken each day at a certain time, but this will not have the significance of an actual closing price...

Source: Investors Chronicle, September 22, 2000.

Technical analysis is sometimes called "charting" for the simple reason that most of the information content of this technique is reduced to the form of charts. Thus, there will be charts for markets, exchanges, commodities, industries and individual company stocks. Figure 7.1, with comments produced by one technical analyst, gives an example of the conclusions which a technical analyst will draw from such a presentation.

Technical analysis is a widely used technique. It has a solid track record and is heavily influenced by market based theory and research. In the hands of experienced analysts it produces potent and profitable insights into share movements and patterns.

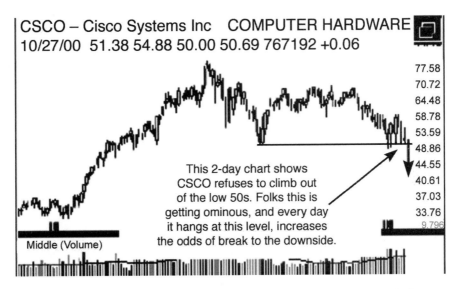

**Figure 7.1   Technical analysis. Source: Smith, G.B. (2000), The Nazz and all that,** ***TheStreet.com*, October 30, 2000.**

## Summary

Fundamental analysis and technical analysis describe two different approaches to information. While technical analysis focuses on market-based data such as historic movements in share price, fundamental analysis turns its attention to fundamentals impacting on a company such as financial performance.

To this end fundamental analysis has identified various techniques and methods which assist in this process. The most potent of these is ratio analysis. Properly understood, ratio analysis forms one part of a five-step process that sees informed decision-making as its goal.

The five elements of this process are:

1. Observation
2. Calculation

3. Analysis

4. Interpretation

5. Decision-making

Techniques such as ratio analysis must be applied with caution and the results interpreted in an appropriate context. Indeed, on occasion, their contribution to the decision-making process may be quite limited, providing nothing more than an initial screening mechanism that identifies factors to be analysed by other means.

Properly used, however, they have proven to be potent and insightful means of extracting meaningful information from financial statements. Reducing often-complex financial data to summary statistical form, they provide a means of contextualizing firm or industry-specific information and of identifying trends. The comparative exercise that they enable is often the key to any considered evaluation of an entity.

## Review Questions

**Question 1**
Identify the principal differences between fundamental analysis and technical analysis.

**Question 2**
Explain the use of common-size statements as a means of identifying trends within a company and of facilitating inter-firm comparison.

**Question 3**
"It can be argued that financial data and their various representations, for example ratios, only acquire their real significance when placed in an appropriate context." Explain what is meant by this statement.

**Question 4**
Explain what each of the following terms mean and list examples of ratios under each:
- Activity
- Liquidity
- Financing
- Profitability
- Investment

**Question 5**
List some of the qualities of ratios and identify some features of ratios that require that they be treated with caution.

**Question 6**
List the five-stages involved in a healthy decision-making process based on accounting data. Identify the role of fundamental analysis in this process.

**Question 7**
Identify at least three features of technical analysis that make it a unique approach to data analysis.

**Question 8**
What were the main features of the theories of Charles Henry Dow that have so strongly influenced modern technical analysis?

## Case Studies

### Case 1

The following is a continuation of the article with which this chapter opened. Discuss some of the conclusions which the members of the Reservoir Dogs Share Club have come to in determining the shares they will invest in.

## Money: Share clubs – The Diamonds and the Dogs

...Using this analysis, several companies are worth considering. A highly exceptional stock is ARC International, a small but rapidly growing chipset developer in the mould of the heavyweight ARM.

ARC has only been on the stock market for 5 weeks. Interesting companies with first-rate technology can get their timing badly wrong. ARC came to the market just as investors started to turn against reliable technology stocks, prompted by continuing fears of a downturn in sales for equipment suppliers to the telephone companies. The timing may be wrong but, like Parthus – a similar stock – a short-term downturn can provide a brilliant buying opportunity.

The other stocks we can subdivide into three categories: interesting but avoid; interesting but watch; interesting and buy now.

Marks & Spencer, at around 200p, sports club group Cannons at 115p and ITNet at 352p, fall into the "interesting but avoid" category. M&S does not represent fair value until it falls below 180p, while Cannons looks good value on the surface but one wonders what's gone wrong with the sports club business. Plenty of chic new centres costing a fortune have appeared across London, which leads us to suspect that there is too much capacity in the short term. ITNet may be worth a closer look as it appears to hold a lucrative franchise in supplying IT support to local government, but recent bad news from a north London contract spells short-term instability.

On a more optimistic note, British Vita heads our "interesting but watch" category. This specialist chemicals company has been caught in a sector – wide down draught but scrutinizing its reports and accounts reveals a company with solid profits growth. Any price below 160p could be a golden buying opportunity.

We are a little less sure about Vita's two other companions. Kingston Communications was once Hull's great white telecoms hope, the David to BT's Goliath. Except, of course, BT has been felled and the entire sector has dived. The shares debuted at 225p a short while ago, climbing as high as 1,600p, but they are back down to 400p. Kingston is an excellent outfit with some interesting projects; any price below 390p could be an irresistible opportunity.

Spring, an IT recruitment and consulting firm, is in a similar situation. Its share price has tanked from a high of 390p to 90p today, owing to a slowdown in the IT services industry. The firm has been radical in recent months, setting up a generous share options programme for its IT consultants. In the medium term, Spring is in the right sector and probably worth buying into below 75p.

According to our analysis, three heroes represent outstanding value. St Ives, one of Britain's biggest printers, has nearly a decade of solid earnings and sales growth, and a dividend of about 3.92%. It is laughably cheap and is notoriously aggressive when it comes to maintaining market share. Printing is increasingly hi-tech and large-scale; St Ives is the biggest and best. Nord Anglia is not quite as obvious a buy but is still an excellent play on government outsourcing. The educational services group has been moving steadily into running educational contracts for local government, an area of business bound to expand. It also boasts a solid pedigree in private-sector learning and education and a growing nursery schools business. Shares have languished around 105p, prompting pretty heavy director buying – a healthy sign.

We also like Asian Technology. No prizes for guessing this investment trust's specialism, and with a share price stuck in the low 30p region you would guess that worries about Asian instability have killed this stock for good. Far from it: Asia represents the next great frontier for technology. The next 2 years may be a bit hairy but the 5–10 year outlook is staggering. The truth is, very few easily accessible unit or investment trusts specifically invest in this sector. One to tuck away for the long term.

Source: Independent on Sunday, October 29, 2000.

## Case 2

Referring to the Tesco plc Annual Report 2000 and to recent share price data for the company, explain how a technical analyst and a fundamental analyst might each approach the task of determining whether or not to invest in the company's shares.

## Case 3

The technical analyst who constructed the chart for Cisco shown earlier in this chapter, reached the conclusion that "This 2-day chart shows CSCO refuses to climb out of the low 50s. Folks this is getting very ominous, and every day it hangs at this level, increases the odds of break to the downside". Explain what is meant by this comment and how the analyst might have reached this conclusion.

When you have completed this chapter you will understand:

- That activity (efficiency) and liquidity are related concepts.
- How to calculate ratios which assist in determining the activity and liquidity levels of a business.
- The difficulties posed by stock and its valuation.
- That cash is the lifeblood of a business and must be managed closely.
- That it is the accounts of the group as a whole that are being analysed.

## Dome May Have Been Trading While Insolvent

### PwC Reports Shows Shortfall in Cash flow Projections, by John House

The Millennium Dome has revealed to Accountancy Online that it may have been trading insolvently when company turnaround specialist David James was appointed non-executive chairman last week (September 5). Dome spokesman Richard Saunders said that a review carried out last week by PricewaterhouseCoopers showed that the New Millennium Experience Company, the government-owned company that runs the Dome, had a £10 million shortfall in its cash flow projections. The shortfall meant that in spite of £43 million lottery money grant received from the Millennium Commission (MC) at the end of August, it could not cover its liabilities. Saunders would not say how long NMEC thought the hole in its accounts had gone undetected.

"David James said as soon as he took the Dome on that NMEC's accounts were not as they should be," said Saunders. "And as soon as the shortfall was detected the (NMEC) board applied to the MC for a £53 million grant."

If NMEC's net assets, in addition to its cash flow projections, had been insufficient to cover its liabilities then it would have been legally insolvent. Saunders refused to confirm or deny whether the company's assets covered their liabilities in spite of the shortfall. NMEC has failed to keep track of its assets, which may make it impossible to tell whether the company was legally insolvent. David Kinnon, HLB Kidson's director of reconstruction and reorganization, says that the law requires a company's board of directors to be aware of insolvency and other financial problems and to act accordingly: "the fact that they did not react to the shortfall reflects badly on them even if the company was not legally insolvent".

NMEC was initially awarded a £47 million lottery money grant by the MC. It was given on condition that Nomura, the Japanese Investment Bank that won the government competition to take over the Dome, would pay £53 million of the £105 million it was offering for the Dome to the MC. The NMEC will still receive the MC grant of £47 million, despite Nomura's decision earlier this week to pull out of the deal. James called in PwC's business regeneration unit last week to report on NMEC's finances. PwC's investigation revealed other irregularities in NMEC's finances. NMEC was set up to operate the Dome from January 1 to December 31, 2000 and on the January 1, 2001 it will be liquidated. On September 5, NMEC did not have sufficient funds to cover its liquidation. The PwC report found that NMEC cannot establish who owns the intellectual property in the Dome's exhibits. It has also failed to keep track of its assets and outstanding payments to sponsors and contractors involved in the construction of the Dome.

Nomura said NMEC's accounts were in "such a mess" that it was impossible to conduct proper due diligence. The bank said this was a deciding factor in its decision to withdraw its £105 million bid for the Dome. Nomura tried to obtain a copy of the PwC report but it says it was refused by NMEC. NMEC says Nomura was shown parts of the report that PwC thought would be relevant to the operating costs of the Dome in the new year.

NMEC is being investigated by the National Audit Office, which will publish a report next month. The company is scheduled to attend a Public Accounts Committee hearing on November 20.

Source: accountancymagazine.com, September 15, 2000.

## Introduction

This chapter is concerned with cash, in particular with identifying short-term funding sources and quantifying the relationship between these short-term sources and the uses to which they will be put. It concentrates, therefore, on liquidity and the efficiency with which liquid resources are managed.

This is a constant challenge for all businesses, whether big or small. And in the case of the Millennium Dome, while the problem can ultimately be traced to poor planning and attendance numbers, the opening extract suggests that management of its cash resources may also have left something to be desired.

Solvency refers to the capacity of a business to meet its debts. Liquidity relates to the short-term solvency of a business and measures the capacity of an entity to meet its immediate commitments, i.e., its ability to produce sufficient cash to pay short-term creditors. This definition has two important elements:

- Liquidity as a concept relates to the availability of cash
- It is tied to the capacity of an entity to produce cash with which to pay short-term debts.

There is, therefore, a relationship between these two considerations: the expectation is that a business will be able to generate sufficient cash from its trading activity to meet debts arising directly from that activity. In other words, the usual business dynamic would see a business generating cash from operating activity which could then be used to meet any indebtedness relating to the purchase of those goods.

This highlights the fact that a strong relationship should exist between the trading activity of the business as summarized in the profit and loss account and its debt paying capacity as summarized in the balance sheet. This short-term debt paying capacity is usually assessed from the "working capital" section of the balance sheet. This is the part of the balance sheet where short-term sources of funds (current assets) and short-term calls on those funds (creditors due within 1 year) are presented.

Before dealing specifically with liquidity, therefore, it is necessary to look at that part of the balance sheet which contains information about the anticipated short-term inflows and outflows of the business.

## Activity

In order for a business to function efficiently there must be funds available to pay debts. This requires that current assets and creditors due within 1 year be managed properly. Activity (or efficiency) ratios quantify the trading activity of the business in a way that recognizes that there is a direct relationship between that activity and the availability of adequate cash resources on an ongoing basis. For instance, they recognize that credit sales recorded in the profit and loss account are directly related to debtors shown in the balance sheet.

Any examination of liquidity and efficiency, therefore, requires an understanding of the "working capital" section of the balance sheet section of the balance sheet, since it is here that the items deriving from trading activity – stocks, debtors and creditors – are found. This requires a fuller examination of working capital's constituent parts, current assets and creditors due within 1 year.

## Current Assets

Current assets can be defined as resources that are held for the short-term. They include cash, debtors, stock, short-term investments and prepayments. The specifics of their accounting treatment have already been covered in Chapter 6. This section is concerned specifically with the management of debtors, stock and cash.

# Debtors

Debtors are claims to future inflows of cash. As Chapter 6 indicated these can be short or long-term, and for each sub-category into which debtors is divided on the face of the balance sheet, the amounts due within 1 year and the amounts due after more than 1 year must be clearly distinguished.

The most common such claim is trade debtors which is the amount of money owing to the business in respect of credit sales. Other claims would be prepayments or amounts still owed to the business in respect of fixed assets sold. Since the claims relate to future inflows the question of valuation arises. However, because the collection period is usually short-term this does not normally pose problems, and discounting is rarely employed.

A more pressing issue is the fact that a debt may be defaulted upon and go unpaid. Consequently, companies are required to make provision for doubtful debts. The figure for debtors should, therefore, be shown net of any such provisions.

### Trade Debtors

Trade debtors due within 1 year is usually the most substantial component of debtors. However, since it derives from credit sales it will only be relevant to those firms that engage in such sales.

In attempting to quantify the financial position of the business it will be important that users of financial information be able to reduce it to a form that enables comparison. One approach commonly used in relation to debtors is to produce an "age profile" of amounts owed to the business at a particular moment in time. This simply involves classifying debts into various sub-sections based on the length of time each debt is outstanding, e.g., less than 30 days, 30–60 days and 60 days or more. The business can take then action appropriate to the length of time the debts are unpaid.

This type of classification can be usefully supplemented by ratios. The ratio most commonly employed for debtors is Debtors' days.

## Debtors' Days

This ratio measures the length of time it takes debtors to pay. Since debtors are a direct consequence of credit sales a useful way of quantifying them will be as the fraction which debtors at the end of a period represent of the total credit sales for a year. This can then be expressed in terms of days by multiplying the resulting fraction by 365.

The formula is:[1]

$$\frac{\text{Closing Trade Debtors}}{\text{Credit Turnover}} \times 365$$

The figure for Tesco based on its accounts for the year ended February 26, 2000 is nil (see note 15 to the accounts) because it does not have any trade debtors as its sales are entirely for cash.

Debtors days is a measure of the length of time being taken by a company's customers to pay their debts. Time such as this, when resources are tied up, represent a cost to a business since it is effectively giving free credit to its customers out of its own resources. Obviously, it must fund this cost itself, for example by undertaking an overdraft. It is in a company's best interests, therefore, to keep this debtors' days period to a minimum:

## Bankruptcy Within 6 Months Threat to Third of London Business

### Late Payments Risk Bankrupting a Third of London's Small to Medium-Sized Businesses in the next 6 Months, Accountants have Warned

The Turnaround Finance Group of the London Society of Chartered Accountants found that 34% of 1,050 businesses are in danger of going bankrupt because of bad debt or payments being withheld. And even though the 1998 Late Payments Act enabled small firms to charge interest on late payments, more than three-quarters of firms are reluctant to use it for fear of scaring away customers. Over a quarter of firms said their average waiting time for payment was 90 days; one in five regularly wait 180 days; one respondent had to wait 515 days.

Doug MacDonald, of the Turnaround Finance Group, said: "Cash flow is the basic life-blood of a business. Managing debtor collections and having an effective accounts system is crucial to the viability of any business, large or small."

"However, with Small, Medium Enterprises (SMEs), management of debtor collections can either create a great cash generating business or push in into insolvency. Factoring and confidential invoice discounting is one of the latest growing forms of SME finance and is an excellent method of financing receivables." He advises businesses to check a customer's credit worthiness before entering large contracts, and to get to know the customer's accounts department.

Source: AccountingWEB, August 31, 2000.

---

[1] This formula obviously indicates the Debtors days figure represented by year-end debtors. The numerator can also be the average level of Debtors during the year (Opening Debtors + Closing Debtors/2). The resulting figure gives the average debtors' days over the course of the year in question.

When interpreting the debtors' days ratio a number of points need to be borne in mind:

1. It is usually not possible to determine the level of credit sales from the Annual Report, as there is no requirement on firms to distinguish between cash and credit transactions. Ironically, it will be easiest to calculate this ratio for those entities which have either all credit sales, such as large contractors, or those with almost no credit sales such as supermarket chains. However, the bulk of firms operate a mix of cash and credit sales and this means that informed estimates as to the credit sales levels may be required.

2. Turnover must be stated VAT exclusive. Trade debtors, however, will be VAT inclusive since the individual debtors are liable to pay the full VAT inclusive debt. This poses problems in terms of the compatibility of a formula that comprises elements which are based on different valuations.

3. Seasonal factors may need to be taken into account when interpreting the result. For instance, a year-end debtors figure where the business is seasonal may not be representative.

4. Most large businesses will have developed fairly advanced credit control systems using age profiles, normally expressed in terms of less than 30, 60, 90 days, etc., to control and target outstanding debts. This will provide useful additional information in analysing the debtors' days figure.

5. Where companies have a small number of debtors there is considerable potential for distortion if even one of these debtors changes its payment habits.

6. Other possible explanations of changes include:

   - Sales volume may have expanded or contracted materially towards the end of the year.
   - Some debtors should more properly be classified as bad or doubtful debts.
   - The company operates an instalment payment method.
   - The sales mix may have changed to include more or less cash or credit sales.
   - The company operates a factoring arrangement.[2]

---

**In practice:**

---

*It Pays to be Prompt*

*Southern Europeans are dilatory while Scandinavians are efficient, according to a report by Grant Thornton showing Europe's payment league tables for small businesses.*

*The European Business Survey showed that Europe's late payment hot spots are still in the Mediterranean region, with Greek SMEs taking 87 days to pay trade debt, compared with the European average of 55 days. Italy, Malta and Spain are also propping up the bottom of the table, with payment day averages of 81, 74 and 72, respectively.*

*The best payers in Europe are the Finns, boasting an average of 26 days. UK companies have reduced payment periods over the last 5 years by 1 week, taking the payment period down to 46 days. With the exception of Belgium and Greece, all countries succeeded in reducing their payment periods...*

*Source: Accountancy International, April 1999.*

---

# Stock

To be classified as stock an item should be intended for resale or should be used or consumed in the course of production of goods for resale. Stock will usually comprise a substantial part of every company's current assets. Consequently the control of stock will normally form a large part of management's responsibilities.

As outlined in Chapter 6, stock consumed and closing stock must be valued at the lower of cost and net realizable value. For many firms the identification and valuation of stock will not be difficult. For instance trading firms, which simply purchase goods and then resell them, will have little problem in identifying closing stock and determining its historic cost or net realizable value where appropriate.

Apart from valuing closing stock, the question also arises as to the value at which stocks should be issued from stores to the factory floor or the consumer. This apparently simple task can often prove quite complex. For example, if materials were purchased exactly as needed or used, the cost of stocks of raw materials used could be fairly easily determined. However, in practice materials are purchased in large quantities at different times and prices and issued to production in small amounts. This can make it extremely difficult to trace the cost of raw materials consumed.

It is because of difficulties such as these that a number of techniques have been developed to assist in valuing stock. These are known as "perpetual inventory systems" because they are methods of recording the receipt and issue of individual items of stock as they occur in terms of quantity and value.

The most widely used of these methods are:

- **First In, First Out (FIFO)**: prices each issue at the price paid for the material first taken into stocks for which there are quantities still remaining.

- **Last In, First Out (LIFO)**: prices each issue at the price paid for the material last taken into stocks for which there are quantities still remaining.

- **Weighted average**: pricing is based on the mix of materials in stock and the prices at which they were acquired.

- **Standard cost**: pricing involves assigning predetermined values/prices to units.

A comprehensive example of the effects of these different valuation methods is provided on the website for this text.

## Stock Days

This measures the length of time items are held in stock before being sold. It recognizes the relationship between the total amounts of stock consumed during the year, i.e., cost of sales, and the amount of that stock held at the end of the year. In businesses where there are finished goods, work-in-progress and raw materials, it will make more sense to calculate figures for each category than to calculate one composite figure.

The formula is:[3]

$$\frac{\text{Closing Stock}}{\text{Cost of Sales}} \times 365$$

Referring to notes 2 and 14 to the accounts, the figure for Tesco is:

$$\frac{636}{17365} \times 365 = 13.4 \text{ days}$$

Alternatively, stock levels can be assessed in relation to Turnover, in which case Turnover is substituted for Cost of Sales in the formula above.

The figure for Tesco is:

$$\frac{636}{18796} \times 365 = 12.4 \text{ days}$$

Businesses will want to ensure that the stock days period is kept as low as possible since a longer stockholding period means extra warehousing and security costs. More critically, it also means additional amounts of cash tied up in stock. However, this will need to be balanced against the need to have stock available as necessary.

---

[3] As was the case with Debtors, the numerator can also be the average stock over the course of the year, i.e., Opening Stock + Closing Stock/2, in which case what is being identified is the stock days figure relevant to the financial year as a whole.

Most large organizations will have complex, computer-based stock control systems that will determine and activate economic order quantities, economic order times and reconcile the cost/benefit implications of various stock-holding permutations. Tesco have indicated that, while their stock days figure is relatively low, they expect a combination of new IT-based stock control systems and more efficient buying and management practices to yield £100 million in savings over the next few years.

When interpreting this ratio a number of considerations need to be borne in mind:

1. The constituent parts of the ratios used may need to be investigated, and allowance may need to be made for VAT.

2. Seasonal factors must be taken into account when interpreting the result. For instance a year end stock figure where the business is seasonal may give an unrepresentative result.

3. Where companies trade in a small number of high value items there is considerable potential for distortion where even one item is unsold.

4. Comparative bases, such as industry averages, must be sensitive to product mix.

5. The following considerations may also need to be taken into account:

   • Sales volume may have increased or decreased materially towards the end of the year.
   • The company may have found it necessary to carry more stock due to changes in customer profile, market changes or new product lines.
   • Because of changes in price, total values may have changed without any change in the underlying stock volumes.
   • Purchasing policy may have changed in the light of discounts for bulk purchases.
   • There may be high levels of deteriorated or obsolescent stock.
   • The company may have introduced a policy designed to move goods through more quickly.

## Stock Turnover

This formula (also known as stockturn) is a variation on stock days, employing the same figures to compute its result, although in a different arrangement. It yields a measure of the number of times that the company has converted its stock into sales. The higher the factor, the quicker the stock is moving through. As with stock days either turnover or cost of sales can be used as the basis of the calculation.

The formula is:

$$\frac{\text{Cost of Sales (or, Turnover)}}{\text{Closing Stock}}$$

Using Cost of Sales as the numerator, the figure for Tesco is:

$$\frac{17365}{636} = 27.3 \text{ times}$$

The critical importance of well-managed stock levels is illustrated by the following example of a company which identified stockturn as a crucial item to be monitored if it was to benefit fully from a large contract.

## Forced to Show its Mettle After Winning that Big Contract

### Juliette Jowit Looks at the Risks Involved in a Materials Supply Deal with BAe

A large contract can make or break many small companies. So when Apollo Metals, a metals management company with annual turnover of £90 million, won a £500 million contract with British Aerospace there was optimism but also concern. The 10-year contract to handle materials supply for BAe's military aircraft and aero-structures division was a big leap forward.

One of the first deals of its kind with an aerospace manufacturer, it could lead to further contracts with other companies in the sector. But large capital investment in a new site and stock poses challenges for a small, highly-geared company. If it works, the company could have set a new industry trend; if it fails, the prospects may be bleak for Apollo.

### Strengths

In the past decade, Apollo has grown six-fold, mostly organically, as it shifted away from more volatile general engineering business to the stronger aerospace sector. The new Tyseley plant has greatly improved efficiency: stockpicking times have been cut from 25–30 min to 9–10 min, with almost 100% accuracy, and wastage is down to 10%.

A new £1.8 million computer system should improve customer communications and planning so Apollo can reduce stockholdings. The company hopes this will raise stockturn from 2.6–3.5 times over 2 years. The company claims the BAe contract is the natural culmination of recent progress, and is now looking forward to guaranteed revenue from it of up to £50 million a year and margins of 5%.

### Weaknesses

Financing the BAe deal could be a problem. Low stockturns for a distribution business tie up large amounts of working capital...

Source: Financial Times, October 25, 1999.

## Operating Cycle

The operating cycle is the time between purchase of stock and the eventual realization of cash from the sale of that item. It represents the length of time that an average good takes to move through the various elements of the trading process before yielding cash. It can be calculated using the Debtors days and Stock days figures.

The formula is:

Stock days + Debtors' days

If, for example, the stockturn period was 60 days after which goods were sold on credit, and the subsequent Debtors days period was 45 days, then the operating cycle would amount to 105 days.

The figure for Tesco is:

$13.4 + 0 = 13.4$ days

## Creditors: Amounts Due Within 1 Year

As indicated in Chapter 6, a large number of items are included under this heading. However, for the purposes of determining efficiency, the most important component will be Trade Creditors.

### Trade Creditors

This is the amount due to providers of goods and services. It is a significant means of finance for most businesses since it represents a relatively cheap source of funds, particularly where payment is within the allowed credit period and penalties are avoided. In fact, even where penalties are incurred it represents a relatively cheap source of funds. Consequently, many firms will exploit its potential to the full.

## Creditors' Days

Creditors result from credit purchases of goods or services, and this ratio provides a measure of the time taken to pay suppliers for those goods or services. The proper figure against which to gauge trade creditors therefore, is credit purchases. However, unless the company uses Format 2 for the profit and loss account this will not usually be available. One commonly used approximation is cost of sales. Alternatively, turnover may be taken as the denominator.

The formula is:[4]

$$\frac{\text{Closing Trade Creditors}}{\text{Cost of Sales}} \times 365$$

Referring to notes 2 and 17 to the accounts, the figure for Tesco is:

$$\frac{1248}{17365} \times 365 = 26.2 \text{ days}$$

Creditors days is a measure of the length of time being taken by a company to pay its customers. This period represents a time in which its suppliers are effectively giving the company free finance. Consequently, the company will want to extend this period where possible, although without compromising other considerations such as its payment reputation and legal requirements.

---

**In practice:**

Some of the more humorous reasons given for late payment are outlined below.

*It's in the Post*

*Accountants' noses should be growing, if we are to believe a new survey listing bizarre excuses given by businesses who fail to pay their debts. "The director's been shot," and "I'll pay you when God tells me to" are just two of the most outrageous excuses listed in a survey published by the Credit Services Association, the debt collection industry body.*

*The commercial sector tends to blame financial problems, and excuses such as "You'll get paid when I do," and "The finance director is off sick" are common. However, those in the consumer sector apparently feel no shame in citing personal relationship problems as the reason for not paying bills.*

*Source: Accountancy, April 2000.*

---

When interpreting this ratio a number of points need to be borne in mind:

1. It is often difficult to determine the level of purchases from the Annual Report, as there is no requirement for firms to provide this information unless Format 2 is being used. Nor is it possible to determine credit purchases, as there is no requirement to distinguish between cash and credit transactions.

---

[4] As was the case for Debtors days and Stock days, the numerator can be changed to Average Creditors (Opening Creditors + Closing Creditors/2) to give the average number of days credit taken by the company during the period in question. If the information is available, the Cost of Sales figure could be adjusted for changes in stock levels and depreciation in order to more closely approximate to goods purchased on credit during the year.

2. VAT will cause complications since the profit and loss account will have VAT exclusive figures while the trade creditors figure will be VAT inclusive.

3. Seasonal factors must be taken into account. For instance a year-end creditors figure where the business is seasonal may yield an unrepresentative result.

4. The following may also need to be considered:

- Purchases volume may have increased or decreased materially towards the end of the year.
- The company may have deliberately withheld payment of certain debts.
- In order to avail of discounts, the company may have made earlier than usual payments.

## Asset Turnover

Thus far this chapter has looked at activity measures in the context of the working capital section of the balance sheet, as this is the section that links the end-of-year position with the profit and loss account. However, management efficiency should also be assessed in relation to overall asset management.

This is normally gauged by measuring asset turnover. This is a measure of the relationship between net assets employed in generating business and the turnover that this yields. The figure for net assets employed can vary, but a common measure is Fixed Assets + Net Current Assets (Liabilities).

The ratio is, therefore:[5]

$$\frac{\text{Turnover}}{\text{Net Assets Employed}}$$

For Tesco the figure is:

$$\frac{18796}{8527 - 2145} = 2.95 \text{ times}$$

This means that for the year in question the net assets employed by Tesco yielded almost three times their balance sheet value. Only when compared against industry averages or other comparative bases can the significance of this be assessed.

### Activity Measures

Activity measures, therefore, are useful techniques for quantifying the relationship between trading activity and the related debtors, stock and creditors figures shown

---

[5] In some cases the net assets figure shown as a total in the balance sheet is used. For Tesco this would be £4,798 million. This is an equally valid denominator and differs from the figure shown above as it includes long term debt and provisions. The reasons for adopting the denominator used above will be explained in more detail in Chapter 10 when asset turnover will be revisited.

in the balance sheet. Indeed, it is as much for the fact that they highlight this inter-relationship as for any results they yield, that it is important to understand and apply them. They also allow the efficiency with which the overall asset portfolio is managed to be assessed.

However, activity ratios can only be fully appreciated when considered in the context of liquidity and the ratios which have been developed to quantify this.

## *Liquidity*

Liquidity relates to the capacity of a business to pays its short-term debts as they become due. Therefore, the focus is on the relationship between current assets and creditors due within 1 year, since these measure short-term sources of cash and short-term calls on that cash.

## Current Ratio

The ratio most commonly used to assess liquidity is the Current Ratio which is a simple assessment of the relationship between the two primary elements of liquidity.

The formula is:

Current Assets : Creditors due within 1 year

or

$$\frac{\text{Current Assets}}{\text{Creditors due within 1 year}} \times 100\%$$

The figure for Tesco is:

$$\frac{1342}{3487} \times 100\% = 38\% \text{ (or, in terms of a ratio : 0.38 : 1)}$$

Traditional approaches to interpreting this ratio have tended to emphasize ratios such as 2:1 or 1.5:1 as prudent. However, more recently, the emphasis has moved away from these simplistic evaluations to considerations such as the age of debtors, the imminence of liabilities, and seasonal factors. These and any relevant points raised earlier when discussing Debtors days, Stock days and Creditors days, should all be taken into account when attempting to interpret the significance of the result yielded.

## Quick Ratio

Because the focus is on the ability to pay debts in the short term, it is sometimes appropriate to exclude trading stock from the equation on the grounds that this will often take a considerable time to translate into cash, particularly where goods are initially sold on credit. This results in the Quick ratio (or Acid Test). (Note: in the case of Tesco its calculation may not be appropriate, as its stock days period is quite low and it does not sell on credit, i.e., its Operating Cycle is low.)

The formula is:

Current Assets − Closing Stock : Creditors due within one year or

$$\frac{\text{Current Assets} - \text{Stock}}{\text{Creditors due within 1 year}} \times 100\%$$

The figure for Tesco is:

$$\frac{1342 - 636}{3487} \times 100\% = 20\% \text{ (or, in terms of a ratio : 0.2 : 1)}$$

As is the case with the Current Ratio, it is not appropriate to think in terms of a "normal" Quick Ratio. The point is that there should be evidence of proper and efficient management. This can usually only be assessed in the light of appropriate benchmarks, such as industry averages.

## Cash Flow Ratios

While the Current and Quick ratios are useful measures of liquidity, analysis of information included in the Cash Flow Statement, particularly Net Cash Flow from Operating Activity, can often provide important additional insights into the liquidity position.

This focus helps to emphasize the importance of cash in relation to both its generation and efficient use. As the following extract highlights, it must always be central to management's planning and to any analysis:

### Cash Machine – by Iveystone

There really is nothing like running your own business to teach you the importance of cash flow and cash management. One develops a keen awareness of payables, receivables and capital investments as each pay-day rolls around (and tax payment day and mortgage payment day, etc.). Cash flow becomes more important than almost anything else, because sometimes just a few hundred or a few thousand dollars a few days earlier can spell the difference between being in business and being out of business.

And when the business achieves a cash flow positive position and outlook, then the business can really be called a success, because its the excess cash that can be used to pay off the debt, provide a return to the shareholders, make acquisitions, but most importantly, not to have to worry about having enough cash for payroll and payroll taxes. Anyone who has started a business or run a business knows what I mean.

Having said that then, the real measure of an investments success, in my humble opinion, is not earnings per share (although important), not market share, not marketing, not new products, not even quality management. But a combination of those things that is measured first, second and third as the ability and potential to generate cash. Period. Give me current cash flow and I am happy. Give me current recurring cash flow and I am ecstatic. Give me current recurring cash flow that is already big and is still growing, and I am in heaven.

Source: The Motley Fool, http://search.fool.com/community/pod/1998/2/pd980609.htm.

## Quality of Profits

In order for a business to survive or to avoid having to constantly raise funds from non-trading sources, it must generate cash from its trading activity. The Quality of Profits ratio provides a critical measure of its ability to do this since it relates the Net (or Operating) Profit, calculated according to accruals principles, to the actual cash flow generated from trading activity. The figure for Net Cash Flow from Operating Activity will be available from the cash flow statement.

The ratio is:

$$\frac{\text{Net Cash Flow from Operating Activity}}{\text{Net (Operating) Profit}}$$

The figure for Tesco is:

$$\frac{1513}{1030} = 1.47 : 1$$

This is a very healthy result, and indicates that Tescos profits yield positive cash flows.

This is increasingly being recognized as a critical measure of the "cash health" of a business since it measures the fundamental link between the basic activity of a business and the cash generated by that activity.

## Cash Flow Adequacy (or Cash Cover)

This is an important measure of the capacity of funds generated by trading to cover payments such as creditors, dividends and short-term debt without having to seek recourse to other sources of funds.

The ratio is:

$$\frac{\text{Net Cash Flow from Operating Activity}}{\text{Creditors due within 1 year}}$$

The figure for Tesco is:

$$\frac{1513}{3487} = 0.43 : 1$$

This is an important complement to the Current and Quick Ratios since it demonstrates whether or not the business needs to generate funds from non-trading sources in order to cover short-term payments. It can also be made specific to one or more individual elements of Creditors due within 1 year, for instance dividends, by inserting this figure as the denominator.

## Cash Cycle

The operating cycle was defined earlier as the number of days it takes to sell goods and subsequently collect the cash. It can be calculated as Stock Days + Debtors Days. To the extent that a business uses credit itself, however, for instance by purchasing these goods on credit, the operating cycle is reduced.

This result is the "Cash Cycle", which is a measure of the length of time that a company has to finance its trading activity from other sources.

This measure is particularly useful in expressing the relationship between stock, debtors and creditors, effectively crystallizing it into one figure. The ambition of every business will be to reduce both the Operating Cycle and the Cash Cycle to as low a figure as possible.

It can be computed as follows:

Stock days + Debtors' days − Creditors' days

The figure for Tesco is:

$$13.4 + 0 - 26.2 = -12.8$$

A positive result indicates that the company must pay for the item before it receives payment. Many businesses will find themselves in this position, as goods will normally have to be paid for before payment is received from customers. This is especially the case where sales are made on credit.

A negative result, on the other hand, indicates that the company is receiving cash from customers before having to pay its own suppliers from whom, presumably, it will have purchased on credit. In other words such companies are essentially receiving funding from their suppliers since they are receiving cash before having to pay it out.

Large retailing operations, such as Tesco, which buy on credit but sell predominantly for cash, are typical of this type of business. The result is that they receive, in effect, interest-free financing which can then be used to finance a considerable part of the entity's operations. This consistent and substantial favourable flow of cash has also been a factor in enabling several large retailing chains to develop various banking-type services using techniques such as "loyalty cards". Tesco, for instance, has developed its Personal Finance activity from this base.

The determination of the Cash Cycle is important for a number of reasons:

- It enables a company to establish whether, on average, it receives cash from customers in advance, or must source funds to pay suppliers.

- If it requires to source funds, then it can quantify the amounts required and the means by which this can be raised. Associated costs, for example interest charges, can be estimated by applying appropriate rates.

- In circumstances where it generates funds prior to payment of suppliers it must initiate an active fund management strategy to ensure efficient use and application of these funds.

- It brings together in one number the results of a variety of company strategies designed to deal with cash management.

## *Summary*

The "working capital" section of the balance sheet requires particular attention when analysing company position and performance. This is because it holds information relating to the liquidity of a business, one of the key determinants of company health. This can be measured using certain tools of fundamental analysis such as ratios, which allow a preliminary insight into the position of the business.

This section of the balance sheet also contains important information regarding the activity levels of the business, i.e., the efficiency with which debtors, stock and creditors are managed. The assessment of efficiency in these areas requires that the information shown in the balance sheet be linked with the information in the profit and loss account to which their origin can be traced. For example, stock can be related to cost of sales to determine the levels of stock turnover.

The inter-relationship that exists between various ratios is an important consideration. This is, perhaps, best illustrated by the way in which the Cash Cycle is constructed from the Debtors days, Creditors days and Stock days figures. When interpreting the results of these ratios, this inter-connectivity must be kept in mind if their usefulness is to be fully exploited.

## Review Questions

### Question 1
Cash has been described as "the lifeblood of business". Explain whether this statement can be justified.

### Question 2
Explain the importance of the "working-capital" section of the balance sheet and the different aspects of corporate financial performance and position that can be highlighted by its proper analysis and interpretation.

### Question 3
Distinguish between liquidity and activity measures, and explain how each targets different aspects of corporate activity.

### Question 4
Identify the particular elements of management efficiency captured by the following:
- Debtors' days
- Stock days
- Stock turnover
- Creditors' days

### Question 5
Comment on the advisability of arguing that there are "normal" results for the Current and Quick Ratios.

### Question 6
Identify the specific aspects of cash-related activity that the following assess:
- Quality of Profits
- Cash Flow Adequacy

### Question 7
Explain the significance and usefulness of the Cash and Operating Cycles and how they add a useful additional perspective when assessing company performance and management efficiency.

### Question 8
Taking the relevant activity and liquidity ratios for Tesco plc from the chapter, discuss what is revealed by these figures and whether they provide sufficient information to allow any meaningful conclusions to be drawn regarding Tesco plc's performance and financial position.

### Question 9
Identify any additional information that would be necessary in order to properly assess Tesco's performance under the headings of liquidity and activity.

# Case Studies

## Case 1

The following article gives advice with regard to the proper analysis and understanding of cash-related activity. Read it and discuss the merits and demerits of the arguments made.

## Help for Investors: How to Spot Trouble, by Nanette Byrnes and Jeffrey M. Laderman in New York

Scott W. Schoelzel is a very successful investor. As manager of the Janus Twenty Fund, he boasts a 3-year average annual return of 28%. Even with this year's rocky market, he has managed to post an impressive 21% gain through August. One reason for his success: The $9.3 billion fund is limited to holding about 30 stocks, so he has time to carefully monitor each one. As a result, he managed to dodge such bullets as Sunbeam Corp., selling his shares long before the collapse that lopped off 86% of its value.

So what are the tricks of the trade? While no one – not even a savvy investor such as Schoelzel – can spot the sort of accounting fraud that led to the collapse of Cendant Corp.'s stock, there are plenty of places investors can check to test how healthy a company really is. If you know where to look in the financial statements, it is not that hard to spot the kind of aggressive accounting that can lead to a financial meltdown. And if you know how to carefully read analysts' reports, they too can be packed with useful information. Here's a short guide on how to look for those elusive clues to a company's changing fortunes.

### Watch the Cash Flow

A company posting strong net income (profit) growth but negative cash flow could be in trouble. You will want to look at cash flow from operations, a breakout of which appears in company quarterly and annual filings. Since this cash flow represents the revenue a company is getting from customers minus its out-of-pocket costs, it is the purest measure of how strong core operations are. If cash flow from operations is growing more slowly than net income, or not at all, management is relying on something else for earnings growth. If that something proves to be accounting gimmickry, trouble may not be far off.

### Compare Revenues and Receivables

Annual reports list sales for the last 3 years on the consolidated statement of operations. Two years of "accounts receivable" (debtors) are found in the consolidated balance sheet. Calculate each rate of growth. If receivables are piling up faster than sales, the company is not getting paid for the revenue it is booking. Any unusual spikes in receivables, up or down, can indicate some kind of revenue manipulation – and that may lead to future earnings problems.

## Get Out the Magnifying Glass

The fine-print footnotes to financial statements can be dry reading. But forge ahead, since they contain important information. The size of a restructuring reserve, along with the details of how much has been spent so far and on what, are broken out in a footnote. This is the place to check if money is being fed back, through the reversal of the charges, to pad income. If so, when the reserves run out, earnings may weaken.

Companies total their in-process R&D write-offs under "operating costs and expenses" on the consolidated statements of income. But there should be a detailed footnote, too. The details are often minimal, though that can change when regulators are watching. After the Securities and Exchange Commission (SEC) started asking questions about such charges at Envoy Corp., management penned five pages of explanation about three deals, points out Pat McConnell of Bear, Stearns and Co. That kind of information can help you assess whether management has made a smart move or just blown a lot of cash.

## Check Beyond Earnings

Looking at a multiple of measures to size up a company will minimize the risks of making an investment based on earnings numbers that have been manipulated. In a slowing economy, professional investors suggest focusing on debt levels (they should not be climbing too quickly), gross margins (if they are falling, a company may be selling goods at fire-sale rates to maintain market share), and inventory levels (growth here could signal a dearth of sales). "No one thing tells you the entire story, but taken together it gives you a good picture," says Schoelzel. Even if you are loath to search through a company's financials yourself – or just love to pore over research reports from your broker – you should not take Wall Street's advice without a very large grain of salt. In going through the analysts' reports, there are a number of things to watch out for as well...

Source: Business Week, October 5, 1998.

## Case 2

The ratios for Tesco have been given throughout this chapter under the various headings covered. Go to the Annual Report at the end of the text and calculate the equivalent figures for the previous year. Where possible begin to identify trends as disclosed by the results for 1999 and 2000.

## Case 3

The following extract is useful in highlighting the variety of issues that attend any valuation of stock. By extension it hints at the underlying information which may be lost when financial data is simply reduced to a ratio or other measure. Discuss the principal points made with specific reference to the difficulties which the considerations raised may pose for auditors and analysts.

---

# Slow-Moving Stocks

Difficult trade conditions recently led Network Technology (computer hardware and software) to report some slow-moving stock lines in the year ended March 31, 2000. Hannelore E Schlieker-Bollmann, Network's commercial director and acting finance director, says in her financial review: "The directors have reviewed the group's stocks and remain confident that they will be sold for at least their book value and, accordingly, no provision has been made against carrying value."

However, she adds that in view of the current state of the market, there must be some uncertainty about NT's ability to realize certain stock items at greater than or equal to book value.

Note 13 to the accounts about stocks mentions also that in reaching their conclusion the directors have considered the rapid rate of technological change in the group's principal markets and the possibility of stock items becoming obsolete before they are sold.

Total stocks in the group balance sheet at March 31, 2000 totalled £4.83 million; equity shareholders' funds as at that date amounted to £6.021 million.

Auditors BDO Stoy Hayward, in a paragraph headed "fundamental uncertainty" in their report to shareholders, write: "In forming our opinion, we have considered the adequacy of the disclosures made in note 13 of the financial statements concerning the uncertainty as to the ability of the group to sell its stocks for at least their carrying value. In view of the significance of this uncertainty, we consider that it should be drawn to your attention, but our opinion is not qualified in this respect."

Source: Accountancy, March 2001.

# FINANCING

When you have completed this chapter you will understand that:

- Businesses must fund long-term requirements in a balanced and appropriate manner.
- There are a number of different sources of long-term funding.
- These can be classified into "Debt" and "Equity".
- New forms of funding are constantly being devised.
- There is significant interplay between long-term solvency and short-term liquidity issues.
- Ratios have been developed that enable the relationship between debt and equity to be captured.

## Time to Split: Behind BT's Failure to Deal With its Debt Problems Lies its Inability to Shake Off the Mentality of a National Monopoly

Who would have thought that the cancellation of a dinner would cause such a fuss? Planned for March 20th, the meal was apparently intended to allow BT's executives and large shareholders to discuss the growing problem of its debt, which currently stands at £30 billion ($43 billion). But the dinner was called off at the last minute. BT would not say why, but the general assumption is that BT's bosses feared that if they went ahead with the dinner, they would find themselves on the menu.

BT, Britain's formerly state-owned former telecoms monopoly, has dug itself into a hole by buying stakes in overseas telecoms firms and paying billions of pounds for licences to operate "third generation" mobile phone networks. In doing so, it has followed the industry wisdom that telecoms firms need to become global and be ready to exploit the anticipated (until recently, at least) boom in Internet-capable mobile phones.

But this strategy has not worked well for BT, for two reasons. First, the company is essentially a conglomerate, with different divisions offering fixed-line, mobile and data services to businesses and consumers. As a result, BT's shares are unattractive compared to those of a more focused, wireless-only firm such as Vodafone. So while Vodafone can pay for acquisitions with its own shares, BT must pay cash, which it has to borrow.

Second, even though it has bought minority stakes in overseas operators, BT has repeatedly failed to turn those minority stakes into controlling interests. True, BT now controls mobile operators in Germany, Ireland and the Netherlands, in addition to its British operator, Cellnet. But with smaller stakes in operators in Japan, India, Malaysia and eight other countries, it is hard to avoid the conclusion that BT spread itself too thin.

Hence the restructuring plan, unveiled last November by BT's chief executive, Sir Peter Bonfield, who proposed splitting BT up into eight divisions and floating off minority shares in some of the sexier bits. In particular, the plan called for 25% of BT's wireless division, BT Wireless, to be sold off in a share offering which was expected to raise £10 billion to go towards the debt. Selling off selected minority holdings in overseas firms was expected to raise another £5 billion or so.

But the slide in telecoms shares has now scuppered this plan. Last month's share offering by Orange, which is owned by France Telecom, raised less than half as much as expected, and the markets' subsequent further decline means that floating off a chunk of BT Wireless is out of the question for the time being. And falling share prices make this a terrible time to sell unwanted foreign assets.

**End of the line**

BT's:

Share price, pence

Net debt, £bn

S O N D J F M A M J J A S O N D J F M
1999         2000         2001

*Estimate

Source: Thomson Financial Datastream; company reports

Another option would be a rights issue, in which existing shareholders would be offered new shares at a discount. Rumour has it that Sir Peter and BT's chairman, Sir Iain Vallance, were going to propose just such a rights issue, to raise £5 billion, at Tuesday's non-dinner; but pulled out for fear that, in return, the shareholders would ask one or both of them to resign. Instead, the firm is now expected to pursue more low-key meetings with individual investors to get them to agree to the plan. But while a rights issue would reduce the debt slightly, it would not be enough to prevent BT's credit rating from slipping. And that in turn would increase BT's annual interest payments by as much as £200 million.

So what can BT do? One possible approach was outlined in a recent research report by Mike Williams, a telecoms analyst at Deutsche Bank. It calls for a £5 billion rights issue to stem the bleeding, plus the sale of selected overseas assets, including BT's stake in Japan Telecom (which the firm recently insisted it had no intention of selling) to raise another £5 billion. But the key to the plan is that BT's wireless and directory divisions should be fully demerged, rather than partially sold off, and that they should have some of BT's debt transferred to them. (The wireless division, for example, would take on £3 billion of debt.) BT would then end up with a debt of £15 billion.

That would be a difficult decision to take. BT, born in 1870 as Britain's telegraph operator, still has the heart of a national monopolist. By spinning off its wireless division, which is where the excitement is and the growth is expected, it would condemn itself to the margins of the business. But that may be one of its few remaining options.

Source: The Economist, March 22, 2001.

## Introduction

One of the most important determinants of a company's capacity to develop is its funding structure. Thus, BT's difficulties in relation to the nature and extent of its funding has left a legacy of long-term constraints on its capacity to invest, and a heavy repayment and interest burden which depletes its cash reserves. This in turn has left a dispirited equity interest which has seen its agenda subordinated to that of the providers of debt. Ironically, this highlights both the commonality of interest and the often divergent agendas of these respective providers of funds.

The liquidity and efficiency ratios covered in Chapter 8 concentrate on determining and quantifying a firm's capacity to satisfy its short-term funding requirements. However, it is also important for a company to be able to assess its capacity to satisfy its long-term commitments. Furthermore, it will be useful if a firm can quantify the source and nature of its long-term funding as this will enable a proper balance to be maintained between, for example, fixed-cost sources such as debentures, and variable-cost sources such as equity.

Likewise, a critical consideration for existing or intending investors will be the financial structure and stability of the company. Thus, potential equity investors will have considerable doubts about investing in company which has high bank indebtedness because their claim on profits will be subordinated to the prior claim of bankers to be paid interest.

# Sources of Finance

While it is true that there is a wide range of funding available, for convenience the various financial (or "capital") instruments on the market can usually be classified as either "equity" or "debt". These classifications are useful in that they allow common characteristics of these sources to be identified.

Equity can be defined as "any issued share capital which has unlimited rights to participate in a distribution of either capital or profits". For practical purposes it is often assumed to mean Ordinary Share Capital together with any associated reserves such as Retained Profits.

Debt, on the other hand can be defined at its most basic as "amounts owed to outsiders". The use of the phrase "outsiders" is significant in that a distinction is being made between providers of debt and "insiders". The implication, not entirely accurate, is that providers of equity, i.e., shareholders, are "inside" the business and, therefore, more susceptible to control by the company.

The real issue is the way in which a company funds its long-term activities, whether by debt or equity, as this will have implications for the company's cost of capital, cash flow and future funding requirements.

Quantifying the relative importance of these sources of funding is important, therefore, because it enables the implications of funding structure and financial risk to be more clearly understood. For example, providers of equity do not normally expect a fixed return, while debt providers such as banks will expect a pre-set return regardless of the level of profits. Since the existence of debt imposes definite obligations on a company, the higher the level of debt the higher the level of interest and repayments. This in turn will impact on the attractiveness of the company for equity investors, since the residual profits from which they draw their return will be correspondingly reduced.

---

**In practice:**

The following example illustrates the importance of quantifying the relative importance of different funding sources.

*If a firm funded entirely by equity generates profits of £500,000 then this amount is available in full to the equity interest. If, however, the company were partly funded by debt which had annual service costs of £300,000 then only £200,000 would be available to equity. The real implications of this financial structure would become apparent if profits before interest and tax suddenly fell to £300,000. In those circumstances the debt providers could still be satisfied in full while the equity interest would receive nothing. The real risk-taker in a company is, therefore, the equity interest.*

---

A company's financial structure has implications, therefore, for the financial and strategic well-being of a company and its providers of finance. This chapter is concerned with introducing techniques that capture the critical features of this structure. First, however, it is necessary to explore in more depth the unique characteristics of equity and debt.

## *Equity*

Equity funding derives from the issue of shares. The share capital of a company can comprise of a number of different types of share:

- **Ordinary Shares** are the most common type of share and almost every company will have such shares. The normal rights of ordinary shareholders are to vote at company meetings and to receive dividends. In some instances ordinary shares without voting rights or with varying rights to dividends may exist. Redeemable ordinary shares can be issued where a company already has some non-redeemable ordinary shares in issue. For reasons that will be explained later in this chapter, the term "equity" normally applies to ordinary shares.

- **Preference Shares** are less common. They entitle the owners to preferential treatment when dividends are being distributed, i.e., they are entitled to receive dividends before ordinary shareholders. Furthermore, the rate of dividends they receive is usually fixed so they attract a regular dividend every year. These characteristics make them very attractive to certain types of investors who may not be attracted to the risk inherent in ordinary shares. They also mean that preference shares exhibit many of the characteristics of debt rather from equity. This is an important consideration when determining and classifying the funding structure of a firm.

There are various sub-categories of preference shares:

- **Cumulative**: in circumstances where the company does not pay preference dividends in one or more years, the payment is merely deferred in respect of such shares as any dividends in arrears accumulate. The existence and amount of such dividends must be disclosed by way of a note to the accounts.
- **Redeemable**: such shares can be redeemed by the company at a specified date.
- **Convertible**: ownership of such shares gives the right to convert preference shares into ordinary shares at a pre-set rate.
- **Participating**: such preference shares may receive additional dividends on top of the normal fixed preference dividends.

## Rights Issues

The way in which companies raise funds by issuing shares was outlined in Chapter 1. It is normal for a company to seek to raise funds in this way at various times in its life. However, Stock Exchange regulations limit the amount that can be raised in this way at any one time. For this reason companies often undertake rights issues.

These are offers of shares to existing shareholders in proportion to their existing shareholding, such as BT was proposing in the article at the start of this chapter. The attraction for existing shareholders is that the shares are offered at a discount to the market price. The attraction for the company, apart from allowing it to circumvent stock exchange restrictions, is that it allows its existing shareholder profile to be maintained. For companies that are satisfied with the balance and make-up of its existing investor base this may be an important consideration.

## Bonus (Scrip) Issues

In circumstances where a company thinks that its share price is too high it may undertake a bonus issue. This involves giving shares to existing shareholders in proportion to their existing shareholding. There is no cash inflow to the company and it simply involves converting some of the company's reserves into share capital.

## Impact of Recent FRSs

The accounting treatment, disclosure, and classification of financial (capital) instruments have been matters of serious concern for accounting regulators for a number of years. This is particularly the case since the late 1980s as an ever-growing range of increasingly complex funding types have appeared on the market. As a result it has become difficult in some cases to determine what is equity and what is debt.

In the UK the ASB has been particularly active in attempting to deal with the emergence of increasingly imaginative capital instruments. FRS 4, *Capital Instruments*, has been a key factor in streamlining accounting and disclosure practice. It defines capital instruments as:

"All instruments that are issued by reporting entities as a means of raising finance, including shares, debentures, loans and debt instruments, options and warrants that give the holder the right to subscribe for or obtain capital instruments."

The main implication of this FRS for reporting companies is that it requires that shares be subdivided between equity shares and non-equity shares.

It defines non-equity shares as those shares possessing any of the following characteristics:

1. Any of the rights of the shares to receive payments (whether in respect of dividends, in respect of redemption or otherwise) are for a limited amount that is not calculated by reference to the company's assets or profits or the dividends on any class of equity share.

2. Any of their rights to participate in a surplus in a winding up are limited to a specific amount that is not calculated by reference to the company's assets or profits and such limitation had a commercial effect in practice at the time the shares were issued or, if later, at the time the limitation was introduced.

3. The shares are redeemable either according to their terms, or because the holder, or any party other than the issuer, can require their redemption.

Under these criteria preference shares are normally categorized as non-equity shares (or debt) while ordinary shares are categorized as equity. This is important when classifying preference shares for the purposes of ratios that seek to quantify the relationship between debt and equity.

## Reserves

The nature of reserves and the distinctions between distributable and undistribu-table reserves were outlined in Chapter 6. For the purposes of this chapter it is sufficient to accept that distributable reserves normally attach to the equity interest in a business. Undistributable reserves may require more consideration in that some elements of these may be directly related to non-equity interests, for example, preference shares. In the absence of information to the contrary, however, it can be assumed that reserves are normally allied to equity.

## *Debt*

Equity, in the form of share capital and reserves, represents one significant, and always-present, element of the financial structure of a company. The other signifi-cant, long-term source of finance for most companies is debt.

Debt is different from equity in that it does not give the provider any ownership rights. It can be short- or long-term; fixed or variable cost; secured or unsecured; convertible, in which case the lender can convert the debt into equity in the company at a pre-set rate, or non-convertible.

## Types of debt

As the following acount of the funding experience of Eurotunnel confirms, there is a vast and ever-increasing array of debt funding available to companies:

## Eurotunnel Hedges Loan Exposure

### Deal Covers Two-Thirds of Junior Debt, by Jane Croft

Eurotunnel, the Anglo-French channel tunnel operator, has agreed hedging contracts to limit its exposure to interest rate rises on its debt between 2004 and 2009. The company is paying a premium of £40 million to enter into hedging contracts covering two-thirds of its junior debt, about £2.3 billion. The shares closed up 1 1/4 p yesterday at 64 3/4 p. The company, which has debts of £6.8 billion, has fixed interest rates on almost all its debt until 2004 under a restructuring agreed in 1998. But after 2004, interest on Eurotunnel's £3.4 billion of junior debt was due to have moved to a variable interest rate plus a margin of 1.25%. Now the interest rates will be capped at 7.25% in sterling for 2004, reaching 8% by 2007–08.

Richard Shirrefs, chief financial officer, said: "This gives us an improved level of stability. There has not been huge pressure from analysts to do this but there was some uncertainty, and we are now in a pretty stable position. We may well come back and do further hedging if the opportunity presents itself". Richard Hannah, analyst at Deutsche Bank, said: "The feeling is that this is a risk-reducing move, but it does suggest the company is going to stick with its existing complex debt structure, which could deter equity investors."

Analysts have signalled recently that it is important for Eurotunnel, which carries six types of debt on the balance sheet, to set out its policy on debt after 2004. In 1999 Eurotunnel paid £349 million in net interest charges of which junior debt accounted for £210 million. The junior debt currently trades at 69% of its face value. Eurotunnel is expected to break even in 2002 and pay a dividend by 2006. Currently, its interest is not fully paid in cash; about 24% is still paid in stabilization notes that are effectively IOUs. The £40 million premium will be financed from Eurotunnel's stabilization facility, which is effectively an overdraft that is interest-free until 2006. The premium will act like an insurance policy that will compensate Eurotunnel if interest rates move above the levels set. Last September, Eurotunnel launched a £150 million rights issue to finance the buy-back of £317 million of debt at a discounted price of £143 million.

Source: Financial Times, August 11, 2000.

However, while there is a large variety in the range of debt available, they can be broadly summarized as follows:

- **Bank loans and overdrafts**: a bank loan is the simplest form of long-term debt. It commits the business to repaying both the interest and capital elements of the loan over a fixed period. That portion of it which is repayable within 1 year must be included in "creditors due within 1 year".

- **Debentures**: these are documents that create company debt. They are usually subject to a fixed rate of interest and are secured on a fixed charge, i.e., with a legal interest in specific assets of the business. They are long-term loans and the years during which they must be repaid are normally specified. Debentures can be issued to various holders or listed on the stock exchange, thus becoming negotiable instruments. They are usually subject to a debenture deed or trust document in which the often-complex legal arrangements surrounding the debenture are outlined.

- **Debenture Stock**: is a variant of a debenture and is a hybrid between equity and debt. It normally has all of the characteristics of a debenture but allows the bearer to take shares in the company at some future date instead of repayment of the debenture. However, until such an option is exercised, it will be classified as debt.

- **Leases**: leasing is a common means of acquiring fixed assets. Long-term obligations in relation to finance leases (see Chapter 12) will appear with long-term loans. Any amount due within 12 months will appear under "creditors: amounts due within 1 year".

- **Bonds**: these are similar to debentures, are negotiable instruments and can be secured against a company's assets. The rights and obligations of the various parties will be covered in a trust deed.

---

### In practice:

*Fixed Income in a Stable World*

*British Investors Have Learned to Stop Worrying About Inflation and Love Corporate Bonds, argues Bill Robinson*

*Seven years ago when UK companies looked for new capital they raised three-quarters of it in equity. Now more than three-quarters comes from bonds. Bond issues by industrial companies virtually doubled last year from £10–20 billion. Was it a one-off? Or are we at last seeing the long-sought renaissance of the corporate bond market?*

*…There is plenty of scope for increasing debt in the UK. The great majority of larger industrial and commercial companies have debt-to-value ratios of less than 30% and the average is less than 25%. Interestingly, there are also wide variations in the level of indebtedness among otherwise similar companies in a given sector, suggesting that many are failing to exploit the tax advantages of debt as fully as their competitors.*

*The gradual spread of best practice, as more companies move to their optimal debt-to-value ratio, is bound to increase the average debt ratio in the UK, still only half that in the US and Europe. A 10 percentage point increase in the UK average, which is entirely feasible, would require extra borrowing of the order of £150 billion. Last year's £20 billion of new issues is only the start of a capital restructuring of UK plc that, driven by the powerful fundamentals identified above, has a long way still to run.*

*The writer is head UK business economist at PricewaterhouseCoopers*

*Source: Financial Times, June 27, 2000.*

- **Derivatives and other new financial instruments**: derivatives are so-called because they derive their value from other underlying items. These could be shares, other types of debt, bonds or currencies. They are essentially means by which companies reduce or cover their exposure to future risks.

The principal techniques used are:

- **Options**: these are contracts which impart the right, although not the obligation, to buy or sell a specified asset at a specified price at a particular time in the future.
- **Swaps**: these are used to allow companies to fix the value of the underlying asset or liability in circumstances where a business is dealing in foreign currency. Thus a firm borrowing in foreign currency for a given period lends the equivalent in sterling for the same period. Essentially a swap involves two entities exchanging cash flows in a way that benefits both.
- **Contracts**: these impose obligations to buy or sell at a specified date in the future. If it is a futures contract then it can be traded on a regulated exchange and there will be a set price. If it is a forward contract there is either a pre-set agreement as to price or it is set at the time of exercise.

Whatever the mechanics of a derivative, the essential characteristic is that the parties are entering into a contract designed to either quantify and/or reduce exposure to risk. The real issue for accounting relates to the fact that the commercial reality of any such transaction is intimately tied to the existence of an underlying asset or liability, and it is this which must be tracked.

FRS 13, *Derivatives and other financial instruments: Disclosures*, recognizes the emergence of derivatives and other capital instruments as key sources of funding over recent years. The market for such instruments is now estimated at $90 trillion. This FRS is mainly concerned with disclosure, however, and consequently its principal impact is on the ways in which financial institutions and others report activity in this area.

The principal elements of the FRS are summarized by the ASB as follows.

## FRS 13, Derivatives and Other Financial Instruments: Disclosures

Some financial instruments, such as cash, debtors and creditors, generally arise as part of an entity's operating and financing activities and tend to be highly visible in the financial statements. Others (such as swaps, forwards, caps and collars, and other derivatives) are entered into in order to manage the risks arising from the operating and financing activities of the entity and are generally less visible.

FRS 13 seeks to improve the disclosures provided in respect of all financial instruments and it does this by focusing on the way in which they are used by the reporting entity. The objective of its disclosures is to provide information about:

1. The impact of the instruments on the entity's risk profile.
2. How the risks arising from financial instruments might affect the entity's performance and financial condition.
3. How these risks are being managed.

FRS 13 applies to all entities, other than insurance companies and groups, that have one or more of their capital instruments listed or publicly traded on a stock exchange or market and all banks and similar institutions.

The FRS requires both narrative and numerical disclosures. The narrative disclosures should include an explanation of the role that financial instruments play in creating or changing the risks that the entity faces in its activities. The directors' approach to managing each of those risks should also be explained, and this should include a description of the objectives, policies and strategies for holding and issuing financial instruments.

The numerical disclosures are intended primarily to show how these objectives and policies were implemented in the period. They focus on:

1. Interest rate risk.
2. Currency risk.
3. Liquidity risk (except for banks and similar institutions, which are covered by existing requirements).
4. Fair values.
5. Hedging activities.

Source: http://www.asb.org.uk/publications/publication146.html.

While disclosure is important, various matters relating to fundamental recognition and measurement issues remain to be resolved. Significantly, this is a project in which various international regulators have common concerns, particularly since these instruments are typically employed by multinational enterprises with large foreign currency exposure and complex contractual arrangements. Recognition and measurement issues are most likely to be resolved, therefore, in the context of moves towards international accounting harmonization. This is discussed in more detail in Chapter 15.

In addition to FRS 13, the ASB has also recently issued a discussion paper entitled *Financial Instruments and Similar Items*, which advocates the measurement of all financial instruments at fair value (i.e., market value). Issued in tandem with several other standard-setting bodies, this suggests that a standard international practice in relation to such instruments may be emerging.

## Ratios

The financial structure of a business is an important consideration is assessing the financial health of any entity. This is particularly so where the long-term viability of a business is being assessed. It will be important for both existing and potential equity and debt investors to quantify the relative importance of each source. A number of ratios have been developed which highlight different elements of the debt/equity relationship.

As indicated already, it may not only be difficult to classify a type of funding, but the focus of the user may itself influence the classification.

For example, consider a situation in which a company enjoys the following sources of funding

| | |
|---|---|
| Ordinary share capital | £1,000,000 |
| Preference share capital | £900,000 |
| Revenue reserves | £2,000,000 |
| Fixed cost 5-year bank loan | £100,000 |
| Variable cost 1-year overdraft | £300,000 |
| Creditors due within 1 year | £200,000 |

It would be possible to construct ratios that assess the nature of the funding structure of the company in a variety of ways, each reflecting different characteristics of the relevant sources and the priorities of the users.

For instance, rather than a straightforward subdivision quantifying the relationship between debt and equity, management might want to quantify the ratio of short-term funding to long-term funding. This would give the following result:

£300,000 + £200,000 : £1,000,000 + £900,000 + £2,000,000 + £100,000

= £500,000 : £4,000,000 (or 1 : 8)

Alternatively, if the user is a potential investor, he or she might be more concerned with the relationship between fixed-cost and variable-cost sources as this would enable an assessment of the likely security of dividends. In this case, since the potential investor would also have a long-term perspective, an argument could be made for removing "Creditors due within 1 year". (Although the "Variable cost 1 year overdraft" remains in the calculation on the grounds that such a facility is usually recurring, a similar argument could be made for its removal.) This would result in the following configuration:

£900,000 + £100,000 : £1,000,000 + £2,000,000 + £300,000

= £1,000,000 : £3,300,000 (or 1 : 3.3)

Alternatively, a bank manager might want to assess the ratio of funds supplied to the company by the bank in which case an entirely different arrangement of these sources would be required. The point is that the ratios employed are flexible and should be configured in a way that respects the actual question being asked of the financial data.

## Gearing Ratio

The most commonly used measure is the Gearing ratio, which quantifies the relationship between debt and equity at its most basic. The Gearing (or Debt/Equity) ratio can be expressed in a number of ways.

The approach most commonly employed quantifies the relationship between those long-term sources of finance bearing fixed costs (Loans, Debentures, Bonds and Preference Shares), and those bearing variable costs (Equity or "Ordinary Shareholders Funds"). The higher the ratio then the more vulnerable the company is perceived to be since there is a high and fixed call on its profits before equity interests can be satisfied.

A company is high-geared if the largest proportion of its funding is in the form of fixed-return (normally debt) sources. It is low-geared if the largest proportion of its funding is in the form of variable-return (normally equity) sources. It has nil gearing if it is financed entirely by equity.

The formula is:

$$\frac{\text{Loans} + \text{Preference Shares}}{\text{Equity}} \times 100\%$$

(Minority Interest would normally be included with Equity.)

Using information from note 18, the figure for Tesco is:

$$\frac{1,559}{4,798} \times 100\% = 32.5\%$$

This result indicates that Tesco, which does not have any preference shares in issue, is a relatively low-geared company since "external" fixed-cost sources of funds only amount to less that one-third of "internal" variable-cost sources.

---

**In practice:**

Notice how in this extract the increase in gearing to 86% is described as "aggressive use of its balance sheet".

*Wyndeham Press Group, the printing and packing firm, seems to be on a bit of a roll. Bryan Bedson, the chief executive, says the traditional autumn rush has led to the group's entire capacity being booked up. He is confident the 10% annual compound earnings per share growth recorded since the early 1990s can continue. Wyndeham receives 85% of its revenue from long-term printing contracts for magazines like Euromoney and The Lawyer, and other recurring work. Around 70% of sales are in printing magazines, with the remainder coming from producing packaging for food and healthcare clients.*

*Yesterday's interim results showed sales rising 18% to £59.3 million, helped by July's £15.2 million acquisition of Print Direct, a firm that services direct mail customers. Pre-tax profit gained 9% to £6.6 million, while operating profit added 13% to £7.6 million.*

*Wyndeham's aggressive use of its balance sheet saw net debt nearly double to £39.2 million, sending gearing to 86%. Free cash flow, however, covers interest costs a reasonable 7.6 times and leaves further room to grow the dividend, which is well covered and rose 11% to 3.1 p for the first-half.*

*With full year earnings expected to be around £16 million, Wyndeham trades at a forward multiple of 10.5 times forecast pre-tax profit this year. With manufacturing stocks back in favour, Wyndeham shares, up 6 p to 269.5 p, have further to go. Buy.*

*Source: The Independent, November 1, 2000.*

## Long-term Debt to Total Long-term Finance Ratio

A variation of this ratio expresses the total long-term debt of the company (including preference shares) as a percentage of the total long-term finance of the company by the company. This is a simple rearrangement of the figures used to calculate "Gearing". It expresses debt as a function of the total funding of the business.

The formula is:

$$\frac{\text{Loans} + \text{Preference Shares}}{\text{Loans} + \text{Preference Shares} + \text{Equity}} \times 100\%$$

The figure for Tesco is:

$$\frac{1,559}{1,559 + 4,798} \times 100\% = 24.5\%$$

This confirms Tesco as a "low-geared" firm in that less that one-quarter of its total funding requirement is provided by "external" fixed-cost sources.

Because they measure such an important element of corporate finance (and because many firms will find that they have little room in which to manoeuvre because of limits on borrowing imposed by debt covenants)[1] these are critical measures which every company will want to present in as positive a light as possible. In outlining future strategy, therefore, it is important for CEOs to indicate the likely impact on measures such as gearing.

---

[1] In order to give themselves greater security, providers of finance will often impose restrictions on companies which limit their capacity to take on additional debt. These restrictions are often incorporated in legal "debt covenants" and are usually expressed in terms of certain ratio measurements. For instance, a bank might require a company to sign a covenant that states that "its gearing will not exceed 75%". In the event that this figure is breached the bank may call in the loan, increase interest rates, or impose such other penalties as the covenant specifies.

## Lasmo Chief Talks Shares Up and Down

Oh, the grand old Duke of York, he had 10,000 shares in Lasmo. He saw them march to the top of the hill and he saw them march down again. When they were up, they were up 8.5 to 154.5 p (on Monday night) and when they were down, they were down 10 p at 143.5 p (last night). But most of the time they were neither up nor down, but bumping along with the rest of the oil exploration and production (E&P) sector despite crude oil prices having doubled in the last 12 months.

In fact it was Joe Darby, Lasmo's downbeat chief executive, who unwittingly led to the original surge. The City believed a radical rethink was on the cards because analysts had been summoned to the company's Bishopsgate headquarters on Monday evening to hear the results of a long period of soul-searching.

The pep talk backfired because there was little dramatic to hear from Lasmo, which merged with Monument Oil & Gas this summer. Merrill Lynch cut its inter-mediate-term investment rating to "neutral" from "accumulate" and another investment house described the briefing as "a damp squib".

Mr Darby did outline a new set of financial targets for his company but stressed they were only for guidance and were modest to say the least. Lasmo is aiming for a non-too-exacting 8–10% return on capital employed by the end of 2001 while main-taining gearing at less than 60% and keeping fixed charge cover over five times...

Source: The Guardian, November 17, 1999.

## Debt to Total Assets ratio

Another ratio that relates to the financial structure of a company is the Debt to Total Assets ratio. This measures the percentage of assets funded by long-term debt.

The formula is:

$$\frac{\text{Total Debt}}{\text{Total Assets}} \times 100\%$$

The figure for Tesco is:

$$\frac{1,559}{8,527 + 1,342} \times 100\% = 15.8\%$$

In other words, only a small percentage of company resources is funded by long-term debt.

(On occasion, this formula uses Net Assets Employed, i.e., Fixed Assets + Net Current Assets (Liabilities) as the denominator.)

An alternative approach understands debt to include all sources, whether long- or short-term.

In this case the figure for Tesco is:

$$\frac{832 + 15 + 1,559}{8,527 + 1,342} \times 100\% = 24\%$$

This gives a slightly different perspective and highlights the fact that almost one quarter of the company's resources are funded by external sources. Note also that the amount above the line (£2,406) reconciles with the gross debt figure indicated in note 19.

## Weighted Average Cost of Capital (WACC)

As the term implies, WACC is a measure of "the cost to the firm of its various sources of funding, computed in a way that respects the mix and relative importance of each type." In other words, it is an attempt to quantify the cost to the company of the funding mix that it employs. This will be different for different companies and industries and provides a useful basis for inter-company comparison.

It is usually computed by calculating the cost of each individual source and then weighting these according to their relative importance. The cost of each individual source can be determined using future projections or past experience. The former would be appropriate when assessing different funding possibilities for future investments, the latter when assessing the cost implications of gearing.

For example, assume that X plc is funded 75% by debt and 25% by equity (it is a "high-geared" company) and that the cost of each source is 10% and 20%, respectively.

The WACC for X plc is:

$$(10\% \times 0.75) + (20\% \times 0.25) = 12.5\%$$

At its most simplistic it is possible to say that X plc requires a return on any investments it makes of at least 12.5% if it employs this funding structure. However, investment appraisal normally requires a more nuanced approach.

For the purposes of this discussion on financing it is sufficient to consider WACC as a useful, single-figure measure of the cost implications of a company's funding structure.

## Interest Cover

Financial ratios examine an entity's capital structure, and, as a result, its ability to satisfy debt obligations. Another, more immediate, measure of this is the Interest Cover ratio. This quantifies the capacity of the firm to meet interest payments due out of operating profits.

The formula is:

$$\frac{\text{Profit before interest and tax (PBIT)}}{\text{Interest expense}}$$

The figure for Tesco is:

$$\frac{1,032}{99} = 10.4 \text{ times}$$

This ratio quantifies the relationship between loan interest obligations and profit before tax and interest. It provides a measure of the confidence with which a lender may expect interest payments to be met. And, as with all ratios, whether this is an "acceptable" ratio or not will depend upon the comparative base against which it is considered.

## Interrelationship Between Activity, Liquidity, Gearing and Cash Flow

It is important when assessing the financial stability of a business to remember that it is the business as a whole that is being assessed, not just its component parts.

For example, focusing solely on the liquidity of a business to the exclusion of other considerations, would ignore the fact that this is only one element in the complex and interrelated financial mix which every business must manage. To concentrate on the gearing structure of a business to the exclusion of other factors would be similarly misguided.

What is required is a holistic perspective that recognizes not only the interplay between liquidity, gearing, activity and other measures, but the need for a balanced portfolio of short, medium and long-term funds.

One consequence of a failure to maintain such a balance is "overtrading". This occurs where a business expands rapidly, but without due care being paid to the ways in which this expansion is financed. Eventually this translates into cash flow problems; usually when the cash flow resulting from trading activity is unable to sustain the repayments due on large and ill-advised loans.

The resulting mismatch can often result in even profitable businesses being forced into retrenchment or liquidation. Such companies are often the targets of corporate "carpetbaggers", speculators who specialize in identifying profitable, but unwisely structured, companies which can be quickly turned around and resold.

Another consequence might the type of financial conundrum in which BT finds itself which is likely to lead to an enforced restructuring of the business.

**In practice:**

*Lex Column: On Borrowed Time*

*BT will have to do more than sell Aeronautical and Maritime to tackle the debt mountain built up by mobile licence payments and the acquisition of Viag Interkom. It is not alone. Every telco in Europe needs to restructure its finances. But this makes BT's task all the more difficult: too many rivals are also trying to raise capital and sell assets. This financial crunch should be the catalyst for BT's long-awaited restructuring. But strategy will be dictated as much by financial necessity as business logic.*

*At current estimates, BT's debt will rise to about £30 billion, a debt/equity ratio of 180%. The market value of its assets far exceeds its liabilities: there is no question of insolvency. But BT's cash flow is increasingly being swallowed up by investment in mobile and internet. As a result, the group is going to have to cut its dividend. But even if the dividend is halved, BT's operating free cash flow would fall below the level needed to service £30 billion of borrowings. It has no choice but to restructure.*

*BT could alter its financial profile by swapping assets, perhaps trading its stakes in Cegetel and/or Airtel for Vodafone's Infostrada. It could spin off its network and load it up with debt. But the regulator may not allow the transfer of enough debt to make this a viable solution on its own. BT therefore needs to raise equity by selling shares in its mobile operations. To enhance their attractiveness, it should consider merging BT Wireless with AT&T Wireless first. This might create value even if BT is not paid a premium over the value of its assets.*

*Source: Financial Times, September 2, 2000.*

## Summary

There is a large and growing range of finance options available to modern businesses. However, for convenience these can be classified as either "equity" or "debt". The key is that businesses must ensure a balanced portfolio.

It will be important for every company to be able to calculate and express its dependence on each of these sources. This is done by means of ratios that quantify the relative weightings of debt and equity in a way that allows a company to assess its risk profile in comparison with other companies.

Such an assessment is one important ingredient in interpreting the position and performance of a business. It allows insights to be gleaned not only into the financial structure of the business, but into the relative power and influence of the providers of debt and equity. This in turn allows a more nuanced appreciation of related corporate governance issues since much of the "balance-of-power" manoeuvring which goes on in companies can be traced to clashes between these two vested interests.

## Review Questions

### Question 1
Explain how BT has managed to become so indebted and outline the consequences of this for its overall business strategy.

### Question 2
"When raising finance, it is imperative that the funding being considered should be appropriate in terms of both time-scale and structure. One would not attempt to fund a new factory with an overdraft". Explain the funding implications of this statement.

### Question 3
Distinguish between "Equity" and "Debt" and explain why this distinction is necessary.

### Question 4
What particular issues are raised by preference shares when considering whether they should be classified as "Equity" of "Debt".

### Question 5
Identify and distinguish between the various types of preference share that a company can issue. Consider the particular challenges posed by "Redeemable Preference Shares" for a company's future funding requirements.

### Question 6
Why is there such a range of preference shares available? Identify intending investors for whom each type might hold attractions?

### Question 7
Explain the significance of FRS 4, *Capital Instruments*, in relation to calculating the gearing ratios of a company.

### Question 8
Derivatives have emerged in recent years as a complex form of financing. Identify the unique characteristics of this type of funding and explain some of the accounting-specific issues that their existence raises. Does FRS 13 adequately address these issues?

### Question 9
Identify the unique characteristics of bonds as a form of funding and explain why they have become so popular in recent years as a source of funding for a variety of companies.

### Question 10
Assess the usefulness of gearing as a measure of risk.

# Case Studies

## Case 1

As the opening vignette explained, one company that has encountered considerable problems in managing its debt is BT. The following article illustrates how this financial concern has affected other structural and strategic issues. Discuss the points made and, in particular, the way in which difficulties in relation to debt have impacted more widely upon the company.

### BT Planning to Demerge Mobile Phones Business, by Andrew Turpin, Deputy City Editor

BT is thought to be considering a possible innovative two pronged disposal of its mobile phones arm, BT Wireless, through a partial flotation to raise new cash followed by a demerger. A partial flotation of BT Wireless, which includes Cellnet in the UK and Viag in Germany, could raise enough cash to allow BT to subsequently demerge it without too big a debt burden, analysts said. But City observers think that in current turbulent equity markets, this hybrid approach could still only cut BT's total debt, which will hit £30 billion by April, by around £5 billion. That is just half its 2001 debt reduction target of £10 billion. A demerger of the mobiles arm into a separate company would also represent a big U-turn in BT's strategy, which has previously consisted of operating both fixed line and mobiles businesses under the same roof.

Shares in BT sank 2.5 p yesterday to 597 p, with analysts viewing the new idea for BT Wireless as creating yet more uncertainty. The disastrous flotation of rival mobile phones group Orange this month has forced BT to rethink its original plan to float 25% of BT Wireless as the key element of its £10 billion debt reduction drive.

Amid widespread investor gloom across the telecoms sector generally, the value of Orange was slashed twice in advance of the flotation, down to £30 billion from the £50 billion hoped for last autumn, and has since fallen further to £26 billion. Faced with such turbulent markets, BT has made clear it is now prepared to consider demerger of its Wireless arm instead. It has said it would only do a rights issue to raise money as a last resort.

However, the new BT group finance director Philip Hampton has also said it may combine a partial flotation with a demerger as a solution. A spokesman for BT said: "There is currently one plan on the table, which is an initial public offering of 25% of BT Wireless by the end of this year. However, anyone sensible keeps an eye on what other options might be. The market may change anyway before anything happens." Another BT source said: "We would not rule anything out. We are likely to structure it in a not straightforward way: a mixture of demerger and IPO is possible, but to say we are considering a full demerger is going too far."

One analyst, Hannes Wittig, at Dresdner Kleinwort Benson, said a flotation of BT Wireless could "realistically" only include its subsidiaries: Cellnet, Viag, the Esat business in Ireland and Telfort in the Netherlands, but not the 26% owned minority owned French business Cegetel or 17.8% stake in Airtel, of Spain.

Source: The Scotsman, February 20, 2001.

## Case 2

Compare and contrast the experience of Vodafone (as outlined in the following extract) and BT (as outlined in Case 1 above) in relation to debt and the opportunities for future expansion which their respective experiences place upon their potential for growth.

## The Anglo-file: Vodafone pays $2.5 Billion for Swiss Role, by Nick Watson

London: The 25% stake that Vodafone bought in Swisscom's mobile subsidiary for $2.5 billion does not sound like much to get excited about, but it does say a lot about how much better Vodafone's position is compared with that of its rivals.

Vodafone continues its spending spree to expand its global footprint as telecommunication companies of all kinds; mobile operators, former monopolies and alternative network carriers are staggering under debt that's pushed down their credit ratings and share prices. In fact, Wednesday's announcement takes Vodafone's spending to $5 billion in little more than a month after it paid $2.5 billion for 2% of China Mobile.

"The strong balance sheet is what sets it apart from the other mobile operators," says Tressan MacCarthy, an analyst at SG Securities, which has no investment banking relationship with Vodafone and rates the shares a strong buy.

"While so many of its competitors are trying to raise money on the debt and equity markets or float their mobile assets, Vodafone can go out and buy what it fancies and is well ahead of the curve in putting together the pieces of this jigsaw," MacCarthy adds.

### The Lure

What Vodafone fancied in this case was Swisscom Mobile. The investment is important because it fills one of the last gaps in Vodafone's European footprint and will also help it acquire a third-generation mobile-phone license in the auction the Swiss government will hold next week. In addition, Vodafone increases its presence in Germany, the world's largest mobile market, through Swisscom's stake in Debitel.

Although Switzerland is a relatively small market, with around 5 million subscribers; of which Swisscom has about 70%, the country's users spend the most in Europe on mobile-phone calls. And Vodafone spends the most in Europe on mobile assets.

It is able to do that thanks in large part to the sale of the UK's second-largest mobile operator, Orange, which Vodafone was required to dispose of after it bought Germany's Mannesmann. Vodafone sold Orange to France Telecom for around 50 billion Euro in cash and stock, about a 50% premium to the price that Mannesmann paid for it a mere 9 months previously.

## Coverage

Assuming that Vodafone sells the first tranche of France Telecom shares after a lockup period, Vodafone will end the year with net debt of less than £10 billion and interest coverage, a measure of how well a company can make payments on its debt, should improve to nine times from this year's low of 3.8 times. This compares with the estimated £30 billion of debt British Telecom will be saddled with by next year and explains why Standard & Poor's in September downgraded BT four notches to A minus, but upgraded Vodafone to A from A minus.

Although debt is not a problem for Vodafone, the operator nevertheless remains vulnerable to the terrible sentiment that surrounds the sector, something that was well illustrated by the 8% fall in its shares on Nov. 2 when its house broker, UBS Warburg, lowered its profit forecasts. However, it turned out that the analyst in question had cut less than 2% off his previous numbers to take into account the amortization of the cost of the third-generation mobile licenses Vodafone has bought.

"You cannot really say a 1% shave off forecasts is a downgrade, it's too emotive a word, says one fund manager, who declined to be named but said he's long Vodafone shares.

Perhaps, but it just goes to show that while Vodafone's debt may not pose a problem, the business the company operates in still does.

Source: TheStreet.com, November 8, 2000.

## Case 3

For each of the ratios covered in this chapter calculate the results for Tesco plc for 1999 using the Annual Report at the end of the text. Use these results to identify any emerging trends in relation to its financing profile.

# PROFITABILITY AND RETURN ON INVESTMENT [10]

When you have completed this chapter you will understand:

- The importance of profits to a business.

- The usefulness of the various profitability ratios that have been developed.

- That return on investment ratios have been developed that enable investors to assess their return.

- The importance, and limitations, of earnings per share (EPS) as a measure of performance.

- The nature and role of dividends.

- The need to consider profitability and return on investment ratios in an overall context.

## Sins of the Suits Lurk Among the Exceptionals

### Ignore the Corporate Blarney. Results from Six of Britain's Most Powerful Companies Expose Declining Profitability, by Edmond Warner

Thursday was a day to treasure for market anoraks. Six of the most powerful pieces on the corporate chessboard released their financial results, providing a timely insight into the state of the global economy and of UK plc. The six were AstraZeneca, Barclays, BT, ICI, Shell and Unilever. Together they span the new and old economies, from ice-cream to oil and from overdrafts to ulcer drugs. Each happens to be wholly or partly domiciled in the UK, but this is a function of history and convenience, for each has an international spread of interests.

The results announcements from this big six bore the stamp of investor relations advisers. No surprise there. The job of the analyst is to take a sheet of coarse sandpaper to the coats of varnish and reveal the truth within. I have no specific interest in the six companies that revealed their varnished truths, aside from a small personal shareholding in Barclays - a hangover from last year's takeover of the Woolwich. So, sandpaper at the ready, I was able to take a gander at their statements unburdened by any prior prejudice.

What struck me first was the vast disparity between the actual profits reported by the six and the profit progression they sought to claim for themselves. In market parlance, I was focusing on actual earnings attributable to shareholders, while the companies were drawing the eye towards their own calculations of "underlying" earnings. The difference between the two measures is typically made up of two factors: the profits of businesses that have been sold during the accounting period, and exceptional profits or losses. A variety of sins can lurk within the exceptionals line in the accounts, from redundancy and other restructuring costs to losses incurred on asset disposals.

On Thursday exceptionals were the order of the day. The average earnings per share of the six companies fell almost 10% relative to the prior accounting period. The greatest culprit was ICI, which swung from profits in 1999 to losses in 2000. It was not alone: Unilever's EPS slumped 59% and BT's 31%. BT's day was a disaster. Its shares dropped 9% as the City boggled at the company's limited options for reducing a projected debt burden of a staggering £30 billion. One hopes for their sakes that BT's beleaguered management saw the opprobrium coming. However, the boards of ICI and Unilever might feel miffed at their post results share falls. Both sought to draw attention away from the costs and charges incurred in reshuffling their portfolios. Indeed ICI flagged "headline" earnings growth of 19% and Unilever of 14%.

Management attempts to exclude exceptionals from analysis of their performance is understandable. It might even be forgivable if such charges did not occur so regularly. Each individual exceptional item may strictly be unique, but collectively their recurrence suggests they have become the norm for most megacorporations.

...The six executive teams waxed with varying degrees of lyricalness about the prospective consequences of corporate action. My award for corporate blarney, however, goes to Matt Barrett, chief executive of Barclays, who skated across "the adoption of value-based goals" to this sign-off: "We have much more to do if we are to achieve our aspiration of being in the top quartile amongst the best in class in the global financial services industry...".

Edmond Warner is chief executive of Old Mutual Securities

Source: The Guardian, February 10, 2001.

## Introduction

While focusing on profitability, this opening article manages to bring together a number of the themes discussed so far in the text. For instance, companies' continuing attempts to "massage" the truth are highlighted. So too is the fact that profit announcements still have the potential to impact share price. There is also a timely reference to the ongoing use of various accounting techniques, in this case exceptionals, as a means of diverting attention from underlying performance indicators. Coupled with the rather downbeat nature of the results disclosed, the picture is one of concern about the capacity of some of these large entities to continue to generate sufficient profits to satisfy those expecting a return.

Providers of funds invest in a company with a view to earning a return on that investment. This return can come in many forms, for example, profits, interest, dividends or capital appreciation. Investors will, therefore, want to assess the performance of the company in this regard. This will require that they examine it under the following headings:

- Profitability
- Return on investment
- Dividend policy

## Profitability

Measures of profitability will be important for a variety of users. For example, shareholders will want to be reassured that the firm will be able to generate and sustain profits from which to distribute dividends. Banks and other lending institutions will also be interested in profitability since it will affect the company's liquidity, its capacity to finance debt and, ultimately, its ability to repay loans.

For this reason a variety of measures and ratios have been developed.

## Gross Profit Rate (Margin)

This is a significant ratio because it focuses on measuring that element of profit over which the firm has greatest control. This has much to do with pricing policy and interpretation of the results will need to be informed by sensitivity to the mix of activities within a company. For this reason it may be advisable to calculate rates for each segment of activity where possible. Industry averages will usually be available.

The formula is:

$$\frac{\text{Gross profit}}{\text{Turnover}} \times 100\%$$

The figure for Tesco is:

$$\frac{1,431}{18,796} \times 100\% = 7.6\%$$

(Gross Profit is given in Note 2 to the accounts.)

It is an important measure of profitability for a number of reasons:

- It provides an easily understandable measure of the profitability of the main activity of the business.
- It would be expected to remain relatively consistent over time.
- Industry averages provide a ready comparative base.

## Operating Profit Rate (Margin)

Operating Profit rate is another important measure of business performance and provides a useful basis for comparing the company's performance with competitors or industry averages.

The formula is:

$$\frac{\text{Operating Profit}}{\text{Turnover}} \times 100\%$$

The figure for Tesco is:

$$\frac{1,030}{18,796} \times 100\% = 5.5\%$$

Operating Profit rate is usually considered to be less informative than the gross profit rate because, given the range of expenses and other income that go into its calculation, it is much more difficult for the business to control. Nevertheless, declines in net margin would suggest poor performance and should be of concern to shareholders, bankers and management.

## Net Profit Rate (Margin)

The structure of a profit and loss account allows for the insertion after Operating Profit of items such as profits or losses on disposal of fixed assets. These are amounts which cannot be directly attributable to operating activity, but which are available for distribution. The resulting profit figure, "Profit on Ordinary Activities before Interest and Taxation" (PBIT), is understood to be the "final" profit figure. Only at that point do those with claims on profits such as lenders (interest) government (taxation) and shareholders (dividends) begin to have their claims recognised.

The formula is:

$$\frac{\text{Profit on activities before interest and taxation (PBIT)}}{\text{Turnover}} \times 100\%$$

The figure for Tesco:

$$\frac{1,032}{18,796} \times 100\% = 5.5\%$$

A refinement of this formula changes the numerator to the profit figure after interest, i.e.,

$$\frac{\text{Profit on activities after interest but before taxation}}{\text{Turnover}} \times 100\%$$

The figure for Tesco:

$$\frac{933}{18,796} \times 100\% = 5.0\%$$

## Return on Investment

While Gross and Net Profit ratios quantify the relationship between profits and turnover, Return on Investment (RoI) ratios look at the link between profits and the investment required to generate them.

This will be an important measure for those who have supplied finance to a firm, whether in the form of equity or debt. Indeed, one of the characteristics of the RoI formula is that it can be used to measure the return on investment as a whole, or the return enjoyed by one particular element of the capital base. To achieve this it is critical that there be a direct relationship between the denominator (capital employed) and the numerator (earnings appropriate to that class).

## Return on Capital Employed (ROCE)

The most commonly employed RoI measure is Return on Capital Employed (ROCE). At its most basic ROCE measures return in terms of the profit before interest and tax (PBIT) as a function of total capital employed. Traditionally, total capital employed has been taken to be total long term funding.[1]

The basic formula is:

$$\frac{\text{PBIT}}{\text{Capital Employed}} \times 100\%$$

---

[1] The figure for capital employed indicated in note 1 to the accounts (6,858) is made up of equity (4,798) + net debt as indicated in note 19 (2,060). Therefore, it includes short-term bank loans and excludes provisions etc. This is equally valid.

The figure for Tesco is:

$$\frac{1,032}{1,565 + 19 + 4,798} \times 100\% = 16.2\%$$

(In every case the denominator can also be the average for the year in question.)

Therefore, this ratio assesses the return earned by the whole class of investor, whether classified as equity or debt. It is particularly useful for inter-firm comparison as it provides a good, albeit crude, assessment of the efficiency with which management in different firms use the funds entrusted to them.

### Relationship Between ROCE and Other Ratios

In the calculation of the ROCE for Tesco plc above "capital employed" includes a figure for "provisions for liabilities and charges" to give a total of £6,382 million. This reconciles with net assets employed of £6,382 million, i.e., fixed assets (£8,527 million) + net current assets/(liabilities) (−£2,145 million).

In other words, ROCE could just as easily be expressed as:

$$\frac{\text{PBIT}}{\text{Net Assets Employed}}$$

From this insight it is possible to demonstrate that ROCE is actually the product of two other ratios: Net Profit Rate and Asset Turnover (which was covered in Chapter 8).

i.e.

$$\text{ROCE} = \text{Net Profit Rate} \times \text{Asset Turnover}$$

i.e.

$$\text{ROCE} = \frac{\text{PBIT}}{\text{Turnover}} \times \frac{\text{Turnover}}{\text{Net Assets Employed}}$$

i.e.

$$\text{ROCE} = \frac{\text{PBIT}}{\text{Net Assets Employed}}$$

This can be demonstrated from the results calculated so far for Tesco:

$$\text{ROCE} = \frac{1,032}{18,796} \times \frac{18,796}{6,382} = \frac{1,032}{6,382} = 16.2\%$$

The significance of this is that it allows the elements that together constitute ROCE to be isolated, enabling a more strategic targeting of particular aspects of company performance. If ROCE can be shown to be a product of net margin and the efficiency with which assets are managed, then obviously improvements in these will automatically lead to an improvement in the overall ROCE.

A variation on the basic ROCE formula includes short-term funding as part of Capital Employed. This means that the denominator is increased to include "creditors: amounts due within 1 year" and has the effect of assessing return in terms of the entire investment incurred in generating it.

The basic formula is:

$$\frac{\text{PBIT}}{\text{Capital Employed (including creditors: amounts due within 1 year)}}$$

The figure for Tesco is:

$$\frac{1,032}{1,565 + 19 + 4,798 + 3,487} \times 100\% = 10.5\%$$

## Return on Equity

The basic ROCE formula can be amended to take account of variations in the denominator. For instance, if what is being assessed is the return earned by equity, then the figure above the line will be the profit available to equity.

In these circumstances the formula will be:

$$\frac{\text{Profit after interest, tax and preference dividends}}{\text{Equity (Ordinary Shareholders Funds)}} \times 100\%$$

The figure for Tesco is:

$$\frac{674}{4,769} \times 100\% = 14\%$$

(Note: Minority Interest is not included here as part of equity on the grounds that the return to Minority Interest would already have been deducted in arriving at the numerator. In any case Minority Interest is not a material concern for Tesco.)

---

**In practice:**

This article outlines recent trends in profitability and returns on investment in the UK.

*LEX: UK Profitability*

*High returns from service companies, low returns from manufacturing and a sharp increase in profitability in the oil industry. The latest figures from the UK's Office for National Statistics paint a familiar picture. Based on accounting numbers and replacement costs, they give a better indication of returns on assets than of returns to investors. What is striking is the extent to which returns from manufacturing have declined since 1998. In 1999 UK manufacturing had a pre-tax return on capital of 7.1% compared with 15.3% in the service sector-a gap of 8.2 percentage points compared with 4.6 percentage points the previous year.*

*The market's desertion of old economy stocks was no fad. Last year UK manufacturing failed to cover its cost of capital. The strength of sterling and the oil price spike were partly responsible. But if 1999 is any guide, it is rational for investors to withdraw capital from the manufacturing sector.*

*Conversely, the figures offer no evidence that profitability has increased as a result of the technology revolution: overall returns are remarkably stable since 1995. Close up, UK corporate profitability fell in the first quarter of 2000, with returns from the service sector falling from 15.3% in the final quarter of 1999 to 14.7%. This could simply be the effect of the millennium hangover. Or it could be an early sign that technology is enhancing competition in services too, putting pressure on margins.*

*Source: Financial Times, July 25, 2000.*

## Earnings Per Share (EPS)

EPS is a widely used, if somewhat crude, measure of business performance. At its simplest it expresses earnings as a function of the total number of ordinary shares in issue. In accordance with FRS 14 *Earnings per Share*, EPS must be disclosed on the face of the profit and loss account.

The formula is:

$$\frac{\text{Earnings (Profit)}}{\text{Number of equity shares in issue}}$$

(The EPS for Tesco is provided in the profit and loss account and the way in which it is calculated is explained in more detail in Note 10.)

In spite of the fact that FRS 14 advises against placing too much dependence upon any single indicator of performance, the use of EPS as a primary ratio is strongly urged by the London Stock Exchange as well as by many prominent analysts and investors.

FRS 14 requires that figures for basic and diluted earnings per share be presented on the face of the profit and loss account in respect of each class of ordinary share that has a different right to share in the profit or loss of the period. The numerators and denominators of the calculations presented should also be disclosed and reconciled to the net profit or loss for the period. It is acceptable for companies to disclose earnings per share figures computed according to other methodologies provided that these are not more prominently presented than those required under the FRS, their calculation is reconciled to the figure required by the FRS and the reasons for their presentation is explained.

### Basic EPS

Basic earnings per share is a measure of past performance, calculated by dividing the net profit or loss attributable to ordinary shareholders by the weighted average number of ordinary shares outstanding during the period.

Under FRS 14 (para. 15) the weighted average number of ordinary shares outstanding during the period should reflect the fact that the amount of shareholders' capital may have changed during the period as a result of a larger or lesser number of shares being outstanding at any time. It is the number of ordinary shares outstanding at the beginning of the period, adjusted by the number of ordinary shares bought back or issued during the period multiplied by a time-weighting factor. The time-weighting factor is the number of days that the specific shares are outstanding as a proportion of the total number of days in the period; a reasonable approximation of the weighted average is adequate in many circumstances.

### Diluted EPS

The inclusion of diluted EPS is a recognition of the fact that most companies now have share option schemes in operation for both executives and employees which, when vested and exercised could have a substantial diluting effect on the earnings per share.

For the purpose of calculating diluted earnings per share, the number of ordinary shares should be the weighted average number of ordinary shares calculated in accordance with the approach used for basic EPS, plus the weighted average number of ordinary shares that would be issued on the conversion of all the dilutive potential ordinary shares into ordinary shares. Potential ordinary shares should be deemed to have been converted into ordinary shares at the beginning of the period or, if not in existence at the beginning of the period, the date of the issue of the financial instrument or the granting of the rights by which they are generated (para. 29).

Refer to Note 10 in the Tesco plc 2000 Annual Return for an illustration of how these EPS figures are calculated, and to the profit and loss account to see how EPS is presented.

The following article reports on trends in the use of EPS since the implementation of FRS 14.

## Earnings Per Share: Additional Computations, More Explanations

Reading a random selection of recently-published interim reports suggests that many companies are now showing additional earnings per share figures as well as the basic and fully diluted computations. FRS 14, Earnings Per Share (applicable for accounting periods ending on or after December 23, 1998, see Accountancy, November 1998, p 148), permits such additional earnings per share figures. But they must be presented on a consistent basis over time and, wherever disclosed, reconciled to the amount required by FRS 14.

The FRS 14 eps figures should be at least as prominent as any additional version presented, and the reason for calculating the additional version should be explained. Wickes (DIY stores) shows in its interims for the half year ended June

30, 2000, at the foot of the consolidated p&l account, eps of 6.8 p, diluted eps of 6.6 p and adjusted eps of 12.9 p. A note reveals how these figures have been computed.

The adjusted eps excludes exceptional costs of 9.7 p (from defending the hostile bid from Focus Do It All group) and is after a notional tax on profit of 3.6 p. United News & Media (interims to June 30, 2000) gives five eps figures: headline 28.1 p, post online business 19.7 p, pre-amortisation of intangible assets and exceptional items 18.8 p, basic (2.2 p) and diluted (2.2 p). A note to the interim statement reconciles the calculation of the different figures. Headline eps before investment in online businesses is based on profits before investment in online businesses and attributable interest, new ventures and related interest, amortisation of intangible assets and exceptional items. Eps post online businesses is based on profits before new ventures and related interest, amortisation of intangible assets and exceptional items.

Fellow media group Pearson (interims to June 30, 2000) publishes four eps figures: adjusted earnings per equity share before internet enterprises 10 p, adjusted (loss)/earnings per equity share after internet enterprises (0.6 p), earnings/(loss) per equity share 14.2 p, diluted earnings/(loss) per equity share 14.2 p and diluted earnings/(loss) per equity share 13.8 p. A whole page of the interim report is devoted to the explanation and calculations of the eps figures. "In order to show results from operating activities on a comparable basis, two adjusted earnings per equity share are presented," it says. "First, an adjusted earnings per equity share is presented which excludes profits or losses on the sale of fixed assets and investments, businesses and associates, year 2000 compliance costs, integration costs in respect of acquisitions of Simon & Schuster and Dorling Kindersley and the accelerated amortisation of a financing fee arrangement. Goodwill amortisation has also been excluded from the adjusted earnings calculation following the prospective implementation of FRS 10, Goodwill and Intangible Assets, in 1998. Due to a significant level of expenditure on new internet enterprises, a second adjusted earnings per equity share is presented in which the results of these are excluded from earnings...".

Source: Accountancy, November, 2000.

A word of caution is important in relation to EPS: it is the least suitable of all ratios for inter-firm comparison. This derives mainly from the fact that the capital base of firms will differ dramatically, with the result that it is not possible to compare like with like. For instance two firms of equal size, with similar profits may have completely different capital structures and, consequently, EPS figures will not provide a suitable comparative base.

Thus, the simplicity of EPS is in many senses offset by its unsuitability for identifying any variations between firms.

## Price/Earnings Ratio

The Price/Earnings (P/E) ratio measures the relationship between the earnings of a company and the stock market price. It is an indication of the market's view as to the future prospects of the company.

The formula is:

$$\frac{\text{Market price per share}}{\text{EPS}}$$

The market price for Tesco plc at the year-end date was 169 p. Over the course of the following 6 months it rose by over 30% to 220 p. The market price used in the following calculations is the year-end price. However, a valid case could be made for a weighted average or a price which more closely approximated to the price when results were issued.

The P/E ratio based on the basic EPS for Tesco is:

$$\frac{169p}{10.07p} = 16.78$$

The P/E ratio based on the diluted EPS for Tesco is:

$$\frac{169p}{9.89p} = 17$$

Essentially, the higher the P/E ratio the faster the market expects the company's EPS to grow. Therefore, a high P/E figure implies high investor confidence with regard to the future prospects of the company. Also since share price is influenced by, amongst other things, EPS and dividend levels, a company's dividend policy will usually impact upon its P/E ratio.

### In practice:

*...When researching a share, you might come across the term price-earnings ratio or P/E ratio. One measure of a company's profitability is its earnings-the profits after tax and any other charges that are attributable to ordinary shareholders. Earnings are reported on a per share basis and the P/E ratio is obtained by dividing the current share price by the earnings per share. It indicates how many years' current earnings the share price represents.*

*The higher the P/E ratio, therefore, the more optimistic investors must be about growth prospects. Say a company had earnings of 10 p per share in 1999, the current share price is 170 p and analysts are predicting that the earnings will be 11 p per share in 2000. The historic P/E ratio is 17, while the prospective P/E ratio, based on anticipated profits, is 15.5. This prospective ratio is more important than the historic one.*

> *Consider the example of a company with earnings of 10 p per share in 1999, a current share price of 90 p and predicted earnings of 5 p per share for 2000. The historic P/E ratio of 9 might seem to represent a bargain. However, the prospective P/E ratio of 18 indicates otherwise.*
>
> *Source: Guardian Unlimited, August 4, 2000.*

## Dividend Policy

Dividends are distributions of profit to shareholders. They are seen as important by most shareholders and, particularly in the case of "old economy" companies, have been critical in maintaining investor loyalty. They encourage investment on the part of those interested in an annual return on their investment as much as any capital appreciation of their shares.

Every firm will need to maintain a balance between payment of dividends and retention of cash for investment. This requires that funds at the disposal of management be used wisely so that cash reserves can be retained. As the following extract highlights, dividend policy can be central to this overall strategy.

### ICI to Cut Dividend for Debt Repayment, by Francesco Guerrera

Imperial Chemical Industries is to cut its dividend for the first time in 20 years in order to free up cash to reduce its £3 billion ($4.4 billion) debt, increase capital expenditure and make acquisitions. The decision to reduce next year's pay-out by about 50% signals the virtual completion of a 3-year transformation of the group from a producer of low-margin commodity chemicals into a speciality chemicals business. Brendan O'Neill, chief executive, said the reduction in the 2001 dividend would give the group "the financial flexibility" to take advantage of its restructuring. The move came as ICI confirmed it was in talks with the Belgian group Ineos to sell the rest of its commodity chemicals businesses.

The dividend cut will save the group about £115 million a year and double its dividend cover to nearly three times, in line with the rest of the chemical industry. This year's dividend will be maintained at 32 p. From 2002 the dividend will be equal to about a third of the group's profits. Some analysts said that the reduction in the 2001 pay-out had been expected and would help the company to fund future growth. "Reducing the dividend and investing in the business is exactly what investors want," said Martin Evans at Credit Lyonnais Securities. However, some US analysts said that the decision could disappoint US-based investors. ICI shares rose 10–427 p.

The company is also set to net £330 million from the sale of its 30% stake in Huntsman ICI, a joint venture with the US chemical group Huntsman, expected to be completed next year. A revaluation of its pension scheme will also result in savings of £90 million a year. Mr O'Neill said the three initiatives would generate cash to be reinvested in the business. Some of the proceeds will be used to reduce its £3 billion debt, part of the £6 billion debt taken on in 1997 to fund the £5 billion acquisition of Unilever's speciality chemicals business. Mr O'Neill said ICI was looking at bolt-on acquisitions in its four core areas of adhesives, paints, fragrances and industrial specialities.

His comments came as the group reported third-quarter figures at the top of analysts' expectations. Pre-tax profits in the group's four core activities before goodwill and exceptionals rose 14% to £122 million while turnover increased 4% to £1.48 billion. Including activities to be sold, pre-tax profits fell to £121 million (£320 million) and sales were flat at £2 billion.

Source: Financial Times, November 3, 2000.

While ICI has gradually moved to a position in which changes in dividend policy have been well signalled, for most businesses payment of dividends remains important. In determining dividend policy a firm will have to give attention to the following considerations:

- Previous dividend policy.
- Competitors' policies.
- Availability of profits.
- Availability of cash.
- Other investment possibilities.
- Market expectations.

The importance of dividends is reflected in the variety of ratios developed to assess a firm's dividend policy. The following are three of the more useful measures.

## Dividend Yield

This quantifies the relationship between dividend per share and market value per share. It is a measure of the return enjoyed by shareholders. The formula is:

$$\frac{\text{Dividend per share}}{\text{Market price per share}} \times 100\%$$

The figure for Tesco, based on note 9, is:

$$\frac{4.48}{169\text{p}} \times 100\% = 2.65\%$$

The dividend included is the total dividend, i.e., the interim dividend received plus the proposed final dividend. Thus, the entire benefit to the shareholder from dividends is incorporated.

## Dividend Cover

This indicates the extent to which a company pays out its profits in the form of ordinary dividends and provides a measure of the scope that a company has to pay dividends. It expresses the dividend paid out as a function of the profit available to ordinary shareholders for this purpose. A high cover indicates that the company operates a conservative dividend policy and does not distribute a large portion of its profits to the equity interest.

The formula is:

$$\frac{\text{Profit after tax} - \text{Preference dividends}}{\text{Ordinary dividend}}$$

The figure for Tesco is:

$$\frac{674}{302} = 2.2 \text{ times}$$

## Dividend Payout

This measures the portion of profit that is actually being distributed in the form of dividends. For young, fast-growing firms this would normally be low as the expectation is that profits would be ploughed back into the business rather than distributed as dividends. Industry averages enable inter-firm and industry comparison.

The formula is:

$$\frac{\text{Ordinary dividend}}{\text{Profit after tax} - \text{Preference dividends}} \times 100\%$$

The figure for Tesco is:

$$\frac{302}{674} \times 100\% = 44.8\%$$

This is a relatively high proportion, but is due to the fact that Tesco has traditionally paid a relatively high proportion of its profits in the form of dividends.

## Summary

Those who provide equity or debt financing for a company do so with a view to earning a return on that investment. Consequently, investors will want to assess the performance of the company in order to gauge the success or otherwise of their investment. To this end a variety of ratios and other measures have been developed which allow various aspects of any return to be quantified and assessed.

As with all such ratios covered in this text the key to their proper use is not necessarily their correct mathematical construction, but an appreciation of what each actually assesses and the identification of a suitable comparative base against which results obtained may be contextualised.

Nor should they be considered in isolation. There will usually, not surprisingly, be a relationship between return on investment and dividends or between profitability and ROCE. However, it will be the ability to identify what the nature of this relationship is, to track any changes and to identify longer-term trends that will be the difference between an informed analysis and one that fails to grasp the bigger picture.

## Review Questions

### Question 1
"It is possible to survive several years of losses, but it is only possible for a business to run out of cash once". Taking this statement as a starting point, and allowing for the fact that it is rather simplistic, consider the relative importance of liquidity and profitability.

### Question 2
Compare and contrast what is measured by the Gross Profit Rate and the Operating Profit Rate.

### Question 3
Explain why it is important to measure Return on Capital Employed (ROCE) and distinguish between the interests of equity shareholders and other investors under this heading.

### Question 4
Identify the reasons for the continued importance assigned to EPS and explain why it has been the subject of so much regulation.

### Question 5
Explain why some investors place such importance on dividends and account for their relative unimportance to investors in so-called "new economy" businesses.

### Question 6
Identify and discuss the various considerations that a board of directors must take into account in determining dividend policy.

### Question 7
Distinguish between the different aspects of dividends that Dividend Yield, Dividend Cover and Dividend Payout attempt to quantify.

### Question 8
Identify the key points made in this quotation taken from the article on ICI contained within the body of this chapter.

"The dividend cut will save the group about £115 million a year and double its dividend cover to nearly three times, in line with the rest of the chemical industry. This year's dividend will be maintained at 32 p. From 2002 the dividend will be equal to about a third of the group's profits. Some analysts said that the reduction in the 2001 pay-out had been expected and would help the company to fund future growth. "Reducing the dividend and investing in the business is exactly what investors want," said Martin Evans at Credit Lyonnais Securities. However, some US analysts said that the decision could disappoint US-based investors. ICI shares rose 10 p to 427 p."

## Case Studies

### Case 1

This extract, describing ICI's decision to reduce its dividend, raises some interesting points, such as the changing place of ICI within the UK economy, the interplay between various financial measures, and the role of signalling in alerting the markets to information and forthcoming developments. Discuss the principal points made in this article and that included in the body of the chapter.

## Talking Stock: From Bellwether to Black Sheep, by Philip Coggan

When ICI cut its dividend in 1981, it was seen as a momentous market event. Back then, ICI was universally described as the market's "bellwether". Nowadays, ICI is a shadow of its former self. It floated off its pharmaceutical side, Zeneca, in the early 1990s. In recent years, it has sold much of its bulk chemicals operations. Even if ICI were still the bellwether of manufacturing industry, that would not have much of an impact on the overall market, manufacturing is only 20% of the UK economy. Today's announcement that ICI will rebase, clearly the modern euphemism for cut, its dividend by half was neither a shock to the market nor to ICI investors. At the time of writing, the shares were barely changed.

A cut in the dividend used to be seen as a signal that things were going drastically wrong at a company. As a consequence, management used to make every effort to maintain the dividend and would not be too aggressive in raising it, to ensure they had a margin for error. This signalling process had its pros and cons. Paying out dividends in cash was a good discipline for a business. But it could of course lead to under-investment, as vital cash was taken out of the business to pay shareholders; this was the theoretical justification for Gordon Brown's tax grab on dividends in his first Budget. Nowadays, companies can return cash to shareholders via share buy-backs as well as by dividends. And private investors seem to have lost interest in payouts, which have paled into insignificance compared with capital gains.

I think this trend has gone too far; investors learn to appreciate their dividends in years like these when the main index has gone backwards. And some companies may yet regret buying back their shares at what turn out to have been excessive prices. As for ICI, the move seems entirely sensible - according to Company Refs, its dividend payout in 1999 was greater than its cashflow and its earnings per share. Does it have a replacement as market bellwether? Vodafone is the largest single stock but is in a business marked by both enormous growth and enormous investment. The oil sector's profits are determined by the crude price, as Shell's bumper figures attest. Perhaps the banks are the nearest to a bellwether sector; their share prices are influenced by interest rates and when the economy gets into trouble, the pain quickly shows up in their bad debt provisions.

Source: Financial Times, November 2, 2000.

## Case 2

The world-wide success of the "Harry Potter" series has been one of the phenomena of the book trade in recent years. The following extract discusses its success in terms of its financial impact and uses several of the performance measures alluded to in this chapter. Use these ratios to discuss the financial success of the books.

## Talking Stock: Take a Pause to peg Potter, by Philip Coggan

Can investors make money out of Harry Potter? The phenomenal success of the latest novel by J.K. Rowling (my local Waterstones had a queue round the block on Saturday morning) has certainly sparked interest in the shares of the book's UK publisher Bloomsbury. Its shares stood last night (Tuesday) at 887.5 p; more than treble their level of a year ago.

That leaves the shares on a price-earnings ratio, based on house broker Beeson Gregory's forecast for 2000 of earnings per share of 16.8 p, of 53. That is a pretty aggressive rating.

Book publishing is not that great a business. The latest Harry Potter novel sells for GBP14.99. But a lot of that, 40% or so, goes to the retailer (hence Amazon.-co.uk's ability to sell the book for GBP8.99) and 10% or so goes to the author. Then there are further discounts for bulk purchases, etc. And Bloomsbury only gets the full benefits of the UK sales of the books. Other non-US sales may only generate a royalty. So even if we assume that Harry Potter novels double their non-US sales to date of 15 million, the revenue to Bloomsbury at best might be GBP 50 million. And there are plenty of costs (printing, marketing) to take out of that.

The whole company has a market capitalisation of around GBP150 million. And, of course, it does other stuff than Harry Potter, in particular, a dictionary joint venture with Microsoft. But if we said arbitrarily that the non-Potter business was valued at GBP100 million or about 590 p per share and the company could even achieve eps of 16.8 p this year without Harry, that would still leave the rest of the business on a P/E of 35. That looks very pricey, given that EMAP is on a P/E of 21.

This is the great problem with buying shares on the back of hot products. By the time the notion has occurred to you that, say, Pokemon is very popular, it has occurred to lots of others as well. The shares have been driven to stratospheric heights. And it is easy to forget that (a) the craze concerned may only be a small part of the company's business and (b) crazes tend to be short-lived (although I would bet that Harry Potter lasts longer than Pokemon).

This is where the PEG ratio (the P/E divided by the growth rate) can be a useful check. To go back to Bloomsbury, the consensus forecast is for 25% earnings per share growth between 2000 and 2001. On a P/E of 53, the PEG is thus more than two, suggesting the growth is more than priced in. What investors should really be looking for is PEGs of one or less.

Source: FT.com site; July 12, 2000.

## Case 3

For each of the ratios covered with in this chapter calculate the results for Tesco plc for 1999 using the 2000 Annual Report. In tandem with insights disclosed by the Historical Summaries and graphs or other visual presentations, use these results to identify any emerging trends in relation to its Profitability and Return on Investment.

## Case 4

The following article recounts evidence from research into profit forecasts. In the process it highlights some of the problems revolving around the use of measures such as P/E ratios and dividend yields. Consider the principal points made and whether they are justified by the research.

## Of Prophets and Profits
## Beware Attempts to Forecast Company Profits

In a witty new advertisement for Charles Schwab, a stockbroking firm, no less a market guru than Sarah Ferguson, the Duchess of York, warns a young princess of the need to understand the "difference between a P/E ratio and a dividend yield". Not long ago, the phrase "price/earnings ratio" and its abbreviation were part of the secret language of professional investors. Now, thanks to the transformation of share trading into America's national pastime, the P/E, the ratio of a company's share price to its profits (i.e., earnings) per share, has become part of the vernacular.

But even if the duchess, along with countless millions of other individual investors, can calculate a P/E ratio, will the knowledge do her any good? A P/E ratio provides a crude yardstick of investor optimism. The higher the P/E, the more investors are betting that the firm's future profits will grow. Whether any given level of optimism is a proper reflection of a firm's prospects will always be open to fierce debate.

Economists have become increasingly active in this debate in recent years, as the long bull market in shares propelled P/E ratios to levels that in most cases remain well above historic norms, even after the stockmarket tumbles of the past year. At the end of March, the average "forward-looking" P/E of American firms (as tracked by IBES, a research firm) was 21, based on forecast profits for the coming year. (A "trailing" P/E uses the past year's profits.) This is well down from a year ago: when share prices were at their peak, the IBES average P/E was 26. But it is, even now, hardly low. Since 1980, the ratio has averaged a mere 15.

Some economists think that such high P/E ratios are symptomatic of a stock-market bubble. Others focus on the relationship between share prices and the returns available on alternative assets, such as bond yields. At a time when bond yields are relatively low, the earnings stream available from shares may be worth paying more for. The flaw here is that, although nominal yields have fallen sharply, so too has inflation. Real bond yields are not especially low by historic standards.

Perhaps there has been a sharp fall in the "equity risk premium", the extra returns that investors require, on average, as a reward for bearing the extra risk involved in buying shares rather than, say, Treasury bonds. A lower risk premium means that investors will pay more for any given expected stream of future profits, i.e., that the P/E will be higher.

Certainly, there are reasons why the premium might have fallen, ranging from an increase in the number of investors with experience of shares to easier access to credit with which to buy shares. On the other hand, current P/E ratios are so high that they seem to imply (implausibly) that investors now think shares are safer than bonds, i.e., the equity premium is negative. Unless, that is, profits are about to grow at a rate never seen before.

Which is precisely what many Wall Street analysts have predicted in recent years, pointing in justification to such blessings as freer markets and the technological transformation of the "new economy". Indeed, despite the deluge of disappointing profits news pouring out of companies so far this year, analysts continue to forecast spectacular long-term profits growth. At the end of March, the average forecast for firms tracked by IBES was of annual profits growth of 19.8% over the coming 3–5 years, barely down from the peak forecast last year of 20.2%. One erstwhile stockmarket darling, Cisco Systems, is still forecast to average 30% annual profits growth during this period.

How plausible are such forecasts? Not very, at least if the past is any guide, concludes a new study by Louis Chan, Jason Karceski and Josef Lakonishok[1]. They analyzed the performance of all active American public companies in 1951–97, and found that the growth now forecast by analysts is way above historic norms. At only one firm in ten did profits grow by 18% or more per year over any 10-year period.

Maybe fundamental economic changes will allow faster growth in future. But, strikingly, the study found no evidence that median long-term profits growth rates have increased in recent years, when those changes presumably started to take effect. Nor is there evidence that analysts are any good at forecasting profits growth. Data on their forecasts for firms in the IBES sample have been available only since 1982. In 1982–98, the median forecast annual growth rate for any 3–5 year period was 14.5%. The median growth rate actually delivered was only 9%. Analysts seem to have been consistently over-optimistic; perhaps because it is in their psyche, or perhaps because they are paid to be that way.

## Picking Losers

Analysts were no better at predicting the performance of individual companies. Just as investors are willing to accept higher P/E ratios for firms that have enjoyed above-average profits growth in recent years, so too analysts typically forecast that recent outperformers will continue to beat the average.

---

[1] "The level and persistence of growth rates". University of Illinois working paper, March, 2001.

In general, the rates of increase of profits have tended to converge. Firms do not remain indefinitely on a high or low growth path, a fact that accords with simple economic intuition. Above-average growth in profits should stimulate competition, which should slow the successful firm's growth. On the other hand, the exit of under-performers from unprofitable lines of business should increase their future growth rate.

The study concludes that, whatever happens to the future growth rates of profits (and it would be a brave man who would bet on them bucking the historic trend), it should be no surprise if the firms enjoying the fastest growth are not those that have grown fastest in the past. Nor will they be those that analysts are tipping for greatness. Nor, the Duchess of York should note, will they be those that have the highest P/E ratios.

Source: The Economist, April 5, 2001.

# SECTION IV

# Issues

Most large companies will have to grapple with more complex accounting issues than those alluded to so far. This is not simply a function of their size, but also of their corporate structure, global focus and wider responsibilities.

Section IV addresses a number of the more common accounting-related issues that arise. These range from the accounting implications of group structures to the more prosaic aspects of accounting for foreign currency transactions.

The section begins with two rather technical chapters, one dealing with business combinations and the other with taxation, pensions, leases and foreign currency transactions. It is important to work through the detail provided as any interpretation will require more than a passing knowledge of these topics.

Three less technical chapters follow. The first deals with creative accounting and identifies past examples, regulatory responses and ongoing problems in this area.

Chapter 14 broadens the debate on governance, revisiting the whole notion of the company as a "corporate citizen" in the context of corporate social reporting.

Finally, Chapter 15 places UK practice in its international context by considering accounting practice and governance regimes in France and Germany. It concludes with a review of the catalysts for international harmonization of accounting practice, together with an examination of the role of the International Accounting Standards Committee in this process.

# BUSINESS COMBINATIONS

When you have completed this chapter you will understand:

- The differences between "mergers" and "acquisitions".

- The circumstances in which accounting policies appropriate to each should be applied.

- That there are ongoing issues and controversies relating to accounting for acquisition and mergers.

- How to account for investments in "associate companies".

- How to account for "joint ventures".

- Why related-party transactions must be disclosed.

## Racing With the Raiding Pack from Buckles to Guns and Buns

### The Years of Conglomerate Adventure

When Greg Hutchings bought a 23% stake in FH Tomkins Buckle Company in 1983, the West Midlands group was making an annual profit of 1.6 million pounds on sales of 17 million pounds. Seventeen years later, an aggressive acquisition programme had created a diversified industrial conglomerate with an annual operating profit of nearly 500 million pounds and sales of more than 5 billion pounds.

The maker of buckles and metal fasteners employing 400 people in seven businesses around Birmingham had grown to employ 66,000 in more than 70 subsidiaries around the world. During the 1980s Tomkins ran with the pack of acquisition-hungry raiders that included Lords Hanson and White, Owen Green's BTR and Nigel Rudd's Williams Holdings. Their technique was to target poorly-performing businesses in unglamorous industry sectors, sell off under-performing assets and apply a fierce financial discipline to what was left.

Mr Hutchings, who became chief executive at FH Tomkins in January 1984, had spent 2 years absorbing this approach to business as an acquisitions manager with Hanson. "Products are not relevant," he said in 1992, when he was bidding for Ranks Hovis McDougall, the bread and food manufacturer. "It does not matter to us whether it's a bicycle, a lawnmower or a cake. Raw materials go in one end and products come out at the other."

But RHM was still a long way off when Tomkins made its first acquisition under the Hutchings regime, paying 2.2 million pounds for Ferraris Piston Service, an automobile parts distributor, in January 1984, the new chief executive's first month in office. The following year, with a market capitalization now risen to more than 60 million pounds and increased confidence in his deal making ability, Mr Hutchings launched a hostile bid for Pegler-Hattersley, a UK maker of taps and valves. After a lengthy bid battle, Tomkins emerged the victor, paying 200 million pounds: more than three times its own capitalization. Mr Hutchings' ambitions now took Tomkins overseas, acquiring Murray Ohio Manufacturing, a US manufacturer of lawnmowers, and Philips Industries, a diversified US group. It also bought Smith&Wesson, the hand-gun manufacturer currently facing legal action over alleged "negligent distribution".

So far, so normal for a stock market used to the aggressive tactics of corporate raiders. But in 1992 Mr Hutchings made a move that unsettled the City and raised a question mark that has hovered over his judgement ever since. Tomkins was already in talks with RHM when Hanson unexpectedly launched a hostile bid for the food manufacturer. Denying that this was a grudge match against his mentor and former employer, Mr Hutchings nevertheless made a successful counter-offer worth 950 million pounds. City concerns centred on Tomkins' move into a consumer company involved in the bread market, where over capacity was rife and prices were volatile. Analysts were also alarmed by Tomkins' decision to charge the cost of the acquisition to its balance sheet instead of its profit-and-loss account.

Acquisitions continued, but by the early 1990s conglomerates were falling out of favour. Hanson broke up in 1995; Williams concentrated on engineering until it announced a demerger this year; BTR merged with Siebe to form Invensys. Tomkins alone defended the conglomerate ethos but it, too, adopted a different tack from 1997, opting to return cash to shareholders through a programme of buy-backs. In July 1999, Tomkins took a formal decision to drop the conglomerate approach, concentrating its resources on the automotive, construction and industrial areas. RHM and the lawnmower interests have been sold in recent months. Only the architect of the strategy remained.

Source: Financial Times, October 13, 2000.

## Introduction

As this opening account illustrates, mergers and acquisitions are particularly important vehicles for corporate growth in the UK. Indeed, it can be argued that the governance structure and the presence of a vibrant stock market combine to encourage growth by acquisition rather than organic growth. The consequence of such activity is that most large UK businesses are actually not individual companies, but complex webs of interrelated entities, with one identifiable "parent" company at the top. Such combinations are normally called "groups".

The importance of groups and the ways in which they can be structured or created was outlined in Chapter 6. This chapter will deal with the accounting implications of these business combinations, looking at mergers, acquisitions, associates and joint ventures.

Because the accounting treatment accorded to groups depends very much on the exact determination of the relationships between a parent company and the other companies in which it has invested, it will be necessary to pay considerable attention to legal definitions and accounting rules. This will be particularly important when attempting to determine whether the relationships have resulted from merger or acquisition activity.

The reason that this is important is that a different set of accounting rules applies to each. And experience has shown that companies seeking to employ the usually more favourable merger accounting method have often deliberately blurred the true nature of these relationships. It is because of this that definitions and criteria assume such an importance. Consequently, this chapter will be particularly concerned with identifying the technical, legal and regulatory provisions that have been introduced in recent years to streamline practice in this area.

## Mergers and Acquisitions

Companies grow by various means. One is organic growth, i.e., by developing business internally. While this will be a factor in the expansion of most entities, another will be growth by acquiring shares in, or merging with, other entities.

More detailed definitions and explanations of mergers and acquisitions will be given later in this chapter. For the time being it is sufficient to think of them as two means by which business combinations, or groups, may be created or expanded.

A merger (called a "pooling of interests" in the US) is essentially a coming together of companies to form a larger entity. Usually, but not always, these companies will be of similar size and none will be seen as aggressively acquiring the other.

An acquisition, on the other hand, usually involves one company actively and often aggressively, acquiring shares in another with a view to obtaining sufficient shares to obtain control (or "dominant influence").

In the Anglo-American world the nature of corporate structure and the governance culture ensure the enduring influence of mergers and acquisitions as means of growth.

## M&A wave may have peaked

Merger and acquisitions (M&A) reached a high-water mark during the first part of the year 2000, with UK transactions and public-to-private deals playing a prominent role, according to recent Big Five studies. KPMG's global corporate finance survey for the first 6 months of the year showed a 60% increase in the value of world-wide M&A activity to $643 billion ($403 billion in January – June 1999).

According to KPMG, Western Europeans spent the largest amount ($492 billion) on cross-border deals. Vodafone's $186 billion acquisition of Mannesmann established the UK as the biggest single buyer, accounting for a 29% share of the total value of cross-border mergers and acquisitions.

The KPMG survey also revealed major shifts in global investment patterns. Where Germany and US were once viewed as major engines of economic development, they have now become the leading attractors of inward investment. The Mannesmann purchase helped Germany to grab $209 billion – 32% of the global total – with the US in second place with $133 billion (down from $167 billion for the comparable period last year), followed by the UK ($118 billion), Canada ($33 billion) and France ($19 billion).

The Asia-Pacific region attracted $34 billion ($63 billion in 1999) in cross-border deals in January – June 2000, against an outward investment of $22 billion. The key buyers in the region were Japan ($8 billion), Australia ($6 billion) and Singapore ($4 billion). The US led investment into the region with deals valued at $10 billion, followed by the UK ($6 billion), Australia ($4 billion) and Norway and Germany (both $3 billion).

Stephen Barrett, vice chairman at KPMG Corporate Finance, noted that the increase in the numbers of deals as well as the overall values was particularly striking. "In the 6 months to June we plotted 3,310 cross-border deals: up 20% on the comparable figure for 1999 – and suggesting the reversal of a 3 year gradual decline in underlying activity. Even though major corporations are grabbing the headlines, the statistics do suggest smaller businesses are back in the M&A chase," he said.

Source: AccountingWEB, July 25, 2000.

Chapter 6 provided a broad outline of the nature of relationships within a business combination. This chapter now explores these in more detail, beginning with acquisitions and then proceeding to mergers.

## Acquisitions

Companies purchase shares in other companies for a variety of reasons. Some do so merely to make effective use of excess cash that is available in the short term. In such circumstances the intention is to hold these shares for a short period, and then divest of them in the hope that the return earned from dividends and any appreciation in value will be greater than would have been gained had the funds merely been left with a bank. Such an investment would be classified as a current asset and treated accordingly.

Another motivation for investing in a company's shares might be to control, or at least influence, the operation of that entity. In such circumstances the intention is to hold any shares acquired for at least the medium term and to attempt to actively shape the way in which that company develops. As indicated in Chapter 6, different levels of investment will result in various levels of influence and involvement. For instance, if company H plc buys 100% of the share capital of S plc then it will have complete ownership of that company and total control of its operations.

Obviously, any stake that gives such control is not just different in degree but also in quality from an interest that is insufficient to give control. For instance, a company that owns 60% of S plc not only owns twice as much as a company that owns 30%, but is in a qualitatively different position in that it can control the operations of S plc because it holds a majority of the voting rights. The point here is that the question of who controls a firm is an important consideration. And this is reflected in accounting practice when accounting for such investments – investments that yield control (or dominant influence) are accounted for in a manner that reflects this commercial reality.

### Definitions

The largest corporate entities in the UK are business combinations, i.e., entities that comprise of a number of companies. And the way in which these entities are accounted for will depend upon the exact classification of the nature of these relationships. If the relationships were established by acquisition, i.e., a parent/subsidiary relationship can be said to exist, then they will be accounted for using the acquisition accounting method. If not, then the more favourable merger method may apply. Much hinges, therefore, on determining whether or not a parent/subsidiary relationship exists.

Previously, determination of parent/subsidiary relationships revolved around very rigid definitions of control. However, Section 258 CA85 (as amended by CA89 S1 and S21(1)) broadens the scope to include the more flexible notion of "dominant influence". Thus, while retaining some of the traditional criteria such as majority voting rights, the law now provides for a set of criteria which might more fairly capture commercial reality. It provides the following guidelines for determining the nature of relationships between companies:

1. The expressions "parent undertaking" and "subsidiary undertaking" in this Part shall be construed as follows; and a "parent company" means a parent undertaking which is a company.

2. An undertaking is a parent undertaking in relation to another undertaking, a subsidiary undertaking, if

- It holds a majority of the voting rights in the undertaking, or
- It is a member of the undertaking and has the right to appoint or remove a majority of its board of directors, or
- It has the right to exercise a dominant influence over the undertaking…
- It is a member of the undertaking and controls alone, pursuant to an agreement with other shareholders or members, a majority of the voting rights in the undertaking…

3. For the purposes of subsection (2) an undertaking shall be treated as a member of another undertaking

- If any of its subsidiary undertakings is a member of that undertaking, or
- If any shares in that other undertaking are held by a person acting on behalf of the undertaking or any of its subsidiary undertakings.

4. An undertaking is also a parent undertaking in relation to another undertaking, a subsidiary undertaking, if it has a participating interest in the undertaking and

- It actually exercises a dominant influence over it, or
- It and the subsidiary undertaking are managed on a unified basis.

5. A parent undertaking shall be treated as the parent undertaking of undertakings in relation to which any of its subsidiary undertakings are, or are to be treated as, parent undertakings; and references to its subsidiary undertakings shall be construed accordingly.

The reason for such a complex set of criteria for determining the nature of the relationship between a holding (parent) company and others in which it has an interest is that companies have devised ingenious schemes intended to cloud the nature of this relationship. Thus, in order to hide liabilities or profits or to avoid tax, companies have exploited previous legislative provisions to ensure that the accounting treatment employed did not reflect the commercial reality. In effect companies were hiding behind complex corporate structures in order to obscure the reality of effective control.

Reflecting the new focus introduced by legislation, the thrust of various recent FRSs, in particular FRS 2, *Accounting for subsidiary undertakings*, has been to move the emphasis away from "control" and onto "dominant influence". Thus, FRS 2 enunciates a broader understanding of control as meaning "the ability of an undertaking to direct the financial and operating policies of another". It also makes the following comments on the concept of dominant influence:

"The actual exercise of dominant influence is identified by its effect in practice rather than the means by which it is exercised. The effect of the exercise of dominant influence is that the undertaking under influence implements the operating and financial policies that the holder of the influence desires…(para 72).'

The application of this concept, which has the effect of emphasizing the commercial reality of one company's relationship with another, rather than the technical, legal nature of that relationship, has effectively prevented many of the abuses that were previously possible.

## Examples of Group Structures

The nature of relationships between companies can be very complex. However, the following simple outlines capture the essence of many such structures

| a | b | c |
|---|---|---|
| H plc | H plc | H plc |
| ↓ | ↓ | ↓ |
| 100% | 51% | 25% |
| ↓ | ↓ | ↓ |
| S1 plc | S2 plc | S3 plc |

a. This structure shows a situation in with a parent company (H plc) owns all of the share capital in another company (S1 plc). In these circumstances S1 can be described as a **wholly-owned subsidiary**.

b. This structure shows a situation in with a parent company (H plc) owns 51% of the share capital in another company (S2 plc). Since this is sufficient to give it a dominant influence over S2 plc, S2 plc can be described as a **partly-owned subsidiary**. The remaining portion of S2 plc is owned by entities or individuals known collectively as the **minority interest**. Significantly, the concept of dominant influence would allow a holding of less than 51% to be considered sufficient to establish a parent/subsidiary relationship.

c. In this situation H plc does not own sufficient share capital in S3 plc to give it control. Thus S3 plc is not a subsidiary.

The following diagram presents a more complicated scenario in which S1, S2 and S3 themselves each have subsidiaries

| a | b | c |
|---|---|---|
| H plc | H plc | H plc |
| ↓ | ↓ | ↓ |
| 100% | 51% | 25% |
| ↓ | ↓ | ↓ |
| S1 plc | S2 plc | S3 plc |
| ↓ | ↓ | ↓ |
| 51% | 51% | 80% |
| ↓ | ↓ | ↓ |
| SS1 plc | SS2 plc | SS3 plc |

Under criterion 3 above the general rule is that a subsidiary of a company which is itself a subsidiary of another company is automatically a subsidiary of that latter company. Thus in examples (a) and (b), where S1 plc and S2 plc are subsidiaries of H plc, their own subsidiaries, SS1 plc and SS2 plc, automatically become subsidiaries (sometimes called "sub-subsidiaries") of H plc by virtue of the "chain of command" principle. SS3 plc is a subsidiary of S3 plc, but is not a subsidiary of H plc since S3 plc is not a subsidiary of H plc.

It is important to distinguish between control (or dominant influence) and interest. In the context of ownership, a company has an interest in another entity if it owns shares in that other entity. H plc, for instance, has a direct interest in S1, S2 and S3. It has an indirect interest in SS1, SS2 and SS3.

Significantly, SS2 is a subsidiary of H despite the fact that H's interest in SS2 is only 26%, i.e., 51% of 51%. This is because the 51% interest in S2 is sufficient to give it the power to control S2's controlling interest in SS2. It is important to remember that the issue is control (or dominant influence) and H is in a position to control SS2 by virtue of its 51% shareholding in S2.

---

**In practice:**

*Leisure management group Kunick describes why it has accounted for Games Network as a subsidiary in its annual report and accounts for the year ended September 30, 1998. During the year Bell-Fruit Manufacturing and JPM International each acquired a one-third share in Games Network, which was set up to develop soft terminals.*

*Both the financial review and the notes to the accounts say that Games Network is considered to be a Kunick subsidiary, Kunick's effective holding arises from a direct shareholding of 33% and an indirect shareholding of 17% through its joint venture Precis. Kunick also holds the casting vote on the board thereby permitting control of the board of Games Network.*

*Source: Accountancy, March 1999.*

---

# Mergers

In an acquisition one company normally achieves control (or dominant influence) over another by acquiring shares in that company for cash. This has the effect of depleting the cash resources of the parent company and, consequently, of the group as a whole. The acquisition accounting method, which will be explained later, reflects both this depletion in cash and the commercial reality of control (or dominant influence).

However, there are circumstances in which two or more companies will come together and agree to form a combination for their mutual benefit. In these circumstances the arrangement might be accomplished by an agreement to create a new entity in which the shareholders in the existing companies receive shares. At the end of this process no resources will have left the new group. This is a merger and the merger accounting method, which will also be explained later, reflects this.

Under FRS 6, *Acquisitions and Mergers*, a merger is viewed as a business combination in which, rather than one party acquiring control of another, "the parties come together to share in the future risks and benefits of the combined entity. It is not the augmentation of one entity by the addition of another, but the creation of what is effectively a new reporting entity from the parties to the combination."

For example, Company A and Company B, both of roughly equal size and operating in the same industry, decide to merge. They have a number of options as to how to structure this, but these can essentially be reduced to two:

- A new company, Company C, could be created with the shareholders in A and B surrendering their existing shares and taking shares, on some agreed basis, in the new entity, or

- One or other of the companies, say Company A, could continue in existence with the shareholders in the other, Company B, taking shares in it on some agreed basis.

Whichever method is adopted one critical feature is that the new combination has not depleted the resources brought to it by the merging companies as there has been no disbursement of cash to existing shareholders.

## Definitions

As with acquisitions, there are strict definitions, provisions and criteria relating to the circumstances in which a merger can be deemed to take place. From an accounting perspective this is particularly important as recent regulations, especially as embodied in FRS 6, have been framed in such a way as to incline business combinations away form merger accounting and towards acquisition accounting.

CA89 (Schedule 2) provides the framework for determining whether a business combination can be considered a merger. The main requirement is that at least 90% of the cost of the acquisition is paid for by shares in the acquiring company.

Reflecting the fact that it was framed after significant manipulation of the merger accounting method in the late 1980s and early 1990s, FRS 6 adopted a much more sceptical view of the nature of many so-called "mergers". Its effect is to place the burden of proof on those arguing for a merger. Where the occurrence of a merger cannot be successfully demonstrated then the acquisition method must be applied.

In determining whether a business combination meets the definition of a merger, FRS 6 provides five criteria. Individually these tests are insufficient but, taken together, they provide an acceptable basis for determining whether a particular business combination meets the definition of a merger and thus can be accounted for by using merger accounting.

The five criteria, all of which must be satisfied, are:

1. It represents a genuine combining of the interests of the parties (para 60).

2. All parties to the combination are involved in determining the management of the combined entity and reach a consensus on the appropriate structure and personnel (para 63).

3. Parties to the merger should be of a roughly similar size (para 67).

4. The consideration that the issuing entity offers the equity shareholders in the other parties must not substantially reduce their rights (para 72).

5. The merger should represent a genuine and mutual sharing of the risks and rewards of the whole of the new entity (para 75).

Significantly, where a combination meets these criteria, acquisition accounting is **not** permitted, as this method would not fairly represent the effect of the combination.

## Accounting for Business Combinations

Essentially the accounting approach is to distinguish between two forms of relationship, each relating to the method in which that relationship was established, and to require radically different accounting approaches for each.

There are, therefore, two ways in which such activity can be accounted for:

1. **Acquisitions**: acquisition accounting method
2. **Mergers**: merger accounting method

## Acquisition Accounting Method

FRS 6 defines an acquisition as "any business combination that is not a merger" and requires that the acquisition method be used to account for this transaction. Once a parent/subsidiary relationship is established, therefore, the acquisition method applies.

Acquisition accounting is an accounting method that has been developed to reflect the essential nature of an acquisition, in particular, that there is one dominant party and that the new combination has had its resources depleted by virtue of consideration being paid to the former shareholders of the new subsidiary.

The following points summarize the main features of the acquisition method:

- The results of the acquired company are brought into the group accounts only from the date of acquisition.

- The identifiable assets and liabilities acquired are included at fair value in the consolidated accounts and are therefore stated at their cost to the acquiring group.

- The fair value of the consideration given is set against the aggregate fair value of the net identifiable assets acquired with any resulting balance being called "goodwill" if positive, or "negative goodwill" if negative.

# 1. Consolidated Balance Sheet

Each company will prepare its own individual set of financial statements. At its most basic a consolidated balance sheet is constructed by amalgamating the individual balance sheets of the parent company and its subsidiaries and then eliminating any corresponding items.

Take the following example where S plc is the wholly owned subsidiary of P plc. P plc bought all of S plc's shares several years ago at par (nominal value). The individual balance sheets of the two companies are shown as follows:

| P plc balance sheet as at December 31, 20X0 | | S plc balance sheet as at December 31, 20X0 | |
|---|---|---|---|
| Tangible assets | 200,000 | Tangible assets | 50,000 |
| Investment in S plc | 100,000[a] | | |
| Net current assets | 150,000 | Net current assets | 50,000 |
| | 450,000 | | 100,000 |
| Share capital | 450,000 | Share capital | 100,000[a] |

[a] Corresponding items that can be eliminated one against the other and neither will appear

The consolidated balance sheet is constructed simply by:

1. Adding together the component parts of the individual balance sheets. For example the Net Current Asset figure in the consolidated balance sheet will be:

$£150,000 + £50,000 = £200,000$

2. Eliminating any corresponding items. Investment in S plc shown in P's balance sheet and the Share Capital figure in S's balance sheet correspond not only in amount but also in nature since it was these shares in S that were actually acquired by virtue of P's investment. These amounts, therefore, can be eliminated one against the other and neither will appear in the consolidated balance sheet

| P plc Group consolidated balance sheet as at December 31, 20X0 | |
|---|---|
| Tangible assets (200,000 + 50,000) | 250,000 |
| Net current assets (150,000 + 50,000) | 200,000 |
| | 450,000 |
| Share capital (450,000 + nil) | 450,000 |

Notice that the share capital figure for the parent company is unaffected. This will always appears in the Shareholders Funds section of the consolidated balance sheet.

## Minority Interest

In instances where the amounts correspond in nature but not amount, for example where the parent company does not own 100% of the subsidiary's share capital, the cancellation procedure is still applied, but will not lead to the complete cancellation of the share capital figure from the subsidiary company's books. This simply means that an amount will be left to be incorporated in the consolidated balance sheet. This is done under the title "Minority Interest", reflecting the fact that entities outside the group own some of the share capital in one of the group subsidiaries.

This is explained by the following example

| P plc balance sheet as at December 31, 20X0 | | Y plc balance sheet as at December 31, 20X0 | |
|---|---|---|---|
| Tangible assets | 120,000 | Tangible assets | 60,000 |
| Investment in Y plc | 80,000[a] | | |
| Net current assets | 200,000 | Net current assets | 40,000 |
| | 400,000 | | 100,000 |
| Share capital | 400,000 | Share capital | 100,000[a] |

[a] Corresponding items that can be eliminated one against the other and neither will appear in the consolidating balance sheet. where P plc acquired 80% of the share capital of Y plc.

The principle of cancelling out corresponding items still applies. However, the amounts do not correspond exactly and so cancellation can only be partially achieved. Once the £80,000 "Investment in Y plc" has been cancelled against a similar amount from "Share Capital" in Y's balance sheet, £20,000 remains in the balance sheet of Y plc.

This element is known as "Minority Interest" and its interest is indicated in the consolidated balance sheet as follows:

| P plc Group consolidated balance sheet as at December 31, 20X0 | |
|---|---|
| Tangible assets (120,000 + 60,000) | 180,000 |
| Net current assets (200,000 + 40,000) | 240,000 |
| | 420,000 |
| Share capital | 400,000 |
| Minority interest | 20,000 |
| | 420,000 |

The basic principles of consolidated balance sheets can be summarized as follows:

1. The basic building blocks are the individual balance sheets of the parent and subsidiaries that comprise the group.

2. Corresponding items are eliminated against one another to the extent possible.

3. Any items remaining after this process are included in the consolidated balance sheet for the group, which is normally given the title of the parent company.

While these principles summarize the practical application of the acquisition accounting method, some specific aspects still needs to be addressed. In relation to the consolidated balance sheet these are:

- Pre-acquisition profits, and
- Goodwill

## Pre-acquisition Profits

While the commercial logic suggests that a company is acquiring all or part of the net assets of another when it invests in it, the accounting approach is to look, not at the net assets, but at the equivalent shareholders funds. In other words, the purchase of shares in a company also entitles the investing company to a share in the reserves that attach to that shareholding.

This raises the question of the level of reserves in a company at the date of acquisition, since the acquiring company will be entitled to a proportionate share of those reserves. Another way of looking at this is to say that in assessing the net assets that were acquired, accounting focuses on the equivalent shareholders funds figure, and reserves form a part of this. These reserves, therefore, must be considered as representative of the capital investment made and this has a number of implications for the accounting policies adopted under consolidation:

1. Reserves which represent part of what was purchased are termed "pre-acquisition profits".

2. They are considered "capital reserves" in nature, i.e., they can only be distributed under certain conditions, because to distribute them implies a reduction in the capital base. The new parent could effectively reimburse itself with all or most of the purchase price if they were to be distributable.

3. Payment of dividends out of pre-acquisition reserves should be set against "cost of acquisition" as it is essentially a partial reimbursement of the purchase price.

4. A distinction between pre- and post-acquisition profits will be meaningless as far as the Minority Interest is concerned.

## Goodwill

As outlined in Chapter 6, FRS 10, *Goodwill and Intangable Assets,* defines goodwill as "the difference between the cost of an acquired entity and the aggregate of the fair values of that entity's identifiable assets and liabilities." In simple terms, goodwill is the premium paid by one entity to acquire the separable net assets of another.

Since goodwill as an accounting issue arises most commonly in the context of an acquisition, i.e., where one entity is acquiring another, it is of particular relevance when dealing with consolidated accounts.

There are two issues:

1. The accounting **treatment** of goodwill. As outlined in Chapter 6, FRS 10 requires that goodwill be capitalized and, where appropriate, amortized.

2. Calculating the **amount** of goodwill. Using the same logic as applied to pre-acquisition profits, the share of shareholders funds acquired is taken as equivalent to the net assets acquired. Therefore the premium paid, i.e., goodwill can be taken to be the difference between the cost of the investment and the share capital plus equivalent reserves acquired as a result. Alternatively, as discussed later, the fair values of the separable net assets can be set against the fair value of the consideration.

Take the following example where P plc acquired 75% of the share capital of Z plc at a cost of £100,000.

| P plc balance sheet as at December 31, 20X0 | | Z plc balance sheet as at December 31, 20X0 | |
|---|---|---|---|
| Tangible assets | 100,000 | Tangible assets | 60,000 |
| Investment in S plc | 100,000 | | |
| Net current assets | 200,000 | Net current assets | 40,000 |
| | 400,000 | | 100,000 |
| Share capital | 300,000 | Share capital | 60,000 |
| Reserves | 100,000 | Reserves | 40,000 |
| Shareholders funds | 400,000 | Shareholders funds | 100,000 |

In this example P paid £100,000 to acquire a 75% share of Z, a company with a book value of only £100,000. Obviously, P has identified that the net assets of Z are worth more than their book value. Assuming book value to be the same as fair value (this is an important consideration and will be discussed later) the premium paid can be calculated as follows:

| Purchase consideration | | | £100,000 |
|---|---|---|---|
| Acquired | 75% share capital (£60,000 × 75%) | £45,000 | |
| | 75% reserves (£40,000 × 75%) | £30,000 | £75,000 |
| Goodwill | | | £25,000 |

Until recently, goodwill was normally written off against Reserves, one of the methods allowed under SSAP 22, *Accounting for Goodwill*. In effect this meant that goodwill rarely appeared on the face of the balance sheet of an acquiring company. FRS 10, *Goodwill and Intangible Assets* and FRS 11, *Impairment of Fixed Assets and Goodwill* require, however, that goodwill be included in the balance sheet and:

- Amortized over its useful economic life, or
- Reviewed on an annual basis for impairment in circumstances where it is decided either not to amortize it, or its useful life is deemed to exceed 20 years.

The impact of FRS 10 on accounting practice is illustrated in the following article.

## How They're Accounting for Goodwill on Acquisition

Davis Service Group (textile maintenance and site services) has attributed an indefinite estimated useful economic life to goodwill arising on the acquisition of Midland Laundry Group in its accounts for the year ended December 31, 1999. The accounting policy note on goodwill states that in accordance with FRS 10, Goodwill and Intangible Assets, goodwill arising on acquisitions from January 1, 1998 is capitalized as an intangible asset. Where such goodwill is regarded as having a limited estimated useful economic life, it is amortized through the p&l account on a straight-line basis over its life. Where it is regarded as having an indefinite life, it is not amortized but is subject to an annual impairment review and any impairment charged to the p&l account. The note goes on to say: "In estimating the useful economic life of goodwill, account is taken of the nature of the business acquired, the stability of the industry, the extent of continuing barriers to market entry and the expected future impact of competition: its life is regarded as indefinite where the goodwill is capable of continued measurement and the durability of the acquired business can be demonstrated."

With the exception of Midland Laundry, the directors consider that all Davis's acquisitions since January 1, 1998 have estimated useful economic lives for goodwill of between 5 and 10 years, depending on the business acquired. The acquisition of Midland Laundry on November 8, 1999 gave rise to goodwill of £24.3 million. In the continuation of the accounting policy note on goodwill, the group explains why this has been treated differently. The directors consider that the nature of the Midland Laundry business in terms of essential products and services supplied, which are not subject to changes in fashion, coupled with the fact that demand from an identified and stable customer base is likely to continue for the foresee-able future, supports the business's durability. This goodwill is therefore regarded as having an indefinite useful life and is not amortized. In order to give a true and fair view, the financial statements depart from the Companies Act's requirement to amortize goodwill over a finite period. Instead, an annual impairment review is undertaken and any impairment identified will be charged to the p&l account. It is not possible to identify the effect of this departure, because no finite life for goodwill can be identified. In line with most other companies, Davis eliminated goodwill arising on acquisitions prior to January 1, 1998 against reserves.

### Per Capita

Certainly some of the disclosures about how companies are accounting for goodwill after implementing FRS 10, for accounting periods ending on or after December 23, 1998, make interesting reading. For example, Capita (support services for the UK's public and private sectors) decided in 1998 to rebut the presumption that the useful economic life of purchased goodwill is limited to 20 years, as allowed under para 19 of the standard. This company's board determined that the goodwill arising on businesses acquired during that year had indefinite useful lives and hence did not amortize the goodwill.

In its financial statements for the year ended December 31, 1999, however, Capita has changed its mind. Accordingly, it has altered its accounting policy for goodwill arising on acquisitions made on or after January 1, 1998 and comparative figures have been restated where applicable. The note to the accounts showing the effect of this restatement states that, "generally, companies applying FRS 10 have chosen not to rebut the presumption that the useful economic life of purchased goodwill is limited to periods of 20 years or less. In addition, the significant number of recent acquisitions made by Capita have exacerbated the difficulty of continuing to measure goodwill as a consequence of those acquired businesses being merged with existing businesses'. The impact of the change in 1999 is a charge against profit of £4.115 million (vs. £0.986 million as restated) in respect of FRS 10....

Source: Accountancy, May, 2000.

## 2. Consolidated Profit and Loss Account

The basic principles outlined for the consolidated balance sheet also apply to the consolidated profit and loss account. Thus, the individual elements of the consolidated profit and loss account are constructed using the figures from the accounts of the individual companies comprising the group. And, once again, corresponding items such as inter-company transactions are eliminated.

Take the following example where the individual profit and loss accounts of H plc and its 100% subsidiary, S plc, are provided. During the year in question S plc sold £80,000 of goods to H plc, all of which H plc had subsequently sold on to outside customers.

|                                    | H plc   | S plc   |
|------------------------------------|---------|---------|
| Turnover                           | 600,000 | 500,000 |
| Cost of goods sold                 | 300,000 | 320,000 |
| Profit on activities before tax    | 300,000 | 180,000 |
| Taxation                           | 100,000 | 60,000  |
| Profit after tax                   | 200,000 | 120,000 |

The consolidated profit and loss account, after eliminating the inter-company trading, would look like this:

|  | H plc |
|---|---|
| Turnover (600 + 500 − 80) | 1,020,000 |
| Cost of goods sold (300 + 320 − 80) | 540,000 |
| Profit on activities before tax | 480,000 |
| Taxation | 160,000 |
| Profit after tax | 320,000 |

As is the case with the balance sheet, there are some specific items that may need to be adjusted for in the consolidated profit and loss account. The more common of these are:

- Minority interest's share of profits
- Inter-company dividends
- Unrealized profits on stocks traded between companies in the same group

## Minority Interest in Profits

The minority interest in a subsidiary will be entitled to a share of any of the profits made by that subsidiary. This will need to be calculated and indicated on the face of the profit and loss account, where it is shown as a deduction from "Profit after Tax".

For instance, assume that the data above apply except that S plc is only an 80% subsidiary of H plc. The calculation of Profit after Tax will remain exactly the same. However, it will be necessary to indicate that 20% of the after-tax profits of the subsidiary ($£120,000 \times 20\% = £24,000$) belongs to the minority interest. This will be presented as follows:

|  | H plc |
|---|---|
| Turnover (600 + 500 − 80) | 1,020,000 |
| Cost of goods sold (300 + 320 − 80) | 540,000 |
| Profit on activities before tax | 480,000 |
| Taxation | 160,000 |
| Profit after tax | 320,000 |
| Minority interest | 24,000 |
|  | 296,000 |

## Inter-company Dividends

Since H plc will hold shares in S plc it will be automatically entitled to receive dividends should these be declared by the subsidiary. Likewise, where a minority interest exists, such as in the last example, it too would be entitled to receive dividends.

Following on from the example above where H plc owns 80% of ordinary shares of S plc, and assuming that S plc declares a dividend of £40,000, the following workings would need to precede the construction of the consolidated profit and loss account:

- The total profit of S plc available for distribution is £120,000. S plc's profit and loss account will show a dividend declared of £40,000.

- Of this £40,000 dividend, £32,000 will go to H plc. This will appear in H plc's profit and loss account as "dividends receivable", but in the consolidation process it will be eliminated against the equivalent "dividend payable" figure in the accounts of S plc. The remaining £8,000 will be recorded in the consolidated account books as a deduction from amounts due to minority interest.

### Unrealized Profits on Stocks Traded Between Companies in a Group

In the example above where S plc sold goods worth £80,000 to its parent it was necessary to eliminate these from the consolidated Turnover and Cost of Goods figures, respectively. The important point was that none of these goods remained within the group, i.e., H plc had sold these goods to outside parties, thus realizing a cash benefit to the group as a whole. If there was no requirement that such inter-company trading be eliminated then the possibility would exist for a group to generate spurious sales/purchases between group companies with resultant inflated trading figures, yet no tangible benefits for the group as a whole.

This is not to suggest, however, that there are not legitimate transactions of this kind. Indeed, such symbiotic trading relationships often explain why one company acquires another. In the normal course of trading relationships between companies within a group, therefore, it is likely that there will be a network of trade dealings. Nevertheless, as far as the commercial reality is concerned, only when there is trading activity with entities outside of the group does any transaction occur which should be shown in the group accounts.

A complication arises, however, in circumstances where one company has supplied goods to another within the group but some of these goods remain in stock at the end of the year. Since inter-company trading is usually conducted at a mark-up, the closing stock figure in the company which has acquired these goods will include an unrealized profit figure, and consequently, an unrealized profit will be included in the group accounts. The amount of such "unrealized profits" must, therefore be removed from the consolidated accounts.

For instance, S plc sells goods costing £300 to its parent, H plc, for £400. However, all of these goods remained in the stock of H plc at the end of the financial year. The sale, purchase and unrealized profit recorded in the individual company accounts of H plc and S plc will not be affected. However, because the group has not realized any change in its resources it will be necessary to eliminate the corresponding sale and purchase. It will also be necessary to adjust for the fact that the closing stock figure of £400 includes an unrealized profit of £100. This will be achieved by simply reducing the closing stock figure to £300 in the consolidated accounts, thus reducing profit and closing stock figure in the consolidated balance sheet.

## Fair Values

One of the problems historically with acquisition accounting was the scope that it gave acquiring companies to manipulate the values of the assets taken over when acquiring another company. The temptation was for companies to understate values such that depreciation charges would be lower, with consequent favourable impact on profits in future years. A related issue was the overstatement of provisions for future losses or reorganization costs in relation to any newly acquired subsidiary. To the extent that such provisions were subsequently shown to be excessive they resulted in credits to the consolidated profit and loss account, again resulting in increased profits.

FRS 7, *Fair values in acquisition accounting*, was introduced specifically to counter these practices. Its objective is "to ensure that when a business entity is acquired by another, all the assets and liabilities that existed in the acquired entity at the date of acquisition are recorded at fair values reflecting their condition at that date; and that all changes to the acquired assets and liabilities, and the resulting gains and losses, that arise after control of the acquired entity has passed to the acquirer are reported as part of the post-acquisition financial performance of the acquiring group".

This process requires the identification of fair values for the identifiable assets and liabilities of the acquired entity as well as the consideration. The difference between these and the cost of acquisition is recognized as goodwill (or negative goodwill) which is treated in accordance with FRS 10.

In determining fair values, FRS 7 sets out a number of guiding principles, the most important of which are:

- The cost of acquisition is the amount of cash or cash equivalents paid and the fair value of other purchase consideration given by the acquirer, together with the expenses of the acquisition.

- Assets and liabilities recognized in the allocation of fair values should be those of the acquired entity that existed at the date of acquisition. They should be measured at fair values that reflect the conditions at the date of the acquisition. These will usually be based on market values.

- Liabilities of the acquired entity should not include provisions for future operating losses.

- Fair values should be based on the value at which an asset or liability could be exchanged in an arm's length transaction. The fair value of monetary items should take into account the amounts expected to be received or paid and their timing.

- Costs of reorganization and integrating the business acquired, whether they relate to the acquired entity or the acquiring group, should be dealt with as post-acquisition costs and should not affect the fair values at the date of acquisition.

As the following example demonstrates, under the provisions of FRS 7 much of the scope for the manipulation of profits and reserves has been eliminated.

P plc acquired 80% of the ordinary share capital of S plc on December 31, 20X0 for £800,000. The net assets of S plc had a book value of £600,000 on that date.

The following information to the net assets of S plc is relevant:

- The factory included in the accounts at a book value of £200,000 has recently been revalued at £400,000, but no entry has yet been made to incorporate this amount.

- The fair value of closing stock is reckoned to be £25,000 less than currently stated in the accounts.

- A decision to close one section of the company's operations has been made. The anticipated costs of this are £20,000 but no provision has yet been made.

Under FRS 7 the fair value of S plc's net assets at the date of acquisition will be:

| | |
|---|---|
| Book value | £600,000 |
| Revaluation of property | £200,000 |
| Revaluation of stock | (£25,000) |
| | £775,000 |

The amount paid was goodwill, therefore, was:

| | |
|---|---|
| Fair value of consideration | £800,000 |
| Net assets acquired | £620,000 (£775,000 × 80%) |
| Goodwill | £180,000 |

This amount will be capitalized and amortized.

## Merger Accounting

Where the criteria outlined in FRS 6 regarding mergers are satisfied, then the merger accounting method can be applied. This is a straightforward and uncomplicated method. Its essential characteristics can be summarized as follows:

- The financial statements of the combining companies are aggregated, and presented as though the combining entities had always been part of the same reporting entity.

- As a result, even in circumstances where the merger takes place during the financial year the group accounts for the merged entity will contain the combined results for the full financial year.

- The accounting policies of the combining entities should be adjusted so that there is uniformity of practice.

- It is not necessary for the assets and liabilities to be amended to their fair values.

- Any difference between the nominal value of the shares issued (plus the fair value of any other consideration given), and the nominal value of the shares received in exchange, is not to be treated as goodwill. Instead, it should be shown as a movement in reserves in the consolidated financial statements.

The following example demonstrates the essentially uncomplicated nature of merger accounting and the corresponding attraction of this approach for companies entering into business combinations.

A plc and B plc, companies working in the same industry, and of roughly equal size, decide to merge. This is to be achieved by the shareholders in B plc, which will subsequently be dissolved, taking shares in A plc on a one-for-one basis.

The balance sheets of the two companies on the date of the merger were as follows

|  | A plc | B plc |
|---|---|---|
| Net assets | 15,000 | 12,000 |
| Ordinary shares (£1) issued and fully paid | 10,000 | 10,000 |
| Reserves | 5,000 | 2,000 |
|  | 15,000 | 12,000 |

The fair values of the net assets at the date of acquisition were:

A plc                £20,000
B plc                £18,000

The merger method will produce the following balance sheet

|  | A plc |
|---|---|
| Net assets | 27,000 |
| Ordinary shares (£1) issued and fully paid | 20,000 |
| Reserves | 7,000 |
|  | 27,000 |

As this example illustrates, the merger accounting method requires little more than an amalgamation of the financial statements of the constituent companies. The attractions of the merger method can be summarized as follows:

1. Goodwill and fair values are not an issue as the view is that there is no "real" change of ownership, simply a pooling of interests.

2. Shares issued in a share-for-share merger are recorded at nominal value, unlike the acquisition accounting method which would raise a share premium account to record any premium in the event of the acquisition being funded in whole or part by an issue of shares.

3. Revenue reserves of the participating companies continue to be classified as distributable. This is an important consideration for many acquiring companies as the acquisition accounting method places considerable restrictions on the capacity of acquiring companies to access these reserves.

## Associates and Joint Ventures

It is possible for companies to enter into relationships with other companies, which, while more formal than arms-length trading relationships, are not sufficiently substantial to rank with those discussed earlier.

## Associates

Companies legislation provides that an entity holding 20% or more of the voting rights in another entity should be presumed to exercise a significant influence over that other entity unless the contrary is shown.

FRS 9, *Associates and joint ventures*, moves away from this rather arbitrary threshold and introduces other criteria. An associate is defined by FRS 9 as "an entity (other than a subsidiary) in which another entity (the investor) has a participating interest and over whose operating and financial policies the investor exercises a significant influence". The two critical terms are, therefore, participating interest and significant influence.

"Participating influence" is defined as "any interest held in the shares of another entity on a long-term basis for the purpose of securing a contribution to the investor's activities by the exercise of control or influence arising from or related to that interest".

An entity is deemed to be exercising "significant influence" if it is "actively involved and is influential in the direction of its investee through its participation in policy decisions covering aspects of policy relevant to the investor, including decisions on strategic issues such as:

1. The expansion or contraction of the business, participation in other entities or changes in products, markets and activities of its investee; and

2. Determining the balance between dividend and reinvestment".

### Equity Accounting

Where such a relationship is established then this must be reflected in the accounts of the investor. The accounting method developed to properly reflect the relationship between an investing entity and an associate is called equity accounting. It has the following characteristics:

- It brings an investment into its investor's financial statements initially at its cost, identifying any goodwill arising.
- The carrying amount of the investment is adjusted in each period by the investor's share of the results of its investee less any amortization or write-off for goodwill, the investor's share of any relevant gains or losses, and any other changes in the investee's net assets including distributions to its owners, for example by dividend.
- The investor's share of its investee's results is recognized in its profit and loss account. The investor's cash flow statement includes the cash flows between the investor and its investee, for example relating to dividends and loans.

The main characteristics of the equity accounting method, therefore, are that it results in the following being included in the investor's accounts:

1. **Profit and loss account**: the share of the associate's profits to which its participating interest entitles it.
2. **Balance sheet**: the net assets that underlie the investment in the associate.

## Joint Ventures

Companies can often join with other companies in order to create another entity. This is termed a joint venture. Usually such an entity is created simply to manage one specific project or contract and is often dissolved immediately upon completion of the project or contract. However, in many businesses, such as project management or construction, joint venture activity can form a substantial part of a company's activity.

For this reason the accounting treatment of joint ventures can often be quite significant. Under FRS 9 a joint venture is one in which the reporting entity "holds an interest on a long-term basis and is jointly controlled by the reporting entity and one or more other venturers under a contractual arrangement."

A reporting entity jointly controls a venture with one or more other entities "if none of the entities alone can control that entity but all together can do so and decisions on financial and operating policy essential to the activities, economic performance and financial position of that venture require each venturer's consent."

### Gross Equity Accounting

Joint ventures must be accounted for using the Gross Equity method. Under this approach investments in joint ventures should be treated as fixed asset investments and shown either at cost, less any amounts written off, or at valuation in the investor's individual financial statements.

In fact, the gross equity method is substantially the same as the equity method used for associates, with the following modifications:

- In the consolidated profit and loss account the investor's share of its joint ventures' turnover should be shown but not as part of group turnover. In the segmental analysis, the investor's share of its joint venture's turnover should be clearly distinguished from the turnover for the group itself.

- In the consolidated balance sheet the investor's share of the gross assets and liabilities underlying the net equity amount included for joint ventures should be shown.

---

**In practice:**

---

*Racal Responds to New Standards*

*Racal Electronics has made a number of changes in accounting policies following the introduction of new standards, and spells them out clearly in note 1 to its interim report for the half year ended October 9, 1998.*

*Racal has implemented FRS 9, Associates and Joint Ventures, during this period, and as a consequence the group's investments in Archer Communications Systems Ltd, International Optical Network LLC and Global Telematics plc are now included in the consolidated p&l account and consolidated balance sheet, respectively. Comparatives have been restated to reflect this change.*

*Source: Accountancy, February, 1999.*

---

## Related Party Transactions

FRS 8, *Related Party Disclosure*, was produced in response to concerns that the "true and fair" requirement was being compromised by companies disguising transactions that were not "arms length", but were in fact with related parties.

Two or more parties are related parties when at any time during the financial period:

- One party has either direct or indirect control of the other party; or

- The parties are subject to common control from the same source; or

- One party has influence over the financial and operating policies of the other party to an extent that that other party might be inhibited from pursuing at all times its own separate interests; or

- The parties, in entering a transaction, are subject to influence from the same source to such an extent that one of the parties to the transaction has subordinated its own separate interests.

A good example of a related party transaction that would need to be disclosed would be the granting of a loan to a director of the company. Another would be trading relationships with an associate company.

## Disclosures

The FRS is concerned primarily with information being provided for users by means of additional disclosure. It requires the following to be disclosed:

- Names of the related parties.

- Description of the relationship.

- The monetary amount involved, along with any outstanding balances or provisions at the balance sheet date.

- Any other information necessary to enable a user to more fully understand the financial statements.

Disclosure is not required in the following circumstances:

- Intra-group transactions and balances eliminated in consolidated financial statements.

- Where a parent undertaking provides related party disclosures in its own financial statements when those statements are presented with consolidated financial statements of its group.

- In the financial statements of subsidiary undertakings, 90% or more of whose voting rights are controlled within the group, in relation to transactions with entities that are part of the group or investees of the group qualifying as related parties provided that the consolidated financial statements in which that subsidiary is included are publicly available.

## *Summary*

Mergers and acquisitions are key vehicles for corporate growth in the UK. Consequently, an understanding of the accounting treatment of the business combinations that result will be critical when trying to analyse and interpret the financial performance and position of large corporate entities. Likewise, the incidence of associates and joint ventures has increased in recent years and played a significant role in generating growth and wealth increases in large companies.

The accounting treatment and disclosure requirements attaching to groups are extensive. To a degree they are also complex, and consolidated accounts can often seem daunting. However, it is important not to lose sight of the fact that consolidated accounts are essentially nothing more than a combination of the individual accounts of the group's constituent companies.

The accounting methods developed to deal with each of these forms of corporate relationship are:

- **Acquisition**: acquisition method
- **Merger**: merger method
- **Associate**: equity method
- **Joint venture**: gross equity method

In analysing and interpreting group accounts it is important to be aware that at a strategic and operational level a group is often more than the sum of its individual parts. Economies of scale, symbiotic trading relationships and the possibilities offered by greater geographic reach must be factored into any consideration of a group's position, performance and prospects. This, however, involves nothing more than what has been consistently advocated by this text: informed and sensitive contextualization.

## Review Questions

### Question 1
Explain why merger and acquisition activity is so prevalent in the Anglo-American world.

### Question 2
Identify the unique characteristics of an acquisition.

### Question 3
Explain the difference between the concepts of "control" and "dominant influence" and the reason for the emergence of the latter as a critical consideration when determining the nature of inter-company relationships.

### Question 4
List the criteria for determining whether or not a company is a parent of another company.

### Question 5
Distinguish between the following:

- Wholly-owned subsidiaries and partly-owned subsidiaries
- Interest and control/dominant influence

### Question 6
Explain the main features of the acquisition accounting method. Give examples of how it operates in practice.

### Question 7
Explain how the acquisition accounting method deals with each of the following and explain the rationale behind the accounting practice:

- Minority interest
- Pre-acquisition profits
- Goodwill
- Inter-company dividends
- Unrealized profits on stocks traded between companies in the same group

### Question 8
List the principal characteristics of the merger accounting method and explain why it can be a more attractive option than acquisition accounting for business combinations.

### Question 9
Define the term "Fair Value" and explain why it is such an important concept in relation to business combinations.

### Question 10
Explain the main provisions of FRS 9, *Associates and joint ventures*.

# Case Studies

## Case 1

Curly plc is a publishing company based in Birmingham. In recent years it has embarked on a programme of growth by acquisition. Based on the following information, prepare a consolidated profit and loss account for the Curly plc group for the year ended December 31, 20X3, together with a consolidated balance sheet as at December 31, 20X3.

On January 1, 20X1 it purchased 300,000 £1 ordinary shares in Wee Ltd for £400,000. At the date of acquisition the balance on Revenue Reserves was £100,000. On January 1, 20X3 it purchased 32,000 £1 ordinary shares in Moe Ltd for £30,000.

You have been provided with the following summarized final accounts for each of the three companies at December 31, 20X3

Balance Sheets as at December 31, 20X3 (£,000)

|                               | Curly plc | Wee Ltd | Moe Ltd |
|-------------------------------|-----------|---------|---------|
| Tangible fixed assets         | 3,300     | 500     | 100     |
| Investments in other companies| 430       | –       | –       |
| Net current assets            | 200       | 90      | 10      |
|                               | 3,930     | 590     | 110     |
| £1 ordinary shares            | 2,000     | 400     | 80      |
| Revenue reserves              | 1,930     | 190     | 30      |
|                               | 3,930     | 590     | 110     |

Profit and Loss Accounts for the Year Ended December 31, 20X3 (£,000)

|                                          | Curly plc | Wee Ltd | Moe Ltd |
|------------------------------------------|-----------|---------|---------|
| Turnover                                 | 6,000     | 2,500   | 600     |
| Operating profit                         | 800       | 400     | 80      |
| Proposed dividend receivable from Wee Ltd| 75        | –       | –       |
| Proposed dividend receivable from Moe Ltd| 4         | –       | –       |
| Interest payable                         | (50)      | (30)    | (10)    |
| Profit before taxation                   | 829       | 370     | 70      |
| Taxation                                 | 400       | 180     | 30      |
| Profit after taxation                    | 429       | 190     | 40      |
| Dividend proposed                        | 300       | 100     | 10      |
| Retained profit for year                 | 129       | 90      | 30      |

You have also been made aware of the following:
1. This holding in Moe Ltd is sufficient to give Curly plc significant influence but not dominant influence. Curly plc does not have the right to appoint or remove a majority of the members of the board of directors of Moe Ltd.
2. Dragon plc, which owns the remaining 25% of shares in Wee Ltd, has approached Curly plc with an offer to purchase its shares in Wee Ltd for £2 per share.

(The answer to this question is available on the web site for this text.)

## Case 2

The Financial Accounting Standards Board (FASB) has recently decided to remove the requirement that firms amortize goodwill. As the following article outlines, this will have an immediate effect on the financial statements of those companies that now choose not to amortize. Discuss the likely implications of this change, the extent to which it is motivated by political considerations and the consequences for international accounting practice.

## A Goodwill Gesture from FASB

### New Amortization Rules May Help Mergers – and Stocks, by David Henry in New York

The economy may be faltering, but corporate earnings are about to get a cosmetic pick-me-up. In the biggest change in accounting rules in years, the FASB has announced that as of July 1 companies will no longer have to amortize goodwill. Gone will be those yearly reductions to earnings to reflect premiums companies paid for assets over fair value. Corporate bottom lines will look better without any change in sales, cash flow, or management.

Wall Street is excited, and for good reason. Investors will see higher stock prices, in part, because more companies will be encouraged to launch take-overs. Now companies hesitate to make deals heavy with goodwill because of the hit to earnings. With that penalty removed, they will have less fear that deals will hurt their stocks. Also, investment bankers expect an easier time persuading corporations to buy one another. "This will drive strong M&A volume," predicts Gary Posternack, managing director at Lehman Brothers Inc.

How much better will earnings look? The impact will vary widely. For companies loaded with goodwill and short on profits, earnings per share could rocket. For Coca-Cola Enterprises Inc., the bottler, earnings should look 122% better this year, according to investment bank UBS Warburg. For Pepsi Bottling Group Inc., the improvement will be only 30%; for PepsiCo Inc., 4%.

## Fess Up

The big gainers skew the picture for the whole market. If the change had happened last year for companies in the Standard&Poor's 500-stock index, the average gain in earnings would have been 17%. But the median gain would have been only 4%, estimates Trevor J. Harris, managing director at Morgan Stanley Dean Witter and a Columbia Business School accounting professor who was instrumental in persuading FASB to make the change. Exact numbers are impossible to get. Many companies have yet to disclose just how much they have been amortizing. UBS Warburg chief global strategist Edward M. Kerschner estimates the S&P will get a 5% to 6% boost.

FASB's new stance is in response to widespread dissatisfaction with accounting for mergers and acquisitions. Most tech companies and analysts who follow them already disregard charges for goodwill amortization. They say current rules wrongly assume goodwill always represents an overpayment that should penalize earnings. Amortizing it obscures real cash profits. The new rule will require companies to show goodwill on their balance sheets. Having it there will help investors hold officers responsible for how much they pay to do deals. If something happens to reduce the value of an acquisition, companies will have to admit it and mark down goodwill with one-time charges. Champion investor Warren Buffett recommended the approach last year. FASB will issue guidelines for when goodwill must be revaluated.

But do not expect stock prices to go up as much as earnings, even in industry sectors that are not already ignoring the amortization. "The companies are the same as before," says Chuck Hill, research director at First Call Corp. "Theoretically, price-earnings multiples should come down instead, but I do not think the market is that sophisticated." While many institutional investors already add back estimates of goodwill amortization, others find that too tedious. Hill predicts a blend of slightly higher stock prices and slightly lower p-e ratios.

Still, some corporate executives remain convinced that their stocks will go up because of the change. Dominion Resources Inc., for instance, has stated that it will increase annual earnings by 8%, or 34 cents. At a price-to-earnings ratio of 13, that could mean an additional $4.45 a share, the company notes on its Internet site. "We are valued on net income and we think we will see a change in valuation," explains Dominion's controller, Steven A. Rogers.

## Shopping Sprees?

Despite all the celebratory tone surrounding the new FASB stance, there is clearly a downside. Since acquiring companies will not have to worry about seeing their earnings per share decline because of goodwill amortization, they will be more likely to make bad deals. And another big risk is that deal-happy executives will try to increase earnings through a flurry of dubious acquisitions, as happened in the 1960s, says David F. Hawkins, a Harvard Business School professor and Merrill Lynch&Co. accounting analyst. "There'll be companies that go on an acquisition binge," says Hawkins. FASB tries to thwart that result in details of the rule. Its success will depend on auditors holding executives to the standard, never a sure bet.

Even so, the new FASB rule will be like a shot in the arm to most companies. And that, in turn, is sure to give a welcome boost to investors.

**Estimated boost to earnings in 2001 from new accounting rules**

| | |
|---|---|
| Coca-Cola enterprises | 122% |
| Tribune | 44% |
| Borg-Warner | 42% |
| Vitesse semiconductor | 41% |
| Pepsi bottling group | 30% |
| International paper | 21% |
| Gannett | 19% |
| Intel | 16% |
| Flextronics | 7% |
| Kimberly-Clark | 3% |

Data: UBS Warburg

Source: Business Week: February 5, 2001.

When you have completed this chapter you will understand:

- The accounting treatment of taxation, pensions, leases and foreign currency transactions.

- That changes have been made or proposed in the accounting treatment of several of these items in recent years.

- That much of the motivation for recent changes in specific areas of accounting practice in the UK has derived from moves towards international harmonisation.

## Removing the Transatlantic Divide

### The Harmonisation of Accounting Standards has Received a Fillip With the Removal of Two Building Blocks of Financial Reporting, by Deborah Hargreaves and Michael Peel

Global harmonisation of accounting standards has taken two transatlantic steps forward with the news that both the UK and US are prepared, in two specific cases, to give up business-friendly domestic rules in the interests of international convergence and more transparent accounting. Both issues; accounting for tax in the UK, and for mergers and acquisitions in the US; are fundamental building blocks of financial reporting. The removal of a transatlantic divide on both offers investors comparability, and perhaps reminds them how uneven the present system is.

Sir David Tweedie, chairman of the UK's Accounting Standards Board, was brutally honest when he announced proposals that would see some leading companies face a sharp drop in reported earnings as they are required to account fully for tax liabilities. This issue, "deferred tax", is one of a handful of accounting treatments jealously guarded by UK business. Sir David's policy, which has the backing of leading companies, is to fight to preserve an "opt out" from international harmonisation, led by the International Accounting Standards Committee, where and when the UK believes its methods are best.

But it is now widely recognised that such an "opt out" is never going to be permanent. The idea is that the UK would lobby to bring the international code into line, using its representation on the IASC. If this proves unsuccessful then the UK would have to join the majority eventually. Harmonisation is seen as an accounting virtue in itself.

The suspicion must be that Sir David wants to save the "opt out" option for things which will really upset UK industry, such as accounting for pensions. So he announced that the UK could no longer "fly in the face" of international practice on tax. Under the proposals UK companies would no longer be able to disregard for accounting purposes tax bills that they judge will not have to be paid on the grounds that they are continuously offset by capital allowances on investments.

This is not just an academic point. While it is too early to estimate the impact on individual UK companies, analysts have in the past forecast that accounting fully for tax could cut the net asset value of some by up to a third. Such alterations reflect only an accounting change, a technical distinction that often fails to impress finance directors let alone investors. But Sir David's proposals do not exactly follow international practice and industry is expected to welcome concessions.

His move was swiftly followed by news that the US Financial Accounting Standards Board (FASB) was to press ahead with its intention to ban "pooling of interests" accounting, a much-loved method which has helped fire the 1990s boom in mergers. Ed Jenkins, chairman of FASB, is as enthusiastic as Sir David. The differences between accounting for M&A activity on either side of the Atlantic have often been cited as an example of how accounting can alter economic behaviour...

...A pattern is emerging. Difficult decisions about the future accounting are being taken at international level, a forum where the standard-setters are free from the pressures of dealing directly with constituents. Then each jurisdiction edges towards the agreed goals. It is a complex procedure, but it is working.

Source: Financial Times, September 16, 1999.

## Introduction

As this text has consistently emphasised, and as this opening account amply demonstrates, accounting rules emerge within a political context. That is, they are not neutral, accurate techniques, but the end result of vigorous lobbying and debate where there is rarely unanimity.

This chapter deals with the generally accepted accounting practices relating to a number of technically difficult areas. However, while some technical detail is supplied, the emphasis is less on the specific requirements and more on the principles involved. The international context within which changes in practice are taking place is also introduced. This will be dealt with in more detail in Chapter 15.

The specific areas covered are:

- Taxation
- Pensions
- Leases (including Sale and Leaseback arrangements)
- Foreign Currency transactions

# Taxation

The importance of taxation and the manner in which it appears in financial statements has been alluded to already in Chapter 6. In this chapter the focus will be on the more detailed aspects of its calculation and presentation.

As they are separate legal entities companies are liable to corporation tax in their own right under the Finance Act 1965, as modified by the Finance Act 1973. The emphasis, therefore, is on this tax rather than PAYE and VAT, which derive not from a company's legal status, but from the fact that it engages in trading or service activity.

## Corporation Tax

The tax to which the corporate profits of UK resident companies are subject is known as Corporation Tax (CT). The system involves the application of a fixed rate of tax to the taxable profits (income and capital gains) of a company. Companies may also have income taxable abroad in which case they will also be liable to overseas tax.

For corporation tax purposes the financial year runs from April 1 to March 31 (unlike the Income Tax year, which runs from April 6 to April 5 following). Corporation Tax rates are normally announced in the preceding budget. If a company's accounting year straddles two financial years, then the profits are subdivided on a time basis and subjected to the rate appropriate to each.

For instance, the Corporation Tax rate for 1999 (i.e., financial year April 1, 1999–March 2000) was 30%. The rate for 1998 was 31%. A company with an accounting year ending December 31 ,1999 and profits of £12 million would attract the following liability:

| | |
|---|---|
| January–March 1999: (£12 million × 3/12) @ 31% | £930,000 |
| April–December 1999: (£12 million × 9/12) @ 30% | £2,700,000 |
| Tax liability | £3,630,000 |

Since 1999 large companies pay their corporation tax quarterly.

Where a company's taxable profits are less than £300,000 the small companies' rate (20% since 1999) applies. In circumstances where taxable profits are greater than £300,000, but less than £1,500,000, marginal relief can be claimed.

# Advance Corporation Tax (ACT)

The UK operates an imputation system of taxation, i.e., it recognises that recipients of dividends receive their money out of profits that have already been subjected to taxation, and therefore, imputes to them a credit in respect of such tax. Until April 1999 companies which distributed dividends were required to pay Advance Corporation Tax (ACT) to take account of the fact that individuals were usually in a position to claim the benefits of such credits before the main CT liability would have been paid.

In effect, ACT required the payment of an element of CT in advance. This could lead to various complicated calculations of amounts recoverable by companies over future periods. From April 1999, however, the position has been simplified and recipients of dividends now simply receive a 10% tax credit. Basic rate taxpayers need pay no further tax while higher rate taxpayers are liable to an extra 25% on the gross dividend, i.e., dividend + tax credit. They are then allowed the tax credit as a deduction from this extra liability.

---

**In practice:**

---

*Abolition of ACT Increased Dividends and Borrowings*

*Companies are borrowing more to continue to maintain a high level of dividend payments even though profits are falling, warns an official report, reveals The Times.*

*Companies borrowed a record £39 billion in 1999, according to an article to be published in the latest issue of Economic Trends. It predicts that borrowing will remain high during 2000, driven partly by the need to pay for the third generation mobile licences auctioned by the Government earlier in the year.*

*Data released by National Statistics at the end of July showed profitability levels falling to a five-year low.*

*The report argues that companies maintaining their dividend payments, despite falling profits, are adding to the funding figures. Dividend payments increased in the second quarter of 1999 after the abolition of advance corporation tax (ACT), and remained steady throughout the rest of the year.*

*The study also revealed that the tax payments by non-financial corporations fell 15% in 1999, although this was mainly because of the abolition of ACT and the fact that utility companies had to pay windfall tax instalments in both 1997 and 1998. The mainstream corporation tax bill rose by nearly a third.*

*Source: AccountingWEB, August 11, 2000.*

---

Until 1999 therefore, the figure for "Taxation" in the profit and loss account comprised of these three elements, i.e., CT, ACT and overseas tax. With the effective removal of ACT this is now not included in the charge.

## FRS 16, Current Tax

In 1999 the ASB introduced FRS 16, *Current Tax*, with effect for accounting periods ending on or after March 23, 2000. This reflected the recent changes introduced by Finance Acts, in particular the fact that the imputation system, upon which much of SSAP 8, *The treatment of taxation under the imputation system in the accounts of companies*, was predicated, was now less significant.

The principal effect of FRS 16 is to change the way in which tax associated with dividend income is accounted for. Thus, dividends received from other UK companies need no longer be reported "gross", i.e., inclusive of the associated tax credit. They need now only be reported "net". In addition, dividends received from overseas need only be reported "gross" where they have been subjected to a withholding tax.

In terms of disclosure FRS 16 provides that the current tax expense (or income) should be analyzed between UK tax and foreign tax, with further analysis indicating amounts estimated for the current period and that portion arising from any prior year adjustments. This supplements the provisions of CA85 which require that tax be shown in the profit and loss account under the following categories:

1. Tax on profit or loss on ordinary activities
2. Tax on extraordinary profit or loss
3. Other taxes

Notes to the accounts are required to provide the following details:

- The amount of UK corporation tax
- The extent of double tax relief
- The amount of UK income tax
- The amount of foreign tax charged to revenue

## Deferred Tax

In many continental European countries the accounting and tax codes are intimately related. If anything, tax codes take precedence. In fact, elements of accounting practice in countries like Germany countries can be shown to have been dictated by tax law.

In the UK, however, and in many other English-speaking countries, there has never been this type of relationship, with the result that tax and accounting principles often diverge. One of the consequences of this is that the "profit" computed by company accountants will be based on principles and concepts not entirely consistent with those employed by the taxation authorities.

Consequently, although they will accept the financial statements as a starting point for their computations, the Inland Revenue will insist on making certain adjustments. For example, the financial accounts may contain a deduction in respect of entertainment expenses, but Revenue will refuse to recognise this and insist that it be added back.

These differences between the Inland Revenue's approach and the accounting approach to the calculation of profit can be classified into two types:

- **Permanent differences**: these are adjustments, such as that made in respect of entertainment expenses which represent amendments which will never be reversed.

- **Timing differences**: these are defined as "differences between profits or losses as computed for tax purposes and results as stated in financial statements, which arise from the inclusion of items of income and expenditure in tax computations in periods different from those in which they are included in financial statements. Timing differences originate in one period and are capable of reversal in one or more subsequent periods." They represent changes made by the authorities that will reverse at some point in the future, i.e., they do not result from differences of principle, but from the basis upon which allowances are granted. The most common example arises from the refusal of the tax authorities to recognise depreciation as a deduction in calculating profits, insisting that their own equivalent, "capital allowances", be substituted. Since the amount claimed under the capital allowances calculation will normally be different from that claimed under the depreciation calculation, the taxable profit (and hence the tax due) will be different. Consequently, the CT liability indicated under "Creditors due within 1 year" may have to be amended as it is possible that some element of the tax charge will be deferred. However, while the amounts under the respective headings may differ in any one year, over the life of an asset it would be expected that they would reconcile. That is, the source of difference is due solely to timing differences. Tax that has been temporarily deferred in this way is known as "Deferred Tax".

The way in which deferred tax arises is illustrated in the following example.

A plc purchased machinery for £100,000 in 20X0. It operates a 50% straight-line depreciation policy for such assets. The capital allowance rates are 80% in year 1 and 20% in year 2 (for illustrative purposes only, these rates do not correspond to actual rates currently available). In 20X0 and 20X1 the company's profits, after depreciation, were £200,000. Assume a corporation tax rate of 30% in each year. Show how this would be accounted for in the accounts of A plc in both years.

**Accounts 20X0**

In this year the accounts show a profit before tax of £200,000. Since the CT rate is 30% the basic CT entry would appear to be.

Dr Profit and Loss a/c    £60,000 (shown in the p&l a/c as "Taxation for year").
Cr Corporation Tax a/c   £60,000 (shown in the balance sheet as "Creditor due
                                            within 1 year").

However, the balance sheet entry would be incorrect, as the amount indicated would not be due within the next 12 months since a portion of it would be deferred. This is because the Inland Revenue will insist on adjusting A plc's calculation of profit as it does not recognise depreciation and insists on replacing this with its own equivalent, capital allowances.

Therefore when A plc receives its CT demand it will be based on the following computation by the Inland Revenue:

| | |
|---|---|
| Profit for year per accounts | £200,000 |
| Add back: disallowed depreciation | £50,000 |
| | £250,000 |
| Less: capital allowances | £80,000 (£100,000 × 80%) |
| Taxable profits | £170,000 |
| Tax @ 30% | £51,000 |

The CT due within the next year therefore is only £51,000. In other words £9,000 is deferred and will only become payable when the advantage accruing to the company this year is reversed. Since CT rates are announced in advance, A plc would be expected to be able to calculate this figure.

Therefore, the proper double entry to reflect taxation for the year would actually be:

Dr Profit and Loss a/c    £60,000 (shown in the p&l a/c as "Taxation for year").
Cr Corporation Tax a/c   £51,000 (shown in the balance sheet as "Creditor due within 1 year").
Cr Deferred Tax a/c       £9,000   (shown in balance sheet as "Provisions for liabilities and charges").

**Accounts 20X1**

The benefit accruing to the company in 20X0 by virtue of the higher rate of capital allowances in that year will begin to reverse in 20X1. The accounts will again show a profit before tax of £200,000. As the CT rate is still 30% the basic CT charge is once again £60,000. However, the Inland Revenue computation will be:

| | |
|---|---|
| Profit for year per accounts | £200,000 |
| Add back: disallowed depreciation | £50,000 |
| | £250,000 |
| Less: capital allowances | £20,000 (£100,000 × 20%) |
| Taxable profits | £230,000 |
| Tax @ 30% | £69,000 |

The CT due within the next year therefore is £69,000, i.e., the £9,000 deferred in 20X0 is now due and must be shown as a liability under "Creditors due within 1 year".

The correct double entry to reflect taxation for the year would be:

Dr Profit and Loss a/c    £60,000 (shown in the p&l a/c as "taxation for year").
Dr Deferred Tax a/c       £9,000 (the balance on this account will now be "nil").
Cr Corporation Tax a/c   £69,000 (shown in the balance sheet as "Creditor due
                                             within 1 year").

---

**In practice:**

*Low Tax Charge Explained*

*In its finance report for the year ended April 30, 2000, Ashtead Group (equipment rental) explains why its tax charge is so low; the consolidated p&l account shows tax of only £4.9 million (10.2%) on a profit before tax of £48.1 million. Finance director Ian Robson notes that the tax rate has fallen from 12.1% in 1998/99 to 10.2% in 1999/2000: "This is a result of the continued investment in assets… with tax depreciation exceeding book depreciation, and the resolution of certain taxation contingencies for which provision had previously been made." Ashtead has continued to take a cautious attitude to deferred tax, and provided 33% (v 25%) of the full potential liability.*

*As far as the future is concerned, Robson explains that capital investment to date has provided the group with considerable tax deferment, both in the UK and the US, which operates similar provisions in respect of capital allowances. It is expected to lead to continued payment of tax at levels lower than the standard rate in the foreseeable future. The taxation note to the financial statements reveals that the £4.9 million tax charge is made up of: UK corporation tax at 30%; current year £1.4 million; adjustment in respect of prior year (£2.4 million); double tax relief (£0.1 million); overseas taxation; current year £0.3 million; and deferred taxation £5.7 million. The deferred taxation note shows a total provision at April 30, 2000 of £13.1 million against a full potential liability of £39.2 million.*

*Source: Accountancy: October, 2000.*

---

# Accounting for Deferred Taxation

Until recently the accounting treatment of deferred tax was covered by SSAP 15 (revised), *Accounting for Deferred Tax*. It was based on the premise outlined above that factors such as timing differences will result in some taxation being deferred.

The calculations in the example above are, however, relatively straightforward and are based on fairly simplistic assumptions about CT rates, capital allowances and whether or not liabilities will be deferred or eventually reverse.

In practice the calculation of deferred tax can be much more complex. Recognising this potential for complexity the literature has identified three different approaches when providing for deferred tax. SSAP 15, paragraphs 7–12, outlined these options as follows:

1. **Nil provision method**: this is based on the notion that only the tax payable in respect of a period should be charged in that period. If this method applies then there will be no provision for deferred tax. The rationale is that a tax liability arises on taxable profits, not accounting profits, and therefore it is necessary to provide tax only on taxable profits. In addition, any liability arising on timing differences will depend on the likelihood of future taxable profits and will therefore be difficult to quantify with any degree of certainty.

2. **Full provision method**: this is based on the principle that financial statements for a period should recognise the tax effects, whether current or deferred, of all transactions occurring in that period.

3. **Partial provision method**: this results in deferred tax being accounted for on the basis of the net amount by which it is probable that any payment of tax will be temporarily deferred as a result of timing differences which will reverse in the foreseeable future without being replaced. The partial provision approach recognises that, in circumstances where an enterprise is unlikely to reduce the scale of its operations significantly, it will usually have a continuing "stock" of timing differences as a result of which some element of tax liability will be deferred on an ongoing basis. Consequently, deferred tax has to be provided only where it is probable that tax will become payable as a result of the reversal of timing differences. It is based on an assessment of what will actually be the position. This method is consistent with the example above.

SSAP 15 adopted the partial provision approach and this is consistent with the earlier worked example. This was strongly supported by British industry which saw in this rather pragmatic scheme a source of competitive advantage over international competitors.

---

**In practice:**

The following extract from the Dixons Group plc 2000 Annual Report demonstrates the disclosures necessary in relation to deferred tax.

*Note 29: Provisions for Liabilities And Charges (Extract)*

| Additional information on deferred taxation | Group (£ million) | | Company (£ million) |
|---|---|---|---|
| | 2000 | 1999 | 2000 |
| *Deferred taxation for which provision has been made* | | | |
| Accelerated capital allowances | 10.4 | 8.7 | (0.1) |
| Other timing differences | 23.7 | 24.4 | (0.4) |
| Totals | 34.1 | 33.1 | (0.5) |
| *Potential amounts of deferred taxation for which no provision made* | | | |
| Accelerated capital allowances | 9.2 | 9.2 | – |
| Other timing differences | 31.9 | 30.1 | – |
| Total | 41.1 | 39.3 | – |

© *Dixons plc.*

## Recent Developments

Since 1978, when SSAP 15 was introduced, there have been considerable changes to the tax system. It has also become obvious that SSAP 15 is not in tune with generally accepted international practice. And while some of these issues have been addressed by means of a revision of SSAP 15, it has long been the intention of the ASB to bring UK practice more into line with international practice.

The first stage in this process was the circulation of a Discussion Paper, *Accounting for Tax*, in March 1995. In line with ASB policy this paper addressed accounting for tax from first principles, and, in the process dealt with the circumstances in which deferred tax arose, the different views of deferred tax and the alternative methods which flowed from such an analysis. These include:

- Flow-through method
- Full provision method
- Partial provision method

The Discussion Paper argued in favour of the full provision method and proposed that SSAP 15 be replaced with an FRS which favoured this approach. This would have the effect of requiring companies to recognise deferred tax if the relevant transactions or events have occurred by the balance sheet date. In other words, the more pragmatic partial provision approach, which sought to anticipate the probability that any payment of tax would be temporarily deferred as a result of timing differences and eventually reverse, was to be replaced. The effect would be to dramatically increase the deferred taxation provisions of many firms and consequently reduce profits.

The general response to the ASB proposals was negative. Most industry represen-tative bodies, in particular, continue to favour the partial provision method.

However, the adoption of a new standard by the IASC in 1996, IAS 12, *Income Taxes*, that required companies applying International Accounting Standards to provide for deferred tax using the full provision method highlighted the fact that the ASB was out of step with international practice.

The ASB found itself in something of a quandary. It admitted that there are certain advantages to the partial provision method. However, it not only conceded some of the arguments made against it, but envisaged a situation in which it becomes more irrelevant and less understood as more and more companies internationally adopt International Accounting Standards.

Anxious to conform to international practice, therefore, the ASB issued FRED 19, *Deferred Tax*, which incorporated the full provision method. In December 2000 this became FRS 19, *Deferred Tax*, which is to be implemented for financial statements relating to accounting periods ending on or after 23 January 2002.

The following extract hints at some of the opposition to this FRS and places it in the context of pressures to conform to the IASC equivalent, IAS 12, *Income Taxes*:

## Deferred Tax Standard Spearheads ASB's Twin Attack

As part of outgoing chairman Sir David Tweedie's plan to "clear the decks", the ASB today issued two new accounting standards, including one on deferred tax which could produce some nasty surprises in corporate balance sheets.

FRS 19 "Deferred Tax" will require companies to provide in full for tax liabilities rather than the partial provisioning they are currently permitted to use. Organisa-tions that have only partially (provided) could find that their paper profits take a hit as they boost the balance sheet liabilities to provide for tax due in the future. As if to soften the blow, the ASB has delayed implementation of FRS 19 until January 23, 2002, giving some breathing room for companies to make the necessary adjust-ments.

Sir David explained that the amendments to the existing deferred tax standard SSAP 15 were necessary because "what we do is banned internationally". He pointed out that the European Commission is pushing for mandatory use of Inter-national Accounting Standards (IAS) by 2005, so it was necessary to make the adjustment.

The ASB chairman's argument would have been more convincing if FRS 19 did not depart from international norms in several areas. The standard does not require deferred tax to be provided for when assets are revalued or adjusted to their market values when a business is acquired and allows long-term tax liabilities to be discounted. It also does not force companies to provide for a tax liability on over-seas profits that are not remitted back to the UK.

ACCA financial reporting expert Richard Martin failed to see the point of the ASB's hybrid approach to harmonisation. "We are not absolutely sure the ASB has made a convincing case to change things. If the ASB went for full harmonisation, that would be a justification. This is a position Sir David Tweedie thinks he may be able to sell over the next few years, in his new role (as IASC chairman), perhaps," said Martin. The 2002 implementation date was "not very long away", Martin added. UK companies would have to introduce the changes and immediately need to think about harmonising with IAS in 2005 if the European Commission's plans came into affect.

FRS 18, "Accounting Policies," was also published today...

Source: AccountingWEB, December 7, 2000.

## Pensions

Pension costs will constitute a substantial charge in the accounts of most companies. For this reason the manner in which they are accounted for can have a significant effect on financial results.

There are two principal types of pension scheme:

- **Defined benefit**: such a scheme guarantees a pension related to the average or final pay of the employee. It is the more common of the two schemes in the UK. Because it depends on future salary levels it is not always possible to estimate whether the contributions to the pension scheme will be sufficient to meet the eventual cost.

- **Defined contribution**: the pension is determined by the level of contributions and is a more straightforward approach for the accounting and actuarial systems. Under this method the employer makes agreed contributions to a pension scheme and the benefits paid will depend upon the funds available from these contributions and any investment earnings thereon. There is, therefore, little of the estimation and actuarial intervention characteristic of the defined benefit scheme.

Accounting for pensions, and especially defined benefit schemes, raises two key considerations:

1. The amount to be charged annually to the profit and loss account.
2. The amount at which the assets in the pension fund should be measured.

SSAP 24, *Accounting for pension costs*, which was the governing standard in this area until recently, required that companies account for pensions by ensuring that the cost of providing for the pension was spread over the working lives of the relevant employees. This strict application of the accruals principle, called the "actuarial approach", meant that even in years when there were no actual contributions, there might still be a charge in the profit and loss account. It also meant that the amount at which the pension funds were included in the balance sheet rarely corresponded to current value.

## FRS 17, Retirement Benefits

One of the grounds upon which SSAP 24 was criticised was that it allowed too many options and estimates in determining the amounts to be included in relation to pensions. Responding to these criticisms, the ASB issued a Discussion Paper, *Pension Costs in the Employer's Financial Statements*, in 1995. It sought responses from interested parties on two alternatives to accounting for pension costs:

- The actuarial approach followed by SSAP 24

- A market value approach

As had been the case with the Board's request for feedback in relation to deferred tax, the responses expressed strong preferences for the existing approach. Nevertheless, in another example of the real nature of standard setting process, when the IASC issued IAS 19 (revised), which provided for a market value approach, the ASB availed of the opportunity and promptly issued a second Discussion Paper, *Aspects of Accounting for Pension Costs*. This set out its response to IAS 19 (revised) and sought views on four specific issues: the use of market values, the discount rate, the treatment of actuarial gains and losses and the treatment of past service costs.

Declaring, after analysing the responses, that a majority now favoured the market value approach, the Board then issued its own FRED 20, *Retirement Benefits*. The extent of the opposition to what the ASB was attempting is hinted at in the following account:

## Tweedie's Gladiator Show: ASB Chief Comes Out Fighting in Defence of Reform of Pensions Accounting Rules

Sir David Tweedie took a trip to the circus this week and found himself the target of an ambush. The venue was Finsbury Circus and the occasion a lunch that turned into an inquisition on Sir David's plan to reform the way companies account for pension schemes.

It made for compelling theatre. The Accounting Standards Board chairman sat like a venerable lion at one end of the table of 12, pawing away questions from actuaries, business people and journalists. By the end, he had provided a revealing snapshot of the ASB's latest thinking on its controversial plan. He gave an idea of where the board might give ground and where it would stand firm. Above all, he growled defiance at those who attacked the proposals on the grounds that they would change the way companies behaved.

The thrust of the ASB plan is to make companies better reflect the true value of assets in their pension funds. Businesses will have to show how this varies with movements in bond and equity markets, rather than smoothing these out from year to year. The result will be greater volatility in accounts and a more revealing picture of whether schemes are operating in deficit or surplus. The board says it has attempted to insulate profits from market liveliness by separating pension fund changes from the main profit and loss account. The movements will be confined instead to the statement of total recognised gains and losses (the "struggle"), the repository for items that affect the value of the company but do not reflect its trading performance.

After initial remarks from Sir David, Chris Lewin, head of UK pensions at Unilever, took on the role of lion-tamer. He wondered why the ASB had taken a different line from other countries, which allowed some kind of smoothing of market fluctuations. "This gets us nowhere near the international standard," he said. On the contrary, replied Sir David, this was the only point on which the ASB differed from international thinking. The board had rejected smoothing because it did not reflect economic realities. "Smoothing doesn't give you an answer," he said. "It gives you numbers but they don't mean anything."

The tamer tried approaching from another angle. Change was all very well, but it was too early to do it. Mr Lewin's view chimed with those of actuaries such as Bacon & Woodrow, which said this week the ASB's plan was "the right standard, but at the wrong time".

Sir David said this proved the old aphorism: conservative accountants say "don't do it" while liberal accountants say "do it, but not yet". The ASB ought to be able to lead global opinion on this issue, although it recognised details of its plan were open to challenge. "If we know there is an asset and liability there then we show it," he said. "There is debate over how you measure it and I fully accept that. That is something we should discuss."

Encouraged by this admission, Mr Lewin cracked the whip more eagerly. The sudden jumps in asset values implied by the plan did not reflect the gradual pace of change of pension costs. The ASB's proposal to take a yearly snapshot fogged a process that needed to be viewed using a longer exposure. The references to fog and sudden jumps made it a loaded question, growled Sir David. Companies should be forced to show market-induced movements in profits. "Don't hide volatility," he said. "Explain it."

David Jackson, finance director of Roche Products, took his cue to step into the ring. He said the pension fund surplus should be kept off the balance sheet, as it was not money shareholders could get their hands on. He added that reflecting market movements in the "struggle" made it hard for companies to plan ahead what their results would be. "You are really in the lap of the gods," he said. Sir David leapt on these unguarded comments. This plan was aimed precisely at stopping companies manipulating their results to best advantage. "Accounting is becoming much more sophisticated," he said. "(Explaining) this is what happened, and this is why"...

Source: Financial Times, February 24, 2000.

FRED 20 provided for the following changes from SSAP 24:

- In line with IAS 19 (revised) the pension scheme assets would be measured at market value at the balance sheet date, rather than at an actuarial value.
- Again in line with IAS 19 (revised) the pension scheme liabilities would be discounted at the current rate of return on a long-term AA corporate bond rate.

- Actuarial gains and losses (variations from regular cost) would be recognised immediately in the statement of total recognised gains and losses rather than spread forward in the profit and loss account. This would mean that the profit and loss account would show the ongoing pension cost based on current market conditions.

- Any surplus (subject to a recoverability test) or deficit in the scheme would be shown on the balance sheet.

In spite of opposition, FRED 20 has since led to FRS 17, *Retirement Benefits*. Introducing the new FRS, David Tweedie articulated the ASB's reasons for championing change:

"Pension cost accounting has for a long time been an impenetrable black box to users of accounts. This new standard will help all interested parties to understand the implications for a company of running a defined benefit pension scheme. It may not be popular with some who would like the present obscurity to remain but transparency of information must be preferable. It should mean that decisions about pension provision are made on a better informed basis. In my view, the UK now has the best standard in the world for accounting for pensions and I would expect it to trigger similar reviews in other countries."

Essentially, the accounting treatment of defined contribution schemes remains unchanged. The main changes are in relation to defined benefit schemes where FRS 17 replaces the use of actuarial values with a market value approach, an approach that is consistent with international practice.

Recognising that this introduces an additional element of volatility, and concluding that dealing with this by averaging the market values over a number of years and/or spreading the gains and losses forward in the accounts over the service lives of the employees is unsatisfactory, FRS 17 provides for an alternative approach. The essential features of this are:

- The profit and loss account will show the relatively stable ongoing service cost, interest cost and expected return on assets measured on a basis consistent with international standards.

- The effects of the fluctuations in market values will be treated in the same way as revaluations of fixed assets, i.e., they will be recognised immediately in the statement of total recognised gains and losses.

- The balance sheet will show the deficit or recoverable surplus on the scheme.

Following pressure from industry, the ASB has decided that FRS 17 will only have to be fully implemented for recounting periods ending on or after 23 June 2003 although earlier implementation is encouraged and disclosures by way of notes to the accounts are required for accounting periods ending on or after 23 June 2001.

---

**In practice:**

---

*UK Businesses Holding Back from FRS17*

*Most UK multinationals are putting off the implementation of controversial accounting standard FRS17, according to a recent survey. Although the Accounting Standards Board recommends that the pensions standard is adopted as soon as possible, only 8% of companies plan an early implementation. With 60% still undecided on timing, and a third choosing to hold back, the study, by consultants William M Mercer, shows that businesses are reluctant to conform to the measure.*

*"Understandably, companies are reluctant to move until they have to," said Paul Kelly, European partner with William M Mercer. "The effect of FRS17 could potentially be detrimental to their profit and loss accounts, knocking millions of pounds off the bottom line profits. Where this is the case, it's not unreasonable to want to delay action until the last minute."*

*In November, the ASB put back the implementation deadline until June 22, 2003 following heated debate over the issue. A quarter of the 61 companies asked, which included FTSE 100 businesses, had reviewed the effect of FRS17 on their overseas pension plans. A third said they were planning a review, with the rest having no immediate plans…".*

*Source: AccountingWEB, March 19, 2001.*

---

## *Leases*

Leases are essentially arrangements under which "a lessee obtains the right to use or purchase assets without legal title to the leased asset actually passing to the lessee". A hire purchase contract is somewhat similar to a lease except that under a hire purchase contract the hirer may acquire legal title by exercising an option to purchase the asset upon fulfilment of certain conditions, usually the payment of an agreed number of instalments.

A lease creates a set of rights and obligations that result directly from the use and enjoyment by the lessee of the leased asset. Such rights are, in effect, the rewards of ownership, whilst the obligations, especially the obligation to continue paying instalments over the period of the lease, constitute the risks of ownership. Significantly, in the light of FRS 5, *Reporting the substance of transactions*, and the *Statement of Principles*, these characteristics require the substance of the transaction, rather than its legal form, to be considered. And the substance is that, while legal title may not pass, the risks, rights and obligations associated with ownership do.

SSAP 21, *Accounting for leases and hire purchase contracts*, sought to deal with this tension by distinguishing between two types of lease:

- **Finance leases**: these usually involve payment by a lessee to a lessor of the full cost of the asset as well as various finance charges. Under a finance lease the bulk of the risks and rewards associated with the ownership of the asset, other than the legal title, are transferred to the lessee. Traditionally, such a transfer was deemed to occur if at the inception of a lease the present value of the minimum lease payments, including any initial payment, amounted to substantially all (normally 90% or more) of the fair value of the leased asset.

- **Operating leases**: involves the lessee paying a rental for the hire of an asset for a period of time which is normally substantially less than its useful economic life. Under this type of lease the lessor retains most of the risks and rewards of ownership of the leased asset.

It then requires a different accounting treatment for each type of lease.

- **Finance leases**: should be accounted for as the purchase of the property by the lessee, and as a sale by the lessor. The result is that an asset is shown on the lessee's balance sheet at the present value of the minimum lease payments while a corresponding liability is recognised, similar to that of debt.

- **Operating lease**: should be accounted for by the asset being retained as an asset of the lessor with the lessee merely including the instalment payments as an expense.

While current thinking about the nature of leases requires a complete reconsideration of the place of operating leases, the SSAP 21 classification scheme means that they cause few problems. In effect, payments made under operating leases are simply expensed to the profit and loss account and the balance sheet is unaffected.

Finance leases, however, require a more considered approach. Essentially the acquisition of an asset and the assumption of a long-term indebtedness must be recognised. The accounting implications of this can best be illustrated by means of an example:

X plc can purchase a machine for £40,000 or lease it under the following terms:

- The period of the lease is 4 years from January 1, 20X1 with lease payments due at the end of each calendar year.

- The minimum lease payments will be £14,000 per annum, i.e., £56,000 in total.

- X plc must pay all maintenance, repair and insurance costs associated with the machine.

- Interest rate applicable is 15%.

X plc decides to lease. This requires the company to compute the present value of the minimum lease payments at the start of the lease. Discounting 4 annual payments of £14,000 commencing at end of year 1 at a rate of 15% shows that the present value is £39,970 (i.e., £14,000 × 2.285). Since this is within 90% of the cost this confirms the leasing arrangement as a finance lease. Therefore, this amount must be shown as an asset and as a corresponding liability from the outset.

The annual lease payment must now be subdivided into the capital repayment element and the financing portion. The total finance charge to be paid over the period of the lease will be £16,030 (£56,000 − £39,970). This must be allocated over the 4 years using one of a number of options. The actuarial method allocates the amount in proportion to the outstanding liability. Adopting this approach leads to the following computations:

| Year Ending | Amount owed at start of year (£) | Finance charge 15% (p&l) (£) | Sub-total (£) | Rental (£) | Amount owed at end of year (£) |
|---|---|---|---|---|---|
| 20X1 | 39,970 | 5,995 | 45,965 | 14,000 | 31,965 |
| 20X2 | 31,965 | 4,795 | 36,760 | 14,000 | 22,760 |
| 20X3 | 22,760 | 3,414 | 26,174 | 14,000 | 12,174 |
| 20X4 | 12,174 | 1,826 | 14,000 | 14,000 | nil |

The finance charge will be charged to the profit and loss account every year. The balance sheet will show an asset of £39,970 (less depreciation in accordance with company policy), and a progressively declining liability as indicated in the right hand column.

## Current Developments

Obviously, the way in which a lease is classified, whether as a financing or an operating lease, will be critical in determining levels of debt. This will directly impact upon performance measures such as profit and gearing. For this reason there has been increasing dissatisfaction at the rather arbitrary way in which SSAP 21 distinguished between these types of lease. Coupled with a maturing conceptual understanding of the nature of assets and liabilities, this has encouraged the ASB to reconsider the accounting treatment of leases. At the same time the FASB and the IASC have been engaged in similar initiatives.

This has resulted in new proposals for dealing with leases which were published in Discussion Paper form in 1999. The main thrust of the new provisions would make it difficult for leases to be classified as anything other than finance leases. In summary, the present value of lease payments would be capitalised and the resulting asset and liability figures would be shown on the balance sheet as demonstrated above.

These proposals have generated considerable debate.

## Accounting for Leases

In last month's column we stated that the ASB was considering the introduction of a new standard requiring greater capitalisation of leases. This was partly due to the development of conceptual thinking as to the nature of assets and liabilities and partly due to the perception that the distinction between operating leases and finance leases was very artificial at the margin. Under the current accounting standard (SSAP 21) fairly minor differences in contractual terms can result in one lease being classified as a finance lease and another very similar lease being classified as an operating lease. Additionally the approach taken by SSAP 21 is an "all or nothing one", broadly speaking assets leased under finance leases are capitalised at fair value whilst those leased under operating leases are not capitalised at all. This is perceived by many analysts as being inadequate to reflect the complexity of many modern transactions.

In December 1999 the ASB issued a Discussion Paper on the subject. The paper suggests that at the beginning of the lease the lessee would recognise an asset and liability equivalent to the fair value of the rights and obligations conferred by the lease. Broadly speaking this means capitalising the present value of the minimum lease payments and accounting for the resulting fixed asset and loan in the normal way.

Unsurprisingly much of the reaction to this has been hostile. Many preparers appear to fear the increasing gearing ratios that such a policy would imply for the balance sheet. However, the ASB may well ride out the adverse reaction. All standard setting bodies that are represented on the G4 + 1 group are publishing similar discussion drafts in their own countries. Therefore we may be about to observe a sea change in accounting for leases; watch this space.

Source: Accounting and Business, February 2000.

The antipathy hinted at in this report was not lost on David Tweedie, who summed up the essence of the ASB policy as based on the ASB's guiding definition of a liability, "Have you an obligation? Can you measure it? If yes; then put it on your balance sheet." It was a simple concept, he said, "But the leasing industry thinks it's the end of civilisation as we know it."

The nature and extent of the opposition to the proposals, the principal effect of which would be to remove the facility for companies to classify leases as "operational", a practice which has traditionally positively impacted gearing measures, are summarised in the following article:

## Doubts Raised About ASB Proposals on Leasing

**PriceWaterhouseCoopers Senior Technical Partner Peter Holgate has Taken the Accounting Standards Board to Task Over its New Approach to Accounting for Leases.**

Responding to the ASB leasing discussion paper issued last December, Holgate voiced concerns about how far the changes should go and whether their implications had been fully thought through. PwC agreed with the ASB's basic principle that the obligations and liabilities incurred as a result of leasing arrangements should be recorded on companies balance sheets at their "fair value", the amount that the entity will be required to pay under the lease.

The leasing proposals have raised fears in aviation and other industries where many operators lease their equipment, explained Holgate. "Retailers are concerned since current operating leases on most high street shops may well come back on to the balance sheet," he said. "And what will it do for property companies? The proposals may leave lessees like retailers wanting shorter leases to lessen their commitments. If they do that, what will it do to value of the properties? The value of property with a good tenant on a 25-year lease will differ from one with a tenant on a 5-year lease. There is a potential impact on the market. It's hard to be sure how serious it will be, but it is not a trivial matter."

Leasing, licensing and lease-back arrangements are becoming increasingly prevalent in the new economy, the firm pointed out. But the ASB's proposals are likely to bring all sorts of intangible assets into the balance sheet should they fall within the proposed leasing definition. By way of example, PwC cited the example of a company that currently pays an annual charge to distribute a product in a particular area. The payment is shown in the accounts as an expense. If the distribution agreement were to be brought within the scope of the leasing proposals, it would create a liability on the balance sheet, together with a "right to distribute product X in area Y" asset. "Where, as often happens, the payments depend on future sales, it is far from clear how these amounts would be determined," PwC warned...

Source: AccountingWEB, June 5, 2000

In spite of this opposition, the fact that SSAP 21 is not consistent with international practice is likely to ensure that the ASB's proposals lead to a new standard.

## Sale and Leaseback Arrangements

Sale and leaseback (or sale and repurchase) arrangements are common transactions and can be constructed in a number of ways. The essential characteristic, however, is that the "seller" of the asset in question does not actually give up all of the rights or obligations of ownership. Thus, under such an arrangement the "seller" may retain actual physical control of the asset, as well as the associated economic benefits and risks. The real question revolves around the substance of the transaction.

> **In practice:**
>
> *A company, A plc, "sells" a portion of its property to another, B plc, for £5 million. However, it retains effective control of the property in question. As part of the arrangement A plc agrees to repurchase the property after 10 years for £8 million.*
>
> *Under FRS 5 the critical issue revolves around the retention of the risks and rewards of owner-ship. In fact, these have not been transferred. The transaction is therefore classified as a financing arrangement and not a sale, since what has happened in substance is that the property has been used to obtain finance.*
>
> *A plc should, therefore, continue to show the property as an asset in its balance sheet. The cash inflow of £5 million would be classified as a loan redeemable after 10 years time. The attendant financing cost, to be treated as interest to be accrued, would amount to £3 million.*

FRS 5 outlines the following basic principles to be considered in determining the nature of such a transaction:

- In a straightforward case, the substance of a sale and repurchase agreement will be that of a secured loan, i.e., the seller will retain all significant rights to benefits relating to the original asset and all significant exposure to the risks inherent in those benefits and will have a liability to the buyer for the whole of the proceeds received. For example, this would be the case where the seller has in effect an unconditional commitment to repurchase the original asset from the buyer at the sale price plus interest. The seller should account for this type of arrangement by showing the original asset on its balance sheet together with a liability for the amounts received from the buyer (B4).

- In certain more complex cases, it may be determined that a sale and repurchase agreement is not in substance a financing transaction and that the seller retains access to only some of the benefits of the original asset and retains only some of their inherent risks. Where this is so, in accordance with paragraph 23, the descrip-tion or monetary amount of the original asset should be changed and a liability recognised for any obligation to transfer benefits that is assumed. It will also be necessary to give full disclosure of these more complex arrangements in the notes to the financial statements (B5).

- The substance of the arrangement may be more readily apparent if the position of both buyer and seller are considered, together with their apparent expectations and motives for agreeing to its various terms. In particular, where the substance is that of a secured loan, the buyer will require that it is assured of a lender's return on its investment and the seller will require that the buyer earns no more than this return. Thus whether or not the buyer earns such a return is an important indi-cator of the substance of the transaction (B6).

The effect of these provisions has been to limit the extent to which sale and lease-back arrangements can be employed as means of "window-dressing" accounts.

Nevertheless, as the following "In practice" box illustrates, such arrangements do provide a useful means by which companies with strong tangible asset portfolios can generate cash for funding long-term operating growth.

---

**In practice:**

*In the operating and financial section of its report and accounts for the year ended November 30, 1998, Bensons Crisps gives a clear explanation of the likely effect on the group of selling and leasing back the freehold of its St. George's Park factory. The sale and leaseback, which shareholders approved, resulted in net cash generation of £4 million after discharging the £2 million bank loan and expenses. The net proceeds from the sale will be used to fund more organic capacity development, complementary acquisitions and further purchases of own shares when considered appropriate.*

*In 1999, Bensons Crisps will incur rental charges under the St. George's Park lease of some £537,000 a year, which will adversely affect operating profit. However, depreciation charges of £125,000 a year will be avoided. There will be a net reduction in operating profit from the transaction, which will be broadly offset by a reduction in financing costs. Until such time as the surplus funds are used to develop the group, there is estimated to be a neutral effect on earnings per share from the transaction.*

*Source: Accountancy, April, 1999.*

---

# Foreign Currency

The globalisation of commerce that has occurred steadily over the past number of decades has made it inevitable that most companies, particularly larger multi-national enterprises, will undertake foreign currency transactions.

The two most obvious means by which this will happen are:

- **Directly** by way of business transactions which are denominated in foreign currencies. In these circumstances these transactions will need to be translated into the "home" currency, i.e., the currency in which the company reports.

- **Indirectly** where foreign operations are executed through a foreign enterprise which maintains its accounting records in a currency other than that of the investing company. In these circumstances it will be necessary to translate the complete financial statements of the foreign enterprise into the "home" currency, i.e., the currency in which the investor company reports, in order to prepare consolidated financial statements for the group.

The treatment of transactions involving foreign currency is covered by SSAP 20, *Foreign Currency Translation.*

The accounting goal of this SSAP is "to ensure that the translation and incorporation of such transactions produces financial results which reflect the effects of rate changes on a company's cash flows and equity. In the case of consolidated accounts, it is necessary to ensure that they reflect the financial results as measured in the foreign currency financial statements prior to translation."

SSAP 20 recognises that there are two exchange rates that can normally be considered when translating a foreign currency transaction or balance:

- Historic rate: the exchange rate applying when the transaction occurred.
- Closing rate: the exchange rate applying at the balance sheet date.

For example, an item purchased for $500,000 when the exchange rate was $1.20 = £1 which has to be incorporated into a balance sheet being prepared when the exchange rate has fluctuated to $1.30 = £1 could be shown at either:

- Historic rate = £416,667, or
- Closing rate = £384,615

Obviously, therefore, the rate chosen can have a significant influence on the amount at which an item is included in the accounts.

SSAP 20 approaches the treatment of foreign currency transactions and operations by distinguishing between the "individual company" stage, which deals with direct transactions, and the "consolidated accounts" stage where the issue is the treatment in the group accounts of a constituent company which operates in a foreign currency.

## Individual Company Stage

As part of their normal activities, most companies will engage in transactions that are denominated in a foreign currency. For instance UK companies will purchase supplies from US companies and receive invoices denominated in US dollars.

This stage deals with the way in which the individual company deals with the transaction or balance in its own accounts. Essentially, foreign currency transactions entered into by companies should be recorded at the date of the transaction using the rate applying on that date.

For those transactions involving non-monetary assets such as fixed assets, no further action is required and they are incorporated in the balance sheet at the values produced by the application of the historic rate. All depreciation figures will be computed with reference to this figure.

However, in the case of monetary items such as debtors, creditors and bank balances, it is necessary to include them in the balance sheet at the closing rate. This is because, in the event of currency fluctuations, they are likely to be settled at a rate different from that applying at the transaction date. Any gains or losses should be taken to the profit and loss account.

For example, on April 30 A plc, a UK company, sold goods to a French customer for FFr50,000 when the rate of exchange was £1 = FFr10.

On the date of sale this should be recorded as:

| Dr | Debtors | £5,000 |
|----|---------|--------|
| Cr | Sales   | £5,000 |

If at the financial year-end, June 30, this balance remained outstanding when the rate is £1 = FFr8, then the following entry would need to be made:

| Dr | Debtors | £1,250 |
|----|---------|--------|
| Cr | p&l a/c | £1,250 |

This would have the effect of showing the amount due as £6,250, the amount which A plc would receive in sterling were it to receive a draft for FFr50,000 on that date.

If the account is subsequently settled on July 11, by which time the rate has fluctuated again to £1 = FFr9, then the company would receive a draft for FFr50,000 which would yield £5,555. This would require the following entries to be made:

| Dr | Cash    | £5,555 |
|----|---------|--------|
| Cr | Debtors | £5,555 |
| Dr | p&l a/c | £695   |
| Cr | Debtors | £695   |

The same approach would apply to other monetary assets such as loans and creditors.

### Hedging Loans

In circumstances where an overseas investment is financed by a loan raised in the same foreign currency SSAP 20 allows a slight change to these rules. Such a transaction is categorised as a "hedging loan" on the basis that any fluctuation in the overseas currency will impact the loan and the underlying equity investment in the same way, i.e., they will "hedge" one another since either both will increase or both will decrease. However, if the provisions outlined above were to apply then different rules would apply to the rates at which the equity investment (a non-monetary item) and the loan (a monetary item) were translated. Reflecting the fact that such arrangements mean the investment and the loan are actually matched, SSAP 20 allows companies to treat equity investments financed in this manner as a monetary item. Consequently, any differences resulting from applying the closing rate to the investment and the loan are taken to reserves where they can be offset. In circumstances where the investment and loan are taken out in different currencies the same procedure applies although offset is limited to differences on translating differences only, any remaining difference being taken to the profit and loss account.

## Consolidated Accounts Stage

When one company acquires a foreign subsidiary it becomes necessary to translate the foreign currency figures so that they can be stated in sterling and then incorporated according to the normal acquisition accounting rules in the consolidated accounts. There are two possible rates that can be used:

- **Temporal (historic) method**: the rate applying at the transaction date. This method should be used in those relatively rare circumstances where the operations of a foreign subsidiary can be described as so closely inter-linked with those of the investing company "that to all intents and purposes its results might be considered as more dependent on the economic environment of the investing company's currency than on that of its own reporting currency."

  An example of such an entity would be one which simply operates as a selling agent, receiving stocks of goods from the investing company and remitting the proceeds back to it. It is essentially being treated as a department within the parent company.

- **Closing rate/net investment method**: the rate applying at the balance sheet date. Under this approach the amounts in the balance sheet of a foreign subsidiary are brought into the consolidated accounts by translating the relevant amounts into the currency of the investing company using the rate of exchange applying at the balance sheet date. Exchange differences will arise if this rate differs from that ruling at the previous balance sheet date or at the date of any subsequent capital injection (or reduction). These will be shown in the statement of total recognised gains and losses. The profit and loss account of a foreign subsidiary can be translated using the closing rate or an average rate calculated for the year as a whole.

In most circumstances the closing rate/net investment method will be most appropriate since this reflects the arms-length relationship that normally exists between a parent and a foreign subsidiary. Only in circumstances where the activities of the parent and foreign subsidiary are inextricably linked should the temporal method be adopted. Whichever rate is used it must be used consistently.

## *Summary*

This chapter has looked at the accounting regulations applying in several areas of accounting practice. The focus has, however, been as much on the broader issues such as international pressures for harmonisation as on any presentation of detailed double-entries. Both emphases are important when interpreting financial statements, as one requires macro-considerations to be taken into account while the other respects the fact that technical accuracy is also important.

In the process of discussing some of the catalysts for change in accounting practice in some of these areas, this chapter has identified the broader "harmonisation" agenda, particularly as espoused by the IASC, as a significant factor. Indeed, it is possible to identify in some recent FRSs a greater leaning towards international practice. This will be discussed in more detail in Chapter 15.

# Review Questions

### Question 1
Identify the principal features of the Corporation Tax code in the UK and the effect on the accounting system of recent changes relating to ACT.

### Question 2
Explain why deferred tax arises and why it is significant in an accounting context.

### Question 3
Distinguish between a "timing difference" and a "permanent difference" in the context of deferred taxation and give examples of each.

### Question 4
Outline the main provisions of FRS 19, *Deferred Taxation*, and explain how it differs from its predecessor, SSAP 15 (revised), *Accounting for Deferred Tax*. What were the principal driving forces behind calls for changes in the way in which deferred tax is accounted for?

### Question 5
FRS 17, *Retirement benefits*, introduces some significant changes, particularly when accounting for defined benefit schemes. Outline these and explain how they will impact on financial statements.

### Question 6
"Lease accounting provides one of the most fertile areas for creative accounting practices". Explain what is meant by this statement.

### Question 7
The Discussion Paper, *Accounting for Leases*, provides for some radical changes in the treatment of leases. Outline what these are and why some representative groups are lobbying so hard to ensure that they are not accepted.

### Question 8
Explain what is meant by a "Sale and Leaseback Arrangement" and provide an illustration of such a scheme.

### Question 9
SSAP 20, *Foreign Currency Translation*, provides for various methods of translation. Outline what these are and the circumstances in which each applies.

# Case Studies

## Case 1

The following article outlines some of the broader contexts within which FRS 19, *Deferred Taxation*, has emerged. Using this as an example, discuss the extent to which international accounting concerns should be allowed to set the agenda for UK accounting standards.

## A Step Closer to Harmony

### A Move to Full Provision Accounting Has Been on the Cards for Several Years, and now it Has Happened, by Joan Brown

The Accounting Standards Board published FRS 19, a new accounting standard for deferred tax, in December. The FRS, which replaces SSAP 15, Accounting for Deferred Tax, requires entities to provide for tax timing differences on a full, rather than partial, provision basis. This change represents a step towards international harmonisation for deferred tax accounting. However, there are differences between the requirements of the FRS and those of the equivalent international standard, IAS 12, Income Taxes. FRS 19 comes into effect for accounting periods ending on or after January 23, 2002. But, as with other new FRSs, earlier adoption is encouraged.

The move to full provision accounting reflects an acceptance of the need to harmonise with international practice in the area of deferred tax. It would have been ideal, therefore, if the requirements of the FRS could have been identical to IAS 12's. However, the ASB does not agree with the rationale underlying the "temporary difference" approach adopted in the IAS and, with the support of the financial community in the UK, has developed a different approach in the FRS.

### Increased Liabilities

In practical terms, the requirements the FRS are similar to IAS 12's. Both standards require deferred tax be provided for in full on most timing differences, including capital allowances in excess of depreciation, pension liabilities and short-term timing differences. The FRS will have the effect of increasing the liabilities reported by entities that at present have large amounts of unprovided deferred tax arising from capital allowances in excess of depreciation. Also, like the IAS, the FRS permits deferred tax assets to be recognised only if there is evidence that there will be taxable profits in future against which the assets can be recovered.

However, unlike the IAS, the FRS does not in general require (or permit) deferred tax to be provided for when:

- Non-monetary assets are revalued (or adjusted to their fair values on the acquisition of a business).
- A taxable gain is rolled over into replacement assets, and will become taxable only if and when the assets are sold.

- Group accounts incorporate retained earnings of associates and joint ventures (which would become subject to further taxation on remittance to the parent company).
- In each of the above cases, the ASB believes that there is no obligation to pay more tax until the entity commits itself to selling the assets or remitting the earnings. Unless or until such a commitment has been made, no deferred tax should be provided for.

A second major difference from international requirements is that the FRS permits entities to discount long-term deferred tax assets and liabilities to take account of the time value of money. The ASB believes that, just as other long-term liabilities (such as provisions and debt) are discounted, so too in principle should long-term deferred tax liabilities. The FRS therefore permits discounting and provides guidance on how it should be done. However, the ASB has stopped short of making discounting mandatory, acknowledging that there is as yet no internationally-accepted methodology for discounting deferred tax and that for some entities the costs might outweigh the benefits. Entities are encouraged to select the more appropriate policy, taking account of factors such as materiality and the policies of other entities in their sector.

The FRS was published for consultation in draft form last year. It received the support of most of those commenting, and only a few changes have been made to the requirements proposed. In addition to the decision to make discounting optional, the more significant changes are:

- An exception to the general requirement not to provide for deferred tax on timing differences created by revaluation gains. The exception requires deferred tax to be provided for when the timing difference arises on assets that are marked to market, with gains and losses recorded in the p&l account. It reflects a view that, when gains and losses are recognised in the p&l, it is because they are for the most part readily realisable; to give a true and fair view of the entity's performance, the additional tax that would be payable on realising the gains should also be recognised.
- Clarification of the treatment required for industrial buildings allowances (which are not repayable if the entity owns the building for more than 25 years and may therefore be regarded as giving rise to permanent rather than temporary differences). The FRS clarifies that deferred tax should be provided for on the difference between the amount of the industrial building allowances and any depreciation charged on the asset until the 25-year period has passed.

## Short-live Standard

If, as is proposed, the EU requires listed companies in the UK to report under International Accounting Standards in a few years' time, FRS 19 might be a short-lived standard. You might therefore ask why the ASB has published it at all. The reason is that the ASB is not alone in disliking the "temporary difference" approach that underpins IAS 12. It hopes that by developing and implementing a credible alternative, it will encourage the International Accounting Standards Committee to think again.

Joan Brown is a project director at the Accounting Standards Board. The views expressed here are her own.

Source: Accountancy: January, 2001.

## Case 2

Foreign Currency, deferred taxation, leasing commitments and pensions are dealt with in Notes 20, 21 and 22 and 26, respectively of the Tesco plc Annual Report 2000. Work through these to see how extensive the disclosure requirements are in relation to each.

## Case 3

On January 1, 20X1 X plc, a UK company, acquired the entire ordinary share capital of Y, a German company, for DM 1,200,000. At the time the rate was DM 5 = £1. The full purchase price was obtained from a French bank at the same time when the rate was FFr 8 = £1.

The draft balance sheet for X plc as at December 31, 20X1 has been prepared and reads as follows:

**Draft Balance Sheet as at December 31, 20X1**

|  | £ |
| --- | --- |
| Fixed assets | |
| Premises | 1,000,000 |
| Investment in subsidiary (FFr 1,200,000 @ FFr 8 = 1) | 150,000 |
| Total | 1,150,000 |
| Net assets | 3,000,000 |
| Total | 4,150,000 |
| Share capital | 2,000,000 |
| Revenue reserves | 2,000,000 |
| Loan (DM 750,000 @ DM 5 = £1) | 150,000 |
| Total | 4,150,000 |

The rates applying at the December 31, 20X1 were: £1 = FFr 7.5; £1 = DM 4. Show how this would be accounted for in the financial statements of X plc.

(The answer to this question is available on the web site for this text.)

When you have completed this chapter you will understand:

- What is meant by the term "creative accounting".
- Some of the ways in which accountants, governments and regulators have attempted to deal with this phenomenon.
- That creative accounting practices persist.
- That the nature and dynamics of the "new economy" create the potential for the emergence of "new" creative accounting practices.
- The role of ethics in accounting practice.

## Going for the Juggler

**Those wishing to juggle their financial results used to have plenty of scope to bend the rules – and they certainly used it. Have the latest set of accounting standards caught up with them at last? by Robert Outram**

...Call it what you will, creative accounting, financial engineering or window-dressing, it is the art of bending flexible accounting rules to present a flattering picture of the business in question. While there is a theory that the efficient market will not be fooled by presentation alone, sadly, the evidence is to the contrary. Witness a report which appeared in the Financial Times on June 26, 1987: "Shares across the stores sector tumbled yesterday on fears of an onset of conservative accounting. The widespread decline was triggered by the Argyll Group's decision to treat the £90 million cost of reorganizing its Presto stores as an exceptional item rather than as an extraordinary one. The move, following the company's £681 million acquisition of Safeway in January, will reduce the company's pre-tax profits and earnings per share over the next 4 years." There had been no underlying economic change affecting the retail sector; shares had slumped purely on a change in the way the accounts were presented.

Sometimes the financial risks which creative accounting concealed were enough in themselves to bring a company down. The collapse of British & Commonwealth (B&C) in 1990 was triggered by one of its acquisitions, Atlantic Computers, which had been making healthy profits – on paper – both before and after B&C took it over. But in 1989, less than a year after buying Atlantic for £416 million, B&C discovered that its acquisition was a black hole into which the whole group threatened to tumble. B&C wrote off £550 million and Atlantic was put into administrative receivership in early 1990, but that was not enough to save its parent and the whole group finally went under a few months later. In their report on the debacle, Department of Trade and Industry inspectors said: "If Atlantic's business had been accounted for on a prudent basis, it is probable that it would not have been able to report any significant profits... at any time from the commencement of its business."

Creative accounting was by no means the only factor contributing to the corporate collapses and near-crashes of the 1980s and early 1990s but it did play a significant part in allowing bad business propositions to look good. Questionable accounting practices also encouraged the acquisition fever of this time. Companies showing a strong earnings per share (eps) growth saw their share prices rocket, and they used that in turn to fund paper and debt-based take-overs of less favoured companies steady and boring ones, that is – on a grand scale. Conglomerates like Hanson and Williams Holdings moved on from one deal to the next, following a logic based less on the concept of synergy and more on the so-called Indian rope trick, where the market's perception rather than actual cash generation was enough to fuel the growth of diversified business empires. As with eastern fakirs, what actually supported the whole share price was a mystery.

Another popular ploy in the 1980s was to ensure that the bottom line – the post-tax profit figure used as the basis for calculating eps – excluded as many costs as possible. Since bottom-line earnings are supposed to represent trading performance, one-off items such as reorganization costs on an acquisition could be classed as extraordinary items. They would be reported below the line so that eps would be unaffected. Exceptional items, on the other hand, went above the line, depressing the eps figure as illustrated in the Argyll Group example above. At the end of the 1980s over half the listed companies in the UK were reporting extraordinary items; the equivalent US figure, supposedly following the same principles, was just 5%. As examples of just how significant this could be, in 1990–1 the Costain Group, Saatchi&Saatchi, Storehouse and Unigate all reported extraordinary costs which actually exceeded their profits for the period.

Few areas in the 1980s provided such scope for creative accounting as acquisitions and mergers, however. Take Coloroll's acquisition in 1988 of textile business John Crowther, for example. Coloroll paid £215 million for Crowther. Since Crowther's assets only amounted to £70 million on paper, Coloroll could have written-off the difference, £145 million, as goodwill (that is, the amount by which the cost of an acquired business exceeds its recorded net assets). But Coloroll actually wrote off £224 million, more than the purchase price. To the original figure was added £75 million in asset write-downs and provisions for costs such as relocation and redundancies, together with a reduction in Crowther's net asset value of £4 million. Coloroll was following accepted UK accounting practice in estimating a "fair value" for its acquisition, with the resultant goodwill being written-off against reserves. This reduced the balance-sheet worth of the acquirer, but had a number of advantages, namely that, because the balance sheet was reduced, return on capital employed looked better; any future impact from writing down the value of stock and assets did not have to be shown in the profit and loss account; and provisions included in the goodwill figure meant that future costs such as redundancies and even trading losses need never appear in the profit and loss account.

Source: Management Today, June 1996.

## Introduction

The litany of creative accounting practices and frauds outlined in this opening account is a timely reminder of the nature and extent of the problems which these practices have posed for both accounting and society as a whole. Long understood by accountants and regulators as a key factor in undermining the credibility of financial reports, efforts have been ongoing for many years to limit the scope of companies to "cook the books". From the South Sea Bubble collapse in the early 18th century to the financial chicanery surrounding the Maxwell Communications Corporation's fraud of the early 1990s, the need for tighter control of accounting practices has been obvious.

Indeed, events such as the collapse of the Maxwell empire and a spate of similar scandals in the late 1980s were critical catalysts in bringing about the establishment of the Accounting Standards Board (ASB). "There were only three things wrong with company accounts in the 1980s," Sir David Tweedie has observed, "the profit and loss account, the balance sheet and the statement of sources and applications of funds (the predecessor of the cash flow statement)." In other words, everything was wrong with the basic financial statements upon which investors were relying for a "true and fair view" of company performance.

The sense of urgency communicated by Tweedie was well warranted. By the late 1980s accounting and auditing regimes were under fire from all quarters in the wake of a series of financial and accounting scandals which implicated them as principal actors in a failed system. The establishment of the ASB was seen by some as a final opportunity for accountants to show that they were intent upon establishing their *bona fides* as practitioners of a discipline that was serious about attacking fraud.

Speaking in 1999, Sir David highlighted the progress that had been made: "When the Board was first formed, it faced two big problems – the 'creative' accounting abuses of the 1980s... and the fact that financial reporting in these islands had been moving away from the international mainstream. The Board has (now) ensured that only genuine assets and liabilities appear on the balance sheet and has put to flight the former profit manipulators."

As the following account verifies, however, creative accounting practices are far from eradicated.'

## Lies, Damned Lies and Managed Earnings

The crackdown is here. The nation's top earnings cop has put corporate America on notice: Quit cooking the books. Cross the line, you may do time. Someplace right now, in the layers of a FORTUNE 500 company, an employee – probably high up and probably helped by people who work for them – is perpetrating an accounting fraud. Down the road that crime will come to light and cost the company's shareholders hundreds of millions of dollars. Typically, the employee will not have set out to be dishonest, only to dodge a few rules. Their fraud, small at first, will build, because the exit they thought just around the corner never appears. In time, some subordinate may say, "Whoa!" But they will not muster the courage to blow the whistle, and the fraud will go on. Until it's uncovered. The company's stock will drop then, by a big percent. Class-action lawyers will leap. The Securities and Exchange Commission will file unpleasant enforcement actions, levy fines, and leave the bad guys looking for another line of work. Eventually someone may go to jail. And the fundamental reason, very often, will be that the company or one of its divisions was "managing earnings" – trying to meet Wall Street expectations or those of the boss, trying also to pretend that the course of business is smooth and predictable when in reality it is not.

Jail? This is not a spot that CEOs and other high-placed executives see themselves checking into, for any reason. Jail for managing earnings? Many corporate chiefs would find that preposterous, having come to believe that "making their numbers" is just what executives do. Okay, so the pressure might lead some of them to do dumb (but legal) things – like making off-price deals at the end of a quarter that simply steal from full-priced business down the road. Who cares? Others might even be driven to make hash of the rules that publicly owned companies are required to abide by, Generally Accepted Accounting Principles (GAAP). Sure, that might mean crossing a legal line, but so what?

Well, the "so what" is Arthur Levitt, chairman of the SEC and the grand enforcer when it comes to GAAP. Last year, with his attorneys and accountants digging into Bankers Trust and Cendant and W. R. Grace and Livent and Oxford Health Plans and Sunbeam and Waste Management – and who knows what other big companies the SEC is not talking about – Levitt finally reached the gag point. He simply declared war on bad financial reporting.

The opening shots came in a New York speech, "The Numbers Game," that Levitt gave last September to CPAs, lawyers, and academics. Lynn Turner, chief accountant of the SEC (and formerly a partner of Coopers&Lybrand), recalls that as Levitt started to speak, waiters whipped around serving salads, and people began to eat. "Then," says Turner, "two amazing things happened. First, people put down their forks and started listening very hard. Then – and this just never happens – they pulled out notepads."

What they heard was the SEC chairman committing his agency in no uncertain terms to a serious, high-priority attack on earnings management. Since then several SEC officials have gone out of their way to state that there are many management's doing their accounting honestly, but that night the chairman spared no one. He roundly criticized a business community that greeted "accounting hocus-pocus" with nothing more than "nods and winks." Among the accounting tactics he blasted were improper revenue recognition, unjustified restructuring charges, and the artifices called "cookie-jar reserves." Accountants know all of these (and more) as "accounting irregularities" – intentional misstatements in financial reports, which Levitt and his team regard as very often the equivalent of fraud.

In a recent conversation with FORTUNE, Levitt left no doubt that he intends to keep the heat on. What is at stake, he says, is nothing less than the credibility of the US financial-reporting system, traditionally thought to be the best in the world. It will not now, he vowed, be undermined by management's obsessed with making their numbers. "It's a basic cultural change we are asking for," he said, "nothing short of that."

In identifying creative accounting as one of the reasons why effective regulation is necessary, both Levitt and Tweedie were reminding their audiences of the difficulties in which accountants had found themselves in the wake of the financial chicanery of the late 1970s and 1980s. In the UK the cumulative effect of corporate collapses in which lax reporting and control practices had been identified as major contributory factors, and the success of books such as Terry Smith's *"Accounting for Growth"*, had forced the profession to acknowledge its partial culpability.

One response in the UK was the setting up of the Dearing Committee which in turn led to the new financial reporting regime outlined in Chapter 1. Under David Tweedie's leadership, this has been an important factor in addressing many traditional creative accounting practices and mindsets. Another has been a determination to deal with creative accounting practices by addressing the deficiencies in fundamental accounting principles and concepts.

## Creative Accounting

Creative accounting has been defined in a number of ways, ranging from "outright fraud" to "the imaginative use of accounting numbers". However, it has probably been best defined as "the use and abuse of accounting techniques and principles to achieve financial statements which, intentionally, do not provide a true and fair view".

This is a preferable definition for a number of reasons:

- It emphasizes the fact that it is an intentional act with a particular goal in mind.

- While recognizing that accounting practices and techniques can be manipulated, it resists the temptation to reduce creative accounting to the manipulation of practices and techniques alone.

- Instead, it extends the definition to embrace the more fundamental point that the problem lies in the fact that accounting principles and concepts are flawed. The implication is that any resolution of the problem of creative accounting must address this reality. This helps to explain the significance which the ASB attaches to its *Statement of Principles* and standards such as FRS 5, *Reporting the substance of transactions*. Creative accounting can only be countered by developing a coherent conceptual framework from which an integrated set of practices emerges. FRS 5 provides an excellent example of the merits of this approach. By concentrating on principles rather than specifics, it has helped to engender a culture more concerned with the application of the spirit, than the letter, of the law. This in turn has greatly reduced the incidence of certain creative accounting practices.

- By considering creative accounting within the context of "true and fair", it provides a measure against which creative accounting practices can be gauged.

- By extending the definition to embrace both "use and abuse" it recognizes that much of what is called creative accounting is actually passive manipulation or "creative compliance". In other words, a mentality exists in which it is seen as legitimate to exploit loopholes or the silence of a standard on a particular issue. Again, such practices will only be countered by developing a reporting culture in which compliance with the spirit, rather than the letter, of the law is championed.

---

### In practice:

*Creative Accounting Leaves £4 million Hole in Wimpey's Profit, by Dan Atkinson*

*Accounting irregularities have torn a £4 million hole in the profits of Wimpey, Britain's biggest house builder, it emerged yesterday. Five senior managers pumped up corporate earnings artificially over a 2-year period by putting off payments on roads, sewerage systems and other infrastructure expenses. Dennis Brant, Wimpey chief executive, said: "It's a one-off situation, it's historical."*

*The five managers have been dismissed and in-depth checks across the company have found no other discrepancies. The irregularities occurred at the northern home counties region of the company's Wimpey Homes subsidiary in Luton, Bedfordshire. The managers decided to "roll forward" costs incurred on supplying infrastructure to housing schemes, inflating the profits for 1997 and last year by £4 million.*

*Mr Brant said that the managers had hoped to make good what was effectively a shortfall at some indefinite date in the future, "they believed they could then just drip it out over future years". But in June Wimpey, using a new system of "enhanced financial controls", came across the discrepancies. Internal accountants began a company-wide investigation which was then double-checked by Wimpey's auditors, PriceWaterhouseCoopers.*

*Source: The Guardian, September 16, 1999.*

---

## Examples

Creative accounting is best explained and understood using examples. The following section recounts some of the more common techniques used in the UK over the last decade, highlighting the place of accounting in a broader culture of manipulative and fraudulent corporate practice:

### Extraordinary and Exceptional Items

As explained in Chapter 6, analysts have used eps as one of the more potent measures of company health and performance. It is an important determinant of share price and will often form the basis of a broker's decision on whether to invest in shares of a company or not. Under SSAP 6, *Extraordinary items and prior year adjustments*, however, companies were able to manipulate the Profit before Tax figure on which eps was based by a simple re-classification of an item from "exceptional" to "extraordinary".

FRS 3, *Reporting Financial Performance*, removed many of the abusive practices associated with this confusion by effectively eliminating extraordinary items and forcing firms to deal in a more transparent manner with expenses that were previously categorized as exceptional.

### Goodwill Write-off

As explained in Chapter 11, when one company acquires another it must incorporate the assets acquired in the consolidated accounts at "fair value". Any remaining difference between cost of acquisition and "fair value" is classified as goodwill. Under SSAP 22, *Accounting for Goodwill*, this goodwill figure could then be written-off against reserves immediately. Thus, no element of this figure ever impinged upon profits. Furthermore, if the acquiring company anticipated reorganization costs arising from the acquisition then provision could be made against any possible reductions in asset values as part of the fair value calculations. Thus possible future costs (or asset write-downs) could be raised in such a way as to impact the balance sheet and not future profit and loss accounts.

FRS 7 and FRS 10 have effectively dealt with this issue as explained in Chapters 6 and 11.

### Revaluation Write-offs

A related problem involved the re-classification of assets from current to fixed or vice-versa. The former was availed of by companies to ensure that any losses on revaluation of certain assets could be written-off directly against reserves rather than being shown as a deduction in the profit and loss account. The latter practice was commonly employed in the 1990s by video rental firms that treated videos variously as current and fixed assets in order to avoid depreciation charges in the profit and loss account.

> **In practice:**
>
> *Trafalgar House*
>
> *One of the most ambitious attempts to re-classify items in this manner occurred in the early 1990s when Trafalgar House reclassified as fixed assets various properties it normally showed as current assets and on which it had suffered a revaluation loss of £102 million. This had the effect of allowing the revaluation loss to be written-off against reserves, rather than being shown as a deduction from profits. Had the loss been shown in the profit and loss account it would have reduced profits from £122 to £20 million.*
>
> *The Financial Reporting Review Panel (FRRP) took a very dim view of what was being attempted and eventually forced the company to restate its figures.*

### Off-balance Sheet Finance and Quasi-Subsidiaries

Off-balance sheet finance describes a process by which assets and/or associated finance are effectively kept off of the balance sheet. The intention is usually to impact upon the gearing figure of the company.

One means by which this was achieved was by exploiting the legal definitions pertaining to parents and subsidiaries in such a way as to ensure that certain companies were technically not required to be included in the consolidated accounts. Chapters 6 and 11 traced the gradual tightening in the definition of "parent" and "subsidiary" that has occurred over the past decade. For instance, "control" has now been displaced by "dominant influence" as a primary means of determining the relationship between one company and another. One reason that this was necessary was that criteria based on "control" could be exploited by those wishing to exclude from consolidated accounts the accounts of companies which were subsidiaries in all but the strict legal sense. Such companies were known as "quasi-subsidiaries".

FRS 5, *Reporting the substance of transactions*, has been crucial in resolving the challenges posed by quasi-subsidiaries. In fact, this FRS has proven one of the most potent weapons of all in undermining an array of creative accounting practices. It has succeeded primarily by requiring that the commercial effect of an entity's transactions, rather than merely the legal form, be recorded in its accounts.

## Going for the Juggler, continued

...While it is often in a company's interest to protect earnings at the expense of the balance sheet, sometimes it is the balance sheet that needs massaging. This is especially so when the issue at stake is gearing. Broadly, a company will try to keep as much debt and other liabilities out of the accounts as it can. There are a number of ways to do this. One is so-called off-balance sheet financing where a vehicle is created to take on liabilities. In the property sector, for example, joint ventures are often still used as a means of financing projects. They will be recorded as investments but the debt, even if it is guaranteed by the parent companies, will only appear in the notes to the accounts, not on the parent company's balance sheets.

Sale and repurchase arrangements can also be – and were – used to mask debt. A whisky distiller, for instance, may have to wait many years before assets are ready for sale. In the meantime, however, it can sell the maturing whisky to a bank, with the obligation to buy it back again at a certain date, at a fixed price. To all intents and purposes, this arrangement is a loan, with the whisky as security, but the debt is presented as a sale.

Debt can also be presented as equity through the use of certain financial instruments. Convertible preference shares, for example, begin as loan stock but may be converted by the holder to equity at a given date and price. Back in the 1980s, companies would routinely report this stock as equity, making the assumption that the decision would be to convert rather than call in the debt.

These and other abuses took place in a framework of rules which were flexible enough to be bent a long way without actually being broken. The mechanism for drawing up standards was often criticized as tortuously slow and, in any case, no independent body existed to enforce the standards that were established. Speaking in 1989 as a partner with accountants KPMG Peat Marwick McLintock, Tweedie warned: "If we do not do something soon about the state of financial reporting, we will end up in a total mess."

Source: Management Today, June, 1996.

## Merger Accounting

The more favourable treatment of pre-acquisition reserves which the merger accounting method allows, makes it more attractive for businesses to use this method than the acquisition method. It was not unusual, therefore, for companies to devise elaborate schemes that sought to hide the true nature of their parent/subsidiary relationship. However, FRS 6, *Acquisitions and Mergers,* has resulted in a considerable reduction in the incidence of merger accounting by introducing strict criteria for its use.

## Reorganization Costs and Fair Values

In the course of a take-over the acquiring company would typically make large provisions for anticipated post-acquisition reorganization costs. This would effectively make available to future periods large credit balances which, if unused, as was often the case, could then be written back to the profit and loss account, increasing profits in the process. Various standards such as FRS 7, *Fair Values in Acquisition Accounting,* have removed the scope for companies to manipulate provisions in this manner. They have also eliminated the related problem of the under-valuation of assets when determining goodwill.

The reason that creative accounting holds such an attraction for those charged with producing financial statements is that it allows manipulation of many key measurement criteria, such as profit, gearing and liquidity. These can then be exploited to obtain additional finance, distract attention from fundamental problems and increase management remuneration.

The manipulation of accounting numbers is not, therefore, an end in itself. The aim is to massage the figures in such a way as to achieve a particular goal, whether by hiding facts, impacting on ratios such as gearing, or distracting from true performance measures.

## Financial Reporting Review Panel

One key element of the current regulatory framework in the UK with direct relevance to attempts to deal with creative accounting is the FRRP. Its brief is to examine departures from accounting standards and accounting-related statutory provisions.

Under the Companies (Revision of Defective Accounts and Report) Regulations 1990 the FRRP has power to require that financial reports be either revised, supplemented or withdrawn in situations where it considers them to be "defective". Significantly, in circumstances where its recommendations are not immediately accepted, it can require that directors be made personally liable for any subsequent costs incurred.

The following review explains the "benign", yet effective, manner in which the FRRP conducts its reviews, as well as the often traumatic consequences of its attentions.

### Waving the Red Flag (Part 1)

**Doreen McBarnet and Christopher Whelan, Authors of a New Book on Creative Accounting, Argue that an Exclusive Reliance on Whistleblowers is Undermining UK Regulators' Efforts to Police Company Accounts**

It seems that creative accounting is a common practice world-wide. Last month in the US, for example, Warren Buffett told shareholders at the annual meeting of his Berkshire Hathaway investment group that many companies' results were "no more credible than bogus golf scores". The downside of creative accounting for investors such as Buffett, of course, is that shortcomings in corporate performance can be hidden and investors exposed to unseen risks. Buffett went on to tell shareholders that he was looking outside the US – Japan and the UK were named – for investment opportunities. One commentator observed that this may be to escape what Buffett called the "deplorable" and dishonest accounting practices of the increasing number of companies in the US that managed earnings.

But creative accounting is attractive not only for the advantages it brings, at least in the short-term. It has also proved very difficult to control. If Buffett invested in the UK, would he fare any better? Aren't British companies still "fiddling their profits" too? Or would Buffett find now that creative accounting is being controlled? Creative accounting is one of the primary targets of the UK's revamped financial reporting regime, spearheaded by ASB chairman Sir David Tweedie. Under his auspices, and backed by law, new weapons have been created to tackle creative accounting. Specific abuses have been targeted. Companies are required to report the "substance" of transactions, even where this differs from the legal form and, most significantly, there is an emphasis on principles rather than rules.

Principles, it is felt, are seen as the only way to capture the complexity of accounting, to fill regulatory gaps and to pre-empt problems such as "creative compliance". That term denotes complying with the specific letter of the law but not its spirit, which triggers the cat-and-mouse game where regulators catch one creative device with a specific rule only to find a new technique taking its place. Armed with these and other new weapons, the FRRP was created to police company accounts. The panel has a "war chest" to back its power to take directors to court. The court can order the revision of accounts and hold directors personally liable for all the costs involved. The panel has been described as the "military wing" of the ASB.

But can creative accounting be controlled? Is the new regime succeeding in curbing the abuses of the 1980s and the practices so deplored by Warren Buffett? Or can companies still escape the web of enforcement in spite of the new regime? For the time being, the jury is still out on the issue. "Watch this space" is the only firm conclusion we can draw. For, as with many other forms of regulatory law enforcement, there are two sides to the story.

On the one hand, the new regime can be presented as very successful. Whenever the panel has required remedial action, the directors have voluntarily agreed to it. Occasionally, the panel has threatened to take a company to court and, at the last moment, the company has conceded. There is a real fear on the part of directors in going to court. This may be because they see that they will lose and fear the consequences of so doing, both personally and for the company. It is just as likely, however, that directors fear the adverse publicity, win or lose, that goes with challenging the regulator in court. Not a single case has gone to court to date and it may take an exceptional set of circumstances to persuade the directors to resist the panel. Indeed, it is conceivable that no case will ever go to court – that when it comes to the crunch, directors will always concede and agree to revise the accounts (or even more than one set of accounts, which happened in one case).

Does this mean the regime has won the battle to control creative accounting? Certainly, there are hopes that this is the case. For some, the very presence of the panel serves as a deterrent. Recently, too, the panel's caseload, arguably never that onerous, has been falling sharply. In the mid-1990s, around 45 cases were drawn to the panel's attention each year. In 1997, though, the number fell to only 24 and in 1998 was still low at 32. For the leaders of the regime, this is evidence of a rise in the level of compliance.

However, there is another way of looking at these figures that undermines the claim that the regime is a success. Take the figures themselves. The panel has deliberately adopted an exclusively reactive rather than proactive approach. It will not monitor or actively initiate scrutinies of company accounts for possible defects. Cases are identified through what the former chair of the panel, Edwin Glasgow QC, termed whistleblowing – via individual or corporate referrals, qualified audit reports, departures from accounting standards or other requirements flagged in the accounts or press comment.

*Creative Accounting and the Cross-Eyed Javelin Thrower*, by Dr C. Whelan and Dr D. McBarnet, is published by John Wiley&Sons.

Source, The Accountant, Lafferty Publications Ltd., 1999.

The FRRP is, therefore, a critical element in the regulatory regime's armoury. The question remains, however, whether regulation is an effective means of countering what is essentially an ethical issue.

## Role of Ethics

While regulatory bodies such as the FRRP and individual standards such as FRS 5, *Reporting the substance of transactions*, have managed to eradicate many of the traditional creative accounting practices, the problem of manipulation of accounting information persists. For instance, the emergence of complex financial instruments such as junk bonds and derivatives has increased the scope for development of new and questionable practices. Likewise, the advent of the "new economy" has brought additional challenges directly related to the relatively unregulated world these firms inhabit.

One of the problems for the accounting profession, as Arthur Levitt described earlier, is that the perpetrators of these practices are usually accountants. Ironically, therefore, those concerned with the role of accountants in the modern commercial world, such as professional accounting bodies, find themselves having to deal with a situation in which accountants occupy the roles of both perpetrator and guardian.

In all of this the role of ethics in the training and professional lives of accountants and auditors assumes a greater importance. An increasing awareness that deficiencies in accounting education, where ethical issues have traditionally been subordinated to technical ability, is slowly resulting in more emphasis being placed on such matters.

Ethics describes that set of moral principles taken as a guide or reference point. Most humans adopt such a set or code in order to relate to the various environments within which they operate. This can range from the individual and personal to the corporate and professional. The problem with introducing an ethical perspective into the equation, however, is that it moves matters out of the technical and practical areas that constitute the "comfort zone" of most accountants, and into a less tangible domain.

Significantly, however, this is not an area unexplored by accountants or accounting bodies. In fact, accountants can take some solace from the fact that a substantial corpus of work relevant to the ethical nature of accounting already exists. Furthermore, the professional contexts within which most accountants already operate come complete with ethical guidelines and boundaries.

For example, the various professional accounting bodies operate a system of self-regulation as part of which they promulgate systems of ethical guidelines within which members are expected to operate. These can cover standards of behaviour, relationships between members and clients, and acceptable practice in particular circumstances. These regulations are supported by a variety of codes, such as the Combined Code on corporate governance, and various statutes, which assist accountants in navigating the often-torrid waters that they find themselves in.

However, as the following report highlights, the presence of such a code does not always resolve the problem for accountants.

## Professional Ethics Called into Question

An accountant's approach to ethical issues could be "inadequate" to meet the needs of good corporate citizenship, a CIMA survey reveals. And although one in three of the respondents identified major ethical issues which may have warranted them "blowing the whistle", all remained silent. Mandie Lavin, director of professional standards at CIMA, estimated that this number could in fact be a little higher – professionals may find it difficult that they have not said anything when they felt they should. "Anecdotally, it's a reasonably sound percentage," she said.

The report compared the ethical attitudes of accountants to human resource management specialists. And the approach of the accountancy profession was to treat ethical issues as "distractions that need to be minimized, neatly packaged, and disposed of". Lavin hoped that the document would spark a more pro-active approach to ethical issues in the profession. "I think it's time to heighten awareness throughout the profession of the value of ethical guidance," she said. The profession needs to be seen to be ethically sound. "It's what the whole thing's founded on," she said.

The report found that being economical with the truth, and bending the rules, were two major concerns. But these were part of the "normal routines of organizational life" – decisions need to be made quickly. Another factor was the undue use of power – bullying. Accountants would stand their ground when the issues involved were "local" – the subject fell within their managerial competence and were clearly covered by rules. But they are more focused on solving problems than doing right, the report notes. Many recognize a bad situation, but will remain neutral. And some will allow the case for business to outweigh the case for the individual, although residual guilt may ensue. The study also states that the Public Interest Disclosure Act, labelled as a "licence to whistleblowers" by some, may not provide the support necessary for those wishing to voice legitimate concerns. "There are limitations to the PIDA," Lavin said. "Some of the media coverage has suggested otherwise. The report tries to redress that balance."

Implementing ethical codes may not be what it should be: both groups thought that "codes had a useful reminding and referencing role, although few could recall an occasion on which they had referred to them."...

Source: AccountingWEB, November 27, 2000 (This article is continued in Case Study 3.)

As the research alluded to in this article notes, one of the problems is that accountants too often take refuge in regulations – "they are more focused on solving problems than doing right." Ethical issues are perceived to be "distractions that need to be minimized, neatly packaged, and disposed of". Such attitudes betray a refusal on the part of many accountants to grapple with the real issues raised by creative accounting practices which are themselves merely symptoms of an attitude that views the end as justifying the means. As Arthur Levitt observed, "It is a basic cultural change we are asking for". The fundamental question is whether this can be fostered by regulation alone. The answer is probably "no".

## Summary

Creative accounting can be defined as "the use and abuse of accounting techniques and principles to achieve financial statements which, intentionally, do not provide a true and fair view". Large financial frauds and scandals in the late 1980s and early 1990s resulting from such practices prompted accounting regulators on both sides of the Atlantic to address the more obvious and common manifestations of creative accounting.

By a mixture of regulations aimed at specific abuses and more fundamental accounting and auditing standards that require the application of the spirit of the law rather than merely the letter, regulators have been successful in eradicating many of these practices.

However, the problem of creative accounting remains one rooted in the belief that it is not the perpetration of such practices which is the problem, but being caught. As the accounting scandals in various dot.coms have demonstrated more recently, while it will never be eradicated, unless it is addressed at a more fundamental ethical level, creative accounting will never be controlled.

The willingness of accountants and their professional bodies to deal properly and ethically with the challenges posed by practices such as creative accounting is open to question. Ironically, the subject matter of the next chapter, Corporate Social Reporting, in which the role of the corporation as "corporate citizen" is considered, offers one area in which the *bona fides* of accountants on ethical issues might be tested.

# Review Questions

### Question 1
Define "creative accounting" and explain why it presents such a potent challenge to accounting regulators and users of accounting information.

### Question 2
SEC commissioner Arthur Levitt argues that what is needed as "a basic cultural change". Explain what he means by this and why creative accounting practices may need to be addressed at such a fundamental level.

### Question 3
Identify some of the more common examples of creative accounting used in the past and explain how recent accounting standards have helped to quash them to some extent.

### Question 4
"Creative accounting is usually intended to support, or even increase, share price. Since this is in the interests of shareholders there is rarely any pressure from this group to eradicate such practices". Explain what is meant by this statement and whether there is pressure from shareholders to abandon certain creative accounting practices.

### Question 5
Explain how, giving examples, the following areas were commonly the focus of creative accounting practice. In each case explain how the ASB had addressed the problem and discuss whether its approach has been successful or not:

- Extraordinary and exceptional items
- Goodwill write-off
- Off-balance sheet finance
- Quasi-subsidiaries

### Question 6
Identify the role of FRS 5, *Reporting the substance of transactions*, in the ASB's strategy for dealing with creative accounting.

### Question 7
Explain the role of the FRRP in combating creative accounting practices.

### Question 8
What is the role of "whistle-blowers" in uncovering creative accounting practices? Should there be greater legal protection for those willing to act in this way?

### Question 9
"Creative accounting has several positive features. It should not just be viewed as something to eradicate." Discuss.

# Case Studies

## Case 1

One of the biggest investigations into creative accounting practices in the UK in recent years has centred on a company called Versailles. The following article identifies what was attempted by the company management and the response of the various regulatory bodies involved. Identify and discuss the key issues raised.

## SFO Chief Orders Inquiry at Versailles Accounts and Shares Sale Under Scrutiny, by Dan Atkinson

Serious Fraud Office director Rosalind Wright last night ordered a full-scale criminal investigation into Versailles, the trading group at the centre of a £50 million-plus accounting scandal. The inquiry is likely to torpedo plans to relist shares in the fallen stock market star by the end of this month. Based on information supplied by the department of trade and industry last year, "there now appears to be sufficient reason... to authorize an investigation into possible serious and complex fraud", Mrs Wright said. Not only is the SFO investigating the company's accounts but it is bound also to look into the sale by founder Carl Cushnie of shares worth £29 million – about 5% of the equity – in autumn last year when he knew, and the market did not, that the company was being examined by a DTI-mandated auditors' inquiry.

In recent days Versailles came close to recruiting a new, high-powered financial adviser to assist its return to a stock market listing. Two top names were on the shortlist, but last night's announcement will probably terminate such discussions. Former advisers Raphael Zorn Hemsley and Teather & Greenwood refused to act further for Versailles in the wake of the December 8 statement in which the company first admitted that up to a third of turnover might have been illusory. Two days later, Versailles said it had lied on December 8 when it claimed to have uncovered the problems itself. It had been the DTI that came across apparent gaps in the accounts of Versailles early last year when it investigated the books of an insolvent company, Telecom Manufacturing Ltd (TML), of Airdrie, Scotland. Ironically, Versailles was a TML creditor, and thus a victim of its bankruptcy.

But, under the companies act, the DTI needed to inspect Versailles's books and in doing so cast doubt on the treatment of its MP product, by which it effectively finances a client's materials purchases. The nature of the product seemed to create double counting as a client's materials moved on and off the books of Versailles several times.

Confidentially, the DTI insisted Versailles commission a special audit to look at the problem. The accountancy firm Baker Tilly took on the job, and when it was unable to give the books a clean bill of health Versailles asked for the shares to be suspended and made its December 8 statement. But by then the chairman, Carl Cushnie, had sold £29 million worth of shares into a market entirely unaware of the DTI-ordered investigation. This sale of 5% of the equity still left him with 53% of

Versailles. Versailles last night noted the SFO statement but said it would be inappropriate to comment further. The company was one of the fastest-rising stars of the 1990s. Founded in 1989, Versailles has boomed in recent years, with particular success during the past 12 months. The shares have roared ahead from a few pence in January 1996 to about 150 p in January this year. On December 8, the shares were suspended at 250 p.

Three banks – NatWest, Royal Bank of Scotland and Barclays – have lent about £65 million to Versailles. They might now activate the "force majeure" clauses that will allow them to demand their money back. Accountancy firm PriceWaterhouse-Coopers is examining the books of Versailles on the banks' behalf. Even before last night's announcement Versailles had been braced for a share price crash of up to 50% when it relisted.

Source: The Guardian, January 19, 2000.

## Case 2

Regulators identify the need to encourage those within a firm who are aware of "creative practices" to come forward at an early stage. However, as the following extract explains, such whistleblowing is often likely to lead to serious consequences for those with the courage to do so. Explain whether and how an environment more conducive to such whistleblowing could be cultivated.

## Whistleblower Anthony Fernandes is Suing for Unfair Dismissal After Being Sacked for "gross misconduct", by Steve Hughes

Evidence in the tribunal case of whistleblowing accountant Antonio Fernandes was summed up late yesterday (Thursday April 6) afternoon, but members of the tribunal were unable to reach a decision due to time pressure. Fernandes claims that he was unfairly sacked after reporting his chief executive for allegedly making improper expense claims. A decision is expected within 4–6 weeks. Fernandes claims that expense payments were made to chief executive and managing director Stephen Woodhouse without any receipts being produced.

Fernandes was dismissed from Reading-based telecommunications consultancy Netcom Consultants UK on December 15, 1999, less than a month after reporting the irregularities to the chairman of Netcom's US sister company.

The decision to sack Fernandes for "gross misconduct" followed an internal inquiry. It is claimed that before he reported the irregularities, Fernandes had signed off expense payments to Woodhouse without supporting business documentation for a period of between 3 and 4 years. The internal inquiry also concluded that Fernandes had failed to make corporation tax payments and had paid employee pension contributions late.

Fernandes won the first round of his legal battle against his employer when an employment tribunal ruled that he should retain his £3,112 monthly salary, back-dated to January 1, pending full evidence. The case was tried under the Public Interest Disclosure Act, which protects individuals who make such disclosures. If Fernandes wins the case, the act allows uncapped compensation to be awarded.

Source: accountancymagazine.com, April 5, 2000.

## Case 3

This chapter has highlighted the role of ethics in eradicating a creative accounting mentality. Using the following article, part of which was quoted earlier in the chapter, discuss the role which ethics might play in countering the culture of accounting manipulation.

## Professional Ethics Called into Question

...The report "does demonstrate the practical difficulties that people face on a day-to-day basis," says Levin. Business moves fast, and reaching for the ethical guide-book is not always top priority. But she predicts that, with the new external regulator in January 2001, and public disciplinary hearings in February, greater public interest will be shown in the ethical judgements of the profession. "There will be greater rigour to ensure that standards are truly being met," she said. "From our point of view, it's fairly untrodden territory, and quite a sensitive area. As professionals, we are expected to know the ethical guidelines," she said. "But in some of these situations there's no perfect answer."

Lavin notes that people may be dealing with ethical issues without being aware of them; pressures of workload can hinder proper consideration. Often students find themselves studying, and try to apply what they have learned in the workplace, she says. Some have expressed concern about the difference between what they have done academically and in practice.

The report concludes: "accountants take a pragmatic approach to ethical questions and... this is maybe inadequate for meeting the demands for good corporate citizenship." It advises CIMA that it should develop codes that use more moral judgement than simple rules and regulations, and encourage forums of debate for professionals to seek informal advice on issues.

Professional bodies should consider ethics as one for the whole of accountancy to address, the study recommends. Lavin agrees; they could give more prescriptive guidance, she says, through a more comprehensive approach to sharing the knowledge gained from particular situations. Judgements from individual cases could be used to set guidelines for others in the profession. Continuing Professional Development is a duty – ethics should play a bigger part, she believes... "CIMA does want to drive forward this area of debate," she says.

The report may be controversial to some, Lavin admits. Professionals may not want to admit to their mistakes. But independent research, such as this study, should encourage more to grasp the ethical nettle. Ethical dilemmas will be open to scrutiny come the new year. How will the profession react, muses Lavin? "We are good at investigating problems, but are we as good at getting it right?" she asked. Good question.

Source: AccountingWEB, November 27, 2000.

# CORPORATE SOCIAL REPORTING (CSR)

When you have completed this chapter you will understand:

- The factors that have led to the emergence of Corporate Social Reporting (CSR).
- The contribution which CSR can make to corporate reporting culture.
- How "environmental accounting" has developed as environmental concerns have increased.
- The difficulties which this new agenda pose for many companies.
- Developments in the theoretical and regulatory supports for CSR.

## Of ethics, indices and the wisdom of the Easter bunny:

### A flurry of events over the past few days demonstrates that companies will have to pay increasing attention to their social responsibilities, whether they like it or not, By Martin Dickson

A dismal Easter weekend, in a land cursed with plague and sodden with so much rain it may signal a new phase of global warming. No better moment, perhaps, to raise our eyes from the workings of mammon and focus on a more uplifting issue: companies' social, environmental and ethical responsibilities.

At first glance this may not seem a very significant subject, particularly in a bear market when the emphasis is on corporate survival rather than do-goodery. Yet the events of the past week show that companies are being forced to pay much more than lip service to their responsibilities – and shareholders will need to keep a close eye on their commitment. Behind this lies a shift in philosophical climate: companies are increasingly expected to be accountable to society for their actions, as well as to shareholders for their financial performance. Until now, this has had little impact on investment decisions and thus on companies' policies. Funds that specialize in "socially responsible investing" – holding stakes in "good" sectors or excluding "bad" ones such as tobacco – are a fraction of the UK market and largely confined to the retail sector.

But the big money represented by institutional investors is starting to become engaged and it is conceivable that within 10 years social responsibility could become almost as hot an issue as corporate governance was in the 1990s.

The trend extends far beyond the UK, but in this country the institutions are being prodded not just by the Zeitgeist but by the government, which last year brought in regulations forcing pension funds to disclose whether they were taking account of environmental, social and ethical questions in their investments. There is no insistence that they do, but it will be an unusual fund that admits to amorality. And having paid lip-service to the principle of ethical investing, a closer examination of corporate words and deeds is likely to follow. This week Morley Fund Management, with £100 billion of assets, set a straw fluttering in the wind when it said that from now on it would vote against the accounts of FTSE 100 companies unless they included an environmental report. At present, only 37 do.

A few companies have seen these pressures building from a long way off – especially big oil groups most exposed by their global operations to complaints of environmental degradation and human rights abuse. Shell and BP Amoco produce annual social reports that are among the benchmarks for corporate Britain. Shell has just published its 2000 effort, promoted this week with irritatingly self-righteous newspaper advertisements that show rows of staff with ears cocked, listening for feedback. The content, however, is rather better. It runs to nearly 40 pages and is a mine of interesting facts, including the company's greenhouse gas emissions (down 11% on 1990), the age of its youngest employee (16), and the number of staff fired for soliciting or taking bribes (7).

It is all very well for a large company such as Shell to amass this data. But many British companies, already irritated by the lengthy disclosures they are now required to make on boardroom pay, may balk at having to provide yet another burdensome report. Yet not doing so may provoke bad publicity that far outweighs the costs involved.

Source: Financial Times; April 14, 2001.

## Introduction

Political and economic developments in recent years, for example, the collapse of the USSR and increasing international trade, coupled with the effects of advances in technology and telecommunications, have acted as catalysts prompting the re-evaluation of many of the long-accepted norms of western society.

One of these norms has been the view that companies exist primarily for the purpose of maximizing profits and, consequently, the wealth of its shareholders. Thus, while the responsibilities of companies to the broader community have been acknowledged, these have been understood to be adequately catered for under the legislative and contractual parameters within which companies operate. However, as the realities of corporate downsizing, take-overs, pollution and fraud have

exposed the frailty of these controls as means of protecting the interests of employees, the local community and other interested parties, the role of the company in
modern society has begun to be re-assessed.

As explained in Chapter 4, one of the consequences of this has been the emergence
of an alternative view of the company as a "corporate citizen" with responsibilities
for, and answerable to, a broader community of "stakeholders". This would include
employees, the local communities within which they operate, and interest groups
such as environmental agencies.

This extended accountability has come to be expressed in a variety of forms.
These include social audits, environmental impact reports and employee-centred
reports which are often, somewhat misleadingly, considered under the overall title
of Corporate Social Reporting.

---

### In practice:

*Making Values Count*

Roger Adams Reports on the trend Towards Increased Social Disclosure by Some of the
UK's Largest Companies

*What do mighty blue chips like Shell, BT, Diageo and Body Shop have in common with relative
minnows like Ben and Jerry's, Traidcraft and Shared Earth? And why has KPMG acquired Body
Shop's ethical audit team and launched a Sustainability Advisory Service at the same time as
PricewaterhouseCoopers is launching a "reputational risk" service for its clients? One answer
lies in the statement made by KPMG's UK senior partner Mike Rake at the time of Body Shop
acquisition. "In recent years", said Mr Rake, "it has become increasingly evident that a wide
range of leading companies recognize that financial performance is not the only yardstick by
which their sustainability should be measured... KPMG seeks to be innovators in this field and by
forming this strategic alliance with the recognized leader in sustainability reporting we shall be
able to provide a unique service to our clients." KPMG estimates that the new activity will be
worth some £20 million in fees within 3 years.*

*The notion that companies have responsibilities to groups other than their immediate share-
holders or lenders is not new, but the late 1990s seem to have marked the point at which the
fringe has become the norm – where what was once deeply suspicious and threatening has become
something keenly sought after by the most unlikely of suitors.*

*Of course, market forces have something to do with this transition. In his public presentations,
John Elkington – Executive Director of SustainAbility Ltd – refers to the "CNN World" in which
we live as a "goldfish bowl" existence where no one and, more relevantly, no company is able to
shield its activities from the public gaze and from society's criticism. Questionable corporate
social and ethical behaviour can be almost instantaneously spotlighted by campaign groups
world-wide. For example, the issue might be environmental (McDonalds) or human rights
(Shell), scientific (Monsanto), indigenous people (ABB) or child labour (Nike). The result,
however, is the same – possibly unwarranted but always unwanted high profile negative publicity. The power of the stakeholder society has never been stronger...*

*Source: www.acca.co.uk/media/features/fa27.html.*

# Corporate Social Reporting (CSR)

CSR is less a set of techniques and more a mindset predicated upon notions of good corporate citizenship and transparency. It re-asserts the role of accounting in the broader context of accountability, seeking to devise and articulate a view of the company as an entity answerable to those whose resources it consumes, whether labour, environment or quality of life.

Thus, while the traditional accounting model champions the priorities of capital, i.e., wealth and profit, CSR seeks a broader frame of reference. It envisages both quantitative and qualitative measures of expression and attempts to capture the "true" cost of corporate activity to the local and global community. For instance, where the current accounting model does not allow for reporting on issues such as the risk of loss of employment or unethical business practices, CSR would deem it imperative that these be identified and reported on, whether in quantitative or qualitative terms.

The extent to which these concerns have begun to filter into the reporting activities of many large companies and onto the agenda of various regulatory bodies can be gleaned from the following report.

## What is Social and Ethical Reporting?

"The practice of social and ethical accounting is emerging as a key tool for companies in the 1990s in response to calls for greater transparency and accountability to different stakeholders, and as a means for managing companies in increasingly complex situations where social and environmental issues are significant in securing business success" (Zadek et al. 1997)... Within the last year, developments within the Ethical and Social Reporting field have resulted in the creation of a new global standard for the reporting of ethical information, Social Accountability 8000 (SA8000), released by the Council for Economic Priorities (CEP). The standard provides an auditable framework for ethical sourcing.

The organization, The Institute of Social and Ethical AccountAbility (ISEA) was established in order to develop social and ethical accounting and auditing within organizations, by promoting the formation of standards. In Canada the "International Code of Ethics for Canadian Business" was released, supported by Canadian Occidental Petroleum. The Hampel committee also looked at applying good corporate governance, instead of completing a checklist, moving away from the detail of the Cadbury and Greenbury codes and concentrating on the reasons for good corporate governance. Graham Mason, CBI's (Confederation of British Industry) Director of Business Environment, said "Good corporate governance can lead to effective accountability of a company's board to its shareholders, but it is not a guarantee of good business performance."

"Vyarkarnam (1992) found that current Corporate Social Responsibility concerns encompass such areas as:

- Environmental protection (e.g., reduction of emissions and waste and the recycling of materials).
- Philanthropy (donating to charities, etc.).
- Involvement in social causes (involving anything from human rights to AIDS education).
- Urban investment (working with local government to regenerate small businesses and the inner city environment generally), and
- Employee schemes (higher standards of occupational health and safety, good standard of staff treatment, job sharing, flexi-time, etc.) (Balabanis *et al.* 1998).

There is huge diversity in volumes of corporate disclosure, with companies such as The Body Shop, Traidcraft and Ben and Jerry's leading the way. Petrochemical companies BP and Shell have recently produced ethical and social reporting documents: BP's 1997 Social Report and Shell's Profits and Principles – Does There Have To Be A Choice? Home Depot, an American company produces a social responsibility report and an ethics guide to growth.

Although Ethical and Social Reporting is some way behind environmental reporting, the recent interest and active participation from companies in sectors such as telecommunications, extractive and retail, bodes well for its development in the future.

Source: http://cei.sund.ac.uk/ethsocial/what.htm.

Because it is more a way of thinking than a set of accounting techniques, CSR will depend heavily upon a theoretical base for its legitimacy and development. While such a theoretical base has been only slowly forming, the emergence of stakeholder theory provides one useful avenue, allowing the competing interests of a more broadly based set of interested parties to be recognized and addressed. Within this paradigm it is possible, for instance, to identify the information requirements of groups not traditionally addressed, such as the local community and employees, and to formulate means by which the company can communicate with these groups through the Annual Report or by other means.

In tandem with the development of a theoretical base, various regulatory bodies, governments agencies and pressure groups have been campaigning to have standards introduced.

## Called to Account, Multinationals are Waking Up to Fact That Social Irresponsibility Can Hit the Share Price, by Roger Cowe

It began with Brent Spar – the oil platform whose bungled disposal left mighty Shell floundering. Then Nike was stung by the exposure of labour conditions in factories where its trainers were made. Monsanto has been humbled over genetically modified food. Now Microsoft has joined the corporate bodies tainted with social irresponsibility. When Shell was confronted with the Brent Spar fiasco in 1995, and then controversy in Nigeria, it was unusual. But it has become increasingly common for companies to be challenged in this way, and the challenges have had an increasing financial impact – as the slump in Monsanto's stock market value testifies.

Prominent multinationals are not the only targets and, as the Microsoft case demonstrated, it is not only campaigners such as Greenpeace hurling the accusations. The UK government's "rip-off Britain" campaign questioned the business practices of high street retailers and Railtrack has been widely attacked since the Paddington rail crash. Questioning the values and activities of the business world – and the inability of the targets to respond adequately – has kick-started the development of "social reporting". That is the process of assessing how a business performs in dealing with customers, employees and other interest groups – in the eyes of the stakeholders.

Until recently this was a minority sport practised only by unusual businesses such as Traidcraft and Body Shop. Now there are more than a dozen top UK companies publishing social reports, including BAA and United Utilities as well as Shell and BT. More, including the normally low-profile British American Tobacco, will join the club in the next 18 months. Abroad, Telecom Italia, Danish pharmaceutical company Norsk Hydro and South Africa's Hollard Insurance, are all interested. Nike will produce its first social and environmental report next year. Sarah Severn, Nike's director of environmental action, predicts that many other US companies will follow suit. "If they are global companies they will have to," she told the recent annual conference, in Copenhagen, of the ISEA, an international body embracing companies and those who seek to hold them to account.

Simon Zadek, who chairs the institute, said there was widespread interest around the world from companies struggling to come to terms with demands to be more accountable and to win the trust of customers, employees and other stakeholders. "Every major global branded multinational is exploring these issues," he said. For Shell and Nike the reasons are not hard to see. They need to win back trust. For others there is a more positive motivation.

Chris Tuppen, BT's social and environmental programmes manager, made clear that profit is still the key element in the bottom line, even if social and environmental issues have crept on to what has been dubbed the "triple bottom line".

Source: The Guardian, November 27, 1999.

## Corporate Report

As with much else, the Corporate Report, a discussion paper commissioned by the Accounting Standards Steering Committee and published in 1975, and which took much of its inspiration from the Trueblood Committee in the US, played a seminal role in extending the business and accounting world's understanding of "accountability" and the expressions this might take.

It achieved this primarily by arguing that, as part of their "public accountability" function, economic entities of "significant size", (which it did not quantify), had a responsibility to report to a variety of users.

As a consequence the Report envisaged the publication of an Annual Report that not only provided financial information but was sufficiently comprehensive that it described an organizations economic activity. While including basic financial statements such as the balance sheet and profit and loss account, it was envisaged that such a report would also include narrative elements and various descriptive statements.

In an attempt to address the information needs of the broad range of users, it suggested that several additional statements be included in the report:

- **Statement of corporate objectives**: by challenging the corporate hierarchy to articulate its goals and objectives it was hoped to encourage the adoption of mission statements which would embrace a wider set of impulses, in the process recognizing the interests of stakeholders other than shareholders.

- **Value-added statement**: this was designed to highlight the various interest groups, for example employees, shareholders and government which benefited from the wealth generated by a business. In the late 1970s these statements were widely produced. However, they have now disappeared almost entirely from UK Annual Reports.

There was never a standard format for these statements. However, the following example illustrates how such a statement might highlight the link between wealth generated and those benefiting:

Value-added statement for X plc for the year ended December 31, 20X1

|  | £ | £ |
|---|---|---|
| *Funds available* | | |
| Sales | | 8,000,000 |
| Less: goods bought in | | 2,000,000 |
| Value added | | 6,000,000 |
| *Applied as follows* | | |
| To employees as wages, pensions and other | 1,500,000 | |
| To government as taxes | 1,000,000 | |
| To providers of capital as dividends | 3,000,000 | |
| | | 5,500,000 |
| Retained by company for capital investment | | 500,000 |

- **Employment report**: this was intended to provide information relating specifically to employees, such as details of gender, training costs, health and safety and other matters.

- **Statement of foreign-currency transactions**: at a time when foreign trade was becoming a more significant element in corporate activity this was designed to highlight the financial implications of foreign currency activity.

- **Statement of monetary exchanges with government**: this was intended to indicate the level of financial interaction with government or government agencies. It was envisaged that it would embrace not only various taxation issues, but also grants and related matters.

- **Statement of future prospects**: while recognizing that there was resistance to such disclosure on the grounds of uncertainty as well as sensitivity to competitors having access to this information, it was felt that where it was intended to engage in activities which would impact upon employees or the local community that this should be disclosed.

For a number of reasons, most significantly a change of government coupled with resistance from business leaders to what were seen as onerous and extensive new disclosure requirements, the recommendations of the Corporate Report were never comprehensively implemented. It did, however, lay the foundation for discussion and research into the nature and role of CSR. And significantly, the current debate articulates many of these same objectives.

## Recent Developments in CSR

Throughout the 1980s the espousal of the primacy of the free market economy by Western governments, particularly in the US under Ronald Reagan and the UK under Margaret Thatcher, resulted in the subordination of concerns about social accounting issues. By the end of that decade, however, the contention that legislative protection was sufficient to protect the interests of stakeholders had been exposed as fallacious by a series of frauds, environmental disasters and huge employment losses resulting from financially-driven mergers and take-overs.

The result was a re-kindling of interest in CSR, which was seen to provide a framework within which this broader set of corporate responsibilities might be considered. The Turnbull Report, which requires boards to consider and assess risks from social, environmental and reputational sources, and to develop appropriate internal controls, has placed CSR firmly in the centre of the accountability agenda. Likewise, the preliminary drafts of the Company Law Review (see Chapter 18) suggest that companies will be required to report on these areas, perhaps in the OFR. In addition, some residue of the Corporate Report does persist in the form of Employee Reports that are still produced by many companies and offer a model for other areas. The whole area of Human Resource accounting also offers scope for development, particularly as the role of intellectual capital as a source of corporate wealth comes to be acknowledged.

Nevertheless, the adoption and assimilation of CSR as a significant element in the corporate reporting culture has been slow and fraught with difficulties. There are a number of reasons for this:

- The attraction of the traditional accounting model
- The lack of a theoretical and conceptual base

- The resistance of some regulatory bodies on the basis of the perceived subjectivity and audit-unfriendliness of qualitative measures and reports

The immediate challenge remains, therefore, the development of a robust theoretical framework and a regulatory sub-structure within which the gains of CSR may be consolidated. With these established the possibility that CSR may emerge as a core reporting requirement in the future remains tenable.

---

**In practice:**

*Canny Companies Come Clean: Firms Are Finding it Pays to Tell the Truth About their Social and Environmental Impact*

*When a company goes to the expense of producing a glossy corporate report, the last thing you expect to see in it are comments such as "this report is greenwash", or "you shut your eyes to political situations as long as you can make money. What hypocrisy!"*

*Welcome to a new generation of corporate reporting, where companies solicit the opinions of friends and foes – employees, suppliers, the communities in which they operate – to gain a warts-and-all picture of how they do business.*

*Social reporting, as it is called, is a fast-growing feature of the corporate landscape. A survey of 98 of the FTSE 100 companies by Pensions and Investment Research Consultants found that 79 report in some way on social and community issues, though only 14 produce dedicated social reports.*

*Source: The Guardian, June 27, 1999.*

---

## Environmental Reporting

With the acknowledgement of the rights of stakeholders other than investors, it has become increasingly difficult for business to sustain a reporting model predicated upon outdated modes of governance. The fact that accounting practice often merely reflects and perpetuates a corporate governance system dedicated to the rights of "owners" means that it too will be impacted by any changes in the culture of organizations. The likelihood is that changes in the corporate governance model induced by macro economic and social changes will force change on accounting and reporting practices.

The human impact on the environment, as measured by, for example, global warming, depletion of the ozone layer and pollution, has focused the minds of governments, regulators, business and ordinary individuals on the costs, both financial and environmental, of human activity. While industries belching out smoke and businesses engaging in environmentally damaging practices for short-term gain may well have been accepted as the inescapable consequences of progress a century ago, this is no longer tolerated.

---

**In practice:**

---

*FTSE-100 Annual Reports Go Green: Another 22 of the FTSE-100 Companies Have Pledged to Publish Annual Environmental Reports, Pushing the Issue of Sustainability Reporting Further Up the Business Agenda, By Michelle Perry*

*The development means companies' environmental and social performance is rapidly becoming a crucial factor as investor interest grows and accountancy firms develop new techniques to measure such performance. Announcing the news, environment minister Michael Meacher said: "Investors, insurers, bankers and others are increasingly aware of business ethics, environmental liabilities and risks. At the heart of this agenda is better environmental reporting."*

*On the back of a recent challenge from the prime minister the DETR wrote to 30 of the FTSE-100 companies urging them to report on environmental and social issues. The 22 will add to the 37 that already produce reports on how they minimize damage to the environment and their local communities.*

*BT and Cable and Wireless are some of the leaders in environmental reporting. Now Orange, Vodafone, Energis and Telewest will also publish their first environmental reports this year. Accountancy firms are playing a major role in developments, too. KPMG and PricewaterhouseCoopers are two of the leaders in this sector. KPMG's UK head of environment Michael Kelly said: "The issues driving this are regulatory compliance, stakeholder and shareholder pressure, the City and investor interest. Operational efficiency is also a driver."…*

*Source: Accountancy Age, February 13, 2001.*

---

Companies were previously able to "externalize" such costs, i.e., impose the burden of bearing such destruction or depletion on the local environment or community, or even customers, in the case of environmentally suspect products such as asbestos. However, they are now being forced to internalize such costs, i.e., to develop accounting procedures that see them incur the costs of their activities.

Prompted by stakeholders, and sensing a certain cache, indeed competitive advantage in adopting a "green" image, as well as more immediate benefits such as decreased liabilities, many companies have willingly embraced the environmental agenda. One of the more obvious of these is The Body Shop which includes a substantial amount of information on social, environmental and ethical issues in its Annual Report.

Whether willingly or otherwise, one consequence of business becoming sensitive to environmental concerns is that new managerial practices must be devised to ensure both operational and financial accountability. In this process accounting can play a key role. Significantly the debate has centred on the capacity of the traditional accounting model to meet these new accounting needs and whether a new accounting model might not need to be developed. As part of this process environmental reporting has become established as a credible and useful element of the financial reporting practices of many companies.

---

**In practice:**

---

*Environmental Reporting - Creating the Right Environment*

*The number of companies publishing some sort of environmental report has increased exponentially over the last 10 years. The bigger corporate polluters in the energy, extraction and construction sectors have been publishing health, safety and environmental data for a long time. Many now produce separate environmental performance reports and, as the environmental bandwagon gathers momentum, other companies have been venturing into social reporting. Both BT and NatWest recently produced their first social reports and Rio Tinto has combined a social and environmental report for some years.*

*Environmental reporting usually involves quantifying the direct impacts of a company's activities on the environment and virtually all reports include data on carbon dioxide, sulphur dioxide and other greenhouse gas emissions. Attempts are being made to move towards "sustainability" reporting, which takes account of a company's indirect impact on the environment, as well as direct impact. The boundaries of sustainability reporting are difficult to draw, however, because indirect impacts include not only the impact of, say, customer and supplier activity, but can extend ad infinitum through the supply chain. "Triple-bottom-line reporting" – the idea that measures of economic and social impact together with measures of sustainability, can be integrated – is still some way off.*

*Even so, each year sees new reporting formats and more companies producing environmental reports for the first time. The environmental reputation of a company still has virtually no effect on its market valuation and there is, therefore, no direct financial benefit to publishing environmental reports. Companies produce environmental reports partly out of a growing concern for the environment, but mostly because they get into trouble if they do not. There is now significant pressure from the government and the environmental lobby for companies to publish environmental and social data, particularly those that operate in the third world, although there are still no mandatory reporting requirements.*

*Source: AccountancyAge.com, June 14, 2000.*

## Sustainability

One catalyst for change in relation to environmental concerns was the Pearce Report (1989). Building upon the earlier Brundtland Report, this sought to identify how economic policies might be aligned to more environmentally sensitive concerns. One way in which this might be achieved, it suggested, was to adopt policies which required that the full cost of consuming environmental resources traditionally considered "free" would be absorbed (internalized) by industry.

This conclusion derives from the concept of "sustainability", a term predicated on a view of resources as limited, some critically so. The Brundtland and Pearce Reports as well as various others had championed the notion of "sustainable" development as a means of grappling with the nature of resources, or capital. In recent years a template has emerged which classifies resources into three categories:

1. Man-made capital, such as machines, roads, etc.

2. Renewable natural capital, i.e., items which are easily renewable such as most animals and plants.

3. Critical (non-renewable) natural capital, such as the ozone layer, non-renewable mineral deposits, tropical forests and rare flora and fauna. A business is considered unsustainable to the extent that it consumes these resources.

On the grounds that profit figures are misleading where they do not include a charge for the depletion of critical natural capital, these and other reports suggested that such a charge be incorporated in computing profit. The environment was now to be regarded as a resource held in trust for future generations, with sustainability understood as a measure of corporate success. The most obvious result would be a charge against profit for those companies that were unsustainable.

For most companies this is a step too far. While willing to disclose amounts incurred to protect the environment from the effects of their activity, this would require that they indicate the cost to the global community of the depletion of non-renewable resources resulting from their activity.

Nevertheless, the implications for accounting are considerable. For a start, as the traditional arbiters of "cost", the understanding is that accountants should devise mechanisms by which such costs would be recognized and measured, i.e., internalized, by business. This approach also challenges the role of accounting in advocating investment appraisal techniques, which, because of their use of high discount rates, incorporate an inherent bias towards short-termism. For example, the more common investment appraisal techniques favour less capital-intensive electricity generating facilities at the expense of those that avail of renewable resource approaches such as wind power because the latter require heavy initial investment and only generate positive NPV cash flows over the long term.

Responding to these initiatives the accountancy bodies, although not, significantly, accounting regulators such as the ASB, have begun to take initiatives in this area. In 1990 the Association of Chartered Certified Accountants (ACCA) sponsored a major report, The Greening of Accountancy: the Profession after Pearce, written by Professor Rob Gray. And it has followed up this initial commitment with an annual award for Annual Reports indicating responsiveness to the "green" accounting agenda.

As part of this process the role of auditors has also been considered, with particular interest focusing on their capacity to report on the degree to which companies have complied with stated environmental policies as well as their role in carrying out environmental audits. This is consistent with a growing appreciation of their role as assessors of internal risk-control measures.

Some of the remaining challenges are highlighted in the following report which, apart from identifying areas of concern, also confirms that advances are being made, albeit slowly, in the regulatory sub-structure.

# How Good Are Green Reports?

## There is a Danger That Readers Are Drawing Too Much Assurance From Environmental Reports, by Katherine Bagshaw

Environmental reporting has come a long way. Gone are the days when chief executives routinely treat environmental issues as an irritating operational problem of no strategic importance and airily dismiss both questioning and criticism on the subject. Environmental pressure groups are now too well-organized, well-informed and adept at manipulating the media for that, and they do not like being patronized. Big oil companies have been producing pages and pages of tough-looking technical data on their greenhouse gas emissions for some years now. The Body Shop, BT and others have pushed the boundaries of social and sustainability reporting with new reporting formats every year. It is all very exciting really, especially for the big environmental consultants and accountants whose job it is to advise on what goes into these reports and what can and cannot be verified.

And the standard of reporting is generally getting better. Open any environmental report, and the same targets, standards and agreements stand out: the Kyoto Protocol, the Rio Summit, the Montreal Agreement, the European Environmental Audit and Management Scheme (EMAS), ISO 14001, the US Toxic Release Inventory, and so on. Companies are even getting better at balanced reporting because they have worked out that two pages of "what went wrong", rather than silence, keeps the critics quiet. It all looks quite promising.

## Regulatory Vacuum

But all of these improvements are underpinned by a precarious combination of corporate integrity and good news to report. There is a complete regulatory vacuum, with no generally accepted reporting formats and no generally accepted reporting standards. At the end of the day, there is no mandatory requirement for any company in the UK to produce any kind of environmental report whatsoever. In the absence of a proper reporting framework, we just do not see the whole picture.

Reporting frameworks are being developed: the Coalition for Environmentally Responsible Economies' (CERES) Global Reporting Initiative, for example, has issued a set of "Guidelines for Sustainability Reporting" as a consultation document. The Fédération des Experts Comptables Européens (FEE) is also working on the subject. But these frameworks lack detail; they are a long way from finalization and even further from general acceptance. Another messy and worrying aspect of environmental reporting is verification. Some environmental reports are verified, others are not; some verifiers are firms of accountants, others are environmental consultants. Visions of auditors out there in hard hats and armed with batteries of Geiger counters and smog meters, are, sadly, somewhat wide of the mark... Katharine Bagshaw is director of GAAP Training Ltd.

Source: Accountancy, April, 2000.

These, however, represent only the beginnings of both a conceptual and a regulatory framework. Indeed, in spite of the fact that a small minority has championed CSR and environmental accounting and reporting for several decades, its viability is constantly being questioned. While it is likely that some element of CSR will always be insisted upon, the challenge will be to extend its sphere of influence so that it becomes less a peripheral element and more a central theme in corporate reports.

## Summary

An increasing acceptance of the rights of a broader set of stakeholders, coupled with a growing awareness that corporate responsibilities extend to social and environment issues, challenges accounting both conceptually and practically. In particular, the notion of sustainable development and the consequent accounting and investment appraisal implications pose huge challenges for accountants.

The traditional accounting model can only be extended to embrace this new agenda with some difficulty. And, despite valiant efforts by some individuals to force the pace on issues such as accounting for environmental costs, progress has been limited.

Nevertheless, the prognosis is good. The extent to which environmental reporting has succeeded in establishing its claims to a place in the accountability debate suggests that there is scope for other elements of the CSR agenda to be accommodated. The likelihood is, however, that this will only be achieved as governments and regulators respond to the more inclusive "stakeholder" paradigm, and to the broader set of demands for good corporate citizenship which this both implies and facilitates.

# Review Questions

### Question 1
Identify and explain the various factors that have given rise to what is now commonly called CSR. Is this a fad or is it likely to influence corporate reporting into the long term?

### Question 2
Explain the role played by The Corporate Report in identifying CSR as an area which was likely to have a considerable impact upon corporate reporting in the future.

### Question 3
What are the principal deficiencies in the traditional accounting model identified by those supporting CSR as a reporting paradigm?

### Question 4
Assess the significance for the nature and role of CSR of each of the following:

- Pearce Report
- Brundtland Report
- ACCA's Environmental Reporting Award

### Question 5
In your opinion how does CSR relate to the whole question of the company as "corporate citizen"?

### Question 6
Discuss the role which stakeholder theory could play in acting as a means by which CSR might be assimilated more fully into the financial reporting agenda.

### Question 7
Account for the fact that environmental accounting has emerged as the one area within CSR capable of establishing a central role for itself in the reporting process.

### Question 8
Explain what is meant by "sustainability" and why this is a central concern in environmental reporting.

### Question 9
"The Turnbull Report may well be remembered as the report which finally established risks related to the environmental and social aspects of corporate life at the centre of the reporting and control agendas." Explain why the Turnbull report could be seen in this light.

# Case Studies

## Case 1

Check the extent to which environmental and social issues are addressed in the Tesco plc Annual Report 2000 and discuss whether the level of disclosure is adequate in view of the range of stakeholders attaching to such a large international enterprise.

## Case 2

Access a copy of the most recent Annual Report for The Body Shop plc and compare the level of social, environmental and ethical reporting in this with that disclosed by Tesco plc.

## Case 3

ACCA has been to the forefront in promoting Environmental and Social Reporting. Using the following article as a reference point, and paying particular attention to the notion of environmental reporting as just the "tip of an iceberg" in terms of the sub-structure which it fosters, discuss whether such a project can achieve any practical results.

## Good Citizen:

### Good Business Environmental Reporting, and the Underlying Accounting and Management Processes Behind it, has Traditionally Been Seen More as a Chore Than as a Benefit. But Companies Have Much to Gain, Not Least a Positive Impact on Their Corporate Reputations, by Sarah Perrin

PIRC's latest survey, Environmental Reporting 2000, shows the disparity between the reporting standards of the 674 All-Share Index companies reviewed. While half of FTSE-100 companies report on environmental improvements and target setting, less than 10% of SmallCap companies do so, despite governmental exhortations. Information technology companies are the worst at reporting on any environmental issues, with only 14% disclosing that they actually have an environmental policy and none describing any improvements in environmental impacts, target setting or that they undertake green audits. However, Tessa Younger, senior researcher at PIRC, expects to see more IT companies reporting on environmental issues next year. "I believe many of them have reports in the pipeline," she says. "This year's result is an indication that many IT companies are quite young and are still gearing up to do it."

The fourth Business in the Environment (BiE) Index of Corporate Environmental Engagement, which looks behind reports to focus on management practices, showed similar findings. The BiE Index requires companies to assess themselves against 10 parameters of environmental management, and therefore requires their willingness to participate. Only one FTSE-listed IT company from a possible 15 participated in its latest Index, published in March. In contrast, all 16 FTSE-350 utilities companies took part, a result reflecting the impact that regulatory and lobby group pressure has had on this sector.

## Chore or Benefit?

The obvious conclusion is that companies still see environmental accounting and reporting as a chore, rather than an activity that can bring positive benefits. When launching the fourth BiE Index, chairman Derek Higgs, commented: "The Index identifies a range of environmental issues that are in fact corporate financial risks. I would sum these up as the potential threat to competitiveness from pursuing a strategy which is not sustainable as regards energy, material or resources or possible future eco-taxes or legislation. If boardrooms take this on board, they will find both their companies' performance, and our environment, improve still further." Belinda Howell, a director at BiE, refers to additional research completed in 1999, which found that 86% of UK adults considered the environment to be an extremely important part of corporate responsibility, and that a company's approach to the environment was the single most important factor in contributing to a positive corporate reputation. "We feel that the environment is pretty high up in terms of how consumers and other stakeholders, including shareholders, regard companies," says Howell. "Riots in Seattle, when the World Trade Organization met last year, show there is an increasing trust deficit between individuals and companies; but if companies show environmental responsibility, that helps to support their corporate reputations."

A positive reputation in environmental affairs has one obvious benefit – it enables a company to attract ethical investors. Jupiter Asset Management has £12.5 billion of funds under management, of which approximately £260 million belongs to various sociably responsible investment funds. To be eligible for investment by such funds, companies must meet varying criteria according to the specific investment product, explains Emma Howard Boyd, head of the environmental research unit. "One of the indicators we look for is the publication of an environmental report or some information in their annual report that gives an indication of their environmental performance," she says. Howard Boyd expects that interest in ethical investment will increase further after new regulations for pension fund trustees come into force in July, under which trustees will be legally required to state the extent to which they consider socially responsible investment criteria when constructing their portfolios. "This is already resulting in a number of institutional investment houses looking at socially responsible investments, perhaps for the first time," she says. "It should mean that companies will be asked more questions in relation to their environmental performance."

Environmental reports, containing quality information showing corporate commitment to reducing environmental impact, can clearly have positive repercussions with consumers and investors. But there are still more advantages from establishing sound environmental accounting practices as Scottish Power, joint runner up in the 1999 ACCA Environmental Reporting Awards, has found. Fred Dinning, corporate environment director, stresses that reporting is only the final part of the environmental accounting process. "There is a grave danger that companies see environmental reporting as an end in itself and that would be a very bad thing," he says. "The report should be the visible top of an iceberg. Below that you have governance processes and risk processes. You are looking at the environmental risks which are arising, you are looking at where your company might be in future and you are linking the vision of that with what sustainable development means in your sector. You are assessing those risks and opportunities and devising a business strategy. The governance processes and the risk evaluation processes will all lead your business down a certain route. Your environmental report is a way of showing publicly what that route may be and it is your way of reporting back on the key performance indicators you have set, although only a limited amount of that can be made public because these days it is becoming increasingly commercially sensitive. So the report is part of a much bigger, more important, dynamic process."

Scottish Power experienced the benefit of its thoroughness in these areas when acquiring US energy company PacifiCorp last year. "Our environmental track record, as set out in our environment report, was of considerable advantage in the PacifiCorp acquisition," says Dinning. "Many of the stakeholders, the interested parties in the US, immediately sought environmental information via such means as the web and contacts with pressure groups over here. Our environmental report provided some publicly available material which was immediately useable. That and the rest of the iceberg (the processes and controls which assisted with the detailed due diligence process) put us in a very strong position to deal rapidly with these enquiries and queries. So, the environmental report is an important public display of the good work you are doing internally. It is that important part of the iceberg for people to see so they will know the other nine tenths are working away happily under the surface."

## Good Corporate Citizenship

Mark Goyder, director of the Centre for Tomorrow's Company, cites B&Q as an example of another company which found tangible advantages from adopting an environmentally responsible approach to sourcing its timber. Although the company adopted the policy in order to be a good corporate citizen, it subsequently found that it was attracting younger customers. The marketing department noted the potential. "Sooner or later even the finance director was quite pleased," says Goyder. "So, yesterday's community problem becomes today's customer issue, and that becomes tomorrow's finance director issue. Community issues are often leading indicators of where the wind is blowing. So in that sense there are positive opportunities for businesses (from adopting a socially concerned stance)." Goyder believes there is a correlation between socially responsible business practices, including environmental concern, and good corporate performance in terms of shareholder value. "We have published evidence which links those kinds of behaviours-an inclusive approach-with shareholder return," he says. "We think the reason there is a correlation is that they are surrogates for good leadership and relationship management." It is a common sense hypothesis, Goyder says.

The benefits may be out there, but David Coles, head of KPMG's Sustainability Advisory services, believes companies are not doing enough to generate positive outcomes from their environmental accounting and reporting. "The (mainstream) investment community, for whom the annual report and accounts is primarily aimed, is not interested in environmental issues because analysts do not yet see the connection between good environmental performance and overall good performance," he says. "That is partly their fault and partly the companies' fault for explaining environmental issues in negative terms-in terms of 'not being as bad a polluter as we used to be' – rather than in terms of what it is done for cost savings for the business, or developing better products. Even companies that are good reporters tend to treat it as something they are getting less bad at, rather than something which is giving them a genuine advantage. The challenge for businesses is to say something about their environmental performance which demonstrates the benefits of good environmental performance, rather than being so defensive. Some are doing that, but they are few in number." Coles cites Baxter, the healthcare and pharmaceuticals group in the US, as a good example. "They have a good website (www.baxter.com/investors/citizenship/environment al/financials98.html) and report on cost-savings – how much money their environmental performance has saved them," says Coles.

Roger Adams, ACCA's head of technical and research, believes a number of factors are coming together that will increase pressures on companies to report on environmental matters in their annual report and accounts. These include the Turnbull recommendations, requiring boards to consider risks arising from social, environmental and reputational sources and report that they are satisfied they have a control structure in place to address those risks. In addition, says Adams: "The Company Law Review team is saying that companies will be expected to comment on social, environmental and reputational issues, when these are significant, and that the appropriate vehicle for doing this is the annual report and accounts and the Operating and Financial Review in particular." Adams also notes the incoming new regulations for pension fund trustees. "If trustees are going to start using social and environmental issues in the (investment) screening process, that information has to come from somewhere," he says. The annual report and accounts could provide some of that information, as could stand alone reports and web-based information. Finally, Adams refers to a new report from the Centre for Tomorrow's Company, The Corporate Reporting Jigsaw, which discusses how companies can achieve more integrated reporting of financial, social and environmental issues. "There is quite a groundswell of opinion that says the annual report and accounts is a useful communication channel and more can be done to maximize its value," says Adams.

The UK and Europe may be ahead of the US in reporting environmental performance. Chris Burgess, head of the environmental services team at Deloitte & Touche in the UK, says that anecdotal evidence from contact with global colleagues suggests that interest in environmental reporting has been slower to take off in the US, as well as in Canada and Japan, when compared to Europe. "In the US this type of reporting has been generally seen as a regulatory and compliance chore," he says. "A lot of businesses only take the first step grudgingly. It is only when they are in the process of preparing their first report do they realize there are benefits. You improve the management information you obtain and it gives you a fresh focus for looking at cost savings."

Opinion is growing that establishing environmental accounting procedures and controls, and then reporting on achievements in a positive light, can have a pronounced impact on corporate reputation and value. However, Burgess has a word of warning for those setting out along the environmental accounting and reporting path. "If businesses are going to get real benefit from reporting, it has to be done wholeheartedly," he says. "If they go into it without considering the implications, benefits, risks and resources required, it will always remain a cost and an overhead. Companies need to invest to get quality information."

Sarah Perrin is an accountant and writer.

Source: Accounting and Business, May, 2000.

# INTERNATIONAL ACCOUNTING AND HARMONIZATION

When you have completed this chapter you will be understand:

- That accounting practice differs significantly between countries.
- Some of the principal features of the German and French accounting and governance systems.
- Why globalization has brought with it calls for greater harmonization of accounting practice.
- The role being played by the International Accounting Standards Committee (IASC) in this process.

## Global Standards Challenge Companies

Investors in Daimler-Benz, the German carmaker, received a shock when the company listed in New York and reissued its accounts to comply with US standards. The Atlantic crossing turned a 1993 profit of DM615 million (198 million pounds) into a loss of DM1.84 billion, the result of a stricter US approach to accounting for expected future losses.

A ground-breaking plan published by the European Commission yesterday aims to end the confusion caused to investors by this kind of wild swing in corporate numbers. The Commission wants to force companies across Europe to offer investors accounts that comply with a single regional standard. The proposal would mean a big cultural change for companies in many European countries, leading to extensive revisions of profits to fit in with tighter pan-regional rules. "The whole thing is just a major challenge," says Mary Keegan, head of the global corporate reporting group at the UK business of PwC, the professional services firm. The new rules would cover 6,700 public companies, of which only 275 claim to follow internationally recognized standards.

The change would mean EU companies have to follow regulations drawn up by the IASC, the body set up by the accounting profession in 1973 to come up with a set of global rules. The Commission says the costs of variations in financial reporting methods in the EU are onerous and stand in the way of developing a single capital market. It wants the new rules in place by 2005 at the latest, with the possibility of extending the requirement to unlisted companies and to preparation of the accounts of individuals.

International standards take a stricter line than most national standards on "earnings management", or the practice of smoothing profits from year to year to avoid the volatility that disturbs investors. A series of IASC rules due to be passed in the next few years are likely to introduce further volatility, by requiring companies to ascribe market values to items such as pension fund assets and share option awards. However, perhaps the biggest shift will be in the amount of disclosure required, with companies required to reveal operational details they had previously kept private.

KPMG, the professional services firm, says Deutsche Bank had to show many more details about the market performance of its derivatives investments once it began using IASC standards. "The (profit) numbers did not change much," says Ted Awty, head of KPMG's UK arm. "But there were huge additional disclosures."

The long-term question that has yet to be resolved is whether the Commission's plan will open the way to a set of global rules allowing companies to list on markets anywhere in the world using one set of accounts. Accountants have raised concerns about a proposal to introduce a filter mechanism to allow the Commission political control over IASC rules. They fear this could give the Commission an effective veto on standards that might prove unpopular with member states. The argument is that this could provoke the US to adopt a similar pick and choose approach, dashing hopes of a set of standards to unite European and American companies. "This will become the death knell for global accounting standards harmonization," says Martin Scicluna, the UK chairman of Deloitte&Touche, the professional services firm.

Regional differences meant Glaxo Wellcome, the British drugs group, saw its profits for the years 1995–7 dip from 4.6 to 2.2 billion pounds because of stricter US rules. If Europe and the US end up at loggerheads over the Commission's plan, there could be more of the same.

Source: Financial Times, June 15, 2000.

## Introduction

Accounting lays great claim to being the "universal language of business". Notwithstanding this, it is regularly confronted by the reality of disparate forms of accounting practice. As the experience of Daimler-Benz demonstrates, significant differences persist across national boundaries and this is inconsistent with the needs of an increasingly global economy. This represents a significant challenge to accounting. But it is one which the discipline and the profession are attempting to address.

While it is a fact that there are significant differences between countries in relation to accounting practice, it is, nevertheless, possible to identify various "schools" of accounting which at least share common origins. For instance, many of those countries that belonged to the British Empire share a similar set of accounting principles and practices. While different in some respects, these can be categorized as part of the Anglo-Saxon (or Anglo-American) tradition. Likewise it is possible to speak of a continental European accounting tradition, albeit with a less clearly defined set of concepts and practices. Marxist accounting, to the extent that it existed, effectively collapsed with the Berlin Wall. Islamic accounting operates within an entirely different frame of reference, espousing quasi-religious values and challenging the developed world to at least acknowledge the existence of different perspectives and imperatives in the developing world.

One of the reasons that it is necessary to consider accounting in its international context is that over the course of recent decades a number of factors have conjoined to extend considerations about accounting practice beyond national, cultural and political boundaries. One of the more important of these has been the huge growth in international trade and the cross-boundary Multi-National Enterprises (MNEs) that have evolved as a consequence. MNEs have a vested interest in promoting more uniform accounting practice and have been significant players in demanding greater harmonization of accounting practice across national boundaries.

Another critical catalyst has been the internationalization of money markets. In a global economy which is developing technology-supported international finance markets, national accounting regimes have come to be viewed as hindrances. The advent of technologies such as the Internet, which do not respect international boundaries, as well as a political vocabulary and ambition which has seen cold war rhetoric replaced by "One World" aspirations, have accelerated this process.

One of the responses of regulators and the accounting profession to these challenges has been to set up bodies charged with considering the implications of globalization and technological change. This has found expression in a number of entities. For instance, the International Federation of Accountants (IFAC), while not originally concerned with issues of accounting practice, has provided a forum within which trans-national issues can be explored. Likewise, the Fédération des Experts Comptables Européens (FEE) has emerged as a voice for the European accounting profession and a strong advocate of harmonization.

By far the most potent expression of accounting's willingness to engage on this issue, however, was the establishment of the IASC, which, since 1973, has been attempting to institute a set of accounting standards with global application. The role of this organization is discussed later in this chapter.

## *European Accounting*

Continental European countries share a particular accounting heritage, finding common origin in the Italian double-entry techniques disseminated throughout

Europe in the Middle Ages. Unlike English-speaking countries, however, for whom capital markets became significant sources of finance from the 18th century, European countries developed a system of small, family-based businesses where the need for extensive financial reporting was not as critical. Accounting practice and financial reporting in Europe did not develop in response to market require-ments, therefore, but to the less exacting requirements of a more focused group of owners and investors. The fact that there was, as a consequence, a relatively under-developed accounting profession meant that there was no professional cadre in a position to articulate a preferred and coherent accounting practice. The result was that a rather legalistic perspective took hold in which tax and accounting law took precedence over the insights of an accounting-driven model.

This unique form of continental European accounting was further reinforced in the early 18th century by the extension throughout Europe of the Napoleonic Code which imposed uniform recording practices and pro-forma statements of account based on conservative valuations and creditor protection. Therefore, while national characteristics undoubtedly persisted, by the 19th century it was possible to identify an accounting culture in Western Europe which was developing a markedly different focus and expression from that emerging simultaneously in the Anglo-American world. This gulf widened over the course of the early part of the 20th century.

## Germany

The dominant role given to the principles of conservatism and prudent valuation in the German accounting system make it markedly different in focus and emphasis from the Anglo-American model. The prominence of these two concepts is a function of both the country's economic history and the relative importance of law and accounting.

A notable feature of the German system is the subordination of accounting to the legal and taxation systems. Until recently accounting was essentially considered to be merely a sub-section of the law and to be capable of control solely by legal and means. Thus, much of Germany's accounting culture and form of practice can be traced to the Napoleonic Code de Commerce which was subsequently extended in 1861 as the German Commercial Code.

This legalistic approach had the effect of placing the development of accounting practice and concepts in the hands of lawyers and officials. Their concerns were more with the application of rules than with the development of a coherent discipline such as that being attempted by the profession in the UK and the US. Allied to an economic history in the first half of the 20th century which was characterized by regular bouts of economic depression and business collapse, this placed a strong emphasis on accounting as a means of assessing business liquidity and security. In this scheme of things issues such as valuation and repayment capacity became the principal concerns.

This automatically put an emphasis onto the balance sheet and the application of conservative and prudent valuation principles as a means of exercising some control over business. A consequence of this was an understanding of "income" as the difference between the "net asset" figures disclosed by successive balance sheets rather than as the difference between revenues and costs calculated by means of a profit and loss account.

The result is a published "commercial balance sheet", the *Handelsbilanz*, which is constructed according to strict and conservative valuation rules. It is intended to facilitate the calculation of a distributable income figure which can be distributed to the owners without compromising the capacity of the business to either satisfy its creditors or to continue as a going concern. One other consequence is the existence of often quite substantial hidden reserves regularly used to indulge in income smoothing.

The focus, therefore, has been on the production of accounting information which satisfies a particular range of users, specifically creditors and government. By extension, the primary emphasis has not been on making available information that facilitates an informed process of decision-making by a wider set of users.

Determination of tax liability is achieved by preparing a special balance sheet, the *Steuerbilanz*, which is constructed mainly in accordance with the principles applying to the *Handelsbilanz*. This principle is called the *Massgeblichkeitsprinzip*, which in effect means that recognition and measurement principles applied in constructing the commercial balance sheet must also be employed in constructing the tax balance sheet. There is therefore, a considerable level of congruence between both the commercial and tax balance sheets, although there are significant differences in relation to depreciation methods.

## Corporate Governance in Germany

In contrast to the governance structures that have emerged in the UK, a large "external" capital market such as the Stock Exchange does not dominate in Germany. This is because traditionally companies have sought funds from institutions such as banks, pension funds, and other industry sources, rather than from the stock market. This explains, in part, the relatively small capitalization of the country's principal stock exchange in Frankfurt.

Thus, ownership structure of German companies is not as disparate, and control of most companies can be traced to a relatively small number of institutions and individuals. As a result, the most common control structure is a "supervisory board" to which management report. This body usually contains representatives of all of the significant investors and employees and means that the company's primary reporting responsibilities can be fulfilled by this form of "internal" disclosure to this board. This explains in part why the external reporting function is not as developed, important or thorough as in the Anglo-American world.

One of the consequences of the relatively stable governance system that has developed in Germany over the last 50 years has been that a focus on long-term planning has been possible. Another has been the concentration of ownership of much of the country's industrial base in a relatively small number of banks, pension funds and conglomerates. For example, banks such as Deutsche Bank have large shareholdings in many of Germany's companies. Likewise, "cross-investment", where investment comes from other enterprises, often from within the same industry, is prevalent.

However, increasing exposure to international markets has highlighted a number of deficiencies in this system. For instance, the concentration of shareholding in such a small number of entities has led to charges of monopoly. In addition, larger German companies such as Daimler-Benz seeking major equity investment have found it necessary to list on foreign exchanges, particularly London and New York, in order to raise the necessary funding. This has caused both government and business leaders to acknowledge the limitations of the German corporate governance model.

## Untangling

### The Traditional Links Between Germanys Banks and its Industrial Companies Are Being Transformed

A small and unremarkable place a few miles outside Frankfurt, Eschborn is an unlikely backdrop for a new era in German capitalism. In a neat little industrial estate on the town's outskirts, tucked next to a do-it-yourself superstore, sit the modest offices of DB Investor. Inside there is little – bar the odd piece of flashy pop art – to suggest any link to high finance. Yet DB Investor is a monster in disguise. It was set up last year to manage DM45 billion-worth ($27 billion) of the big-name industrial holdings amassed over several decades by Deutsche Bank, the world's largest bank ranked by assets.

Germany developed a post-war brand of capitalism based on close ties between banks and industry. Banks not only lent to companies, but also bought into them, sometimes out of choice, sometimes because the client might otherwise go bust. These ties guaranteed patient, long-term finance but also led to complacency and conflicts of interest. For many years this mattered little. But German banks now worry as much about pleasing their shareholders as buttering up their clients, and their shareholders do not much care for industrial holdings... It is not hard to see why the old system is breaking down. The banks have realized that, by selling their industrial holdings or managing them more actively, they can curry favour with the stock market, especially in America, where Deutsche and Dresdner plan to list their shares.

...Despite the occasional big purchase, German banks' overall industrial portfolios are likely to keep shrinking – in number of holdings if not in value. Some banks, to be sure, may want to hold on to their brightest jewels: it is hard to see West LB wanting to sell its long-held stake in Preussag, for instance. The engineering-turned-tourism group is a model restructurer and continues to impress the market. Nor is relationship banking dead enough for Deutsche to consider selling all its 12% stake in DaimlerChrysler quite yet.

> More activist banks, however, will no longer be such friendly, forgiving share-holders to the companies they own. ''We have to pressure managers rather than invest and go to bed,'' says Mr Pfeil. Enough to give some executives sleepless nights.
>
> Source: The Economist, August 14, 1999.

## Recent Developments

Experiences such as that of Daimler Benz when seeking to list on the New York Stock Exchange, coupled with a realization that its capital market and corporate governance structures are limiting their capacity to operate efficiently in a global market, have forced both the business community and the government to reconsider many of the traditional elements of German commercial and accounting culture.

And these internal and external pressures have resulted in some changes. For instance, the authorities are now more amenable to both international accounting rules and to EU attempts to advance harmonization, while many large companies have already adopted International Accounting Standards (IAS) for reporting purposes.

However, one of the principal constraints in ensuring the development of a modern accounting system remains the absence of a developed accounting profession in the sense that this is understood in the Anglo-American world. As a consequence of its governance model in which capital markets have traditionally played little or no part, external reporting has never been a strong feature of the German accounting landscape. This, coupled with the legalistic approach which the subordination of the accounting agenda to the legal and taxation agendas has fostered, has meant that the conditions within which a vibrant public accounting practice culture might emerge have not existed. Thus the two principal auditing and accounting professional bodies in Germany, the *Wirtschaftsprüferkammer* (WP) and the *Vereidigte Buchprüfer* (vBP) have neither the social nor the professional influence of their colleagues in the English-speaking world. Consequently, there is a lack of leadership in initiating change and much of the responsibility has devolved on state and federal governments and, increasingly, on the EU.

---

**In practice:**

---

*German Car-maker VW Looks for New Accounting Model*

*German car manufacturer Volkswagen is preparing to abandon German accounting standards for IAS, according to Chief Financial Officer (CFO) Bruno Adelt. Adelt told journalists the change could come when the company switches its base accounting currency to the Euro in 2001.*

*VW is the last of the top 30 German companies to use German accounting standards, which put more emphasis on recording historical costs in a prudent manner. More rapid depreciation charges, greater scope for provisioning and lower asset and liability valuations combine to depress profits compared to Anglo-American accounting practices. Changing its accounting methods would help VW revive the company's share performance, where gloomy profit forecasts have seen it become the weakest performer in Germany's top 30 Dax share index.*

*The impact of Germany's accounting standards on its multinational companies cannot be under-estimated. Discrepancies between UK and German practice were highlighted last year when losses at BMW's subsidiary Rover were cited as the reason for BMW's threat to stop building cars at the Rover Longbridge plant. Rover's accounts, compiled under UK GAAP and filed at Companies House, showed it made profits of £147 million between 1994 and 1997. BMW's consolidated accounts prepared following German GAAP showed Rover making a loss of £363 million in the same period.*

*Source: AccountingWEB, February, 2000.*

## France

Not surprisingly, given their common European heritage, accounting practice in France shares many of the characteristics of the German system, most noticeably in the central role adopted by the state in its formulation and regulation. Increasingly, however, the profession and other interested parties are becoming proactive in articulating the need for change.

The most obvious expression of the centralizing role of the state is the *Plan Comptable General* (PCG). Ironically, given the unifying role of the Napoleonic code over 100 years previously, this has its origins in an initiative by the Vichy regime in the 1940s, initiated in an attempt to harmonize accounting practice with the German code.

The most recent version of the code was produced in 1982 and incorporates or anticipates several of the key ideas incorporated in the relevant EU accounting instruments dating from that period such as the Fourth and Seventh Directives.

The PCG, which is the responsibility of the *Conseil National de la Comptabilite*, adopts an essentially bureaucratic approach to the whole accounting function. In its current form it is produced as a book of over 400 pages with prescriptive rules determining the way in which specific items should be accounted for. It is presented in three parts.

Part 1: general rules, principles and terminology together with the account codes and entry classifications to be adopted.

Part 2: valuation and measurement rules together with financial statement formats.

Part 3: management accounting rules (this is not part of the regulatory system).

The PCG is supplemented by a legal framework which embraces various accounting-specific statutes and by the Commercial Code.

The effect of the PCG approach is to produce balance sheets and profit and loss accounts which are consistent not just between accounting periods, but across industries. These statements also incorporate concepts such as consistency, accruals and matching, going concern and historic cost. While cash flow statements can be prepared, they are not obligatory.

In this relatively structured approach, the schematic nature of the recording process and the important role played by the state as regulator represent important similarities between the French and German systems.

However, there are also a number of important differences:

- The prominence given to tax law in Germany is not reflected in the French system. A strong tax code is in place, but the congruence expected in Germany between financial and tax accounts does not occur in France. Instead, while there are important rules regarding the availability of depreciation and the calculation of taxable profit which ensure a strong measure of compatibility, the accounting rules applicable under the PCG take precedence over tax law.

- There is scope within the French system for incorporating assets at values other than historic cost. Thus, replacement cost can be used to value certain assets in consolidated accounts.

## Corporate Governance

The lack of a strong capital market is a consequence of the corporate governance model adopted historically in France where small family-centred businesses have always been, and remain, significant engines of growth.

However, probably the most unique characteristic of French corporate governance is the extent of state ownership of many enterprises in the country. Coupled with the influence of banks and the cross-ownership of shares by one company in another, this has the effect of limiting the range of investors and consequently the users of accounts. The result has been a financial reporting regime not unlike that in operation throughout much of Western Europe, in which demands for extensive external reporting have been muted.

France has not, however, been immune to the same influences that have caused the UK to reconsider several aspects of its corporate governance culture. For instance, the consequences of operating in a global market, coupled with a stream of financial scandals involving several of its largest companies, have forced the French authorities to embark on a process similar to that undertaken in the Anglo-American world.

---

**In practice:**

---

*France Lags in Applying Corporate Governance Principles: French Requirements are Same as UK, But Not Applied as Fully*

*France has some progress to make in applying corporate governance principles, despite having published the Vienot reports (1994, 1999) and the Marini report in 1996 – the equivalent of Cadbury, Turnbull and Treadway in the UK. Corporate governance has become a major issue in France due to a growing number of financial scandals, increasingly globalized markets, and the influence of Anglo-Saxon pension funds which own 30% of shares in French companies.*

*John Kennedy, a Paris-based UK chartered accountant, expert comptable, commissaire aux comptes and associate professor at the Paris business school ESCP, told delegates at an IIR international seminar in London last week that despite France having made gigantic leaps over the past 8 years in bringing its financial reporting requirements up to international standards, its application of corporate governance principles has not been "100%".*

*The Vienot and Marini reports indicated the need to change from the traditional French-style of management, particularly in: the appointment of non-executive directors; use of specialized committees; separation of powers between the president of the board and chief executive; and the need for a more active board on strategic decisions, as opposed to mere ratification decisions.*

*A survey based on the 100 largest commercial and industrial companies has shown that only: 54 groups refer to corporate governance principles in their annual reports; 14 groups report to shareholders within 60 days; 10 groups have appointed non-executive directors; nine groups give details on directors' shareholding; 14 groups give the age of directors; 63 groups give information on specialized committees; and 89 groups give information on directors' remuneration, but not on the bases. Kennedy said: "The application of corporate governance principles is not as well developed in France yet as it is in the UK and US."*

*Source: accountancymagazine.com, November 27, 2000.*

---

## Recent Developments

The influx of foreign MNEs, the fact that French companies are now experiencing the constraints of an underdeveloped domestic capital market and the impact of new technologies, have forced the government and other interested parties to address the question of accounting practice in a larger context.

As in other European countries this has found expression in support for EU initiatives in this area as well as the emergence of a more proactive profession, the *Ordre des Experts Comptables.* This has been given added momentum by the creation in 1998 of the *Comite de Reglementation Comptable* charged with the reform of accounting standards and regulation and the development of a policy in relation to the place of international standards in French practice.

As with most continental European countries, however, the greatest catalyst for change has been the broader global agenda for harmonization, particularly as mediated by the IASC and the EU.

## Globalization and Harmonization

For a variety of economic, social and historical reasons, by the mid-20th century the most powerful trading nations in the world were functioning under different accounting regimes. Thus the US and the UK were operating under an accounting scheme which could be broadly categorized as Anglo-American, while countries such as Germany, France and Italy operated under a loosely titled "Continental European" approach. This, however, was inconsistent with the needs of a new international business phenomenon that paid little heed to national and cultural boundaries. For these MNEs one of the primary goals was greater accounting compatibility across borders.

Over recent decades the role and power of MNEs and capital markets have increased. This, in turn, has led to greater international capital flows, the internationalization of capital markets and increased funding by stock exchanges. This is confirmed by the following statistics which give some idea of the scale of this international trade and the range of financing sources availed of by most large companies. For instance, Table 15.1 confirms the increasing turnover in foreign equity on the London Stock Exchange, while Table 15.2 shows that, in spite of a recent decline, foreign issuers still account for over two-thirds of the equity value.

**Table 15.1. Domestic-Foreign Equity Turnover, London Stock Exchange, 1993–98 (Billions of £)**

|      | UK companies | Foreign companies | Foreign % |
|------|--------------|-------------------|-----------|
| 1993 | £564         | £580              | 50.7      |
| 1994 | £606         | £718              | 54.2      |
| 1995 | £646         | £791              | 50.0      |
| 1996 | £742         | £1,039            | 58.3      |
| 1997 | £1,013       | £1,443            | 58.7      |
| 1998 | £1,037       | £2,183            | 67.8      |

**Table 15.2. Domestic-Foreign Equity Value, London Stock Exchange, 1993–99 (Billions of £)**[a]

|  | Number of UK companies | Number of foreign companies | Foreign as % of total | Market value of UK companies £ billion | Market value of foreign companies £ billion | Foreign as % of total |
|---|---|---|---|---|---|---|
| 1993 | 1,927 | 485 | 20.1 | 810 | 1,918 | 70.3 |
| 1994 | 2,070 | 464 | 18.3 | 775 | 1,983 | 71.8 |
| 1995 | 2,078 | 525 | 20.2 | 900 | 2,357 | 72.4 |
| 1996 | 2,171 | 533 | 19.7 | 1,012 | 2,388 | 70.2 |
| 1997 | 2,157 | 526 | 19.6 | 1,251 | 2,429 | 66.0 |
| 1998 | 2,087 | 522 | 20.0 | 1,423 | 2,804 | 66.3 |
| 1999 | 1,945 | 499 | 20.4 | 1,820 | 3,578 | 66.3 |

[a] Source: www.londonstockex.co.uk.

## Harmonization

One of the responses to the process of globalization has been an attempt by various professional and regulatory accounting bodies to push a "harmonization" policy. As distinct from standardization, which implies the application of exactly similar rules everywhere, "harmonization" is generally understood to mean "the reduction of reporting differences between countries". It is, therefore, sensitive to the fact that for historical and cultural reasons a complete uniformity of accounting practice is probably unrealistic, at least in the short to medium term.

The essential nature of harmonization and its possible benefits are outlined in the following extract.

### Global Consequences of International Accounting Diversity, by Professor Frederick Choi

Professor Choi describes a number of reasons why he believes international harmonization is critical for the future of accounting:

1. Language – "As an example, consider the word 'current'. When translated into the Japanese language, the Japanese equivalent word is similar to 'present'. While these two words appear to convey the same meaning, such may not be the case when they are used in an asset valuation context. Thus, valuing off-balance sheet interest rate swap obligations at current value does not necessarily connote the same measurement yardstick as present value. The former normally implies a market valuation concept; the latter a discounted cash flow measure. Both could yield very different measurements."
2. Format – "Account classifications often vary quite considerably in international reporting. In the US, analysts are used to seeing multiple step income

statements that break out important expense categories, such as cost of sales. In countries such as Germany, analysts must often impute cost of sales as expenses tend to be disclosed by type rather than function, i.e., wages are aggregated whether they relate to production or distribution."

3. Currency – "As a convenience to foreign readers, reporting companies in some countries, notably Japan, will translate their financial statements to another currency. Foreign readers are provided with two sets of comparative figures, one in Japanese yen, the other usually in US dollars. The exchange rate used is the year-end rate and simply involves multiplying all statement items by a constant. This is known as a 'convenience translation'. Readers can therefore conduct their analysis in foreign currency or utilize a convenience translation methodology. Those adopting the former approach have little cause for concern as financial ratios that transform nominal (interval) measurements to percentage relationships are independent of the currency of denomination. A debt to equity ratio computed from a French balance sheet expressed in francs is no different from a debt to equity ratio computed from the same financial statements translated into dollars using a convenience translation rate. Analysts preferring to work with convenience translations, however, must be careful when analysing time series data. Use of convenience-rates to translate foreign currency amounts can distort underlying trends because of changes in exchange rates over time."

4. Disclosure and measurement – "Despite the progress that has been made in international reporting, disclosure levels still vary considerably both between and within countries. Interviews with large institutional investors in Frankfurt, London, New York, Tokyo and Zurich reveal the following areas where international disclosure practices are considered most wanting: segmental information, methods of asset valuation, foreign operations disclosures, frequency and completeness of interim information, description of capital expenditures, hidden reserves, and off-balance sheet items".

Source: AccountingWEB, October 30, 1998 (originally printed in Accounting and Business).

The main arguments in favour of harmonization are, therefore, that it would remove communication barriers, encourage cross-border trade, facilitate the creation of a more efficient capital market and, of particular interest to entities such as the EU, promote regional integration.

Critics counter that harmonization will not offer the advantages claimed, pointing out that it will impose extra costs on small and medium entities, while the only ones for whom the project is relevant are large MNEs. Others, critical of any project that further secures the role of the capital markets in the order of things, point out that there are far greater social, environmental and cultural issues at stake, particularly in developing countries, where a capital-markets driven project is simply unsuitable and unsustainable.

# International Accounting Standards Committee/Board

Accountant regulators have expressed no such qualms. Realizing that significant catalysts for change existed, representatives from various professional bodies and regulatory agencies came together in 1973 to form the IASC, which by 1999 had representatives from accounting bodies in over 90 countries.

The IASC , now the IASB, has set itself the task of developing and disseminating a globally acceptable set of accounting standards for financial reporting. While the ambition of standardization has never been surrendered, for the time being the goal is one of harmonizing accounting practices across borders and accounting blocs. To this end it issues IASs. One of the principal criticisms of early IASs was that, in allowing great diversity of choice, they undermined the goal of comparability. The IASC countered that its initial priority was the elimination of unacceptable practices, a process that would have to precede any attempt at the development of a global accounting standards regime.

As with any body attempting to operate in such an international context, the IASC faces various challenges. For instance, as it seeks to bind continental Europeans into the standard-setting process there is unease at what is often misleadingly called an Anglo-Saxon bias – the dominance of the US, UK and Commonwealth countries. Thus, Karel Van Hulle, the European Commission's senior accounting official, recently told a round table discussion in Warsaw: "The Anglo-Saxons should accept that if they want the IASC to be an international organization they should have a little bit more respect for other cultures."

For their part, US regulators fear a move away from their rule-based, prescriptive approach, to a more principles-centred scheme that allows for subjective application and interpretation. Confident that they have held the initiative as the possessors of the most developed GAAP in the world, the SEC and FASB have consistently proposed that US standards should form the core of any new global scheme. This, in turn, has led to considerable tension between FASB and IASC as both compete for the "prize" of framing an acceptable global standard.

In 1995, however, the IASC project received a substantial boost when it signed an agreement with the International Organization of Securities Commissions (IOSCO) to develop a set of new standards which, subject to the agreement of IOSCO, would form an acceptable basis for reporting purposes for companies with cross-border listings. This, in turn, has seen the IASC emerge as favourite to succeed in its "tussle" with FASB.

More recently, under the leadership of Sir Brian Carsberg, and in response to pressure from the US, the IASC has adopted a structure intended to broaden its governance and decision-making structure and accommodate a more technical bias. This has been instrumental in providing FASB with the necessary comfort to acknowledge the potential for the IASC project to succeed. While not yet willing to surrender, the US has at least indicated its intention not to resist the IASC.

And, as the following article explains, this has led to endorsement from IOSCO as well as qualified approval from the EU and US.

## The Glass is Half Full

### The European Commission and IOSCO Have Given IAS the Credibility They Needed, by Ted Awty

Accounting rarely stirs the blood, but in the space of a few days we have just seen two of the most significant announcements of my professional career. The first was IOSCO's endorsement of Inter-national Accounting Standards; the second was the European Commission's decision to require listed companies throughout the European Union to use IASs from 2005. The benefit of this decision is both European and international. Second, Fourth and Seventh Directives notwithstanding, European accounting standards remain highly fragmented. The decision provides critical support to the process of bringing European capital markets together, for which comparable and reliable financial data is the lifeblood.

### Winners and Losers

From a UK perspective, the move to IASs will inevitably create both winners and losers. It can be argued that some UK standards are more intellectually sound than IASs. But, by and large, there is much similarity, and the differences are relatively small and identifiable. The wider benefits of harmonization outweigh intellectual parochialism and a degree of compromise must be accepted. Given the choice between having to produce two sets of figures, one UK and one international, with a reconciliation between them, or simply one set based on IASs, I am convinced that UK finance directors would prefer the latter.

But this of course ignores an even more important issue. The real battle in the world of accounting is between US GAAP and the rest. No one could seriously deny the credibility of US GAAP and the immense amount of thought that goes into individual standards. But they suffer from two fundamental draw-backs, both of which are structural in nature. The first is the rule-based mentality; the second is the constituency to which the standard setters are answerable. IAS provide the solution to both these problems.

By throwing its weight behind the IASC, the Commission has given IASs the vital credibility they need in order to become truly inter-national GAAP. There is of course the inevitable small print – in both announcements. The Commission's proposal indicates that "in order to provide legal certainty", the EU will adopt a two-tier endorsement mechanism – one technical, one political – to confirm the standards to be applied. I might regard this as just a safety net, but have to accept that there may be a more sinister intent. The mechanism could well be used to develop IASs into a separate body of European accounting standards, which would be applied perhaps solely within the EU. This would have two most unfortunate consequences. First, we could then see three accounting bodies battling it out for global domination, with US GAAP, IASs and EU GAAP preserving the need in different jurisdictions for unnecessary reconciliation from one to the other. Second, it could deal a fatal blow to the credibility of IASs internationally and, most importantly, in the US...

Ted Awty is KPMG's head of assurance.

Source: Accountancy, July, 2000.

The fact that the EU will endorse a "two-tier" mechanism is significant in illustrating the tensions that remain. Nevertheless, the future for the harmonization project seems assured, even if its final contours cannot yet be finally determined. It seems certain that the twin drivers of increased international commerce and the voracity of capital markets will be sufficient to maintain momentum.

However, significant challenges still remain, not least the political pressures that attend any such project. Nor is it likely that tensions within the EU will subside entirely. The fact that, as the following account indicates, not all countries are as proactive as others, and that considerable legislative and statutory hurdles remain, mean that the EU deadline for application of IASs by 2005 is by no means assured.

---

### In practice:

#### UK Lags Behind Europe on International Standards

*British finance directors are lagging behind their European counterparts in their support for IAS, PricewaterhouseCoopers has found. The firm's survey of 717 European CFOs found that 79% supported the European Commission's decision to make IAS mandatory for European listed companies by the year 2005. In the UK, the level of support ran at 65%. UK respondents to the survey were less familiar with IAS and were the most patriotic accountants, with 61% preferring UK GAAP.*

*Because the Companies Acts do not permit the use of IAS, the UK's experience of using international standards is limited to subsidiaries of continental companies that use IAS for group reporting, PwC's analysts explained. "Given the very limited UK experience of IAS, it is not surprising that UK CFOs are concerned about the likely consequences of change. Support for IAS among UK CFOs is based on strategic considerations rather than accounting issues," the firm said.*

*International comparability and raising finance were the key benefits of IAS identified by the survey. PwC's head of global corporate reporting, Mary Keegan, commented: "The use of the Internet is probably the key driver for change. CFOs know that international investors access and analyse Internet information for investment decisions – but that data is not valid for cross-border comparison because almost all the world's governments currently require companies to follow unique national rules. Companies, just like investors, support a single global set of rules so that valid comparisons can be made."*

> *Keegan warned that making the transition to IAS "is not a push-button" exercise, and said that companies should start preparing now to meet the 2005 deadline. National governments could help, she added, by allowing companies to use IAS for reporting group financial accounts in their countries. Currently this is only allowed in Austria, Belgium, Finland and Germany. However, the possibility of such a reform has been raised in the current review of UK company law.*
>
> *The survey covers technical knowledge and understanding, boardroom attitudes, what business people think of the IAS standards themselves and of the European Commission's proposal to create an endorsement mechanism that could lead to a European variant of IAS.*
>
> *Source: AccountingWEB, November 27, 2000.*

## Summary

For a variety of historical, cultural and economic reasons accounting practices differ across national and regional boundaries. Thus, the accounting regimes in France and Germany, while similar in some respects, demonstrate considerable divergences. These in turn exhibit considerable differences from the principles and practices characteristic of the Anglo-American model.

As business becomes more global, abetted by technological innovation and an ascendant capital market economy, the need for accounting to respond appears self-evident. As a result, accounting regulators such as the IASC have attempted to advance a harmonization project that seeks to minimize differences between different national accounting codes.

With the recent imprimatur of the US, EU and IOSCO this IASC project has received a considerable boost. However, potential pitfalls remain and the project must still negotiate a maze of national, political and cultural obstacles before coming to fruition.

# Review Questions

**Question 1**
Identify the main catalysts for change in international accounting practice and assess how these might impact differently on developed and developing countries.

**Question 2**
List some of the common characteristics, if any, of continental European accounting.

**Question 3**
Explain how accounting practice has developed in Germany to date and identify some of the principal characteristics of the German accounting system.

**Question 4**
"German accounting can be best described as conservative". Explain.

**Question 5**
Identify the principal characteristics of the corporate governance culture in Germany and explain how it differs from that operating in the UK.

**Question 6**
What is the role of the *Plan Comptable General* (PCG) in French accounting practice?

**Question 7**
Compare and contrast the accounting systems in Germany and France. Pay particular attention to identifying common features which distinguish them from the Anglo-American system.

**Question 8**
Distinguish between harmonization and standardization as means by which accounting might address the needs of international business.

**Question 9**
Why has the EU opted for "two-tier" endorsement mechanism in relation to IASs? Does this suggest that there will be greater conflict in coming years as the US and the EU vie for supremacy?

**Question 10**
The US has expressed some reservations about the IASC project. Having developed a very prescriptive set of regulations it is, understandably, reluctant to surrender the initiative to a body which it sees as too anxious to compromise on quality in order to reach consensus. Explain whether this position can be sustained by the US and its representatives.

## Case Studies

### Case 1

The following article summarizes many of the issues (and tensions) surrounding the harmonization project, particularly the difficulties for the IASC, EU and US with regard to compromises that must be made. Discuss the key points raised and consider the prospects for the success of the IASC approach.

### A Tip From Alexander the Great: After a Deadlock Lasting Decades, a Global Standard of Accounting is at Last in Prospect, by Michael Peel

Those fighting for rules that will allow companies to list on any stock market in the world using a single set of accounts have found an unlikely inspiration in Alexander the Great. The Macedonian general's strategy of creating a trade zone to unite economies from Gibraltar to the Punjab holds lessons for latter-day administrators of the world's corporate empires, says Graham Ward, president of the Institute of Chartered Accountants in England and Wales. "(Alexander) was an example at an early stage of taking a global view of an empire, rather than a micro-management, command-and-control approach," he says.

Mr Ward's vision is that accounting should likewise no longer be fragmented, but should abide by a single world-wide set of standards. And, thanks to shifts in the political geography of accounting earlier this summer, that vision looks as if it may become reality.

Sir Bryan Carsberg, secretary-general of the IASC, set up by the profession in 1973 to press for global rules, says this means not merely modifying traditional accounting, but ushering in "a whole new approach".

This accounting lingua franca should produce huge benefits. Accountants will gain from having better tools to help them judge the status of a business. Investors will gain new information about companies, especially new-economy start-ups that they complain today's accounting rules leave in obscurity. Even companies will gain: although they will have to divulge more about the business (including details they would rather never saw the light of day), the confidence of investors should lower their cost of capital.

Despite this, global standards still face formidable barriers before they are accepted: accounting is a conservative profession; companies do not relish disclosure; national regulators want to protect their turf. Yet just about everyone agrees that the rules should change to reflect the shift in the global economy from traditional manufacturing to high-technology services. Most importantly, conventional accounts are backward-looking, measuring historic costs of exchange transactions between the company and other parties, such as suppliers and customers. Many accountants argue that this is becoming less relevant with the arrival of high-tech companies that have no past record. Since investors are backing an unproven business model, the argument goes, they need to see forward-looking data such as trading forecasts.

Also, these days more corporate assets such as staff goodwill and brand names are intangible. The intangible items clearly have value, but just how much is a moot point: most have never had a price put on them, unlike machinery which was bought from a manufacturer.

One solution is to include more narrative in financial statements, letting companies explain their prospects and how the value of items such as brands is changing. Some argue this is a "dumbing down" of the accounts, in which numerical precision and rigour are sacrificed for a subjective discussion of future performance.

Sir Bryan retorts that traditional accounts are full of judgements about likely events – even a "fact" such as the statement of cash reserves assumes the central bank will honour its promise to pay on demand. "I would not ever use the term: 'These accounts are accurate'," he says.

This view is guaranteed to irritate US standard-setters, who argue precision can be achieved by a prescriptive approach that offers companies little leeway for interpretation. "Most of the numbers that get put out today are very firm numbers," says one US standard-setter. "These accountants who have never been a controller or a CFO simply do not understand." It is a philosophical difference that has made the US suspicious of some European national standards. For many years, this made the US reluctant to support the drive for global rules. It feared they would inevitably be inferior to American standards.

The big change is that now the US is prepared to put its faith in the international system. This is partly thanks to a restructuring of the IASC in May, which introduced an influential group of trustees, headed by Paul Volcker, a former head of America's Federal Reserve. The new IASC should be practical rather than theoretical – and friendly to business. The IASC gained further momentum in the same month when its proposed global standards gained the backing of Iosco, the club of world stock market regulators, which includes the US Securities and Exchange Commission.

The IASC's new rules would bring far-reaching changes – although national regulators would continue to embellish the international norms with extra rules of their own designed to reflect local business life. One of its big ideas is "fair value" – that is, giving companies the duty to reveal the economic effects of all their activities. One controversial plan being floated internationally is to make companies ascribe market values to holdings of derivatives, rather than accounting for them at historic cost. This has caused uproar among banks, which argue it will cause their balance sheets to become more volatile and obscure trends in profits and cash flow.

On the other hand, fair value should help stop companies concealing bad news by manipulating the numbers. It should also end anomalies that arise because different regulators set different standards. Often significant variations arise between the US, which proclaims the primacy of the investor and full corporate disclosure, and Europe, where there is often more flexibility for companies to manage their profit levels to best advantage. When Daimler-Benz, the German carmaker, listed in New York and reissued its accounts to comply with US standards, it saw a 1993 profit of DM615 million (182 million pounds) become a loss of

DM1.84 billion, the result of a stricter US approach to accounting for expected future losses.

David Cairns, a former secretary-general of the IASC, says more hard revelations for companies may be on the way. For instance, European banks boost profits in lean years by deploying hidden reserves.

"If and when they move to (international rules), there will be some unpleasant revelations in bad years," he says.

It has taken years for the principle of international rules to be accepted. But once they are, further reform could be relatively swift. One reason is that business lobbies will find it harder to derail initiatives on the grounds that they would make company accounts look less flattering – which was the fate of proposals in the US in the mid-1990s to charge share options as an expense on the profit and loss account. "It might be more difficult to overrule an independent international body on an issue like that," says Allan Cook, technical director of Britain's Accounting Standards Board.

National accounting bodies could also help promote change, by acting as a kind of brains trust. They would flag up emerging issues and identify deficiencies in existing IASC rules. "If there were an enormous problem, even if it arose in only one country, the international body would have to do something," says Mr Cook.

However, despite this year's progress, global accounting standards are not here yet. For a start, the European Commission was unhappy about the structural changes at the IASC, which it thought were driven by the US. It has announced plans for common European rules based on IASC standards to be in place by 2005 but "filtered" by the commission. Accountants fear this represents an attempt by the EU to pick and choose from the global rules, though the Commission denies this.

The US has issues to resolve, too. Despite Iosco's endorsement of international standards, the SEC has insisted on a wide-ranging public consultation gauging how the standards measure up to US regulations. The US will ignore any attempt to bounce it into accepting rules it sees as inferior to its own. "We think we have the highest quality and most competitive standards," says the US standard-setter. "If the European markets want to go towards lower quality financial reporting, let them go."

In short, much work remains to be done. Much will depend on how successfully the IASC can resolve political and philosophical differences such as those that exist between Europe and the US. Enthusiasts for global rules are likely to need all the skills of improvisation and adaptation for which Alexander the Great was noted.

Source: Financial Times, October 26, 2000.

## Case 2

The following case provides a very practical and useful example of how the introduction of IASs may influence accounting practice, particularly in finally enabling a more informed comparison of companies across national boundaries and industries. Identify what the issues are and the implications of improved comparability.

# More Uniformity, Please

## Might Nestlé and Unilever One Day Present Similar Information Similarly? by Trevor Pjiper

The FTSE Eurotop 300 "Food Producers & Processors" sector is dominated by Nestlé and Unilever, which together account for over 70% of the total capitalization. The Swiss company reports under IAS and the twinned parents of the Anglo-Dutch multinational use a blended version of UK and Netherlands GAAP. IAS and UK GAAP are regarded as having a lot in common, but the differences in the 1999 financial information presented by the two sector leaders would tax the skills of even an experienced accountant.

In 1999, Nestlé's trading profit represented 10.6% of sales. The company's chairman and CEO commented that "the improvement in trading margins is in line with our policy in recent years and our explicit intention to do whatever is necessary to sustainably raise the group's overall performance levels". Unilever's 1999 accounts reveal an almost identical operating margin of 10.5%, with the joint chairmen noting that "we have made good progress pursuing our strategy of category focus and margin improvement against a challenging economic and competitive background". Similar results for companies in the same sector, one might think.

However, the apparent similarity in the two companies' margins is in stark contrast to their published returns on equity. In 1999, Nestlé achieved a return of 20% whereas Unilever's equivalent is an eye-popping 43%. Footnote (b) beneath the relevant table in Unilever's annual report cautions that the "return on shareholders' equity is substantially influenced by the group's policy prior to 1998, of writing off purchased goodwill in the year of acquisition as a movement in profit retained". Note 21 to the accounts reveals that the cumulative amount of goodwill so written off is £6,313 million, compared with equity shareholders' funds of £3,892 million. If the ratio is meaningless, why bother to calculate it?

In the above circumstances, help can sometimes be sought from the page entitled "Additional information for US investors". This reveals Unilever's approximate net income and approximate capital and reserves under US GAAP, whereby goodwill and identifiable intangibles are capitalized and amortized. The 1999 return on average equity works out at 14%, compared with Nestlé's 20%. This is perhaps an unduly harsh result because Unilever's US GAAP capital and reserves figure includes £859 million of 10 cents preference share capital. The preference shareholders' entitlement to a dividend of 65% of the 6 months Euribor interest rate makes this look rather more like a debt instrument.

## Possible to Adjust Margins?

Unilever's US GAAP information also allows a revised operating margin to be calculated. Amortizing the previously eliminated goodwill against profit reduces the operating margin from 10.5–9.7%, compared with Nestlé's 10.6%. So is Unilever trailing some way behind Nestlé?

Nestlé's calculation of a 20% return on average equity does not contain a health warning similar to that in Unilever's accounts. However, careful study of Nestlé's accounting policies reveals that it has also eliminated purchased goodwill against reserves. The policy of capitalizing and amortizing goodwill commenced only in 1995. Unlike Unilever's accounts, there is no equivalent disclosure of the amount of goodwill eliminated against reserves. There is also no "Additional information for US investors". The suspicion remains that Nestlé's ratios might not be that far ahead of Unilever's, but even rough comparability is thwarted by a lack of readily available information.

In addition to the treatment of purchased goodwill described above, there are other pitfalls in the path of users seeking to compare the headline margins. Nestlé's 10.6% benefits from the exclusion of charges for the impairment of tangible fixed assets and goodwill amounting to SFr585 million in 1999. By contrast, Unilever has included an impairment charge of £115 million on fixed assets in arriving at its 10.5%. Then again, Unilever's practice of including business disposal profits in operating profit (£328 million in 1998 which contributed towards an operating margin of 10.9%) is not adopted by Nestlé. The Swiss company deems these gains to be "non-trading" income.

Unilever deals with the distorting effect of exceptional items on the published operating margin by providing an additional ratio (11% in 1999) which strips these out. However, this is itself controversial because restructuring charges are added back. Nestlé eschews such practice. This might be because these charges are of a recurring nature. Nestlé's chairman and CEO point out that "optimization measures are part of a long-term process and require a permanent openness to change". They note that "our industrial sector is still far from having finished restructuring". Unilever takes the practice of stripping out exceptional items to its logical conclusion by disclosing that earnings per share rose by 9% before such items. The pre-exceptional eps figures disclosed for 1999 and 1998 show an increase of just under 7%, but the joint chairmen's 9% is calculated at constant exchange rates.

## Segmental Reporting Lacks Depth?

Readers keen to examine the performance of the component parts of the two multinationals' portfolio will notice another difference in presentation. Unilever uses the traditional UK approach of splitting the overall totals into different geographical areas on the one hand and different businesses on the other. However, this tends to even out good and bad performances. For example, we are told of "a mixed year in North America: Home and Personal Care achieved excellent results, but our Foods business returned a weaker performance".

Nestlé is closer to achieving the more informative so-called "matrix presentation" because its primary segment disclosure splits the Food business into three geographical segments. IAS 14, Segment Reporting, requires a two format approach to segmental reporting – a primary format and a secondary format. Surprisingly, Nestlé has dedicated only two pages of narrative to its primary format but allocated over 25 pages of discussion to its secondary format. More financial information is required in respect of the primary format, which should normally reflect the group's management structure.

Readers curious about the two companies' performance in ice cream, where they are direct competitors, will be disappointed. For financial reporting purposes, Unilever combines its ice cream business with beverages (like Brooke Bond and Lipton). Nestlé uses an enlarged segment entitled "Milk products, nutrition and ice cream". In the absence of numbers for ice cream, we are told by Unilever that "overall volumes were flat and operating profits were slightly below 1998". Nestlé reports that "results also improved for nutrition products and for ice cream, as the group consolidates its performance in these areas".

The May 2000 landmark agreement by stock market regulators potentially paves the way for companies to list on stock markets anywhere in the world using one set of accounts. It remains to be seen whether this will ultimately result in sector leaders providing readily comparable information about their financial performance.

Trevor Pijper, a member of Ernst and Young's Financial Reporting Group in London, is a former investment analyst.

Source: Accountancy, July, 2000.

# SECTION V

## Interpretation

The goal of this text is to equip readers with the skills and insights necessary to analyse and interpret financial information and reports, specifically that contained in an Annual Report. This has necessitated a review of the various contexts within which accounting information emerges, a consideration of the information content of financial reports and an investigation of some of the more advanced provisions relating to accounting practice. A variety of techniques have also been introduced which underpin the Fundamental Analysis paradigm adopted by this book.

These themes are now brought together in one section which applies the various techniques and perspectives covered thus far to Tesco plc.

The Annual Report 2000 for this company is included as an appendix at the rear of the text and should be referred to throughout.

# TESCO PLC 2000 [16]

When you have completed this chapter you will be able to:

- Analyse, contextualise and interpret the performance and position of Tesco plc as disclosed by the Annual Report 2000.
- Draw on a variety of other sources to inform your analysis.
- Produce a report to that effect.

## Listening to customers and learning from mistakes:

### Tesco's well-executed domestic and international strategy has helped eliminate the valuation gap that once separated it from large continental rivals, By Martin Dickson

At the end of a week of deep market gloom, here is a happier story. A decade ago you could have raised a laugh in the city by suggesting Tesco of all companies was destined to be Britain's prime contender for membership of an elite of international retailers. It was an organization in shock, with its prices out of kilter with its customers as it tried to take on JSainsbury, the leading UK food retailer. And while Marks and Spencer was busily expanding in continental Europe and North America, the wider world did not figure large at Tesco's modest Hertfordshire headquarters.

Today, while Sainsbury and M&S flounder, Tesco has a seemingly impregnable lead as the UK's largest and slickest food retailer (as well as e-tailer) and is busily recycling cash from this mature business into rapid expansion in the emerging markets of eastern Europe and Asia. Its UK dominance will be underscored on April 10 when it is expected to report another year of solid sales and profits growth. Its increasing international stature is demonstrated by the elimination of the valuation gap that once separated it from its large continental rivals, notably Carrefour of France, the first company to take standardized hypermarkets into the developing world.

Just 18 months ago, Tesco shares stood at a 30% discount to the likes of Carrefour, making the company a potential bid target. Now, on some measures, Tesco stands at a 10% premium. Carrefour has been plagued with problems since its merger 2 years ago with French rival Promodes while Tesco has hardly put a foot wrong. Its eerily smooth progress under Terry Leahy, chief executive since the mid-1990s, raises two questions: what has it done right? And what could now derail it?

Perhaps the most important factor in its UK success is that, having lost touch with its customers at the start of the 1990s, it began listening to them intently. It focused on value for money, while simultaneously stretching its brand upmarket by offering quality products. This was reinforced by strong managerial and technical skills (notably in ordering and distribution) that produced the efficiencies underpinning its price cuts. Its ability to learn from mistakes – a seemingly rare quality among large UK retailers – has been just as important internationally. Its first foray was an acquisition in the mature French market but when that proved unsuccessful it sold out and concentrated on organic expansion in fast-growing emerging markets such as Hungary and Thailand.

It may have been copying Carrefour, but Tesco has adopted a less imperial approach, making sure its hypermarkets are developed with local partners and adapted to local conditions. With 140 stores outside western Europe, Tesco still trails Carrefour, with 745, but its rapid expansion means by the end of next year it should have nearly half its selling space outside the UK. Its foreign operations are barely in profit, but double-digit growth is in prospect.

There are three main threats to this happy picture. First, emerging markets entail greater risks as well as rewards. They have volatile economies and hypermarket shopping is still a relatively new idea that could fall out of favour if times get hard. Second, Tesco's UK stronghold could come under attack from Wal-Mart, the huge US retailer that bought Asda 2 years ago. So far Wal-Mart has not posed a great threat. It has trouble in Germany, where the credibility of its European expansion is on the line, and seems to prefer a quiet life in the UK. Finally, Tesco's management might get complacent, the fate that befell Sainsbury and M&S. Or, buoyed by its share price, it could make an arrogant, unwise acquisition in western Europe, where economies of scale are creating a single regional market.

For now this looks unlikely. The management seems healthily haunted by ghosts of failures past. But as they fade, overconfidence could develop – a danger with all strong-cultured companies. As for the share price, it has performed so well over the past year there is little justification for a further rerating relative to its peers.

Source: Financial Times, March 24, 2001.

## Introduction

One of the problems when studying financial information analysis in the traditional way is that the exercise can seem to consist of nothing more than the application of various techniques to masses of accounting data. This rather limited perspective is often reinforced by an approach which seems to present ratio calculation as an end in itself.

One of the key themes running through this text, however, has been the need to constantly contextualise accounting information, whether it is within relevant industries, governance cultures, past performance or other appropriate criteria. The point has been repeatedly made that accounting information only acquires its real significance when placed within a context that allows its full meaning to be properly explored.

And that will be the theme of this chapter, an interpretation of Tesco plc in a way that brings together the various skills covered in previous chapters and yet is sensitive to the fact that the resulting ratios are only one step on the way to a more informed and holistic understanding of the company. The opening vignette provides one example of such a context, enabling the company's future to be considered in an international context where it is possible to view it as a target for takeover rather than a predator.

Of necessity this chapter is structured slightly differently from previous chapters. The focus is on producing a report on Tesco plc based on the Annual Report 2000 which is provided in an appendix at the rear of this text.

## *Report*

The tenor and content of any such report will depend to a large extent on the audience being targeted. In this case the assumption is that the report is being prepared by a large stockbroking firm whose primary audience will be existing or potential investors in Tesco plc. This means that the concerns addressed will be those of shareholders, whether current or future.

However, it also means that the report adopts the perspective of a particular interest group. A report produced on behalf of a competitor, an environmental pressure group or a trade union would adopt an entirely different approach and reach some radically different conclusions.

The analyst's report that forms the core of the chapter is presented in a manner which separates computational detail from the body of the report. Thus, while ratios, percentages and trends are obviously central to the conclusions reached, their presentation has been relegated to supporting appendices. This is a standard approach and enables the report writer to concentrate on themes and argument without having to digress into the specifics of ratio construction.

There are no standard formats for such a report. Nor is there a list of areas and topics which must be covered. However, it is possible to devise a number of sub-headings that might form the core of any analysis and interpretation. These would include:

- Background, including reference to macro-economic and industry contexts
- SWOT (Strengths, Weaknesses, Opportunities and Threats) analysis
- Management efficiency: activity and liquidity analysis

- Profitability and returns
- Financing
- Strategic objectives
- Other relevant issues
- Conclusion: Buy/Sell/Hold recommendation
- Supporting appendices

Every report will normally begin with an introduction outlining the focus of the report and have an Executive Summary at the outset in which the main points of the report are summarised.

There is no standard length for such a report. However, they should be readable and to the point. It is generally unusual to see a report, such as the one intended here, which is greater than 2,000 words in length. Where further detail or analysis is required then more detailed reports can be commissioned.

## Tesco plc (Group) 2000

### Introduction

*The following report is based on information provided in the Tesco plc Annual Report 2000, other information made available by the company during the year as well as industry and peer group data. Reference should be made throughout to Appendix 1 where performance measures are summarised.*

### Executive Summary

*Tesco plc continues to be the UK market leader in the food retail sector. All industry and firm-specific indicators suggest that it will sustain this position into the medium-term. At 169 p its share price represents good value and the shares are now being accorded "moderate buy" status by this firm.*

*The following points are the key conclusions drawn, and observations made, in the body of this report:*

- *Operating profit of £1,032 million exceeded market expectations.*
- *The company remains market leader with sales (excluding VAT) of £18,796 million.*
- *This represents a market share of 15.6%.*
- *The company's expansion into Europe has progressed well although sales there only account for 7% of the total.*
- *South-east Asia is a focus of particular attention, although only 2.5% of group sales occur there.*
- *The company is the world leader in online grocery shopping.*
- *It has increased its non-food turnover considerably.*
- *The company is exploiting its technological and operational capabilities to move into the profitable financial services area.*
- *The strategy of the company is well-suited to current macro- and micro-economic conditions.*
- *Funding exists for growth by acquisition.*

## Background

*Over the course of the last two decades Tesco has transformed itself from an exponent of the "pile it high, sell it cheap" policy of its founder Jack Cohen, to a quality retailer specialising in out-of-town outlets with a reputation for quality and value. It is a policy which means that it can compete with peers which concentrate on price (for example, Asda) and those which emphasise quality (such as J. Sainsbury).*

*In 1994 Tesco overtook J. Sainsbury as the market leader in the UK food retail market, a market which by December 1999 was worth £96.6 billion. It did this through a combination of aggressive and sustained price-cutting, the introduction of its Clubcard customer loyalty scheme, flexible store formats and innovative management practices. This position has been secured in recent years as the company has exploited its core competencies to develop the Tesco Personal Finance initiative and become a world leader in online grocery sales.*

*It has since secured this position by virtue of sustained expansion and the development of its online grocery shopping trade. Its market capitalisation is now over £15 billion (Sainsbury, £6 billion) and its market share 15.6% (Sainsbury, 11.8%). However, the rate of growth has slowed in a saturated UK market from year-on-year 12.4% in 1998 to 7.4% in 2000.*

*The company strategy is to build market share by cutting prices (2000 price cuts = £340 million). This increases volume, which in turn enables discounted purchasing. It has yet to see this policy replicated successfully overseas.*

*This is clearly consistent with the food policy of successive government's which has been to ensure that food is made available as cheaply as possible. An ongoing Competition Commission investigation into the food retail sector is unlikely to lead to significant changes in this policy. With the exception of some parts of Eastern Europe, the group operates in low inflation zones.*

*The company had 845 stores at the end of February 2000, occupying 24 million square feet. During 2001 this is anticipated to increase by 17% to over 28 million square feet. Only 1 million square feet of this increase will be in the UK. It is projected that by end 2001 over one-third of floor space will be outside of the UK. This will involve capital investment of over £1 billion. The financing implications of this are considered later in this report.*

*The group currently employs in excess of 135,000 people world-wide.*

### SWOT Analysis

*Strengths:*

- *The company is in a market leadership position in the UK.*
- *It has a committed and capable management team.*
- *It has the strategy and resources to fulfil its ambition to become a global force.*
- *It is a world leader in online grocery shopping.*

*Weaknesses:*

- *Its principal market is highly competitive with little scope for organic growth.*
- *Opportunities for global expansion are limited and require heavy initial capital investment.*

- *Security of supply chain cannot yet be guaranteed in some overseas markets.*

*Opportunities:*

- *Online grocery shopping business offers significant market leader possibilities.*
- *Liquidity difficulties of several UK and European competitors means that some may become attractive takeover candidates for Tesco.*
- *Share of non-food retail sector can grow significantly.*

*Threats:*

- *A Competition Commission review of the retail industry in the UK threatens restrictions.*
- *The company may itself become a target of several international buyers.*
- *Investments in some Asian economies may not yield returns for several years.*
- *The acquisition of UK competitor ASDA by US giant Wal-Mart may increase competition.*

### Activity and Liquidity

*A cash cycle of 12.8 days (1999: 11.6) testifies to the favourable cashflow enjoyed by the company. The absence of debtors coupled with efficient stock (stock days = 13.4 days) and creditor management (creditors days = 26.2 days) ensure that the company enjoys a favourable cashflow from trading activities.*

*Much of the group's success in its Personal Finance initiative is built on this consistent and favourable cashflow profile.*

*The high-quality management practices implemented by the company in relation to its working-capital will be sustained by virtue of recent investment in stock management technologies. It is anticipated that this investment will yield cost savings in excess of £100 million in the coming year. This will allow the virtuous circle of cost savings facilitating price-cuts which in turn yield greater economies of scale and increased turnover to be perpetuated.*

*Low current ratios are not a problem in this industry as turnover rates are high. The Quality of Profits ratio of 1.47:1 (1999: 1.41:1) confirms that operating activity produces cash quickly and efficiently.*

### Financing

*The company has funded the bulk of its expansion through equity investment and cashflow from operating activity. Therefore, it is a low-geared company with a gearing ratio of 0.32:1. This is a slight increase on the figure for 1999 (0.28:1). This is as a result of increased investment on overseas expansion. This is also reflected in a slightly reduced asset turnover ratio of 2.95 (1999: 3.05) which derives from increased capital expenditure in areas which have yet to yield turnover rates commensurate with other parts of the group.*

*As a consequence of its low gearing, the group has relatively low fixed interest charges and satisfies the bulk of its funding by means of dividends. Interest cover of 10.4 times (1999: 10.3) confirms the healthy financing structure of the company and the fact that scope exists for additional external funding to be raised if necessary.*

*The company is confident that it can finance the bulk of its projected expansion into Eastern Europe and South-east Asia by means of internally generated funds. However, some element of external funding may well be required, but it is unlikely that this will materially affect gearing.*

*Profitability and Return on Investment*

*A sustained policy of price-cutting, which was initiated by Tesco in the early 1990s, has resulted in the industry margin declining over recent years. As a pioneer of the price-cutting strategy and with the advantage of its Clubcard customer loyalty scheme, and its Personal Finance facility, Tesco has been in a position to cut margins while increasing profitability by a combination of increased sales, greater efficiencies and increased economies.*

*Gross Profit margins of 7.6% (1999: 7.6%) and Operating margins of 5.5% (1999: 5.4%) exceed those of all other major competitors. Allied to a low-gearing which gives Tesco lower financing costs than many of its rivals, this has allowed return on investment to remain strong with an ROCE of 16.2% (1999: 16.6%).*

*The segmental analysis shows that, of overseas operations, only the Republic of Ireland is producing profits. The expectation is that Eastern Europe and South-East Asia will begin to yield profits by 2002/3.*

*EPS continues to show healthy growth. From 7.6 p per share in 1996 adjusted diluted EPS has increased steadily to 10.18 p for 2000. Projected EPS for 2001 is 11.1 p. Dividends have increased correspondingly from 3.20 p per share in 1996 to 4.48 p. Dividend cover has decreased slightly.*

*Online Shopping*

*One of the potentially most lucrative and profitable activities of the company is its online shopping business, where it now ranks as a world leader. Annualised sales at current weekly turnover rates are in excess of £300 million. This business has worked successfully in the UK because of high population densities. The company has indicated that it intends to operate this function under a new company to be known as Tesco.com. The intention is to replicate the success of this activity in other parts of the world.*

*Future Strategy*

*Chief Executive Terry Leahy has outlined the following strategic objectives for the group:*

- *45% of sales and £100 million profits to derive from overseas operations by 2002. This will require capital investment in existing and new stores as well as funding for acquisitions.*

- *Online grocery shopping via Tesco.com to consolidate company's position as the leading global online food retailer.*

- *More stores to be modelled to suit local retailing conditions: these range from hypermarkets (Extras) to small convenience stores (Express) to forecourt garage outlets (Metros).*

- *Concerted effort to capture larger element of non-food market which currently accounts for 15% of turnover. Pricing strategy has been devised with the aim of undercutting Boots and Dixons.*

- *Management have devised policies intended to ensure that the company stays in touch with customers so as not to repeat mistakes of some competitors.*

- *Double-digit annual earnings growth.*

*Recommendation*

*With forecast profits of £1.05 billion for 2001, and shares currently at 210 p, shares are on a prospective earnings multiple of 20. This yields a return of 2.2%. Moderate BUY.*

---

**Appendix 1: Summary of Performance Measures**

*All of the company specific ratios and performance measures alluded to in this report have been covered in the body of the text and can be accessed there.*

*Industry specific data can be accessed at www.igd.com/, which is the site for the Institute of Grocery Distribution. Performance data for competitors can be accessed at individual company websites. The competitor against which Tesco plc should be set is J. Sainsbury plc.*

---

## Other Persectives

The report above adopts the perspective of a firm of investment advisers preparing a briefing for its own clients. Its perspective is, therefore, investor specific.

However, a number of other stakeholding groups could also prepare reports. For instance, a more community-aware, environmental protection lobby group would have an entirely different agenda and focus.

The following points summarise the issues that such a group might focus on in their analysis of Tesco plc.

---

**Tesco plc**

- *The cheap food policy which the UK government has traditionally espoused has meant that health and safety issues have been subordinated to price. Thus, unlike several continental European countries, quality has often suffered at the expense of quantity. This is best illustrated by the various health scares in the meat industry where farmers operating under a regime which insists on ever lower prices have been producing products steadily declining in quality.*

- *Large-scale overseas investment in Eastern Europe and South-east Asia has seen the shopping culture of these areas affected by an influx of large bulk-buying entities. This brings much-needed employment, but often at a cost. The company has, however, committed itself to sourcing more of its products locally.*

- *The company has a good record in relation to health and safety of employees. It has introduced many local, national and global initiatives that have seen employees benefit from improved wage rates and conditions.*

- *The projected building programme of the group is of great concern. This will take place in both the UK and abroad. The likelihood that this will lead to the further use of the ubiquitous "Essex Barn" type of building is of particular concern.*

- *Unlike companies such as the Body Shop and Shell, Tesco does not produce an environmental report. It would be useful to have greater disclosure of social, environmental and cultural issues of concern to local communities.*

- *Overall, Tesco is an excellent company and a good employer, but has yet to make environmental issues central to its strategic outlook.*

## *Summary*

The main report produced here is, of necessity, limited in both its scope and its ambition. However, it does highlight what such a report might contain and indicates the general points that might be made.

The concerns of investors are dramatically different from those of other interest groups, as suggested by the outline of a report aimed at a group coming from the perspective of those more interested in corporate social reporting and environmental reporting.

The key point to remember is that both the data available and the perspective of the user will influence every report. Regardless of this, the techniques and principles covered thus far in the text can be gathered together to present a useful insight into the business with a view to facilitating the decision-making process.

## Review Questions

### Question 1
"The tenor and content of any report will depend to a large extent on the audience being targeted." Explain what this means and give examples of how user perspective will influence conclusions drawn from data.

### Question 2
Explain why financial ratios should not be allowed to form the core of any report on a company.

### Question3
"Since analysts make their money by encouraging investors to buy shares, it is hardly surprising that the vast bulk of such reports conclude with BUY recommendations." Explain the role of analysts in the encouraging investment, sometimes unwisely, by investors.

### Question 4
The executive summary is probably the most important section of an analyst's report. Explain why this is so and give illustrations of the type of comments that might be found in that section.

### Question 5
"Analyst's reports should be concise and to the point. There is no point in a rambling account of company performance and position. An analyst who cannot produce a report that presents a coherent analysis and recommendation in less than 2,000 words should be fired.' Is this tenable?

### Question 6
List the elements of the Tesco plc Annual Report that would be of most interest to a member of a local community concerned at the possibility that a new store might be built in his or her locality.

### Question 7
List the principal ratios that should be included or referred to in any report that attempts to discuss the efficiency of management.

### Question 8
Explain how the task of financial information analysis has been made so much easier by the availability of vast amounts of information on company web sites. Identify some problems with depending exclusively on information from such sites when attempting an analysis of a company.

### Question 9
Chapter 7 provided a five-point scheme to be adopted when undertaking financial information analysis. Consider the extent to which the main report in this chapter conforms to this outline.

## Case Studies

### Case 1

The following article comments on the Tesco preliminary results for the year ended February 2001. In the light of the information disclosed reconsider the report included in this chapter.

## Piling Up the Profits

Marks and Spencer's failings underline Tesco's success. This week, Britain's largest supermarket group reported a 13% increase in its pre-tax profits to over a billion pounds. Until now, M&S was the only British retailer to have beaten a billion. The press responded with its usual enthusiasm for Britain's business successes, and decried the profits as evidence of Tesco's rapacity.

boxTesco had a ready riposte. Operating profit margins in Britain remained steady in the year ending February 2001 at about 6%. Tesco says that it has spent £250 million in the past year cutting prices. Last year, the Competition Commission cleared supermarkets of making excessive profits.

boxIrritating though it is to its detractors, Tesco's success comes from consistently good management and close attention to what customers want. This formula has turned a supermarket group once legendary for the "pile 'em high, sell 'em cheap" approach of its founder Jack Cohen into one that combines high quality and competitive prices. In 1995, Tesco toppled Sainsbury off its perch as the biggest supermarket chain. Since then Tesco's lead over the other supermarkets has increased steadily.

boxLike other British retailers, Tesco is operating in a testing environment. Food prices are falling; across the range of goods that Tesco sells, prices are stable. The company is responding by extending its range of products. Its 304 superstores devote 40–50% of their shelf space to non-grocery items such as clothes and products for the home. In the past year, Tesco, which is also Britain's biggest independent petrol retailer, has opened up a new front in electronic retailing, selling televisions, DVD players and mobile phones.

Despite such initiatives, the scope for growth in Britain is limited by Tesco's already commanding share of the market. Its real challenge at home is to fend off the competition, which is intensifying. Under the leadership of Sir Peter Davis, Sainsbury is fighting back. Wal-Mart, the world's biggest retailer, has gained a strategic foothold through its purchase of Asda, Britain's third-largest supermarket.

So Tesco's growth prospects now depend upon expanding overseas. Its ambition is to emulate the success of Carrefour, the French supermarket group, in becoming an international retailer. Tesco is concentrating on two principal areas, Central Europe and East Asia. It already has 68 giant hypermarkets overseas and is planning to increase this to 130 by 2002. Overseas sales currently amount to 13% of total turnover, but by 2003 this share is planned to rise to 30%.

Terry Leahy, Tesco's chief executive, revealed encouraging figures about the strategy this week. Total international sales grew last year by 43% to £2.9 billion. In Asia, they jumped by 85% to almost a billion pounds. Altogether, overseas operations contributed £74 million to group profits last year, an increase of almost half. Tesco's operations in Hungary and Thailand moved into profit.

Abroad has generally been a disaster for British shops. Only this week, Sainsbury announced that it was pulling out of Egypt. It lost over £100 million there. M&S is closing its overseas stores, including those in France. Tesco itself made a short-lived foray into the French market in the early 1990s when it bought and then disposed of the Catteau food chain. The difficulty for retailers is that their brands are generally difficult to transfer across frontiers. However, Tesco possesses genuine strengths in logistics and retail management which can be exploited in fast-growing emerging economies that are ill-served by traditional retailing outlets. Tesco could be the first British chain to prove itself a winner abroad as well as at home.

Source: The Economist, April 12, 2001.

## Case 2

One of Tesco's major competitors is Marks and Spencer. It was also the first retailer before Tesco to generate profits in excess of £1 billion. However, since that point it has been embroiled in trouble and has seen its market leadership position disappear.

Drawing on Marks and Spencer's experience as outlined in the following article, as well as more recent financial results which can be accessed at the company's web site, identify potential opportunities and pitfalls for Tesco in the years ahead.

## Two British Retailers are in Trouble

Marks and Spencer is under attack because it is making too little money. Tesco is under attack because it is making too much.

What has gone wrong for Marks and Spencer, once the icon of British retailing? A classic mid-life crisis, by the look of it. When it got into trouble in the late 1990s it compounded its difficulties by a desperate and doomed attempt to look young and exciting. Now its latest internal estimates suggest that the profit for the year just ended will turn out to be barely £430 million, lower than forecast only a few months ago.

Three years ago Marks and Spencer was riding high. During the 1990s, with Sir Richard Greenbury as chairman and chief executive, profits doubled to £1.16 billion ($1.9 billion) in 1997–98. It was in competition with Wal-Mart for the title of the most profitable chain store in the world.

But investors wanted the top jobs split, so in February 1999, Sir Richard gave up being chief executive, and stayed on as chairman. Then things started to go wrong.

Profits fell in 1998–99. Much of it was put down at the time to special factors, such as "overbuying to support expansion", costs associated with buying Littlewoods stores and a fall in overseas profits caused partly by the strong pound. But with hindsight, the company's reach may have exceeded its grasp.

Sir Richard resigned a year early in June 1999, because he could not get along with the new chief executive, Peter Salsbury. Mr Salsbury announced big reorganisations including a new global supply chain designed to get garments made wherever costs were lowest in the world. He was also seeking to turn the company into a global retailer. But profits continued to fall. Most of the problems have been in clothing, which makes up 60% of M&S's business. Clothing sales are falling even though the market is growing. A new chairman, Luc Vandevelde, was brought in 15 months ago, with a bonus of £650,000 unrelated to the company's financial performance. He promised to turn the company round in two years, but when things still seemed to be going off the rails he fired Mr Salsbury last October.

Yet another reorganisation was announced last month, with some stores closing as a new boss of British retailing was hired. Now Mr Vandevelde is pulling out of France and selling Brooks Brothers in America, despite signs that the overseas bits are quite healthy. The French shut-down was announced so brutally that it broke local labour law, and has caused a national outcry in France.

M&S's fall is being used as evidence to support a range of different prejudices. One columnist says it is a sign the British can no longer manage anything; railways, hospitals or shops. Another says it is because M&S pared things to the bone, cutting costs in the boom years, to boost profits and please the City (tut-tut), thus storing up trouble for the future. A more prosaic interpretation, based on what insiders say, is that the management over-reacted to the first fall in profits. Mr Salsbury brought in no fewer than 12 teams of management consultants, including one whose job was to advise on the use of management consultants.

Most of the top managers on the buying side have been ousted. The consultants have been reorganising everything in sight. Staff, many of whom have been obliged to re-apply for their own jobs, are demoralised. The supply-chain reorganisation was botched. It upset suppliers. Deliveries, coming from farther and farther away, became harder to control. Distribution costs rose. Quality fell. "They've lost control of their supply chain in terms of quality and cost, that's the big problem," says a former executive.

Between them, the management and the consultants came up with all sorts of exciting new ideas. The company rushed to develop new brands, and to bring in exciting new designers. The fashion magazines were enthusiastic about the new stuff, and gave it plenty of publicity; the (oldish) customers were less keen. Now Mr Vandevelde says the company is going back to its old business of selling classic clothes. It looks as though he may have run out of new ideas. Perhaps that is a good thing.

Source: The Economist, April 12, 2001.

## Case 3

Write a report on Tesco plc from the perspective of a trade union representative. Comment in particular on information which would be of interest to employees, but which is not included in the Annual Report 2000.

# SECTION VI

---

# Challenges and Opportunities

Section I of this text outlined some of the larger contextual issues which should inform any analysis of accounting information.

Section II then augmented this with specific information as to the accounting and disclosure requirements governing Annual Reports.

Section III introduced a range of ratios and other fundamental analysis techniques that have been developed to facilitate the extraction of key items of information from financial statements. The point was made repeatedly that these techniques were merely a means to an end, that end being an informed decision-making process.

Section IV dealt with some advanced accounting matters and, in the process introduced related issues such as Corporate Social Reporting and Creative Accounting, topics which must also be kept in mind when assessing the quality and dependability of any accounting information.

Section V brought these various themes together by applying them to Tesco plc.

Section VI, the final section, extends beyond the rather limited confines of the accounting world. Recognising that the text has thus far adopted a financial information-focused view of the firm, Chapter 17 introduces a range of alternative approaches which have emerged in recent years as the limitations of the accounting-centred approach have become evident. Finally, Chapter 18 outlines the challenges and opportunities presented by the dynamics of the "New Economy" and the information and technological revolutions which have given rise to it.

# ALTERNATIVE APPROACHES [17]

When you have completed this chapter you will understand that:

- Financial measures cannot capture every area critical to the long-term health of a business.

- A number of models have been developed which try to redress this imbalance.

- The Balanced Scorecard (BSC) challenges businesses to identify and measure areas typically not measured by the traditional financial model.

- Economic Value Analysis (EVA) is another approach that attempts to broaden the frame of reference.

- Multi-variate analysis techniques have been developed to assist in predicting bankruptcy.

- Ideally, financial and non-financial measures should complement one another.

## Performance Anxiety

**New Performance Measurement Approaches Might Be Coming Thick and Fast, But it Does Not Mean You Can Throw Away the Old Ones. Alison Classe Asks How Finance Functions Are Coping**

In their quest to "add value" to their organisations, finance directors are naturally interested in measurement techniques that promise demonstrable improvements to business performance; and which one doesn't? But at the same time, they are increasingly sceptical about the possibility of a "magic bullet".

Like many other organisations, BT has adopted a balanced scorecard (BSC) approach, but manager of strategy process Ian Isaac regards scorecards as a way of approaching the performance measurement task, rather than a unique break-through: Every company needs a method of setting strategic objectives and measuring performance against them, but whether you use a balanced scorecard or just a list of objectives probably doesn't make a great deal of difference. "What's important is the balance, a healthy company looks at a range of financial and non-financial objectives, weighting them appropriately. It's when you decide what weightings are important that it gets complex. To do that properly requires a detailed business strategy," says Mr Isaac.

Using a framework like a balanced scorecard can actually help with this process of definition, according to Andy Neely, director of the centre for business performance at the Judge Institute of Management Studies, Cambridge University. "The process of deciding what to measure forces you to clarify your business strategy. The balanced scorecard forces you to think about areas where you may not have measures, such as innovation and learning. But you shouldn't just take a standard balanced scorecard. You should think about whether the categories are right for you. For example, in the case of a manufacturing company 50%-60% of costs may be represented by bought-in parts, so measurements relating to suppliers would have to be added to the scorecard," advises Dr Neely.

## Business Drivers

There again, you don't have to start with a score-card at all. Robert Bittlestone, managing director of Metapraxis and member of the Council of the Foundation for Performance Measurement suggests that a technique called "business driver maps" can have similar benefits. "They're a unifying discipline bringing together a variety of other approaches including economic value analysis, some aspects of activity-based costing, plus common sense." This is the approach gas transportation company Transco has taken.

At BT, has the adoption of scorecards led to any startling findings? It's more of a shift of emphasis, Mr Isaac says. "Since privatisation, we'd already been through an evolutionary process, reflecting a realisation of the need to look beyond purely financial measures: there had been programmes designed to increase customer focus, like total quality management; process re-engineering programmes; the creation of the internal market to increase the entrepreneurship of business units, and so on. "Rather than introduce many new measurements that weren't already in place, the balanced scorecard idea has helped us to consolidate a lot into one model. We're using it to check that the measurements we do collect are those that we need to support our strategy."

## Satisfying Stakeholders

The Royal Mail is rethinking its performance measurement and management approach to support recent strategy. "We need to focus more on stakeholders and their needs," says project manager George Wilson. "We're looking at where our business needs to go from here, and how we can communicate our aims to everyone in the organisation."

At present, Mr Wilson explains, there is a plethora of measurements being collected, but they're not fully tied to strategy, nor are they closely enough linked to staff behaviour and appraisals to translate policy into action. "Our objective is to produce a clear hierarchy of linked measures, supported by appropriate information systems." To help it do this, the Royal Mail is applying techniques such as balanced score-cards and driver analysis tables, but these are only used insofar as they shed useful light on the task in hand...

Source: Accountancy, March 1999.

## Introduction

The experiences of companies such as BT and the Royal Mail are not unusual. Traditional financial measures, however complex and comprehensive, are simply incapable of allowing users to form a comprehensive view of a firm's performance, strategic challenges and opportunities. Companies realise that a more broadly constituted set of performance indicators is required. The Balanced Scorecard (BSC), Economic Value Analysis (EVA), and other business analysis techniques alluded to in this opening vignette, while incorporating some financial elements, do offer a more holistic alternative.

Responding to the intuitions and experiences of various stakeholders, a variety of alternative approaches have been developed over recent decades. These range from relatively straightforward measures that identify areas requiring attention, through more holistic templates such as that supplied by the Balanced Scorecard (BSC), to complex integrated systems such as Total Quality Management (TQM).

Whatever their focus, these approaches add the perspective of strategy as well as emphasising the need for a company to manage, measure and control all of its resources over the short, medium and long term. In particular, they bring a renewed emphasis on the customer, on quality and innovation and on specifically human concerns such as employee morale, knowledge and potential.

However, these approaches do not seek to displace the traditional financial reporting and control model. Instead, they should be viewed as a means by which financial measures can be augmented and informed. Nor are these non-financial measures complete in themselves. As Ian Isaac comments above, "What's important is the balance, a healthy company looks at a range of financial and non-financial objectives, weighting them appropriately."

Whichever method is adopted it is important to remember that, like financial indicators, these systems only provide information for decision-making purposes. Like ratios and other forms of information, they are merely means to an end and must be contextualised and interpreted properly.

Two of the more common alternatives are the Balanced Scorecard (BSC) and Economic Value Analysis (EVA).

## Balanced Scorecard

Businesses must measure and control more than financial flows. Business success derives in the long-term from efficient and effective operational processes and cultures. Thus, financial measures on their own only provide a limited perspective. Attention has increasingly focused, therefore, on recognising, measuring and managing non-financial elements of business activity.

The Balanced Scorecard (BSC) was developed in the early 1990s by Robert Kaplan and David Norton. The BSC broadens the frame of reference to incorporate four key aspects of performance. These are:

- Financial perspective
- Innovation and learning perspective
- Customer perspective
- Business process perspective

In relation to each of these a business is encouraged to determine those measures that best capture and reflect operations deemed to be critical to future success.

Thus, Kaplan and Norton outline how one company addressing its Customer and Learning Perspectives might develop the following sets of measures to track and control the goals it has set:

| Customer perspective | | Learning perspective | |
|---|---|---|---|
| Goals | Measures | Goals | Measures |
| New products | % sales from new products | Technology leadership | Time to develop products |
| Responsive supply | On-time delivery | Manufacturing learning | Process time to maturity |
| Preferred supplier | Ranking by key accounts | Product focus | % products = 80% of sales |
| Customer partnership | No. of co-operative efforts | Time to market | New product introductions |

The significant point, of course, is that this process identifies key areas of strategic importance that the traditional financial measurement process will usually overlook. The following extract describes the implementation of such a system:

## Balanced Scorecard

### Thou Shalt Not Fail: Balanced Scorecard Implementation Does Not Have to Be Difficult; Just Obey the 10 Commandments, by Liz Fisher

Since it was first described in the Harvard Business Review in 1992, the balanced scorecard has become one of the hottest topics on the management conference circuit. Perhaps this is an indication of how small is the number of people who really understand what the balanced scorecard is designed to achieve. It has become such a high-profile management tool that companies are rushing to implement it without a deep understanding of why, or even being sure what benefits they are hoping to gain. According to KPMG Management Consulting, which has worked with many companies implementing the balanced scorecard approach, many of the projects fail because of the same repeated mistakes. As a result of its experiences, the firm has produced what it calls the 10 commandments of balanced scorecard implementation.

### To Do or Not to Do

KPMG has split the list into five "dos" and five "don'ts" of implementation. It defines a successful implementation as an operation during which there was evidence that the scorecard was firmly anchored in the organisation's planning and control cycles, with periodic reporting and discussion of its contents. Obeying all 10 commandments is not a watertight recipe for success, but it will greatly improve your chances.

First, the "do's":

- Use the scorecard as an implementation pad for strategic goals, because it can be an ideal vehicle for rolling corporate strategy down through the organisation.
- Ensure the goals are in place before the scorecard is implemented. If you invent the strategy as you go along, the scorecard will drive the wrong behaviour.
- Ensure that a top-level, non-financial sponsor backs the project, and that relevant line managers are committed to it. Implementing a scorecard is a major task and should be nothing less than a top priority. Never leave it to accountants.
- Implement a pilot before introducing the new scorecard; you could learn some valuable lessons, and you'll avoid the risk of a Big Bang.
- Carry out an entry review for each business unit before implementing the scorecard. This allows you to customise the project to suit your organisation's needs.

And now the "don'ts"

- Don't use the scorecard to obtain extra top-down control; people will rebel.

- Don't attempt to standardise the project. A ready-made scorecard will not fit any organisation. It must be tailor-made to fit your company.
- Don't underestimate the need for communication and training in using the scorecard. Implementing the scorecard brings about huge changes that have to be dealt with.
- Avoid paralysis by analysis. Don't look for complexity.
- Putting the new routine in place will take longer than you think. Don't underestimate the extra administrative workload and costs of scorecard reporting.

Companies that have succeeded in implementing a balanced scorecard that is rooted in their planning and control processes have obeyed most of the commandments and have kept the scorecard as a priority throughout implementation. Those that failed did not obey the commandments or took their eye off the scorecard ball before it was in place. According to KPMG, scorecard implementation projects must adhere to at least six of the commandments to succeed...

Source: Accountancy, September, 1998.

The BSC, therefore, offers a different and more comprehensive perspective of the business to which it is being applied. It forces management to recognise and incorporate strategic and human factors into its business planning and control models. It also provides a means by which intangible resources can be recognised and measured, usually in non-financial terms. In an economy in which intangible drivers of value such as intellectual capital and knowledge are emerging as the key sources of competitive advantage, such attributes can only increase in importance.

As with any other technique, it has its limits. It must be sensitively applied and users must be aware of both its potential and its limitations. A cost/benefit analysis should normally precede any attempt to apply it and the template adopted should be sensitive to the unique value drivers of the firm. Finally, the way in which inter-firm comparison can be compromised by virtue of the uniqueness of each business's strategic and operational mix must be appreciated.

## Economic Value Analysis

Economic Value Analysis is predicated on the notion that "accounting profits" adopt a very limited perspective when assessing performance. The economic understanding of profit on the other hand is informed as much by opportunity cost and the use of scarce resources as by any notion of "the excess of revenue over costs".

EVA is a performance measurement and analysis technique that focuses on "economic profit" as distinct from financial profit and stresses the importance of cash flow increments over and above the market-determined weighted average cost of capital (WACC). As Chapter 9 illustrated, WACC is the sum of the implied or required market returns of each component of a corporate capitalization, weighted by that component's share of the total capitalization. EVA is attempting, therefore, to incorporate a more economic notion of profit into the assessment criteria applied to business.

It is calculated as: Net Operating Profit after Tax and Weighted Average Cost of Capital (WACC).

For example, assuming a company has an Operating Profit after Tax of £10 million and a capital base of £100 million with a WACC of 8%, its economic profit under EVA would be: £10 million − £8 million (£100 × 8%) = £2 million. Further informed by cashflow information, this return would be compared with alternatives in order to see whether the money could be more profitably invested elsewhere.

As the following extract explains, EVA has been widely adopted and has as one of its primary effects the imposition of a stricter budgetary discipline on management.

## Economic Value Analysis, by Dawne Shand

Remember Microeconomics 101? Maybe not. At any rate, the class would typically start with the professor striding slowly to the front of the room and announcing that "accounting profits are not economic profits." He would peer over his spectacles to see if any wide-eyed freshman had even a glimmer of the profundity of this statement, then he would sigh. No one gets it at first. Unfortunately, it's a tenet that often confuses many business and information technology managers as well.

Basic accounting practices define a profit as revenue minus costs. If you spent $10 million on a new plant and earned $10.5 million from the sales of the products it produced, you would claim an accounting profit of $500,000. But that same investment might have generated $11 million or more if it had been invested elsewhere. Suddenly, that $500,000 accounting profit doesn't look so compelling, especially to investors.

According to economic theory, capital eventually moves to the investment opportunities with the best returns because investors want to maximize their profits. An economic profit means that a business generates returns similar to an investment in the stock market. Getting decision-makers to think about economic profits as they evaluate new business opportunities is the purpose of using economic value added (EVA). Michael Contrada, executive vice president at Balanced Scorecard Collaborative Inc. in Lincoln, Mass., explains that "revenue minus costs doesn't tell you much about the cost of resources, such as equity and debt."

EVA says that assets used by a line of business have opportunity costs. Investments in one arena (such as distribution) detract from another (such as manufacturing) that may hold an opportunity for bigger returns. For example, London-based Diageo PLC, which owns United Distillers & Vintners Ltd., used EVA to gauge which of its liquor brands generated the best returns. The analysis determined that because of the time required for storage and care, aged Scotch didn't generate as much profit as vodka, which could be sold within weeks of being distilled. As a result of the EVA analysis, management at United Distillers began to emphasize vodka production and sales...

Source: Computerworld, October 30, 2000.

While EVA does take financial information as its starting point, it is normally classified as a non-financial measure on the basis that it forces management attentions onto "economic profit". This requires that budgetary systems, strategic plans and investment appraisal techniques acknowledge a more rigorous assessment criteria than is imposed by purely financial measures. The effect in many of those businesses in which it has been applied has been to identify those areas which are more profitable, and ensure than marginal funds are directed there. This in turn has positively impacted upon return on investment.

## Multi-Variate Analysis and Corporate Failure Prediction

One area in which traditional financial measures and non-financial indicators have found common ground is that of company failure prediction. Considerable research has been carried out in this area in recent years and several studies have indicated that the models developed can be used with a certain degree of confidence.

The ability to predict corporate failure will be of particular importance to bankers and suppliers. It will also be of interest to auditors attempting to establish the degree to which a company can be considered a going concern. It will obviously also be critical for companies themselves as a means of identifying their own viability and of assessing the stability of suppliers and customers.

There are several principal causes of insolvency and corporate failure:

- Failure to respond to market changes
- Overtrading
- High gearing in anticipation of growth which does not materialise

Most corporate failure prediction models focus on the use of key ratios to highlight prospective difficulties such as these. They usually calculate a "score" for the company and then compare this with a "pass mark" which has been determined by previous study to be appropriate to entities operating in the business sector.

### Altman's Z-Score

This was the original corporate failure prediction model and was developed in the late 1960's. It uses financial ratios as a means of predicting bankruptcy. The Z-score for a business is the product of a weighted average of five separate ratios. These weightings and ratios were derived from a major empirical study.

The formula is:

$$Z = 1.2X1 + 1.4X2 + 3.3X3 + 0.6X4 + 1.0X5$$

$$X1 = \frac{\text{Working Capital}}{\text{Total Assets}}$$

$$X2 = \frac{\text{Retained Earnings}}{\text{Total Assets}}$$

$$X3 = \frac{\text{Profit before interest and tax}}{\text{Total Assets}}$$

$$X4 = \frac{\text{Market capitalisation}}{\text{Book value of debts}}$$

$$X5 = \frac{\text{Sales}}{\text{Total Assets}}$$

Companies which score a Z-score of $> 2.7$ are considered to be going concerns, at least in the short- to medium-term. A score below 1.8 indicates potentially serious problems.

There have, however, been criticisms of the Z-score model on the following grounds:

- Lack of commonality of definition of similar items between companies
- Use of historic data
- Lack of conceptual base
- Lack of sensitivity to time scale of failure

Nevertheless Altman's Z-score approach (modified in several instances to take account of local conditions, for example, Taffler's model in the UK) is widely used by those wishing to assess the stability and solvency of companies.

## Taffler's Model

Taffler's model for quoted UK companies, which is open to the same criticisms as Altman's Z-score, has also been widely employed.

The formula is:

$$Z = 0.53X1 + 0.13X2 + 0.18X3 + 0.16X4$$

$$X1 = \frac{\text{Profit before tax}}{\text{Current Liabilities}}$$

$$X2 = \frac{\text{Current Liabilities}}{\text{Total Liabilities}}$$

$$X3 = \frac{\text{Current Liabilities}}{\text{Total Assets}}$$

$$X4 = \frac{\text{Immediate Assets} - \text{Current Liabilities}}{\text{Operating Costs} - \text{Depreciation}}$$

A negative score means that the company has a score similar to that of previously failed companies.

## Argenti's Failure Model

This model was developed primarily through discussion with bankers, businessmen and investors, as well as a wide-ranging review of cases of failure. As a result it depends less upon financial information than an assessment of various aspects of a companies controls and systems.

The model requires that scores be assigned under the following headings:

|  |  | Score |
|---|---|---|
| *Defects* |  |  |
| *Management* | Autocratic chief executive | 8 |
|  | Chief executive is also chairman | 4 |
|  | Unbalanced skill/experience on board | 2 |
|  | Passive board | 2 |
|  | Weak finance director | 2 |
|  | Lack of professional managers | 1 |
| *Accounting systems* | Budgetary control | 3 |
|  | Cash flow plans | 3 |
|  | Costing systems | 3 |
| *Response to change* | Products, processes, markets, etc. | 15 |
|  | **Total possible** | **43** |
|  | **Danger mark** | **10** |
| **Mistakes** | Over-trading | 15 |
|  | Excessively high gearing | 15 |
|  | Impending project failure | 15 |
|  | **Total possible** | **45** |
|  | **Danger mark** | **15** |
| **Symptoms** | Deteriorating ratios or Z-scores | 4 |
|  | Signs of creative accounting | 4 |

*(continued)*

| | Score |
|---|---|
| Decline in quality, morale, market share, etc. | 3 |
| Resignations | 1 |
| **Total possible** | 12 |
| **Overall total possible** | 100 |
| **Danger mark** | 25 |

The main rules of interpretation are:

- Total $< 25$: company not in imminent danger.
- Total $> 25$: company may fail within 5 years.
- Defects score $> 10$: management likely to make potentially fatal mistake.
- Mistakes score $> 15$ (and Defects score $< 10$): management somewhat risky.

Like the Z-score, Argenti's model can be criticised on a number of grounds:

- The mix of indicators may be inappropriate
- The weighting given to indicators may be unsuitable
- Time factors may not be fully respected

## Application of Failure-Prediction Models

While these prediction models have been widely applied, some scepticism remains as to their efficacy, as suggested by the following report.

### Predicting Failure: A failure in Prediction?

#### Just How Useful Are Bankruptcy Prediction Models? by Richard Morris

Most investment and credit analysts are well aware of the existence of so-called "failure prediction" models, if only because their forecasts are published by company data services and debt rating agencies. Clearly, if their predictions are correct, those who ignore their existence are in the short term likely to lose money for their clients, and in the longer term to find their advice spurned and themselves out of a job.

But it is not only financial advisers who ought to be interested in the forecasts of such models. Accounting practitioners must also decide from time to time if and when to enter going concern audit qualifications. Indeed, a research partner in one of the Big Six firms has even suggested that the models' forecasts should be published alongside company accounts as indicators of financial risk.

## At Least Since the Thirties

There is nothing new in trying to predict corporate bankruptcy. Formal procedures using accounting ratios to distinguish between failing and surviving businesses have existed for almost 70 years. Like the alchemists of old who sought to turn base metals into gold, generations of researchers have tried to find a way to predict accurately which companies are on the road to bankruptcy.

Their motive is easy to understand, since investors and creditors, and the agents who work on their behalf, search endlessly for a novel procedure that might give them a narrow (and presumably short-lived) advantage. If they were successful, analysts and their clients would stand to make a lot of money; or, at least, in the case of the latter, not to lose heavily! It is therefore quite easy to believe that each innovation that makes for more accurate predictions will be well worthwhile. But what is more difficult to accept is that a new approach will continue to be successful in terms of earning abnormal risk-adjusted returns once everybody knows that it exists and analysts are able to mimic its forecasts. Its prophecies should then become self-fulfilling.

In fact, what successions of academics have succeeded in doing since the mid-1960s is to apply new statistical and simulation-based techniques to an ever-wider set of potentially critical indicators. The former include procedures that purport to assess the compound probabilities of companies reporting a sequence of losses; the likelihood of a company failing in the next accounting period; and how long each company is likely to survive.

Most recently, so-called "neural network" techniques have been using computers to simulate thought processes and identify behaviour patterns. As for the variables examined, these now embrace a variety of non-quantitative measures, even including word structures used in chairmen's reports to shareholders. However, despite these efforts, the success rates claimed for new models are not usually substantially above those recorded for their predecessors, even when applied to wider sets of potentially critical indicators...

Source: Accountancy, December, 1997.

As with all ratio analysis, the interpretation of scores and results requires experience and sensitivity to the general economic environment as well as specific industry and national contexts. Nevertheless, properly used, these approaches have proven helpful in predicting corporate failure.

## Summary

Alternative approaches have emerged in response to the rather limited perspective which financial measures both adopt and encourage. An appreciation on the part of various stakeholders that such indicators would enrich the data flow for decision-makers and other users has resulted in their widespread use.

Significantly, such models are at their most useful when they are employed in tandem with financial measures. Indeed, those approaches such as BSC which recognise the potency of accounting information by including a financial perspective within the model offer more enriching insights into the role of financial information within the overall strategic vision of the business. The key is to ensure a balanced approach in devising any system of assessing a business, whether this is for the purposes of planning, control or failure prediction.

# Review Questions

### Question 1
Explain why approaches that emphasise non-financial factors would be attractive to the management of many corporate entities.

### Question 2
Identify some advantages and disadvantages of such approaches.

### Question 3
"The starting point is understanding a company's value drivers, the factors that create stakeholder value. Once known, these factors determine which measures contribute to long-term success and so how to translate corporate objectives into measures that guide managers' actions." Explain what is meant by this statement.

### Question 4
Outline the key features of the Balanced Scorecard approach and list the four "perspectives" which it encourages. Suggest at least three measures that might be employed under each of these perspectives.

### Question 5
Explain what is meant by Economic Value Analysis (EVA) and how it operates.

### Question 6
"EVA seeks to jog managers' memories by deducting from a firm's net operating profit a charge for the amount of capital it employs. If the result is positive, then the firm created value over the period in question; if the EVA is negative it was a 'value destroyer'. Providing a company knows how much capital its operating units use, it can work out their EVA too. For example, if a division's capital is $100 million and its cost of capital is 10%, its target rate of return will be $10 million. If it earns $50 million, then its EVA will be $40 million." Explain this statement.

### Question 7
Explain the use of bankruptcy prediction models, specifically, the $Z$-Score and Argenti models.

### Question 8
"There is nothing new in trying to predict corporate bankruptcy. Formal procedures using accounting ratios to distinguish between failing and surviving businesses have existed for almost 70 years. Like the alchemists of old who sought to turn base metals into gold, generations of researchers have tried to find a way to predict accurately which companies are on the road to bankruptcy."

This quotation, taken from an extract earlier in this chapter, suggests that the author is somewhat sceptical about the claims made for these bankruptcy prediction models. Discuss the issues raised by such models and identify their merits and demerits.

# Case Studies

## Case 1

The following article provides an excellent overview of the place of non-financial measures in the complex array of indicators that must be incorporated and monitored when assessing a company's performance and potential. Discuss, in particular, its contention that "By supplementing accounting measures with non-financial data about strategic performance and implementation of strategic plans, companies can communicate objectives and provide incentives for managers to address long-term strategy."

## A Bigger Yardstick for Company Performance

### Financial Data Has Limitations as a Measure of Company Performance. Other Measures Such as Quality May be Better at Forecasting, But Can be Difficult to Implement, say Christopher Ittner and David Larcker

Choosing performance measures is a challenge. Performance measurement systems play a key role in developing strategy, evaluating the achievement of organisational objectives and compensating managers. Yet many managers feel traditional financially oriented systems no longer work adequately. A recent survey of US financial services companies found most were not satisfied with their measurement systems. They believed there was too much emphasis on financial measures such as earnings and accounting returns and little emphasis on drivers of value such as customer and employee satisfaction, innovation and quality.

In response, companies are implementing new performance measurement systems. A third of financial services companies, for example, made a major change in their performance measurement system during the past two years and 39% plan a major change within two years.

Inadequacies in financial performance measures have led to innovations ranging from non-financial indicators of "intangible assets" and "intellectual capital" to "balanced scorecards" of integrated financial and non-financial measures. This article discusses the advantages and disadvantages of non-financial performance measures and offers suggestions for implementation.

### Advantages

Non-financial measures offer four clear advantages over measurement systems based on financial data. First of these is a closer link to long-term organisational strategies. Financial evaluation systems generally focus on annual or short-term performance against accounting yardsticks. They do not deal with progress relative to customer requirements or competitors, nor other non-financial objectives that may be important in achieving profitability, competitive strength and longer-term strategic goals. For example, new product development or expanding organisational capabilities may be important strategic goals, but may hinder short-term accounting performance.

By supplementing accounting measures with non-financial data about strategic performance and implementation of strategic plans, companies can communicate objectives and provide incentives for managers to address long-term strategy.

Second, critics of traditional measures argue that drivers of success in many industries are "intangible assets" such as intellectual capital and customer loyalty, rather than the "hard assets" allowed on to balance sheets. Although it is difficult to quantify intangible assets in financial terms, non-financial data can provide indirect, quantitative indicators of a firm's intangible assets.

One study examined the ability of non-financial indicators of "intangible assets" to explain differences in US companies' stock market values. It found that measures related to innovation, management capability, employee relations, quality and brand value explained a significant proportion of a company's value, even allowing for accounting assets and liabilities. By excluding these intangible assets, financially oriented measurement can encourage managers to make poor, even harmful, decisions.

Third, non-financial measures can be better indicators of future financial performance. Even when the ultimate goal is maximising financial performance, current financial measures may not capture long-term benefits from decisions made now. Consider, for example, investments in research and development or customer satisfaction programmes. Under US accounting rules, research and development expenditures and marketing costs must be charged for in the period they are incurred, so reducing profits. But successful research improves future profits if it can be brought to market.

Similarly, investments in customer satisfaction can improve subsequent economic performance by increasing revenues and loyalty of existing customers, attracting new customers and reducing transaction costs. Non-financial data can provide the missing link between these beneficial activities and financial results by providing forward-looking information on accounting or stock performance. For example, interim research results or customer indices may offer an indication of future cash flows that would not be captured otherwise.

Finally, the choice of measures should be based on providing information about managerial actions and the level of "noise" in the measures. Noise refers to changes in the performance measure that are beyond the control of the manager or organisation, ranging from changes in the economy to luck (good or bad). Managers must be aware of how much success is due to their actions or they will not have the signals they need to maximise their effect on performance. Because many non-financial measures are less susceptible to external noise than accounting measures, their use may improve managers' performance by providing more precise evaluation of their actions. This also lowers the risk imposed on managers when determining pay.

## Disadvantages

Although there are many advantages to non-financial performance measures, they are not without drawbacks. Research has identified five primary limitations. Time and cost has been a problem for some companies. They have found the costs of a system that tracks a large number of financial and non-financial measures can be greater than its benefits. Development can consume considerable time and expense, not least of which is selling the system to sceptical employees who have learned to operate under existing rules. A greater number of diverse performance measures frequently requires significant investment in information systems to draw information from multiple (and often incompatible) databases.

Evaluating performance using multiple measures that can conflict in the short term can also be time-consuming. One bank that adopted a performance evaluation system using multiple accounting and non-financial measures saw the time required for area directors to evaluate branch managers increase from less than one day per quarter to six days.

Bureaucracies can cause the measurement process to degenerate into mechanistic exercises that add little to reaching strategic goals. For example, shortly after becoming the first US company to win Japan's prestigious Deming Prize for quality improvement, Florida Power and Light found that employees believed the company's quality improvement process placed too much emphasis on reporting, presenting and discussing a myriad of quality indicators. They felt this deprived them of time that could be better spent serving customers. The company responded by eliminating most quality reviews, reducing the number of indicators tracked and minimising reports and meetings.

The second drawback is that, unlike accounting measures, non-financial data are measured in many ways, there is no common denominator. Evaluating performance or making trade-offs between attributes is difficult when some are denominated in time, some in quantities or percentages and some in arbitrary ways.

Many companies attempt to overcome this by rating each performance measure in terms of its strategic importance (from, say, not important to extremely important) and then evaluating overall performance based on a weighted average of the measures. Others assign arbitrary weightings to the various goals. One major car manufacturer, for example, structures executive bonuses so: 40% based on warranty repairs per 100 vehicles sold; 20% on customer satisfaction surveys; 20% on market share; and 20% on accounting performance (pre-tax earnings). However, like all subjective assessments, these methods can lead to considerable error.

Lack of causal links is a third issue. Many companies adopt non-financial measures without articulating the relations between the measures or verifying that they have a bearing on accounting and stock price performance. Unknown or unverified causal links create two problems when evaluating performance: incorrect measures focus attention on the wrong objectives and improvements cannot be linked to later outcomes. Xerox, for example, spent millions of dollars on customer surveys, under the assumption that improvements in satisfaction translated into better financial performance. Later analysis found no such association. As a result, Xerox shifted to a customer loyalty measure that was found to be a leading indicator of financial performance.

The lack of an explicit causal model of the relations between measures also contributes to difficulties in evaluating their relative importance. Without knowing the size and timing of associations among measures, companies find it difficult to make decisions or measure success based on them.

Fourth on the list of problems with non-financial measures is lack of statistical reliability, whether a measure actually represents what it purports to represent, rather than random "measurement error". Many non-financial data such as satisfaction measures are based on surveys with few respondents and few questions. These measures generally exhibit poor statistical reliability, reducing their ability to discriminate superior performance or predict future financial results.

Finally, although financial measures are unlikely to capture fully the many dimensions of organisational performance, implementing an evaluation system with too many measures can lead to "measurement disintegration". This occurs when an overabundance of measures dilutes the effect of the measurement process. Managers chase a variety of measures simultaneously, while achieving little gain in the main drivers of success.

## Selecting Measures

Once managers have determined that the expected benefits from non-financial data outweigh the costs, three steps can be used to select and implement appropriate measures.

## Understand Value Drivers

The starting point is understanding a company's value drivers, the factors that create stakeholder value. Once known, these factors determine which measures contribute to long-term success and so how to translate corporate objectives into measures that guide managers' actions.

While this seems intuitive, experience indicates that companies do a poor job determining and articulating these drivers. Managers tend to use one of three methods to identify value drivers, the most common being intuition. However, executives' rankings of value drivers may not reflect their true importance. For example, many executives rate environmental performance and quality as relatively unimportant drivers of long-term financial performance. In contrast, statistical analyses indicate these dimensions are strongly associated with a company's market value.

A second method is to use standard classifications such as financial, internal business process, customer, learning and growth categories. While these may be appropriate, other non-financial dimensions may be more important, depending on the organisation's strategy, competitive environment and objectives. Moreover, these categories do little to help determine weightings for each dimension.

Perhaps the most sophisticated method of determining value drivers is statistical analysis of the leading and lagging indicators of financial performance. The resulting "causal business model" can help determine which measures predict future financial performance and can assist in assigning weightings to measures based on the strength of the statistical relation. Unfortunately, relatively few companies develop such causal business models when selecting their performance measures.

## Review Consistencies

Most companies track hundreds, if not thousands, of non-financial measures in their day-to-day operations. To avoid "reinventing the wheel", an inventory of current measures should be made. Once measures have been documented, their value for performance measurement can be assessed. The issue at this stage is the extent to which current measures are aligned with the company's strategies and value drivers. One method for assessing this alignment is "gap analysis". Gap analysis requires managers to rank performance measures on at least two dimensions: their importance to strategic objectives and the importance currently placed on them.

Our survey of 148 US financial services companies found significant "measurement gaps" for many non-financial measures. For example, 72% of companies said customer-related performance was an extremely important driver of long-term success, against 31% who chose short-term financial performance. However, the quality of short-term financial measurement is considerably better than measurement of customer satisfaction. Similar disparities exist for non-financial measures related to employee performance, operational results, quality, alliances, supplier relations, innovation, community and the environment. More important, stock market and long-term accounting performance are both higher when these measurement gaps are smaller.

## Integrate Measures

Finally, after measures are chosen, they must become an integral part of reporting and performance evaluation if they are to affect employee behaviour and organisational performance. This is not easy. Since the choice of performance measures has a substantial impact on employees' careers and pay, controversy is bound to emerge no matter how appropriate the measures. Many companies have failed to benefit from non-financial performance measures through being reluctant to take this step.

## Conclusions

Although non-financial measures are increasingly important in decision-making and performance evaluation, companies should not simply copy measures used by others. The choice of measures must be linked to factors such as corporate strategy, value drivers, organisational objectives and the competitive environment. In addition, companies should remember that performance measurement choice is a dynamic process, measures may be appropriate today, but the system needs to be continually reassessed as strategies and competitive environments evolve.

Christopher D. Ittner is associate professor of accounting and David F. Larcker is Ernst & Young Professor of Accounting at the Wharton School of the University of Pennsylvania.

**Further Reading**

Baum, G. et al. (2000) "Introducing the New Value Creation Index", Forbes ASAP, April 3, 140–143.
Ittner, C. and Larker, D. (1998) "Are Non-financial Measures Leading Indicators of Financial Performance?", Journal of Accounting Research, supplement, 1–35.

Source: Financial Times, October 16, 2000.

## Case 2

Assuming a WACC of 12% for Tesco, analyse the company's financial performance over recent years using the EVA approach.

## Case 3

Referring to the Tesco plc Annual Report 2000, identify appropriate sets of measures to track and control the goals the company could set for itself under each of the following headings:

- Financial perspective
- Innovation and learning perspective
- Customer perspective
- Business process perspective

Consider how the incorporation of these into the company's reporting and control regime might affect its self-assessment and strategy formulation.

When you have completed this chapter you will understand:

- Some of the social, economic and commercial implications of the emergence of the "new economy".

- That the term "new economy" embraces changing wealth-creation dynamics enabled by new technologies and attitudes to knowledge.

- That, as a social discipline, accountancy must accommodate itself to this new paradigm.

- That history teaches that accounting can adapt, evolve and mutate to meet new challenges.

- Some of the strategies already being adopted by accountants and regulators to address these new dynamics.

## New Millennium Brings New Economy, by Don Tapscott

### Changed Rules of the Game Will be Found Woven in the Web

Happy new economy! Are you ready for the most dramatic changes in history to wealth creation and the diffusion of knowledge? What will happen during our lifetime will make the developments of the previous two millennia pale in comparison. For a year I have resisted millennium madness. But given today's date it is appropriate to step back a few thousand years and put today's changes in historical context.

For many millennia the basic mode of wealth creation was hunting and gathering. By 2000 years ago, this had been replaced in many parts of the world by slavery. Vast empires from the Romans and Greeks to China and South America harnessed the physical power of people by owning them. A thousand years ago, this had been replaced by feudalism, where kings, nobles and clerics ran an economy based on the farming of serfs, tied to the land and compensated for their labour by receiving part of what they produced.

The first stage of the enterprise was the vertically integrated Industrial Age corporation – with supply driven, command-control hierarchies, division of labour for mass production, lengthy planning cycles, and stable industry pecking orders. Henry Ford's company – the first archetypal industrial age firm – did not just build cars. It owned rubber plantations to produce raw materials for tires, power plants to generate electricity and marine fleets for shipping materials on the Great Lakes. Employees were treated as extensions of the machine. In Ford's factories, immigrant workers spoke 50 different languages and had little education. They were expected to follow orders and not to take much initiative – if any. Management was based on mistrust, command, and control.

The industrial economy depended on physical goods and services. In the new economy, many products, such as software and electronic entertainment, are knowledge-based and non-physical. Even the value of physical items like pharmaceuticals and cars increasingly depends on the knowledge embedded in their design and production. The Internet is enabling new models of economic activity and fusing the intellectual energies of people and organizations around the world. While one cannot predict precisely what will happen, the new economy's general contours are starting to become clear. The basic institution to tomorrow's wealth creation is the business web. As Nobel prize winning economist Ronald Coase explained 60 years ago, wealth creation was organized into firms because of transaction costs. The costs of co-ordination, planning, and allocating resources was lower within the boundaries of the firm than out in the open marketplace.

The Net is changing all of this. Based on a publicly available network infrastructure, the costs of many kinds of transactions have been dramatically reduced, and sometimes approach zero. Large and diverse sets of people can now, easily and cheaply, gain near real-time access to the information they need to make safe decisions and co-ordinate complex activities. As a result, we can increase wealth by adding knowledge value to a product or service – through innovation, enhancement, cost reduction or customization – at each step in its lifecycle. In the digital economy, business webs bring together sets of contributors – suppliers, distributors, commerce services providers, infrastructure providers, and customers – via the Internet to create value for customers and wealth for their shareholders. In the most effective b-webs, each participant focuses on a limited set of core competencies – the things that it does best.

B-webs like Ebay, ETrade, Cisco, Linux and Enron are inventing new value propositions, transforming the rules of competition, and mobilizing people and resources to unprecedented levels of performance. Economies determine not just the mode of wealth creation but also its distribution. Over the next decades ownership of wealth will also change. And not just in the sense that a majority of people participate in the stock market. Rather, b-webs create value for customers using brains not brawn. Intellectual capital not land, plant or even money is now the most important form of capital. Firms will have to view their employees as investors of intellectual capital rather than as a variable cost – the way labour was viewed and measured in the industrial economy. These investors of know-how and brain power will come to expect a return on their investment – to share in the wealth they create. Expect new approaches to compensate employees based increasingly on the value they create. This will precipitate a profound democratization of corporate ownership. Further, many individuals and teams can participate in production and commerce without having to work for a large company. Entrepreneurializm will continue to grow.

Also expect to see profound changes in governance, the nature of the state and relationships between citizens and their governments. Just as the printing press led to the distribution of knowledge, the rise of a new economy and new structures of governance the Net enables new forms of social and political organization. The nation state itself was based on the national economy. But as the skin of networks that surrounds the planet becomes ubiquitous and full of functionality, economic walls and soon political walls will fall as well.

But there is nothing inherent in the technology that ensures that all will work out well. People will determine the future, not technology. If we do this right, this will be an age of vast new opportunity where all aspects of society advance.

Source: Financial Post, January 1, 2000.

## Introduction

A point made consistently throughout this text is that accounting is a social science. That is, it is not a set of unchangeable techniques, but rather a discipline that is responsive to the political, cultural and social environments in which it finds itself. In other words it can change and evolve. And just as the primary means of wealth creation has changed over time, so too accounting has managed to adapt to new challenges. For instance, over recent decades alone it has moved from a purely stewardship function to one in which it is now a primary supplier of information for decision-making purposes.

As the opening article suggests, the advent of networking technology, the dramatic reconfiguration of transaction and information cost economics, and processes of globalization and knowledge democratization, provide the catalysts for a new set of economic, commercial and political models. These will have profound social consequences and will only be worked out over coming decades.

This chapter begins with a look at the role of accounting in this new economy and at some of the specific challenges it faces. It then identifies some of ways in which traditional reporting practices will be revolutionized by the innovative forms of delivery which new media and changing information economics allow. Finally, it looks at some external regulatory forces for change, such as the ongoing Company Law Review, which promise significant change in the nature and focus of financial reporting.

## Role of Accounting

The nature and dynamics of the new economy offer both great opportunities and significant threats to accounting. Some of these relate to specific aspects of accounting practice such as the way in which share option schemes or bartering should be accounted for. Others derive from the fundamental challenges posed by intellectual capital and issues relating to access to information and corporate governance. As the following extract explains, these are matters which accounting is finding it difficult to incorporate into traditional models and paradigms.

---

### Regulators Are Struggling to Come to Terms With Issues

#### Internet Companies Are Moving into Areas Where Accounting Rules Do Not Exist, say Caroline Daniel and Michael Peel

The wobbles in Internet stocks across Europe this week reveal a market crying out for more information. Investors are starting to ask the killer question already posed by their US counterparts: how reliable is the performance data underlying hefty Internet valuations?

The emerging concerns are numerous and fundamental. They have been stirred up by cases of dubious accounting, the use of share options as a form of pay and the lack of independent scrutiny both on dot.com boards and among the analyst community. "When it is all cock-a-hoop, people do not tend to care that much about these issues," says one analyst. "But once there are difficulties, investors will start to ask who is really looking after their best interests."

Regulators are struggling to come to terms with these issues, hampered by the lack of historical examples to guide them. Financial reporting rules geared to profitable, revenue-earning companies are of little help to investors trying to work out if a dot.com will succeed. "The big question is: should you apply any different accounting rules?" says one auditor. "Regulators are saying the rules should not be any different. But the consequence is that the picture you give of these companies is wrong."

The worry for regulators is that Internet companies are venturing into areas for which accounting rules simply do not exist. This means a lack of consistency in the information dot.coms produce, to the disadvantage of investors...

Source: Financial Times, March 25, 2000.

---

Significantly, however, accounting does already possess a set of principles and practices which, albeit somewhat limited, allows it to tackle some of the more obvious challenges of this revolution. For instance, it still produces and mediates much of the information used by management and investors to make decisions. It also produces, via internal and external reports, a range of measures that allow corporate performance to be gauged and interpreted.

The extent to which accounting is meeting the challenge can be gauged from the way it is dealing with three specific topics that are central to the new economy. These range from practical issues such as the way in which revenue and stock options should be accounted for, to the more fundamental conceptual problems raised by "intellectual capital". Each of these is treated in turn.

## 1. Revenue Recognition

Most e-businesses operate at a loss in their early years. Nor, as many successful IPOs demonstrate, does this appear to deflect potential investors. The key concerns in start-ups appear to be non-financial measures such as website hits, customer base and the commitment of the founders.

To the extent that they are employed, a consensus is emerging that the two most dependable financial indicators of likely survival and success are turnover and cash-consumption (burn) rate. There is, therefore, considerable pressure on businesses to maximize the turnover figure shown in the profit and loss account.

With these pressures have come a variety of questionable accounting practices intended to inflate the turnover figure. Examples include:

- Showing gross turnover figures where GAAP would suggest that net figures are more appropriate.

- Booking licence fees immediately.

- Incorporating gross value of sales facilitated in circumstances where the company is only acting as an agent, for example, a travel agent booking the gross value of flights arranged rather than the commission earned.

Current accounting practice in these areas revolves around the concept of revenue recognition which emphasizes the need to satisfy the twin elements of revenue: that it must be earned, i.e., a good or service must have been delivered, and realized, i.e., cash must have been received or be likely to be received.

However, the fact that there is no current UK standard dealing specifically with revenue has allowed several firms to exercise a certain license. In addition, many such businesses have insisted that practices designed to cope with an industrial economy are incapable of dealing with revenue recognition and measurement issues raised by new technologies and ways of doing business.

---

**In practice:**

---

*Internet Companies Are Moving Into Areas Where Accounting Rules Do Not Exist, say Caroline Daniel and Michael Peel*

*…One big issue is barter advertising, where websites swap advertising slots without exchanging money, but book the transaction as if money had been received. Since most investors expect Internet companies to be loss making, bolstering sales has attained much importance as a way to justify high valuations. The result is, in the words of one analyst, an "impressive creativity" in dot.com accounting for advertising.*

*The concern is greater in Europe than in the UK, where analysts say there are fewer cases, with barter advertising accounting for more than 10% of revenues. But the fear remains that abuse is possible. "Maliciously co-operating websites could overvalue their barter advertisements," says Peter Bradshaw of Merrill Lynch. "This would leave their gross profits unchanged, but would increase the revenue line even further." This latent worry seems certain to prompt a regulatory clampdown.*

*The Accounting Standards Board (ASB) says any like-for-like transaction cannot be counted as revenue, as the benefit gained is not readily realizable for cash. "When you exchange something for another type of the same thing it's not really revenue," says Allan Cook, technical director.*

*Dot.coms could take another regulatory impact over revenue sharing agreements, which form the bulk of e-commerce agreements between sites. One site may agree to hand over 50% of any sales generated to a partner site that has helped deliver the customer to them. Some sites may book more than 50% of the sale and count the partner's share as costs. This makes no difference to gross profit, but again results in higher revenue. Another trick that Internet companies use to boost revenues is to include sales made by third parties. An example would be a company that booked as turnover the value of a holiday sold through its website, even though it only earned commission on the deal…*

*Source: Financial Times, March 25, 2000.*

---

## 2. Stock Options

A stock (share) option is a right to purchase a share at a pre-set price. Many companies, both public and private, now use stock options to remunerate staff. In fact, the government is actively encouraging more companies to offer these schemes to all employees.

Assuming the market price of the share increases, it effectively allows grantees to purchase shares at a price lower than market price. The attraction for companies is that they are able to compensate their employees without having to record it as an expense in the profit and loss account.

The anomaly of a situation in which remuneration given to an employee in the form of cash is recorded as an expense while that given in the form of share options is not, raises obvious questions. As Warren Buffett, the renowned American investor has remarked: "Accounting principles offer management a choice: pay employees in one form and count the cost, or pay them in another form and ignore the cost. Small wonder then that the use of options has mushroomed... If options are not a form of compensation, what are they? If compensation is not an expense, what is it? And, if expenses should not go into the calculation of earnings, where in the world should they go?"

The ASB, following an initiative on the part of the G4 + 1, has recently issued a discussion paper which recommends that the "fair value" of such options be recorded as a charge in the profit and loss account. This would have an immediate and negative impact on the results of most companies.

Not surprisingly the reaction has not been entirely enthusiastic. Technology companies and representative bodies such as the Institute of Directors and the Hundred Group of Finance Directors have expressed strong opposition. The National Association of Pension Funds, on the other hand, was broadly supportive. The likelihood is that it is an issue that will only be solved at a supra-national level. For this reason responsibility to devise an acceptable solution may devolve to the IASB.

## 3. Intellectual Capital

The emphasis on knowledge as a key source of competitive advantage has led to a realization that the resource base of an entity comprises of far more than its tangible assets. Indeed, the principal wealth-creating source in most non-traditional industries is now viewed as consisting of its intangible assets such as people competencies, relationships with customers and internal processes. These have come to be called the "Intellectual Capital" of a business.

However, as explained in Chapter 6, because this is an internally generated intangible asset it is neither recognized nor measured by the current accounting model.

The reason for this is that accounting has traditionally focused its attentions on capturing and representing items that are tangible. Knowledge and people are, however, outside the comprehension of this model. Thus the largest source of revenue generation goes unrecognized in the balance sheet of most knowledge-intensive firms. As Bill Gates has remarked, "Our primary assets, which are our software and our software-development skills, do not show up on the balance sheet at all. This is probably not very enlightening from a pure accounting point of view".

Consequently, accounting's capacity to fulfil its function as supplier of relevant information has diminished as it has struggled to come to terms with items to which its limited conceptual framework can assign neither value nor tangible existence.

Recognizing that allowing a situation to persist in which a large element of the resource base of many firms is not shown in the accounts would simply undermine the credibility of accounting, accountants and regulators have recently begun to suggest remedies. One is the introduction of a separate statement of intellectual capital. Another is that the Operating and Financial Review (OFR) could be extended to incorporate narrative detail specific to internally generated intangibles.

## ICAEW 2020 Group Calls for New OFR to Cover Intangibles

ICAEW president Graham Ward has raised the possibility of reporting intangible assets such as corporate reputation and human capital in a new-look OFR. The suggestion comes in "Human Capital and Corporate Reputation: Setting the Board-room Agenda", a report from the ICAEW's 2020 Vision project. Boards of major companies need to reassess "the challenges and risks inherent in the growth in importance of intangibles, in particular human and reputational capital", Ward warned.

Has the board formulated appropriate strategies for creating and sustaining human capital and does it publish sufficient information about staff recruitment, training and skill levels, he added. Social and environmental policies can also influence the organization's reputation and should be evaluated. These issues are currently not covered by financial accounts. However, the ICAEW group spotted that the company law review is putting considerable thought into defining new elements that should be included in listed companies' OFRs – and subjecting the content to an auditor's review.

Glaxo Wellcome finance director and 2020 steering group member John Coombe explained the reasoning behind the report. "Under the present accounting model, there is a growing gap between companies' market values, as reflected in the share price, and their book values." The gap is biggest for companies – such as Glaxo Wellcome – that invest most in innovation. In Coombe's case, his company has net assets of just over £3 billion, but its market value is many times that amount. The main source of this "value gap" is the value of unrecognized and inter-related intangible assets such as human and reputational capital, investment in research and development and new products and brands in the pipeline.

As a director of a company that spends heavily on R&D, Coombe is frustrated that under current accounting treatments, expenditures have to be written off as expenses rather than as value-adding investments. "This provides a narrow, short-term view of financial performance. When times are hard, a reduction in R&D spending can improve short-term profits, yet damage long-term value," he argued. Glaxo Wellcome devotes considerable attention to R&D activities in its OFR, he continued, including time-tables and target dates for submitting new drugs for regulatory approval.

The new OFR, Coombe argued, should build on current best practice and provide relevant, forward-looking information to help investors assess performance and potential. "Coverage of intangible assets would be an important aspect of the review," he concluded. Peter Murray, chief executive of the Railways Pension Trustee Company, added his weight to the debate. "Traditional published accounts focus on past and present performance, not on what the organization might achieve in the future,' he said. Investors should be given more forward-looking information and it should be organized and published in a way which non-professional investors can access it conveniently on a timely basis.

Source: AccountingWEB, July 31, 2000.

The extent to which people are coming to be seen as assets rather than costs suggests that one way in which intellectual capital might be accommodated would be by revisiting the whole concept of Human Resource Accounting. This would involve developing new templates and conceptual approaches that recognize employees as the principal asset of a business.

This links to another related consequence of the dynamics of the knowledge economy – the changes being induced in corporate governance models. The existing corporate model strongly favours the providers of financial capital. However, in an environment in which the primary resource is seen as knowledge embedded in people, the existing model will be challenged to embrace a stakeholder approach which recognizes the claims of employees to a share of ownership since they provide the primary value-creating resource.

Nor is this likely to be satisfied by stock option schemes that are predicated upon notions of reward. A governance model that has traditionally linked ownership to provision of capital may be forced to recognize the consequences of this paradigm in an economy in which intellectual capital is provided by employees, not financial capitalists. It is also likely that as part of this process the attempts of financial capitalists to capture and establish ownership of knowledge by means of patents will be resisted by employees. The nature of relationships internally will also be affected, with influence correlating more closely to knowledge and knowledge networks than to hierarchy.

Finally, the new economy emphasizes the importance of teams, knowledge flows, processes and collegiality as facilitators of value creation. This requires the development of internal management techniques that recognize and encourage these traits, as well as reporting methodologies which distinguish between entities in which these traits are increasing and those in which they are decreasing. To achieve their purpose these techniques will need to recognize the often chaotic and intuitive process of creativity and ideas. This will require imagination and experimentation on the part of accountants, the traditional gatekeepers of internal management and reporting practices. However, this is territory worth capturing.

## New Forms of Delivery

Quite apart from the accounting-specific issues that the wealth creation dynamics of the new economy raise, technology is itself a catalyst for change, challenging communicators to adapt in terms of content, access and speed of delivery. Commercial, technological and cost factors are combining to ensure that accounting reporting practices are not immune from the momentum towards real-time, widely disseminated, user-specific information that media such as the Internet facilitate.

In response, task forces in both the UK and the US are exploring the implications for accounting of the technological revolution. Governments and regulators have already begun to take steps to ensure that web-reporting is both facilitated and regulated. For instance, in the UK the Companies Act (Electronic Communications) Order, 2000 removes legal obstacles to companies communicating in this manner with its shareholders in a number of specified areas; the IASC has released a draft that paves the way for more substantial online reporting; the ICAEW and ASB are engaged in similar exercises; the Auditing Practices Board has published *Bulletins 2001/1* and *2001/2* which provide guidance for auditors in relation to electronic reporting.

More important than the use of new media to disseminate traditional reports, however, are the possibilities which the Internet and new approaches to reporting and disclosure might together enable. There is every possibility that the combined effect of electronic media, corporate governance changes which respect stakeholder theory, and an insatiable appetite for information on the part of global capital markets, may lead to radical change in financial reporting culture.

Indeed, in a Report produced for the ICAEW in 1997 a group chaired by Sir Brian Jenkins was already outlining the possibilities which existed.

"We must now begin without delay to focus more clearly on the issues of what information should be provided and the ways in which it can best be transmitted to fulfil the needs of the 21st century capital markets." Effective communication with a company's shareholders and other stakeholders is a vital constituent of good governance and it is essential that interested parties be given a clear and balanced view of a company's performance.

Until a few years ago, the annual report was very much a set menu with no choices. The one report was the primary document given to all shareholders. The focus was on financial information and by and large continues to be so although the OFR has been a very worthwhile innovation. Then, summary financial statements were introduced. Many more companies have started to introduce them in recent years, especially those such as mine with a very large shareholder register. With technology, a whole new vista of opportunities is, however, opening up and we are in the world of à la carte with potentially infinite alternative menus of information able to be given to users of financial data. The principal limitation will be companies' ability or willingness to provide additional disclosures.

Whilst technology is an enabler, if its potential is to be realized, many businesses will need to change their approach to providing information, moving away from primarily seeking statutory compliance and towards meeting market needs. And there is a variety of different markets including, for instance, financially sophisticated investors who may have large or small holdings, those more interested in non-financial performance information and users primarily interested in social accountability issues.

There will undoubtedly be challenges to be faced in the new era such as deciding how to strike the balance between transparency and not giving away too much competitively sensitive information as well as determining how frequently information should be updated. These issues must be addressed but they are not reasons for staying where we are. In this new world, the notions of what information should be included on performance measures will also be subject to substantial change with more sought on non-financial performance indicators and on, for example, the value of a company's intangible assets, including its human resources and customer satisfaction ratings, the key drivers of wealth in many companies. We must now begin without delay to focus more clearly on the issues of what information should be provided and the ways in which it can best be transmitted to fulfil the needs of the 21st century capital markets.

Source: The Institute of Chartered Accountants in England and Wales, 1997.

Significantly, Jenkins highlighted the need for a change in a culture which has traditionally been characterized as "disclosure averse" if the full potential of new media was to be fully realized. In fact, this very metamorphosis may be forced on businesses as the democratizing nature of the Internet takes hold. The new economics of information and the speed with which it can now be disseminated, contain within themselves the seeds of an information revolution which will see attitudes to accounting information changed as one part of a societal shift.

### In practice:

Some of the possibilities and opportunities for accounting offered by new media and attitudes to information dissemination are outlined in the following account of recent developments.

#### Online and Bespoke
*Reporting on the Internet Has Expanded the Amount of Information Available to All Comers, and Has Democratized the Process, by Peter Holgate*

*Many large companies now put some or all of their annual report and accounts on their website, despite company law and accounting standards being developed in the context of printed reports. Many also put their interim's and prelims there too. But putting the existing paper reports on the website is just the starting point. A democratic development is emerging whereby some companies, such as Boots and 3i, put their analysts' presentations there too. This addresses a major recent concern, namely that limited numbers of professionals have been privy to inside information ahead of its general release.*

*The information posted is not confined to financial reporting. For example, BT has an area concerned with social reporting, which includes statements about communication with employees, results of employee surveys, and gender and ethnicity analysis of recent recruits. Rentokil Initial is among those that have a facility for readers to email the investor relations department. It is also an example of the cautious reporters. It has a well-signposted legal statement that disclaims liability to visitors. Inclusion of share price information is also an emerging trend. For example, BT's website shows its almost-current share price: like a good train, another one comes along every 15 minutes.*

**Interactive Reports**

*Excellent though all this is, it is, perhaps inevitably, a pale shadow of what is provided by Microsoft, whose website shows accounting information on various GAAPs (US, Canadian, UK, Australian, French, German), and in the equivalent currencies. It contains Bill Gates' letter in various languages (the same, plus Dutch, Italian, Spanish, etc.). And, for analysts and insomniacs, it provides an Excel spreadsheet so that visitors can download data and do their own modelling of results: what if we increase R&D spend by 20%, etc.? These and other exciting developments are all very recent and for the most part are occurring in an unregulated environment.*

*Nevertheless, various regulators are already taking an interest. The US Financial Accounting Standards Board has published a study entitled Electronic Distribution of Business Reporting Information (see Accountancy, March, p 9). The IASC has published Business Reporting on the Internet, and plans to follow this up with the development of a code of conduct. The ASB has discussed the implications of the Internet in its recent discussion paper on year-end financial reporting (see p 110). Many regulatory issues arise, particularly in the area of investor protection and quality control. For example, how does a company ensure that the information is accurate? How do we guard against companies wishing to publish through a "rose-tinted screen", showing only, for example, results before exceptional items? What about the risk of unauthorized changes made by company officials or external hackers? How is the status of information made clear – for example, as to what is audited, statutory information. What, indeed, are the responsibilities of the auditors?...*

*Source: Accountancy, April, 2000.*

## Company Law Review

Paralleling these attempts by regulators and the accounting profession to address the issues raised by the advent of these new technologies, the Department of Trade and Industry has been sponsoring a review of company law aimed at outlining a new approach.

As the chairman of the review group argued in the wake of the publication of an early draft, this process is not only long-overdue, but likely to result in significant changes in the reporting process and culture:

## Put Gladstone to Rest: Review of Company Law Unveiled Last Week is Long Overdue, writes Martin Scicluna

...Transparency is about a dialogue. It is important that the dialogue is timely, that all shareholders can participate in it at the same time and that they can understand what it is about. Directors, shareholders and auditors all have a role to play. Get the balance of accountability right by encouraging them to take on their fair share of responsibility and you get a healthier business and a healthier economic environment. The proposals achieve this by re-focusing the structure of statutory reporting. The emphasis will be on the preliminary results – the document that really moves the markets.

Under the proposals the prelims will be e-mailed to all shareholders within 70 days after the year-end. They will be required to contain market-sensitive information, but can be supplemented by the "glossy" information companies believe shareholders want to hear. Alternatively, shareholders might choose not to receive the prelims, but instead get even simpler financial information in a "glossy" version that will be sent to them at a later date. The full story will still be told in the annual report, but not the annual report as we know it. It will become a filing document and will be required within 90 days after the year-end. It will be a full story – in addition to financials it will talk about a company's principal drivers of performance.

These are its key relationships with employees, customers and suppliers; environmental policies and performance and "soft" assets like intellectual capital and brands. Most importantly, the story told will be from a company's perspective, describing the effect of these wider factors on its performance and future prospects. Companies with effective stakeholder relations have a better chance of success long-term. This is not just hot air. When a company tells a full story to its shareholders they understand it better, and they understand the factors influencing its performance and future prospects. This, in turn, means a cheaper cost of capital. Companies will be required to place their annual report and prelims on their website. Some do already. We are talking about making this mandatory. This means instant access for everybody. They will be able to analyse information and compare it from one year to another and from one company to another. The Electronic Communications Bill, currently before Parliament, takes us a step closer to where we want to be. It will allow electronic distribution of information and electronic filing of some statutory returns.

We want to go further. Mandatory electronic filing opens many opportunities. It can help cut the cost of good analytical research. Once the data is in electronic form it can be codified in such a way that anybody can search and interrogate it, and drill down into the set of financial statements not just of one company but across companies. For example, it would be possible to see how intangibles are treated in the companies in your sector, or what the average gearing ratio across the sector is, or how much your competitors sell overseas. Clearly, the wider the range of companies required to file electronically, the broader the scope for the analysis.

This is not the end of the story. We live in the electronic age. Financial communications tomorrow might look very different to what we have today or what is proposed as a reporting structure by the review. Real-time reporting and the ability to "drill" down to the actual source data are not the inventions of science fiction. The accessibility and depth of information will be of great importance to shareholders of the future. I believe the legal framework we have proposed is flexible and responsive to ever-changing business needs and practices. It will allow us to deliver on the expectations of shareholders in the world of e-commerce.

Martin Scicluna, chairman of Deloitte&Touche, chaired the high-level reporting issues group of the company law review.

Source: Financial Times; March 23, 2000.

In response to the Company Law Review group's first set of proposals the ASB issued a discussion paper, "Year-end Financial Reports: Improving communication", which proposed that companies would have the option of sending summarized financial reports to shareholders, while making the Annual Report available on request. The intention is to respond to the needs of a variety of stakeholders. As David Tweedie remarked, "Detailed accounts are prepared by accountants for accountants – a relatively small minority," The ASB was aiming for companies to get the message across to "Aunt Aggie, who wants to know what's happened to the BA share price, the size of her dividend and whether the company is still solvent."

In February 2001 the Company Law Steering Group issued its final consultation paper, *Modern Company Law for a Competitive Economy: Completing the Structure*. It made several far-reaching proposals. Among those proposals specifically relating to accounting and financial reporting are the following:

- Listed companies to post preliminary announcements on their websites.
- Public companies to file accounts and lay them before members within 150 days of the year-end.
- Listed companies to publish full accounts on websites within 90 days of year-end.
- Summary financial statements to be retained.
- OFR to become an expanded statutory statement for all listed companies.
- Detailed accounting requirements to be removed from legislation and delegated to a "Standards Committee" which would then replace the ASB.
- Financial Reporting Review Panel to be replaced by a "Monitoring and Enforcement Committee".
- Financial Reporting Council to be replaced by a "Companies Commission".

The scope of the recommendations made, ranging from reporting formats to regulatory regimes to the use of new technologies, hints at the significant impact which this report will have if and when implemented.

---

### In practice:

*European law firm Eversheds published some alarming statistics yesterday (March 5) related to the Company Law Review's consultation document, Completing the Structure, including that over half of respondents in a survey of UK companies were unaware of the main proposals emerging from it.*

*Overall, Eversheds found that 38% of quoted companies, 50% of unquoted plcs and 77% of private companies that participated in the survey, stated that they were unaware of the proposals. The survey also found that 81% of respondents believed that the proposals emerging from the Review would make Britain less attractive for directors as a place to incorporate their business.*

*When asked about specifics, 57% of public companies said they felt that a new OFR would be of no benefit to the company, although 67% thought that it would be of benefit to shareholders. However, 100% of private companies that would have to produce an OFR under the proposals, all public companies with a turnover of more than £5 million and all private companies with a turnover in excess of £500 million would have to produce a new-style OFR instead of the existing directors' report.*

*Nearly 1/5th of quoted public companies said that it would not be practical to place their full audited annual report and accounts on a website within 90 days of their period end (as proposed by the Company Law Review Steering Group), and 11% said that they did not even have a suitable website!*

*The ASB, for one, has been quick to indicate its general support and has worked with the review group to expand on its proposals issued in response to the earlier draft. Professional bodies have also been proactive in indicating support for what is being proposed.*

*However, while there has been broad acceptance of these proposals, there has been resistance. Some accountants, for instance, have expressed reservations about what may be an overly legalistic and prescriptive approach.*

*But these are precautionary reservations. In general the proposals are seen as offering a considered response to the challenges of the new economy and the technologies underpinning it. Paralleling work by the ASB, IASC and various other regulatory bodies, it offers a structure and vision within which accounting may accommodate itself.*

*Source: AccountancyMagazine.com, March 6, 2001*

## Summary

The implications of the technological revolution, the dynamics of the "new economy", and the changes these are inducing in the reporting and governance cultures of companies are already having a significant impact on accounting information and the means of its dissemination. The resulting democratization of the information dissemination process will in turn cause further moves in this direction.

The challenges for accounting are considerable. They extend from basic matters of practice to more fundamental issues such as the implications of "free" information available in real time.

These issues are being responded to by a wide variety of professional bodies and regulators. However, it is likely to be some time before they are resolved. In fact, the notion of resolving such issues may itself have to surrender to the implicitly fluid and mutating nature of new economic paradigms. The certainty with which accounting was once able to approach its world may no longer be sustainable.

## Review Questions

### Question 1
Explain what is meant by the term "new economy".

### Question 2
Explain why the dynamics and nature of the "new economy" offer opportunities and pose threats to accounting's traditional role within the business world.

### Question 3
What is meant by "real-time" access? Outline its implications for the financial reporting process in general and for accountants and auditors in particular.

### Question 4
What is meant by "Intellectual Capital"? Why is it such a crucial concept?

### Question 5
Identify the critical challenges that the emergence of knowledge and intellectual capital as key wealth generators pose to accounting.

### Question 6
"People represent the greatest resource of any business. Under any definition they must be considered an asset and accounted for as such." Explain what the implications of viewing people in this way would be for the accounting model.

### Question 7
Describe some of the strategies being adopted by accountants in order to exploit the opportunities offered by new media for disseminating information.

### Question 8
"Our notion of how corporations should be governed, and, in particular, the way in which 'knowledge-workers' will be accommodated, will be dramatically impacted by the democratizing influence of the Internet and the way in which employees are no longer viewed as costs, but resources". Explain some of the ways in which accounting will be impacted by these developments.

### Question 9
"A governance model that has traditionally linked ownership to provision of capital may be forced to recognize the consequences of this paradigm in an economy in which intellectual capital is provided by people who are not financial capitalists in the traditional sense. It is also likely that as part of this process the attempts of financial capitalists to capture and establish ownership of knowledge by means of patents or its physical expression in the form of recipes and manuals will be resisted by employees." Identify the principal arguments being made here and whether or not they are sustainable.

# Case studies

## Case 1

The following case outlines some accounting issues relating to dot.coms in both the UK and the US. Identify the key points made and discuss the implications for the accounting profession of what is proposed.

## Accounting for the New Economy: Mind the GAAP

America Online's $3.5 million fine following the discovery of accounting irregularities in its advertising accounts is hardly a flash in the pan; accounting for the Internet has never been a straightforward matter.

Successful dot.coms strive to show a semblance of profitability, and it is the accountant's job to help. But gaps are starting to appear as regulators try to put a reality check to the web pioneers. And one day, just one day, the pressure on accounting practice could give, and bring the whole dot.com revolution crashing down around its ears.

In the UK, the chairman of the ICAEW Audit Faculty has suggested the Auditing Practices Board is out of touch with e-commerce. Gerry Acher wrote to the ICAEW council: "We consider that auditing standards and guidance have not kept pace with the auditing implications of e-commerce and that, at a minimum, there should be a review of all standards to ascertain whether they are, and will still be, relevant over the coming years."

But unsurprisingly, it's the States that are leading the way in the apparent clampdown on Internet accounts. PricewaterhouseCoopers recent embarrassment over software company MicroStrategy's accounts, which saw a $12.6 million profit turned into a $35 million loss, was due to its treatment of sales and profits, both crucial areas for web wonders wanting to describe their own success story.

Priceline.com, roughly the US equivalent of our own bedraggled lastminute.com, recently reported it made $152 million in revenues – but used the top-end figure of how much customers paid for flights, hotel rooms, etc., and put how much the firm paid for them down as "product costs". These costs came to $134 million, but you can imagine which figure the Internet group wanted the public and investors to know.

Several other "tricks of the trade" have been employed in the murky world of Internet accounting. One is barter; one firm exchanges advertising space on web pages in return for ads elsewhere. Some firms derive up to half their revenues from barter – VerticalNet posts around 18% using this system.

Discounts also enter the fray. Giveaways and the like are rife on the web – it's a good way to boost traffic. But how to account for the discount? Perhaps you can post the full price of the item as revenues and write off the rest as marketing expenses. Such expenses can also encompass shipping costs and warehousing.

Revenues are the key; the higher the revenue, the bigger the headline figure, the happier the investor. But all's not well in the state of dot.com, Mark. Revenue recognition cases arose in only one in five securities fraud lawsuits in 1998, according to US research. In the first half of 1999, it was one in two.

It comes as no surprise that Arthur Levitt's SEC is highly sceptical. Levitt voiced his doubts last year, saying some companies operate "in the grey area between legitimacy and outright fraud... where the accounting is being perverted... In the numbers game integrity may be losing out to illusion." The Financial Accounting Standards Board is trying to get to the bottom of this Net numbers game. It has set the Emerging Issues Task Force on how GAAP should be applied in the dot.com haze. It is due to report later in the year; whatever the result, the World Wide Web revolution will have to sit up and take notice.

But regulators are one thing; accountants are another. And there is some sign that firms are taking common sense into their own hands and making a stand against this apparent madness. Arthur Andersen pre-empted SEC inquiries by declaring that it had "substantial doubt" that web retailer CDnow – the 33rd most visited site on the Net – could survive as a going concern. And Ernst&Young ditched IT software supplier SCB's audit after doubts were raised about the suitability of revenue and sales postings.

How many more firms will stick their heads above the parapet before the SEC hammer comes crashing down? It is impossible to tell. But one thing is for sure; the luck that has blessed the Internet revolution so far is about to run out. And when the dot.com bubble bursts, the accountant will be holding the pin.

Source: AccountingWEB, May 16, 2000.

## Case 2

The following article sums up many of the themes covered in this text, ranging from regulatory concerns to social reporting issues. Use it as an opportunity to review and discuss the major themes which have been raised throughout, such as the political nature of regulation, the globalization of accounting, the impact of stakeholder theory and the increasing importance of corporate social reporting.

## New Financial Era Dawns With Public Protests Over Globalization and Ethical Business, by Roger Davis

...The advance of corporate reporting will require innovation and experimentation rather than rule setting. The portrait of a company in a new era of accountability means crafting the picture, rather than painting by numbers. That should represent the professional skills in the new era. No company ever went bust because of a technical accounting rule; many have done so because the picture didn't make sense. "Bean counters" is a fun tag but we need to take the perception seriously. Does the term "accountant" mean only the ability to count? Should it not mean expertise in accountability? No contest again. The new era of accountability will not be based on precision. The profession will need to come away from its comfort zone.

Now apply this to the specifics. Take international accounting standards first. An approach which relies on many detailed rules may obscure the underlying principles and encourage the attitude that an approach may be adopted if it is not prohibited by a rule. Those are not my words, but the recommendation of the outgoing International Accounting Standards Committee to its successor.

The 10 Commandments have stood the test of millennia remarkably well. But, if you write a 100 page standard on the meaning of adultery, somewhere in it you will find an excuse for a fling. Of course, the world's accounting standards cannot be written on just one tablet. Underlying the achievements of the Anglo-Saxon standard setters is a vast body of thought on seemingly intractable problems of accounting for the incredibly complex business transactions which are now the way of the world. And none more so than in the US. But somehow we will have to find a compromise between the extraordinary rigidity of a legally driven US accounting code and something appropriate to the rest of the world.

Contemplate using the US approach as a world standard, and how many more volumes would need to be added to deal with other countries' fiscal systems, pension arrangements and so on. Sadly, the UK has already given up its pragmatic deferred tax accounting in the interests of international convergence; we now have precise numbers, but in my view they are precisely wrong for the UK. What the rest of the world has to do is convince the US authorities that our professional judgement on a more flexible code can be relied upon. The UK can take a lead; the recent SEC hearings noted our system of professional regulation.

Now to the UK company law review. Its cornerstones are: – Excluding from the law all that which does not require parliamentary scrutiny, including the corporate governance code and the vast majority of accounting requirements – therefore concentrating the law on directors duties, and their accountability through the new OFR – the proposed Companies Commission of investors, directors, professional advisers and others with a stake in corporate governance to take it forward.

It is an excellent package. Corporate governance codes can be concentrated on their principal purpose of wealth creation, as well as investor protection which initially drove them. And whoever heard of a "rule" for the creation of wealth? Delegating accounting to a largely non-statutory mechanism recognizes the extraordinary potential and pace of technology. The next generation of "Aunt Agathas" will have been brought up on the Internet – or will they still want the glossy on the hall table? Many people over simplify the effects of technology: it is said, for example, that all companies will put last week's sales on screen. Maybe they are an indicator of shareholder value for a fashion retailer but they will mean nothing for a pharmaceutical company where value is in products in the pipeline. We do not know how it will all pan out so we need the flexibility.

Technology years are like dog years, but regulatory days tick by like years. That is why we need principles rather than rules. And the centrepiece of the law review is surely the new OFR of the real drivers in shareholder value. The profession has been saying for years that value cannot be read off the historical accounts. Now is our chance – do we take it forward or leave it to the lawyers as is the custom for the US Management Discussion or Analysis? The New OFR is not intended as an account of corporate social responsibility *per se*.

But it does not stop there. The failure of the first attempt at the next trade round in Seattle, the rise of the NGOs, the protests at any world economic gathering (anarchists apart) and, perhaps most importantly, dinner party discussions of business leaders, show that corporate social accountability is moving from political correctness to serious consideration by companies. Now there is no rule for that.

Roger Davis is the ICAEW's representative on the company law consultative committee and head of professional affairs at PricewaterhouseCoopers.

Source: AccountancyAge, February 7, 2001.

# BIBLIOGRAPHY

Arnold, J., Hope, T., Southworth, A. and Kirkham, L., *Financial Accounting*, 2nd ed., Prentice Hall, Hemel Hempstead, 1995.

Alexander, D. and Britton, A., *Financial Reporting*, 6th ed., ITP, London, 2001.

Bernstein, L.A. and Wild, J.J., *Financial Statement Analysis: Theory, Application and Interpretation*, McGraw Hill, Boston, 1998.

Blake, D., *Financial Market Analysis*, 2nd ed., Wiley, Chichester, 2000.

Bloom, R. and Elgers, P.T. (eds.), *Foundations of Accounting Theory and Policy*: A Reader, Drydon Press, Fort Worth, 1995.

Bromwich, M., *Financial Reporting, Information and Capital Markets*, Pitman, London, 1992.

Davies, M., Paterson, R. and Wilson, A., *UK GAAP*, 5th ed., Macmillan, London, 1997.

Clarkson, M.B.E. (ed.), *The Corporation and its Stakeholders: Classic and Contemporary Readings*, UTP, Toronto, 1998.

Deegan, C., *Financial Accounting Theory*, Irwin/McGraw Hill, Roseville, 2000.

Elliott, B., and Elliott, J., *Financial Accounting and Reporting*, 4th ed., Financial Times/Prentice Hall, 2000.

Fridson, M.S., *Financial Statement Analysis: A Practitioner's Guide*, Wiley, New York, 1991.

Gibson, C.H., *Financial Statement Analysis: Using Financial Accounting Information*, 5th ed., South-Western Publishing Co., Cincinnati, 1992.

Gray, R., Owen, D. and Adams, C., *Accounting and Accountability: Changes and Challenges in Corporate Social and Environmental Reporting*, Prentice Hall, London, 1996.

Hartman, B.P., Harper, R.M., Knoblett., J.A. and Reckers, P.M.J., *Intermediate Accounting*, West Publishing Company, Minneapolis, 1995.

Helfert, E.A., *Techniques of Financial Analysis: A Modern Approach*, 9th ed., Irwin/McGraw Hill, Boston, 1997.

Holmes, G. and Sugden, A., *Interpreting Company Reports and Accounts*, 7th ed., London, Financial Times/Prentice Hall, 1999.

Hutton, W., *The Stakeholding Society: Writings on Politics and Economics*, David Goldblatt (ed.), Polity, Cambridge, 1999.

Knapp, M.C., *Financial Accounting: A Focus on Decision Making*, West Publishing Company, Minneapolis, 1996.

Lawrence, S., *International Accounting*, 1st ed., ITP, London, 1996.

Lewis, R. and Pendrill, D., *Advanced Financial Accounting*, 6th ed., Financial Times / Pearson, London, 2000.

Mathews, M.R. and Perera, M.H.B., *Accounting Theory and Development*, Chapman and Hall, London, 1991.

McBarnett, D. and Whelan, C., *Creative Accounting and the Cross-Eyed Javelin Thrower*, Wiley, 1999.

McKenzie, W., *Unlocking Company Reports and Accounts*, Financial Times/Pitman, London, 1998.

Munro, R. and Mouritsen, J., eds., *Accountability: Power, Ethos and the Technologies of Managing*, 1st ed., ITP, London, 1996.

Naser, K.H.M., *Creative Financial Accounting: Its Nature and Use*, Prentice Hall, London, 1993.

Parker, R.H., *Understanding Company Financial Statements*, 5th ed., Penguin, London, 1999.

Pendlebury, M. and Groves, R., *Company Accounts: Analysis, Interpretation and Understanding*, 5th ed., ITP, London, 2001.

Rees, B., *Financial Analysis*, 2nd ed., Prentice Hall, London, 1995.

Revsine, L., Collins, D.W. and Johnson, W.B., *Financial Reporting and Analysis*, Prentice Hall, New Jersey, 1998.

Roslender, R., *Sociological Perspectives on Modern Accountancy*, Routledge, London, 1992.

Rutherford, B.A., *An Introduction to Modern Financial Reporting Theory*, Paul Chapman, London, 2000.

Rutterford, J. *Financial Strategy: Adding Stakeholder Value*, Wiley, Chichester, 1998.

Samuels, J.M., Brayshaw, R.E. and Craner, J.M., *Financial Statement Analysis in Europe*, 1st ed., Chapman and Hall, London, 1995.

Schaltegger, S., Muller, K. and Hindrichsen, H., *Corporate Environmental Accounting*, Wiley, Chichester, 1996.

Schroeder, R.G. and Clark, M., eds., *Accounting Theory: Text and Readings*, 5th ed., Wiley, New York, 1995.

Tryfos, P., *Methods for Business Analysis and Forecasting: Text and Cases*, Wiley, New York, 1998.

Walton, P., Haller, A. and Raffournier, B., *International Accounting*, ITP, London, 1998.

White, G.I., Sondhi, A.C. and Fried, D., *The Analysis and Use of Financial Statements*, 2nd ed., Wiley, New York, 1997.

**TESCO PLC ANNUAL REPORT AND FINANCIAL STATEMENTS 2000**

## CONTENTS

# Accelerating growth through our customer focused strategy

· **Strong UK core business** continues to grow

· **Non-food** growing market share

· **Following the customer** providing new products and services such as e-commerce and Tesco Personal Finance

· **International business** achieving real scale

This publication includes the operating and financial review, the Directors' report, the corporate governance statement, the accounts and the auditors' report for the 52 weeks ended 26 February 2000. The Chairman's statement and review of the business are contained in a separate statement entitled Annual Review and Summary Financial Statement 2000.

These Annual Accounts together with the Annual Review and Summary Financial Statement 2000 comprise the full Annual Report and Accounts of Tesco PLC for 2000, in accordance with the Companies Act 1985. Copies may be obtained, free of charge, by writing to the Company Secretary, Tesco House, Delamare Road, Cheshunt, Hertfordshire EN8 9SL. Telephone 01992 632222.

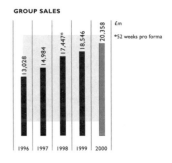

**GROUP SALES**

# financial highlights

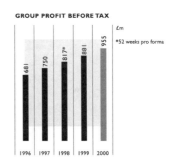

**GROUP PROFIT BEFORE TAX**

| | |
|---|---|
| Group sales | up 9.8% |
| Group profit before tax† | up 8.4% |
| Earnings per share†‡ | up 8.6% |
| Dividend per share | up 8.7% |

**EARNINGS PER SHARE**

| | 2000 52 weeks | 1999 52 weeks | 1998* 52 weeks (pro forma) |
|---|---|---|---|
| Group sales (including value added tax) (£m) | 20,358 | 18,546 | 17,447 |
| Group operating profit (prior to integration costs and goodwill amortisation) (£m) | 1,043 | 965 | 895 |
| Profit on ordinary activities before tax† (£m) | 955 | 881 | 817 |
| Group enterprise value (market capitalisation plus net debt) (£m) | 13,591 | 13,528 | 12,556 |
| Adjusted diluted earnings per share†(p) | 10.18 | 9.37 | 8.70 |
| Dividend per share (p) | 4.48 | 4.12 | 3.87 |
| Number of stores | 845 | 821 | 781 |
| Retail selling area (000 sq ft) | 24,039 | 21,353 | 18,254 |

† Excluding net loss on disposal of fixed assets, net loss on disposal of discontinued operations, integration costs and goodwill amortisation.

‡ Adjusted diluted.

* 1998 was a 53 week year. For comparison purposes a pro forma 52 week profit and loss account has been used.

**OPERATING CASH FLOW AND CAPITAL EXPENDITURE**

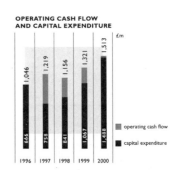

1

# operating and financial review

| Group summary | 2000 £m | 1999 £m | Change % |
|---|---|---|---|
| Group sales (including value added tax) | 20,358 | 18,546 | 9.8 |
| Group operating profit (prior to integration costs and goodwill amortisation) | 1,043 | 965 | 8.1 |
| Profit on ordinary activities before tax† | 955 | 881 | 8.4 |
| Adjusted diluted earnings per share† | 10.18p | 9.37p | 8.6 |
| Dividend per share | 4.48p | 4.12p | 8.7 |

† Excluding net loss on disposal of fixed assets, integration costs and goodwill amortisation

This operating and financial review analyses the performance of Tesco in the financial year ended 26 February 2000. It also explains certain other aspects of the Group's results and operations including taxation and treasury management.

### Group performance

**Group sales** including VAT increased by 9.8% to £20,358m (1999 – £18,546m).

**Group profit before tax** rose by 10.8% to £933m. Excluding the net loss on disposal of fixed assets, goodwill amortisation and integration costs, Group profit before tax increased 8.4% to £955m.

**Group capital expenditure** was £1,488m (1999 – £1,067m) with £989m in the UK, including £579m on new stores and £182m on extensions and refits. Total international capital expenditure was £499m including £186m in Asia. In the year ahead we see Group capital expenditure increasing to £1.6bn.

**Group net debt** in the year increased by £340m to £2,060m (1999 – £1,720m), with gearing increasing to 43% (1999 – 39%).

### Group interest and taxation

**Net interest payable** was £99m (1999 – £90m). Interest on our additional borrowings, reflecting the cost of our investment plans, was partially offset by lower interest rates.

**Corporation tax** has been charged at an effective rate of 27.8% (1999 – 28.1%). Prior to accounting for the net loss on disposal of fixed assets, integration costs and goodwill amortisation, our underlying tax rate was 27.4% (1999 – 27.8%).

### Shareholder returns and dividends

**Adjusted diluted earnings per share** (excluding the net loss on disposal of fixed assets, integration costs and goodwill amortisation) increased by 8.6% to 10.18p (1999 – 9.37p).

The Board has proposed a **final net dividend** of 3.14p giving a total dividend for the year of 4.48p (1999 – 4.12p). This represents an increase of 8.7% and dividend cover has been maintained at 2.27 times.

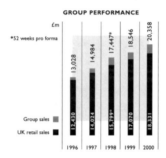

**GROUP PERFORMANCE**

£m

*52 weeks pro forma

Group sales ▨
UK retail sales ■

| | 1996 | 1997 | 1998 | 1999 | 2000 |
|---|---|---|---|---|---|
| Group sales | 13,028 | 14,984 | 17,447* | 18,546 | 20,358 |
| UK retail sales | 12,430 | 14,024 | 15,799* | 17,070 | 18,331 |

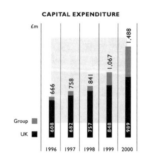

**CAPITAL EXPENDITURE**

£m

Group ▨
UK ■

| | 1996 | 1997 | 1998 | 1999 | 2000 |
|---|---|---|---|---|---|
| Group | 666 | 758 | 841 | 1,067 | 1,488 |
| UK | 608 | 682 | 757 | 848 | 989 |

**TESCO SHARE PRICE**

Pence

177.0

169.0

| Mar 99 | Jun 99 | Oct 99 | Dec 99 | Feb 00 |

Shareholders' funds, before minority interests, increased by £387m. This was due to retained profits of £372m and issue of new shares less expenses of £51m, offset by losses on foreign currency translation of £36m. As a result, return on shareholders' funds was 20.9%.

Total shareholder return, which is measured as the percentage change in the share price plus the dividend, has been 19.4% over the last five years, compared to the market average of 18.9% and has been 18.3% over the last three years, compared to the market average of 15.4%. In the last year, total shareholder return in Tesco has been (0.5)% compared to the market average of 8.5%.

## UK

**UK sales** (excluding property development sales) grew by 7.4% to £18,331m (1999 – £17,070m) of which 4.2% came from existing stores and 3.2% from net new stores.

Inflation in our UK business totalled 1.0% for the year due entirely to duty increases on petrol, tobacco and alcohol. Through our significant price investment we have seen volume gains and deflation in our core business.

This year we experienced tough trading conditions. In this environment Tesco continues to perform well above the market and was one of the very few major retailers to deliver continued profit growth.

**UK operating profit** was 8.1% higher at £993m (1999 – £919m) with an operating margin held broadly flat at 5.9%.

**Store development and capital expenditure** UK capital expenditure included £579m on opening 38 new stores comprising one Extra, 13 Superstores, 14 Compact stores and ten Express stores. We also spent £182m on our refit and extension programmes. In total we opened 1.2m sq ft of new space and expect to open a similar amount in the current year.

**TOTAL SHAREHOLDER RETURN**

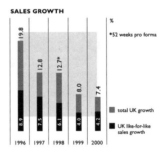

**SALES GROWTH**

**UK SALES AREA**

## UK fact file

| | |
|---|---|
| POPULATION | 59m |
| MARKET SHARE | 15.5% |
| NUMBER OF STORES | 659 |
| SQUARE FOOTAGE 000s | 16,895 |
| STORES OPENED/SQ FT ADDED | 38 / 1,216,500 |
| CAPITAL EXPENDITURE £m | 989 |
| TURNOVER £m | 18,331 |
| OPERATING PROFIT £m | 993 |

| UK performance | 2000 £m | 1999 £m | Change % |
|---|---|---|---|
| Retail sales (including value added tax) | 18,331 | 17,070 | 7.4 |
| Operating profit | 993 | 919 | 8.1 |

# operating and financial review continued

| Rest of Europe performance | 2000 £m | 1999 £m | Change % |
|---|---|---|---|
| Retail sales (including value added tax) | 1,527 | 1,285 | 18.8 |
| Operating profit | 51 | 48 | 6.3 |

## Rest of Europe fact file

| | |
|---|---|
| POPULATION | 68m |
| NUMBER OF STORES | 167 |
| SQUARE FOOTAGE 000s | 4,887 |
| STORES OPENED/SQ FT ADDED | 11 / 1,264,000 |
| CAPITAL EXPENDITURE £m | 313 |
| TURNOVER £m | 1,527 |
| OPERATING PROFIT £m | 51 |

| Asian performance | 2000 £m | 1999 £m | Change % |
|---|---|---|---|
| Retail sales (including value added tax) | 497 | 170 | 192 |
| Operating loss | (1) | (2) | 50 |

## Asian fact file

| | |
|---|---|
| POPULATION | 130m |
| NUMBER OF STORES | 19 |
| SQUARE FOOTAGE 000s | 2,257 |
| STORES OPENED/SQ FT ADDED | 5 / 502,000 |
| CAPITAL EXPENDITURE £m | 186 |
| TURNOVER £m | 497 |
| OPERATING LOSS £m | (1) |

## Europe

**In the Rest of Europe** total sales rose by 18.8% to £1,527m (1999 – £1,285m) and contributed an operating profit of £51m up from £48m last year.

Retail sales in the Republic of Ireland in local currency grew by 6.1%. We have now re-branded nearly 50 stores and our customers continue to benefit from the extended range, improved service and better value.

In Central Europe total sales at constant exchange rates were up 76.8%. This represents strong growth from our increasing number of hypermarkets in the region. We opened 11 new hypermarkets in the year giving us 19 in total with 2m sq ft.

## Asia

Our Tesco Lotus business in **Thailand** now comprises 17 hypermarkets and has shown strong sales growth of 96% on last year to £357m. We currently have 2.1m sq ft of selling space in Thailand which will increase to 2.8m sq ft by the end of 2000.

On 23 March 1999 we announced we had formed a partnership with the Samsung Corporation to develop hypermarkets in **South Korea**. Tesco has now invested a total of £142m, including costs of £4m, for an 81% controlling interest. In the 32 weeks to 31 December 1999 the two acquired trading stores contributed £140m to Group sales.

In 1999, our Asian businesses contributed sales of £497m, nearly 200% up on the previous year and made a small loss of £1m (1999 – £2m loss). However, we anticipate Thailand moving into profit in 2000 with the region as a whole being profitable soon after as our development programme gathers pace.

We are continuing with our research in Taiwan and Malaysia and plan to open our first stores in Taiwan in 2001. New research projects are also underway in China and Japan.

## Joint ventures

Our total share of profits from joint ventures was £11m compared to £6m last year.

Within this, Tesco Personal Finance has made good progress. We have increased the offer and value for our customers and incurred a small loss of £4m (1999 – £12m loss). Other joint ventures contributed an operating profit of £15m this year.

## Treasury management and financial instruments

Group Treasury is formally authorised by the Board to manage the Group's treasury operations. The authority establishes the objectives of Group Treasury and the strategies and policies to be applied. It also defines limits to those operations, which are reviewed at least annually by the Board and formally monitored. Group Treasury activity is routinely reported to members of the Board and is subject to review by the internal and external auditors. In accordance with Group policy, Group Treasury does not engage in speculative activity.

The main financial risks faced by the Group relate to credit, liquidity, interest rates and foreign exchange. Objectives, strategies and policies for managing these risks are summarised below. These objectives, strategies and policies are consistent with those in the previous year. The balance sheet positions at 26 February 2000 are representative of the positions throughout the year.

## Credit risk

The objective is to reduce the risk of loss arising from default by dealing counterparties. The strategy is to avoid high exposure to any single counterparty by spreading such risk across a number of banks or similar institutions of high credit quality. For each dealing counterparty, exposure limits, established normally by reference to the major credit rating agencies and by deal type, are reviewed at least annually by the Board. Mandates, defining the Group's dealing practices are agreed with these institutions prior to deals being arranged.

## Liquidity and interest rate risk

The objective is to ensure continuity of funding at low cost and to avoid significant exposure to changes in interest rates. The strategy is to maintain a portfolio of debt that is commensurate with future cash generation and complements the Group's trading operations by reducing overall business risk.

Operating subsidiaries are financed by a combination of retained profits, bank borrowings, commercial paper, medium term notes, long-term debt market issues and leases.

Exposure to debt refinancing risk is managed through modest gearing and adequate interest cover; by arranging for short-term borrowings and commercial paper issuance to be fully backed by committed bank facilities; by limiting the amount of debt repayable in any one year; and by smoothing the debt maturity profile and extending it in line with increased gearing levels.

At the year end, undrawn committed bank facilities amounted to £765m (1999 – £510m) of which £110m (1999 – £25m) expire within one year, £55m (1999 – £210m) between one and two years and £600m (1999 – £275m) in more than two years.

Derivatives, predominantly forward rate agreements and interest rate swaps and caps, are used to establish our desired mix of fixed and floating rate debt. The policy is to fix or cap between 30% and 70% of the interest cost on outstanding debt although a higher percentage may be fixed within a 12 month horizon.

The average rate of interest paid during the year was 6.8% (1999 – 7.1%). A 1% rise in interest rates would reduce profit before tax by less than 2%.

## Foreign currency risk

The objective is to reduce the risk to short-term profits of exchange rate volatility. Relevant short-term transactional currency exposures are therefore hedged.

The Group also seeks to mitigate the effect of structural currency exposures by borrowing, where cost effective, in the functional currencies of its main overseas operating units. In managing its structural currency exposures, the Group's objectives are to maintain a low cost of borrowing and retain some potential for currency related appreciation while partially hedging against currency depreciation.

Financial instruments used for these purposes are predominantly foreign currency borrowings, forward exchange rate transactions and swaps.

5

# operating and financial review continued

## Year 2000

Tesco has been working on the Year 2000 issue for over three years
and we achieved our key objective of 'Shopping as Normal' for our
customers over the millennium period. Additionally, there were no
significant issues surrounding the recognition of the leap day at the
end of February 2000.

The actual spend on the Year 2000 programme of £30m over
three years was in line with the original budget.

## Economic Monetary Union

Our aim is for all the relevant parts of the Group to be able to
handle business in euros when required. Project teams continue
to address the issues arising from EMU and current progress is in
line with the timetable set by the Group.

We are gaining valuable experience of the EMU process from
Tesco Ireland. We will draw upon this learning if and when other
Group companies are impacted by the introduction of the euro.

## Going concern

The Directors consider that the Group and the company have
adequate resources to remain in operation for the foreseeable
future and have therefore continued to adopt the going concern
basis in preparing the financial statements. As with all business
forecasts the Directors' statement cannot guarantee that the going
concern basis will remain appropriate given the inherent uncertainty
about future events.

# directors' report

The Directors present their annual report to shareholders on the affairs of the Group together with the audited consolidated financial statements of the Group for the 52 weeks ended 26 February 2000.

## Principal activity and business review

The principal activity of the Group is the operation of food stores and associated activities in the UK, Republic of Ireland, France, Hungary, Poland, Czech Republic, Slovakia, South Korea and Thailand. A review of the business is contained in the Annual Review which is published separately and, together with this document, comprises the full Tesco PLC Annual Report and Financial Statements.

## Group results

Group turnover excluding VAT rose by £1,638m to £18,796m, representing an increase of 9.5%. Group profit on ordinary activities before taxation, integration costs, loss on disposal of fixed assets and goodwill amortisation was £955m compared with £881m for the previous year, an increase of 8.4%. Including integration costs, loss on disposal of fixed assets and goodwill amortisation, Group profit on ordinary activities before taxation was £933m. The amount allocated to the employee profit-sharing scheme this year was £41m as against £38m last year. After provision for tax of £259m and dividends, paid and proposed, of £302m, profit retained for the financial year amounted to £372m.

## Dividends

The Directors recommend the payment of a final dividend of 3.14p per ordinary share to be paid on 30 June 2000 to members on the Register at the close of business on 25 April 2000. Together with the interim dividend of 1.34p per ordinary share paid in December 1999, the total for the year comes to 4.48p compared with 4.12p for the previous year, an increase of 8.7%.

## Tangible fixed assets

Capital expenditure amounted to £1,488m compared with £1,067m during the previous year. In the Directors' opinion, the properties of the Group have a market value in excess of the book value of £6,969m included in these financial statements.

## Acquisitions

During the year, Tesco acquired for a consideration of £142m, a majority holding in a newly incorporated company in South Korea. Details of this acquisition are set out in note 32 to the financial statements.

## Share capital

The authorised and issued share capital of the company, together with details of the shares issued during the period, are shown in note 23 to the financial statements.

## Company's shareholders

The company is not aware of any ordinary shareholders with interests of 3% or more.

## Directors and their interests

The names and biographical details of the present Directors are set out in the separately published Annual Review.

Mr J A Gardiner, Mr D E Reid, Mr R S Ager, Mr A T Higginson and Mr J W Melbourn retire from the Board by rotation.

Mr J M Wemms and Baroness O'Cathain will retire from the Board on 15 June 2000 and will not offer themselves for re-election.

The service contracts of Mr D E Reid, Mr R S Ager and Mr A T Higginson are terminable on two years' notice from the company.

Mr J A Gardiner and Mr J W Melbourn do not have service contracts.

The interests of Directors and their immediate families in the shares of Tesco PLC, along with details of Directors' share options, are contained in the Report of the Directors on Remuneration set out on pages 12 to 16.

At no time during the year did any of the Directors have a material interest in any significant contract with the company or any of its subsidiaries.

# directors' report <sub>continued</sub>

## Employment policies

The Group depends on the skills and commitment of its employees in order to achieve its objectives. Company staff at every level are encouraged to make their fullest possible contribution to Tesco success.

A key business priority is to provide First Class Service to the customer. Ongoing training programmes seek to ensure that employees understand the company's customer service objectives and strive to achieve them.

The Group's selection, training, development and promotion policies ensure equal opportunities for all employees regardless of gender, marital status, race, age or disability. All decisions are based on merit.

Internal communications are designed to ensure that employees are well informed about the business of the Group. These include a staff magazine called 'Tesco Today', videos and staff briefing sessions.

Staff attitudes are frequently researched through surveys and store visits, and management seeks to respond positively to the needs of employees.

Employees are encouraged to become involved in the financial performance of the Group through a variety of schemes, principally the Tesco employee profit-sharing scheme, the savings-related share option scheme and the profit-related pay scheme.

## Political and charitable donations

Contributions to community projects and to charity amounted to £1,485,000 (1999 – £1,301,000). There were no political donations.

## Supplier payment policy

Tesco PLC is a signatory to the CBI Code of Prompt Payment. Copies of the Code may be obtained from the CBI, Centre Point, 103 New Oxford Street, London WC1A 1DU. Payment terms and conditions are agreed with suppliers in advance.

Tesco PLC has no trade creditors in its balance sheet. The Group pays its creditors on a timely basis which varies according to the type of product and territory in which the suppliers operate.

## Auditors

PricewaterhouseCoopers have expressed their willingness to continue in office. In accordance with section 384 of the Companies Act 1985, a resolution proposing the reappointment of PricewaterhouseCoopers as auditors of the company will be put to the Annual General Meeting.

## Annual General Meeting

A separate circular accompanying the Annual Accounts explains the special business to be considered at the Annual General Meeting on 15 June 2000.

This report was approved by the Board on 10 April 2000.

By Order of the Board

**Rowley Ager**
Secretary
10 April 2000

Tesco PLC
Registered Number: 445790

# corporate governance

## Statement of application of principles of the Combined Code

The Group is committed to high standards of corporate governance. This statement describes the manner in which the company has applied the principles set out in Section 1 of the Combined Code on Corporate Governance which have been incorporated in the Listing Rules of the London Stock Exchange.

## Directors

The Board of Tesco PLC comprises nine Executive Directors and six independent Non-executive Directors. The Board is chaired by Mr J A Gardiner, an independent Non-executive Director, who has primary responsibility for running the Board. The Chief Executive, Mr T P Leahy, has executive responsibilities for the operations, results and strategic development of the Group. Clear divisions of accountability and responsibility both exist and operate effectively for these positions. In addition, Mr G F Pimlott is the senior Non-executive Director. The Board structure ensures no one individual or group dominates the decision-making process.

The full Board meets ten times a year and, in addition, annually devotes two days to a conference with senior executives on longer term planning giving consideration both to the opportunities and risks of future strategy. The Board manages overall control of the Group's affairs by the schedule of matters reserved for its decision. Insofar as corporate governance is concerned, these include the approval of financial statements, major acquisitions and disposals, authority levels for expenditure, treasury policies, risk management policies and succession plans for senior executives. In order that the Board is able to make considered decisions, a written protocol exists and has been communicated to senior managers ensuring that relevant information is presented to all Board members five days before Board meetings. All Directors have access to the services of the Company Secretary and may take independent professional advice at the company's expense in the furtherance of their duties.

The Board delegates day-to-day and business management control to the Executive Committee which comprises the Executive Directors. This meets formally every week and its decisions are communicated throughout the Group on a regular basis. The Executive Committee is responsible for implementing Group policy, the monitoring and performance of the business and reporting to the full Board thereon.

The Executive Committee conducts a risk assessment to the achievement of the Group's objectives at least annually which is then discussed with the full Board and any appropriate actions taken.

Appointments to the Board for both Executive and Non-executive Directors are the responsibility of the Nominations Committee which is chaired by Mr J A Gardiner and whose members are set out in the table on page 11.

As exemplified by the section on 'Directors and their interests' within the Directors' Report on pages 7 and 8, the company's Articles of Association ensure that on a rotational basis Directors resign every three years and, if so desire and being eligible, offer themselves for re-election.

The Board has also established a Compliance Committee whose purpose is to ensure that the Board discharges its obligations to avoid civil and criminal liability. The Committee, comprising two Executive Directors and three members of senior management, normally meets four times a year.

## Directors' remuneration

The Board has a long-established Remuneration Committee, composed entirely of Non-executive Directors, now chaired by Mr C L Allen, with effect from 10 April 2000, in succession to Baroness O'Cathain. The members are set out in the table on page 11. The responsibilities of the Remuneration Committee together with an explanation of how it applies the Directors' remuneration principles of the Combined Code are set out in the Report of the Directors on Remuneration on pages 12 to 16.

## Relations with shareholders

The Board attaches a high importance to maintaining good relationships with all shareholders and, primarily through the Investor Relations department, ensures that shareholders are kept informed of significant company developments. During the year, Directors have met with more than 65 of our leading shareholders representing over 45% of the issued shares of the company.

While the focus of dialogue is with institutional shareholders to whom regular presentations are made on company direction, care is exercised to ensure that any price-sensitive information is released to all shareholders, institutional and private, at the same time as in accordance with London Stock Exchange requirements.

The Board regards the Annual General Meeting as an opportunity to communicate directly with private investors and actively encourage participative dialogue. The Chairman, Executive Directors and chairpersons of the Audit and Remuneration Committees attend the Annual General Meeting and are available to answer questions from shareholders present.

# corporate governance <small>continued</small>

## Relations with shareholders <small>continued</small>

Each year end, every shareholder may choose to receive a full Annual Report and Financial Statements or an abbreviated Annual Review and Summary Financial Statement. At the half year, all shareholders receive an Interim Report. These reports, together with publicly made trading statements, are available on the company's website (www.tesco.co.uk).

## Accountability and audit

The Group has an Audit Committee, chaired by Mr J W Melbourn and consisting entirely of Non-executive Directors, which meets a minimum of three times a year. Membership of the Audit Committee is set out in the table on page 11. Its terms of reference represent current best practice. The Audit Committee's primary responsibilities include monitoring internal control throughout the Group, approving the Group's accounting policies and reviewing the interim and annual financial statements before submission to the Board. In terms of financial reporting, an assessment of Group performance is set out in the Operating and Financial Review on pages 2 to 6.

## Internal financial control

The Combined Code introduced a requirement upon Directors that they report on the effectiveness of the whole system of internal control, including financial and all other controls together with the risk management process. As permitted by the London Stock Exchange letter of 27 September 1999, the Board has decided to adopt the transitional arrangements in respect of principle D.2 of the Code. As a result, the Board will continue to report on internal financial control in accordance with the guidance to Directors issued by the Rutteman Working Group in December 1994. However, the Directors are of the view that they have established the procedures necessary to implement the requirements of the Combined Code relating to internal control as reflected in the September 1999 guidance 'Internal Control: Guidance for Directors on the Combined Code'.

The Board has overall responsibility for the systems of internal financial control. Implementation and maintenance of the internal financial control system is the responsibility of executive management. The Board, through the Audit Committee, has reviewed the effectiveness of the systems of internal financial control for the accounting year and the period to the date of approval of the financial statements. It should be understood that such systems are designed to provide reasonable but not absolute assurance against material misstatement or loss.

The Group has an established framework of internal financial controls, the key features of which are as follows:

**Organisational structure** The responsibilities of the Board set out above are designed to ensure effective control over strategic, financial and compliance issues.

**Financial framework** The Group operates a comprehensive system of financial reporting to the Board and senior management, based upon an annual budget and regular forecasts. Weekly and periodic reports of actual results together with key performance indicators are produced. The Group monitors financial performance along with other non-financial objectives through a balanced scorecard approach ensuring overall alignment of goals and objectives.

**Policies and procedures** The Group employs 220,000 people including over 1,500 senior managers. Management control is formalised at all levels and is regulated by cascading limits of authority. Formal policies and procedures also exist for areas that are identified, by their nature, as being significant risk areas. Policies and procedures are regularly subject to compliance audits.

**Quality and integrity of personnel** The Group attaches high importance to the values of trust, honesty and integrity of personnel in responsible positions and operates a policy of recruiting and promoting suitably experienced personnel with clearly defined accountabilities.

**Investment appraisal** The capital investment programme is subject to formalised review procedures with key criteria requiring to be met. All major initiatives require business cases to be prepared, normally covering a minimum period of five years. Post investment appraisals are also carried out.

**Control monitoring** Our external auditors, PricewaterhouseCoopers, contribute an independent perspective on certain aspects of the internal financial control system arising from their audit work and annually report their findings to the Audit Committee. The Group also maintains an internal audit function whose work is focused on areas of perceived high risk, as identified by risk analysis, and who regularly provide reports to the Audit Committee.

## Pension fund

The assets of the pension funds established for the benefit of the Group's employees are held separately from those of the Group. Both the Tesco PLC Pension Scheme and the Tesco PLC Money Purchase Pension Scheme are managed by a trustee company. Its Board comprises one Executive Director, four senior managers and four members appointed from staff and pensioners. Management of the assets of the Tesco PLC Pension Scheme is delegated to a number of independent fund managers. Contributions to the Tesco PLC Money Purchase Pension Scheme are paid into insurance policies administered by the Equitable Life Assurance Society. There has been no self-investment in Tesco shares or property occupied by the Tesco Group. Details of pension commitments are set out in note 26 to the financial statements on page 37.

## Statement of compliance with the Code Provisions in the Combined Code

Throughout the year ended 26 February 2000 the Group has been in compliance with all the Code Provisions set out in Section 1 of the Combined Code on Corporate Governance, except as with regard to provision B.1.7 on the length of Directors' service agreements. The Remuneration Committee considers that the current length of two years is both appropriate and necessary although it reviews the matter every year.

| BOARD COMMITTEE MEMBERSHIP | Nominations Committee | Remuneration Committee | Audit Committee | Compliance Committee |
|---|---|---|---|---|
| **Independent Directors** | | | | |
| Mr J A Gardiner | * | * | * | |
| Mr G F Pimlott | * | * | * | |
| Mr J W Melbourn | * | * | * | |
| Baroness O'Cathain | * | * | | |
| Mr C L Allen | * | * | * | |
| Dr H Einsmann | * | | | |
| **Executive Directors** | | | | |
| Mr T P Leahy | * | | | |
| Mr R S Ager | | | | * |
| Mr P A Clarke | | | | * |

# report of the directors on remuneration

## Directors' remuneration policy

The remuneration packages, including contract periods, of Executive Directors are determined by the Remuneration Committee ('the Committee'). It ensures that the remuneration package is appropriate for their responsibilities, taking into consideration the overall financial and business position of the Group, the highly competitive industry of which the Group is part and the importance of recruiting and retaining management of the appropriate calibre. The remuneration of the Non-executive Directors is determined by the Board as a whole on the recommendation of the Executive Committee after considering external market research.

## Compliance

The Committee is constituted and operated throughout the period in accordance with the principles outlined in the Stock Exchange Listing Rules derived from Schedule A of the Combined Code. In framing the remuneration policy, full consideration has been given to the best practice provisions set out in Schedule B, annexed to the Listing Rules. The auditors' report set out on page 17 covers the disclosures referred to in this report that are specified for audit by the London Stock Exchange.

Details of Directors' emoluments and interests, including executive and savings-related share options, are set out on pages 13 to 16.

The following summarises the remuneration packages for Executive Directors. Copies of the Executive Directors' contracts of employment are available for inspection by shareholders as required.

## Base salary and benefits

The base salary, contract periods, benefits (which comprise car benefits, life assurance, disability and health insurance) and other remuneration issues of Executive Directors and other senior executives, are normally reviewed annually by the Committee, having regard to competitive market practice supported by two external, independent surveys.

## Profit-sharing

The Group operates an approved employee profit-sharing scheme for the benefit of all employees, including Executive Directors, with over two years' service with the Group at its year end. Shares in the company are allocated to participants in the scheme on a pro rata basis to base salary earned up to Inland Revenue approved limits.

## Executive incentive scheme

The company operates performance-related award schemes designed to provide a growing element of variable reward to reflect the performance of the Group. The executive incentive scheme introduced in March 1993 was designed and introduced for this purpose.

Long-term share bonuses are awarded annually, based on improvements in earnings per share, achievement of strategic corporate goals and comparative performance against peer companies including total shareholder return. The maximum long-term bonus is 50% of salary. Shares awarded have to be held for a period of four years, conditional upon continuous service with the company. The share equivalent of dividends which would have been paid on the shares is added to the award during the deferral period.

Short-term share bonuses are awarded annually, based on improvements in earnings per share and on the achievement of strategic corporate goals. The maximum short-term bonus payable is 25% of salary, which is augmented by up to a further 12.5% of salary if the participants elect for the trustees of the scheme to retain the fully paid ordinary shares awarded for a minimum period of two years, conditional upon continuous service with the company. The share equivalent of dividends which would have been paid on the shares is added to the award during the deferral period.

The Committee sets performance targets annually for the incentive scheme for each of the criteria noted above, confirms achievement of performance and awards to be made under the scheme and directs the general administration of the scheme. The Executive Committee has adopted a policy of extending the Group Board executive incentive scheme to a wider body of senior executives within the Group. The scheme rules and awards of this extension are administered on a consistent basis as previously set out for the Executive Directors.

The holding period for both the long-term and short-term shares may be extended to seven and five years respectively by the scheme members. During this holding period, the shares held are increased by 12.5% at the beginning of each year based on the scheme shares held. This holding period may be extended only subject to personal share-holding targets set by the Committee being met by the scheme members and conditional upon continuous employment with the company.

## Share options

Executive Directors are included in an approved executive share option scheme (ESOS), and are eligible to join the employees' savings-related share option scheme (SAYE) when they have completed one year's service.

Executive options granted since 1995 may be exercised only subject to the achievement of performance criteria related to growth in earnings per share, in accordance with ABI guidelines.

## Pensions

Executive Directors are members of the Tesco PLC Pension Scheme which provides a pension of up to two-thirds of base salary on retirement, normally at the age of 60, dependent upon service. The scheme also provides for dependants' pensions and lump sums on death in service. The scheme is a defined benefit pension scheme, which is approved by the Inland Revenue.

## Service agreements

Executive Directors have service contracts with entitlement to notice of 24 months. This notice period is renewed annually by the Remuneration Committee and is regarded as an essential part of the remuneration package, designed to retain key executives within the company.

## Non-executive Directors

Non-executive Directors do not have contracts but each appointment is subject to review every three years. Non-executive Directors receive a basic fee plus an additional sum in respect of committee membership. Mr J A Gardiner and Baroness O'Cathain each have the benefit of the use of a company car.

**TABLE 1** Directors' emoluments

| | Salary £000 | Profit sharing £000 | Benefits £000 | Incentive scheme Short-term £000 | Incentive scheme Long-term £000 | Total 2000 £000 | Total 1999 £000 |
|---|---|---|---|---|---|---|---|
| Mr J A Gardiner | 300 | – | 5 | – | – | 305 | 300 |
| Mr T P Leahy | 648 | 8 | 41 | 231 | 245 | 1,173 | 901 |
| Mr D E Reid | 557 | 8 | 65 | 195 | 228 | 1,053 | 836 |
| Mr R S Ager | 379 | 8 | 18 | 131 | 162 | 698 | 590 |
| Mr C L Allen | 35 | – | – | – | – | 35 | 3 |
| Mr P A Clarke | 249 | 6 | 23 | 95 | 61 | 434 | 85 |
| Dr H Einsmann (a) | 24 | – | – | – | – | 24 | – |
| Mr J Gildersleeve | 504 | 8 | 66 | 174 | 212 | 964 | 782 |
| Mr A T Higginson | 378 | – | 46 | 134 | 86 | 644 | 553 |
| Mrs L James (b) | 303 | – | 4 | – | – | 307 | 427 |
| Dr M G Jones (c) | – | – | – | – | – | – | 10 |
| Mr T J R Mason | 381 | 8 | 22 | 134 | 135 | 680 | 567 |
| Mr J W Melbourn | 38 | – | – | – | – | 38 | 37 |
| Baroness O'Cathain | 33 | – | 7 | – | – | 40 | 44 |
| Mr G F Pimlott | 38 | – | – | – | – | 38 | 30 |
| Mr D T Potts | 314 | 8 | 13 | 104 | 66 | 505 | 116 |
| Mr J M Wemms | 422 | 8 | 48 | 146 | 177 | 801 | 658 |
| | 4,603 | 62 | 358 | 1,344 | 1,372 | 7,739 | 5,939 |

a  Dr H Einsmann was appointed to the Board on 1 April 1999.

b  Mrs L James retired from the Board on 30 April 1999. Included in her salary is a payment of £258,000 upon retirement.

c  Former Director.

# report of the directors on remuneration continued

**TABLE 2** Gains made on share options

| | Number of shares at exercise price (pence) | | | | | Value realisable | |
| | 61.7 | 90.3 | 104.0 | Total | Price at exercise (pence) | 2000 £000 | 1999 £000 |
|---|---|---|---|---|---|---|---|
| MrT P Leahy | — | — | — | — | — | — | — |
| Mr D E Reid | 11,058 | 194,835 | 557,712 | 763,605 | 181.5 | 623 | — |
| Mr R S Ager | — | — | — | — | — | — | 386 |
| Mr P A Clarke | — | — | — | — | — | — | 153 |
| Mr J Gildersleeve | — | — | — | — | — | — | 781 |
| Mr A T Higginson | — | — | — | — | — | — | — |
| Mrs L James | — | — | — | — | — | — | 466 |
| MrT J R Mason | — | — | — | — | — | — | 594 |
| Mr D T Potts | — | — | — | — | — | — | 410 |
| Mr J M Wemms | — | — | 566,603 | 566,603 | 188.5 | 479 | 232 |
| Date of grant | 27 May 1993 | 27 April 1995 | 13 October 1995 | | | | |

The value realisable from shares acquired on exercise is the difference between the fair market value at exercise and the exercise price of the options, although the shares may have been retained. Where individual Directors exercised options on different dates and sold the shares, the price at exercise shown represents an average of the prices on these dates weighted to the number of options exercised. The market price of the shares at 26 February 2000 was 169p. The share price during the 52 weeks to 26 February 2000 ranged from 156p to 197p.

**TABLE 3** Pension details of the Directors

| | Age at 26 Feb 2000 | Years of service | Increase in accrued pension during the year (a) £000 | Transfer value of increase during the year £000 | Accrued total pension at 26 Feb 2000 (b) £000 |
|---|---|---|---|---|---|
| MrT P Leahy | 44 | 21 | 38 | 407 | 229 |
| Mr D E Reid | 53 | 15 | 34 | 508 | 247 |
| Mr R S Ager | 54 | 14 | 18 | 274 | 180 |
| Mr P A Clarke | 39 | 25 | 4 | 39 | 76 |
| Mr J Gildersleeve | 55 | 35 | 24 | 379 | 281 |
| Mr A T Higginson (c) | 42 | 2 | 14 | 138 | 28 |
| Mrs L James (d) | 50 | 15 | 18 | 283 | 82 |
| MrT J R Mason | 42 | 18 | 17 | 166 | 127 |
| Mr D T Potts | 42 | 27 | 5 | 47 | 96 |
| Mr J M Wemms (e) | 60 | 28 | 23 | 240 | 276 |

a  The increase in accrued pension during the year excludes any increase for inflation.

b  The accrued pension is that which would be paid annually on retirement at 60 based on service to 26 February 2000.

c  Part of Mr A T Higginson's benefits, in respect of pensionable earnings in excess of the earnings limit imposed by the Finance Act 1989, are provided on an unfunded basis within a separate unapproved arrangement.

d  Mrs L James took early retirement on 30 April 1999 and is receiving her pension. Transfer values do not apply in these circumstances. The value of increase during the year has been calculated on a basis consistent with transfer values. The accrued total pension shown is her pension immediately after retirement.

e  Mr J M Wemms' pension commenced on 8 February 2000 at his normal retirement age.

**TABLE 4** Share options held by Directors and not exercised at 26 February 2000

Executive share options schemes (1984), (1994) and (1996)    Number of shares at exercise price (pence)

| | 61.7 | 61.7 | 70.0 (a) | 81.0 (a) | 66.0 | 90.3 | 104.0 | 98.3 | 117.7 | Sub-total |
|---|---|---|---|---|---|---|---|---|---|---|
| Mr T P Leahy | 62,211 | 51,150 | 417,144 | 471,372 | – | 398,523 | 248,256 | 523,728 | – | 2,172,384 |
| Mr D E Reid | – | – | 11,427 | – | – | – | – | 223,728 | – | 235,155 |
| Mr R S Ager | – | 51,153 | 75,714 | – | 106,833 | – | – | 250,170 | 94,335 | 578,205 |
| Mr P A Clarke | – | – | – | – | – | – | – | 165,504 | – | 165,504 |
| Mr J Gildersleeve | – | – | – | – | – | – | – | 122,034 | – | 122,034 |
| Mr A T Higginson | – | – | – | – | – | – | – | – | – | – |
| Mrs L James (b) | – | – | – | – | 42,813 | – | – | 113,646 | – | 156,459 |
| Mr T J R Mason | – | – | – | – | – | – | – | 284,745 | – | 284,745 |
| Mr D T Potts | – | – | – | – | – | – | – | 97,581 | – | 97,581 |
| Mr J M Wemms | – | – | 87,141 | – | – | – | – | 275,643 | 50,994 | 413,778 |
| Date exercisable (d) | 29 October 1995 | 27 May 1996 | 10 June 1997 | 12 August 1997 | 29 September 1997 | 27 April 1998 | 13 October 1998 | 3 July 1999 | 17 April 2000 | |

| | Sub-total b/f | 151.7 | 160.3 | 176.7 | 164.0 | 178.0 | 179.4 (c) | 173.0 (c) | Total |
|---|---|---|---|---|---|---|---|---|---|
| Mr T P Leahy | 2,172,384 | 120,660 | – | – | 126,832 | – | – | 228,901 | 2,648,777 |
| Mr D E Reid | 235,155 | 601,305 | – | – | 90,245 | – | 425,827 | 117,920 | 1,470,452 |
| Mr R S Ager | 578,205 | 299,904 | – | 89,433 | 26,831 | 149,171 | – | 36,994 | 1,180,538 |
| Mr P A Clarke | 165,504 | 76,281 | – | 17,718 | 29,946 | 146,991 | – | 277,170 | 713,610 |
| Mr J Gildersleeve | 122,034 | 504,999 | – | 150,564 | 56,100 | 364,092 | – | 73,988 | 1,271,777 |
| Mr A T Higginson | – | – | 411,642 | 373,584 | 63,415 | – | – | 76,301 | 924,942 |
| Mrs L James (b) | 156,459 | 225,150 | – | – | 19,514 | 113,263 | – | – | 514,386 |
| Mr T J R Mason | 284,745 | 198,669 | – | 149,076 | 63,415 | 255,796 | – | 87,861 | 1,039,562 |
| Mr D T Potts | 97,581 | 119,238 | – | – | 38,756 | 288,730 | – | 199,827 | 744,132 |
| Mr J M Wemms | 413,778 | 154,944 | 34,731 | 65,658 | – | – | – | – | 669,111 |
| Date exercisable (d) | | 7 October 2000 | 17 November 2000 | 21 May 2001 | 30 September 2001 | 28 January 2002 | 24 May 2002 | 30 November 2002 | |

a  In the case of Mr T P Leahy 25% of the options, and in the case of Mr D E Reid and Mr R S Ager 100% of the options at 70.0p and 81.0p respectively may be exercised at 59.7p and 69.0p respectively as targets related to growth in earnings per share in accordance with ABI guidelines have been achieved.

b  Position as at Mrs L James' retirement on 30 April 1999.

c  Options granted in the year.

d  Date of expiry is seven years from date exercisable, with the exception of the 98.3p, 117.7p, 151.7p and 160.3p options which expire four years from date exercisable.

15

# report of the directors on remuneration continued

**TABLE 5** Share options held by Directors and not exercised at 26 February 2000

| Savings-related share option scheme (1981) | | | Number of shares | | | Value realisable | |
|---|---|---|---|---|---|---|---|
| | As at 27 Feb 1999 | Granted | Exercised | As at 26 Feb 2000 | Exercise price pence | 2000 £000 | 1999 £000 |
| Mr T P Leahy | 25,095 | 2,235 | 16,782 | 10,548 | 83.0-151.0 | 17 | – |
| Mr D E Reid | 19,575 | 2,235 | 5,592 | 16,218 | 83.0-151.0 | 7 | – |
| Mr R S Ager | 15,253 | 2,235 | 10,290 | 7,198 | 136.0-151.0 | 9 | 18 |
| Mr P A Clarke | 19,344 | 2,235 | 5,592 | 15,987 | 83.3-151.0 | 6 | 5 |
| Mr J Gildersleeve | 19,692 | 2,235 | 11,187 | 10,740 | 121.7-151.0 | 11 | – |
| Mr A T Higginson | – | 2,235 | – | 2,235 | 151.0 | – | – |
| Mrs L James (a) | 19,500 | – | – | 19,500 | 61.7-83.0 | – | 9 |
| Mr T J R Mason | 20,475 | 2,235 | 11,187 | 11,523 | 83.3-151.0 | 11 | – |
| Mr D T Potts | 20,700 | – | – | 20,700 | 83.3 | – | – |
| Mr J M Wemms | 25,095 | 2,235 | 16,782 | 10,548 | 83.0-151.0 | 17 | – |

a  This shows the movement of options up to the date of Mrs L James' retirement on 30 April 1999.

The subscription price for the savings-related share option scheme granted during the year was 151.0p and the option matures in either 2003 (three-year scheme) or 2005 (five-year scheme). The shares relating to options exercised in the year were all retained.

Between 26 February 2000 and 10 April 2000 there have been no changes in the number of share options held by the Directors. For further details on the company share option schemes see note 25.

**TABLE 6** Disclosable interests of the Directors, including family interests

| | 26 Feb 2000 | | 27 Feb 1999 | |
|---|---|---|---|---|
| | Ordinary shares | Options to acquire ordinary shares | Ordinary shares | Options to acquire ordinary shares |
| Mr J A Gardiner | 496,848 | – | 353,325 | |
| Mr T P Leahy | 1,527,914 | 2,659,325 | 1,233,415 | 2,444,971 |
| Mr D E Reid | 1,689,528 | 1,486,670 | 1,418,418 | 1,709,885 |
| Mr R S Ager | 995,063 | 1,187,736 | 797,067 | 1,158,797 |
| Mr P A Clarke | 103,553 | 729,597 | 65,145 | 455,784 |
| Mr J Gildersleeve | 1,009,829 | 1,282,517 | 771,244 | 1,217,481 |
| Mr A T Higginson | 179,595 | 927,177 | 60,512 | 848,641 |
| Mrs L James (a) | 847,948 | 533,886 | 737,681 | 533,886 |
| Mr T J R Mason | 623,396 | 1,051,085 | 452,596 | 972,176 |
| Mr J W Melbourn | 9,690 | – | 6,570 | – |
| Baroness O'Cathain | 46,473 | – | 46,473 | – |
| Mr G F Pimlott | 26,724 | – | 26,134 | – |
| Mr D T Potts | 212,503 | 764,832 | 157,588 | 565,005 |
| Mr J M Wemms | 983,456 | 679,659 | 765,054 | 1,260,809 |

a  Position at Mrs L James' retirement on 30 April 1999.

Options to acquire ordinary shares shown above comprise options under the executive share option schemes (1984), (1994), (1996) and the savings-related share option scheme (1981) (note 25).

Between 26 February 2000 and 10 April 2000 there were no changes in the number of shares held by the Directors.

# directors' responsibilities for the preparation of the financial statements

The Directors are required by the Companies Act 1985 to prepare financial statements for each financial year which give a true and fair view of the state of affairs of the company and the Group as at the end of the financial year and of the profit or loss for the financial year.

The Directors consider that in preparing the financial statements on pages 18 to 39 the company has used appropriate accounting policies, consistently applied and supported by reasonable and prudent judgements and estimates, and that all accounting standards which they consider to be applicable have been followed.

The Directors have responsibility for ensuring that the company keeps accounting records which disclose, with reasonable accuracy, the financial position of the company and which enable them to ensure that the financial statements comply with the Companies Act 1985.

The Directors have general responsibility for taking such steps as are reasonably open to them to safeguard the assets of the Group and to prevent and detect fraud and other irregularities.

# auditors' report to the members of Tesco PLC

We have audited the financial statements on pages 18 to 39 which have been prepared under the historical cost convention and the accounting policies set out on pages 22 and 23, and the information on Directors' emoluments and share details included on pages 13 to 16.

## Respective responsibilities of Directors and auditors

The Directors are responsible for preparing the Annual Report. As described above, this includes responsibility for preparing the financial statements, in accordance with applicable United Kingdom accounting standards. Our responsibilities, as independent auditors, are established in the United Kingdom by statute, the Auditing Practices Board, the Listing Rules of the London Stock Exchange and our profession's ethical guidance.

We report to you our opinion as to whether the financial statements give a true and fair view and are properly prepared in accordance with the United Kingdom Companies Act. We also report to you if, in our opinion, the Directors' report is not consistent with the financial statements, if the company has not kept proper accounting records, if we have not received all the information and explanations we require for our audit, or if information specified by law or the Listing Rules regarding Directors' remuneration and transactions is not disclosed.

We read the other information contained in the Annual Report and consider the implications for our report if we become aware of any apparent misstatements or material inconsistencies with the financial statements.

We review whether the statement on page 11 reflects the company's compliance with the seven provisions of the Combined Code specified for our review by the London Stock Exchange, and we report if it does not. We are not required to consider whether

the Board's statements on internal control cover all risks and controls, or to form an opinion on the effectiveness of the company's or the Group's corporate governance procedures or its risk and control procedures.

## Basis of audit opinion

We conducted our audit in accordance with Auditing Standards issued by the Auditing Practices Board. An audit includes examination, on a test basis, of evidence relevant to the amounts and disclosures in the financial statements. It also includes an assessment of the significant estimates and judgements made by the Directors in the preparation of the financial statements, and of whether the accounting policies are appropriate to the company's circumstances, consistently applied and adequately disclosed.

We planned and performed our audit so as to obtain all the information and explanations which we considered necessary in order to provide us with sufficient evidence to give reasonable assurance that the financial statements are free from material misstatement, whether caused by fraud or other irregularity or error. In forming our opinion we also evaluated the overall adequacy of the presentation of information in the financial statements.

## Opinion

In our opinion the financial statements give a true and fair view of the state of affairs of the company and the Group at 26 February 2000 and of the profit and cash flows of the Group for the year then ended and have been properly prepared in accordance with the Companies Act 1985.

PriceWaterhouseCoopers

Chartered Accountants and Registered Auditors
London 10 April 2000

# group profit and loss account
52 weeks ended 26 February 2000

| | note | 2000 £m | 1999 £m |
|---|---|---|---|
| Sales at net selling prices | 1 | 20,358 | 18,546 |
| Value added tax | | (1,562) | (1,388) |
| Turnover excluding value added tax | 1/2 | 18,796 | 17,158 |
| Operating expenses | | | |
| – Normal operating expenses | | (17,712) | (16,155) |
| – Employee profit-sharing | 3 | (41) | (38) |
| – Integration costs | 2 | (6) | (26) |
| – Goodwill amortisation | 11 | (7) | (5) |
| Operating profit | 1/2 | 1,030 | 934 |
| Net loss on disposal of fixed assets | | (9) | (8) |
| Share of operating profit of joint ventures | 1 | 11 | 6 |
| Profit on ordinary activities before interest | | 1,032 | 932 |
| Net interest payable | 7 | (99) | (90) |
| Profit on ordinary activities before taxation | 4 | 933 | 842 |
| Profit before integration costs, net loss on disposal of fixed assets and goodwill amortisation | | 955 | 881 |
| Integration costs | | (6) | (26) |
| Net loss on disposal of fixed assets | | (9) | (8) |
| Goodwill amortisation | | (7) | (5) |
| Tax on profit on ordinary activities | 8 | (259) | (237) |
| Profit on ordinary activities after taxation | | 674 | 605 |
| Minority interest | | – | 1 |
| Profit for the financial year | | 674 | 606 |
| Dividends | 9 | (302) | (277) |
| Retained profit for the financial year | 24 | 372 | 329 |
| | | Pence | Pence |
| Earnings per share | 10 | 10.07 | 9.14 |
| Adjusted for integration costs after taxation | | 0.06 | 0.27 |
| Adjusted for net loss on disposal of fixed assets after taxation | | 0.13 | 0.12 |
| Adjusted for goodwill amortisation | | 0.10 | 0.06 |
| Adjusted earnings per share | 10 | 10.36 | 9.59 |
| Diluted earnings per share | 10 | 9.89 | 8.93 |
| Adjusted for integration costs after taxation | | 0.06 | 0.26 |
| Adjusted for net loss on disposal of fixed assets after taxation | | 0.13 | 0.12 |
| Adjusted for goodwill amortisation | | 0.10 | 0.06 |
| Adjusted diluted earnings per share | 10 | 10.18 | 9.37 |
| Dividend per share | 9 | 4.48 | 4.12 |
| Dividend cover (times) | | 2.27 | 2.27 |

Accounting policies and notes forming part of these financial statements are on pages 22 to 39.

## statement of total recognised gains and losses

52 weeks ended 26 February 2000

| | Group | | Company | |
|---|---|---|---|---|
| | 2000 £m | 1999 £m | 2000 £m | 1999 £m |
| Profit for the financial year | 674 | 606 | 42 | 209 |
| Loss on foreign currency net investments | (36) | (19) | (3) | – |
| Total recognised gains and losses relating to the financial year | 638 | 587 | 39 | 209 |

## reconciliation of movements in shareholders' funds

52 weeks ended 26 February 2000

| | Group | | Company | |
|---|---|---|---|---|
| | 2000 £m | 1999 £m | 2000 £m | 1999 £m |
| Profit for the financial year | 674 | 606 | 42 | 209 |
| Dividends | (302) | (277) | (302) | (277) |
| | 372 | 329 | (260) | (68) |
| Loss on foreign currency net investments | (36) | (19) | (3) | – |
| New share capital subscribed less expenses | 30 | 147 | 54 | 256 |
| Payment of dividends by shares in lieu of cash | 21 | 22 | 21 | 22 |
| Net addition/(reduction) to shareholders' funds | 387 | 479 | (188) | 210 |
| Shareholders' funds at 27 February 1999 | 4,382 | 3,903 | 2,699 | 2,489 |
| Shareholders' funds at 26 February 2000 | 4,769 | 4,382 | 2,511 | 2,699 |

Accounting policies and notes forming part of these financial statements are on pages 22 to 39.

# balance sheets
26 February 2000

| | note | Group 2000 £m | Group 1999 £m | Company 2000 £m | Company 1999 £m |
|---|---|---|---|---|---|
| **Fixed assets** | | | | | |
| Intangible assets | 11 | 136 | 112 | – | – |
| Tangible assets | 12 | 8,140 | 7,105 | – | – |
| Investments | 13 | 79 | 102 | 5,200 | 5,001 |
| Investments in joint ventures | 13 | 172 | 234 | 124 | 252 |
| | | 8,527 | 7,553 | 5,324 | 5,253 |
| **Current assets** | | | | | |
| Stocks | 14 | 744 | 667 | – | – |
| Debtors | 15 | 252 | 151 | 1,183 | 1,924 |
| Investments | 16 | 258 | 201 | 21 | 2 |
| Cash at bank and in hand | | 88 | 127 | – | – |
| | | 1,342 | 1,146 | 1,204 | 1,926 |
| Creditors: falling due within one year | 17 | (3,487) | (3,075) | (2,525) | (3,292) |
| **Net current liabilities** | | (2,145) | (1,929) | (1,321) | (1,366) |
| **Total assets less current liabilities** | | 6,382 | 5,624 | 4,003 | 3,887 |
| Creditors: falling due after more than one year | 18 | (1,565) | (1,230) | (1,492) | (1,188) |
| **Provisions for liabilities and charges** | 21 | (19) | (17) | – | – |
| **Total net assets** | | 4,798 | 4,377 | 2,511 | 2,699 |
| **Capital and reserves** | | | | | |
| Called up share capital | 23 | 341 | 339 | 341 | 339 |
| Share premium account | 24 | 1,650 | 1,577 | 1,650 | 1,577 |
| Other reserves | 24 | 40 | 40 | – | – |
| Profit and loss account | 24 | 2,738 | 2,426 | 520 | 783 |
| **Equity shareholders' funds** | | 4,769 | 4,382 | 2,511 | 2,699 |
| Minority interest | | 29 | (5) | – | – |
| **Total capital employed** | | 4,798 | 4,377 | 2,511 | 2,699 |

Accounting policies and notes forming part of these financial statements are on pages 22 to 39.

**Terry Leahy**
**Andrew Higginson**
Directors

Financial statements approved by the Board on 10 April 2000.

# group cash flow statement
52 weeks ended 26 February 2000

| | note | 2000 £m | 1999 £m |
|---|---|---|---|
| Net cash inflow from operating activities | 31 | 1,513 | 1,321 |
| **Returns on investments and servicing of finance** | | | |
| Interest received | | 58 | 34 |
| Interest paid | | (188) | (162) |
| Interest element of finance lease rental payments | | (1) | (1) |
| Net cash outflow from returns on investments and servicing of finance | | (131) | (129) |
| **Taxation** | | | |
| Corporation tax paid (including advance corporation tax) | | (213) | (237) |
| **Capital expenditure and financial investment** | | | |
| Payments to acquire tangible fixed assets | | (1,296) | (1,032) |
| Receipts from sale of tangible fixed assets | | 85 | 27 |
| Purchase of own shares | | (18) | – |
| Net cash outflow for capital expenditure and financial investment | | (1,229) | (1,005) |
| **Acquisitions and disposals** | | | |
| Purchase of subsidiary undertakings | 32 | (61) | (184) |
| Disposal of subsidiary undertaking | | – | (4) |
| Net cash acquired with subsidiary undertaking | | – | 2 |
| Received from/(invested in) joint ventures | 30 | 62 | (69) |
| Net cash inflow/(outflow) from acquisitions and disposals | | 1 | (255) |
| **Equity dividends paid** | | (262) | (238) |
| **Cash outflow before use of liquid resources and financing** | | (321) | (543) |
| **Management of liquid resources** | | | |
| Increase in short-term deposits | | (68) | (7) |
| **Financing** | | | |
| Ordinary shares issued for cash | | 20 | 42 |
| Increase in other loans | | 322 | 719 |
| New finance leases | | 29 | – |
| Capital element of finance leases repaid | | (20) | (15) |
| Net cash inflow from financing | | 351 | 746 |
| (Decrease)/increase in cash in the period | | (38) | 196 |
| **Reconciliation of net cash flow to movement in net debt** | | | |
| (Decrease)/increase in cash in the period | | (38) | 196 |
| Cash inflow from increase in debt and lease financing | | (331) | (704) |
| Loans acquired with subsidiary undertaking | | – | (19) |
| Cash used to increase liquid resources | | 68 | 7 |
| Amortisation of 4% unsecured deep discount loan stock | | (4) | (3) |
| Other non-cash movements | | (30) | – |
| Foreign exchange differences | | (5) | (6) |
| Increase in net debt | | (340) | (529) |
| Net debt at 27 February 1999 | 33 | (1,720) | (1,191) |
| Net debt at 26 February 2000 | 33 | (2,060) | (1,720) |

Accounting policies and notes forming part of these financial statements are on pages 22 to 39.

# accounting policies

## Basis of financial statements

These financial statements have been prepared under the historical cost convention, in accordance with applicable accounting standards and the Companies Act 1985.

The Group has adopted Financial Reporting Standard 15, 'Tangible Fixed Assets', and Financial Reporting Standard 16, 'Current Tax', during the year.

## Basis of consolidation

The Group profit and loss account and balance sheet consist of the financial statements of the parent company, its subsidiary undertakings and the Group's share of interests in joint ventures. The accounts of the parent company's subsidiary undertakings are prepared to dates around 26 February 2000 apart from Global T.H., Tesco Polska Sp. z o.o., Tesco Stores ČR a.s., Tesco Stores SR a.s., Samsung Tesco Co. Limited and Ek-Chai Distribution System Co. Ltd which prepared accounts to 31 December 1999. In the opinion of the Directors it is necessary for the above named subsidiaries to prepare accounts to a date earlier than the rest of the Group to enable the timely publication of the Group financial statements.

The Group's interests in joint ventures are accounted for using the gross equity method.

## Stocks

Stocks comprise goods held for resale and development properties, and are valued at the lower of cost and net realisable value. Stocks in stores are calculated at retail prices and reduced by appropriate margins to the lower of cost and net realisable value.

## Money market investments

Money market investments are stated at cost. All income from these investments is included in the profit and loss account as interest receivable and similar income.

## Fixed assets and depreciation

The Group has adopted Financial Reporting Standard 15, 'Tangible Fixed Assets', during the year.

Following the adoption, interest paid on funds specifically related to the financing of assets in the course of construction, which was previously capitalised net of tax relief, is now capitalised gross. The impact of this change in accounting policy on the current and prior year is not material, and accordingly prior period figures have not been restated.

Depreciation is provided on a straight line basis over the anticipated useful economic lives of the assets, at the following rates:

- Land premia paid in excess of the alternative use value on acquisition – at 4% of cost.
- Freehold and leasehold buildings with greater than 40 years unexpired – at 2.5% of cost.
- Leasehold properties with less than 40 years unexpired are amortised by equal annual instalments over the unexpired period of the lease.
- Plant, equipment, fixtures and fittings and motor vehicles – at rates varying from 10% to 33%.

## Goodwill

Goodwill arising from transactions entered into after 1 March 1998 is capitalised under the heading 'Intangible assets' and amortised on a straight line basis over its useful economic life, up to a maximum of 20 years.

All goodwill from transactions entered into prior to 1 March 1998 has been written off to reserves.

## Impairment of fixed assets and goodwill

Fixed assets and goodwill are subject to review for impairment in accordance with Financial Reporting Standard 11, 'Impairment of Fixed Assets and Goodwill'. Any impairment is recognised in the profit and loss account in the year in which it occurs.

## Leasing

Plant, equipment and fixtures and fittings which are the subject of finance leases are dealt with in the financial statements as tangible assets and equivalent liabilities at what would otherwise have been the cost of outright purchase.

Rentals are apportioned between reductions of the respective liabilities and finance charges, the latter being calculated by reference to the rates of interest implicit in the leases. The finance charges are dealt with under interest payable in the profit and loss account.

Leased assets are depreciated in accordance with the depreciation accounting policy over the anticipated working lives of the assets which generally correspond to the primary rental periods. The cost of operating leases in respect of land and buildings and other assets is expensed as incurred.

## Deferred tax

Deferred taxation is provided on accelerated capital allowances and other timing differences, only to the extent that it is probable that a liability will crystallise.

## Pensions

The expected cost of pensions in respect of the Group's defined benefit pension schemes is charged to the profit and loss account over the working lifetimes of employees in the schemes. Actuarial surpluses and deficits are spread over the expected remaining working lifetimes of employees.

## Post-retirement benefits other than pensions

The cost of providing other post-retirement benefits, which comprise private healthcare, is charged to the profit and loss account so as to spread the cost over the service lives of relevant employees in accordance with the advice of qualified actuaries. Actuarial surpluses and deficits are spread over the expected remaining working lifetimes of relevant employees.

## Foreign currencies

Assets and liabilities in foreign currencies are translated into sterling at the financial year end exchange rates. Profits and losses of overseas subsidiaries are translated into sterling at average rates of exchange. Gains and losses arising on the translation of the net assets of overseas subsidiaries, less exchange differences arising on matched foreign currency borrowings, are taken to reserves and disclosed in the statement of total recognised gains and losses. Gains and losses on instruments used for hedging are recognised in the profit and loss account when the exposure that is being hedged is itself recognised.

## Financial instruments

Derivative instruments utilised by the Group are interest rate swaps and caps, cross currency swaps, forward rate agreements and forward exchange contracts and options. Termination payments made or received in respect of derivatives are spread over the life of the underlying exposure in cases where the underlying exposure continues to exist. Where the underlying exposure ceases to exist, any termination payments are taken to the profit and loss account.

Interest differentials on derivative instruments are recognised by adjusting net interest payable. Premia or discounts on derivative instruments are amortised over the shorter of the life of the instrument or the underlying exposure.

Currency swap agreements and forward exchange contracts are valued at closing rates of exchange. Resulting gains or losses are offset against foreign exchange gains or losses on the related borrowings or, where the instrument is used to hedge a committed future transaction, are deferred until the transaction occurs or is extinguished.

# notes to the financial statements

**NOTE 1** Segmental analysis of sales, turnover, profit and net assets

The Group's operations of retailing and associated activities and property development are carried out in the UK, Republic of Ireland, France, Hungary, Poland, Czech Republic, Slovakia, South Korea and Thailand. The results for South Korea, Thailand and continental European operations are for the year ended 31 December 1999.

| | 2000 | | | | 1999 | | | |
|---|---|---|---|---|---|---|---|---|
| | Sales including VAT £m | Turnover excluding VAT £m | Profit £m | Assets £m | Sales including VAT £m | Turnover excluding VAT £m | Profit £m | Assets £m |
| **Continuing operations** | | | | | | | | |
| Retailing – UK | 18,331 | 16,955 | 993 | 5,685 | 17,070 | 15,814 | 919 | 5,392 |
| Property development | 3 | 3 | – | 28 | 21 | 21 | – | 32 |
| Total UK | 18,334 | 16,958 | 993 | 5,713 | 17,091 | 15,835 | 919 | 5,424 |
| Retailing – Rest of Europe | 1,527 | 1,374 | 51 | 771 | 1,285 | 1,167 | 48 | 522 |
| Retailing – Asia | 497 | 464 | (1) | 374 | 170 | 156 | (2) | 151 |
| | 20,358 | 18,796 | 1,043 | | 18,546 | 17,158 | 965 | |
| Integration costs | | | (6) | | | | (26) | |
| Goodwill amortisation | | | (7) | | | | (5) | |
| Operating profit | | | 1,030 | | | | 934 | |
| Net loss on disposal of fixed assets | | | (9) | | | | (8) | |
| Share of operating profit from joint ventures | | | 11 | | | | 6 | |
| Net interest payable | | | (99) | | | | (90) | |
| **Profit on ordinary activities before taxation** | | | 933 | | | | 842 | |
| Operating margin (prior to integration costs and goodwill amortisation) | | | 5.5% | | | | 5.6% | |
| Capital employed | | | | 6,858 | | | | 6,097 |
| Net debt (note 33) | | | | (2,060) | | | | (1,720) |
| **Net assets** | | | | 4,798 | | | | 4,377 |

The analysis of capital employed by geographical area is calculated on net assets excluding net debt. Inter-segmental turnover between the geographical areas of business is not material. Turnover is disclosed by origin. There is no material difference in turnover by destination. The Group's share of sales in the joint ventures which is not included in the numbers above is £74m (1999 – £49m).

**NOTE 2  Analysis of operating profit**

| | 2000 Continuing operations £m | Acquisitions £m | Total £m | 1999 Continuing operations £m | Acquisitions £m | Total £m |
|---|---|---|---|---|---|---|
| Turnover excluding VAT | 18,666 | 130 | 18,796 | 17,002 | 156 | 17,158 |
| Cost of sales | (17,242) | (123) | (17,365) | (15,695) | (155) | (15,850) |
| Gross profit | 1,424 | 7 | 1,431 | 1,307 | 1 | 1,308 |
| Administration expenses | (394) | (7) | (401) | (371) | (3) | (374) |
| Operating profit/(loss) | 1,030 | – | 1,030 | 936 | (2) | 934 |

Cost of sales includes distribution costs and store operating costs. Integration costs, goodwill amortisation and employee profit-sharing are included within administration expenses.

The charge made for integration costs relating to our Irish businesses is £6m (1999 – £26m).

**NOTE 3  Employee profit-sharing**

This represents the amount allocated to the trustees of the profit-sharing scheme and is based on the UK profit after interest, before net loss on disposal of fixed assets and taxation.

**NOTE 4  Profit on ordinary activities before taxation**

| | 2000 £m | 1999 £m |
|---|---|---|
| Profit on ordinary activities is stated after charging the following: | | |
| Depreciation | 428 | 401 |
| Goodwill amortisation | 7 | 5 |
| Operating lease costs (a) | 158 | 159 |
| Auditors' remuneration (b) | 1 | 1 |
| Employment costs (note 5) | 1,865 | 1,736 |

a  Operating lease costs include £37m for hire of plant and machinery (1999 – £35m).

b  Auditors' remuneration amounted to £0.8m (1999 – £0.7m) and includes £0.1m (1999 – £0.1m) for the company. The auditors also received £3.6m (1999 – £1.9m) in respect of non-audit services of which £2.0m (1999 – £1.1m) related to overseas operations. These fees were principally in respect of acquisitions, taxation advice and systems implementation and training.

**NOTE 5  Employment costs**

| | 2000 £m | 1999 £m |
|---|---|---|
| **Employment costs during the year** | | |
| Wages and salaries | 1,677 | 1,558 |
| Social security costs | 106 | 105 |
| Other pension costs (note 26) | 82 | 73 |
| | 1,865 | 1,736 |

**Number of persons employed**

The average number of employees per week during the year was: UK 169,500 (1999 – 164,471), Rest of Europe 24,665 (1999 – 19,497), Asia 11,051 (1999 – 6,133) and the average number of full-time equivalents was: UK 108,409 (1999 – 104,772), Rest of Europe 18,573 (1999 – 16,489) and Asia 7,914 (1999 – 5,653).

# notes to the financial statements <sub>continued</sub>

**NOTE 6** Directors' emoluments and interests

Details of Directors' emoluments and interests are given in the Report of the Directors on Remuneration on pages 12 to 16.

**NOTE 7** Net interest payable

|  | 2000 | | 1999 | |
| --- | ---: | ---: | ---: | ---: |
|  | £m | £m | £m | £m |
| Interest receivable and similar income on money market investments and deposits |  | 56 |  | 22 |
| Less interest payable on: |  |  |  |  |
| Short term bank loans and overdrafts repayable within five years | (73) |  | (46) |  |
| Finance charges payable on finance leases | (7) |  | (8) |  |
| 4% unsecured deep discount loan stock 2006 (a) | (9) |  | (8) |  |
| 10⅜% bonds 2002 | (21) |  | (21) |  |
| 8¾% bonds 2003 | (17) |  | (17) |  |
| 7½% bonds 2007 | (25) |  | (21) |  |
| 5⅛% bonds 2009 | (19) |  | (1) |  |
| 6% bonds 2029 | (2) |  | – |  |
| Medium term notes | (15) |  | (17) |  |
| Interest capitalised | 41 |  | 35 |  |
| Share of interest of joint ventures | (8) |  | (8) |  |
|  |  | (155) |  | (112) |
|  |  | (99) |  | (90) |

a  Interest payable on the 4% unsecured deep discount loan stock 2006 includes £4m (1999 – £3m) of discount amortisation.

**NOTE 8** Taxation

|  | 2000 £m | 1999 £m |
| --- | ---: | ---: |
| UK taxation: |  |  |
| Corporation tax at 30.1% (1999 – 31.0%) | 287 | 257 |
| Share of joint ventures | – | (2) |
| Prior year items | (40) | (32) |
| Deferred taxation (note 21) – current year | (1) | 5 |
| – prior year | – | 2 |
|  | 246 | 230 |
| Overseas taxation: |  |  |
| Corporation tax | 10 | 7 |
| Deferred taxation (note 21) | 3 | – |
|  | 259 | 237 |

**NOTE 9** Dividends

|  | 2000 Pence per share | 1999 Pence per share | 2000 £m | 1999 £m |
| --- | ---: | ---: | ---: | ---: |
| Declared interim | 1.34 | 1.25 | 90 | 83 |
| Proposed final | 3.14 | 2.87 | 212 | 194 |
|  | 4.48 | 4.12 | 302 | 277 |

NOTE 10 Earnings per share and diluted earnings per share

Earnings per share and diluted earnings per share have been calculated in accordance with Financial Reporting Standard 14, 'Earnings per Share'. The standard requires that earnings should be based on the net profit attributable to ordinary shareholders. The calculation for earnings, including and excluding integration costs, net loss on disposal of fixed assets and goodwill amortisation, is based on the profit for the financial year of £674m (1999 – £606m).

For the purposes of calculating earnings per share, the number of shares is the weighted average number of ordinary shares in issue during the year of 6,693m (1999 – 6,627m).

The calculation for diluted earnings per share uses the weighted average number of ordinary shares in issue adjusted by the effects of all dilutive potential ordinary shares. The dilution effect is calculated on the full exercise of all ordinary share options granted by the Group, including performance based options which the Group consider to have been earned. The calculation compares the difference between the exercise price of exercisable ordinary share options, weighted for the period over which they were outstanding, with the average daily mid-market closing price over the period.

| | 2000 | 1999 |
|---|---|---|
| Weighted average number of dilutive share options (million) | 124 | 153 |
| Weighted average number of shares in issue in the period (million) | 6,693 | 6,627 |
| Total number of shares for calculating diluted earnings per share (million) | 6,817 | 6,780 |

NOTE 11 Intangible fixed assets

| | 2000 £m | 1999 £m |
|---|---|---|
| **Cost** | | |
| At 27 February 1999 | 117 | – |
| Additions at cost | 31 | 117 |
| At 26 February 2000 | 148 | 117 |
| **Amortisation** | | |
| At 27 February 1999 | 5 | – |
| Charge for the period | 7 | 5 |
| At 26 February 2000 | 12 | 5 |
| **Net carrying value** | | |
| At 27 February 1999 | 112 | – |
| **At 26 February 2000** | 136 | 112 |

Goodwill arising on the purchase of our businesses in South Korea and Thailand has been capitalised and amortised over 20 years in accordance with the provisions set out in Financial Reporting Standard 10, 'Goodwill and Intangible Assets'.

During the year, our Thailand business increased its share capital by rights issues and the Group purchased shares generating additional goodwill of £25m. As a result of this, the Group shareholding has increased from 75% to 93%.

# notes to the financial statements continued

**NOTE 12** Tangible fixed assets

| | Land and buildings £m | Plant equipment fixtures and fittings and vehicles £m | Total £m |
|---|---|---|---|
| **Cost** | | | |
| At 27 February 1999 | 6,918 | 2,533 | 9,451 |
| Currency translation | (32) | (22) | (54) |
| Additions at cost (a) | 1,105 | 383 | 1,488 |
| Purchase of subsidiary undertaking | 80 | 7 | 87 |
| | 8,071 | 2,901 | 10,972 |
| Disposals | (66) | (93) | (159) |
| **At 26 February 2000** | 8,005 | 2,808 | 10,813 |
| **Depreciation** | | | |
| At 27 February 1999 | 886 | 1,460 | 2,346 |
| Currency translation | (3) | (10) | (13) |
| Charge for period | 167 | 261 | 428 |
| | 1,050 | 1,711 | 2,761 |
| Disposals | (14) | (74) | (88) |
| **At 26 February 2000** | 1,036 | 1,637 | 2,673 |
| **Net book value** (b) (c) | | | |
| **At 26 February 2000** | 6,969 | 1,171 | 8,140 |
| At 27 February 1999 | 6,032 | 1,073 | 7,105 |
| **Capital work in progress included above** (d) | | | |
| **At 26 February 2000** | 189 | 49 | 238 |
| At 27 February 1999 | 124 | 21 | 145 |

a  Includes £40m in respect of interest capitalised principally relating to land and building assets. The capitalisation rate used to determine the amount of finance costs capitalised during the period was 8.5%. In 1999 the amount of interest capitalised £24m is stated net of tax relief of £9m.

b  Net book value includes capitalised interest at 26 February 2000 of £319m (1999 – £288m). The 1999 net book value includes capitalised interest net of tax relief.

Plant, equipment, fixtures and fittings and vehicles subject to finance leases included in net book value are:

| | Cost £m | Depreciation £m | Net book value £m |
|---|---|---|---|
| At 27 February 1999 | 179 | 157 | 22 |
| Movement in the period | 97 | 70 | 27 |
| **At 26 February 2000** | 276 | 227 | 49 |

c  The net book value of land and buildings comprises:

| | 2000 £m | 1999 £m |
|---|---|---|
| Freehold | 6,022 | 5,130 |
| Long leasehold – 50 years or more | 553 | 557 |
| Short leasehold – less than 50 years | 394 | 345 |
| **At 26 February 2000** | 6,969 | 6,032 |

d  Capital work in progress does not include land.

**NOTE 13** Fixed asset investments

| | Group | | | | Company |
|---|---|---|---|---|---|
| | Joint ventures (b) £m | Own shares (c) £m | Share in Group undertakings (a) £m | Loans to Group undertakings £m | Joint ventures (b) £m |
| At 27 February 1999 | 234 | 102 | 2,001 | 3,000 | 252 |
| Additions | 40 | 11 | 199 | – | 44 |
| Share of profit of joint ventures | 3 | – | – | – | – |
| Disposals | (105) | (34) | – | – | (172) |
| **At 26 February 2000** | 172 | 79 | 2,200 | 3,000 | 124 |

a  The company's principal operating subsidiary undertakings are:

| | Business | Share of equity capital | Country of incorporation |
|---|---|---|---|
| Tesco Stores Limited | Retail | 100% | Registered in England |
| Tesco Property Holdings Limited | Property Investment | 100% | Registered in England |
| Tesco Insurance Limited | Insurance | 100% | Guernsey |
| Tesco Distribution Limited | Distribution | 100% | Registered in England |
| Spen Hill Properties Limited | Property Development | 100% | Registered in England |
| Tesco Ireland Limited | Retail | 100% | Republic of Ireland |
| Global T.H. | Retail | 99% | Hungary |
| Tesco Polska Sp. z o.o. | Retail | 98% | Poland |
| Tesco Stores ČR a.s. | Retail | 100% | Czech Republic |
| Tesco Stores SR a.s. | Retail | 100% | Slovakia |
| Samsung Tesco Co. Limited | Retail | 81% | South Korea |
| Ek-Chai Distribution System Co. Ltd | Retail | 93% | Thailand |
| Tesco Stores Hong Kong Limited | Purchasing | 100% | Hong Kong |

All principal subsidiary undertakings, none of which are owned directly by Tesco PLC, operate in their country of incorporation.

b  The Group's joint ventures are:

| | Business | Share of issued share capital, loan capital and debt securities | Country of incorporation and principal country of operation |
|---|---|---|---|
| Shopping Centres Limited | Property Investment | 50% | Registered in England |
| BLT Properties Limited | Property Investment | 50% | Registered in England |
| Tesco BL Holdings Limited | Property Investment | 50% | Registered in England |
| Tesco British Land Property Partnership | Property Investment | 50% | Registered in England |
| Tesco Personal Finance Group Limited | Personal Finance | 50% | Registered in Scotland |
| Tesco Personal Finance Life Limited | Personal Finance | 50% | Registered in Scotland |
| Tesco Personal Finance Investments Limited | Personal Finance | 50% | Registered in Scotland |
| Tesco Home Shopping Limited | Mail Order Retail | 60% | Registered in England |

The Group's share of gross assets and gross liabilities of the joint ventures is disclosed below:

| | 2000 £m | 1999 £m |
|---|---|---|
| Gross assets | 958 | 821 |
| Gross liabilities | (786) | (587) |
| | 172 | 234 |

c  The investment in own shares represents 71 million 5p ordinary shares in Tesco PLC with a weighted average value of £1.11 each. These shares are held by a qualifying employee share trust (QUEST) in order to satisfy options under savings-related share option schemes which become exercisable over the next few years. The carrying value of £79m (market value £120m) represents the exercise amount receivable in respect of these shares subscribed for by the QUEST at market value. Funding is provided to the QUEST by Tesco Stores Limited, the company's principal operating subsidiary. The QUEST has waived its rights to dividends on these shares.

# notes to the financial statements continued

**NOTE 13** Fixed asset investments continued

|  | 2000 £m | 1999 £m |
|---|---|---|
| The net funds/(borrowings) of the joint ventures, as at 26 February 2000, were as follows: | | |
| Cash and deposits | 1,445 | 979 |
| Debenture stock – repayable 2001 | (40) | (38) |
| Term bank loan – repayable 2003 | (135) | (134) |
| Other loans | (1,225) | (900) |
|  | 45 | (93) |

There is no recourse to Group companies in respect of the borrowings of the joint ventures, apart from £16m (1999 – £15m) which has been guaranteed by Tesco PLC (note 29).

Details of transactions and balances with the joint ventures are set out in note 30.

**NOTE 14** Stocks

|  | Group | | Company | |
|---|---|---|---|---|
|  | 2000 £m | 1999 £m | 2000 £m | 1999 £m |
| Goods held for resale | 636 | 595 | – | – |
| Development property | 108 | 72 | – | – |
|  | 744 | 667 | – | – |

Additions to development property include £1m (1999 – £2m) of interest capitalised. Accumulated capitalised interest at 26 February 2000 was £15m (1999 – £14m).

**NOTE 15** Debtors

|  | Group | | Company | |
|---|---|---|---|---|
|  | 2000 £m | 1999 £m | 2000 £m | 1999 £m |
| Amounts owed by Group undertakings | – | – | 705 | 1,690 |
| Prepayments and accrued income | 37 | 31 | 419 | 202 |
| Other debtors | 178 | 100 | 22 | 12 |
| Amounts owed by undertakings in which the company has a participating interest | 37 | 20 | 37 | 20 |
|  | 252 | 151 | 1,183 | 1,924 |

**NOTE 16** Investments

|  | Group | | Company | |
|---|---|---|---|---|
|  | 2000 £m | 1999 £m | 2000 £m | 1999 £m |
| Money market deposits | 256 | 199 | 19 | – |
| Bonds and certificates of deposit (market value £2m, 1999 – £2m) | 2 | 2 | 2 | 2 |
|  | 258 | 201 | 21 | 2 |

**NOTE 17** Creditors falling due within one year

| | Group | | Company | |
|---|---|---|---|---|
| | 2000 £m | 1999 £m | 2000 £m | 1999 £m |
| Bank loans and overdrafts (a) (b) | 832 | 811 | 1,327 | 1,341 |
| Trade creditors | 1,248 | 1,100 | – | – |
| Amounts owed to Group undertakings | – | – | 905 | 1,733 |
| Other creditors | 603 | 446 | 19 | 3 |
| Corporation tax (c) | 282 | 236 | 33 | – |
| Other taxation and social security | 78 | 92 | 1 | – |
| Accruals and deferred income (d) | 217 | 177 | 28 | 21 |
| Finance leases (note 22) | 15 | 19 | – | – |
| Proposed final dividend | 212 | 194 | 212 | 194 |
| | 3,487 | 3,075 | 2,525 | 3,292 |

a  Bank deposits at subsidiary undertakings of £746m (1999 – £767m) have been offset against borrowings in the parent company under a legal right of set-off.

b  Includes £11m (1999 – £9m) secured on various properties.

c  The prior year comparative includes relief for advance corporation tax recoverable within one year.

d  A gain of £45m, realised in a prior year, on terminated interest rate swaps is being spread over the life of replacement swaps entered into at the same time for similar periods. Accruals and deferred income include £6m (1999 – £6m) attributable to these realised gains with £6m (1999 – £12m) being included in other creditors falling due after more than one year (note 18).

**NOTE 18** Creditors falling due after more than one year

| | Group | | Company | |
|---|---|---|---|---|
| | 2000 £m | 1999 £m | 2000 £m | 1999 £m |
| 4% unsecured deep discount loan stock 2006 (a) | 90 | 87 | 90 | 87 |
| Finance leases (note 22) | 51 | 8 | – | – |
| 10¾% bonds 2002 (b) | 200 | 200 | 200 | 200 |
| 8¾% bonds 2003 (c) | 200 | 200 | 200 | 200 |
| 7½% bonds 2007 (d) | 325 | 325 | 325 | 325 |
| 5⅛% bonds 2009 (e) | 350 | 150 | 350 | 150 |
| 6% bonds 2029 (f) | 200 | – | 200 | – |
| Medium term notes (g) | 127 | 226 | 127 | 226 |
| Other loans (h) | 16 | 22 | – | – |
| | 1,559 | 1,218 | 1,492 | 1,188 |
| Accruals and deferred income (note 17) | 6 | 12 | – | – |
| | 1,565 | 1,230 | 1,492 | 1,188 |

a  The 4% unsecured deep discount loan stock is redeemable at a par value of £125m in 2006.

b  The 10¾% bonds are redeemable at a par value of £200m in 2002.

c  The 8¾% bonds are redeemable at a par value of £200m in 2003.

d  The 7½% bonds are redeemable at a par value of £325m in 2007.

e  The 5⅛% bonds are redeemable at a par value of £350m in 2009.

f  The 6% bonds are redeemable at a par value of £200m in 2029.

g  The medium term notes are of various maturities and include foreign currency and sterling denominated notes swapped into floating rate sterling.

h  Secured on various properties.

# notes to the financial statements continued

**NOTE 19** Net debt

|  | Group | | Company | |
|---|---|---|---|---|
|  | 2000 £m | 1999 £m | 2000 £m | 1999 £m |
| Due within one year: Bank and other loans | 832 | 811 | 1,327 | 1,341 |
| Finance leases | 15 | 19 | – | – |
| Due within one to two years: Bank and other loans | 266 | 137 | 127 | 127 |
| Finance leases | 13 | 4 | – | – |
| Due within two to five years: Bank and other loans | 272 | 477 | 272 | 465 |
| Finance leases | 11 | 4 | – | – |
| Due wholly or in part by instalments after five years: |  |  |  |  |
| Finance leases | 27 | – | – | – |
| Due otherwise than by instalments after five years: |  |  |  |  |
| Bank and other loans | 970 | 596 | 1,093 | 596 |
| Gross debt | 2,406 | 2,048 | 2,819 | 2,529 |
| Less: Cash at bank and in hand | 88 | 127 | – | – |
| Money market investments and deposits | 258 | 201 | 21 | 2 |
| Net debt | 2,060 | 1,720 | 2,798 | 2,527 |

**NOTE 20** Financial instruments

An explanation of the objectives and policies for holding and issuing financial instruments is set out in the Operating and Financial Review on pages 2 to 6. Other than where these items have been included in the currency risk disclosures, short-term debtors and creditors have been excluded from the following analyses.

**Analysis of interest rate exposure and currency of financial liabilities**

The interest rate exposure and currency profile of the financial liabilities of the Group at 26 February 2000 after taking into account the effect of interest rate and currency swaps were:

|  | Floating rate liabilities £m | Fixed rate liabilities £m | 2000 Total £m | Floating rate liabilities £m | Fixed rate liabilities £m | 1999 Total £m |
|---|---|---|---|---|---|---|
| **Currency** |  |  |  |  |  |  |
| Sterling | 1,186 | 512 | 1,698 | 1,172 | 487 | 1,659 |
| Euro | 104 | 147 | 251 | 16 | 162 | 178 |
| Thai baht | 235 | – | 235 | 190 | – | 190 |
| Other | 222 | – | 222 | 21 | – | 21 |
| Gross liabilities | 1,747 | 659 | 2,406 | 1,399 | 649 | 2,048 |

|  | Fixed rate financial liabilities | | | |
|---|---|---|---|---|
|  | Weighted average interest rate 26 Feb 2000 % | 2000 Weighted average time for which rate is fixed Years | Weighted average interest rate 27 Feb 1999 % | 1999 Weighted average time for which rate is fixed Years |
| **Currency** |  |  |  |  |
| Sterling | 6.7 | 15 | 9.0 | 6 |
| Euro | 5.8 | 3 | 5.9 | 4 |
| Weighted average | 6.7 | 12 | 8.2 | 5 |

Floating rate liabilities bear interest at rates based on relevant national LIBOR equivalents. Borrowing facilities are shown in the Operating and Financial Review on pages 2 to 6. The interest rate profile of the Group has been further managed by the purchase of interest rate caps with an aggregate notional principal of £100m (1999 – £100m), an average strike price of 8.3% and a two year maturity. The current value of these contracts, if realised, is nil (1999 – nil).

**NOTE 20** Financial instruments continued

### Analysis of interest rate exposure and currency of financial assets

The interest rate exposure and currency profile of the financial assets of the Group at 26 February 2000 were:

| | Cash at bank and in hand £m | Short-term deposits £m | Other £m | 2000 Total £m | Cash at bank and in hand £m | Short-term deposits £m | Other £m | 1999 Total £m |
|---|---|---|---|---|---|---|---|---|
| Sterling | – | 75 | 37 | 112 | 62 | 49 | 20 | 131 |
| Other | 88 | 183 | – | 271 | 65 | 152 | – | 217 |
| Total financial assets | 88 | 258 | 37 | 383 | 127 | 201 | 20 | 348 |

Other financial assets are in respect of amounts owed by undertakings in which the company has a participating interest, which attracts a rate of interest of 6.7%. Surplus funds are invested in accordance with approved limits on security and liquidity and bear rates of interest based on relevant LIBOR equivalents. Cash at bank and in hand includes non interest bearing cash and cash in transit.

### Currency exposures

Within the Group, the principal differences on exchange arising which are taken to the profit and loss account, relate to purchases made by Group companies in currencies other than their reporting currencies. After taking into account hedging transactions, there were no significant balances on these exposures at year end. Rolling hedges of up to one year's duration are maintained against the value of investments and long-term intercompany borrowings in overseas subsidiaries, and to the extent permitted in SSAP20, differences on exchange are taken to the statement of total recognised gains and losses.

### Fair values of financial assets and financial liabilities

| | 2000 Book value £m | Fair value £m | 1999 Book value £m | Fair value £m |
|---|---|---|---|---|
| **Primary financial instruments held or issued to finance the Group's operations:** | | | | |
| Short-term borrowings | (847) | (847) | (830) | (830) |
| Long-term borrowings | (1,559) | (1,563) | (1,218) | (1,335) |
| Short-term deposits | 258 | 258 | 201 | 201 |
| Cash at bank and in hand | 88 | 88 | 127 | 127 |
| **Derivative financial instruments held to manage the interest rate and currency profile:** | | | | |
| Interest rate swaps and similar instruments | – | 4 | – | 24 |
| Forward foreign currency contracts | (9) | (9) | (4) | (4) |
| Swap profit crystallisation | (12) | (12) | (18) | (18) |
| | (2,081) | (2,081) | (1,742) | (1,835) |

Other significant financial instruments outstanding at the year end are £44m (1999 – £222m) nominal value forward foreign exchange contracts hedging the cost of foreign currency denominated purchases. On a mark-to-market basis, these contracts show a profit of nil (1999 – nil). The fair values of the interest rate swaps, forward foreign currency contracts and long-term sterling denominated fixed rate debt have been determined by reference to prices available from the markets on which the instruments are traded. The fair values of all other items have been calculated by discounting expected future cash flows at prevailing interest rates.

### Hedges

Unrecognised gains and losses on instruments used for hedging and those recognised in the year ended 26 February 2000 are as follows:

| | Unrecognised Gains £m | Losses £m | Total net gains/(losses) £m | Deferred Gains £m | Losses £m | Total net gains/(losses) £m |
|---|---|---|---|---|---|---|
| At 27 February 1999 | 58 | (34) | 24 | 18 | – | 18 |
| Arising in previous years and recognised in the year ended 26 February 2000 | (17) | 15 | (2) | (6) | – | (6) |
| Arising in the period to be recognised in future years | (27) | 9 | (18) | – | – | – |
| At 26 February 2000 (a) | 14 | (10) | 4 | 12 | – | 12 |
| Expected to be recognised in the year ended 24 February 2001 (a) | (3) | 2 | (1) | (6) | – | (6) |

a Gains and losses to be recognised through the profit and loss account.

# notes to the financial statements continued

**NOTE 21** Provisions for liabilities and charges

|  | Deferred taxation £m |
|---|---:|
| At 27 February 1999 | 17 |
| Amount charged in the year | 2 |
| At 26 February 2000 | 19 |

|  | Amount provided | | Potential amount for deferred tax on timing differences | |
|---|---:|---:|---:|---:|
|  | 2000 £m | 1999 £m | 2000 £m | 1999 £m |
| **Deferred taxation** |  |  |  |  |
| Excess capital allowances over depreciation | 1 | – | 358 | 315 |
| Capital gains deferred by rollover relief | – | – | (6) | (8) |
| Short-term timing differences | 18 | 17 | 18 | 12 |
|  | 19 | 17 | 370 | 319 |

Deferred taxation balances relate principally to short-term timing differences.

Where possible, taxation on capital gains has been or will be deferred by rollover relief under the provisions of the Taxation of Chargeable Gains Act 1992.

**NOTE 22** Leasing commitments

### Finance leases

The future minimum finance lease payments to which the Group was committed
at 26 February 2000 and which have been guaranteed by Tesco PLC are:

|  | £m |
|---|---:|
| Gross rental obligations | 81 |
| Less: finance charges allocated to future periods | (15) |
|  | 66 |

|  | 2000 £m | 1999 £m |
|---|---:|---:|
| Net amounts payable are: |  |  |
| Within one year | 15 | 19 |
| Between one and five years | 24 | 8 |
| After five years | 27 | – |
|  | 66 | 27 |

### Operating leases

|  | 2000 £m | 1999 £m |
|---|---:|---:|
| Group commitments during the 52 weeks to 24 February 2001, in terms of lease agreements expiring, are as follows: |  |  |
| Within one year | 4 | 4 |
| Between one and five years | 18 | 10 |
| After five years | 147 | 135 |
|  | 169 | 149 |

**NOTE 23  Called up share capital**

| | Ordinary shares of 5p each | |
|---|---|---|
| | Number | £m |
| Authorised at 27 February 1999 | 9,200,000,000 | 460 |
| Authorised during the year | – | – |
| Authorised at 26 February 2000 | 9,200,000,000 | 460 |
| Allotted, issued and fully paid: | | |
| Issued at 27 February 1999 | 6,770,197,098 | 339 |
| Scrip dividend election | 11,286,890 | – |
| Share options exercised | 41,535,371 | 2 |
| Issued at 26 February 2000 | 6,823,019,359 | 341 |

During the year, 52.8 million shares were issued for an aggregate consideration of £75m, which comprised £21m for scrip dividend and £54m for share options.

Between 26 February 2000 and 10 April 2000, options on 5,131,917 ordinary shares and 6,616,704 ordinary shares have been exercised under the terms of the savings-related share option scheme (1981) and the executive share option schemes (1984, 1994 and 1996) respectively.

As at 26 February 2000 the Directors were authorised to purchase up to a maximum in aggregate of 682,301,935 ordinary shares.

**NOTE 24  Reserves**

| | Group | | Company | |
|---|---|---|---|---|
| | 2000 £m | 1999 £m | 2000 £m | 1999 £m |
| **Share premium account** | | | | |
| At 27 February 1999 | 1,577 | 1,528 | 1,577 | 1,528 |
| Premium on issue of shares less costs | 52 | 248 | 52 | 248 |
| Bonus issue on 3 July 1998 | – | (221) | – | (221) |
| Scrip dividend election | 21 | 22 | 21 | 22 |
| **At 26 February 2000** | 1,650 | 1,577 | 1,650 | 1,577 |
| **Other reserves** | | | | |
| At 26 February 2000 and 27 February 1999 | 40 | 40 | – | – |
| **Profit and loss account** | | | | |
| At 27 February 1999 | 2,426 | 2,225 | 783 | 851 |
| Loss on foreign currency net investments | (36) | (19) | (3) | – |
| Issue of shares | (24) | (109) | – | – |
| Retained profit for the financial year | 372 | 329 | (260) | (68) |
| **At 26 February 2000** | 2,738 | 2,426 | 520 | 783 |

Other reserves comprise a merger reserve arising on the acquisition of Hillards plc in 1987.

In accordance with section 230 of the Companies Act 1985 a profit and loss account for Tesco PLC, whose result for the year is shown above, has not been presented in these accounts.

The cumulative goodwill written off against the reserves of the Group as at 26 February 2000 amounted to £718m (1999 – £718m). During the year, the qualifying share ownership trust (QUEST) subscribed for 21 million shares from the company. The amount of £24m shown above represents contributions to the QUEST from subsidiary undertakings.

# notes to the financial statements continued

## Company schemes

The company had five principal share option schemes in operation during the year:

i  The savings-related share option scheme (1981) permits the grant to employees of options in respect of ordinary shares linked to a building society/bank save-as-you-earn contract for a term of three or five years with contributions from employees of an amount between £5 and £250 per month. Options are capable of being exercised at the end of the three and five year period at a subscription price not less than 80% of the middle market quotation of an ordinary share immediately prior to the date of grant.

ii  The executive share option scheme (1984) permitted the grant of options in respect of ordinary shares to selected executives. The scheme expired after ten years on 9 November 1994. Options were generally exercisable between three and ten years from the date of grant at a subscription price determined by the Board but not less than the middle market quotation within the period of 30 days prior to the date of grant. Some options have been granted at a discount of 15% of the standard option price but the option holder may take advantage of that discount only if, in accordance with investor protection ABI guidelines, certain targets related to earnings per share are achieved.

iii  The executive share option scheme (1994) was adopted on 17 October 1994. The principal difference between this scheme and the previous scheme is that the exercise of options will normally be conditional upon the achievement of a specified performance target related to the annual percentage growth in earnings per share over any three year period. There will be no discounted options granted under this scheme.

iv  The unapproved executive share option scheme (1996) was adopted on 7 June 1996. This scheme was introduced following legislative changes which limited the number of options which could be granted under the previous scheme. As with the previous scheme, the exercise of options will normally be conditional upon the achievement of a specified performance target related to the annual percentage growth in earnings per share over any three year period. There will be no discounted options granted under this scheme.

v  The international executive share option scheme was adopted on 20 May 1994. This scheme permits the grant to selected non-UK executives of options to acquire ordinary shares on substantially the same basis as their UK counterparts. Options are normally exercisable between three and ten years from their grant at a price of not less than the average of the middle market quotations for the ordinary shares as derived from the London Stock Exchange Daily Official List for the three dealing days immediately preceding their grant and will normally be conditional on the achievement of a specified performance target determined by the Remuneration Committee when the options are granted. There will be no discounted options granted under this scheme.

The company has granted outstanding options in connection with the five schemes as follows:

### Savings-related share option scheme (1981)

| Date of grant | Number of executives and employees | Shares under option 26 Feb 2000 | Subscription prices (pence) |
|---|---|---|---|
| 22 October 1993 | 5 | 14,136 | 53.7 |
| 26 October 1994 | 1,903 | 5,513,787 | 61.7 |
| 27 October 1995 | 15,288 | 32,043,763 | 83.3 |
| 31 October 1996 | 12,943 | 30,222,135 | 83.0 |
| 30 October 1997 | 33,377 | 43,007,253 | 121.7 |
| 29 October 1998 | 51,763 | 63,999,669 | 136.0 |
| 28 October 1999 | 55,501 | 49,059,538 | 151.0 |

### Executive share option scheme (1984)

| Date of grant | Number of executives | Shares under option 26 Feb 2000 | Subscription prices (pence) |
|---|---|---|---|
| 17 May 1991 | 4 | 60,000 | 91.3 |
| 29 May 1992 | 72 | 2,772,503 | 92.3 |
| 29 October 1992 | 2 | 78,663 | 72.3 |
| 27 May 1993 | 3 | 184,425 | 72.3 |
| 10 June 1994 | 137 | 3,117,726 | 70.0 |
| 12 August 1994 | 1 | 471,372 | 81.0 |
| 29 September 1994 | 9 | 346,242 | 77.3 |

**NOTE 25** Share options continued

### Executive share option scheme (1994)

| Date of grant | Number of executives | Shares under option 26 Feb 2000 | Subscription prices (pence) |
|---|---|---|---|
| 27 April 1995 | 7 | 741,954 | 90.3 |
| 13 October 1995 | 312 | 7,924,787 | 104.0 |

### Executive share option scheme (1996)

| Date of grant | Number of executives | Shares under option 26 Feb 2000 | Subscription prices (pence) |
|---|---|---|---|
| 3 July 1996 | 22 | 2,624,106 | 98.3 |
| 23 September 1996 | 593 | 16,018,351 | 99.7 |
| 17 April 1997 | 1,012 | 19,760,589 | 117.7 |
| 7 October 1997 | 40 | 4,662,588 | 151.7 |
| 17 November 1997 | 2 | 446,373 | 160.3 |
| 21 May 1998 | 1,287 | 21,859,618 | 176.7 |
| 30 September 1998 | 36 | 1,521,695 | 164.0 |
| 28 January 1999 | 1,358 | 22,025,669 | 178.0 |
| 24 May 1999 | 8 | 882,044 | 179.4 |
| 9 November 1999 | 43 | 2,356,085 | 184.0 |
| 30 November 1999 | 8 | 1,098,962 | 173.0 |

### International executive share option scheme

| Date of grant | Number of executives | Shares under option 26 Feb 2000 | Subscription prices (pence) |
|---|---|---|---|
| 7 October 1997 | 117 | 1,869,690 | 151.7 |
| 21 May 1998 | 284 | 2,775,000 | 176.7 |
| 28 January 1999 | 359 | 3,727,500 | 178.0 |
| 24 May 1999 | 18 | 520,746 | 179.4 |

**NOTE 26** Pension commitments

The Group operates a funded defined benefit pension scheme for full-time employees in the UK, the assets of which are held as a segregated fund and administered by trustees. The total cost of the scheme to the Group was £60m (1999 – £55m).

An independent actuary, using the projected unit method, carried out the latest actuarial assessment of the scheme at 5 April 1999. The assumptions that have the most significant effects on the results of the valuation are those relating to the rate of return on investments and the rate of increase in salaries and pensions.

The key assumptions made were:

| | |
|---|---|
| Rate of return on investments | 7.25% |
| Rate of increase in salaries | 4.50% |
| Rate of increase in pensions | 2.75% |

At the date of the latest actuarial valuation, the market value of the scheme's assets was £1,297m and the actuarial value of these assets represented 96% of the benefits that had accrued to members, after allowing for expected future increases in earnings. The actuarial shortfall of £53m will be met via increased contributions over a period of 11 years, being the expected average remaining service lifetime of employed members.

The Group also operates a defined contribution pension scheme for part-time employees which was introduced on 6 April 1988. The assets of the scheme are held separately from those of the Group, being invested with an insurance company. The pension cost represents contributions payable by the Group to the insurance company and amounted to £19m (1999 – £17m). There were no material amounts outstanding to the insurance company at the year end.

The Group operates a number of pension schemes worldwide, most of which are defined contribution schemes. The contributions payable for non-UK schemes of £3m (1999 – £1m) have been fully expensed against profits in the current year. A defined benefit scheme operates in the Republic of Ireland. At the latest actuarial valuation carried out at 1 April 1998, the market value of the scheme's assets was £42m and the actuarial value of these assets represented 129% of the benefits that had accrued to members, after allowing for expected future increases in earnings.

# notes to the financial statements continued

**NOTE 27  Post-retirement benefits other than pensions**

The company operates a scheme offering post-retirement healthcare benefits. The cost of providing for these benefits has been accounted for on a basis similar to that used for defined benefit pension schemes.

The liability as at 24 February 1996 of £10m, which was determined in accordance with the advice of qualified actuaries, is being spread forward over the service lives of relevant employees and £1m (1999 – £1m) has been charged to the profit and loss account. An amount of £4m (1999 – £3m) is being carried in the balance sheet. It is expected that payments will be tax deductible, at the company's tax rate, when made.

**NOTE 28  Capital commitments**

At 26 February 2000 there were commitments for capital expenditure contracted for but not provided of £303m (1999 – £260m).

**NOTE 29  Contingent liabilities**

Certain bank loans and overdraft facilities of joint ventures have been guaranteed by Tesco PLC. At 26 February 2000, the amounts outstanding on these facilities were £16m (1999 – £15m).

The company has irrevocably guaranteed the liabilities as defined in Section 5(c) of the Republic of Ireland (Amendment Act) 1986 of various subsidiary undertakings incorporated in the Republic of Ireland.

**NOTE 30  Related party transactions**

During the year there were no material transactions or amounts owed or owing with any of the Group's key management or members of their close family.

During the year the Group traded with its eight joint ventures: Shopping Centres Limited, BLT Properties Limited, Tesco British Land Property Partnership, Tesco BL Holdings Limited, Tesco Personal Finance Group Limited, Tesco Personal Finance Life Limited, Tesco Personal Finance Investments Limited and Tesco Home Shopping Limited. The main transactions during the year were:

 i  Equity funding of £42m (£41m in Tesco Personal Finance Group Limited and £1m in Tesco Home Shopping Limited).

 ii  The sale of nine properties formerly held in the British Land Property Partnership to subsidiaries of Tesco BL Holdings Limited, a limited company owned 50:50 by Tesco PLC and British Land PLC. A bank loan of £210m was raised against the properties and the company received £105m, reducing the aggregate investment by Tesco in the Property Partnership and the new joint venture to £63m. Additionally, the Group made rental payments of £16m (1999 – £13m) to Tesco British Land Property Partnership.

 iii  The Group made rental payments of £3m (1999 – £3m) and £11m (1999 – £11m) to Shopping Centres Limited and BLT Properties Limited respectively.

 iv  The Group has charged Tesco Personal Finance Limited (a 100% subsidiary of Tesco Personal Finance Group Limited) an amount totalling £12m in respect of services, loan interest and assets transferred, of which £2m was outstanding at 26 February 2000. Tesco Personal Finance Limited received fees totalling £3m from the Group for managing certain financial products. In addition, an amount of £4m, the majority of which relates to group relief was outstanding at 26 February 2000.

 v  The Group has charged Tesco Home Shopping Limited an amount totalling £3m in respect of services, loan interest and assets transferred, of which £1m was outstanding at 26 February 2000.

 vi  The Group made loans totalling £17m (£10m to Tesco Personal Finance Group Limited and £7m to Tesco Home Shopping Limited).

**NOTE 31 Reconciliation of operating profit to net cash inflow from operating activities**

|  | 2000 £m | 1999 £m |
|---|---|---|
| Operating profit | 1,030 | 934 |
| Depreciation and goodwill amortisation | 435 | 406 |
| Increase in goods held for resale | (47) | (69) |
| (Increase)/decrease in development property | (40) | 13 |
| Increase in debtors | (45) | (12) |
| Increase in trade creditors | 156 | 81 |
| Increase/(decrease) in other creditors | 24 | (32) |
| Decrease/(increase) in working capital | 48 | (19) |
| Net cash inflow from operating activities | 1,513 | 1,321 |

**NOTE 32 Acquisitions**

Effective 1 May 1999, Tesco acquired a 51% controlling interest in a newly incorporated company, Samsung Tesco Co. Limited for a cash consideration of £81m and incurred fees of £4m.

Subsequently the company paid £57m to increase its holding in Samsung Tesco Co. Limited to 81% on 30 June 1999. Net assets amounted to £138m. A subsequent fair value adjustment revised this to £136m. The impact of this acquisition on the results for the year was immaterial.

**NOTE 33 Analysis of changes in net debt**

|  | At 27 Feb 1999 £m | Cash flow £m | Other non cash changes £m | Exchange movements £m | At 26 Feb 2000 £m |
|---|---|---|---|---|---|
| Cash at bank and in hand | 127 | (34) | – | (5) | 88 |
| Overdrafts | (31) | (4) | – | – | (35) |
|  | 96 | (38) | – | (5) | 53 |
| Money market investments and deposits | 201 | 68 | – | (11) | 258 |
| Bank and other loans | (780) | (19) | (4) | 6 | (797) |
| Finance leases | (19) | 4 | – | – | (15) |
| Debt due within one year | (799) | (15) | (4) | 6 | (812) |
| Bank and other loans | (1,210) | (303) | – | 5 | (1,508) |
| Finance leases | (8) | (13) | (30) | – | (51) |
| Debt due after one year | (1,218) | (316) | (30) | 5 | (1,559) |
|  | (1,720) | (301) | (34) | (5) | (2,060) |

# five year record

| Year ended February | 1996 | 1997 | 1998 [1] | 1999 | 2000 |
|---|---|---|---|---|---|
| **Financial statistics £m** | | | | | |
| **Turnover excluding VAT** | | | | | |
| UK | 11,560 | 13,118 | 14,971 | 15,835 | 16,958 |
| Rest of Europe | 534 | 769 | 1,481 | 1,167 | 1,374 |
| Asia | – | – | – | 156 | 464 |
| | 12,094 | 13,887 | 16,452 | 17,158 | 18,796 |
| **Operating profit** [2] | | | | | |
| UK | 713 | 760 | 875 | 919 | 993 |
| Rest of Europe | 11 | 14 | 37 | 48 | 51 |
| Asia | – | – | – | (2) | (1) |
| | 724 | 774 | 912 | 965 | 1,043 |
| **Operating margin** [2] | | | | | |
| UK | 6.2% | 5.8% | 5.8% | 5.8% | 5.9% |
| Rest of Europe | 2.1% | 1.8% | 2.5% | 4.1% | 3.7% |
| Asia | – | – | – | (1.3)% | (0.2)% |
| Total Group | 6.0% | 5.6% | 5.5% | 5.6% | 5.5% |
| Share of profit/(loss) from joint ventures | – | – | (6) | 6 | 11 |
| Net interest payable | (43) | (24) | (74) | (90) | (99) |
| **Underlying profit** [3] | 681 | 750 | 832 | 881 | 955 |
| Ireland integration costs | – | – | (63) | (26) | (6) |
| Goodwill amortisation | – | – | – | (5) | (7) |
| Net loss on disposal of discontinued operations [4] | – | – | (8) | – | – |
| Net loss on disposal of fixed assets | (6) | – | (1) | (8) | (9) |
| Profit before taxation | 675 | 750 | 760 | 842 | 933 |
| Taxation | (209) | (230) | (228) | (237) | (259) |
| Minority interest | – | – | – | 1 | – |
| **Profit for the financial year** | 466 | 520 | 532 | 606 | 674 |
| Adjusted diluted earnings per share [3] | 7.30p | 7.83p | 8.84p | 9.37p | 10.18p |
| Adjusted earnings per share | 7.50p | 8.03p | 9.05p | 9.59p | 10.36p |
| Dividend per share | 3.20p | 3.45p | 3.87p | 4.12p | 4.48p |
| Net worth – £m [5] | 3,588 | 3,890 | 3,903 | 4,377 | 4,798 |
| Return on shareholders' funds [6] | 20.4% | 20.1% | 21.3% | 21.3% | 20.9% |
| Return on capital employed [7] | 16.9% | 17.1% | 18.7% | 17.2% | 16.1% |
| Net assets per share [8] | 56p | 60p | 59p | 65p | 70p |
| **UK retail productivity £** | | | | | |
| Turnover per employee [9] | 143,3359 | 146,326 | 149,799 | 151,138 | 156,427 |
| Profit per employee [9] | 8,841 | 8,478 | 8,755 | 8,771 | 9,160 |
| Wages per employee [9] | 13,948 | 14,222 | 15,079 | 15,271 | 15,600 |
| Weekly sales per sq ft [10/11] | 18.31 | 19.74 | 20.48 | 21.05 | 21.43 |
| **UK retail statistics** | | | | | |
| Market share in food and drink shops [12] | 13.4% | 14.2% | 14.8% | 15.4% | 15.5% |
| Number of stores | 545 | 568 | 618 | 639 | 659 |
| Total sales area – 000 sq ft [11] | 13,397 | 14,036 | 15,215 | 15,975 | 16,895 |
| Average store size (sales area – sq ft) [13] | 25,600 | 26,300 | 26,600 | 26,654 | 27,720 |
| Full-time equivalent employees [14] | 80,650 | 89,649 | 99,941 | 104,772 | 108,409 |
| **Group statistics** | | | | | |
| Number of stores | 734 | 758 | 781 | 821 | 845 |
| Total sales area – 000 sq ft | 15,114 | 16,747 | 18,254 | 21,353 | 24,039 |
| Full-time equivalent employees | 84,918 | 98,463 | 119,127 | 126,914 | 134,896 |
| **Share price (pence)** | | | | | |
| Highest | 113 | 123 | 180 | 202 | 197 |
| Lowest | 82 | 88 | 113 | 157 | 156 |
| Year end | 90 | 116 | 172 | 177 | 169 |

notes
1. 53 week period.
2. Excludes integration costs and goodwill amortisation. Operating margin is based upon turnover exclusive of VAT.
3. Underlying profit, adjusted and adjusted diluted, earnings per share excludes net loss on disposal of fixed assets, loss on disposal of discontinued operations, Ireland integration costs and goodwill amortisation.
4. Represents loss on disposal of discontinued operations.
5. Total capital employed at the year end.
6. Underlying profit divided by weighted average shareholders' funds.
7. Operating profit divided by average capital employed.
8. Based on number of shares at year end.
9. Based on turnover exclusive of VAT, operating profit and total staff cost per full-time equivalent employee.
10. Based on weighted average sales area and turnover inclusive of VAT excluding property development.
11. Store sizes exclude lobby and restaurant areas.
12. Based on Tesco food, grocery, non-food and drink sales and Institute of Grocery Distribution/Office for National Statistics data for the year to the previous December.
13. Average store sizes exclude Metro and Express stores.
14. Based on average number of full-time equivalent employees in the UK.

# INDEX

Weighted average cost of
capital (WACC), 242,
423–424, 436
Weighted-average costing
method, 212
Wheat, Francis, 32
Whistleblowers, creative
accounting, 344–347
Wholly-owned subsidiaries,
140–141, 279–280
Wimpey, 340

Work-in-progress, 143,
155–156
Working capital, 207–218,
406, 425
World Bank, 14–15
World Trade Organization
(WTO), 371
Written-off investments, 169
WTO *see* World Trade Orga-
nization

**Y**

Yellow Book, 20–25, 97–102,
119

**Z**

Z-score model, 424–425